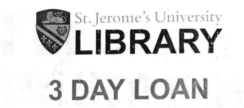

HISTORICAL DICTIONARIES OF RELIGIONS, PHILOSOPHIES, AND MOVEMENTS
Edited by Jon Woronoff

Historical Dictionary of Catholicism

Historical Dictionaries Of Religions,
Philosophies, And Movements, No. 12

WILLIAM J. COLLINGE

The Scarecrow Press, Inc.
Lanham, Md., & London
1997

SCARECROW PRESS, INC.

Published in the United States of America
by Scarecrow Press, Inc.
4720 Boston Way
Lanham, Maryland 20706

4 Pleydell Gardens, Folkestone
Kent CT20 2DN, England

British Cataloguing-in-Publication Information Available

Library of Congress Cataloging-in-Publication Data

Collinge, William J.
    Historical dictionary of Catholicism / by William J. Collinge.
        p. cm. — (Religions, movements, philosophies ; no. 12.)
    Includes bibliographical references and index.
    ISBN 0–8108–3233–X (alk. paper)
    1. Catholic Church—Dictionaries. 2. Church history—Dictionaries.
I. Title. II. Series: Historical dictionaries of religions, philosophies, and movements ;
no. 12.
BX945.2.C65   1996
282'.03—dc20   MAR 1 1 1999   95–30421
                                                                CIP

ISBN 0–8108–3233–X (cloth : alk.paper)

The paper used in this publication meets the minimum requirements of
American National Standard for Information Sciences—Permanence of
Paper for Printed Library Materials, ANSI Z39.48–1984.
Manufactured in the United States of America.

Contents

Editor's Foreword

Catholicism, if you just look at the numbers, is the world's premier religion, with more than a billion faithful. But it is yet more significant when you consider its impact well beyond that circle. It is closely, ever more closely, related to many Christian denominations, including those that broke away in the past. It influences other religions of entirely different traditions as they define what they believe and do not believe and what they regard as right and wrong. It even has an effect on philosophies and ideologies that claim to be indifferent to or deny religion and end up competing with it. How then could this series of *Historical Dictionaries of Religions, Philosophies, Movements* be complete without a volume on Catholicism?

But ... Catholicism in one book? It would seem impossible that a religion with such a long history and such a vast tradition and one that is still very active in today's concerns, spiritual and secular, should be summed up so briefly. That is probably true. Yet this one book does an exceptional job of bringing together essential information on Catholicism, its history and tradition, its beliefs and concepts, the various forms it has adopted over the centuries, many of the tasks that exercise it today, the persons who have contributed heavily to its action in the past and at present. This long history is easier to follow, thanks to the chronology. And its many facets are easier to grasp, thanks to numerous concise entries in a handy format. Those who want to know more can find it in the many other books listed in an extensive, if still selective, bibliography.

And ... Catholicism by one author. True, William J. Collinge did turn to others for advice. And he consulted the most authoritative written sources. But it would also seem impossible for any one person to describe so many aspects. Be that as it may, Dr. Collinge has done an exceptional job of presenting a broad and deep image of Catholicism in learned but readily accessible language. This may come from more than two decades of teaching theology and philosophy, most of this at

Mount Saint Mary's College. Whatever the cause, Dr. Collinge has managed to fill a major gap in our series with this *Historical Dictionary of Catholicism*.

Jon Woronoff
Series Editor

Abbreviations

Books of the Bible[1]

Acts	Acts of the Apostles
Am	Amos
Bar	Baruch
1 Chr	1 Chronicles
2 Chr	2 Chronicles
Col	Colossians
1 Cor	1 Corinthians
2 Cor	2 Corinthians
Dn	Daniel
Dt	Deuteronomy
Eccl	Ecclesiastes (Qoheleth)
Eph	Ephesians
Est	Esther
Ex	Exodus
Ez	Ezekiel
Ezr	Ezra
Gal	Galatians
Gn	Genesis
Hab	Habakkuk
Heb	Hebrews
Hg	Haggai
Hos	Hosea
Is	Isaiah
Jas	James

---

[1]These are the abbreviations used in the New American Bible translation, except that the NAB uses "Hb" for Habakkuk.

Jb	Job
Jdt	Judith
Jer	Jeremiah
Jgs	Judges
Jl	Joel
Jn	John
1 Jn	1 John
2 Jn	2 John
3 Jn	3 John
Jon	Jonah
Jos	Joshua
Jude	Jude
1 Kgs	1 Kings
2 Kgs	2 Kings
Lam	Lamentations
Lk	Luke
Lv	Leviticus
Mal	Malachi
1 Mc	1 Maccabees
2 Mc	2 Maccabees
Mi	Micah
Mk	Mark
Mt	Matthew
Na	Nahum
Neh	Nehemiah
Nm	Numbers
Ob	Obadiah
Phil	Philippians
Phlm	Philemon
Prv	Proverbs
Ps (Pss)	Psalms
1 Pt	1 Peter
2 Pt	2 Peter
Rom	Romans
Ru	Ruth
Rv	Revelation (Apocalypse)
Sir	Sirach (Ecclesiasticus)
1 Sm	1 Samuel
2 Sm	2 Samuel
Sg	Song of Songs

Tb	Tobit
1 Thes	1 Thessalonians
2 Thes	2 Thessalonians
Ti	Titus
1 Tm	1 Timothy
2 Tm	2 Timothy
Wis	Wisdom
Zec	Zechariah
Zep	Zephaniah

Other Abbreviations

AA	Vatican II, *Apostolicam actuositatem (Decree on the Apostolate of the Laity)*
AG	Vatican II, *Ad gentes (Decree on the Missionary Activity of the Church)*
b.	born
Bl.	Blessed
ca.	*circa*, "approximately"
CCC	*Catechism of the Catholic Church* (1992)
CCD	Confraternity of Christian Doctrine*
CDF	Congregation for the Doctrine of the Faith* (Roman Curia*)
CELAM	Consejo Episcopal Latino-Americano (Latin American Bishops' Conference)
d.	died
DH	Vatican II, *Dignitatis humanae (Declaration on Religious Freedom)*
DS	Denzinger-Schönmetzer: Henricus Denzinger and Adolfus Schönmetzer, *Enchiridion Symbolorum Definitionum et Declarationum de Rebus Fidei et Morum*, 34th ed. (Freiburg im Breisgau: Herder, 1965)
DV	Vatican II, *Dei verbum (Dogmatic Constitution on Divine Revelation*
Ed(s).	Editor(s); edition(s)
Engl	English
Fr	French

GE   Vatican II, *Gravissimum educationis (Declaration on Christian Education)*

Ger   German

Gk   Greek

GS   Vatican II, *Gaudium et spes (Pastoral Constitution on the Church in the Modern World)*

Heb   Hebrew

Ital   Italian

LG   Vatican II, *Lumen Gentium (Dogmatic Constitution on the Church)*

Lt   Latin

LXX   Septuagint (Greek version of Old Testament, made in late B.C. centuries)

NA   Vatican II, *Nostra aetate (Declaration on the Church's Relation to Non-Christian Religions)*

NAB   The New American Bible

NCCB   National Conference of Catholic Bishops (see article EPISCOPAL CONFERENCES)

NT   New Testament

O.F.M.   *Ordo Fratrum Minorum* ("Order of Friars Minor") = Franciscans

O.P.   *Ordo Praedicatorum* ("Order of Preachers") = Dominican

Op.T.   Vatican II, *Optatam totius (Decree on Priestly Formation)*

OT   Old Testament

PO   Vatican II, *Presbyterorum ordinis (Decree on the Ministry and Life of Priests)*

Port   Portuguese

RB   *Rule of Saint Benedict*

SC   Vatican II, *Sacrosanctum concilium (Constitution on the Sacred Liturgy)*

S.J.   *Societas Iesu* ("Society of Jesus") = Jesuit*

Sp   Spanish

St.   Saint

ST   *Summa theologiae* of St. Thomas Aquinas; references are to Part, Question, Article, and Reply to Objection (if relevant); thus, "ST 1.3.4 ad 2" refers to First Part, Question 3, Article 4, Reply to Objection 2.

	"1-2" and "2-2" designate, respectively, the First Part of the Second Part (*Prima secundae*) and the Second Part of the Second Part (*Secunda secundae*), so "ST 1-2.94.3" refers to the First Part of the Second Part, Question 94, Article 3.
Tr.	Translated, translator
UR	Vatican II, *Unitatis redintegratio (Decree on Ecumenism)*
USCC	United States Catholic Conference
WCC	World Council of Churches*
*	Indicates cross-reference

Notes to Users

Finding a term. The main body of this book, the Dictionary, is composed of more than five hundred entries, arranged alphabetically. If you do not find what you are looking for in the Dictionary, please look in the Index. If that fails, consult the list of other reference books at the beginning of the Bibliography.

Cross-References. An asterisk (*) is used for cross-references. Normally, a cross-reference is indicated only at the first prominent use of a term within an entry. Cross-references are not made to very commonly used terms (e.g., "God," "church," "Vatican Council II") that have entries in the book, unless there is some substantive reason for the cross-reference. Cross-references are sometimes made to forms that are grammatically cognate to a term that is the subject of an entry, e.g., "infallible*" when the entry is INFALLIBILITY.

Boldface. Boldface used within an article designates either a major division of the subject or else a subordinate topic. Thus, for instance, in the article VESTMENTS, individual vestments (alb, cincture, etc.) and liturgical colors are named in boldface.

Preface

"Catholicism" comes from a Greek root meaning "universal," and anyone trying to write a single volume on Catholicism soon finds that virtually everything in the universe has some claim for inclusion. So a few words are in order as to what this book does and does not try to do.

First off, it is a historical dictionary of Catholicism, not a dictionary of the history of Catholicism. I have made some attempt to encompass all seven of Ninian Smart's dimensions of religion as they apply to Catholicism: practical-ritual, experiential-emotional, narrative-mythic, doctrinal-philosophical, ethical-legal, social-institutional, and material (artifacts) (*The Religious Experience* [New York: Macmillan, 1989]), with primary emphases on doctrine, theology, and liturgy.

"Catholicism," as I explain in the Introduction, here means primarily Roman Catholicism. This work covers the whole history of Catholicism, including the periods of Christian history prior to the present divisions into Catholic, Orthodox, and Protestant, but within the earlier periods it focuses on the "story line" that leads to Catholicism in the Roman Rite, and particularly to Roman Catholicism in the United States.

I must explain one important exclusion. Though Catholicism is a preeminently biblical religion, this book for the most part does not cover biblical topics, persons, or places. There are entries on the Bible* and biblical criticism*, and biblical backgrounds to theological and liturgical themes are considered, but for entries on specifically biblical themes and individuals, the reader is directed to the reference works on the Bible listed under "Reference Works" or "Bible" in the Bibliography.

Besides my home, I have lived and worked in three milieux during the time I have been preparing this book, and they correspond to three intended audiences. I teach undergraduates at Mount Saint Mary's College, Emmitsburg, Maryland; I had college teachers, students, and librarians primarily in mind as I wrote. I did most of the research for this book in the library of the Lutheran Theological Seminary, Gettysburg, Pennsylvania (could a book on Catholicism have been researched at a Lutheran seminary even a generation ago?); I hope this book will be useful to Lutherans and individuals of all other religious backgrounds who desire to learn more about Catholicism. I worship and participate in parish life at St. Francis Xavier Church in Gettysburg, and I hope that this volume will be valuable to religious educators at St. Francis and in other Catholic parishes and dioceses and to Catholics who desire to learn more about their tradition.

Reflecting the current state of language in the daily life of the Catholic Church in the United States, I have made three choices that some readers will regard as unduly conservative: (1) I make some use of the masculine pronoun in reference to God; (2) I speak of dates as B.C. and A.D. ("Before Christ" and *Anno Domini* ["in the year of the Lord"]) rather than B.C.E. and C.E. ("Before the Common Era" and "Common Era"); (3) I speak of the "Old Testament" rather than the "Hebrew Scriptures." I believe all three choices are theologically defensible, and I defend the third a little under BIBLE, but my primary rationale is simply that these are the terms commonly in use (1 Cor 11.16).

I have many debts to acknowledge to individuals, institutions, and published sources.

I want to thank, first of all, Professor Berard L. Marthaler, O.F.M. Conv., of the Catholic University of America, who steered this project my way and has overseen my progress in it. He is the author of the articles CATECHISM and CREED in this volume. Elizabeth Watts read the entire first draft and made many helpful stylistic and substantive suggestions. Throughout its gestation, this book has been twinned with her neo-Confucian commentary on the *I Ching*. My colleague Patricia McDonald, S.H.C.J., has similarly reviewed the second draft. I am very grateful to both of them for their help on this book and for their continuing friendship.

William Portier, my department chairman, provided assistance with a number of the entries below as well as much support for my work generally. I would also like to thank William Buckley, Ann Miriam Gallagher, R.S.M., Carl Glover, Frederick M. Jelly, O.P., Christopher Kauffman, Jean Smith Liddell, Ronald G. Roberson, CSP, Paul Russell, and Michael Steltenkamp, S.J., for advice in specific topic areas. I am grateful to my brother, Paul Collinge, of Heartwood

Books, Charlottesville, Virginia, for the gift of sourcebooks I would
have been unable to afford. My wife, Susan H. Collinge, has reviewed
and commented on many of the articles below. I would like to thank
her for her comments as well as for her ongoing support in
innumerable ways and her patience in sharing a room (and a husband)
for the better part of four years with the stacks of books assembled for
this project. (Daniel, you can use the computer now.) And finally, I
would like to thank my parents, William and Rita Collinge, who more
than anyone else are responsible for the formation in Catholicism that
is the deepest substrate of this book.

I am indebted to Mount Saint Mary's College for a sabbatical leave
in the fall of 1994 to pursue this project, to the staff in Information
Technology at Mount Saint Mary's for help in preparing the
manuscript, and to the library staffs at Mount Saint Mary's and
Gettysburg Seminary for assistance in locating sources. I would like to
thank representatives of the Knights of Columbus, the Legion of Mary,
Worldwide Marriage Encounter, Maryknoll, Pax Christi USA, and the
Society of St. Vincent de Paul for information about their
organizations.

In writing this book, I have used all manner of sources, from texts
in Greek to telephone conversations. But anyone who writes a one-
volume reference work on a subject as vast as Catholicism is going to
make considerable use of other reference works. The conventions of
writing dictionaries preclude much footnoting, so I want to
acknowledge my indebtedness especially to the *New Catholic
Encyclopedia* (1967, with four later supplementary volumes) and to the
four-volume series published by Michael Glazier and, later, by
Liturgical Press: *The New Dictionary of Theology*, *The New Dictionary
of Sacramental Worship*, *The New Dictionary of Catholic Spirituality*,
and *The New Dictionary of Catholic Social Thought*. For "facts and
figures" about the Catholic Church, I have relied on several years'
volumes of *The Catholic Almanac*, published by Our Sunday Visitor.

The Bible is quoted in the New American Bible translation. The
documents of the ecumenical councils of the Church are quoted as
translated in Norman P. Tanner, S.J., ed., *Decrees of the Ecumenical
Councils*, two volumes (Washington, D.C.: Georgetown University
Press, 1990). I have made some slight modifications in spelling,
capitalization, and punctuation to accord with American conventions.
Some other church documents are quoted from *The Teaching of the*

Catholic Church as Contained in her Documents (Staten Island, New York: Alba House, 1967), from the two-volume set, *Vatican Two: The Conciliar and Post-Conciliar Documents*, edited by Austin Flannery (Northport, New York: Costello, 1975-82), and from *Origins*, the weekly periodical of the United States Catholic Conference, Washington, D.C.

Introduction

Worshiping on Sunday, all Eastern Orthodox* and many Protestant* Christians use the words of one of the ancient creeds* to profess their faith in the "holy catholic Church." But if given a form on which to specify their religious affiliation, they would not check the box for "Catholic." Thus, the historian of Catholicism faces a dilemma at the outset. "Catholic" comes from a Greek word meaning "universal" or "comprehensive" (*see* CATHOLICITY). As first used of the Christian Church, it referred to the whole community of followers of Jesus Christ*. But it is also the name of a particular church or "denomination." These are not simply two distinct meanings of a word, on the analogy of "friends" and "Society of Friends" (Quakers). Rather, as the Second Vatican Council says, they are two aspects of one complex reality. "The unique church of Christ, which in the creed we profess to be one, holy, catholic and apostolic ..., subsists in the Catholic Church, governed by the successor of Peter and the bishops in communion with him, although outside its structure many elements of sanctification and of truth are to be found, which, as proper gifts to the church of Christ, impel towards catholic unity" (*Dogmatic Constitution on the Church [Lumen Gentium]* 8). It is one Church, though Vatican II does not explain exactly what is the relation designated by "subsists in." Thus, in a sense, the history of Catholicism embraces the whole of Christianity.

This book in fact covers a millennium of church history in which the Eastern Orthodox and Western Catholics were one church, and a further half millennium of Western church history that is common to Catholics and Protestants. But, as the quotation from Vatican II suggests, its focus is on "the Catholic Church, governed by the successor of Peter...," that is, the pope*, who is the bishop of Rome*. Thus, "Roman Catholicism" is an alternate name for the subject of this book. Certainly, acceptance of the authority of the pope is what distinguishes those labeled "Catholic," in the sense used in the title of

1

this book, from all others. But many Catholics object to the designation, "Roman Catholic." Some hold that it disparages the Eastern Catholic Churches*, which are in union with the pope but follow distinctive traditions of worship, theology, and church order. Others claim that it overly particularizes the catholicity of the Church and elevates its distinguishing feature into its central feature. Though acknowledging that other options are defensible, this book will, for the most part, use "Catholicism" and "Roman Catholicism" interchangeably, adding "Roman" only when necessary for clarity. (For articles on other Christian churches with some claim to the title, "Catholic," *see* ANGLICAN COMMUNION, EASTERN ORTHODOX CHURCHES, OLD CATHOLICS, ORIENTAL ORTHODOX CHURCHES.) The particular "story line" to be followed is determined by the location in which this book is written: it concentrates on the history that leads to the Catholic Church in the Roman Rite (*see* RITE) in the United States at the close of the twentieth century.

The German Jesuit theologian Karl Rahner* once divided the history of the Church into three epochs of unequal length. The first is the period of Jewish Christianity, before the proclamation of Christ to the Gentiles. The second is the period of Western Christianity, Christianity as shaped by the thought forms and social structures of Greco-Roman culture and its historical successors. The third phase began, in an obscure and rudimentary way, with the Second Vatican Council (1962-65), which Rahner called "the first major official event in which the Church actualized itself precisely as a *world Church.*"[1] The present book focuses on the second epoch, which spans most of Catholic history. A historical dictionary of Catholicism written a century from now is likely to contain many more entries on African, Asian, Latin American, and Eastern European persons, places, and ideas than this book does.

This introduction will address the three epochs, using the standard division of the second into antiquity, the middle ages, and modernity.

---

[1]Rahner, Karl, S.J., "Towards a Fundamental Theological Interpretation of Vatican II," *Theological Studies* 40 (1979): 717.

I. Jewish Christianity

The Church began in the band of disciples* who gathered around Jesus of Nazareth. Older Catholic books of Church history depicted Jesus as explicitly founding the structure of the Church much as we know it today, with Peter as the pope (Mt 16.13-20), the Twelve apostles* as bishops*, and seven sacraments*. Contemporary Catholic scholarship sees Jesus as having *laid the foundations* for the Church in his ministry and his call of the disciples, but not to have founded it in an explicit sense.[2] Jesus proclaimed a "Kingdom of God"* or "Reign of God," which was to be, at least first and foremost, a renewed Israel. Though later Christians could legitimately claim that a mission to the Gentiles (non-Jews) was an extension of the inclusiveness that Jesus showed in his ministry, it was to the Jews that Jesus himself spoke. After Jesus' resurrection, the disciples understood this kingdom to have begun to come to pass in Jesus' life, death, and resurrection. They were energized by the Holy Spirit* to proclaim that Jesus is the Messiah, the "Christ," that is, the "anointed one" whom God was to send to save Israel (Acts 2.36). But at first they preached only to the Jews, and Luke portrays them as gathering regularly in the Temple (e.g., Acts 2.46). The proclamation of Christ to the Gentiles ("Greeks") probably originated in Antioch* (Acts 11.20). It was there that the disciples were first called "Christians" (Acts 11.26) by a Gentile public, which did not recognize the religious significance of the title "Christ" ("Messiah") and took it to be a proper name.

The proclamation of Jesus to the Gentiles was spearheaded by a Jewish convert named (in Hebrew) Saul and (in Greek) Paul. His message that salvation comes by faith in Christ—accessible to Jew and Gentile alike—and not through the works of the Jewish Law (Gal 2.16) carried the day in the Christian movement, though not without opposition. Luke (perhaps conflating several events) portrays the decisive moment as a council of the "apostles and elders" at Jerusalem around A.D. 50 (Acts 15.1-29), at which it was decided that Gentile converts to Christianity did not have to follow the Jewish Law (it is assumed that Jewish Christians still lived according to the Law). This

---

[2]Richard McBrien, *Catholicism*, New Edition (San Francisco: HarperSanFrancisco, 1994), 577-79.

meeting was not as universally decisive as Luke portrays it, and other New Testament writings reflect different approaches to the question; but due to developments both in Christianity and in Judaism*, Jewish Christianity had nearly died out by the end of the first century.[3]

II. The Western Church

Imagine what the shape of Christianity might have been if the Persian Empire rather than the Roman Empire had controlled Palestine in the time of Jesus, so that the natural route for the expansion of Christianity was to the east rather than the west. Christianity did, in very early times, spread to the east, reaching India by the second century, if not the first.[4] But political circumstances made it natural for Christian missionaries chiefly to travel westward, in the Mediterranean basin, where the lingua franca was Greek and Greek philosophy shaped the conceptual patterns of every intellectual.

A. Antiquity

The Christians faced sporadic persecution* from the Roman authorities because of their refusal to worship Roman gods. Veneration of the martyrs*, whose death made them one with Christ, became very prominent in the Church; it was the foundation of the later cult of the saints*. Despite persecution, the Church continued to grow, for reasons that are varied and not always clear. One incentive for conversion to Christianity was the Church's willingness to include people of all social classes, including slaves. Christian practice of love and mutual hospitality* was another incentive. The example of the martyrs and the moral quality of the lives of many ordinary Christians inspired others to convert. Christianity's rivals in the Empire were relatively weak: the traditional local cults were often in decay, and the "mystery religions"

---

[3]Terrance D. Callan, *Forgetting the Root: The Emergence of Christianity from Judaism* (New York: Paulist, 1986).

[4]Samuel Hugh Moffett, *A History of Christianity in Asia*, vol. 1: *Beginnings to 1500* (San Francisco: HarperSanFrancisco, 1992): 24-44.

from the East tended to be secretive and elitist.[5] In the second century, the Apologists* defended the respectability of Christianity and enhanced its appeal to intellectuals by giving expression to Christian faith in the language of Greek philosophy. (This project was continued and extended by the Fathers of the Church* and the medieval theologians.)

Internally, the second-century church was threatened by the many movements that are known collectively as Gnosticism*. These groups claimed to possess a secret tradition of Jesus' teaching, different from that handed down in the major churches. They took a negative stance toward the physical world and taught their adherents formulas for delivering their souls from imprisonment in the body and the cosmos. It became necessary for the leaders of the Church to establish some norms of doctrinal authority, that is, of establishing what it is that the Church believes and professes. The bearers of doctrinal authority that were firmly established in the second century have been central to the Church ever since, even if at times—especially in the Protestant Reformation—they were set in opposition to one another. They are the scriptures and the teaching of the bishops of the apostolic churches.

The **canon** of the scriptures was (for the most part) settled in the second century. Despite the attacks of Marcion* against the Old Testament and its God, the Church accepted the Old Testament as Christian scriptures, reading them as testimony to the Christ who was to come. From the collections of apostolic writings then in circulation, the Church accepted the four gospels, the Acts of the Apostles, and the Pauline writings (some disputes remained about the rest of our New Testament into the fourth century). These came to be regarded as distinctively Christian scriptures (*see* BIBLE), inspired by God. The most important criteria for the selection of scriptural books (that is, the NT) were apostolic origin, use in the major apostolic churches, and coherence with the faith of those churches. In an important sense, tradition preceded scripture, but the scriptures served as a norm for Church tradition. The function of the **bishop*** as official spokesperson for a local church became more prominent, and the bishops of the major apostolic churches were guardians of the apostolic tradition. By the end of the second century, all churches had a threefold ministry of bishop, presbyter (elder, priest*), and deacon*. The arguments for the

---

[5]Robin Lane Fox, *Pagans and Christians* (San Francisco: Harper and Row, 1988): 265-335.

authority of the scriptures and the tradition of the apostolic churches were put most clearly by Irenaeus*, bishop of Lyons in France in the late second century. Already for Irenaeus, the church of Rome* had a preeminence above the other churches, owing to its origins in Peter and Paul and to its location in the capital. This preeminence developed into the primacy of the bishop of Rome (the pope) within the whole Church. The church modeled its internal structure on the society of the Empire; division into "orders"*, most importantly into clerics* and laity*, dates from the third century.

The status of Christians in the Empire changed radically when Constantine* came to power in the West in 312 and into sole power in the Empire in 324. He favored Christianity and extended it toleration and a quasi-official status (it became officially the religion of the Empire under Theodosius I in 380). Though it was not perceived so at the time, this was a mixed blessing for the Church. On the one hand, persecutions ended and the Church gained large numbers of members. On the other, many of these new members joined the Church more for reasons of social conformity than personal faith, and Constantine began an entanglement of Church leaders with political authority, which has continued in some ways until the present time. Monasticism* gained momentum at this time as a protest against the laxity of imperial Christianity and an effort to recapture something of the heroic spirituality of the martyrs.

The fourth and fifth centuries saw controversies that led to the formulation of central doctrines that the Church has held ever since. The progress of these doctrinal controversies was partly the result of increasing sophistication in theology and partly the result of the emperors' desire for religious uniformity in the empire. It was now possible for church leaders from throughout the Empire (or large parts of it) to gather in **ecumenical councils***, summoned by the Emperor, to resolve issues of Christian faith and practice. The Councils of Nicaea I* (325) and Constantinople I* (381) established the basis of the doctrine of the Trinity*, defending the full divinity of the Word of God and the Holy Spirit. The Councils of Ephesus* (431) and Chalcedon* (451) stated the Church's belief in the divinity and humanity of Jesus, one single person who was the Word of God and the son of Mary. These conciliar decisions did not put an end to all controversy. Their authority was established only gradually, and churches still exist that do not accept the decisions of Ephesus (*see* ASSYRIAN CHURCH OF THE EAST) or Chalcedon (*see* ORIENTAL ORTHODOX

CHURCHES). The work of the great theologians of this period, Fathers of the Church such as Athanasius*, the Cappadocian Fathers*, Ambrose*, and Augustine*, remains one of the chief sources on which Christian theology draws today.

B. The Middle Ages

1. The Byzantine Church

Already by the fourth and fifth centuries the beginnings of the division between Greek East and Latin West were appearing. In 330, Constantine moved the seat of the Empire to Byzantium, which he renamed Constantinople*. The Empire was formally divided after the death of Theodosius in 395. In the West, it was besieged by Germanic tribes, and the last emperor (Romulus Augustulus) was deposed by the Goths in 476. The Empire survived in the East until 1453. Political and cultural forces combined with religious differences to produce a gradual estrangement that led to the schism between Catholic and Eastern Orthodox, which continues to the present time.

The Empire in the East came to be known as the Byzantine Empire. In it, there developed a vision of a Christian state, in which Church and Empire were closely united. More often than not, the emperor was the most powerful figure in the Church, though there were many conflicts between emperors and Patriarchs of Constantinople. Religious conflicts always had a political dimension, and most often political conflicts had a religious dimension. At first, the Byzantine Church was deeply involved in conflicts over Monophysitism*, which had the sympathy of some emperors and much of the population of the patriarchates of Antioch and Alexandria. These conflicts were settled in the Empire by the Second and Third Councils of Constantinople* (553 and 680-681). They persist today in the division between the Eastern Orthodox and Oriental Orthodox churches. Meanwhile, Christianity was put on the defensive against Islam*, as Arab armies overran the Middle East and North Africa, conquering the ancient patriarchal sees of Antioch and Jerusalem in 638 and Alexandria in 642-643. Constantinople finally fell to the Muslim Turks in 1453.

From 726 to 843, the Byzantine church was preoccupied by the conflict over iconoclasm*, which was finally resolved in favor of the use of images. The leading opponents of iconoclasm were the monks, whose position in the leadership of the church was secured as a result of the controversy. The mission to the Slavs began under the patriarch Photius* with the sending of Cyril and Methodius* to Moravia in 862. Missionaries also went to the Kievan Rus (Russians) at this time. By the end of the tenth century, the Rus were converted, beginning the rich tradition of Russian Orthodoxy.

Meanwhile, relations with the Western church worsened. There were disputes about who had authority over churches in border regions, differences of custom (e.g., Western use of unleavened bread in the eucharist, married priests in the East) elevated into church-dividing issues, and a genuine theological disagreement over the *filioque**, the procession of the Holy Spirit* from the Son as well as the Father in the Trinity*. Politically, the pope's crowning of Charlemagne (see below) as Emperor gave offense to Constantinople, whose emperor still claimed sovereignty in the West. After the ninth century, belief in the primacy of the pope waned in the East. "Nothing that happened ever seemed irremediable, but from the eighth century onwards every impulse to disunity had a disproportionate effect because the political and social situation allowed no contrary impulses to survive."[6] In 1054, following a dispute over church customs such as the use of unleavened bread, Patriarch Michael Cerularius and legates of Pope Leo IX excommunicated one another. This is taken traditionally as the date of the schism between the Eastern and Western churches, though it was not regarded as decisive at the time. Whatever chance of reunion there might have been was ended when Western crusaders sacked Constantinople in 1204 and installed a Venetian as Patriarch (*see* CRUSADES). The Second Council of Lyons* (1274) and the Council of Florence* (1439) developed formulas of reunion that were accepted by the Emperor and the Patriarch, but never by the clergy and laity of the Byzantine Church at large.

2. The Medieval Church in the West

While in the East the persistence of the empire led to a close alliance between emperor and patriarch, with the emperor usually the senior partner, in the West the collapse of the empire led to a power vacuum that was eventually filled by the pope. The Germanic tribes

---

[6]R. W. Southern, *Western Society and the Church in the Middle Ages*, The Pelican History of the Church 2 (Harmondsworth: Penguin, 1970): 66.

that overran the West were mostly Arians*, followers of the heresy that had been condemned at the Council of Nicaea. Under Justinian*, the empire briefly reconquered Italy and other parts of the West, but it was unable to hold on to them. After a period of chaos, Pope Gregory I* emerged as the functional ruler of central Italy. Gregory has often been called the "founder of the medieval papacy." He strengthened the authority of the pope in the Western church and, by dispatching St. Augustine of Canterbury in 596 to convert Anglo-Saxon England, began a pattern in which missionary monks would establish a loyalty to Rome among Christians in the farther reaches of Europe. The greatest figure in these efforts was St. Boniface (ca. 675-754), who led the Christianization of Germany.

Gregory was himself a monk and a great admirer of St. Benedict*. Partly through his influence, Benedictine monasticism became the dominant form of religious life in early medieval Europe. After the educational system of the Empire had collapsed, the monasteries were the principal centers of cultural life. They were crucial in preserving literacy and literary texts. Still, the period from the seventh through the tenth centuries in the West was a "Dark Age" in which schools were few, literacy was rare, and little creative work was done in literature, philosophy and theology.

A key point in the preservation of Catholicism in the West was the conversion of Clovis, king of the Franks, in 496. An alliance formed between the pope and the Franks in the eighth century. In 754, Pope Stephen II granted Pepin, the Frankish ruler, the title "Patricius Romanorum," "protector of the Romans," an act that effectively broke the link between the pope and the Byzantine Emperor. In turn, Pepin in 756 granted the pope sovereignty over central Italy; this was the beginning of the Papal States*, which survived until 1870. In 800, Pope Leo III crowned the Frankish king Charlemagne* as Holy Roman Emperor. The gesture of crowning was meant to show the pope's authority over the emperor, but in practice until the eleventh century the emperor often had the upper hand. More locally, the monasteries and dioceses became enmeshed in the system of rights and obligations known as "feudalism." Bishops and abbots became feudal lords themselves, often subservient to higher secular authorities. This was dramatized in the ceremony of lay investiture*, in which the secular ruler gave a new bishop or abbot the staff and ring that symbolized spiritual authority.

Around the middle of the eleventh century, Western European society underwent a general reawakening. Economic activity expanded, new lands were settled, the urban population grew, the West began to assert itself militarily, and intellectual activity flourished in monasteries and cathedral schools. This revival was accompanied by a growth of the power of the pope in church and society. Pope Gregory VII* (1073-1085) combatted lay investiture and reformed the clergy, strengthening their independence from secular rulers. His *Dictatus papae* (1075) put forward a theory of absolute papal monarchy in the Church and the right of the pope to depose kings and absolve their subjects from allegiance. As canon law* grew, more and more ecclesiastical and political business went through the papal court. In the late twelfth and early thirteenth centuries, the pope was the most powerful political figure in Europe. Thereafter, the popes' power declined, as they lacked effective means to enforce their claims against resistant secular rulers.

The Crusades* (1096-1291) were an effort to divert Europe's rising military forces to the service of spiritual ends, specifically the liberation of the Holy Land from the Muslims. In practice, spiritual and political aims were deeply entangled, and the resulting spectacle was often disedifying, not least when the Fourth Crusade sacked Constantinople. At the same time, the military power of the Christian states began more often to be turned against Jews, who had lived in relative peace, and heretics.

Many new spiritual movements arose in the twelfth and thirteenth centuries. The Cistercians were founded in 1098 as a reform of Benedictine monasticism. Their spirituality was articulated and championed by St. Bernard of Clairvaux*, the most important church figure of the twelfth century. The mendicant orders* represented a new form of religious life*, breaking with monasticism. "Friars" were not attached to a specific monastic house but traveled as needed for their ministry and, initially, lived by begging (hence, "mendicant"). Most prominent among the mendicant orders were the Franciscans, founded by St. Francis of Assisi* in 1209, and the Dominicans, founded by St. Dominic* in 1210.

Part of the appeal of the mendicants was the contrast between their evangelical poverty and the wealth and splendor of the hierarchy*. Other movements of the time extended the critique of ecclesiastical wealth to the point of heresy, or at least of suspected heresy. These included the beguines* and the poverty* movements, in particular the Waldensians*, who sounded some of the themes later taken up by the

Protestant Reformers. More clearly heretical were the partisans of a sort of Gnostic religious outlook who are collectively known as Cathars*. It was against these movements that the various forms of inquisition* were established in the thirteenth century and the execution of suspected heretics became common.

The twelfth and thirteenth centuries were the high point of medieval culture, a culture that was thoroughly Catholic. The great Gothic cathedrals (*see* ARCHITECTURE) date from this period, as do the major universities of Europe, of which Paris was the premier. Theological study prospered in the universities, renewed by the recovery of the corpus of the works of Aristotle*. The mendicants were attracted to the university towns, and most of the major theologians of the thirteenth and fourteenth centuries were Franciscans (e.g., Bonaventure*, Duns Scotus*, William of Ockham*) or Dominicans (e.g., Albert the Great*, Thomas Aquinas*, Meister Eckhart*). The great systems of scholastic theology, of which that of Aquinas was pre-eminent, displayed a confidence in the harmony between faith and reason in their synthesis of the Western Christian heritage with Aristotelian philosophy. Yet the excessive enthusiasm for Aristotle shown by some university teachers led to a series of ecclesiastical condemnations in the late thirteenth century and to a diminished estimate of the value of reason in subsequent theology.

The leading theological movement in the universities of the fourteenth century was nominalism, whose most important representative was William of Ockham. The nominalists curbed speculative reason in the interest of preserving God's sovereign freedom. They concentrated on narrow technical issues and produced some real advances in logical theory, as well as making increased room for experimental rather than deductive natural science. Their work, however, was considered spiritually sterile (Thomas More* later drew the analogy of seeking bodily nourishment by milking a he-goat[7]). The perceived sterility of rational theology was one factor in the rise of an experiential, mystical spirituality in the fourteenth century. Three of the many important fourteenth-century mystics were Meister Eckhart*, St. Catherine of Siena*, and Julian of Norwich*. The latter two reflect the increasing prominence of women spiritual writers at this time.

---

[7]Owen Chadwick, *The Reformation*, The Pelican History of the Church 3 (Harmondsworth: Penguin, 1964): 36.

The "breakdown of the medieval synthesis"[8] in theology was part of a larger process of the disintegration of medieval culture. The vision of a politically united Europe with the pope at its head gave way to warring nation states. Pope Boniface VIII* (1294-1303), whose claims for papal power were among the most extreme ever made, was imprisoned by the French king Philip IV (the Fair). In 1309, under Philip's influence, the papacy was moved from Rome to Avignon*. The pope's return to Rome in 1378 was soon followed by the Great Western Schism*, in which there was one line of popes at Rome, a second at Avignon, and, after 1409, a third line at Pisa, all with plausible claims to legitimacy. The schism was settled at the Council of Constance* in 1417, but at the cost of greatly strengthening the movement of conciliarism*, which held that a general council is superior to the pope. The popes of the fifteenth century succeeded in overcoming conciliarism, but the papacy lost strength as the Renaissance* popes neglected spiritual leadership in favor of political and dynastic intrigues.

Not only was the papacy weakened, but bishops and abbots frequently acquired their offices as political favors and did not reside in their dioceses or abbeys. Priests were often poorly educated. The liturgy* had lost its original character as a celebration by the whole community and had become primarily an action performed by a priest in order to dispense spiritual benefits. Often it was corrupted by superstitious practices. There was a widespread demand in the Church for "reform in head and members," but, fearing conciliarism, the popes did not wish to call for a reforming council.

C. The Reformation and Modernity

When reform did come, it split the Church rather than healing it. The Protestant Reformation is traditionally dated from October 31, 1517, when Martin Luther circulated his *Ninety-Five Theses* in Wittenberg, Germany. The reforming movement took different shapes in Switzerland, the Low Countries, and England, reflected in the differing Protestant Churches* today (*see also* ANGLICAN COMMUNION). The theologies of the Reformers were various, but all

---

[8]David Knowles, *The Evolution of Medieval Thought*, second edition, ed. by D. E. Luscombe and C. N. L. Brooke (London: Longmans, 1988): 263.

took issue with the "system of spiritual mediation"[9] between the human being and God that the medieval church had developed. The issue that evoked Luther's protest, namely, indulgences*, was typical. The relation of the individual to God was mediated through the hierarchical order of the Church, with the pope at its head, and through the established rituals of the sacraments, whereby one secured one's standing before God. In contrast, the Reformers emphasized (1) the sovereignty of God, and the freedom of God in giving the grace* of salvation; (2) the importance of the scriptural word of God, over against the tradition of the Church; (3) the direct participation of believers in enacting their relationship with God, over against the mediation of the hierarchy. The latter emphasis led to the translation of the liturgy and the Bible into vernacular languages, to an increase in congregational participation in worship, and to a repudiation of sacramental confession*. The early Reformers did not intend a break with the Catholic Church, but their own radicalism, the intransigence of church authorities, and social and political developments made division inevitable.

A reforming council was finally called by Pope Paul III. It met at Trent*, beginning in 1545 (twenty-eight years after Luther's reform movement began), off and on until 1563. It produced a document on justification*, which might well have satisfied Luther, but it restated other controverted doctrines (e.g., the number of the sacraments, the sacrificial character of the eucharist) without much argumentation or any accommodation of Protestant objections. It took steps to curb abuses in the church, requiring bishops to live in their dioceses and ordering the institution of seminaries* for the education of priests. "Sale" of indulgences (giving indulgences for monetary donations) was ended. The council asked the pope to reform the mass*, and the result was a uniform order of the mass to be followed strictly everywhere in the Latin Rite (with some very few exceptions for local customs). This "Tridentine Mass" was familiar to Catholics until after the Second Vatican Council (1962-1965). No concessions were made to Protestants regarding congregational participation or the use of vernacular languages in the liturgy.

---

[9]John S. Dunne, *A Search for God in Time and Memory* (New York: Macmillan, 1967): 76.

The period after Trent is called the **Counter-Reformation*** period. In many respects, Catholicism defined itself over against Protestantism so that the Church often spoke and acted in a defensive spirit. But Catholic life was also renewed in ways that did not always have a direct reference to Protestantism. The Society of Jesus (Jesuits*), founded by St. Ignatius Loyola* in 1540, revitalized Catholic education and led the Church's expansion into foreign missions*. The sixteenth-century Spanish Carmelites, St. Teresa of Avila* and St. John of the Cross*, wrote classics of mystical spirituality and reformed their order. In the seventeenth century, Saints Francis de Sales*, Jane Frances de Chantal, and Vincent de Paul* did much to enrich the spirituality of the church in France and—through the religious communities that they founded or inspired—the rest of the world. Baroque art* and music* reflected the splendor and vigor of the Tridentine church.

At the same time, Europe was expanding its power throughout the world. The great age of explorations began in the late fifteenth century. It was led by the Spanish and Portuguese, whose explorers and conquerors were accompanied by Catholic missionaries. Franciscans reached the Americas in 1493, the year after their discovery by Europeans. In Central and South America and the southern part of North America, native populations were evangelized by Spanish and Portuguese missionaries, mostly Franciscans, Dominicans, and Jesuits. Unfortunately, the mission effort was closely tied to the effort by the colonizing powers to subjugate the natives (*see* NATIVE AMERICANS). The Jesuit St. Francis Xavier* established a school at Goa in India in 1542, and from there he and others went out to preach in south Asia, the East Indies, the Philippines, and Japan. Jesuits led by Matteo Ricci reached China in 1581. The strategy of the Jesuits in China (and also in India) was to adapt Catholicism as much as possible to the forms of native culture, and this led to the Chinese rites controversy* in the seventeenth and eighteenth centuries, which resulted in a curbing of the Jesuits and a setback to missionary efforts generally. In most parts of the world outside Europe and North America, not much progress was made in development of a native clergy and hierarchy until the twentieth century.

Between the reformation and the middle of the seventeenth century, Europe was recurrently torn by "wars of religion" between Catholic and Protestant powers. The last and worst of these was the Thirty Years' War (1618-1648) in Germany, concluded by the Peace of Westphalia in 1648. It reaffirmed the formula of the Peace of Augsburg

(1555), *cuius regio eius religio*, that is, the ruler of a territory is to determine the religion of that territory. Catholics controlled the central and southern parts of Western Europe (in particular, France, Spain, Italy, and Austria-Hungary) and also Poland, while the northern parts (e.g., England, Scotland, the Netherlands, most of Germany, the Scandinavian countries) were mainly Protestant.

In the seventeenth and eighteenth centuries, Western Europe underwent a major cultural shift, introducing what is now called "modernity." Like all such shifts, it is difficult to trace cause and effect relations among its component parts.[10] Its intellectual component is known as the **Enlightenment***. Enlightenment thought exalted the methods of mathematics and natural science and disparaged knowledge claims—such as Christian claims about Jesus—that depended on tradition. Influenced by the spectacle of the wars of religion, it rebelled against the political power of church authorities and favored religious toleration, giving rise to the idea of separation of church and state. It tended toward political theories that understood political and other communities as constructions or compacts by humans who were essentially individual units, rather than seeing the human being as essentially constituted by relations within social and political communities. Thus, on the whole, it favored democratic (or at least republican) forms of government. The economic reality corresponding to Enlightenment thought was the rise of capitalism* with its market economies.

The two political revolutions at the end of the eighteenth century, the American and French, could be seen as culminations of more than a century of Enlightenment thought, and their differences underlay differing evaluations of the Enlightenment heritage among Catholics on the two sides of the Atlantic. In Europe, Catholic thought, already on the defensive against Protestantism, was put increasingly on the defensive by the Enlightenment's challenges to tradition and authority. After the French Revolution* attacked the Church and sought to extirpate Christianity from France, Ultramontanism* gained sway in the Church, especially among the popes. Against the perceived chaos of the modern age, Ultramontanism took refuge in an ideal of a restored

---

[10]Charles Taylor, a Canadian Catholic philosopher, traces the origins and development of one of modernity's central concepts, that of the human self, in *Sources of the Self* (Cambridge, Mass.: Harvard University Press, 1989).

medieval Christendom, headed by a strong pope. It favored restoration of monarchies and opposed "liberalism"*, the nineteenth-century term for movements toward democracy, capitalism, and religious freedom*. Ultramontanism did not win out all at once. There was an important movement of Catholic liberalism in Europe in the first half of the nineteenth century, which had some early influence on Pope Pius IX* (1846-1878). But the pope soon turned toward Ultramontanism as he fought off challenges to his authority over the Papal States. His *Syllabus of Errors* (1864) took an intransigent stand against "progress, liberalism, and modern civilization," and in particular against religious freedom. In 1870 he lost the Papal States but, within the Church, registered his greatest triumph, when Vatican Council I* declared his infallibility*. He took other steps to centralize authority in the papacy, especially in increasingly reserving to himself the right to select bishops, previously often the prerogative of the local church (and often influenced by local secular rulers).

The identification of Church teaching authority (magisterium*) with the authority of the pope dates from the early nineteenth century, and Roman oversight of theologians was consolidated by a series of condemnations, e.g., of traditionalism* and ontologism*. Nineteenth-century popes allied themselves with the rising Roman school of Neo-Thomism (*see* THOMISM, SCHOLASTICISM), which endeavored to establish a firm foundation for the defense of Catholicism and the refutation of the errors of modern philosophy. In 1879, Pope Leo XIII*, in his encyclical *Aeterni Patris*, gave Thomism a quasi-official status in theology. Neo-Thomism sought to establish a timeless system of truths and had little or no appreciation of the historical character of meaning and truth (*see* HERMENEUTICS), whereas outside the Church the discovery of the importance of history was perhaps the most important characteristic of nineteenth-century thought. A movement in the Church that sought to take history into greater account in the interpretation of scripture and dogma* and to place more emphasis on human experience than was allowed by Neo-Thomism came to be called **Modernism***. Modernism was condemned in strong terms by Pope Pius X* in 1907. While some Modernist opinions were clearly at odds with the faith of the Church, the way in which Modernism was suppressed created a climate of suspicion and fear among theologians, which retarded Catholic intellectual life for decades.

The Church had grown slowly in the lands that became the United States. It was first brought to the North American continent by early sixteenth-century Spanish missionaries (*see* NATIVE AMERICANS), who founded the first parish church in North America at St. Augustine, Florida, in 1565. The first English Catholics in the American colonies landed in Maryland in 1634. Catholicism flourished during times of religious toleration in Maryland and Pennsylvania, but at other times and places it was severely restricted. Accordingly, Church leaders in the new American republic, beginning with Bishop John Carroll*, were by and large comfortable with its separation of church and state and the liberty thereby afforded the Church. They tended toward a more conciliar style of church governance, as epitomized in a series of seven provincial and three plenary councils at Baltimore between 1829 and 1884. Lay trusteeism*, influential in the first half of the nineteenth century but eventually suppressed by the bishops, was a movement for a measure of democracy in the Church. John England, bishop of Charleston, South Carolina, from 1820 to 1842, instituted a quasi-republican system of church government in his diocese, giving clergy and laity considerable authority in church affairs. Most American bishops initially opposed the movement to define papal infallibility, regarding it as at best "inopportune" or untimely, though all of them eventually accepted the doctrine. This relatively "liberal" and republican Catholicism gave rise to the movement known as "Americanism"*, censured by Pope Leo XIII in 1899. Too often, those associated with this trend in the nineteenth-century American Church were insufficiently critical of American society. For instance, no American bishops before the Civil War spoke out against slavery*.

By the end of the nineteenth century, a different tradition was dominant in American Catholicism. As large numbers of Catholic immigrants entered the United States throughout the nineteenth century, beginning with the Irish in the 1830s and followed by Germans, Italians, and Poles and other Slavs, America was increasingly torn by anti-immigrant and anti-Catholic sentiment. Within the Church, a more defensive spirit regarding the surrounding American culture competed with the accommodating trends mentioned earlier. American Catholicism developed a cohesive alternative culture which aimed, at one and the same time, to promote the participation of Catholics in American society and to preserve Catholic distinctiveness. Primary among the agencies of this alternative culture were the Catholic schools*, which grew to number more than thirteen thousand by 1965. Catholic hospitals* and religious houses also proliferated. A spirituality that emphasized devotions* to the Sacred Heart*, Mary and the saints magnified the differences between Catholics and Protestants. By the beginning of the twentieth century, the ultramontanist cast of American Catholicism, especially the personal cult of the popes, was strengthened by the increasing number of American bishops trained at the North American College in Rome.[11] The cohesive culture of the American "Catholic ghetto" lasted, despite numerous cracks and strains, until the Second Vatican Council, and many American Catholics still feel a sense of loss from its passing.[12]

Meanwhile, new trends were developing in Europe, which would eventually break down the Counter-Reformation synthesis and its twentieth-century American particularization. Pope Leo XIII's encyclical *Rerum novarum* (1891) began the modern era of Catholic social teaching*. While it still looked back to an idealized middle ages, it defended the rights of workers in modern industrial society. As Catholic social teaching developed in the teaching of subsequent popes, it acquired a more accepting (though never uncritical) stance toward modern society than had characterized the writings of Pius IX. Encouraged by these documents, Catholics became more involved in labor movements and organizations promoting social change. The encyclicals of Pope John XXIII* applied the principles of Catholic social teaching to the international order. Catholic biblical scholarship, though retarded by the suppression of Modernism, continued steadily to the point where it gained a charter of approval in the encyclical *Divino afflante spiritu* of Pope Pius XII in 1943. The liturgical movement* was recovering the ancient sources of the liturgy and recognizing the limitations of the Tridentine model. Catholic historians were increasingly acknowledging how much the Church had changed through the centuries, undermining the popular Counter-Reformation picture of the Church as a changeless rock of stability. Stimulated by the work of textual scholars, theologians in the mid-twentieth century undertook a *ressourcement* ("return to the sources"), bypassing Neo-Thomism in favor of a renewed appreciation of the thought and idiom

---

[11]On the themes of this paragraph, see Patricia Byrne, C.S.J., "American Ultramontanism," *Theological Studies* 56 (1995): 301-326.

[12]Its spirit is memorably captured in Richard Rodriguez, *Hunger of Memory* (New York: Bantam, 1983): 75-110.

of the Fathers of the Church*. All of these movements were to bear fruit in the Second Vatican Council.

III. Toward a World Church

Pope John XXIII took the Church by surprise when, in 1959, he announced his intention to call a council. His aim, he said, was aggiornamento*, or "updating" the Church to strengthen it for its mission in a changed world. Among the changes in the world since Vatican I was the unification of the globe through modern means of transportation and communication. Most of the approximately 800 bishops at Vatican I were European. Bishops could not travel to Vatican I by airplane, nor could they telephone home once they got there. No one could hear or see radio and television reports of the council. But all of this was possible at Vatican Council II*, which met in four sessions from 1962 to 1965. Of the approximately 2,800 bishops who took some part in the council, more than 40 percent were not from Europe or North America. People were aware of the unity of the world in more threatening ways as well. Two "world wars" had been fought within the previous fifty years, and the global conflict between the West and the Communist powers, together with the existence of atomic weapons, held out the prospect that a third world war could destroy all human life on earth—something that humans had not had in their power since the very beginning of the species.

The bishops, theologians and scholars who most shaped the Council were Europeans and North Americans (including some, such as Yves Congar* and John Courtney Murray*, who had previously suffered ecclesiastical censures and silencings), but their work did much to free the Church from the Western cultural forms it had assumed over the centuries. The Council's use of a biblical and patristic style of writing broke the hold of scholasticism. Its teaching on the collegiality* of the bishops with the pope reversed the emphasis on "papal monarchy" which dated back to Gregory VII in the eleventh century. Its treatment of the Church as first and foremost the entire "people of God" challenged the tendency, prevalent since the middle ages, to identify the Church with the hierarchy. Its openness to the use of vernacular languages led within a few years to the translation of the liturgy into Asian and African languages and other indigenous languages in which it had never before been celebrated. It encouraged diverse expressions of Christian faith in the many human cultures, thus implicitly separating Christianization from Westernization (*see* INCULTURATION). Its endorsement of the principle of religious freedom* reversed the teaching of nineteenth-century popes and, in an important sense, ended an era in church-state relations that dated from Constantine. Its document on the non-Christian religions took steps to end centuries of hostility toward Jews and set the Church on the path of dialogue with the non-Western religions, a dialogue that holds out the prospect that Catholicism might engage itself with the great religious heritages of India, China, and Japan as fruitfully as it has with the heritage of Greece and Rome.

Within the West, the Council committed the Church to the pursuit of ecumenism* with other Christians. Its portrait of the Church as the people of God and of the bishops as sharing the highest authority in the Church was more congenial to the Eastern Orthodox than earlier papal centralism had been. Its emphasis, in its documents on revelation* and liturgy, on the importance of scripture, its willingness to speak of all the faithful as possessing a "priesthood," and its call for intelligibility and congregational participation in liturgy addressed some of the central concerns of the Protestant Reformers. Since the council, ecumenical dialogues* have been the occasion for some of the most important developments in Catholic theology, and Catholics have become far more accustomed to joining with other Christians for prayer, study, and action. The Council's *Pastoral Constitution on the Church in the Modern World (Gaudium et spes)* replaced the Church's earlier stance of hostility and defensiveness toward modern Western cultural and political developments with a new attitude indicated by the key words, "dialogue" and "service."

In the Western European and North American Church, the years immediately after the Council were a time of rapid change. Changes in the liturgy were felt the most immediately by most Catholics, but institutional structures, religious life, theology, and social action also changed, sometimes drastically. Some found it a time of unprecedented excitement, while others were dismayed, and still others both excited and dismayed. In the American Church, the effect of the changes introduced by the Council was magnified by two other factors, so that three waves of change were superposed. One was the fact that the Church had just at that point gone from a primarily immigrant to "mainstream" status, as indicated by the election in 1960 of the first Catholic President, John F. Kennedy. The other was the changes going on in American society independently of the Church and known generally as "the Sixties." The structures of the cohesive Catholic culture that had lasted from the late nineteenth century began to give way. The number of diocesan priests dropped 20 percent between 1966 and 1985, as many men left the priesthood and fewer men entered seminaries. By 2005, there are projected to be only three-fifths as many diocesan priests in the United States as in 1966, even though the Church will be larger. The number of religious sisters dropped even more precipitously (38 percent between 1962 and 1988), leading to closings of, or major changes in, the institutions that they had staffed, chiefly schools* and hospitals*.

The Church in the West has experienced much conflict over sexual morality*. The Catholic tradition has seen the procreative dimension as primary, or at least as indispensable, in sexual relations, though it has shown increasing appreciation of the dimension of interpersonal love. Western secular thought, on the other hand, has tended to regard sexual relations as primarily personal transactions between autonomous partners. The development of effective means of birth control* has made a separation of the interpersonal from the procreative dimension of sexuality possible for heterosexuals, and if such a separation is morally permissible the primary argument against homosexual intercourse is removed. Immediately before and during Vatican II, there was much debate within the Church as to whether the use of the newly invented contraceptive pill could be morally acceptable. Pope John XXIII appointed a commission, which included married laymen and women, to study the issue, and it became known that the commission overwhelmingly favored a change in the traditional teaching. When a final decision against any change was issued by Pope Paul VI* in 1968 in the encyclical, *Humanae vitae*, it provoked a crisis. Many Catholics saw the pope's action as violating the consultative, collegial style of decision making that they saw as encouraged by the Council, and as rejecting the voice of the laity. Widespread public dissent* broke out, and married couples in large numbers ignored the teaching, claiming the right to follow their own consciences*. Dispute has continued over the related issues of premarital sex and homosexuality*, as well as over abortion*, which the Catholic tradition treats as an issue of the taking of innocent human life but Western secular culture tends to consider as a supplement to contraception as a means of birth control. In these cases as in that of contraception, the official teaching of the Church is rejected or ignored by large numbers of Western Catholics, especially the young.

The dominant figure in the last two decades of Church history has been Pope John Paul II*. Nothing more graphically illustrates the arrival of a "world Church" than the pope's highly publicized journeys to almost all parts of the world and the accolades he receives in the places he visits. Pope John Paul was instrumental in the fall of Communism in Eastern Europe, beginning in his native Poland, and he has also criticized Western society, especially its sexual mores and social injustice. He does not reject Vatican II's standpoint of dialogue with the world, but he subsumes "dialogue" under "evangelization"*, which is the term he prefers for the mission of the Church to the world. His vision calls for an increasingly centralized and disciplined Church. Though he professes to be faithful to Vatican II's ideal of collegiality*, he has strengthened the centralization of authority in the pope, for instance in the appointment of bishops, and he seems to resist any movements toward greater autonomy of local churches from Rome. He has taken measures to control the teaching of theology and to discipline theologians who dissent from official teachings. At the same time, he has strongly endorsed ecumenism, any progress in which would in all likelihood require some decentralizing of Church authority.

By 1993, almost half of the Catholics in the world lived in Africa, Asia, and Latin America. Increasingly, theologians in these areas begin not with the challenges to Christian faith posed by modern science and culture, but rather with the devastating poverty in which most people live. Shortly after the Council, liberation theology* began to develop as an outgrowth of the reflection and action of the base communities* in Latin America. It later developed Asian and African varieties, and it has influenced theologians in Europe and North America. Pope John Paul has been ambivalent toward liberation theology, sometimes using its language in calling for justice for the poor and oppressed, but opposing its use of Marxist categories and any challenges it makes to the institutional Church.

The Church cannot be truly a world Church if it neglects the voices of half of humanity. The most profound challenge that the Church faces today is posed by the movement of women toward full equality. Church authorities have endorsed women's rights (excluding any right to abortion) in the secular arena. But within the Church, the issue is more contested. In most of Christian history, men's voices have been dominant. This book contains eighty entries on individual Christians (including two on two individuals and one on four), plus seven more on "isms" named after individuals who are not the subject of articles as individuals. Of these ninety-two persons, selected for their impact on Catholic thought and institutional history, only nine are women. Almost all of the men selected were in holy orders; most were popes or bishops. Women's relative lack of influence on Catholic theology and institutions is closely connected with their exclusion from the sacrament of order*. Thus, the ordination of women* has been a central point of debate after Vatican II, though it did not arise at the Council itself. A 1976 Roman document, *Inter insigniores,* held that the nature of the priesthood, as intended by Christ, is such that women are ineligible for it, and Pope John Paul has declared the question of the ordination of women to the priesthood to be closed. While acknowledging the importance of the ordination issue, Catholic feminism* does not focus narrowly on it. Rather, it extends a far-ranging challenge to the Church to rethink its entire heritage of thought and practice, the original formation of which did not adequately attend to the experience of women.

In the United States it is popular to portray the Church as polarized over issues of sexuality, gender, and authority. Books have appeared with such titles as *The Battle for the American Church*[13] and *Holy Siege.*[14] When one turns from the mass media and the academy to local parishes, one finds that American Catholics are indeed often confused and divided over these issues. But here as elsewhere in the world, one also finds a desire for a living relation with God, a loyalty to the Church as community, an acceptance of the reforms of Vatican II, and, encompassing all the rest, a struggle to be faithful to Jesus within the particular cultural circumstances in which Catholics find themselves.[15] That struggle, its triumphs and its failures, will shape the Church in its next millennium as it has in the two millennia that this book surveys.

---

[13]By George A. Kelly (Garden City, N.Y.: Doubleday, 1979).

[14]Kenneth A. Briggs, *Holy Siege: The Year that Shook Catholic America* (San Francisco: HarperSanFrancisco, 1992).

[15]See, for instance, Andrew M. Greeley, *The Catholic Myth: The Behavior and Beliefs of American Catholics* (New York: Scribner, 1990).

Chronology

(All dates are A.D., unless otherwise noted)

ca. 4 B.C.-30 or 33   Life of Jesus (the standard B.C.-A.D. chronology devised by Dionysius Exiguus in the sixth century sets the birth of Christ at least four years too late).

50-120   Composition of New Testament Books.

ca. 50-100   Gradual separation of Christianity from Judaism.

ca. 64-67   Martyrdom of Saints Peter and Paul at Rome.

ca. 100-750   "Patristic period," i.e., the period of the Fathers of the Church, major early theologians.

ca. 100-300   Formation of the canon of scripture and the typical authority structure of the Church: bishop, priest, deacon. Challenge of Gnosticism.

ca. 130-200   Life of Irenaeus, theologian and bishop of Lyons.

ca. 184-254   Origen, theologian of Alexandria.

285   St. Antony withdraws into the desert; founder of monasticism.

312   Constantine becomes sole ruler in the West. He declares toleration for Christianity in 313 and gives it a favored status. From this point on, Christianity is the dominant religion in the Empire, and the Church and the state become closely intertwined.

325	First Council of Nicaea. First ecumenical council. Condemns Arianism. Declares that the Word of God is "one in being" with the Father. Original source of "Nicene Creed."
330	Constantinople, the "new Rome," dedicated on site of ancient Byzantium.
381	First Council of Constantinople. Source of final (or almost final) version of Nicene Creed. Declares divinity of Holy Spirit and the full humanity of Jesus.
354-430	St. Augustine. Greatest theologian of antiquity. Bishop of Hippo in North Africa. Author of *Confessions* and *City of God*.
431	Council of Ephesus declares, against Nestorius, that Mary is the "Mother of God."
ca. 432	St. Patrick begins missionary work in Ireland.
440-61	Reign of Pope Leo I ("the Great").
451	Council of Chalcedon declares, against the Monophysites, that Jesus is "one person in two natures," human and divine.
476	Fall of the Roman Empire in the West.
496	Baptism of Clovis, king of the Franks.
ca. 500	Benedict (ca. 480-547) writes his rule for monks; foundation for medieval Western monasticism.
500-1300	Feudalism. Church in the West closely tied to feudal system. The Pope eventually (by the eleventh century) becomes the most powerful political figure in Europe.
553	Second Council of Constantinople.

590-604	Reign of Pope Gregory I ("the Great").
680-81	Third Council of Constantinople.
727-843	Iconoclast controversy in East.
756	"Donation of Pepin": Frankish king grants pope sovereignty over territory in central Italy, which comes to be known as "Papal States."
768-814	Charlemagne comes to power in the West; declared Emperor in 800. Cultural revival in the West.
787	Second Council of Nicaea. Last council recognized as ecumenical by the Eastern Orthodox.
862	Cyril and Methodius undertake mission to the Slavs.
988	Conversion and baptism of St. Vladimir and the Kievan Rus, foundation of Christianity in Russia.
1033-1109	St. Anselm ("faith seeking understanding"). Greatest Western monastic theologian.
1054	The Patriarch of Constantinople and the delegates of the Pope solemnly excommunicate each other. Traditional date for the split between the Eastern Orthodox and the Roman Catholics.
1059-1122	Controversies over lay investiture.
1073-85	Reign of Pope Gregory VII (Hildebrand).
1096-1291	The Crusades.
1098	Foundation of Cistercian Order.
ca. 1100-1200	Foundation of universities in Europe.

1200-1350	High point of medieval theology. The great theologians are university teachers, e.g., Albert the Great (ca. 1200-1280); Bonaventure (1217-1274); Thomas Aquinas (1226?-1274); Duns Scotus (1266-1308); William of Ockham (ca. 1285-1347). Intellectually, this period is characterized by the rediscovery of Aristotelian thought and its integration into the Christian theological tradition.
1209	Founding of first mendicant order, the Order of Friars Minor (Franciscans), by St. Francis of Assisi (1182-1226).
1216	Foundation of second mendicant order, the Order of Preachers (Dominicans), by St. Dominic (1170-1221).
1231	Papal Inquisition established by Pope Gregory IX.
ca. 1300	Rise of nation states in Europe. Conflicts between kings and popes.
1309-77	Pope lives in Avignon, France; much under influence of King of France.
1347-50	Black Death devastates Western Europe.
1378-1417	Great Western Schism; rival popes in Rome and Avignon; after 1409, a third rival pope in Pisa.
1414-18	Council of Constance settles Great Western Schism; high point of conciliarism (council more powerful than pope).
ca. 1300-1500	Increasing corruption of late medieval and Renaissance Church; increasing demands for reform.
1431-45	Council of Basel-Ferrara-Florence. Move to Ferrara and Florence secures papal victory over conciliarists. Formula of union between Western Catholics and

Eastern Orthodox signed 1439, but not accepted in Eastern Church at large. Conciliarist party continue council at Basel, and later Lausanne, until 1449.

ca. 1452   Pope Nicholas V establishes Vatican Library.

1453   Constantinople falls to the Turks, ending Byzantine Empire.

1492   European discovery of the American continents; opens great age of exploration, missionary work, colonization.

1517   Martin Luther (1483-1546) circulates the *Ninety-Five Theses*, beginning the Protestant Reformation. Other major Reformation figures: Ulrich Zwingli (Zurich) (1484-1531); John Calvin (Geneva) (1509-1564).

1534   Act of Supremacy declares King Henry VIII head of the Church in England; beginning of English Reformation.

1539   Archbishop Juan de Zumárraga of Mexico publishes a catechism, the first book published in the Americas.

1540   Foundation of Society of Jesus (Jesuits).

1542   Francis Xavier arrives at Goa in India, establishes base for missionary work in Asia.

1545-63   Council of Trent reforms the Catholic Church, correcting many abuses but also sharpening the differences between the Catholic Church and the Protestants.

1555   Peace of Augsburg ratifies division of Europe along religious lines with principle *cuius regio eius religio*.

1565   Foundation of first Catholic parish in what is now the United States, St. Augustine, Florida.

1582   Pope Gregory XIII reforms the calendar.

1583   Matteo Ricci establishes mission in China.

1633   Condemnation of Galileo by the Inquisition.

1634   First English Catholics arrive in the American
                colonies, landing in Maryland in the *Ark* and the
                Dove.

1648   The Peace of Westphalia ends the Wars of Religion
                in Europe.

ca. 1650-1800   Enlightenment. Challenges belief in traditional history
                and in the supernatural (e.g., miracles). Catholic
                theology between Trent and Vatican II was largely
                defined in reaction against the Reformation and the
                Enlightenment.

1732   St. Alphonsus Liguori founds the Redemptorists.

1742   Pope Benedict XIV forbids the "Chinese Rites."

1769   Junipero Serra founds first mission in California, at
                San Diego de Alcalá.

1773   Pope Clement XIV suppresses the Jesuit order.

1789-99   French Revolution overthrows power of the Church
                in France, seeks to destroy Catholicism itself in
                France.

1789   John Carroll named bishop of newly created see of
                Baltimore; first Catholic bishop in the United States.

1809-14   Pope Pius VII held captive by Napoleon in France.

1830   Apparitions of Mary to St. Catherine Labouré,
                revealing Miraculous Medal, inaugurate modern
                Marian apparitions.

1854	Pope Pius IX declares dogma of the Immaculate Conception of Mary.
1864	Pope Pius IX, in the *Syllabus of Errors*, condemns many tendencies of modern society, including freedom of religion.
1869-70	First Vatican Council declares that the pope is, in certain circumstances, infallible.
1870	Papal States fall to Italian armies.
1884	Third Plenary Council of Baltimore mandates a standard catechism for United States.
1891	Pope Leo XIII publishes landmark social encyclical, *Rerum Novarum*, on the rights of labor.
1899	Pope Leo XIII sends letter *Testem benevolentiae* to Cardinal Gibbons, censuring "Americanism."
1907	Pope Pius X issues condemnation of Modernism in encyclical *Pascendi dominici gregis*.
1917	*Code of Canon Law* promulgated for Roman Rite.
1929	Lateran Pacts between the Holy See and the government of Italy establish sovereign state of Vatican City.
1943	Pope Pius XII, in his encyclical *Divino afflante Spiritu*, opens the way for the Catholic use of modern biblical scholarship.
1950	Pope Pius XII declares dogma of bodily Assumption of Mary.
1959	Pope John XXIII calls for Second Vatican Council.

1962-65   Second Vatican Council: The Church restates its
               nature and mission; affirms openness to other
               Christians, non-Christians, and the modern world;
               initiates reform of liturgy.

1968   Latin American bishops, meeting in Medellin,
               Colombia, espouse option for the poor; origin of
               liberation theology.

1968   Pope Paul VI, with his encyclical *Humanae vitae*,
               condemning artificial birth control, sparks a crisis of
               authority in the Church.

1977   Pope Paul VI canonizes Elizabeth Anne Bayley
               Seton, the first American-born saint, and Czech-born
               John Nepomucene Neumann, fourth archbishop of
               Philadelphia, the first American man named a saint.

1978   Pope Paul VI is succeeded by Pope John Paul I, who
               dies after a month in office. Cardinal Karol Wojtyla,
               archbishop of Krakow, succeeds him as Pope John
               Paul II, the first non-Italian pope in four hundred
               years.

1980   Archbishop Oscar Romero of San Salvador, El
               Salvador, assassinated.

1983   Revised *Code of Canon Law* promulgated for Roman
               Rite. Revised code for Eastern Catholic Churches
               promulgated 1990.

1992   *Catechism of the Catholic Church* approved.

1994   Pope John Paul II convenes Synod of the African
               Bishops in Rome.

1994   Pope John Paul II, in apostolic letter *Ordinatio
               sacerdotalis*, says ban against ordination of women as
               priests is "to be definitively held."

A

ABBOT, ABBESS, ABBEY (Aramaic *abba*, "father"). An abbot is superior of a monastic* community in the Benedictine tradition and a few other orders. (The corresponding terms in the Eastern Rites are "hegumen" or "archimandrite.") The equivalent title in a community of women is "abbess." A community headed by an abbot or abbess is an abbey. Otherwise, it is headed by a prior or prioress and called a priory (a priory may be independent or "dependent," that is, subject to the authority of an independent community). The difference between an abbey and an independent priory is largely a matter of words today, though in the past there have been differences in canon law. The older, larger houses are more likely to be called abbeys.

The word "abbot" derives from the custom among the early monks of the desert of addressing spiritual leaders as "Father" (*abba*) (*see* DESERT FATHERS AND MOTHERS). It became prominent in the West through its use in the Rule of St. Benedict* (sixth century). The Rule describes the ideal abbot as a nurturing spiritual parent or shepherd, who "holds the place of Christ in the community" and must take responsibility for the community. Most Benedictine abbots are elected for life, while in other communities abbots and abbesses are elected for specified terms. Elections must be confirmed by the local bishop or the pope. Abbots are exempt from control by the local bishop in regard to the affairs of their abbeys. An **abbot nullius [diocesis]** (an office mostly suppressed in 1976) has actual episcopal jurisdiction over his abbey and the surrounding territory, though he cannot ordain priests. Some medieval abbesses had similar quasi-episcopal powers; the last such arrangement was abolished in 1810.

The superior of a congregation consisting of several monasteries is called an **abbot general** or **archabbot**. The **Abbot Primate** is the head of the Benedictine Confederation.

ABELARD (ABAILARD), PETER (1079-ca. 1142). A leading intellectual figure of the twelfth century. Born at Pallet, near Nantes, he became a celebrated teacher of dialectic and theology at Paris. His love affair with his pupil Héloise led to his castration by agents of Héloise's uncle and guardian, Fulbert, and he retired to a monastery. He continued to write controversial works of theology, and some of his propositions were condemned at councils of Soissons (1121) and Sens (1140), the latter at the instigation of Bernard of Clairvaux*.

His importance lies especially in his introduction of dialectical methods into theology. His work, *Sic et non* (ca. 1122), uses seemingly contradictory texts from Scripture and the Fathers of the Church* as material for exercises in explanation and harmonization. Subsequent scholasticism* bears the mark of his influence. He also made contributions in logic (in the theory of universals), in ethics, where he emphasized the importance of the agent's intentions, and in the theory of the atonement*, where he saw Christ's work as bringing salvation chiefly through the example set by his life and the way it manifested God's love. Though bold and incautious in his use of logic, he was not, at least not in his intentions, guilty of heresy* or rationalism*.

ABORTION (procured abortion). The deliberate termination of pregnancy before the fetus is able to survive outside the womb or in such a way as to render the fetus unable to survive outside the womb.

There is little reference to abortion in the OT and none in the NT, but Catholic tradition, beginning in the first century (*Didachē* 2.2), is virtually uniform in condemning the act. The ground of the condemnation is that abortion is a direct attack upon human life; whether or not it was judged "homicide" depended on beliefs regarding the time of ensoulment or "animation" of the fetus. Arguments against contraception (*see* BIRTH CONTROL) also hold force against abortion; however, Catholic teaching regards abortion as primarily an issue of life-taking rather than of sexual morality. Official Catholic teaching, while not taking a position on the exact time of ensoulment, strongly opposes all direct abortion. Thus, according to the 1974 Vatican *Declaration on Procured Abortion*, "From the time that the ovum is fertilized, a life is begun which is neither that of the father nor of the mother; it is rather the life of a new human being with his own growth....Even if a doubt existed concerning whether the fruit of conception is already a human person, it is objectively a grave sin to dare to risk murder....Divine law and natural reason, therefore, exclude all right to the direct killing of an innocent man" (12-14). In the encyclical *Evangelium vitae* (1995), Pope John Paul II*, using language close to that of an infallible pronouncement, declared that "direct abortion ... always constitutes a grave moral disorder" (62). According to canon law, "A person who procures a successful abortion incurs an automatic excommunication" (Canon 1398). What is sometimes known as indirect abortion—termination of pregnancy as an unintended side effect of a medical procedure, such as removal of a cancerous uterus, done to save the life of the mother—is allowable.

Abortion became a subject of serious controversy in the Catholic Church after the liberalization of abortion laws in Western countries (e.g., the 1973 *Roe v. Wade* decision of the U.S. Supreme Court). Catholic theological opinion is in general supportive of official teaching on abortion, with some authors regarding this teaching as infallible. Yet emphasis on women's right to reproductive freedom and continued doubt as to the moral status of the human fetus have led to some dissent. Thus, for Charles Curran, abortion may be justified to save human life "or for a value commensurate with life itself." Daniel Maguire holds for a "moral right" to abortion in a broad range of cases. The organization Catholics for a Free Choice represents a pro-abortion position. Continuing doubts about the time when conception occurs and the status of the preembryo (zygote, morula, blastocyst) and early embryo, the availability of drugs that terminate pregnancy, and ecumenical dialogue with Protestant churches (which generally take a more liberal position on abortion) are factors that promise to complicate the abortion debate within North American Catholicism in the foreseeable future. One important emphasis in recent Catholic treatments of the abortion issue is on consistency in defense of life, as in Cardinal Joseph Bernardin's "seamless garment" ethic, which opposes abortion, euthanasia*, capital punishment*, and nuclear war*, while promoting public support for the hungry, unemployed, or otherwise needy.

Catholic authorities have generally insisted that abortion be forbidden or restricted by civil law and have in some cases publicly criticized or even excommunicated Catholic politicians who favor a right to abortion. *Evangelium vitae* says that laws permitting abortion are not true laws and may not be obeyed or supported. Church authorities, however, have not insisted on any specific course of action in regard to the legal restriction of abortion.

ABSOLUTION. The ritual act of remission of sins, which completes the sacrament of penance or reconciliation*. The formulary for absolution is "God, the Father of mercies, through the death and resurrection of his Son has reconciled the world to himself and sent the Holy Spirit among us for the forgiveness of sins; through the ministry of the Church may God give you pardon and peace, and I absolve you from your sins in the name of the Father and of the Son and of the Holy Spirit." This combines the **deprecatory** form of absolution ("may God give you pardon and peace") and the **declarative** form ("I absolve you"); the latter is regarded as essential. Normally, absolution follows individual confession*; however, in the Third Form of the Revised Rite of Penance of the Roman Ritual (1973), it follows a general confession of sins on the part of the congregation. This rite as a whole (the use of which is restricted) is sometimes referred to as "General Absolution." The term *absolution* is also applied to the remission of canonical censures, such as excommunication*.

ABSTINENCE. From eating meat, *see* **FAST AND ABSTINENCE**. From sexual activity, *see* **BIRTH CONTROL, CELIBACY**.

ACOLYTE (Gk *akolouthos*, "follower"). A minister who assists the priest* (and deacon*) at the altar*. This ministry* requires formal installation but does not make one a member of the clergy. It was created in its present form in 1972, before which time acolyte was the fourth and highest of the "minor orders" through which a man passed in preparation for priesthood. Ordinarily, the duties of an acolyte are carried out by **altar servers**, who are not formally installed, though they are sometimes informally called "acolytes." The ministry of acolyte is restricted to men, but in 1994 women were permitted to be altar servers in the Roman Rite.

ADVENT (Lt *adventus*, "coming"). The season of the liturgical year* that prepares for Christmas*. It begins with Evening Prayer I of the Sunday nearest to November 30 and ends on December 24. The earliest accounts of a celebration of Advent come from Spain and Gaul in the fourth century. Pope Gregory I* (590-604) established the four-week length of Advent. Since the eighth or ninth century, Advent has been regarded as the beginning of the liturgical year. The predominant theme in the Advent liturgy is anticipation or expectation, but from early times it has also had a penitential cast, associated with the coming of

Christ in the last judgment*. Since the twelfth century, it has been customary to speak of Advent as celebrating Christ's three comings: in the past (the Incarnation*), the present (grace*), and the future (the Parousia*). Gospel readings for Advent move from Jesus' discourses about the last times, through the stories of John the Baptist, to stories of Mary from the infancy narratives. OT readings emphasize prophecies (especially from Isaiah) of the coming of Christ.

AFRICAN AMERICAN CATHOLICISM. The first Black Catholics in what is now the United States were slaves who accompanied sixteenth-century Spanish explorers. A settlement of free Black Catholics was established near St. Augustine, Florida, in the late seventeenth century. In Maryland, the one English colony settled by Catholics, African slaves were imported from the 1630s onward. Many were owned by the Jesuits*, who operated large plantations. In Louisiana, ruled by the French from 1699 to 1763, Catholics imported Black slaves from the Caribbean. Catholic slave owners baptized and catechized their slaves and often made the other sacraments available to them. Catholics, including some bishops and religious communities, continued to hold slaves until the Civil War. Few Catholics, and no bishops, spoke out for abolition of slavery*.

The first community of Black religious sisters was the Oblate Sisters of Providence, founded in Baltimore in 1829. They opened a school for Black girls. The second was the Sisters of the Holy Family, founded in New Orleans in 1842. White religious communities generally did not admit Blacks until the twentieth century. A society of Black laity met weekly in Baltimore between 1843 and 1845.

The Catholic Church did not vigorously evangelize the newly freed Blacks after emancipation, though a few schools for Blacks were opened. The first Black bishop was James Augustine Healy, appointed bishop of Portland, Maine, in 1875. The first Black priest to work among African Americans was Augustus Tolton, ordained in Rome in 1888. In 1871, Mill Hill Missionaries arrived from England to work among African Americans. From them arose the Society of St. Joseph (Josephites), which nurtured vocations among Blacks. The Josephite Charles Randolph Uncles was the first Black priest ordained in the United States (1891). Inspired by Daniel Rudd, publisher of the Black-oriented *American Catholic Tribune*, five congresses of Black Catholic laity were held between 1889 and 1894. A second movement of lay Black Catholics was initiated by Thomas Wyatt Turner (1877-1978), who founded the Committee for the Advancement of Colored Catholics, later the Federated Colored Catholics, in 1919. An outgrowth of this group was the Catholic Interracial Council, founded by John LaFarge, a White Jesuit, in 1932. The 1930s saw the beginnings of serious efforts by Catholics to desegregate their own institutions. The task of integrating Catholic schools in the South was accomplished only in the 1960s, against great resistance. Major Catholic universities, such as Georgetown and Notre Dame, accepted African American students only in the 1950s.

The second African American bishop, Harold R. Perry, auxiliary of New Orleans, was appointed in 1966. In 1968, the National Black Clergy Caucus and the National Black Sisters Conference were founded. These and other organizations sponsored the National Black Catholic Congress, founded in 1985, which holds annual assemblies of African American Catholics and those who work with them. The National Office for Black Catholics, founded in 1970, is a central agency that aims to promote the participation of African Americans in the Church and the recognition of the Black heritage within Catholicism. The National Association of African American Catholic Deacons was formed in 1993.

Some Black Catholics have urged the creation of a separate rite for African Americans. An effort in this direction led to schism* in 1989, when Father George A. Stallings of Washington, D.C., formed the African American Catholic Congregation. Stallings was later consecrated an Old Catholic* bishop.

By 1994, there were around one million African American Catholics in the United States, including about three hundred priests and twelve bishops. In 1984, the Black Bishops issued a pastoral letter, *What We Have Seen and Heard,* announcing that "the black Catholic community in the American church has now come of age." The bishops declared, "There is a richness in our black experience that we must share with the entire people of God." Racism*, however, "remains ... the major impediment to evangelization* in our community."

AGGIORNAMENTO. (Ital "updating," from *giorno*, "day"). A term used by Pope John XXIII* to characterize the change in the Church which he hoped would be accomplished through Vatican Council II*.

ALBERT THE GREAT (ALBERTUS MAGNUS), ST. (before 1200-1280). One of the central intellectual figures of the thirteenth century.

He was the only man in the high middle ages to be called "the Great." He was born perhaps as early as 1193, probably in Lauingen in Germany, and entered the Dominican order probably in 1229. He taught in Paris and Cologne, in both of which Thomas Aquinas* was among his students. From 1260 to 1262 he was bishop of Regensburg in the Salzburg province. Today he is remembered chiefly as Thomas Aquinas's teacher, but in his own day his fame rested on his mastery of the newly rediscovered works of Aristotle*. He paraphrased (and supplemented) the works of Aristotle, seeking to make them "intelligible to the Latins." He wrote extensively in the areas of logic, natural science, philosophy, biblical commentary, and theology. The process of his canonization was impeded in the fifteenth century by false charges of involvement in sorcery and magic. He was beatified in 1622 and canonized and named a Doctor of the Church* in 1931. In 1941 he was named the patron saint* of natural scientists. His feast is celebrated on November 15.

ALBIGENSIANS. *See* CATHARS.

ALEXANDRIA. A major seaport on the Mediterranean coast of Egypt. Founded by Alexander the Great in 331 B.C., it became a leading intellectual and religious center. From its large Jewish community came the OT Book of Wisdom, the Septuagint (Greek translation of the OT), and the writings of Philo of Alexandria. Tradition has it that St. Mark brought Christianity to Alexandria and died there; clearly, Markan influence was felt there. Gnostic* teachers, among them Basilides and Valentinus, flourished in Alexandria in the second century. Late in the second century a Christian school was founded there by Pantaenus, whose successors included Clement of Alexandria and Origen*. In the fourth century, Arianism* arose in Alexandria; its chief opponent was Athanasius*, bishop of Alexandria from 328 to 373.

Alexandrian theology was strongly influenced by Platonism*, and its exegesis of the Bible tended toward the mystical and allegorical, in the tradition of Philo. It emphasized the divinity over the humanity of Christ. In all of these respects, it stood in contrast to the rival school of Antioch*. Alexandria-Antioch conflict reached its height in the fifth century with the attack by Cyril of Alexandria (bishop 412-444) on the theology of Nestorius*. Cyril's own theology of the "one divine nature" of Christ was developed into monophysitism* by Eutyches, and the latter was condemned at Chalcedon* in 451. After Chalcedon, monophysitism remained strong among the patriarchs (bishops) and people in Alexandria, leading to today's Coptic Church (*see* ORIENTAL ORTHODOX CHURCHES). In 538, a rival line of orthodox patriarchs was established, known as "Melchites" (from a Syriac word meaning "imperial") because of their loyalty to the emperor in Constantinople. Monothelitism*, an effort on the part of the orthodox patriarch to reconcile the two parties, was condemned by the Third Council of Constantinople* in 680.

ALL SAINTS. This feast, November 1, celebrates the whole Church, especially those who now enjoy eternal life. It developed in the eighth century from feasts of all martyrs*, which existed since at least the fourth century and were celebrated, in different places, on Easter Friday, the Sunday after Pentecost, and May 13. The latter date was chosen for the dedication of the Roman Pantheon to Christian use in 609. The earliest evidence for the date of November 1 for this feast comes from the late eighth century. That date may have arisen in the British Isles, where it was the date of the Celtic festival of Samhain, which marked the beginning of winter and was a time when the souls of the dead were said to return to earth. Relics of the customs of Samhain are found in the customs of modern **Halloween** (All Hallows' Eve = All Saints' Eve). The liturgy of All Saints celebrates the unity in Christ of the Church in heaven and on earth.

ALL SOULS. A feast, November 2, which is closely associated with All Saints*, but which adds an emphasis on prayer for the dead in purgatory*, who do not yet enjoy the fullness of eternal life. The earliest evidence for a liturgy for all the "faithful departed" is from the seventh century. The date of November 2 became standard when imposed by Abbot Odilo of Cluny on all Cluniac monastic houses in 998. In the liturgy, as reformed after Vatican Council II, the theme of hope* for eternal life through the resurrection of Jesus predominates over the somberness formerly characteristic of the feast.

ALTAR (Lt *altare*, probably cognate with *altus*, "high"). A place where sacrifice* is offered. It is ordinarily a raised place, as indicated by the derivation of the word. In a Catholic church, the altar combines the symbolism of (1) the sacrificial place, as in the altars in the Jewish Temple, only now related to the sacrifice of Jesus on the cross, and (2) the table on which Jesus and his disciples shared the Last Supper and post-Resurrection meals. It especially symbolizes Christ, who is high priest, sacrifice, and altar (Heb 13.10), and it is a focal point of Christ's eucharistic presence. In the Mass*, the priest moves to the altar to celebrate the liturgy of the eucharist.

The eucharistic table was first called an altar in the second century. In the fourth century, churches began to have fixed rather than movable altars. From early times, altars were often associated with martyrs*, e.g., by being built over their graves. In the Middle Ages it became customary (and eventually mandatory) for altars to contain relics*. In early churches, the altar was prominent in the apse or nave (*see* ARCHITECTURE, CHURCH), but in fifth-century Gaul it began to occupy a position at the apse wall. This change in position became general, partly due to the presence of large reliquaries (and later *retables*, decorated panels) behind altars. Liturgical reforms after the Second Vatican Council emphasized the eucharist as meal as well as sacrifice and the altar as table. The altar has been restored to a central position, closer to the congregation (often at the crossing of nave and transepts). It is freestanding, so that the priest may face the congregation across it in the celebration of the eucharist*.

Originally, there was only one altar in a church. Starting in the fifth century, the practice grew of having additional "side altars," as repositories for relics and to accommodate the increased number of masses being said. Recent liturgical directives have re-emphasized the single altar as symbol of the unity of the church and its worship. Side altars, if they exist, should be in separate chapels.

AMBROSE, ST. (ca. 339-397). Bishop and Doctor of the Church*. Born in Trier, the son of an imperial official, Ambrose became the governor of the province of Aemilia-Liguria, with seat at Milan. In controversy following the death of Auxentius, the Arian-sympathizing bishop of Milan, Ambrose was chosen bishop by popular acclamation, though he was still a catechumen. He was promptly baptized and, within a few days, ordained. He opposed Arianism* and the attempted revivals of paganism. He promoted the power of the Church over the state and the supremacy of Christian moral principles over the wishes of the Emperor. In 390, he succeeded in compelling the emperor Theodosius to do public penance for a massacre at Thessalonika. Although he was not an original thinker, he read Greek fluently and introduced much of the thought of the Greek Fathers into the West. His allegorical, somewhat Platonic scriptural interpretations were influential in the conversion of St. Augustine*. His extant writings include numerous treatises, sermons, and letters, as well as several hymns. His best-known works are *De officiis ministrorum (The Duties of the Clergy)*, which is based closely on Cicero's *De officiis*, and *On the Sacraments*. He promoted asceticism and monasticism and introduced the antiphonal chanting of psalms into the West. His feast is celebrated on December 7.

AMERICAN INDIAN MISSIONS. *See* NATIVE AMERICANS.

AMERICANISM. A movement within the late nineteenth-century American Catholic church. Its context was the question of sustaining the faith of immigrant Catholics in the environment of American culture. Leading Americanists were John Ireland, archbishop of St. Paul, Minnesota, John J. Keane, bishop of Richmond and later rector of The Catholic University of America, and Denis O'Connell, rector of the North American College in Rome. The Americanists favored adaptation of Catholicism to American culture, holding that there was no fundamental conflict between the two. In time, they adopted a form of the American Puritan idea of the messianic mission of America; in the Americanist version, the American Catholic church was to lead the Catholic Church into a new democratic age. The Americanists favored Catholic acceptance of religious freedom*, separation of church and state, and openness to labor movements, to people of other faiths, and to modern science and culture. In these concerns, they allied themselves with liberal movements in European Catholicism and they can be seen as forerunners of Vatican Council II*. However, their reformism was entangled with their espousal of American political expansionism, as represented in the Spanish-American War.

In their understanding of the mission of America, the Americanists developed some ideas of Isaac Hecker (1819-1888) (*see* PAULISTS), whom they saw as a sort of founding father. A French version of Walter Elliott's biography of Hecker provoked a controversy in Europe in 1897, and this ultimately led to a censure of "Americanism" by Pope Leo XIII* in the apostolic letter, *Testem Benevolentiae*, in 1899. The letter censured the theses that the Church must adapt its doctrines to modern civilization and that greater religious liberty should be introduced into the Church. It insisted that only the Church, and not individuals within the Church, could adapt church practices to cultural circumstances, and it censured several theses on nature and grace that were thought to be associated with Hecker. It is debatable whether Hecker or any of the major Americanists actually taught the ideas censured in *Testem Benevolentiae*, but the document effectively put an end to the movement as a force in American and European Catholicism.

ANATHEMA. A Greek word meaning "accursed." In the LXX it translates the Hebrew word meaning "under the ban," a status that could entail the destruction of a city and its inhabitants. St. Paul uses it in various senses of "accursed"; Gal 1.9 most clearly approximates the later use of the term: "If anyone preaches to you a gospel other than the one that you received, let that one be accursed." In the Church, the term comes to refer to those whose opinions are judged to be heresy*; they are "anathema," which is equivalent to being under excommunication*. The earliest recorded instance of "anathema" in this sense is at the Council of Elvira in Spain in 306.

ANCHORITE (fem., **ANCHORESS**) (Gk *anachorein*, to withdraw). Someone who lives the religious life* in solitude, as contrasted with a cenobite*, who lives in community. Sometimes "anchorite" is synonymous with "hermit"; a hermit, however, may live some distance from a community, while an anchorite normally lives in a cell near a community. Thus, medieval anchorites and anchoresses, such as Julian of Norwich*, often lived in cells built against the walls of churches.

ANGELS (Gk *angelos*, "messenger"). Created spiritual beings who serve God, especially as messengers to human beings. The OT speaks often of angels as messengers from God or manifestations of God, as well as of their worship of God in heaven. It does not speculate on their nature or origin. The NT speaks similarly, with the Letter to the Hebrews emphasizing Christ's superiority over all angels. The story of a sin of the angels prior to human history arises in the Judaism of the late OT period; it is not reflected in the OT, but it is presupposed in the NT in 2 Pt 2.4 and Jude 6.

Christian tradition has always insisted on the angels' creation by God and their subordination to God. Some early Christian writers, e.g., Augustine*, described them as having aerial or ethereal bodies, but from the time of Pseudo-Dionysius* (sixth century) they have been described as pure spirits. Pseudo-Dionysius also produced the standard medieval classification of angels into nine choirs: cherubim, seraphim, thrones, dominations, virtues, powers, principalities, archangels, angels. The scholasticism of the thirteenth century, notably Thomas Aquinas*, combined biblical and traditional teaching on angels with Aristotelian and Arabic speculation on separate intelligences to produce a complex theory of angels as pure spirits whose intellects have no need of sensory powers.

Belief in **guardian angels** draws on Jewish and pagan beliefs about guardian spirits. Jesus presupposes such a belief in Mt 18.10, and it is generally found in Christian tradition, but it is not developed clearly in theology until the middle ages.

According to the *Catechism of the Catholic Church*, "The existence of the spiritual, non-corporeal beings that Sacred Scripture usually calls 'angels' is a truth of faith" (328). The Fourth Lateran Council* (1215) declared God to be the creator of angels ("God ... created from nothing both spiritual and corporeal creatures, that is to say angelic and earthly ...." [DS 800]). But some theologians argue that IV Lateran did not *assert* the existence of angels but merely presupposed them in its intent to assert that God is the creator of whatever there is. Of theologians who hold that position, some hold the existence of angels nonetheless to be a matter of faith (in which belief is required) as an inseparable part of the teaching of scripture and tradition. Others hold it to be a nonessential presupposition of what is taught as binding in faith.

The principal feast on which the Church honors angels is that of Saints Michael, Gabriel, and Raphael, Archangels, on September 29. These are the only three angels named in the Bible. This feast originated not later than the sixth century as a feast of St. Michael, on the anniversary of the dedication of a basilica in his honor at Rome. Since 1670, October 2 has been celebrated as the feast of the Guardian Angels.

ANGELUS (Lt "angel"). A prayer based on the Annunciation scene in Luke 1.26-38. It consists of three verses ("versicles") and responses, each followed by a "Hail Mary," then a fourth versicle and response, and a concluding prayer. The first versicle, "The angel of the Lord declared unto Mary," gives the prayer its name. Traditionally, this prayer is said at 6 A.M., noon, and 6 P.M., and church bells ring to indicate these times for prayer. The elements of this practice developed gradually, perhaps beginning in the eleventh century with the recitation of three Hail Mary's at the ringing of the curfew bell. The prayer reached its standard form in the sixteenth century.

ANGLICAN COMMUNION. The Anglican Communion comprises those churches in communion with the see of Canterbury and recognizing the spiritual leadership of the Archbishop of Canterbury. It includes the Church of England, the Episcopal Church in the U.S.A., the Anglican Church of Canada, and more than twenty other national and regional churches. The bishops of the Anglican Communion assemble once every ten years for the Lambeth Conference (named for the London palace of the Archbishop of Canterbury).

The separation of the Church of England from the Catholic Church began over the issue of the divorce of King Henry VIII of England from Catherine of Aragon. After Pope Clement VII refused to issue a decree of nullity for their marriage, the Act of Supremacy was passed in 1534, making the King the "supreme head in earth of the Church of England." Growing Protestant* influence under King Edward VI (1547-1553) was followed by restoration of papal supremacy under Queen Mary (1553-1558). The present shape of the Church of England, independent of Rome but fairly traditional in structure and worship, was largely achieved under Queen Elizabeth I (1558-1603). The Oxford (or Tractarian) Movement (1833-1845) promoted Catholic elements in the Anglican churches and popularized the term *Anglo-Catholic*; a number of its leaders, including J. H. Newman*, eventually became Roman Catholics.

The churches of the Anglican Communion retain the orders of bishop*, priest*, and deacon*, the creeds* of the early Church, and a liturgy, traditional in form, set forth in the Book of Common Prayer. From the Roman Catholic point of view, dispute over the validity* of Anglican ordinations was settled in the negative in 1896 by Pope Leo XIII's* apostolic letter, *Apostolicae Curae*. The finality of this decision has been questioned in recent theology and ecumenical documents, but at present Anglican priests who wish to become Catholic priests must be reordained.

Ecumenical relations between the Anglican and Roman Catholic churches have proceeded actively since Vatican Council II. A Common Declaration by Pope Paul VI* and Archbishop Michael Ramsey of Canterbury in 1966 led to the establishment in 1970 of the Anglican-Roman Catholic International Commission (ARCIC). This commission produced "agreed statements" on the eucharist (1971), ministry (1973), and authority in the Church (1976 and 1979). Its Final Report appeared in 1982. The official Vatican response, prepared jointly by the Congregation for the Doctrine of the Faith* and the Pontifical Council for Promoting Christian Unity, was issued in 1991 and expressed numerous reservations, chiefly having to do with authority* in the Church. Meanwhile, in 1982, Pope John Paul II* and Archbishop Robert Runcie of Canterbury appointed ARCIC-II, which has produced agreed statements on "Salvation and the Church" (1986) and "Church as Communion" (1991). In the United States, the official Anglican-Roman Catholic consultation (ARC/USA) has produced a series of agreed statements, including ones on the ordination of women* and on Anglican orders (1990). There have been many covenants and joint activities between Catholic and Episcopal dioceses and parishes in the United States.

While much progress has been made toward full communion between the Anglican and Roman Catholic churches, the issues of papal authority and Anglican orders remain stumbling blocks. More prominent obstacles in practice recently have been the ordination of women in many churches of the Anglican Communion (including the Episcopal Church in the United States in 1974 and the Church of England in 1994) and disagreements over moral issues.

ANNULMENT of a marriage*. The issuance of a Declaration of Nullity or the process leading to the issuance of such a declaration. A Declaration of Nullity is an official statement that a presumed marriage did not exist as a sacramentally valid union. Some of the grounds recognized in the 1983 Code of Canon Law for annulment of a marriage are lack of ability to give valid consent at the time of marriage, lack of ability to carry out the obligations of marriage, reservations that preclude full consent to marriage, deception, coercion, and failure to observe proper form of marriage ceremony. Declarations of Nullity are normally issued by a diocesan tribunal*. Annulment should be distinguished from official dissolution of an acknowledged marriage (*see* DIVORCE). The distinction between annulment and dissolution, and Catholic practice in regard to both, have evolved along with changing understandings of what constitute the sacramental validity* and indissolubility of marriage. Present practice is substantially based in sixteenth-century papal documents, adapted in the canon law* codes of 1917 and 1983.

ANOINTING OF THE SICK. A sacrament* administered to Catholics in serious illness or old age. Two New Testament texts refer to anointing. Mark 6.13 speaks of how the Twelve, sent out by Jesus, "anointed with oil many who were sick and cured them." James 5.14-15 provides more direct background to later sacramental practice: "Is anyone among you sick? He should summon the presbyters [elders] of the church, and they should pray over him and anoint [him] with oil in the name of the Lord, and the prayer of faith will save the sick person, and the Lord will raise him up. If he has committed any sins, he will be forgiven." Scattered patristic texts indicate that the oil, blessed by the bishop, was taken home and applied externally or drunk by the sick person, or applied by others to him or her. The purpose was physical or spiritual healing or both. The Carolingian reform of the ninth century associated the anointing ritual with the growing practice of deathbed penance* and hence restricted the ministry of anointing to priests. This trend continued in the Middle Ages. The term *extreme unction* became widespread in the twelfth century—the anointing (*unctio*) is the last (*extrema*) received by a Christian (the anointings of baptism and confirmation having preceded), and it is received at the end of life (*in extremis*). The Council of Trent*, in response to Protestant Reformers' criticisms of Catholic practice of the sacrament, declared (1551) that extreme unction is a genuine sacrament instituted by Christ, that it confers grace, forgives sins, comforts the sick, and can bring about physical healing, and that its proper minister is the ordained priest. It refused to limit the sacrament to the dying, but said it was to be administered "to the sick, especially those who are so desperately ill that they seem near to death." The Second Vatican Council in its *Constitution on the Sacred Liturgy* (1964) says, "'Extreme unction,' which can also and better be called 'anointing of the sick,' is not a sacrament exclusively for those who are involved in the final crisis of life and death" (73). Viaticum* is to be regarded as the sacrament for the dying and is to be administered after anointing.

The present rites for this sacrament are found in English in *Pastoral Care of the Sick: Rites for Anointing and Viaticum* (1982). It includes communal rites within and outside mass and a rite for use in a hospital or institution. There is an abbreviated rite for emergencies. The sacrament is intended for "the faithful whose health is seriously impaired by sickness or old age." Emphasis is no longer on the sacrament as preparation for dying. Hence the terms "extreme unction" and "last rites" are to be avoided; however, the sacrament is not to be administered indiscriminately to those not seriously ill. The reformed rituals emphasize the involvement of the whole Church in healing* and the fact that the sacrament is a liturgical act. Communal celebration, which comprises an introductory rite, a liturgy of the word, a liturgy of anointing, and an optional communion service, is accordingly encouraged. The purpose of the sacrament is to bring the saving power of Christ to the sick person and accordingly to effect spiritual and perhaps physical healing. In accordance with the Council of Trent, the sacrament must be administered by a priest. Some theologians and pastoral ministers, however, argue in favor of allowing deacons or specially designated laypeople, such as hospital chaplains, to administer the sacrament.

ANSELM, ST. (1033-1109). One of the leading theologians of the Middle Ages, called by some the founder of scholasticism*. Born in Aosta in the Piedmont, he entered the Benedictine monastery of Bec in Normandy in 1059, becoming its prior in 1063 and abbot in 1078. He became Archbishop of Canterbury in 1093.

His theological work combines the Augustinian and Benedictine traditions with Aristotelian logic or dialectic, which was being revived in the schools of his day. He left numerous writings, of which the most important are the *Proslogion (Address)*, originally titled "Faith Seeking Understanding" (1077), and *Cur Deus homo (Why God Became Man)* (1098). The *Proslogion* introduces the famous "ontological argument" (the name originates with Immanuel Kant) for God's existence: God is that-than-which-a-greater-cannot-be-thought. If one denies that that-than-which-a-greater-cannot-be-thought exists, one can still *think* of it as existing, but, since to exist is greater than not to exist, one is then *thinking* of something *greater* than that-than-which-a-greater-*cannot-be-thought*. Hence, to deny God's existence involves one in a self-contradiction. *Cur Deus homo* offers the classic medieval theory of the atonement* in arguing that only a God-man can make the satisfaction that God's justice requires for human sin.

Anselm's tenure as Archbishop of Canterbury was marked by recurrent conflict with kings William Rufus and Henry I over the revenues of the church of Canterbury and the relative authority of pope and king. As a result, Anselm was exiled twice, for about six years in all.

Anselm's feast is celebrated on April 21. He was declared a Doctor of the Church* in 1720.

ANTIOCH. City in ancient Syria on the Orontes River (now Antakya in Turkey). It was the third-ranking city in the Mediterranean world, behind Rome* and Alexandria*, and a leading Christian center. Acts 11.19-26 records the founding of the church at Antioch, where the disciples were first called "Christians." At Antioch, Gentiles were first received into the Christian community without having to be circumcised. This became a source of great conflict and a turning point in the history of the Church (Acts 15). St. Paul was a "prophet and teacher" in the church at Antioch (Acts 13.1) and began his first missionary journey from there. St. Peter was also prominent in the Church at Antioch, and later tradition makes him its first bishop. The Gospel of Matthew may have been written at Antioch. In the second century, bishop Ignatius of Antioch* strongly defended the church order centered on a single bishop in each local church (the "monepiscopate").

In contrast with the rival school of Alexandria, Antiochene theology in the third through fifth centuries tended toward a relatively literal, historical reading of Scripture and an emphasis on the humanity of Jesus. Paul of Samosata (bishop of Antioch, 260-268) was condemned for teaching that the human Jesus was only a man, on whom the Word of God rested. Nestorius, an Antiochene who became bishop of Constantinople, was condemned in 431 for his resistance to calling Mary "Mother of God" (*theotokos*) (*see* NESTORIANISM). The greatest Antiochene theologian was Theodore of Mopsuestia (ca. 350-428). Antiochene theology is also reflected in the preaching of John Chrysostom*. Antioch declined as a Christian center after a sack by the Persians in 540 and conquest by the Arabs in 638.

APOCALYPTIC (Gk *apocalypsis*, "revelation" or "unveiling"). A genre of literature that grows out of OT prophecy. Apocalyptic literature flourished from about 200 B.C. to about A.D. 200. Typically, it is pseudonymous, attributed to great figures of the past. It employs symbolic visions to portray the victory of God over the powers that govern the present world order. The primary examples of apocalyptic literature in the Bible are the Book of Daniel in the OT and the Book of Revelation (or "Apocalypse") in the NT. There are numerous apocryphal* Jewish and Christian apocalyptic writings. *See also* ESCHATOLOGY.

APOCRYPHA (Gk "things hidden"). (1) Term used mainly by Protestants for Old Testament books that were not included in the Hebrew canon but were included in Greek versions of the Old

Testament, such as the Septuagint. While most Protestants do not regard these works as belonging to the canon of Scripture, the Catholic Church officially declared at the Council of Trent* in 1548 that most of them belonged to the canon. Catholics usually call these books **deuterocanonical books** (*see* BIBLE). (2) "New Testament apocrypha" denotes works similar in form to the NT writings, but of later date (second to fourth century) or lesser authenticity or dubious orthodoxy*, or some combination of these. NT apocrypha include gospels, acts of the apostles, letters, and apocalyptic writings*.

APOLLINARIANISM. A Christological heresy* named for its founder, Apollinaris (or Apollinarius) (ca. 310-ca. 390). Apollinaris was a strong opponent of Arianism* and a friend of St. Athanasius*, to whom he gave hospitality during the latter's exile. He became bishop of Laodicea in Syria in 361. In defending the divinity of Christ, he held that in Christ the divine word (*logos*) was joined to a human body or flesh (*sarx*). Christ possessed a human "sensitive soul" (the part of the soul that governs sensation and body functions), but in him the *logos* took the place of the human "rational soul" or mind. This is not very different from the position that Athanasius took unreflectively through most of his career, but once Apollinaris made it explicit, it became evident that it denied the true humanity of Christ, and thus broke the link between the savior and those he saved. Apollinaris went into schism* in 375. His Christology* was condemned at a synod in Rome, circa 377, and at the ecumenical First Council of Constantinople* in 381.

APOLOGETICS (Gk *apologia*, "a speech for the defense"). The branch of theology that is concerned with the defense of the truth or reasonableness of Christian faith. Apologetics always presupposes some existing framework of thought, within which or in opposition to which the reasonableness of faith must be established. The early Apologists* defended Christian faith within the culture of pagan antiquity, often arguing that the Christian religion achieved the ideals of the Greek and Roman philosophers better than Greek and Roman religion did. Some early apologetics, for instance in Justin Martyr*, defended Christianity against Jewish criticisms, arguing that Christianity was the fulfillment of Jewish prophecies. Some of the principal works of medieval apologetics, notably the *Summa contra Gentiles* of St. Thomas Aquinas*, were directed against Islam*. After the Protestant*

Reformation, much Catholic apologetics was directed against Protestant claims; thus, the themes of the pope, sacraments, and tradition* were prominent. From the eighteenth into the twentieth centuries, Catholic apologetics (with some noteworthy exceptions, such as John Henry Newman* and Maurice Blondel) tended to assume a rationalistic, quasi-scientific form, grounded in "human reason" or assumptions supposedly acceptable to every reasonable person. The influential apologetic work of Giovanni Perrone (1794-1876), for instance, sought on such a basis to establish (1) the possibility of revelation*, (2) the necessity of revelation, (3) the actuality of revelation (including a defense of the historical reliability of the Gospels, and, on this basis, of the divinity of Christ), and (4) the authority of the Catholic Church as the true Church of Christ. In the twentieth century the assumptions on which such works were based came under much criticism, as did the very idea of arguing to the conclusions of Christian faith from a neutral, "rational" standpoint. At present, the term *apologetics* is somewhat out of use, and the concerns of apologetics are assumed into the discipline of "fundamental theology." This seeks to establish the reasonableness (but not necessarily the truth) of Christian faith within the assumptions of contemporary thought, or to challenge some of those assumptions on Christian grounds, or to display Christian assumptions as a no less reasonable alternative. The importance for apologetics not only of rational argument but also of Christian practice is increasingly recognized; a major consideration in the defense of the claims of Christian faith is the quality of life such faith makes possible.

APOLOGIST. Anyone who does apologetics*. Capitalized, "Apologists" designates a group of second- and third-century writers who defended Christian faith in the context of the pagan culture, especially the philosophy, of the Roman Empire. The Apologists include Quadratus, Aristides, Athenagoras, Justin Martyr*, the author of the anonymous letter to Diognetus, Tatian, Theophilus of Antioch, Tertullian*, and Minucius Felix.

APOPHATIC (Gk *apophēmi*, "say no"). The apophatic or negative way (*via negativa*) in Christian spirituality uses negative language to emphasize the transcendence of God, the vast difference between God and creatures. It complements the affirmative or **kataphatic** way, which uses language or images drawn from the world of creatures in order to give some expression to the mystery* of God the creator.

APOSTASY (Gk *apostasis*, "a standing away from"). Defined in canon law as "the total repudiation of the Christian faith" (by someone who formerly believed) (Canon 751). It is distinguished from heresy* and schism*. Apostasy was regarded in the early Church as an unpardonable sin. Later, it could be forgiven after public penance*. Contemporary theologians are more willing to recognize mitigating conditions in the mind or heart of the apostate.

APOSTLE (Gk *apostellein*, "to send"). Literally, "one who is sent" (equivalent to Heb *shāliach*). In the NT it refers to those who were witnesses to the risen Jesus and given by him the mission and power to proclaim the gospel as his representatives. Although it is customary to speak of the "twelve apostles," this expression is used in the gospels only at Mt 10.2. The Twelve were an inner circle among Jesus' disciples, chosen by Jesus to correspond to the twelve tribes of Israel and thus to show the continuity of Jesus' kingdom with the Israelite people of the OT (Lk 22.30). Luke-Acts usually identifies the "apostles" with the Twelve, although Luke twice speaks of Paul and Barnabas as "apostles" (Acts 14.4,14). Paul probably includes the Twelve among the apostles, but uses "apostle" more broadly (e.g., 1 Cor 15.5-7) and insists on his own credentials as an apostle (1 Cor 15.9-10). In Romans 16.7, he may refer to a woman, Junia, as an apostle.

Apostles had great authority* in the Church. Acts presents them as being empowered by the Holy Spirit to witness to Jesus (1.8), working wonders (5.12), supervising the Jerusalem community (6.2), and resolving disputes in other churches (15.2,6). Paul sees apostleship as a charismatic gift, first in rank in the Body of Christ (1 Cor 12.28-29). The Pauline Letter to the Ephesians speaks of the apostles, along with the prophets, as the "foundation" of the Church (2.20).

APOSTOLIC SEE. *See* HOLY SEE.

APOSTOLICITY. One of the four marks of the Church mentioned in the Nicene Creed*. It means oneness in belief and practice with the faith of the apostles*. An essential sign of this apostolicity, according to Catholic tradition, is the **APOSTOLIC SUCCESSION** of bishops*. This means both that there is an unbroken line of descent from the apostles to the bishops of the present and that "by divine institution the bishops have succeeded to the place of the apostles as shepherds of the

Church, and the one who hears them hears Christ, but whoever rejects them rejects Christ and him who sent Christ (see Lk 10.16)" (Vatican II, LG 20).

Historians think it unlikely that the apostles ordained successors and called them "bishops." Rather, the apostles made some provisions for the continuity of authority after their death, perhaps different arrangements in different places, and the office of bishop and the institution of ordination (*see* ORDER, SACRAMENT OF) emerged over the course of time as the most effective way to guarantee such continuity. Theologically, this process can be seen as having been guided by the Holy Spirit*. By ca. A.D. 95, the First Letter of Clement of Rome speaks of the Apostles as having "tested in the Spirit their first converts in order to make of them bishops and deacons for those who would later come to believe" (42.44). Irenaeus*, writing ca. 180, strongly defends the apostolic succession of bishops as a mark of the true Church and a guarantee of the true faith.

The Catholic Church holds that ordination by a bishop in apostolic succession is necessary for a valid priestly ministry and hence a valid eucharist*. This is an obstacle to Catholic recognition of the ministry and eucharist in Protestant* churches, most of which have not preserved the succession of bishops. It is currently under discussion by theologians, especially in ecumenical dialogues*, whether apostolic succession, in the sense of orderly transmission of the beliefs, practices, and ministry of the Church, might be adequately or partially preserved in some of these churches without the outward sign of the succession of bishops.

APOSTOLIC FATHERS. Authors of orthodox* Christian writings contemporary with or slightly later in time than the New Testament, but not included in it. These writings include the *Didache** (ca. A.D. 70-110), the *Letter of Barnabas* (ca. 70-130), the *First Letter of Clement* (ca. 95), the letters of St. Ignatius of Antioch* (ca. 108-117), the letter of Polycarp (ca. 110?), the fragments of Papias (ca. 130?), the *Martyrdom of Polycarp* (155-56), the *Shepherd of Hermas* (ca. 140-155), and the homily known as the *Second Letter of Clement*, probably dating from the middle of the second century. Sometimes the *Letter to Diognetus* is also classed with these writings (*see* APOLOGISTS).

APPARITION. An appearance of Jesus*, Mary*, an angel*, a saint*, or other sacred personage. Apparitions of Mary have had the greatest impact on the life of the Church and are the focus of this article. An apparition is a sort of vision (*see* MYSTICAL PHENOMENA). The term *apparition* implies authenticity and tends to be used when some authenticating factor is present, such as simultaneous vision by a group of people. Important apparitions of Mary in modern times include that at Guadalupe in Mexico in 1531, that to St. Catherine Labouré revealing the Miraculous Medal in 1830, that at La Salette in France in 1846, those at Lourdes in France in 1858, those at Fatima in Portugal in 1917, and those at Medjugorje in Yugoslavia (now Bosnia) beginning in 1981. The official Church is cautious in its judgment of alleged apparitions. Normally, the evaluation is left to the local bishop, but the Vatican or national episcopal conferences* may become involved. In arriving at a judgment, the Church considers the origin of the alleged apparition, looking for any evidence of fraud, delusion, or error; the character of the visionaries; the message of the apparition and the extent of its consistency with the faith of the Church; and the effects of the apparition for sacramental life and the promotion of Christian virtue. Official judgments range from condemnation, through declaration that there is no clear evidence of supernatural activity (perhaps the most common finding), through acceptance in some way, such as approval of prayers and devotions, through formal declarations of approval, to the establishment of a feast. Thus, for instance, February 11 is the feast of Our Lady of Lourdes. The Church never requires belief in the authenticity of any alleged apparition, however well attested, as a matter of faith.

ARCHBISHOP. In the Latin Church, a title that, in most cases, denotes a **metropolitan**, that is, the ordinary (bishop having jurisdiction) of the principal diocese* in an ecclesiastical province. This diocese is called an **ARCHDIOCESE**. The archbishop possesses certain powers of supervision over the other dioceses in the province but does not govern them directly. He has the power to convoke and preside over a provincial council*. Bishops who are not metropolitans are sometimes awarded the title of archbishop, for reasons of honor or service in the Roman Curia* or papal diplomatic corps. The title has been in use in the West since the ninth century.

ARCHITECTURE, CHURCH. The earliest Christians met for worship in private homes (Acts 2.46). The first church buildings were simply houses set apart for worship. The earliest known Christian church is the church-house found at the excavation of Dura Europos in Syria, dating from ca. 230-250. In the fourth century, when Christianity moved from being a clandestine, sometimes persecuted sect to having official approval and encouragement, Christians began to build churches modeled on the public halls called **basilicas***. Basilicas were rectangular, with a central space (*nave*) and aisles on the side surrounded by columns. They were often richly furnished inside, for instance, with mosaics. There was some variation as to the location of the altar*, the lectern, and the benches for the clergy. In the **Byzantine** churches, beginning in Constantinople* under Justinian* in the sixth century, the basilica was covered by a wide central dome. The classic example of Byzantine church architecture is Hagia Sophia in Constantinople (Istanbul), built 532-537. Its dome, which has no internal supports, affords a spectacular display of light through its many windows. Later variations on Byzantine style multiply the number of domes. The interiors of Byzantine churches were decorated with extensive mosaics, which came to take on a systematic pattern reflecting the divine and earthly hierarchy*. The building as a whole was an earthly representation of the heavenly mysteries.

Few churches survive from the early Middle Ages in the West, after the fall of the Roman Empire. The most celebrated are small monastic chapels in remote areas. The **Romanesque** style developed in larger monasteries and then cathedrals between 950 and 1150. Romanesque churches retained the basic basilica plan, surrounded by thick, fortress-like walls, and having exterior towers. Ceilings were vaulted, with round arches. Relatively little light could be admitted. Buildings were often decorated with stone sculpture, an art lost in the West in preceding centuries. The **Gothic** style originated in France in the twelfth century. It is characterized by great heights of open spaces, enabled by a new mastery of the pointed arch. Flying buttresses on the outside of buildings carried weight downward toward the ground, removing the need for thick walls. The walls became something like a skeletal frame, allowing space for extensive stained glass windows, with the play of colored lights creating a numinous interior atmosphere. Classic examples of thirteenth-century French Gothic architecture are the cathedrals at Chartres, Amiens and Nôtre-Dame at Paris. The style spread to Germany, England, and Spain, where it developed local variations.

Gothic took relatively little hold in Italy, which in the early fifteenth century saw a revival of classical Roman styles, leading to **Renaissance*** architecture. Renaissance style favored geometrical patterns and mathematical symbolism. Its ideals of symmetry, clarity, and harmony were seen as reflecting the perfections of God. A representative feature was the dome on a circular drum. St. Peter's Basilica* in Rome is a Renaissance church, but with Baroque decoration in the interior. The **Baroque** style, which began to develop in the late sixteenth century and predominated in Italy, France and Spain through the eighteenth century, is distinctive more for its internal decor in painting and sculpture (discussed under ART) than for the structural forms used. It is not easy to draw a line between structure and ornament in Baroque churches, as spatial effects joined with painting and sculpture (often by means of visual illusion) to evoke a dramatic response. Some of the most striking Baroque churches are in the New World, such as the Sagrario of the cathedral of Mexico City. Revivals of Greek, Roman, and Gothic style characterized the churches, Catholic and Protestant, of the nineteenth century.

Twentieth-century Catholic church architecture has been affected by the availability of new building materials in reinforced concrete, glass, iron and steel, and by changes in liturgy*. The axiom of **modern architecture**, "Form follows function," cohered well with the liturgical movement's* emphasis on the liturgical action. More than those of earlier eras, modern churches tend to focus attention on the action and are designed to foster congregational participation. This is particularly true of those that have been built since Vatican Council II's* liturgical reforms. The altar, lectern, and baptismal font are more centrally located, and visibility and audibility are important considerations (in some respects, the reforms have restored features of the early basilicas). The U.S. Bishops' Committee on the Liturgy's document, *Environment and Art in Catholic Worship* (1978), states well the principles governing contemporary church architecture at its best: "The environment is appropriate when it is beautiful, when it is hospitable, when it clearly invites and needs an assembly of people to complete it …, when it brings people close together so that they can see and hear the entire liturgical action, when it helps people feel involved and become involved" (24).

ARIANISM. A heresy* that takes its name from Arius (ca. 256-ca. 336), a priest of Alexandria*. Arius' doctrine arose from an attempt to reconcile the belief that God had to suffer in order to save humankind with the belief that the high God could not suffer. Arius held that the divine in Christ, the Word (*Logos**) or Son of God, was less than fully divine, but rather was a creature (*ktisma*)—although the first among creatures—through whom the others were made. In Christ, this Word took on a human body, but not a human soul. Thus the Arian Christ was neither fully divine nor fully human. The doctrine of Arius was condemned by his bishop, Alexander, and later condemned at the first ecumenical council*, convoked by the emperor Constantine* at Nicaea in 325. The First Council of Nicaea* proclaimed that the Son of God is *homoousios*, "one in being," with the Father. The council did not settle the issue, and controversy raged through the fourth century, with what has been called a phantasmagoria of synods and councils embracing the Arian position (though not under that name), the Nicene position, and various positions in between. The dispute, complicated enough theologically, was further complicated by the involvement of contestants for power in the Christian empire after Constantine. The Nicene position was championed by St. Athanasius* and later by the Cappadocian Fathers*, but its opponents felt that it threatened the distinction between the Father and the Son. Opposing positions included: (1) that of Eunomius, called "anomoian" (from *anomoios*, "unlike") by its opponents, which held that the Son was unlike the Father in being; (2) the "homoians," who held that the Son was "like" (*homoios*) the Father; and (3) the "homoiousians" (later called "Semi-Arians") who held that the Son was "like in being" (*homoiousios*) to the Father. Eventually, the controversy was settled in the empire in favor of the Nicene position at the First Council of Constantinople* in 381. Yet, due to the work of the Arian bishop Ulfilas (ca. 311-383), who translated the Bible into Gothic, Arianism remained prominent among Germanic tribes for the next several centuries.

ARISTOTELIANISM. The philosophy of Aristotle (384-322 B.C.), along with Plato* the greatest of the Greek philosophers. At first a pupil of Plato, Aristotle diverged from his teacher in assigning primary reality to the particular thing rather than to the general "form" of a class of things. Some characteristics of Aristotelian thought are generalization from observation, the use of syllogistic reasoning, and the search for purposes or "final causes" in nature. Aristotle left a large body of writing (much of it in the form of lecture notes) covering most of the fields of study known in the ancient world. Particularly influential were his treatises on logic, biological and physical science, metaphysics, ethics, and politics.

Partly because Aristotle's philosophy was judged less useful for religious and spiritual ends and partly because of accidents in the transmission of texts, it was not as prominent in antiquity as was Plato's. Only a few of his works (some treatises dealing with logic) were translated into Latin in late antiquity, and these were all that the medieval West possessed until the twelfth century. Aristotle's works were preserved, translated, and studied in the centers of Islamic culture during the Middle Ages, and it was from there—especially Spain—that they arrived in a culturally resurgent Western Europe in the twelfth century. By late in the thirteenth century, almost all of Aristotle's works had been translated. Their arrival coincided with the rise of universities* and sparked an intellectual revolution, changing both the methods and the content of study (*see* SCHOLASTICISM).

Theology* always involves the interpretation of religious tradition in a philosophical or cultural matrix, and for Christian theology in the West that matrix had been mainly Platonic since the second century. The task of integrating the newly discovered Aristotelian material into a Christian view of the world and of rethinking Christian theology in an Aristotelian framework fell to the theological masters of the thirteenth century, chiefly St. Thomas Aquinas*, but also St. Bonaventure* and St. Albert the Great*, among others. This enterprise was threatened both by conservative resistance to Aristotle and by the extreme positions taken by a group now called "radical Aristotelians," whose leading figure was Siger of Brabant (ca. 1240-1283/4). These thinkers held that the conclusions of Aristotle (as interpreted by Jewish and Islamic commentators, notably Ibn Roshd [or Averroes; 1126-1198]) were the necessary conclusions of reason, though we might know by faith that some of them, e.g., that the world is everlasting and that the individual soul* is not immortal, are not true (some of these thinkers may not have made, or seriously made, this last proviso). The result was a series of ecclesiastical condemnations of Aristotelian positions, the most important condemning 219 propositions (some of them probably asserted by Thomas Aquinas) by the bishop of Paris in 1277.

Despite this opposition, Aristotelian thought continued to dominate the Western intellectual world through the fourteenth and fifteenth centuries. Thereafter, the Protestant* Reformation challenged Aristotelianism in theology, and the Renaissance* and the rise of modern science dislodged Aristotle from his central position in the humanities and sciences. Aristotelianism, however, in the form of scholasticism, remained dominant in Catholic theology until the twentieth century. Though no longer as central to theology as in previous centuries, Aristotelianism, as one of the fountainheads of the Western intellectual tradition, is likely to continue to be a source of new inspirations. Thus, for instance, the revival of the Aristotelian ethics of the virtues* in late twentieth-century philosophy has led to a new appreciation of the virtues in Catholic moral theology.

ART. This article concerns mainly the visual arts of painting, mosaic, and sculpture, especially as they are used in church buildings. On other arts, *see* ARCHITECTURE, DANCE, MUSIC, VESSELS, VESTMENTS. Even among visual arts, readers should be aware of the great range of artistic media, from calligraphy to videotape, put to service in the Church but not mentioned specifically here.

According to the *Constitution on the Sacred Liturgy* of Vatican Council II* (1963), "The fine arts are very rightly reckoned among the most noble expressions of human creativity—and especially religious art .... The Church has always been a friend of the fine arts. ... The chief purpose for this has been so that the things which form part of liturgical worship can be suitable, dignified, and beautiful—signs and symbols of things above" (SC 122). "The Church has not regarded any style of art as its own," but draws and should draw on all styles and traditions that are suitable for worship (123). The United States Bishops' Committee on the Liturgy's *Environment and Art in Catholic Worship* (1978) adds that, in light of the incarnation*, "Christians have not hesitated to use every human art in their celebration of the saving work of God in Jesus Christ" (4). The document adds that the liturgy draws on "all human faculties: body, mind, senses, imagination, emotions, memory" (5). Such principles, though contemporary, provide a framework for understanding the great expanse of Catholic uses of the visual arts over the centuries.

Early Christian art. In Judaism, representational religious art is forbidden as idolatry ("You shall not carve idols"—Ex 20.4), though this prohibition was not observed as universally in the Judaism of early Christian times as later. As Christianity moved into the Gentile world, it soon dropped such strictures, probably because of belief in the incarnation. Much of the earliest Christian art we possess comes from the **catacombs**, underground tunnels used for burials in Rome and other parts of Italy. There we find paintings from the early third century, combining biblical and pagan motifs, e.g., Christ as the good shepherd or as Orpheus. There are also sculptures, some with Christian symbolism, e.g., the fish. Once Christianity became publicly accepted under Constantine* in 313, its art became more stately. Church buildings were basilicas*, designed on the model of a public audience hall. **Mosaics**, consisting of small pieces of colored stone embedded in cement on a wall, decorated the basilicas, often depicting biblical narratives. **Frescoes** (painted on plaster while still wet) are also found, as at Dura Europos in northern Syria, where a Christian church-house dating from the early third century was discovered.

A distinctive **Coptic** tradition in art, sculpture, and architecture, blending Greco-Roman and Egyptian elements, developed in Egypt in the third century, lasting until the thirteenth. One characteristic is distortion of the proportions of figures through emphasis on large colored areas. The **Byzantine** tradition flourished at Constantinople* from the fourth century to the thirteenth. Its churches featured prominent wall and ceiling mosaics. As time passed, the mosaics concentrated more on timeless truths of theology than on biblical narratives. Images of Christ enthroned as *pantocrator* ("ruler of all") often held a dominant place. Images became flat, figures faced the viewer, and bright colors were used—features that were transferred to the painted icon*. The great crisis of Christian art was centered in Constantinople: the controversy over iconoclasm*. In two periods, 730 to 787 and 815 to 843, the iconoclasts, who rejected the use of sacred images, were in power. Once they were decisively vanquished, the theology of the victors, which interpreted the icon as an earthly participation in a heavenly reality, led in the East to a canonization of the particular form of the icon as it existed in the ninth century and thus to a failure to develop other styles of religious art.

The fall of the Roman Empire in the West interrupted classical traditions in the arts. Little painting or sculpture survives from the early Middle Ages in the West. One art that flourished in the period was manuscript illumination, of which Celtic monks in Ireland produced two classics: the *Book of Kells* and the *Lindisfarne Gospels* (both eighth century), while the Ardagh Chalice is a classic of metalwork from the same period.

Tenth-century Germany under the Ottonian emperors was the site of important sculpture in ivory. Sculpture in stone was revived in the church buildings of the **Romanesque** period of the eleventh and twelfth centuries, often using images of animals from ancient mythology. Images of biblical figures and the saints and images teaching moral lessons are also found. The **Gothic** cathedrals, which were built first in France and then all over Europe from the twelfth through the fifteenth centuries, were ornamented inside and out with stone sculpture, more realistic in its depiction of human figures than the preceding period. The central visual feature of the interior of Gothic churches was the play of light through stained glass windows, an art that reached its peak at this time.

The **Renaissance***, which began in Italy in the fourteenth century, was a "revival" or "rebirth" (terms that were not used of it until the sixteenth century) of classical forms and styles in the arts and, increasingly, a birth of new styles. Features of Renaissance art include greater verisimilitude in painting, the use of visual perspective, and increased use of variation in shading. Though it became more secularized in its later phases, Renaissance art was chiefly religious, both in its themes and in its locations. A great classic of Renaissance religious art is the ceiling of the Sistine Chapel in the Vatican, painted in fresco by Michelangelo from 1508 to 1512.

The Protestant* Reformers de-emphasized the visual aspect of church buildings in favor of the Word of Scripture and preaching. Though religious art flourished in parts of Protestant Europe, Protestant church buildings were austere in their decoration. In contrast, **Baroque** art developed in Catholic countries, especially Italy and Spain, in the seventeenth and eighteenth centuries. In Baroque art, the classical forms of the Renaissance gave way to a greater sense of movement in painting and sculpture, a freer play of imagination, and much use of visual illusion. Baroque art was closely tied to the piety of the Counter-Reformation*, its proliferation of images contradicting Protestant austerity and often focusing on the themes least congenial to Protestants, for instance the saints. After the high point of the Baroque era, there was a greater separation between the Catholic church and the development of the arts, as artists sought independence from religious authorities and the latter regarded developments in art with caution and suspicion. The nineteenth century was not a period of great originality in Catholic religious art.

The greatest force for change in Catholic attitudes toward art in the twentieth century has been the liturgical movement*, which held that art in liturgical settings is meant to serve and enhance the experience of liturgical worship. The styles of art most compatible with the liturgy as reformed after Vatican II are abstract forms that do not draw attention away from the liturgical action. Vatican II called for moderation in the number of images used in churches and for the removal of works of art "which are offensive to a true religious sense … whether this is because of the decadence of the forms, or because the art is below standard, mediocre and pretentious" (SC 124). The Church has been increasingly open to the styles and materials of all forms of modern art and to non-European as well as European traditions. Wherever the Church is inculturated*, Catholics may say, as does the U.S. Bishops' Committee, "Contemporary art is our own … and belongs in our celebrations as surely as we do" (33).

ASCENSION of Jesus. The "raising up" of Jesus to be with God in heaven*. This signifies the end of Jesus' appearances after his resurrection* and his transition from earthly life to a new mode of existence with God "in glory." Most NT texts that refer to the Ascension do not describe it nor situate it at a fixed point in time. Luke, however, describes it in his gospel as occurring on Easter Sunday (24.50-51) and in Acts 1.3-11 as occurring forty days after the resurrection. As often in the Bible, the "forty" should be regarded as a round number, here indicating a period of preparation (in this case, for Jesus' departure and the coming of the Holy Spirit*). Initially, the Ascension was celebrated together with Pentecost*, but since the late fourth century it has been celebrated on the Thursday that occurs forty days after Easter, in accordance with the account in Acts. In some regions, the celebration of the Ascension is transferred to the Sunday following that Thursday.

ASCETICISM (Gk *askēsis*, "exercise, training, discipline"). Spiritual self-discipline and self-denial. Asceticism is found in all religions; in Christianity, it specifically refers to removing obstacles to following Christ. Typically, but not necessarily, it involves such practices as fasting*, giving up of property, and celibacy* or sexual abstinence. Christian asceticism has been affected by world-rejecting or body-rejecting philosophies and religions such as Gnosticism* and Neo-Platonism, but at its most authentic shows a respect for the goodness of bodily creation. Individual Christian ascetics or small communities of ascetics (e.g., virgins*) are known from the early days of Christianity. At first, they were associated with local Christian communities. Beginning in the early fourth century, there was considerable movement to the desert in Egypt and Palestine (*see* DESERT FATHERS AND MOTHERS), first among individuals and small groups, then among organized communities (*see* MONASTICISM). The fourth century also saw the development of a temporary period of asceticism during the catechumenate*. In scholastic theology of the modern period, **ascetical theology** referred to the branch of spirituality* that dealt with what could be accomplished by human effort (aided by grace*). Asceticism, in the broad sense of spiritual training and discipline, is an essential part of any Christian life.

ASSUMPTION of the Blessed Virgin Mary. A dogma* of the Catholic faith proclaimed by Pope Pius XII* in the apostolic constitution *Munificentissimus Deus* in 1950 as follows: "We proclaim and define it to be a dogma revealed by God that the immaculate mother of God, Mary ever Virgin, when the course of her earthly life was finished, was taken up body and soul into the glory of heaven" (DS 3904). Mary, in other words, has already attained the final bodily resurrection* that is promised to all faithful Christians, and thus, in Mary, the Church has already reached its ultimate salvation. It is left as an open question whether Mary died or was raised to eternal life without bodily death.

This doctrine is not stated explicitly in the Scriptures. Rather it makes explicit something that is implicit in the Scripture and tradition when studied in the light of faith. The "sense of the faithful"* (*sensus fidelium*) is the crucial factor in the development of this doctrine, in which liturgy seems to have preceded theology. A feast of Mary's "birthday into heaven" was celebrated on August 15 in the fifth century. It came to be called the "Dormition", or "falling asleep", of Mary and was adopted at Rome around 650. Since the eighth century the feast has been called the Assumption; it is still celebrated on August 15. A homily, dating from the mid-sixth or seventh century, by Theoteknos, bishop of Livias on the Jordan River, discusses the Assumption by name (in Greek, *Analepsis*). The doctrine was strongly defended by John Damascene (d. 739) and accepted in the East since his time. It was slower to be accepted in the West (partly due to the opposition to it by a ninth-century treatise falsely attributed to Jerome*) but was generally accepted by the thirteenth century. Prior to defining the doctrine of the Assumption, Pius XII polled all the bishops of the Church as to whether it should be defined, receiving an overwhelmingly positive response.

ASSYRIAN CHURCH OF THE EAST (CHURCH OF THE EAST). The oldest surviving church to have split from the mainstream Catholic tradition. Centered in Edessa, Persia ("East Syria"), this church rejected the Council of Ephesus* (431) and its condemnation of Nestorianism's* denial that Mary is *theotokos* (God-bearer, Mother of God). It has therefore often been called "Nestorian," but in 1984 its Patriarch, Mar Denkha IV, requested that this name not be used, and it is doubtful how Nestorian the church's theology is. The church flourished in medieval times, extending to India and China, with its patriarchal see in Baghdad, but was almost annihilated during the invasions of Tamerlane in the fourteenth century. In the sixteenth century, many of its members entered communion with Rome, becoming the Chaldean Church. The church survived to modern times chiefly in Kurdistan, from which Turkish persecution drove many members into Iraq and other parts of the world, especially the United States, in the early twentieth century. The Patriarch now resides in Morton Grove, Illinois. In November 1994, Mar Denkha IV and Pope John Paul II* signed a common Christological declaration at Rome.

ATHANASIUS, ST. (ca. 297-373). Bishop of Alexandria* 328-373 and Doctor of the Church*. Athanasius is best known for leading the defense, against Arianism*, of the doctrine of the First Council of Nicaea* (325) that the Son of God is *homoousios*, or "one in being", with the Father. In later years, he also wrote in defense of the divinity of the Holy Spirit*. His involvement in doctrinal, ecclesiastical, and political controversies caused him to be exiled four times from his see at Alexandria. His major works include *Against the Pagans* and *On the Incarnation of the Word* (335-336), two or perhaps three *Orations against the Arians* (339-345), and the *Life of Antony* (357), a classic of monastic biography. His feast is celebrated on May 2.

ATHEISM. The denial of the existence of God*. It is to be distinguished from **agnosticism** (a word coined by Thomas H. Huxley in the late nineteenth century), which is the claim that the existence of

God is unknown or unknowable. "Atheism" often refers to the denial of the existence of God or gods conceived in a particular way; thus, Socrates in the fifth century B.C. and the early Christians were called "atheists" because they rejected their societies' common beliefs about the gods. The Jain religion and some traditions of Hinduism* and Buddhism* are called "atheistic" because of their denial of a personal (and sometimes even an impersonal) supreme being. These traditions, however, for the most part remain religious, in that they affirm a transcendent reality, state (e.g., Buddhist nirvana), or dimension of the human soul. Atheism in the context of modern Western Christianity begins in the eighteenth century in such figures as Denis Diderot (1713-1784) and Paul Henri d'Holbach (1723-1789), who claimed that the natural world can be explained sufficiently in its own terms, without reference to God. In the nineteenth century, this argument is combined with the contention that belief in God prevents human beings from asserting the freedom that is properly theirs. These two arguments combine, in different proportions, in the leading figures of modern atheism, namely Ludwig Feuerbach (1804-1872), Karl Marx (1818-1883), Friedrich Nietzsche (1844-1900), and Sigmund Freud (1856-1939).

Recent Church documents, especially Vatican II's *Pastoral Constitution on the Church in the Modern World* (GS 19-21), combine a strong rejection of atheism with a recognition of the genuine values that often motivate atheism. They call for dialogue with atheists, for the sake of greater knowledge of truth, removal of misunderstandings of Christian faith, and promotion of shared values of human freedom and dignity.

ATONEMENT (Engl, to make "at one"). In the Old Testament, ritual acts that overcome sin* or the effects of sin and reconcile human beings to God (thus, *Yom Kippur*, the "Day of Atonement"). In Christian theology, "atonement" refers to the overcoming of sin and the reconciliation of human beings with God through the life, death, and resurrection of Jesus. The Catholic Church affirms the fact of atonement by Jesus, but does not proclaim any dogma* of how atonement is accomplished. The so-called "classical" theory, put forward by Irenaeus* in the second century, identifies the atoning work of Jesus with his victory over the devil*, who had held humans in his power. Other significant theories were developed by Anselm* and Abelard*. *See also* REDEMPTION.

AUGUSTINE, ST. (354-430). Bishop and Doctor of the Church*, the greatest of the Western Fathers of the Church*. His thought gave shape to the theology of the Western Church for the millennium after his death. Born in Thagaste, Numidia (now in Algeria), of a pagan father and a Christian mother, St. Monica, Augustine was not baptized as an infant nor given much education in the Christian faith. He studied rhetoric and later taught it at Carthage, Rome, and Milan. While a student, he became an adherent of the dualistic religion of Manichaeism*. Gradually he became disaffected from both Manichaean theology and its moral code. These difficulties, together with the preaching of St. Ambrose* and a discovery of neo-Platonic philosophy (*see* PLATONISM), led to Augustine's conversion to Catholic Christianity and his baptism at Milan in 387. He tells the story of his early life and conversion, combining it with a theology of the fall and return of the soul, in his *Confessions* (397-401).

Augustine returned to North Africa, becoming a priest in 391 and a bishop at Hippo (in modern Tunisia) in 395. He dedicated much of his life to preaching and writing, and among his extant works are close to one hundred books, more than two hundred letters, and in excess of four hundred sermons. His early writings are strongly neo-Platonic, but over time the Scriptures (especially the Pauline letters) and the life of the Church came to be the primary influences. Besides the *Confessions*, his most influential works were *The City of God* (413-426), which criticizes pagan religion and philosophy and narrates the origin, progress, and destiny of the City of God (united in love of God) and the city of man (which prefers self to God), and *On the Trinity* (ca. 399-419), which takes biblical, logical, and speculative approaches to the doctrine. He engaged in three major theological controversies: against the Manichaeans, he defended the essential goodness of all that is; against the Donatists*, he argued that the efficacity of the sacraments* is based on the power that Christ gave the Church, rather than on the character of the minister of the sacrament; against the Pelagians*, he insisted on the necessity of divine grace* for the doing of any act that leads toward salvation, and he developed theories of original sin* and predestination*. His monastic rule, written originally for his priests at Hippo, was adopted by canons regular in the twelfth century and later followed by Augustinians, Dominicans*, and Servites, among others. His feast is celebrated on August 28.

AUTHORITY IN THE CHURCH. Philosophers distinguish *epistemic* authority (authority in regard to knowledge, such as that possessed by an expert) from *deontic* authority (authority in regard to action, such as that possessed by a ruler or military commander). The concept of authority in the church combines both of these, but draws on a third, more fundamental sense: authority as a spiritual gift, empowering one to speak or act on behalf of God. This is the sense in which the gospels often speak of Jesus' authority (*exousia*, also translated "power"), e.g., to teach (Mt 7.29), to forgive sins (Mt 9.6), and to cast out demons (Lk 4.36), as well as the authority he gives to the apostles to cast out demons (Mk 3.15).

Authority or empowerment to take part in the work of Jesus is given first of all to all Christians (Vatican II, LG 10-12). Authority belongs in a special sense, however, to those with certain charismatic gifts (see, e.g., 1 Cor 12.28) and saints* and holy people, and in another sense to those ordained for leadership in the institutional Church (*see* ORDER, SACRAMENT OF). Charismatic and institutional authority, although often in tension throughout history, should not be seen as fundamentally opposed. First among charismatic gifts is that of being an apostle* (1 Cor 12.28), which confers an authority to "build up" the Church (2 Cor 10.8). The Catholic Church sees bishops*, with the pope* at their head, as successors to the authority given by Jesus to the apostles (*see* APOSTOLICITY). Vatican Council II* characterizes it as authority to teach, to make holy, and to govern.

Authority to teach is called *magisterium**. This term, in modern usage, applies specifically to the authority that is entrusted to bishops to speak in the name of Christ, and is to be distinguished from the ordinary epistemic authority (also called *magisterium* in earlier usage) belonging to scholars and theologians. In this context, the authority of living persons is related and in some cases subordinate to the authority of texts, firstly that of the Scriptures, written under the inspiration* of the Holy Spirit*, secondly that of documents expressing the judgment of authoritative bodies (such as councils*) or individuals (such as popes).

Jesus insists that authority to govern among his followers must be exercised not as domination but as service (Mk 10.43-45, Lk 22.25-27). Vatican II renews this emphasis in its treatment of the authority of bishops (LG 27).

AVIGNON. City in southern France on the Rhône River. From 1309 to 1377 it was the residence of the popes. Pope Clement V (elected 1305), though remaining Bishop of Rome, established his court at Avignon as a temporary measure because of strife in Italy and conflict between the papacy and the French king, Philip IV. Although Avignon was not technically in France, the kings of France had great influence over the Avignon popes. A papal palace was built in Avignon and endowed luxuriously. To build it and to support the magnificence of their court, the Avignon popes developed a system of papal taxation, which caused much tension in the late medieval Church. Gregory XI returned the papacy to Rome in 1377, dying there in 1378. He was succeeded at Rome in 1378 by Urban VI, but later that year the cardinals repented of their choice and elected Clement VII, who reigned as pope (antipope) in Avignon, while Urban remained pope in Rome. This was the beginning of the Great Western Schism*, with claimants to the papacy in Rome and Avignon (and later Pisa) simultaneously. The schism was officially ended at the Council of Constance* in 1417, but the Avignon pope, Benedict XIII, refused to resign and fled to Spain, where he died without a successor in 1423.

B

BAPTISM (Gk *baptizein*, "to dip" or "to immerse"). The fundamental sacrament* of Christian initiation*. It involves a ritual immersion of candidates or pouring water over them. The remote ancestor of Christian baptism was Jewish ritual washings, especially a ritual bath of proselytes, but the immediate background was the baptism of John the Baptist, which Jesus himself underwent (Mt 3.13-17). It is unclear whether Jesus baptized (Jn 3.22, 4.2), but the NT clearly shows that baptism has from the earliest times been the ritual of initiation to the community of Jesus' followers (e.g., Acts 2.38). In Mt 28.19, Jesus mandates baptism "in the name of the Father, the Son, and the Holy Spirit." Though probably not the actual words of Jesus, this text shows a trinitarian baptismal formula in use in the early apostolic community. The NT speaks of baptism as being "for the forgiveness of your sins" (Acts 2.38) (a phrase repeated in the Nicene Creed), as incorporating one into the body of Christ in the Holy Spirit (1 Cor 12.12-13), and as joining the baptized person with Christ's death (Rom 6.3). The *Apostolic Tradition* of Hippolytus, from Rome around A.D. 215, describes baptism as preceded by a catechumenate*, or period of instruction, lasting up to three years. Candidates gathered with the whole assembly, led by the bishop, at the Easter* Vigil. They were baptized naked by immersion in water, then clothed and anointed with the oil of thanksgiving, then anointed again before the assembly, finally admitted to the eucharist*. With the entry of large numbers of people into the Church after the conversion of the Empire under Constantine*, the catechumenate declined and infant baptisms increased. It ceased to be the custom for baptisms to be done at Easter in a large gathering before the bishop; this eventually led to the separation of confirmation* from baptism.

Infant baptism may well be implied in NT passages that speak of the baptism of a whole household (e.g., Acts 16.33). It was an established custom by the second century but not the dominant practice until the fifth century. St. Augustine's* theology of original sin* was partly devised as a rationale for the existing practice of infant baptism but in turn gave it a great impetus. Baptism had earlier been understood as incorporating the baptized into the Christian Church and as forgiving personal sins (a purpose that did not apply to infants); it now was also seen as saving infants and others from the damnation that would otherwise be theirs as a result of the inherited sin of Adam. Infant baptism, apart from communal assembly, became the norm throughout the Middle Ages. The Council of Trent* (1547) reaffirmed infant baptism against the teaching of some Protestant* reformers (called "Anabaptists"), who held that only the baptisms of adult believers were valid.

Vatican Council II (1963) called for a restoration of the catechumenate and for revision in the rites for the baptism of infants and of adults. In consequence, the *Rite of Baptism for Children* appeared in 1969 and the *Rite of Christian Initiation for Adults*, including the restored catechumenate, in 1972 (*see* INITIATION, CHRISTIAN). In both cases, there is a blessing of baptismal water, a renunciation of sin and a profession of faith (spoken by the parents and godparents in the case of infants), a baptism by immersion or the pouring of water, an anointing after baptism, and a clothing with a white garment. There are some shorter rites for special circumstances. The baptismal formula in the Latin rite is, "I baptize you in the name of the Father, and of the Son, and of the Holy Spirit." The ordinary minister of baptism is a bishop, priest, or deacon. Catechists or others may be deputed by a bishop to baptize, and laypersons may baptize in cases of emergency. The Catholic Church regards baptisms performed by non-Catholic Christians to be valid, so long as the intention is to do what the Church does in baptizing and the trinitarian formula is used. Baptism "in fact or at least in intention" (Canon 849) is regarded as necessary for salvation. Martyrdom*, or "baptism of blood," is considered to suffice for baptism. "Baptism in intention" or "baptism of desire" must be construed broadly to include implicit forms of intention, in the light of Vatican II's affirmation of the possible salvation of nonbelievers (e.g., LG 16) (*see* SALVATION OUTSIDE THE CHURCH).

BASE (or **BASIC**) **CHRISTIAN COMMUNITIES** (Portuguese or Spanish *comunidades eclesiais* [Port; Sp: *eclesiales*] *de base*; hence the abbreviation, CEB). Small Christian communities that gather for prayer, bible study, social and political action, and other purposes. CEBs originated in Latin America in the 1960s and proliferated in the 1970s, especially in Brazil, where their growth was fostered by the hierarchy and their number may have reached 100,000 (though there is no sharp boundary between CEBs and informal gatherings of Christians). The adjective *eclesiais* (ecclesial) indicates a connection with the institutional Church; such communities tend to be answerable to the local pastor and bishop. In some countries (e.g., Nicaragua), however, there has been tension between the base communities and the hierarchy. "Base" indicates both the base or "grassroots" of the Church and the base or bottom of the social pyramid, since, in Latin America at least, base communities are usually made up chiefly of the rural or urban poor. CEBs range from small, family groupings to "mini-parishes" of 150 persons or more, which carry on a broad range of liturgical, educational and social ministry. They vary in their emphasis, some mainly devotional, some political, some both. Latin American liberation theology* draws extensively on the experience of base communities. Base communities were endorsed by the Latin American Conference of Bishops (CELAM) in their meetings at Medellin (1968) and Puebla (1979), and also (with some cautions) by Pope Paul VI* in *Evangelii nuntiandi* in 1975. They have spread from Latin America to Africa, Asia (especially the Philippines), Eastern and Western Europe, and North America, and from the Catholic Church to Protestant churches. In the United States, they are prominent among Hispanic Catholics and also have served as a model for the renewal of middle-class parishes.

BASEL (or **BASLE**), **COUNCIL OF** (1431-1449). An ecumenical council* convoked by Pope Martin V at Basel, Switzerland, and continued under his successor, Eugenius IV. It represented the high point of conciliarism* in the Church. It reaffirmed the teaching of the Council of Constance* on the superiority of a council over the pope, and required the papal representatives to take an oath to this effect. It aimed to reform the Church, but its members could agree only on reform of the papacy and Roman Curia*. By orders of the council, the pope was deprived of most of his sources of revenue. The council was temporarily successful in working out a reconciliation with the Hussites in Bohemia but foundered on the question of reconciliation with the Greeks (*see* EASTERN ORTHODOX CHURCHES). The Eastern Emperor was then seeking reunion, partly in order to secure Western support against the Turks. Eugenius wanted the reunion council to be held in Italy, to which the Greeks agreed, but the Council of Basel insisted that the site be Basel or Avignon. A minority agreed with Eugenius, and with their support and that of the Greeks, he moved the council to Ferrara in 1437. In 1439 it moved to Florence*. Meanwhile, the remainder of the council continued to meet at Basel, and in 1439 they deposed Eugenius and elected an antipope, Felix V. Thereafter, the council lost support and was eventually transferred to Lausanne in 1448, where it dissolved itself in 1449.

BASILICA (Gk *basilikē*, "royal"). An early form of Christian church building, modeled after Roman public buildings of the same name. Typically, the Christian basilica consisted of a rectangular *nave* (the main part) with two or four aisles (or "ambulatories"). At one end—from the fifth century onward this was almost always the east—was the *apse*, a semicircular space that contained the bishop's throne. The altar* stood in front of the apse. At the opposite end of the nave were the main doorways, and beyond them the *narthex* or porch, beyond that often an *atrium* or courtyard. The basilica was the principal form of Christian church building, especially in the West, in the centuries following the legalization of Christian public worship in A.D. 313 and has had an influence on church architecture* ever since.

"Basilica" is also used as a title of honor, conferred by the pope, on a church regardless of its architectural structure. There are four "major basilicas" in Rome (St. John Lateran, St. Peter's*, St. Paul's Outside the Walls, and St. Mary Major) and numerous "minor basilicas" throughout the world.

Outside the Walls, and St. Mary Major) and numerous "minor basilicas" throughout the world.

BEATIFIC VISION. The direct knowledge of God and the happiness enjoyed by the blessed in heaven*. The image of "vision" draws especially on 1 Cor 13.12 ("we see [God] ... then face to face") and 1 Jn 3.2 ("we shall see him as he is"). It highlights the role of knowledge. Such an emphasis was congenial to many medieval scholastics, especially Thomas Aquinas*, who saw the intellect as the supreme human power. They were careful, however, to say that the beatific vision is the fulfillment of the entire human person, not the intellect only. It is given by God's grace*, not attained through our nature (Council of Vienne* [1311-1312]). For the soul of one who is saved, the vision begins immediately after death or the cessation of purgatory*. This was solemnly declared by Pope Benedict XII in 1336 against the personal opinion of his predecessor, John XXII, who held that it began only after the final resurrection*. The teaching was repeated by the Council of Florence* in 1439. It is commonly held that the beatific vision includes not only knowledge of God but also knowledge of created things as they are in God.

BEGUINES (probably from "Albigensian," in the broad meaning of "heretic"; see CATHARS). Formed what Caroline Walker Bynum has called the first women's movement we can identify in Christian history. The beguines lived austere, celibate lives, combining prayer and manual labor (such as handicrafts or care of the sick) in small communities or, later, in larger ones called "beguinages." Unlike nuns, they did not take permanent vows* and did not constitute an order nor live under a rule. Men who lived in similar communities were called **BEGHARDS**; they were never as numerous as beguines. Beguines began around 1210 and were concentrated in the towns of the Low Countries, the Rhineland, and northern France. For the most part, they came from the new urban bourgeoisie and lower nobility. Beguine spiritual literature displays an affective, mystical and visionary spirituality, emphasizing the experience of the love of God, which is often described in erotic language. Important beguine spiritual writers included Beatrice of Nazareth (ca. 1200-1268), Hadewijch (mid-thirteenth century), Mechtild of Magdeburg (1207-1282), and Marguerite Porete, burned as a heretic in Paris in 1310. As the last example illustrates, beguines were suspected of heretical tendencies, and they and the beghards were suppressed by the Council of Vienne* in 1311, but in ambiguous terms, which allowed them to continue to some degree. Beghards survived till the French Revolution, beguines to the present day, mainly in Belgium.

BELLARMINE, ROBERT, ST. (1542-1621). A leading theologian of the sixteenth and seventeenth centuries. Born in Tuscany, he entered the Jesuits* in 1560. He became a professor at the Louvain and later at Rome, where he wrote his most important work, the *Disputationes de controversiis Christianae fidei contra hujus temporis haereticos* (1586-93), a defense of the Catholic Church against the Protestant* Reformers. He was named a Cardinal in 1599 and served at Rome the remainder of his life, except for an appointment as Archbishop of Capua from 1602 to 1605. He defended the power of the pope*, but emphasized that it was primarily spiritual; the pope's temporal power was only indirect, derived from the spiritual. In 1616, on behalf of the Holy Office, he had to deliver an admonition to Galileo*, for whom he had some sympathy. He unsuccessfully proposed a compromise, whereby the heliocentric model of the universe could be regarded as a useful calculating device but not a true representation of reality. His canonization was delayed until 1930, held up by those who regarded his theory of papal power as too minimal. He was named a Doctor of the Church* in 1931. His feast is celebrated on September 17.

BENEDICT, ST. (ca. 480-ca. 547). Considered the founder of Western monasticism*. His life is known only from a biography written about fifty years after his death by St. Gregory the Great*, which combines history and legend. He was born in Nursia, northeast of Rome, and at around the age of twenty withdrew to live in solitude near Subiaco, where he later founded several monastic communities. Later, he established a monastery at Monte Cassino, where he composed his monastic rule. This rule draws heavily on earlier sources, but its distinctive simplicity, moderation, and wisdom made it the dominant monastic rule in the West from the century after his death up to the present time. His feast is celebrated on July 11.

BENEDICT XV, POPE (1914-1922) (Giacomo della Chiesa, b. 1854). Born in Genoa, he rose through the papal diplomatic service to undersecretary of state. He became Archbishop of Bologna in 1907. As pope, he sought to make peace during World War I but was allowed no official role in the process. He eased tensions in the Church following the condemnation of Modernism* by Pius X* and actively promoted missions.

BENEDICTION. A blessing. The term commonly refers to **Benediction of the Blessed Sacrament**, a ritual of eucharistic adoration dating from around the fourteenth century. Benediction has often been criticized in modern times for separating the eucharistic host (wafer) from the eucharistic meal, the mass*, but the present "Rite of Eucharistic Exposition and Benediction" emphasizes that eucharistic adoration is to be properly related to the mass. After prayers, hymns, and readings, the celebrant, who may be a priest or a deacon, blesses the congregation by a sign of the cross*, made with the host in a *monstrance*, a special vessel* for the exposition of the eucharist, or a ciborium, the vessel in which the eucharistic hosts are contained during mass. See also EUCHARIST, DEVOTION.

BERNARD OF CLAIRVAUX, ST. (1090-1153). Most prominent churchman and writer of the twelfth century. He was born in Burgundy and in 1112 became a monk of Cîteaux, the mother house of the Cistercian Order. In 1115, he was sent to found a house at Clairvaux in Champagne. Largely through his influence, the order grew to around 350 houses by the time of his death. At the Council of Troyes (1128), he succeeded in gaining recognition of the Knights Templars*. Between 1130 and 1138, he helped to settle a schism* in the Roman church, when Pope Innocent II was opposed by an antipope, Anacletus. At a council at Sens (1140) and in correspondence afterward, he attacked the teaching of Abelard*. He had great influence over Pope Eugenius III (pope 1145-1153), who had been a Cistercian monk. From 1146 to 1148 he led the preaching of the Second Crusade (*see* CRUSADES), which was unsuccessful. The interior life, however, was his chief interest. He combined the monastic tradition with a new emphasis on affectivity, in which the dominant theme is the love* of God, which flows out into love of neighbor. His writings inaugurate an increased emphasis on love in Christian spirituality. His best-known works are *De diligendo Deo (On Loving God)* (ca. 1125) and eighty-six *Sermons on the Song of Songs* (1135-1153). He was canonized in 1174 and declared a Doctor of the Church* in 1830. His feast is celebrated on August 20.

BIBLE (Gk *biblia*, "books"). The collection of sacred writings ("Scripture") understood to be inspired by God. Christians divide it into two sections, called **Old Testament** (OT) and **New Testament** (NT). "Testament" translates the Greek word *diathēkē*, which can also be rendered "covenant"; one might say that the two testaments are witnesses ("testifiers") to two "covenants" or stages in God's relationship with the people of God*, first with Israel, second with the Christian community. The use of the terms "Old Testament" and "New Testament" dates from the early third century, and indicates both the continuity and the distinction between the two. (Some Christians prefer to use "Hebrew Scriptures" in place of "Old Testament." Use, however, of "Old Testament" indicates that these writings are, from a Christian point of view, properly to be considered among the Christian as well as the Jewish scriptures. "Old" should be taken in the sense of "former" or "earlier," not of "obsolete." The terms "First" and "Second Testament" are becoming more common.)

The **canon** of Scripture is the list of books recognized by the church as being the inspired word of God. For the Catholic Church, the canon of the Old Testament includes forty-six books. Of these, thirty-nine books (all written in Hebrew except for a few passages in Aramaic) were included in the Jewish canon, established in the early A.D. centuries. These works are accepted as Scripture by all Jews and Christians.

Seven other books, which were part of the Greek versions of the Old Testament commonly read by early Christians, are regarded by Catholics as part of the Old Testament. These are now called **deuterocanonical books**; they are the books of Baruch, Tobit, Judith, Wisdom, Sirach, and 1 and 2 Maccabees. Parts of the books of Daniel and Esther are also deuterocanonical. For the most part, the deuterocanonical books were regarded as part of Scripture by the early Church, and they appear in the earliest statements of the canon; there remained, however, some question about them throughout the early Church and the medieval period. The Protestant Reformers, following the lead of Martin Luther, excluded them from the canon, calling them "apocrypha"*. For the Catholic Church, their status as Scripture was affirmed by the Council of Trent* in 1546. (The Eastern Orthodox* have a still larger canon.)

The New Testament includes twenty-seven books: the Gospels* of Matthew, Mark, Luke, and John, the Acts of the Apostles, thirteen letters ascribed to St. Paul, the anonymous Letter to the Hebrews, seven letters ascribed to apostles* other than Paul (two to Peter, one each to James and Jude, three to John), and the Book of Revelation. The canon of the NT was established for the most part in the second century, but there was some dispute about Hebrews, 2 Peter, James, Jude, 2 and 3 John, and Revelation as late as the fifth century, and some other writings now considered apocrypha or as belonging to the Apostolic Fathers* were at times considered part of the NT. A final statement of the NT canon occurred only at Trent.

Versions of the Bible. Most early Christians read the Bible in Greek, using, for the Old Testament, mainly the **Septuagint**, a translation that originated in the Jewish community in Alexandria in the third and second centuries B.C. and underwent many later revisions. Latin versions of the Bible, translated from the Greek, were current as early as the second century. St. Jerome*, translating from the original languages in the late fourth century, produced the **Latin Vulgate**, which became the standard Latin version from then on (the Vulgate versions of works of the NT other than the Gospels may not be by Jerome). Other important early versions are in the Syriac, Coptic, and Ethiopic languages. The Council of Trent declared that the Latin Vulgate was "the authentic text in public readings, debates, sermons, and explanations" (DS 1506). Therefore, Catholic translations into other languages were based on the Vulgate until after 1943, when the encyclical *Divino Afflante Spiritu* of Pope Pius XII* encouraged translation from the original languages. The standard Catholic translation of the Bible into English was for many years the **Douay-Rheims** version, made by English Catholic exiles in France, and published in 1582 (NT) and 1609 (OT). It was revised considerably by Bishop Richard Challoner, coadjutor in London, between 1749 and 1763. The most important Catholic translations from the original languages into English are *The New American Bible*, published in the United States in 1970 (with a revised NT, 1987), and *The Jerusalem Bible*, which was based on the French *Bible de Jérusalem* of 1948-1954 and published in 1966, appearing in a revised edition as *The New Jerusalem Bible* in 1985. These and the *Revised Standard Version*, produced in 1946 to 1952 (revised 1990) under Protestant auspices but officially approved for use by Catholics, are the English versions most commonly used by Catholics.

Catholic teaching about the Bible. The Catholic Church has always recognized the authority* of the Bible as the inspired word of

God, but the respective roles of Scripture and the tradition* of the Church have been the subject of controversy, especially since the Protestant* Reformation and its insistence on the authority of "Scripture alone." The *Dogmatic Constitution on Divine Revelation* (DV) of the Second Vatican Council (1965) expresses the authoritative Catholic teaching on the role of the Bible. It states, "Sacred tradition and sacred scripture ... both flow from the same divine wellspring, merge together to some extent, and are on course towards the same end" (DV 9). They "form a single sacred deposit of the word of God" (10), not two separate and distinct expressions of the word of God. Official interpretation of the Bible is the task of the *magisterium** or teaching office of the Church; "This teaching function is not above the word of God but stands at its service" (10). The document goes on to explain Catholic teaching on the inspiration* and inerrancy* of the Bible. It follows *Divino Afflante Spiritu* in endorsing the use of modern biblical criticism*, directs that all the faithful be given easy access to the Scripture, continues to encourage translation from the original languages, and specifies that clergy should be well trained in the Scriptures and that preaching should be based in them. Together with other documents of Vatican II, it led to an increased emphasis on Scripture in the liturgy (for instance, a lectionary* that included a greatly increased amount of the biblical text) and in the life of the Church generally.

BIBLICAL CRITICISM. The scholarly endeavor to understand biblical texts. There are many types of criticism. **Textual criticism** seeks to ascertain, by way of such activities as the comparison of manuscripts and early versions, exactly what the original text of the Bible is. **Literary criticism**, in a broad sense, refers to the effort to specify the meaning of a text and the ways in which it conveys its meaning. In a narrower sense, it refers to the study of a biblical book as a whole, rather than dividing it into smaller units or seeking to chart its history. **Historical criticism** involves situating a text in its historical context, e.g., employing archaeology or parallels with non-biblical texts in order to clarify the meaning of a text. It also refers to the effort to determine the historical value of a biblical text, e.g., to specify the actual events that underlie biblical narratives. Some important types of biblical criticism combine the literary and the historical. Thus, **form criticism** seeks to determine the literary form (e.g., letter, parable) of a biblical text and how this shapes the content; it also asks questions about the context ("setting in life", or *Sitz-im-Leben*) in which such forms would have been used and what these settings contributed to the content. **Redaction criticism** explores the work of the final author or editor ("redactor") of a text; it investigates how the text is affected by the concerns of the author and the author's audience.

In all ages of the Church, some forms of biblical criticism have been practiced in order to understand and interpret the text of the Bible. "Biblical criticism," however, commonly refers to the approaches to the Bible, such as those described above, which came into use in the eighteenth century, when the Enlightenment sought to replace reliance on tradition with reliance on reason or "scientific" history. Particularly since the use of these techniques was often accompanied by a skepticism about traditional Christian claims (e.g., the divinity of Jesus and the possibility of miracles*), the Catholic Church did not encourage the development of modern biblical criticism until the mid-twentieth century. Official Church documents first pay attention to modern biblical criticism in the late nineteenth century, taking a cautionary or negative note. Decrees of the Pontifical Biblical Commission between 1905 and 1915 defended the literal historical accuracy of the first chapters of Genesis and the claim that Moses is the author of the Pentateuch (first five books of the Bible). In 1943, however, the encyclical *Divino Afflante Spiritu* of Pope Pius XII* authorized Catholic biblical interpreters to make full use of historical study and the study of literary forms. This position was confirmed by the *Dogmatic Constitution on Divine Revelation* of the Second Vatican Council. Catholic scholars, then, so long as they uphold the inspiration* and inerrancy* of the biblical text as these are understood by the Church, may and do make free use of all the critical methods of modern biblical scholarship.

BIRTH CONTROL. Any form of intentional regulation of human reproduction. A distinction can be made between **contraception**, or artificial methods of birth control, and natural methods. Abortion* can be used as a method of birth control, but it involves special moral issues and is usually discussed separately, as here. Artificial methods of contraception involve an intentional mechanical or chemical interference with the reproductive power or with the act of sexual intercourse in order to prevent conception. These include withdrawal, or coitus interruptus, the condom, the diaphragm, the anovulant (ovulation-preventing) contraceptive pill, the intrauterine device (IUD), spermicides, and morning-after pills. **Sterilization** of either a man or a woman, when done for contraceptive purposes, may be classed with the artificial means. Some contraceptives, such as the IUD and the morning-after pill, which work by preventing the implantation of the fertilized egg on the uterine wall, might better be regarded as abortifacients (agents that cause abortion). Natural methods of birth control include complete abstinence from sexual intercourse and the restriction of intercourse to those times in a woman's menstrual cycle when she is infertile. An early and ineffective form of the determination of such periods by the use of a calendar was known as **rhythm**. More accurate contemporary methods for the determination of infertile periods rely on measurements of the woman's body temperature and vaginal mucus. Such methods are known as **Natural Family Planning**.

Early Christian opinion (without making the natural/artificial distinction) condemned contraception. Reasons included its association with magic and pagan sexual laxity, the lack of a clear distinction between contraceptives and abortifacients (so that the use of either was seen as an offense against human life), and Christian adoption of the principle of Stoic* philosophy that sexual intercourse was only for purposes of procreation. Medieval and modern arguments focused on contraception as destroying potential human life and violating the purpose of marriage and sexual intercourse. Such opinions held sway among Catholic authorities and other Christians until the beginning of the twentieth century, which saw both increased pressure for population control and development of more effective contraceptive devices. Partly in response to liberalized Protestant opinion, Pope Pius XI* in the encyclical *Casti Connubii* (1930) strongly reasserted the traditional condemnation of contraception and also discouraged natural methods of birth control, though permitting them for grave reasons.

During the mid-twentieth century, theologians began to emphasize the importance of marital love as a reason for sexual intercourse, and this emphasis was reflected in Vatican Council II's* treatment of marriage (GS 47-52) (1965). This development, together with dissatisfaction with rhythm by those using it, and arguments that the newly developed contraceptive pill required a reexamination of the morality of contraception, led in the 1960s to pressure for change in Church teaching. A commission appointed in 1963 by Pope John XXIII* responded in 1966 overwhelmingly in favor of Church acceptance of contraception in some cases. In 1968, however, Pope

Paul VI* issued the encyclical *Humanae Vitae* (HV), which reaffirmed the traditional teaching. According to HV, "Each and every marriage act [act of intercourse] must remain open to the transmission of life" (11). This principle excluded artificial birth control but allowed for the use of natural means.

After HV, the issue of contraception became the focus of widespread dissent*. The teaching of HV was challenged by many theologians and not followed by the majority of the laity, at least in Europe and North America. It has been strongly supported by Pope John Paul II*, who has disciplined some theologians, e.g., Charles E. Curran, who oppose it. The majority of theological opinion continues to support artificial contraception in some circumstances, seeing no morally relevant distinction between artificial and natural means of birth control. Others, e.g., Germain Grisez, support the teaching of HV on philosophical and theological grounds. Some of these theologians hold that the condemnation of contraception has been infallibly proclaimed by the ordinary magisterium (*see* INFALLIBILITY.)

BISHOP (Gk *episkopos*, "overseer, supervisor"). Someone who has received the fullness of the sacrament of order*. Bishops are the successors of the apostles* (*see also* APOSTOLICITY) and as such possess (when in union with the whole Church through communion with the pope) the highest power to teach, to make holy, and to govern their local churches (*see* AUTHORITY IN THE CHURCH). They possess as well (when in union with the pope) a share in the supreme power to teach, to make holy, and to govern the universal Church (*see* COLLEGIALITY).

The term *episkopos*, which became "bishop" in English, is used infrequently in the NT and seems more or less synonymous with *presbyteros,* which means "elder" and became "priest"* in English. Probably, some local churches did not use the term *episkopos*; where used, it probably referred to a member of the board of elders who governed the local church, or to the leaders of that board (e.g., 1 Tm 3.2, Titus 1.7). By the end of the first century, the Church was moving toward having only one bishop in each local church, but this institution (called the **monepiscopate** or **monarchical episcopate**) was not universal till the mid-second century. The role of the local bishop, according to second-century writers, is to safeguard the unity of the local church and its preservation of the faith of the apostles, to preside over the community in the eucharist*, to instruct and to baptize new members, and to represent the local church in relations with other churches and the Church as a whole. Vatican Council II, in its *Dogmatic Constitution on the Church (Lumen Gentium)* (also in its *Decree on the Bishops' Pastoral Office in the Church*) restored this early theology, against tendencies to see the bishop as merely a local representative of the pope. "The individual bishops are the visible principle and foundation of unity in their own particular churches....In and from these particular churches there exists the one unique Catholic Church" (LG 23).

What is said above applies primarily to the **diocesan bishop** or **local ordinary**, to whom is entrusted care of a diocese*. There are also **coadjutor** and **auxiliary bishops**, who assist the diocesan bishop in the performance of his duties. A coadjutor differs from an auxiliary bishop in having the right of succession to the seat of the diocesan bishop. A coadjutor or auxiliary bishop is made **titular bishop** of a local church, usually in the Near East, which no longer has a bishop (nor a vacant episcopal seat), but he has no power over that church.

Besides the duties mentioned above, a bishop is the ordinary minister of the sacraments of confirmation* and order*. (*See also* EPISCOPAL CONFERENCE.)

BLACK CATHOLICS. *See* AFRICAN AMERICAN CATHOLICISM.

BONAVENTURE, ST. (1217-1274). A leading theologian of the Middle Ages. Born John of Fidanza in Bagnoregio, Italy, he received the name Bonaventure upon his entry into the Franciscan order in 1243. He became a master of theology at Paris in 1253 or 1254 and minister general of the Franciscan Order in 1257. As minister general, his task was to reconcile the spirit of Francis with the increasingly institutionalized and intellectual character of the order. In theology, he combined Aristotelianism* with a greater faithfulness to the tradition of St. Augustine* than was observed by St. Thomas Aquinas*, his chief contemporary theological rival. He left many writings, of which the best known is the *Itinerarium Mentis in Deum (The Soul's Journey into God)* (1259), which combines philosophy, theology, and mystical spirituality. His *Legenda maior (Life of St. Francis)* (1263) became the order's official biography of its founder. Bonaventure was canonized in 1482 and named a Doctor of the Church* in 1588. His feast is celebrated on July 15.

BONIFACE VIII, POPE (1294-1303) (Benedetto Caetani). Born ca. 1235 at Anagni. He persuaded Pope Celestine V to resign and was elected as Celestine's successor, whereupon he had Celestine imprisoned. His reign was marked by his extravagant claims on behalf of the papacy, while at the same time a turning point was being reached in the decline of papal power over the secular rulers of Europe. In his bull*, *Unam sanctam* (1302), he declared, "It is altogether necessary for salvation for every human creature to be subject to the Roman pontiff." This bull was issued in the course of a long, losing struggle with King Philip IV (the Fair) of France over taxation of the clergy and related matters. In 1303, Philip placed him under arrest, and although he was rescued, his health was broken and he died soon afterward. The French king's power over the papacy increased, and six years later the papacy moved to Avignon*.

BREVIARY. *See* HOURS, LITURGY OF THE.

BROTHER, RELIGIOUS. A male, unordained (in most cases) member of a religious community. Brothers take vows* or make some other form of profession of the evangelical counsels* of poverty, chastity, and obedience. Some brothers belong to "clerical communities," societies whose members are mostly priests (e.g., the Jesuits*), but most brothers belong to nonclerical or lay communities, such as the Christian Brothers. A few nonclerical communities allow some brothers to be ordained priests, for service to the community. Moreover, a small number of brothers have been ordained permanent deacons*. Brothers engage in a wide variety of ministries, especially in education. (See also MONASTICISM, MENDICANT ORDERS, RELIGIOUS LIFE.)

BUDDHISM. A family of religious traditions that trace their origin to Siddhartha Gautama, called the Buddha ("enlightened one"), who lived in India around 563 to 483 B.C. Buddhism spread to south and southeast Asia, to Tibet, China, and Japan. Vatican Council II summarizes Buddhist teaching as follows: "In Buddhism, according to its various forms, the radical inadequacy of this changeable world is acknowledged and a way is taught whereby those with a devout and trustful spirit may be able to reach either a state of perfect freedom or, relying on their own efforts or on help from a higher source, the highest illumination" (NA 2).

The first Christian writer to mention Buddhism was Clement of Alexandria (early third century), but Catholic-Buddhist contact was limited until fairly recent times. Since Vatican Council II, Catholic-Buddhist dialogue has been widespread. The main settings for such dialogue have been (1) theology, as Catholic theologians and Buddhist thinkers have examined one another's traditions (this has been especially prominent in Sri Lanka, Japan, and the United States); (2) monasticism, as monks of both traditions have explored and in many cases shared in one another's practices; (3) social concerns, as representatives of both faiths have searched for common ground and mutual enlightenment on such issues as world peace and the environment. Many Catholics have adopted (or adapted) techniques of meditation* from Buddhism. In 1989, the Vatican Congregation for the Doctrine of the Faith* warned against excesses in the use of such practices but did not forbid the practices. The first official dialogue between Catholics and Buddhists in the United States, cosponsored by the Archdiocese of Los Angeles, began in 1989.

BULL. A papal letter of special importance, sealed with a leaden *bulla* (Lt "seal") or a red ink imprint of the seal.

BURIAL AND CREMATION. Following Jewish custom, the early Christians buried their dead. Cremation, though common in the ancient world, was discouraged because of the belief in the resurrection* of the body. The Church officially forbade cremation in 1886 because its promotion at that time was associated with denial of the resurrection of the body. Cremation was allowed in 1963, though burial is still preferred. The Order of Christian Funerals (1969) provides for a Rite of Committal to be celebrated at the grave, tomb, or crematorium, expressing hope in the final resurrection. *See also* FUNERAL.

C

CALENDAR, LITURGICAL. The liturgical calendar divides and sanctifies the week and the year, relating them to the mysteries of salvation in Christ.

The week. Christians took over the seven-day week from Jewish tradition, and the earliest Christians continued Jewish Sabbath observances. Because Jesus rose on "the first day of the week" (Mt 28.1), Christians observed this day as well. Acts 20.7 records a gathering on this day for the "breaking of the bread" (the eucharist), and Sunday* observance, featuring the eucharist*, soon became a defining mark of Christians. Other days in the week were subordinate to Sunday. Early sources (e.g., the *Didachē**, probably late first century) record Wednesday and Friday fasts, to which Rome later added Saturday. Some tradition of Friday fasting survives to the present (*see* FAST AND ABSTINENCE).

The year. The Christian year combines a lunar calendar, used for the computation of Easter* and the feasts depending on it, and a solar calendar, used for feasts* depending on Christmas* and for feasts of the saints. The cycle that depends on Easter is called the **temporal cycle**. Easter is celebrated in the West on the Sunday following the first full moon after the spring equinox. The cycle based on annual calendar dates for the feasts of the saints and other feasts is called the **sanctoral cycle**. Annual, as distinct from weekly, celebration of Easter dates from the second century, while celebration of Christmas on December 25 dates from the third or fourth century, although the related feast of the Epiphany*, January 6, originally a nativity festival, dates from the second century. The liturgical year begins with the First Sunday of Advent* (the fourth Sunday before Christmas), then continues with the Christmas season till the Sunday after Epiphany. Lent* begins on Ash Wednesday (the Wednesday before the sixth Sunday before Easter) and ends on Holy Thursday (the Thursday before Easter), when the Easter Triduum* begins. The Easter Season begins with the Easter Vigil and concludes with Pentecost*. The weeks between the Christmas Season and Lent, and those between Pentecost and Advent, are called Ordinary Time. While preserving this ancient framework, Vatican Council II mandated a reform of the liturgical year, emphasizing the priority of Sunday and the liturgical seasons over the feasts of the saints and other celebrations.

For further information on the liturgical year, see the entries on ADVENT, CHRISTMAS, EPIPHANY, LENT, HOLY WEEK, EASTER TRIDUUM, EASTER, and PENTECOST.

CANON LAW (Gk *kanōn*, "rule, measure"). Church law, as distinct from civil or secular law. Individual laws are called *canons*. The need for some sort of legislation in the Church is evident as early as the Pauline letters and is reflected in early church orders, e.g., the *Didachē** (first century). Early councils passed canons to deal with disciplinary matters, with those of Nicaea* especially important. Collections of church laws began to appear in the fifth century. One of the most important was that of Dionysius Exiguus (early sixth century), who gathered papal **decretals** (letters having the force of law) as well as the canons of councils. Collections continued to be made through the Middle Ages, until the entire field of canon law was transformed by the work of Gratian (ca. 1140). Gratian, who taught at Bologna, used the method of Abelard* to marshal and reconcile texts apparently on opposing sides of a given issue; hence, his collection was called the *Concordia discordantium canonum (Harmony of Discordant Canons)* or *Decretum.* It drew considerably on Roman law, the study of which was then being revived in the universities*, and became the standard text used in the schools and courts of the Middle Ages. Gratian's text and several further collections of decretals that supplemented it in the later Middle Ages were brought together as the *Corpus Iuris Canonici* around 1500. This collection received official approval in 1580 and became the basis of Church law until 1917, when the first unified *Codex Iuris Canonici (Code of Canon Law)* was promulgated, systematizing the earlier *Corpus* and later legislation. A revised *Code of Canon Law,* reflecting the reforms of the Second Vatican Council, appeared in 1983. It comprises 1,752 canons in seven books, dealing in turn with "General Norms," "The People of God," the Church's offices of teaching and sanctifying, Church property, sanctions, and trials and procedures. This code applies only to the Latin Rite. A parallel *Code of Canons of the Oriental Churches (Codex Canonum Ecclesiarum Orientalium)* was promulgated in 1990. It is largely based on the Latin code but draws on the distinctive traditions of the Eastern Catholic Churches*.

CANONIZATION. The official declaration that a deceased person is a saint*. The process leading to canonization begins with an investigation on the part of the local bishop, considering the candidate's life and writings. If this investigation establishes the candidate's orthodoxy* and martyrdom* or outstanding Christian virtue, the case is sent to the Congregation for the Causes of Saints, in the Roman Curia*. There the candidate's life is given an extensive further consideration. The occurrence of a miracle* attributable to his or her intercession must also be established (except in the case of martyrs). The successful outcome of this process is **beatification**: the pope declares that the candidate may be called "Blessed" and may be honored in the liturgy locally. Another miracle (or a first miracle in the case of martyrs beatified without one) must then be authenticated, after which the pope may declare the candidate to be a saint, worthy of veneration in the universal Church.

In the early centuries of the Church, the process leading to the veneration of a saint was informal and locally based. Abuses led to increasing centralization. The first documented canonization was that of St. Ulrich of Augsburg in 993 by Pope John XV. In 1170, Pope Alexander III declared that all local veneration of saints required papal approval. The *Decretals* of Pope Gregory IX in 1234 made the jurisdiction of the pope over canonization a matter of canon law, but the pope assumed complete control over the process only under Urban VIII (1623-44). The definitive treatment of canonization was published by Prospero Lambertini, the future Pope Benedict XIV, in five volumes from 1734 to 1738. The process was reformed and simplified in 1983. It is often said that solemn canonizations are infallible (*see* INFALLIBILITY), but this has never been formally declared, and some theologians dispute it.

CAPITAL PUNISHMENT. The putting to death, by an agent of a legitimate authority, of someone legally condemned by that authority. Third-century sources (e.g., Tertullian*, Minucius Felix, Hippolytus) forbade Christians to take part in the practice. From the fourth century, when Christianity became the state religion, through the Middle Ages, Christian writers conceded (often with misgivings) the right of the state to take human life. Thus, Thomas Aquinas held that a criminal who was dangerous to the community could be killed in order to safeguard the common good (ST 2-2.64.2). Medieval authorities prohibited clergy from participating in executions and forbade the ordination of those who had done so (this provision remained in canon law until 1983). Movements opposing the death penalty began in Europe in the eighteenth century and led eventually to its abolition in most European and some Latin American countries, as well as some American states. Though some theologians supported this movement, Catholics were not prominently involved in it, nor did it receive official backing. The U.S. bishops, in a series of statements beginning in 1974, have opposed capital punishment. In 1980, they rejected the death penalty on grounds, among others, of human dignity, God's lordship of life, the example of Jesus, and evils and injustices involved in the carrying out of the penalty, but conceded that support of capital punishment is not "inconsistent with the Catholic tradition." The 1992 *Catechism of the Catholic Church* affirmed, "The traditional teaching of the Church has acknowledged the right and duty of legitimate public authority to punish malefactors by means of penalties commensurate with the gravity of the crime, not excluding, in cases of extreme gravity, the death penalty" (2266). It added, though, "If bloodless means are sufficient ... to protect public order and the safety of persons, public authority should limit itself to such means, because they better correspond to the concrete conditions of the common good and are more in conformity to the dignity of the human person" (2267). In his 1995 encyclical *Evangelium vitae*, Pope John Paul II* strengthened the presumption against the death penalty, holding that cases where it is necessary are "very rare if not practically nonexistent" (56). Some theologians argue that capital punishment should be condemned on the same grounds on which suicide*, murder, abortion*, and euthanasia* are condemned—that it is immoral directly to take a human life, except in cases of immediate self-defense.

CAPITALISM. The following passage from Pope John Paul II's* encyclical, *Centesimus annus* (1991), can serve as both a definition and a statement of current official teaching on capitalism: "Can it perhaps be said that, after the failure of communism, capitalism is the victorious social system, and that capitalism should be the goal of the countries now making efforts to rebuild their economy and society? ... The answer is obviously complex. If by 'capitalism' is meant an economic system which recognizes the fundamental and positive role of business, the market, private property and the resulting responsibility for the means of production, as well as free human creativity in the economic sector, then the answer is certainly in the affirmative.... But if by 'capitalism' is meant a system in which freedom in the economic sector is not circumscribed within a strong juridical framework which places it at the service of human freedom in its totality, and which sees it as a particular aspect of that freedom, the core of which is ethical and religious, then the reply is certainly negative" (42). This quotation, and the encyclical from which it is taken, is somewhat more affirmative toward capitalism than the tradition of Catholic social teaching* had previously been. Earlier encyclicals, beginning with Leo XIII's* *Rerum novarum* (1891), always affirmed a right to private property* and rejected Marxist socialism*, but viewed capitalism (called "liberalism"*), as it existed in Western Europe and America, with suspicion. The popes were critical or suspicious of capitalism for subordinating the common good to individual pursuit of wealth, degrading the dignity of working people and the poor, and pursuing material goods at the expense of spiritual goods. Outside the zone of official teaching, theological opinion ranges from extolling "democratic capitalism" as the economic system best suited to Catholic values (Michael Novak) to arguing on Christian grounds for some form of socialism (most liberation theologians*).

CAPPADOCIANS. The **Cappadocian Fathers**, three great defenders of Trinitarian orthodoxy in the late fourth century, and St. Macrina, the sister of two of them, all from Cappadocia in Asia Minor (now central Turkey). The Cappadocian Fathers supported the creed of Nicaea* against the Arians*, gave standard form to the doctrine of the Trinity*, and argued for the divinity of the Holy Spirit* against the Macedonians (or "Pneumatomachi"). (1) **St. Basil** (ca. 330-379), bishop of Caesarea from 371 to his death, was the author of monastic "rules" (really precepts or conferences) that form the basis of the rule still followed by most Eastern Orthodox monks. He left many letters, homilies, and treatises. (2) **St. Gregory of Nazianzus** (329-389), son of Gregory, bishop of Nazianzus, was a friend of Basil. He was the greatest rhetorician of the Cappadocian Fathers but was unreliable under pressure of public life. He became bishop of Sasima ca. 372 but never went there. In 381, during the First Council of Constantinople*, he was made bishop of Constantinople and presided over the council, but resigned the position while the council was still in progress. He left important collections of orations (especially the "Five Theological Orations") and letters, as well as an autobiography in verse. (3) **St. Gregory of Nyssa** (ca. 335-ca. 395), brother of St. Basil and St. Macrina, was the most profound theologian of the three, well-versed in Platonic philosophy and much influenced by Origen*. He became bishop of Nyssa in 371. The most important of his many works are *Contra Eunomium* (380-83), against the form of Arianism promoted by Eunomius, the *Catechetical Oration* (after 381), and the *Life of Moses* (ca. 390), a classic of mystical theology. (4) **St. Macrina** (called "the Younger" to distinguish her from her maternal grandmother) (ca. 327-

379) left behind no written works but her theological insight is reflected in some of the works of Gregory of Nyssa. She founded an ascetic community with her widowed mother on the family estate. The feast of Basil and Gregory of Nazianzus is celebrated on January 2, that of Gregory of Nyssa on March 9, and that of Macrina on July 19. All three Cappadocian Fathers are considered Doctors of the Church*.

CARDINAL (Lt *cardo*, "hinge"). A bishop chosen by the pope to be a member of a "college" (collective body) whose special responsibility is to elect the pope. The term *cardinal* had a variety of uses in the Middle Ages; by the eighth century it had come to mean the Roman clergy and the bishops of certain dioceses (called "suburbicarian") near Rome. The College of Cardinals achieved an organized form in the eleventh century, and in 1179 the Third Lateran Council* gave it the exclusive right to elect the pope. The title "cardinal" was restricted to members of this college only in 1567. Though in 1918 it was required that all cardinals be priests and in 1962 that they be bishops, there remains a ranking of "cardinal bishops" (the bishops of the suburbicarian dioceses and the oriental patriarchs*), "cardinal priests" (cardinals who are bishops of dioceses outside Rome), and "cardinal deacons" (cardinals who are not diocesan bishops but serve within the Roman Curia*). The major offices of the Roman Curia are headed by cardinals. The cardinals may be called together at the pope's discretion. When the papacy becomes vacant, they meet in **conclave**, or closed session, to elect the new pope. A two-thirds majority is required. Cardinals over the age of eighty may not vote.

CARDINAL VIRTUES. The moral virtues* on which other virtues hinge (*see* CARDINAL). The tradition of Catholic moral theology draws here ultimately on Plato* and Aristotle*. There are four cardinal virtues: **prudence** (or practical wisdom) is the ability to recognize the good in particular situations involving choice; **temperance** is the ability to submit one's desires (particularly bodily appetites) to the control of reason; **fortitude** (or strength of character) is the ability to overcome fears and other tendencies that discourage one from pursuit of what is good; **justice***, as defined by Thomas Aquinas*, is "a habit whereby one renders to each one his due by a constant and perpetual will" (ST 2-2.58.1). The cardinal virtues are distinguished from the theological virtues* in that the cardinal virtues lead to our natural fulfillment and are attainable by our natural powers (if the effects of sin are not taken into consideration), while the theological virtues require a special infusion of divine grace*.

CARROLL, JOHN (1735-1815). The first Catholic bishop in the United States. Born in Upper Marlboro, Maryland, he entered the Jesuits* in 1753. He was ordained priest in 1761 (or perhaps 1769) and taught in Europe until the suppression of the Jesuits in 1773. He returned to America in 1774. In 1776, he accompanied Benjamin Franklin to Canada in an effort to secure Canadian support of the American Revolution. The pope named him superior of the American missions in 1784. In 1789, he was elected bishop by the clergy of Baltimore. He was ordained bishop in 1790 and named archbishop in 1808, when the diocese of Baltimore, initially covering the entire United States, was subdivided into five dioceses. He supported religious liberty* and the cooperation of the Church with the secular authorities and with members of other religions. He deserves much credit for establishing the foundations of the Church in the new republic.

CATECHESIS (Gk *katechein*, to instruct). Instruction in the doctrines and life of the Church. **CATECHETICS** is the academic study of the goals and methods of catechesis. Catechesis differs from apologetics* in that it presupposes, in its audience, faith or at least interest in becoming a member of the Church. It is distinguished from theology* in that it is instruction in the Christian faith rather than systematic reflection upon it. As part of the process of Christian formation, catechesis is closely related to liturgy* and not sharply distinguished from evangelization*. Catechesis was initially bound up with the catechumenate*, but, after the decline of the catechumenate and the rise of infant baptism, it mainly involved post-baptismal instruction, especially of children. From the sixteenth century to the twentieth it was focused on teaching children the contents of printed catechisms*. A revival of catechetical studies in the twentieth century led to a broader view of catechesis, reflected in the *General Catechetical Directory*, issued by Rome in 1971. The principles of this document are adapted and applied to the situation of the United States in *Sharing the Light of Faith: National Catechetical Directory for Catholics of the United States*, issued by the National Conference of Catholic bishops in 1979. These documents describe the aim of catechesis as the fostering of mature faith and thus see all forms of catechesis as oriented in some way to the catechesis of adults.

CATECHISM. A manual that summarizes Church teachings. The catechism, originally an oral presentation of Christian doctrine, came with the advent of printing to be identified with books and booklets. The genre was popularized by Martin Luther, who regarded the catechism as an instrument of reform in combatting ignorance of the faith. He wrote both a large catechism for use by pastors and preachers and a short catechism as a means to instruct children and the uneducated (both 1529). The latter was in the form of questions and answers. Catechisms such as Luther's Large Catechism, the *Heidelberg Catechism* (1563), and the Westminster Catechism (1647) were confessional statements accepted as normative of the Lutheran, Reformed (Calvinist) and Presbyterian traditions, respectively.

From the sixteenth century onward Catholics have produced a steady flow of catechisms. Early Jesuits, notably St. Peter Canisius (d. 1597) and St. Robert Bellarmine* (d. 1621), produced catechisms that exercised wide influence throughout the Catholic world, including English-speaking countries. Many Catholic catechisms, such as that of Edmund Auger (1591) in France, were polemical in nature, while others, such as that of St. Toribio de Mongrovejo in Peru, were used as means of evangelization*. Several bishops in the United States, e.g., Frederic Baraga of Marquette, Michigan, and Francis Norbert Blanchet of Oregon City, compiled catechisms for Native Americans*. Others imported and adapted European catechisms for Irish, French, German, Polish, and Italian Catholics. The great diversity of catechisms caused the American bishops at the Third Plenary Council of Baltimore (1884) to mandate a standard text for the whole country. Despite criticisms leveled against it, the "Baltimore Catechism" gradually displaced most other catechisms. It was revised in 1941 and continued to be the accepted text for children as well as adults until the Second Vatican Council.

Before Vatican II almost all Catholic catechisms in the United States and elsewhere belonged to the genre of "small catechisms." Only the Catechism of the Council of Trent (1566), also known as the "Roman Catechism," for pastors and preachers, was regarded as a "major" or "large catechism."

In 1992 Pope John Paul II* promulgated the *Catechism of the Catholic Church*. The CCC follows the structure of the Trent catechism, but reflects the teachings of Vatican II and addresses contemporary issues in the light of Catholic teachings. By way of introduction to the catechism, the pope gives a brief account of its genesis, sources, structure, purpose, and intended audiences in the apostolic constitution *Fidei depositum*. The Catechism's 2,865 numbered paragraphs are divided into four parts under the traditional headings of the creed, the liturgy and sacraments, moral life and commandments, and prayer. In the words of John Paul, it is "a sure norm for teaching the faith." The catechism is to serve the church's pastors (the bishops) and publishers of catechetical materials as an "authentic reference text for teaching catholic doctrine and particularly for preparing local catechisms."

CATECHUMEN (Gk *katechoumenos*, "person being instructed"). A person preparing for baptism*. According to the *Apostolic Tradition* of Hippolytus of Rome (A.D. 215), the **CATECHUMENATE** could last as long as three years. It involved many rituals, leading up to baptism and admission to the eucharist* at the Easter Vigil (*see* EASTER). Because the catechumens were excluded from the eucharist, they attended the mass* only up through the homily*; hence, what is now called the Liturgy of the Word was in the past called the Mass of the Catechumens. The catechumenate declined in the fourth century, as candidates often postponed baptism till later in life, in order to avail of its forgiveness of sins. In practice, the catechumenate was shortened to a final preparatory period in the weeks before baptism. When infants began to form the great majority of those baptized, the catechumenate disappeared.

In 1963, Vatican Council II called for the restoration of the catechumenate, and this became part of the *Rite of Christian Initiation of Adults* (1972) (*see* INITIATION). It includes a Rite of Acceptance into the Order of Catechumens, followed by a period of instruction and training (the catechumenate proper) of indeterminate length, which closes with a Rite of Election or Enrollment of Names, in which the Church formally "elects" or accepts the catechumens as candidates for initiation. There follows a Period of Purification and Enlightenment, normally coinciding with the Lent* preceding baptism. Three rites of self-examination and repentance, called "Scrutinies," each including a rite of exorcism*, are celebrated, normally during the masses of the Third, Fourth, and Fifth Sundays of Lent. A formal presentation of the Creed occurs during the week following the third scrutiny, and the catechumenate concludes with rites on Holy Saturday preparatory to the celebration of the sacraments of initiation at the Easter Vigil.

CATHARS (Gk *katharos*, "pure"). A group of dualistic heretical movements in Europe between the eleventh and fourteenth centuries. Cathars were found in Italy, Germany, and France, especially in the south of France, where they were known as **Albigensians**, from the city of Albi. The Cathars had affinities with Gnosticism* and Manichaeism*. There may have been a direct connection with Manichaeism by way of the **Bogomils** ("beloved of God"), a dualistic sect that appeared in the Balkans in the tenth century and influenced European Cathars at least from the mid-twelfth century. Cathars tended to say that Satan created the material world and to identify Satan with the God of Genesis. Some held that Christ did not truly have a material body. The Cathars' ethical code was strongly ascetical, rejecting sexual relations and the begetting of children as well as the eating of meat and animal products. Much of Cathar life was centered on the "Perfect," an elite who kept the ethical code in all its rigor. All of this resembles Manichaeism.

The Cathars were condemned at a number of local councils and at the Fourth Lateran Council* in 1215. In 1209, Pope Innocent III* declared a crusade* against the Albigensians, which became at least as much a struggle of the French kings for power over the south of France. Fighting continued till 1229. In 1233 or 1234, Gregory IX instituted the papal inquisition* against the Cathars. Inquisitors, chiefly Dominicans, had power to interrogate and to judge, and after 1252 to use torture. Many suspected Cathars were turned over to the secular government to be burned. As a result of the use of force and the persuasive power of Dominican and Franciscan preachers, the Cathars disappeared by the middle of the fourteenth century.

CATHEDRAL (Gk *kathedra*, "throne", or "seat"). The principal church of a diocese*, where the bishop* preaches and conducts services. It is the location of the bishop's throne (Greek *kathedra* or Latin *cathedra*), one of the most ancient symbols of the bishop's authority.

CATHERINE OF SIENA, ST. (Caterina di Benincasa, 1347-1380). Catherine from an early age lived a life of solitude and mystical prayer, entering the Third Order of St. Dominic at the age of eighteen and afterward devoting herself to service of the poor and needy of Siena. She gathered a circle of disciples and wrote them many letters of spiritual counsel. Due to her reputation for sanctity, she became influential in public life, working to bring peace between Florence and the papacy, to bring the pope back to Rome from Avignon*, to avert what became the Great Western Schism*, and to promote a crusade*. Her most important written work is the *Dialogue* (between the soul and God), based in large part on a mystical experience she had in 1377. She was canonized in 1461 and in 1970 was named a Doctor of the Church*, one of two women to be so named (the other was Teresa of Avila*). Her feast is celebrated on April 29.

CATHOLIC CHARITIES USA. Founded in 1910 as the National Conference of Catholic Charities, this organization assumed its present name in 1986. It assists in coordinating the efforts of diocesan charitable agencies and provides information to them. It also engages in advocacy on public policy issues and is responsible for Catholic programs of disaster relief in the United States. It represents U.S. charities in Caritas Internationalis, the international conference of Catholic Charities. In its earlier years, it was concerned to promote the professionalization of social work. Later, like their counterparts in Catholic hospitals* and universities*, members became concerned lest professionalization cause a loss of religious motivation for service. The 1,200 member agencies of Catholic Charities provide a wide range of social services, including food, shelter, and counseling, to the needy, irrespective of religion. In all, more than twelve million people received assistance in 1991. Deteriorating conditions for America's poor have resulted in a great increase in the proportion of member agencies' services dedicated to basic food and shelter, from 23 percent in 1981 to 68 percent in 1991.

CATHOLIC RELIEF SERVICES (CRS). The official overseas relief and development agency of the Catholic Church in the United States. It is a separately incorporated organization, administered by a board of bishops appointed by the U.S. Catholic Conference (*see* EPISCOPAL CONFERENCE). It was founded in 1943 as War Relief Services—NCWC [National Catholic Welfare Conference], and its mission was to provide aid to refugees, prisoners of war, and nations damaged by World War II. In 1954 it assumed its present name. It now operates in more than seventy countries worldwide, and has regional offices for Africa, the Middle East, Southeast Asia, India, Central America, and South America. It provides emergency and disaster assistance, for instance in the recurrent famines in sub-Saharan Africa, and sponsors development programs for the elimination of the long-term causes of poverty and hunger. There are no religious restrictions as to who may receive aid. The agency is funded chiefly by private donations, especially through the CRS Annual Appeal. From the U.S. government it receives food for distribution and some transportation assistance and other grant support.

CATHOLIC WORKER. A movement founded in New York in 1933 by Dorothy Day (1897-1980) and Peter Maurin (1877-1949). Maurin, a French immigrant, brought a social vision shaped by the papal social encyclicals and French Catholic thought. Day, who had converted to Catholicism in 1927, brought a background of experience in American radical movements, as well as leadership and journalistic talents. The Catholic Worker (CW) is a loose federation of communities, not a centralized organization. In keeping with Maurin's vision, CW communities operate *houses of hospitality*, providing meals ("soup kitchens"), lodging, and other services to the urban homeless and needy. CW farms, though never achieving Maurin's ideal of large farming communes or "agronomic universities," promote a simple and self-sufficient life on the land and serve as rural houses of hospitality. Under Day's influence, the CW has maintained a firm pacifism*, and CW members, including Day, have often been involved in demonstrations and acts of civil disobedience protesting war, military industry, and civil defense programs. Especially through the newspaper, *The Catholic Worker*, edited by Day until her death and still published by the New York CW community, the CW has had a significant impact on American Catholic intellectual life, even among those who do not share its radicalism and pacifism. The May 1996 issue of *The Catholic Worker* listed around 150 CW houses, including eleven farms, in the United States, three houses in Canada, and eight in other countries. Several of these houses publish newspapers of their own.

CATHOLICITY (Gk *katholikos*, "universal"). "Universality, comprehensiveness"; one of the "marks of the Church," mentioned in the Nicene Creed*. The term is first attested in Ignatius of Antioch* (early second century), for whom it referred to the whole Church rather than the local church. Later it meant the authentic Church as distinct from heretical sects. Cyril of Jerusalem (ca. 350) explained the Church's catholicity as its extension throughout the world, its incorporation of every class of human being, and the completeness of its possession of saving doctrines, virtues, and spiritual gifts. St. Augustine*, opposing the Donatists* in the early fifth century, spoke of catholicity as communion with the Church throughout the world.

The relation between catholicity as a mark of the Church and "Catholic" as the name of a church is problematic. The Eastern Orthodox* speak of their church as Catholic, and many Anglicans* and Protestants* also do so, or at least regard catholicity as essential to the church. After the divisions between the churches, especially between the Protestant Reformation and the Second Vatican Council (1962-1965), Roman Catholic writers tended to treat the catholicity of the Church as its worldwide extension, united under a single visible head, the pope*. Vatican II acknowledged that the divisions among Christians were obstacles to the Church's full expression of its catholicity. It described catholicity as a unity in diversity, wherein "the individual parts bring their own gifts to the other parts and to the whole church." The pope, it said, "presides over the universal communion in charity and safeguards legitimate differences, while taking care that what is particular not only does no harm to unity but rather is conducive to it" (LG 13).

CCD. *See* CONFRATERNITY OF CHRISTIAN DOCTRINE.

CELIBACY. Abstention from marriage* and sexual activity. The term usually is applied to such abstention when it is permanent and for a religious purpose (frequently object of a vow*). Celibacy is found in many religions and has a variety of rationales, e.g., transformation of sexual energy, a sign of otherworldly commitment, or avoidance of involvement in a physical or bodily realm that is seen as evil. It is not found in Judaism of the OT period, except among small groups such as the Essenes, around the time of Jesus. Jesus' own celibacy, and similarly that of Paul (1 Cor 7.8, 32), can be understood in terms of their overriding commitment to the kingdom of God. Most of the other apostles, notably Peter, were married (e.g., 1 Cor 9.5). Celibates (virgins*) of both sexes are attested in second-century sources, and the practice of celibacy increased in the fourth century when monasticism* replaced martyrdom* as the most revered form of the imitation of Christ. A movement toward celibacy of the clergy is first seen in the early fourth century. The Synod of Elvira (ca. 306) required (perhaps for reasons of ritual purity) that bishops, priests, and deacons abstain from sexual relations with their wives. The First Council of Nicaea (325) forbade deacons, priests, and bishops to marry, though those already married could enter these orders. Efforts to enforce clerical celibacy in the West lost ground between the fifth and tenth centuries but became more successful in the eleventh century. The First Lateran Council* (1123) forbade priests, deacons, or subdeacons to live with wives or concubines, and the Second Lateran Council (1139) declared the marriages of clerics and religious to be invalid. This rule was firmly reiterated by the Council of Trent* (1563), after clerical marriage continued to be practiced in parts of Europe in the later Middle Ages. It remains the norm in the Roman Rite: married men may not be ordained priests, though they may be ordained deacons*. No one may marry after ordination. Some exceptions have been made in recent times to allow married men who become Catholics after having been ministers in other churches (in most cases, churches in the Anglican Communion*) to be ordained as Catholic priests in the Roman Rite. In the Eastern Rites (with some exceptions), as among the Eastern Orthodox*, married men may be ordained priests, but not bishops; marriage after ordination is forbidden.

Although Vatican II acknowledged that celibacy "is not ... required by the very nature of the priesthood" (PO 16), it is defended in recent Church documents as a symbol of Christ's love of the Church, as a sign of the priest's total dedication to service of Christ and the Church, and as a means of freeing the priest for this complete dedication. Though few in the Church challenge the value of celibacy, many question the obligation of celibacy for diocesan priests (as distinct from those in religious communities), especially in the light of the current shortage of priests.

CENOBITE (COENOBITE) (Gk *koinos bios*, "common life"). A religious* who lives in community under vows*, as contrasted with an anchorite*. Cenobite monasticism* dates from the work of Pachomius (ca. 286-346) in the Egyptian desert.

CHALCEDON, COUNCIL OF (451). A council whose purpose was to settle the continuing controversy over the divinity and humanity of Jesus Christ*. The Council of Ephesus* in 431 had condemned the view attributed to Nestorius* that Mary was not to be called "God-bearer" (*theotokos*), which seemed to imply that the human Jesus, born of Mary, was different in person from the Word of God. In opposition to Nestorianism, Eutyches, a monk of Constantinople, so stressed the divinity of Jesus that he seemed to deny that his flesh was truly human; the humanity was, so to speak, absorbed into the divinity. This and related positions were called **monophysitism***, from the Greek words for "one nature." After Flavian, Patriarch of Constantinople, condemned Eutyches, a second council at Ephesus in 449 (later known as the "robber synod") was strong-armed by Dioscorus, patriarch of Alexandria, into rehabilitating Eutyches and banishing Flavian. Pope Leo I* supported Flavian, sending him the *Tome*, defending the two natures of Christ, but this was not read at the council in Ephesus. In 450, the Emperor Theodosius died, and power was assumed by his sister Pulcheria, a supporter of Leo. Her husband Marcian became Emperor and soon called a new council to settle the Christological controversy. The council met in October 451 at Chalcedon, across the Bosporus from Constantinople. It affirmed the teaching of Cyril of Alexandria against Nestorianism and the *Tome* of Leo against monophysitism. After restating the teachings of the Councils of Nicaea I*, Constantinople I*, and Ephesus* (431), the council used Leo's language to declare that the one Christ is "acknowledged in two natures which undergo no confusion, no change, no division, no separation; at no point was the difference between the natures taken away through the union, but rather the property of both natures is preserved and comes together into a single person (*prosōpon*) and a single subsistent being (*hypostasis*)...." From the last-mentioned term, this doctrine is called that of the **hypostatic union**: the union of the two natures (divine and human) in the one person or hypostasis of Jesus Christ. The teaching of Chalcedon was eventually accepted in East and West, except in much of Egypt, where monophysite sympathies remained strong, and in Armenia and parts of the Syrian church. The Oriental Orthodox* churches of today are the descendants of those who did not accept Chalcedon.

CHALLENGE OF PEACE, THE. A pastoral letter* published by the United States bishops on May 3, 1983, on war* and peace* in the contemporary world. The first chapter explores biblical perspectives on war and peace, develops the traditional just-war theory (*see* WAR), and praises the witness of nonviolence (*see* PACIFISM). The second chapter applies Catholic teaching to problems of nuclear* war; it condemns acts of war directed at civilian populations, opposes the initiation of nuclear war, voices skepticism about the possibility of limited retaliatory nuclear war, and expresses serious moral reservations about nuclear deterrence, without condemning it outright. The third chapter discusses ways of making the world more peaceful, while the fourth and concluding chapter explores spiritual and pastoral responses to the challenge of peacemaking in a nuclear age. Perhaps more than any other agency, the letter introduced discussion of nuclear war as a *moral* issue into American political discourse. Within the Church, many saw the letter, both in its contents and in the extensive consultative process that went into its making, as a model for how the Church should deal with moral and social issues.

CHARISMATIC RENEWAL. A spiritual movement that grows out of American Pentecostalism. Pentecostalism, which began in the United States in 1901, emphasized a strong experience of "baptism in the Holy Spirit," the outward sign of which was speaking in tongues (glossolalia*). The influence of the Pentecostal movement spread from the specifically Pentecostal churches into the "mainline" Protestant churches, where it came to be called "neo-Pentecostalism" or the "charismatic movement," from the **charisms** or special graces given to the Church and described in St. Paul's letters, especially 1 Corinthians 12. Besides tongues, these gifts included prophecy, healing*, and the discernment* of spirits. The Catholic charismatic renewal began in 1967 at Duquesne University in Pittsburgh and quickly spread to other parts of the United States and the rest of the world. Baptism in the Spirit is understood as a conscious experience of the Holy Spirit*, who has already been given in baptism* and confirmation*; speaking in tongues is not regarded as a necessary sign of it. There were an estimated 5000 charismatic prayer groups in the United States in 1992 and many more worldwide. Centers of charismatic renewal activity include Ann Arbor, Michigan, the Franciscan University of Steubenville, Ohio, and the Pecos Benedictine Abbey, New Mexico. Some charismatics live together in structured "covenant communities," including single and married people. The International Communications Office of the Catholic Charismatic renewal is in Rome. The movement has received a favorable but cautious reception from Church authorities, including Popes Paul VI* and John Paul II*. Problems have arisen because of a tendency of some charismatics to interpret the Bible in a fundamentalist* way and because of the authoritarian structure of some charismatic communities.

CHARITY. *See* LOVE.

CHARLEMAGNE ("Charles the Great") (742-814). King of the Franks and first Holy Roman Emperor. The son of King Pepin III, he ruled jointly with his brother Carloman from 768 till Carloman's death in 771 and was sole ruler thereafter. He conquered surrounding peoples, establishing rule over what is now France, the Low Countries, Germany, Switzerland, Austria, and parts of Italy and other adjoining countries. He endeavored to create an orderly society in the midst of the chaos of early medieval Europe. He continued the religious reform begun under his predecessors and did not hesitate to intervene to resolve theological disputes. Though illiterate himself, he promoted education, especially of the clergy, and presided over the "Carolingian renaissance," a revival of Latin learning that continued under his successors through the ninth century. This revival was centered in the palace school at Aachen, headed at first by Alcuin of York (735-804). On Christmas day, 800, at St. Peter's Basilica in Rome, Pope Leo III crowned Charlemagne emperor, successor to the ancient Roman emperors in the West. Neither Leo nor Charles acknowledged the authority of the Empress Irene, then ruling in Byzantium. Coronation by the pope may have been meant to show the pope's superiority to the emperor, but in fact, Charlemagne and his successors saw themselves as the supreme temporal rulers of Christendom, responsible for the spiritual as well as material welfare of Christian society. They overshadowed many popes in the exercise of power in the Church, until their status was reduced by the reforms under Gregory VII* (1073-1085) and the resolution of the investiture* crisis. Politically, the Empire declined under Charlemagne's successors but was revived by Otto I in 962. In the twelfth century it acquired the title Holy Roman Empire. It survived in some form until it was dissolved under Napoleon in 1806.

CHINESE RITES CONTROVERSY. A result of the work of the Jesuit* Matteo Ricci (1552-1610), the founder of the modern Christian mission to China. Ricci became learned in Chinese culture and sought to express Catholicism in a manner acceptable to Chinese intellectuals. Controversy arose when members of other religious orders besides the Jesuits entered China after 1630. These missionaries, who tended to work with the rural populace rather than the urban intellectuals, saw in the Jesuits' adaptations the introduction of superstition and idolatry into

Catholicism. Controversy focused on veneration of the sage Confucius (ca. 551-479 B.C.), veneration of dead ancestors (particularly the ceremonial bow [*kowtow*] to tablets containing their names), and the use of the Chinese terms *Tien* (Heaven) and *Shangti* (High God) as translations for "God." A papal commission studied the issue from 1697 to 1704. Its decree in 1704 prohibiting the controversial usages was confirmed by Pope Clement XI but not immediately promulgated in China. The issue was finally settled by the Apostolic Constitution *Ex quo singulari*, issued by Pope Benedict XIV in 1742, forbidding the usages and imposing an oath against them on all missionaries. This decision severely curtailed the spread of the Catholic Church in China, as the ritual veneration of ancestors was a central bond of Chinese family and civic life. Changed political and social circumstances led to an instruction by Pope Pius XII* in 1939 lifting most of the prohibitions and suppressing the oath. *See also* INCULTURATION.

CHRISM (Gk "oil for anointing," from *chriein*, "to anoint"). The holy oil used for anointing in the sacraments of baptism*, confirmation*, and order*. Normally a mixture of olive oil and balsam, it is consecrated by the bishop at the Chrism Mass on Holy Thursday (*see* HOLY WEEK).

CHRISTMAS (Engl "Christ mass"). The celebration of the birth of Jesus. Although the date of Jesus' birth is unknown, it has been observed on December 25 in the West since the third or early fourth century. The dating of December 25 has received two explanations. (1) It was chosen to coincide with the festal day, *dies natalis solis invicti* ("birthday of the unconquered sun"), established at the winter solstice by the Roman emperor Aurelian in 274. (2) It was computed from the date of the passion of Jesus. The latter explanation draws on an ancient supposition that the crucifixion occurred on March 25, Friday the 14th day of Nisan in the year A.D. 29. Adapting a Jewish tradition that the birth of a great man occurred on the same date as his death (so that he lived an exact, non-fractional, number of years), the *conception* of Jesus was located on March 25 (the present Feast of the Annunciation), and hence the birth on December 25. A comparable pair of explanations are available for the feast of the Epiphany*, January 6, which was a nativity festival in the Eastern churches (as it still is for the Armenian Church). Between the fourth and sixth centuries, the

December 25 date of the nativity celebration became standard in the East.

A four-week Advent*, preparatory to Christmas, dates from the sixth or seventh century. On Christmas itself, there are three eucharistic liturgies, for mass at midnight, dawn, and later in the day. These are vestiges of a fifth- or sixth-century Roman custom of celebrating mass at different churches in the city. In the fourth to sixth centuries, the feasts of St. Stephen, St. John, and the Holy Innocents were established on the three days immediately following Christmas. The Feast of the Holy Family was established in 1921 and situated on the Sunday after Christmas (when Christmas is not a Sunday) in 1969. An octave day for Christmas was added in the seventh century as a feast of Mary, January 1. In the West the feast of the Epiphany became a celebration of the manifestation of Jesus to the Gentiles, symbolized by the Magi of Matthew 2.1-12. The Christmas season concludes with the feast of the Baptism of the Lord, on the Sunday after Epiphany.

CHRISTOLOGY. The branch of theology that treats the person and mission of Jesus Christ*. "Christology" refers especially to the study of the divinity and humanity of Jesus. The study of his work as savior is called **soteriology**, or the theology of the atonement*. These two investigations, however, cannot proceed apart from each other. The primary data for Christology are the NT records of Jesus' words and deeds and of the early Church's reflection on the meaning of Jesus, read in the context of the Church's life and liturgy. This reflection continued beyond the NT period and resulted in the dogmatic definitions of the first ecumenical councils*: Nicaea I* (325), which affirmed the divinity of Jesus against Arianism*; Constantinople I* (381), which affirmed against Apollinarianism* that Jesus had a fully human soul; Ephesus* (431), which affirmed the unity of divine and human in Jesus, against Nestorianism*; and Chalcedon* (451), which affirmed against monophysitism* the distinction of the divine and human natures joined in the one person of Jesus. These doctrines should not be seen as providing a full Christology for the Church, but rather as setting some limits within which Christology must proceed. The revival of biblical studies in the twentieth century has led to significant work in Christology by Catholic theologians, notably Karl Rahner*, Edward Schillebeeckx, and Walter Kasper.

CHURCH (Gk *kyriakos*, "of the Lord," an adjective modifying a noun designating a building). While in English "church" can indicate a building, its theologically more important senses occur when it is a translation of Gk *ekklēsia*, "assembly," specifically the assembly of God's people. In this sense, it may refer to a local or regional Christian community, a "denomination" (e.g., the Methodist Church), the Christian community as a whole, or the leadership of the community.

The documents of Vatican Council II* represent the Catholic Church's most authoritative expression of its own self-understanding as Church. The Council's *Dogmatic Constitution on the Church (Lumen Gentium)* emphasizes that the primary sense of "Church" is the whole community of the "People of God"*. It thereby counteracts the trend in the modern period to use the term "Church" primarily to refer to Church leaders (pope and bishops). It also states that the whole Church is present in each local church (LG 26). The latter is not simply a subdivision of the universal Church, but rather the universal Church is a communion of local churches.

The Catholic Church understands itself to be more than just a denomination within the whole Christian community; indeed, the whole Church of Christ "subsists in" it (LG 8). Yet Christian bodies separated from the Catholic Church also partake in the reality of the Church of Christ in many respects, for instance, in their possession of a valid baptism, and Vatican II does not withhold from them the name of "churches" (*see* ECUMENISM). Hence, the Church of Christ cannot be said simply to coincide with the Catholic Church.

See also ECCLESIOLOGY.

CHURCH OF THE EAST. *See* ASSYRIAN CHURCH OF THE EAST.

CLERIC, CLERGY (Gk *klēros*, "lot, portion"). A cleric is one who is set apart for ministry in the Church. The clergy are the collective body of clerics, as distinguished from the laity*. The use of "clerical" and "lay" as opposing terms dates from the third century. It was bound up with the introduction into the Church of the Greco-Roman concepts of order (*ordo*), meaning a distinct class within society, and "ordination" as admission to such a class. Today, the sacrament of order* is the admission to the clerical state, which thus is limited to deacons*, priests*, and bishops*. Before 1972, those in minor orders (*see* ORDER, SACRAMENT OF) were considered clerics. In the middle ages, **tonsure** (later, "first tonsure"), a ceremonial cutting of the hair, rather than ordination, was the ritual of admission to the clerical state. First tonsure was abolished in 1972.

COLLEGIALITY. The doctrine that the bishops*, with the pope* at their head, form a "college" or corporate body, sharing supreme authority* in the Church. This was a controversial theme at Vatican Council II* in that it challenged tendencies toward "papal monarchy" or concentration of all authority in the pope. Vatican II develops the idea of collegiality as follows: "Just as, by the Lord's decree, St. Peter and the other apostles constitute one apostolic college, so in a similar way the Roman Pontiff, Peter's successor, and the bishops, successors of the apostles, are joined together.... The order of bishops, which succeeds the college of apostles in teaching authority and pastoral government, and indeed in which the apostolic body continues to exist without interruption, is also the subject of supreme and full power over the universal Church, provided it remains united with its head, the Roman Pontiff, and never without its head ..." (LG 22). Collegiality is expressed solemnly in an ecumenical council* but may be expressed in other ways. In an extended sense, "collegiality" refers to the shared responsibility of the bishop and pastors, or of the pastor and people.

COLORS, LITURGICAL. *See* VESTMENTS.

COMMUNION OF SAINTS. This phrase, which forms part of the Apostles' Creed (*see* CREED), first appears in creedal statements toward the end of the fourth century in the West. It does not appear in Eastern creeds. The Latin original, *communio sanctorum,* is ambiguous, meaning "communion of holy things" or "communion of holy persons." There is a similar ambiguity in the corresponding Greek phrase, *koinōnia tōn hagiōn.* If, however, as scholars now incline to surmise, the phrase is originally Greek, its primary meaning is "communion of holy things," meaning the sharing on the part of the members of the Church in the eucharist*, especially, and the other sacraments*, sacramentals*, etc. If the phrase is originally Latin, it primarily refers to holy persons. In either case, the reference is to the Church*. As the interpretation of the phrase developed in the West, "communion of saints" denoted primarily the union of all those who share in Christ's salvation and the gift of the Holy Spirit*, both those now living and those who have died. It was customary to explicate the communion of saints as comprising the Church Militant (those still living), the Church Suffering or Church Expectant (in purgatory*), and the Church Triumphant (in heaven*), but these expressions are no longer commonly used.

CONCILIARISM. A late-medieval theory of church authority*, which held that authority is given through the Holy Spirit* to the Church* as a whole, and that an ecumenical (general) council* is the best organ for exercising that authority. The judgment of such a council could overrule that of a pope*. Conciliarism was first developed in the fourteenth century by John (Quidort) of Paris, Marsilius of Padua, William of Ockham*, Jean Gerson, and others, and received its fullest statement in the *De concordantia catholica* (1433) of Nicholas of Cusa*. It gained momentum in the late fourteenth century with the Great Western Schism (1378-1415)*, when there were two and then three claimants to the papacy, all with some claim to legitimacy. It was given expression in the decrees of the Council of Constance* (1414-1418), which resolved that schism: *Haec sancta* (1415) declared that the council, as a general council, had its power directly from Christ, and that the pope must obey it, while *Frequens* (1415) required that councils be convened at regular intervals in the future. Conciliarism lost support in the contention surrounding the Council of Basel* (1431-1449) and was condemned by Pope Pius II in 1460. It survived in Gallicanism* but was excluded by Vatican Council I's* declaration of full and supreme papal jurisdiction over the Church. Vatican II's teaching on episcopal collegiality* responds to some of the concerns of conciliarism, but insists that the college of bishops exercises supreme authority only when acting together with the pope.

CONFESSION (Lt *confessio*, "acknowledgement, avowal"). (1) The sacrament of penance or reconciliation*, or, more properly, that part of the sacramental rite that consists of the penitent's recitation of sins to the confessor (the priest who is minister of the sacrament). Confession is normally to be done individually, with specification of the number and kind of serious sins. Absolution* may follow a general confession of sins only under restricted circumstances; in such a case the penitent is to seek individual confession as soon as possible. Catholics are obliged to make sacramental confession of any serious sins at least once a year. The **seal of confession** binds a confessor never to reveal what is told to him by a penitent in confession.

(2) A profession of faith, especially a formally stated profession, such as the Augsburg Confession of 1530 (Lutheran). This usage, more common among Protestants than Catholics, has led to the use of "confession" as a designation for a Protestant religious body.

(3) The tomb of a martyr* (deriving its name from martyrdom as a confession of faith), or the crypt that contains the martyr's relics* beneath the high altar* of a church.

CONFIRMATION. The second of the sacraments* of Christian initiation*, in which believers receive the Holy Spirit* in a special way. "This giving of the Holy Spirit conforms believers more fully to Christ and strengthens them so that they may bear witness to Christ ..." (Introduction to the *Rite of Confirmation* [1971]). Some distinction between baptism* and what later became confirmation may be inferred from the sequence of baptism and the descent of the Holy Spirit in the gospel narratives of the baptism of Jesus, from the story of Pentecost in Acts 2, and from Acts 8.12-17 and 19.1-7, which distinguish baptism from a post-baptismal laying on of hands that confers the Holy Spirit. The *Apostolic Tradition* of Hippolytus of Rome (A.D. 215) portrays a post-baptismal anointing of the baptized by the bishop* before the whole assembly. By the fifth century, the number of those baptized was such that they no longer could all be baptized in a single ceremony by the bishop but were baptized at various times by priests. The custom in the East came to be that the priest performed the anointing ("chrismation"), although with chrism* blessed by the bishop. In the West, those baptized were to be anointed later by the bishop. The term "confirmation" was first used in the early fifth century in Gaul to refer to the bishop's confirmation (in the sense of ratification) of baptism. In parts of Europe, the bishop was remote, and the interval between baptism and confirmation widened. The intimate connection between baptism and confirmation was lost. When the number of sacraments was fixed at seven in the twelfth century, confirmation was one of the seven. This was made official at the Council of Trent* (1547).

Between 450 and 470, Bishop Faustus of Riez (in Gaul) preached a Pentecost sermon in which he spoke of confirmation as "strengthening" (the literal meaning of "confirm") the baptized, giving them "arms for battle." Because parts of Faustus' sermon were circulated under the name of a (nonexistent) fourth-century pope, his theology, including the military image, had great influence on subsequent medieval and modern theology of confirmation.

Late-medieval theology held that confirmation should be received at the "age of discretion," which has usually been taken to be around twelve. Normally, confirmation was to precede first communion, but this sequence was reversed in eighteenth-century France, and then more generally in 1910 when Pope Pius X* set the normal age of first communion at seven. In the Eastern Rites of the Catholic Church, as among the Eastern Orthodox, confirmation is conferred immediately after baptism.

Vatican Council II directed, "The rite of confirmation is ... to be revised. The point of this revision is that the very close connection of this sacrament with the whole process of Christian initiation may become more clearly visible" (SC 71). The 1972 *Rite of Christian Initiation of Adults* (RCIA) restores this connection, so that, as in the early Church, a catechumen* is confirmed immediately after baptism and before first communion, while a candidate who is validly baptized but newly received into the Church is confirmed before first communion. The disharmony between this practice and that followed for those baptized in infancy and raised Catholic reflects a discrepancy between the ancient and contemporary theology of confirmation on the one hand and the medieval/modern theologies on the other. It is likely to be a source of further liturgical change in the future.

The ordinary minister of confirmation is the bishop, except that in the RCIA the priest confirms. Priests may be delegated to confirm in other circumstances as well. The age of confirmation is to be "about the age of discretion unless the conference of bishops determines another age" or for grave cause. In the United States, the National Council of Catholic Bishops has left the decision to the local bishop. In the rite of confirmation, the celebrant stretches his hands over the group to be confirmed and prays for the Holy Spirit to be sent upon them. He then anoints each individually with chrism, saying, "N., be sealed with the gift of the Holy Spirit."

CONFRATERNITY OF CHRISTIAN DOCTRINE (CCD). A confraternity is an organization or association of Catholics, under the supervision of Church authority, for some religious purpose. The Confraternity of Christian Doctrine began in Rome around 1560 as an association of priests and laymen who taught children and adults. Pope

Pius V recommended it to all bishops in 1571, and in 1905 Pope Pius X* ordered the establishment of the Confraternity of Christian Doctrine in every parish. At that time, the CCD was conceived as a distinct organization, headed locally by the pastor, and affiliated with the Archconfraternity of Christian Doctrine in Rome. In the United States, the CCD exists as a distinct organization on the national level, separately incorporated and governed by a board of trustees from the United States Catholic Conference. It holds the copyright for the New American Bible translation and licenses the publication of this translation and certain other religious literature. On the parish level, however, CCD became simply the designation of one of the ministries of the parish, namely, programs of religious instruction for children who do not attend Catholic schools. These programs are under the supervision of a parish CCD coordinator and/or a Director or Minister of Religious Education who has responsibility for a broader range of programs. They are overseen by the pastor, and coordinated by a diocesan Office of Religious Education or the equivalent and, at the national level, by the Division of Catechesis/Religious Education of the United States Catholic Conference.

CONGAR, YVES, O.P. (1904-1995). French Dominican theologian, whose ecclesiology was very influential at Vatican Council II*. Born at Sedan, France, he was ordained a Dominican priest in 1930. He was one of the first Catholics to participate actively in the ecumenical movement, and his *Divided Christendom* (1937) was a landmark of Catholic ecumenical theology. In *Lay People in the Church* (1953), he wrote of the Church as the "People of God" and of the importance of the laity within it. His *Vraie et fausse réforme dans l'Eglise (True and False Reform in the Church)* (1950) described the church as always in need of reform; it was suppressed by ecclesiastical authorities and never translated into English. In 1954, pressure from the Holy Office (*see* CONGREGATION FOR THE DOCTRINE OF THE FAITH) caused him to be removed from all teaching, lecturing, and publishing. But Pope John XXIII* appointed him a theological adviser at Vatican II (1962-1965). All of the Council's major documents reflect his thought, and some central passages are from his hand. After the council, his most important work was the three-volume *I Believe in the Holy Spirit* (1979). He was named a cardinal* by Pope John Paul II* in 1994.

CONGREGATION FOR THE DOCTRINE OF THE FAITH (CDF). One of the nine congregations of the Roman Curia*. Its responsibility is to examine questions of doctrine* and to evaluate books and other expressions of theological opinion. It has in recent times been involved in several well-publicized cases of censure of theologians. It originated as the Congregation of the Inquisition or Holy Office in 1542 (*see* INQUISITION), became the Congregation of the Holy Office in 1908, and acquired its present name in 1965. It is advised by the Pontifical Biblical Commission and the International Theological Commission.

CONSCIENCE. The human ability to make judgments of moral right and wrong. It is not just one of several factors in the formation of moral judgment; rather, it is itself one's best moral judgment, or, perhaps better, it is oneself in the act of making moral judgments. According to Thomas Aquinas*, conscience has three dimensions: (1) the ability to know and do good (*synderesis*); (2) recognition of what is good or evil in a particular situation (practical reasoning); (3) the specific judgment of what one must do in the situation (*conscientia*). Catholic moral theology recognizes an obligation to follow one's conscience, which simply means to follow one's best judgment. It acknowledges, however, that one's conscience may be "erroneous," in regard either to objective moral principles or to the facts of a situation or to the relation of the principles to the facts. Hence, there is an obligation not only to follow one's conscience, but also to *form* one's conscience in order to judge correctly. The Second Vatican Council stresses the dignity of conscience (GS 16) and bases its teaching on religious freedom* on that dignity (DH 2-3).

CONSCIENTIOUS OBJECTION. Refusal, on religious or moral grounds, to participate in war. Usually the term refers to objection to all wars (*see* PACIFISM). **Selective conscientious objection** is religious or moral objection to some but not all wars; it is based on just-war reasoning (*see* WAR). Some authors use the term **situational conscientious objection** to designate refusal to obey a specific order deemed immoral in a war one considers just. In the early centuries of the Church there are many examples of Christians refusing to fight, either out of a refusal to kill or because of the idolatrous ceremonies required of Roman soldiers. Medieval just-war theories entail the possibility of selective and situational conscientious objection; in practice, the issue was usually resolved in favor of obedience* to legitimate authority. Modern Western law on conscientious objection was crafted in response to pacifist Protestant churches, e.g., Quakers and Mennonites. Modern Catholic teaching prior to Vatican Council II did not allow room for general conscientious objection, although there were some individual Catholic conscientious objectors earlier in the twentieth century. But Vatican II held, "It … seems just that laws make humane provision for the case of those who refuse on grounds of conscience to bear arms, provided they consent to another way of serving the human community" (GS 79). In the United States, the Catholic bishops declared in 1968 and more strongly in 1971 that Catholics could be general or selective conscientious objectors. They have repeatedly called for extension of legal recognition to the latter as well as the former category.

CONSTANCE, COUNCIL OF (1414-18). An ecumenical council* that settled the Great Western Schism*. Constance is in present-day Switzerland. The council was convoked by John XXIII, pope in the Pisa line, under pressure from the Emperor Sigismund. Early in 1415, it passed the decree *Haec sancta*, declaring its supremacy over any pope. It proceeded to depose John XXIII. Then the council induced the Roman pope, Gregory XII, to resign; as a condition for his resignation, he was allowed to officially convoke the council, making it legitimate in his eyes. In 1417, the council deposed the Avignon* pope, Benedict XIII, after failing to secure his resignation. Finally, it resolved the schism by electing Pope Martin V in November 1417. The council's decrees *Haec sancta* and *Frequens* (1417), which required the calling of future councils at regular intervals, represent a high point for the influence of conciliarism* in the Church. The council also condemned the teaching of John Wyclif (ca. 1330-1384) of England, who had challenged papal power and eucharistic transubstantiation (*see* EUCHARIST), and Jan Hus (John Huss) (ca. 1372-1415) of Bohemia, who was accused of supporting Wyclif's ideas. Hus came to the council under a safe-conduct from Sigismund but was tried and found guilty of heresy by the council and turned over to the secular authorities to be burned at the stake on July 6, 1415.

CONSTANTINE I (THE GREAT) (ca. 280-337). The Roman Emperor first responsible for the toleration and official encouragement of the Christian religion. He was the son of Constantius (the "Caesar" or second-in-command in the West in the empire as divided by Diocletian) and St. Helena. Upon Constantius's death in 306, his troops proclaimed Constantine "Augustus" (primary ruler) in the West. He achieved sole power in the West with his victory over Maxentius at the Milvian Bridge near Rome in 312, a victory he attributed to the Christian God. This solidified Constantine's support of the Christian Church, with which he probably already had vague sympathies. Though he postponed baptism till his deathbed, his adherence to Christianity became clearer over time. Meeting with Licinius, Emperor in the East, at Milan in 313, he extended toleration to all religions, thus ending the persecution* of Christians. This came to be called the Edict of Milan, though it may not have been formally an edict. After defeating Licinius at Chrysopolis in 324, he attained sole power. He moved the capital of the Empire to Byzantium, which he had renamed as Constantinople* in 330.

His policies favored Christianity in many ways. He established Sunday* as a day of rest, built numerous churches, mitigated laws governing treatment of children, slaves, criminals, and celibates, and exempted Christian clergy from military service and burdensome civic duties. He saw it as his duty to preserve unity in the Church (and thereby continue to secure the favor of God on the Empire). Perhaps the peak of his influence came when he called and presided over the First Council of Nicaea* in 325. Historians now regard Constantine's reign as an ambiguous turning point in Church history. On the one hand, it ended persecution and enabled the Church to flourish in the Empire; on the other, it began the close involvement of secular with ecclesiastical power, which was to last through the Middle Ages and beyond.

CONSTANTINOPLE. City on the west bank of the Bosporus where it joins the Sea of Marmara, now Istanbul (from Gk *eis tēn polin*, "into the city") in Turkey. This was the town of Byzantium, renamed after Constantine I* transferred the capital of the Empire there in 330. It remained the capital of the Eastern (hence "Byzantine") Empire until it fell to the Turks in 1453. The First Council of Constantinople* (381) gave the bishop of Constantinople "the privileges of honor after the bishop of Rome" because Constantinople is the "new Rome"; the Council of Chalcedon* (451) made Constantinople second only to Rome in jurisdiction as well, though Rome did not accept this. In the sixth century the bishop of Constantinople began to use the title,

"Ecumenical Patriarch," originally meaning patriarch of the Empire, a title still used today. Since the Middle Ages, the churches of Constantinople and Rome have been separated from one another (*see* EASTERN ORTHODOX CHURCHES). The Patriarch of Constantinople has the highest jurisdiction in the Greek Orthodox Church and is accorded a primacy of honor by all the Eastern Orthodox churches.

CONSTANTINOPLE, COUNCILS OF. Four councils* of Constantinople are usually reckoned as ecumenical by Catholics:

I (381): Called by the Emperors Theodosius I and Gratian to settle the Arian* controversy. No Western bishops attended this council, but it was later acknowledged as ecumenical in the West as well as the East. It adopted what is now known as the "Nicene" or "Niceno-Constantinopolitan Creed," a restatement and expansion of the original creed of the First Council of Nicaea* in 325 (*see* CREED). It defended the divinity of the Holy Spirit* and, against Apollinarianism*, the presence in Christ of a truly human soul. It proclaimed the see of Constantinople* to be second in honor only to Rome*.

II (553): In an effort to squelch remaining tendencies toward Nestorianism* and to reconcile the monophysites*, the Emperor Justinian* called this council to condemn the "Three Chapters"—the person and writings of Theodore of Mopsuestia, the writings of Theodoret against Cyril of Alexandria, and the letter of Ibas of Edessa to Maris—as tainted with Nestorianism. Pope Vigilius had previously refused to agree to these condemnations. They were, however, accepted by the council, after which the pope reluctantly accepted them as well. The name of Origen* is included in a list of heretics condemned by this council, but this is now regarded as a later interpolation.

III (680-681): Called by the Emperor Constantine IV, this council condemned monothelitism*. It declared that there are two wills, divine and human, and likewise two "energies" or operations in Christ "inseparably, immovably, undividedly, and unconfusedly." It deposed Patriarch Macarius of Antioch and condemned Pope Honorius I (625-638). The decisions of the council, including the condemnation of Honorius, were approved by Pope Leo II.

IV (869-870): Anathematized the deposed Patriarch of Constantinople, Photius*, who in a synod in 867 had anathematized Pope Nicholas I, and reaffirmed the primacy of Nicholas. Photius was restored by the Emperor's order upon the death of his successor in 877, and a council at Constantinople in 879-880 appears to have approved the restoration and to have revoked the decision of the 869-870 council. The Eastern Orthodox* do not accept the ecumenicity of IV Constantinople, and some Catholic writers question it as well.

CONTEMPLATION. In Catholic spirituality*, this is a form of mental prayer* that consists in a simple dwelling upon God or dwelling in God's presence. It is contrasted with meditation*, when the latter term designates a succession of mental acts requiring effort of some sort. Some writers speak of **acquired contemplation**, which comes as a result of effort by our own natural powers. **Infused contemplation**, by contrast, is understood to be a direct gift of God, a self-communication of God in which the person having the experience is passive. The term *contemplation* suggests a subject intent upon an object, but in the actual experience of contemplation, this subject-object distinction tends to be overcome in a sense of unity.

CONTRACEPTION. *See* BIRTH CONTROL.

CONVERSION (Lt *conversio*, "turning around"). A change of mind and heart, a reorientation of one's life away from sin* and toward God in Christ. This is the broader and more traditional meaning of a term formerly used narrowly to refer to a case when a person, having previously belonged to another religious body or to none, makes a choice to join the Catholic Church. NT terms rendered as "conversion" are *epistrophē*, which emphasizes the element of turning or change, and *metanoia*, which emphasizes the taking up of new ways of thinking and feeling. While Christian literature often recalls dramatic examples of conversion, such as those of St. Paul (Acts 9) and St. Augustine* (described in his *Confessions*), contemporary theology and liturgy also recognize conversion as a continual need and ongoing process for all Christians and for the Church collectively. In this sense, the term and concept are prominent in recent Church documents and in the liturgies for the restored catechumenate* and the sacrament of reconciliation*.

COUNCIL. A meeting of Church leaders to discuss and to decide matters of doctrine and discipline. Particularly for earlier periods in Church history, there is no clear distinction between a council and a synod*. The term *council* usually designates the more important meetings. Councils may be **particular** or **ecumenical (general)**. Particular councils are divided in contemporary canon law into **provincial** councils, for all the churches in a province or region, and **plenary** councils, for all the churches belonging to a given episcopal conference*. Ecumenical councils are gatherings of the bishops of the whole church (though, at the discretion of the pope, others may be invited and even given a vote). According to Vatican Council II*, an ecumenical council is a solemn expression of the collegiality* of bishops in exercising supreme authority over the whole Church. Against conciliarism*, however, the Council adds, "There is never an ecumenical council which is not confirmed as such or at least accepted as such by the successor of Peter [the pope]. It is the prerogative of the Roman Pontiff to convoke these councils, to preside over them, and to confirm them" (LG 22). An ecumenical council may speak with infallibility* on matters of faith and morals.

It is sometimes difficult to determine whether a council is ecumenical. In earlier times, the pope did not always convoke or even attend councils now considered ecumenical, though at least his representatives took part in them. At times, the acknowledgment of a council as ecumenical seems to have been determined by its reception* by the whole Church. There is no official list of ecumenical councils, nor an official statement of the criteria that make a council ecumenical. Catholic lists normally recognize twenty-one ecumenical councils, however, from Nicaea I* (325) to Vatican II (1962-1965) (see the list of ecumenical councils in Appendix II). The Eastern Orthodox* recognize the ecumenicity of only the first seven of these councils, through Nicaea II* (787).

COUNTER-REFORMATION. A period of reform in the Church, lasting from the sixteenth into the eighteenth century, largely in response to the Protestant* Reformation. Catholic historians often prefer **Catholic Reformation** as a name for this period, to emphasize that it was not entirely a reaction against Protestantism and indeed began before Martin Luther's break with the Church. A principal agency of reform was the Council of Trent* (1545-63), which restated Catholic doctrine on justification* and on the sacraments* in opposition to the Protestants and, assisted by the popes of the period, curbed many of the abuses (e.g., the sale of indulgences*) that had significantly contributed to the success of the Protestant movements. The theology, and especially the liturgy and devotion of the period, tended to emphasize precisely those aspects that the Protestant Reformation had challenged, e.g., papal authority, the Mass in Latin, eucharistic adoration, devotion to the saints*. In this respect, the Counter-Reformation did not end until Vatican Council II* (1962-1965), which sought common ground with Protestants (*see* ECUMENISM) and made reforms that addressed their more central concerns.

The Counter-Reformation saw a major revival of spirituality*, led especially by religious orders founded (in particular, the Jesuits*) or reformed (e.g., the Carmelites) in the period. Prominent spiritual figures of the time include Saints Ignatius of Loyola*, Teresa of Avila*, John of the Cross*, Francis de Sales*, and Vincent de Paul*. This was also a time of great missionary expansion, led by the religious orders, especially to the lands of Africa, Asia, and the Americas, newly explored by Europeans. Finally, the period was marked by the achievements of baroque art*, architecture*, and music*.

CREATION. The doctrine of creation has to do with the relation of the finite world, both material and spiritual, to the transcendent God*. The idea of creation is based in the Old Testament, especially in Deutero-Isaiah (Isaiah 40-55) (sixth century B.C.) and the first chapter of Genesis (fifth century B.C.). The Genesis narrative borrows some features from the Babylonian creation epic, *Enuma Elish*, but these very borrowings highlight its differences from the *Enuma Elish* and similar myths: Genesis affirms that the world is created by one God, by word alone without struggle or sexual generation, and all that is made is good. To these OT themes, the NT adds the relation of creation to Jesus Christ*: it is through the Word of God, who became flesh in Jesus, that all things were made (Jn 1.1-14); "all things were created through him and for him" (Col 1.16). Catholic doctrine on creation develops the biblical themes, with three particular emphases:

(1) God is the creator of all that is. This was affirmed especially against all forms of Gnosticism*, which tends to hold that the material world is not from the supreme God. Thus, from the second century onward, the language of creation *ex nihilo* (from nothing) has been used, to exclude the position (not excluded in the OT) that God shaped the world from a preexisting formless matter.

2) All that is is good. Though there is genuine evil*, this evil is secondary, not part of the fundamental nature of what is. Against Gnosticism the fundamental goodness of all things, as deriving from the one, good God, is affirmed.

(3) The created world is truly distinct from God; pantheism* is rejected. The world does not emanate necessarily from God's nature, but is created freely.

These teachings were pronounced in their most authoritative form at the Fourth Lateran Council* (1215) and (particularly the third teaching) at Vatican Council I* (1870).

Catholic teaching is compatible with belief in evolution*, considered as the manner whereby God creates new species of living beings, but it has insisted that the human soul*, in its spiritual nature, is not a product of prior material causes. This has most often been expressed in terms of God's special creation of each human soul. Belief in such special creation is often called **creationism** in Catholic theology and is to be distinguished from the "creationism" that is a rejection of the theory of evolution. In contemporary theology, the doctrine of creation is being reconsidered for the light it can shed on the environmental crisis (*see* ECOLOGY).

CREED (Lt *credo*, "I believe"). An authoritative statement of religious belief. Over the centuries, Christians have formulated many creedal statements, but the two classic creeds are the *Apostles' Creed* and the *Niceno-Constantinopolitan Creed*. The basic structure of both is based on the threefold profession of faith made by Christians at baptism: belief in God as Father, Son, and Holy Spirit. An early form of the baptismal creed used in Rome, dated in the late second century, is the prototype of all the Western (Latin) creeds, including the *Apostles' Creed*. The common form of the creed in the Eastern (Greek) churches is the *Niceno-Constantinopolitan Creed*. It is often referred to simply as the "Nicene Creed" because it expresses the anti-Arian doctrine of the Council of Nicaea* (A.D. 325), but in fact the text, based on a baptismal creed from Syria, was promulgated by the Council of Constantinople* (381). Thus it is also called "the creed of the 150 fathers," the number of bishops in attendance at the Council of Constantinople. The Roman Catholic Church follows the ancient custom of reciting the Nicene Creed during the eucharist on Sundays and other major feasts. Texts of the Apostles' Creed and the Nicene Creed may be found in Appendix V.

In the twentieth century, the Faith and Order Commission of the World Council of Churches* has undertaken to have all Christian churches recognize the Nicene Creed as the expression of their common faith. The effort has led to a reconsideration of the phrase *filioque** ("and from the Son") that was added to the Latin text of the Creed in the sixth century. The Eastern churches object to the phrase on several counts, especially the unilateral decision on the part of the Western church to insert it.

The *Athanasian Creed,* a strongly anti-Arian* profession of faith in metrical form, has a place in the Lutheran, Anglican, and (until the 1960s) Roman Catholic liturgical books. Once attributed to St. Athanasius*, it is now thought to have been composed in Latin about A.D. 500 by someone greatly influenced by St. Augustine*, perhaps St. Caesarius of Arles or someone in his circle. It is also known as the *Quicunque vult* from its opening words ("Whoever wishes [to be saved] ...").

CREMATION. *See* BURIAL AND CREMATION.

CROSS, CRUCIFIX. The cross is a universal, pre-Christian symbol, but in Christianity it symbolizes the crucifixion of Christ. Though crucifixion was the most painful and disgraceful form of execution in the Roman Empire, for Christians the cross represented Christ's victory. Use of the cross as a symbol dates from at least the second century. As long as Christianity was illegal, the cross was often disguised or combined with another symbol, such as the X-shape of the Greek letter *chi,* first letter in *Christos,* "Christ." Once Christianity came into favor, with Constantine* in the early fourth century, cross symbols were more widespread and public. Impetus was given to devotion to the cross by the legendary finding of the true cross by St. Helena, mother of Constantine, on September 14, 326. September 14 is still celebrated as the Feast of the Triumph of the Cross.

A **crucifix** is a cross that bears the figure of the crucified Christ. The first depictions of the crucifixion date from the fifth century. The Third Council of Constantinople* (681) decreed that the crucified Jesus be portrayed, to emphasize his true humanity, against the monothelite* heresy. Realistic crucifixes date from the thirteenth century, when there was a movement toward increased devotion to Christ's humanity.

A ceremony of veneration of the cross (or crucifix) is part of the liturgy for Good Friday (*see* EASTER TRIDUUM).

See also SIGN OF THE CROSS, STATIONS OF THE CROSS.

CRUSADES. In its primary meaning, this term refers to a series of military expeditions under religious auspices, mounted by European forces against Islamic powers in the Near East in the eleventh through thirteenth centuries. According to Frederick Russell, "The medieval crusade as event and institution was a strange hybrid of holy war, just war, pilgrimage, and vow that defies neat categorization." The word *crusade* (French *croiserie*) appears only in the thirteenth century and derives from the fact that the warriors wore a cross as a sign of their vow. Initially there was no clear distinction between a crusade and a pilgrimage*. This fact points to the religious nature of the crusades; religiously, their central elements were papal authorization, a vow* taken by the crusaders to visit the Holy Sepulchre as part of an organized expedition, and a plenary indulgence*, like that offered to pilgrims to the Holy Land. Economic and political factors, however, were also prominent.

The First Crusade (1096-1099) was preached by Pope Urban II at the Council of Clermont in 1095. The most successful of the Crusades, it conquered Edessa, Antioch*, and Jerusalem*, and set up Latin "Crusader States" in these places. After the Muslims took back Edessa in 1144, the Second Crusade (1147-1148) was proclaimed by Pope Eugenius III and preached by St. Bernard of Clairvaux*. It ended in an unsuccessful siege of Damascus. Saladin's capture of Jerusalem in 1187 was followed by the Third Crusade (1189-1192), led by Kings Richard I (the Lion-Hearted) of England, Philip II of France, and the Emperor Frederick Barbarossa. It recaptured much territory along the coast of Palestine, but not Jerusalem; Richard, however, negotiated with Saladin and achieved safe passage for pilgrims to visit Jerusalem. The Fourth Crusade (1202-1204) was diverted to Constantinople* when the crusaders made alliance with a claimant to the imperial throne, Alexios IV. When Alexios was killed by a rival, the crusaders stormed and sacked the city, establishing a Latin empire that lasted till 1261. This episode sealed the schism* between the Eastern and Western Churches. Further crusades in the thirteenth century had little success, although a crusade under the Emperor Frederick II recovered Jerusalem from 1229 to 1244. The **Children's Crusade** in 1212 resulted from a popular movement in France and Germany. Unarmed young people set out for Provence or Italy to sail to the Holy Land. Few set sail, and some may have been sold into slavery. The fall of the last part of the Latin kingdom in Palestine in 1291 ended crusade activity in the Holy Land, but a series of smaller crusades were launched against the Turks in the fourteenth and fifteenth centuries. Crusade indulgences were used for other expeditions against Muslims as late as the seventeenth century.

Crusades likened to those to the Holy Land and bearing the same indulgences were proclaimed for other purposes: among others, against the Albigensians in France in 1209 (*see* CATHARS), against the Greeks at Constantinople in 1237 and 1261, against the political enemies of the Papal States* at various times, against the Hussites between 1421 and 1435, even by rival claimants to the papacy against one another during the Great Western Schism*.

CURIA (Medieval Lt, "court"). A **diocesan curia** is the administrative offices of a diocese*. Its chief officers are the Vicar General of the diocese and the Chancellor. The **Roman Curia** is the central administrative offices of the Church. As reorganized under Pope Paul VI* in 1967 and further reorganized under Pope John Paul II* in 1988, the Roman Curia consists of the Secretariat of State, nine congregations (governing agencies), three tribunals*, twelve councils, and a number of offices, commissions, committees, and other agencies. The Roman Curia originated in various assemblies or synods of Roman clergy and assumed something resembling its present form in the sixteenth century.

CYRIL, ST. (826/8-869), **and METHODIUS, ST.** (ca. 815-885). Greek brothers from Thessalonika who came to be known as "the Apostles of the Slavs." The younger brother's given name was Constantine; he took the name "Cyril" only upon becoming a monk the year before his death. In 862 they were sent as missionaries to what is now Moravia and Slovakia by Emperor Michael in response to a request from Rastislav, Duke of Greater Moravia. There Cyril devised an alphabet for the Slavonic language (the alphabet now called "Glagolitic" rather than that now called "Cyrillic," though the two are of comparable age and similarly based on the Greek alphabet), and the two developed a Slavonic liturgy (which received papal approval in 867) and translated the Bible into Slavonic. Pope John Paul II* in 1980 named them co-patrons of Europe. His 1985 encyclical, *Slavorum apostoli*, held them up as a model of inculturation*. Their feast is celebrated on February 14.

D

DANCE, LITURGICAL. Dance is "liturgical," as distinct from other types of religious dance, when it is an integral part of a liturgical service. Dance is mentioned often in the OT, almost always in a religious context, e.g., Miriam leading the women in dance after the Exodus (Ex 15.20) and David dancing before the Lord (2 Sm 6.14). The Fathers of the Church* are ambivalent about dancing, sometimes speaking favorably of the dance as an anticipation of heaven*, at other times disparaging it because of its association with pagan or Jewish worship, or simply out of a negative attitude toward the body. In the Middle Ages, especially between about 1100 and 1400, religious dance was common, often within the liturgy, but it had almost disappeared by 1700. After Vatican Council II*, whose *Constitution on the Sacred Liturgy* (1963) emphasized worshipers' "active participation" in the liturgy, there has been a renewed interest in liturgical dance. This accompanies a heightened awareness of the importance of bodily movement and gesture in prayer more generally, along with a realization that the line between dance and other liturgical gestures and movements is not sharp. Ambivalence remains in Church documents. A 1978 document of the U.S. Bishops' Committee on the Liturgy, *Environment and Art in Catholic Worship*, says, "Processions and interpretations through bodily movement (dance) can become meaningful parts of the liturgical celebration if done by truly competent persons in the manner that benefits the total liturgical action" (59). The 1988 missal* approved for Zaire includes dance as integral to the liturgy, comparable to music. On the other hand, a 1975 document published by the Vatican Congregation for Sacraments and Divine Worship disapproves of liturgical dance in Western cultures, because there dance is "tied with love, diversion, profaneness, and unbridling of the senses."

DANTE ALIGHIERI (1265-1321). Italian poet and philosopher, whose *Divina Commedia (Divine Comedy)* (1307/8-1321) is one of the classics of Catholic, and indeed of world, literature. Dante was born in Florence. In 1274, he met the woman he loved, whom he called "Beatrice" (probably Bice, the wife of Simone dei Bardi). Her death in 1290 led to a crisis in his life, which bore ultimate fruit in the *Divina*

Commedia. Dante's involvement in Florentine politics led to exile from 1302 to the end of his life. His *De Monarchia* (ca. 1310) expressed support for the Emperor (then Henry VII) against the temporal claims of the pope. The three parts of his masterwork, the *Divina Commedia*, depict a journey by Dante in 1300 through hell*, purgatory*, and heaven* (in Italian, *Inferno, Purgatorio, Paradiso*). The Roman poet Virgil is his guide through the first two parts, Beatrice through most of the third. The poem combines popular medieval eschatology with scholastic philosophy and theology and reflects much influence of classical poetry, especially Virgil, but the resulting vision is uniquely and personally the poet's. It is the first major work to appear in Italian, and it exerted much influence on the subsequent development of the language.

DEACON (Gk *diakonos*, "servant, helper"). The lowest of the three levels of ordained clergy (see ORDER, SACRAMENT OF). The ministry of the deacon is called the **DIACONATE**. **Transitional deacons** are ordained to the diaconate in the course of training for the priesthood. Vatican Council II* envisioned a restoration of the **permanent diaconate** (LG 29), and this was done by Pope Paul VI* in 1967. Permanent deacons are to be at least twenty-five years old if unmarried and thirty-five years old if married. They may not marry or remarry once ordained to the diaconate. Deacons may baptize, distribute the eucharist, bring viaticum* to the sick, read the Scripture and preach at eucharistic liturgies, lead the prayer of the faithful, and preside at weddings and funerals. They often have duties of administration or service in the Church. Some are entrusted with the pastoral care of a parish* that lacks a priest*. Few permanent deacons are full-time employees of the Church; most serve without pay. Of the approximately 18,000 permanent deacons in the world in 1993, around 11,000 were in the United States.

Traditionally, the appointment of the "Seven" in Acts 6.1-6 is seen as the origin of the diaconate, although the word *diakonos* is not used in this passage. The earliest reference to deacons as officers in the Church is in Phil 1.1. There is more detailed discussion in 1 Tm 3.8-13. On Rom 16.1, see DEACONESS. Deacons were very prominent in the Church of the second and third centuries, both in liturgy and in the administration of the Church. The **archdeacon** was the bishop's principal administrative officer. The Council of Nicaea (325)* curbed the power of deacons, and thereafter the importance of deacons yielded to that of presbyters (priests). In the West after the sixth century and in the East after the eleventh century, the diaconate survived mainly as a stage on the way to ordination to the priesthood.

DEACONESS (Gk *diakonos* with feminine article, later *diakonissa*). An officially designated ministry of women in the early Church, similar but perhaps not identical to that of male deacons*. Romans 16.1 speaks of Phoebe as a *diakonos* of the Church at Cenchreae, but it is not clear whether this is the name of a specific office or a general term meaning "helper." 1 Tm 3.11 speaks of "the women" in a passage on deacons, and it seems more likely these are women deacons than deacons' wives. The Roman governor Pliny the Younger, writing to the Emperor Trajan around A.D. 112, speaks of Christian *ministrae* ("deaconesses"). The most detailed descriptions of deaconesses are in the *Didascalia* (third century) and the *Apostolic Constitutions* (fourth century). At least in some churches, deaconesses were ordained by laying on of hands, but it is not clear if this was considered the same as the ordination of a male deacon. Their ministry was chiefly to women: they cared for poor and sick women, helped in the preparation of women for baptism, and played a major role in the baptism of women (for reasons of propriety due to baptismal nudity). The distinction between the office of deaconess and that of widow* is not always clear. The office of deaconess was suppressed by several councils in the West in the fifth and sixth centuries but lasted into the eleventh century in the East and here and there in the West.

DEAD SEA SCROLLS. Scrolls, written in Hebrew, Aramaic, and Greek, found between 1947 and 1956 in caves on the northwest shore of the Dead Sea, mainly at **Qumran**, where there are extensive ruins indicative of a communal or monastic settlement. Many scholars associate the scrolls and the ruins with the **Essenes**, a Jewish "sect" mentioned by the Jewish writers Josephus and Philo and by the Roman writer Pliny the Elder. The Essenes took a radically purist and separatist stance in regard to the influence of Greek culture and Roman rule in Palestine. The scrolls date from the first century B.C. to the first century A.D. They contain fragments, at least, from all of the OT books except Esther; these are among our earliest textual witnesses of the OT. They also contain fragments of the OT apocrypha* and documents concerning the beliefs and practices of the Qumran sect. The latter documents are important sources of information about Judaism (particularly Jewish apocalypticism*) as it existed at the time of the origin of Christianity. They do not mention Jesus or the Christian movement, but their imagery resembles that of the NT (especially the Johannine writings) at times, and the structure of their community shows some similarities to the early Christian community as described in the Acts of the Apostles. John the Baptist may have been a link between the Qumran community and Jesus.

DEATH. The end of our bodily life on earth. The Church has adopted Plato's* definition of death as the separation of the soul* from the body. This event is invisible; the Church generally accepts current medical criteria of death (e.g., the cessation of brain activity) as evidence that it has occurred. Some biblical texts see death as natural (e.g., Gn 25.7-11, 2 Sm 14.14), but others speak of it as a consequence of sin* (Gn 2.17, Rom 5.12-21). The latter point has been the focus of Church pronouncements; in 418, the provincial Council of Carthage condemned the opinion of Caelestius, associated with the Pelagian* movement, that Adam would have died even if he had not sinned, and the connection between sin and death was reiterated by the Second (regional) Council of Orange (529) and by the Council of Trent* (1546) (DS 222, 372, 1511). Usually, this connection has been taken literally: humans, though mortal by nature, would have been given immortality by God had they not sinned. The tendency in contemporary theology, however (following Karl Rahner*), is to see physical death as natural but to understand its darkness, its character as enemy, to be the result of sin. Were it not for sin, Rahner held, death would be a free act of self-surrender to God. This is what the death of Jesus was (Lk 23.36), though Jesus also experienced death in its darkness (Mk 15.34). For the Christian, the victory over death is through uniting oneself with the death of Jesus and sharing in his resurrection*. *See* ESCHATOLOGY.

Preparation for death in one sense occupies one's entire life, but when death is near, the Church commends: (1) the sacrament of reconciliation*; (2) the sacrament of anointing* of the sick; (3) viaticum*—holy communion for the dying. The ritual books also provide prayers for the "Commendation of the Dying." After death, the funeral* rite entrusts the dead person to God's mercy.

DEMON (Gk *daimōn*, "god, spirit"), **DEVIL** (Gk *diabolos*, "accuser, slanderer"). The earlier OT books contain only scattered references to evil spirits (e.g., Dt 32.17, Is 34.14). Judaism of the late OT period, drawing on Mesopotamian traditions, developed an extensive demonology. Found chiefly in apocryphal* books (especially Enoch), this demonology is in the background of some OT books and of the NT. Demons were seen to form a kingdom, with **Satan** as their leader. "Satan" means "accuser" or "adversary"; *diabolos* is a Greek translation of this title or name. In Job 1-2, "the Satan" is one of the "sons of God" (angels*), who has the task of testing humans. It is only in the apocryphal literature that he becomes an evil figure. The principal theme of NT demonology is the victory of Christ over the demonic kingdom. Jesus' exorcisms* are signs of the power of God's kingdom, overcoming the power of Satan (e.g., Lk 11.20). Paul and other NT writers see the world as being held in the sway of demonic powers, which Christ vanquishes (e.g., 1 Cor 15.24, Col 2.15, 1 Pt 3.22).

Belief in demons was pervasive in the Greco-Roman world, and early Christian demonology was affected by it. The Church Fathers* often understood the pagan gods to be demons in reality. Evils and disasters of all sorts were ascribed to demons. The Fathers took over the identification of demons with fallen angels, which originated in Jewish apocryphal literature. The Fathers at first inclined to see the angels' sin as lust (following Genesis 6.1-4); later Origen* and Augustine* identified it as pride. Origen speculated that eventually the devil might be saved; this opinion was condemned in a synod at Constantinople in 543 (DS 411). Official Church teaching on demons and the devil is quite limited and concerned mainly to combat a Manichaean* view of the devil as a power independent of and rival to God. Rather, the devil and demons were created by God and are good by nature, but wicked by their own choice (Lateran Council IV* [1215], DS 800). As in the case of angels, most theologians hold that the existence of demons is asserted by the Church or is inseparable from what the Church asserts; some, however, see it as an incidental part of the worldview presupposed in the ancient and medieval Church. Belief in demons implies that the reality of malice in the world is not reducible to that of our own human wills; it is all subject to the providence of God, however, and it is all overcome in Christ. The mystery of God's toleration of demonic evil is parallel to that of God's permission of our own evil*.

The chief activity ascribed to demons or the devil is **temptation**, or enticement to sin. The devil (or demons) is not the only source of temptation, nor does diabolic temptation remove the sinner's responsibility for sin. In rare cases, someone is said to be **possessed** by a demon (not by the devil); *see* EXORCISM.

DESCENT INTO HELL. According to some versions of the Apostles' Creed (*see* CREED), Jesus, after he "died and was buried," "descended into hell." This phrase first appeared in a creed drafted at Sirmium (on the Danube) in 359. Its purpose may have been simply to underscore the reality of Jesus' death. "Descended into hell" translates the Latin, *descendit ad inferna*. The official text and translation now read *descendit ad inferos*, "descended to the dead." "Hell" is not the hell* of the damned but the underworld (Sheol, Hades), the place of the dead. That Jesus was in the underworld between his death and resurrection* is a very early Christian belief, found in Ignatius of Antioch* (d. ca. 110) and elsewhere. From an early time, this belief has been connected to the puzzling texts in 1 Pt 3.19 and 4.6, in which, in his spirit, Jesus "preached to the spirits in prison" and "the gospel was preached to the dead." Later tradition identifies the part of the underworld to which Jesus descended as the *limbus patrum*, the "limbo* of the fathers," where the virtuous people from antiquity were detained until original sin* could be forgiven.

DESERT FATHERS AND MOTHERS. Beginning in the late third century, many Christian men and women took to the desert, especially in Egypt but also in Palestine and Syria, in order to pursue prayer and asceticism*. This was an important phase in the development of Christian monasticism*. An impetus was given to this movement by the end of persecution* and the Christianization of the empire, with the attendant routinization of Christian life in the cities. St. Antony (ca. 251-356), who was made famous in a *Life* by St. Athanasius*, was regarded as the founder of the movement. Typically, the ascetics lived alone, perhaps sometimes coming together for communal prayer and liturgy. Less-experienced ascetics would gather around more experienced ones for spiritual direction*. Some lived in community; Pachomius (ca. 286-346), in Egypt, organized the first cenobite* community, living under a rule. Collections of sayings (called "apophthegms") of and stories about the Desert Fathers and Mothers circulated in Greek, Coptic, and Latin.

DEVIL. *See* DEMON.

DEVOTIONS. "Devotion" means the dedication of the will to God, or else the emotional or affective side of religion. "Devotions" or "popular devotions" are acts of worship meant to enhance and express devotion. Devotions are distinct from the official liturgy* of the Church, although they bear some relation to it. They are also distinct from private prayer* in that they are often done publicly; even when private, they tend to emphasize religious objects and formulas of prayer that are common to many devotees. Devotions, in their present sense, arose in the Middle Ages in connection with the Liturgy of the Hours*. For example, the 150 Hail Mary's of the rosary* substituted for the 150 psalms, and the Little Office of the Blessed Virgin was often prayed in place of the canonical hours. Devotions flourished during the Counter-Reformation* period. The liturgy, especially the mass*, was closely regulated, allowed little room for congregational participation, and was in Latin, a language understood by few worshipers. Devotions met the needs for flexibility, participation, and intelligibility that the liturgy did not meet. They were especially prominent among English-speaking Catholics in the nineteenth and early twentieth centuries. Devotions that were important in that period included the rosary*, Benediction* of the Blessed Sacrament, exposition of the eucharist*, Stations of the Cross*, novenas*, devotions to the Sacred Heart* of Jesus, devotions associated with the scapular* and miraculous medal, and devotions to St. Anthony of Padua and to St. Jude. When, as a result of Vatican Council II* (1962-1965), the liturgy was translated into the vernacular languages and more congregational participation was introduced, devotions declined in importance. Ecumenism* also contributed to this decline, since devotions tended to stress elements in Catholicism that Protestants* found offensive; devotional Bible services became more common, however. Vatican II itself commended devotions but insisted that they harmonize with the liturgy and liturgical year (SC 13).

DIDACHE (Gk, "teaching") or *Teaching of the Twelve Apostles*. A very early church manual. Scholarly opinions as to its date range from before A.D. 70 to the mid-second century, with the late first century seeming most probable. It is a composite work, including some considerably earlier material. It was discovered in 1873 (in a manuscript dating from 1056) and published in 1883. It probably originated in a Jewish-Christian community in Syria. The text opens with a description of the "two ways" of life and death, the former based on the commandments of the gospel and on the ten commandments (this section closely parallels part of the first or second century *Letter of Barnabas)*. There follow a description of the baptismal ritual, teachings on fasting and prayer, thanksgiving prayers for eucharistic celebrations or *agapē* meals associated with them, and some directives on church order. These directives portray a relatively fluid church structure in which itinerant prophets have an important role. The text concludes with warnings about the second coming of Christ. The *Didachē* is important as an early witness to Christian teaching and liturgical practice.

DIOCESE. (Gk *dioikēsis*, "administration"). In the Roman Rite, "A portion of the People of God which is entrusted for pastoral care to a bishop ..." (Canon 369). The corresponding term in the Eastern Churches* is **eparchy.** The diocesan bishop* has **ordinary jurisdiction,** that is, he governs in his own name and not as the representative of another. A diocese is normally a territorial unit, but there may be non-territorial dioceses, such as the Archdiocese for the Military Services, U.S.A. A diocese was a division of the Roman Empire, especially as reorganized under Diocletian (emperor 294-305); once the term came into church use, by the fourth century, it took some time for it to develop the precise meaning it now has. The whole of the Church is considered to be present in each local diocese (LG 26).

DISCERNMENT OF SPIRITS (Lt *discernere*, "to separate, to distinguish"). The process of determining whether or not an experience, desire, impulse, etc., is from God. Sometimes "spirits" refers primarily to external angelic or demonic spirits; more often, in contemporary usage, the term refers to inner "movements of the spirit." "Discernment" can designate a special spiritual gift or a more ordinary process fostered by prayer, self-knowledge, and the study of spirituality*. Several NT texts speak of discernment, e.g., 1 Jn 4.1: "Test the spirits to see whether they belong to God" (similarly Paul in 1 Thes 5.21). Both John and Paul identify a good spirit as one that leads to faith in Jesus (1 Jn 4.2; 1 Cor 12.3). Paul provides contrasting lists of the "works of the flesh" and the "fruit of the Spirit" in Gal 5.19-23. Criteria for discernment of spirits were refined in the early monastic tradition, especially by John Cassian (ca. 360-435), and given classic formulation by St. Ignatius Loyola* in his *Spiritual Exercises* (1548). In general, for Ignatius, the "good spirit" leads to greater love of God and desire for service, to growth in virtue, and to inward courage and peace, while "the evil spirit" weakens love of God and causes inward turmoil and outward strife. Contemporary writers expand the discussion of discernment to include not only inner movements but also social trends and conditions.

DISCIPLE, DISCIPLESHIP (Lt *discipulus*, "pupil, one who is taught," translating Gk *mathētēs*). A follower of Jesus. The OT does not use the word "disciple," but it is common in the Gospels, probably coming from Rabbinic Judaism. Unlike the rabbis, Jesus calls the disciples; the complete and total response to a call from Jesus is one of the characteristics of a disciple (e.g., Mk 1.18, Mt 8.18-22). The call is inclusive, addressed to ordinary people, even those rejected by society, e.g., tax collectors (e.g., Lk 5.27-32). The disciples include women (e.g., Lk 8.2) as well as men. Disciples are admitted into intimacy with Jesus and given a share in his mission (Lk 9.1-6). They are called upon to imitate Jesus, even to the point of death (Mk 8.34-35). The Gospels show the disciples as flawed, often lacking faith or understanding, but loved and forgiven by Jesus. In all of these respects, the disciples are an image of subsequent Christians. There are several "inner circles" among the disciples, notably the "Twelve" (*see* APOSTLE). In recent times, many Church documents and theologians have revived "discipleship" as a term for all of Christian life. Contemporary treatments of discipleship tend to emphasize the imitation of Jesus, solidarity* with the poor and marginalized, and, often, a contrast between the life of Christians and that of the surrounding society.

DISSENT. In a broad sense, disagreement (particularly if expressed in a public way) by a member of the Church with official teaching of the Church. It is limited to teachings which are not infallible*; to deny a teaching that is infallibly proclaimed is heresy*. A narrower sense of "dissent" is found in some Church documents: here "dissent" refers specifically to disagreement publicly expressed in mass media or through organized groups. Often the term is used with the dissent of theologians specifically in mind, but it is not limited to them.

According to Vatican Council II*, the authoritative but non-infallible teachings of the pope and bishops (see MAGISTERIUM) should be accepted by the faithful in *obsequium religiosum* (LG 25; translations vary: "due respect," "loyal submission," and "religiously motivated obedience" illustrate the range). This does not necessarily exclude limited private disagreement; long before the Council, authorized theological textbooks had allowed some possibility for such disagreement, and the Council's Theological Commission made reference to this. After the Council, some theologians, citing the Council's call for the faithful to contribute to the Church's teaching office by making their opinions known, particularly where they have expertise (LG 37), argued that there is a right and may be a duty to dissent publicly at times. Dissent became a major issue after Pope Paul VI's* reassertion of the Church's condemnation of contraception (see BIRTH CONTROL) in 1968, in the encyclical* *Humanae Vitae*. For instance, shortly after this encyclical was released, more than six hundred theologians, led by Charles E. Curran of The Catholic University of America, signed a statement expressing their disagreement with it, and the large majority of Catholics in the West to whom its teaching is relevant have not abided by it. Subsequently, dissent has been frequent on other issues, such as abortion*, homosexuality*, and some issues of social ethics. Under Pope John Paul II*, Church authorities have taken strong steps to curb dissent, especially as construed in the narrow sense mentioned above. Disciplinary measures have included the removal of Curran from his teaching position in 1987. Condemnations of dissent are found, among other places, in the encyclical *Veritatis Splendor* (1993) and the Congregation for the Doctrine of the Faith's "Instruction on the Ecclesial Vocation of the Theologian" (1990).

DIVINE OFFICE. *See* HOURS, LITURGY OF THE.

DIVORCE. The legal dissolution of a marriage*. Divorce is a civil, not an ecclesiastical, procedure. An annulment*, which is the issuance of an ecclesiastical declaration that a sacramentally valid marriage never existed, is normally preceded by a civil divorce. Canon law (Canons 1141-1155) also speaks of two forms of "separation of spouses," both of which would normally be accompanied by civil divorce: (1) "Dissolution of the marriage bond" can be granted in some cases in which either the marriage partners were not baptized or the marriage was not "consummated," i.e., sexual intercourse did not occur; it cannot be granted in the case of a consummated marriage between two baptized persons. It leaves the partners free to marry again. (2) "Separation while the bond endures" can occur in cases of adultery or when a partner causes "serious danger of spirit or body" to a family member "or otherwise renders common life too hard"; it may be undertaken by the innocent spouse but should be submitted to the judgment of church authority. Except in cases of annulment or dissolution of the bond, Catholics are not permitted to remarry after divorce, so long as the original marriage partner is living. Catholics in such circumstances who have remarried are excluded from communion, though no longer formally excommunicated.

The Church's opposition to divorce stems from Jesus' prohibition of divorce, found in Luke 16.18 and parallel passages; in Mt 19.5, Jesus ties the indissolubility of marriage to God's original purpose in creating humans as male and female (Gn 2.24). In the Christian tradition this is reinforced by Paul's comparison of marriage to Christ's relation to the Church (Eph 5.21-33). Already in the NT, there is evidence of attempts to mitigate this prohibition in cases to which it was seen not to apply. Thus, Mt 19.9 makes an exception for *porneia* ("unchastity"), which may have meant marriages within forbidden degrees of kinship, while in 1 Cor 7.15 Paul allows a divorce in the case when one partner receives baptism and the other partner, unbaptized, does not wish to continue living with the baptized partner. Paul does not mention remarriage, but from the fourth century appeal has been made to this text to justify remarriage in such cases. This is called the "Pauline privilege," allowed by canon law. (There are other, similar cases in which the pope may dissolve a consummated marriage in which only one of the partners was baptized; these are called "favor of the faith" or "Petrine privilege" cases.)

From around the tenth century, the Eastern church, appealing to the *porneia* clause in Matthew's version of Jesus' words, has allowed divorce and remarriage, first in cases of adultery, later in a wider range of cases. This is the practice in the Eastern Orthodox churches* today, though marriages after the first are not considered sacramental. Protestant* churches generally accept remarriage after divorce. In 1563, the Council of Trent* strongly reaffirmed the indissolubility of marriage and condemned those who held that the Church erred in not allowing divorce in cases of adultery or similar circumstances. This condemnation was directed at the Protestant reformers and has never been taken to condemn the Eastern Orthodox churches.

History shows that the Church has had to interpret and adapt Jesus' prohibition of divorce in order to apply it to the situations in which it has found itself. In contemporary Western society, Catholics divorce at a rate close to that of the general public, and there is considerable theological and pastoral support for a relaxation of the prohibition of the admission of divorced, remarried Catholics to the sacraments. This is proposed in recognition of the difficulties of sustaining a marriage in contemporary society, but is opposed partly on the grounds that any such relaxation would further contribute to the forces weakening marriage in our time.

DOCETISM (Gk *dokein*, "to appear"). The belief that Jesus only *appeared* to be human but was not truly human. Docetism was already combatted in the NT (e.g., 2 Jn 7). It was common in Gnosticism*, which sought to minimize the involvement of divinity in the material world. "Docetism" does not name a distinct movement, but rather a tendency or temptation within Christology*. It can still be found today, when, explicitly or implicitly, one does not take the humanity of Jesus with full seriousness.

DOCTOR OF THE CHURCH (Lt *doctor*, "teacher"). A title given to certain theologians from whose teaching the Church has greatly benefited. The criteria for designating someone a Doctor of the Church were set forth by Pope Benedict XIV in 1738; they are great sanctity, great learning, and declaration by a pope or ecumenical council. Four Doctors were recognized in the West from the eighth century: Sts. Gregory I* (the Great), Ambrose*, Augustine*, and Jerome*. Later Sts. Basil, Gregory Nazianzus (*see* CAPPADOCIANS), John Chrysostom*, and Athanasius* were added as Eastern Doctors. Since the sixteenth century, popes have added twenty-four more Doctors, most recently the first two women Doctors, Sts. Teresa of Avila* and Catherine of Siena*, named by Pope Paul VI in 1970.

DOCTRINE (Lt *doctrina*, "instruction"). Jaroslav Pelikan defines "doctrine" as "what the Church of Jesus Christ believes, teaches, and confesses on the basis of the word of God." Doctrines are taught by the Church in many ways (*see* MAGISTERIUM) and with various degrees of authority (*see* THEOLOGICAL NOTES). Those taught most authoritatively are called "dogmas"*. *Doctrina* for Augustine* referred to the activity of Christian teaching; for Thomas Aquinas*, *sacra doctrina* ("sacred doctrine") referred to the academic discipline of theology*. The use of "doctrine" to mean all that is taught by the

Church or individual propositions taught by the Church dates from the Counter-Reformation*.

Like all linguistic expressions, doctrines can be expressed only in the language and conceptual framework of a given time and place. As efforts to give expression to the transcendent mystery* of God and God's revelation* in Christ, they necessarily fall short of adequacy, though not of truth. Over the course of time, they are subject to development, a point most clearly emphasized in the nineteenth century by J. H. Newman*. Several understandings of **development of doctrine** have been proposed. From an understanding of doctrines as chiefly propositions came the idea that doctrines develop through the unfolding of their logical implications. This was supplanted in Newman and others by an understanding of development as an organic process in which the Church, guided by the Holy Spirit*, became increasingly aware of the meaning of what it believed. More recently, doctrinal development has been seen (e.g., by Avery Dulles) as a result of encounters between the Church's tradition and new historical and cultural situations, which both pose new challenges to traditional doctrines and offer new resources for understanding God's revelation.

DOGMA (Gk, "that which seems right," from *dokein*, "to appear, to seem"). A truth proclaimed by the Church as divinely revealed. It must be based in Scripture or tradition and be proclaimed by the Church either by a solemn declaration or in its ordinary and universal teaching (Vatican Council I, DS 3011). To deny a dogma is heresy*. This sense of the term *dogma* has been current since the eighteenth century. Among the Fathers of the Church*, the term can refer to any opinion or teaching, pagan or heretical as well as orthodox. Still earlier, e.g., Acts 16.4, it meant an official decision.

DOMINIC, ST. (ca. 1170-1221), **DOMINICANS** (Order of Preachers). Dominic was born at Calereuga in Castile. He became a canon (cathedral priest) at Osma about 1196. Traveling with his bishop, Diego, he encountered the Albigensian heretics (*see* CATHARS) in France. At Montpellier in 1206, Diego proposed that, if they were to succeed against the Albigensians, preachers should adopt a life of apostolic poverty, begging for their sustenance. Diego and Dominic proceeded to do so, and after Diego's death in 1207, Dominic and a small group of associates continued the work of preaching against the Albigensians. In 1215, Dominic asked Pope Innocent III* to recognize his community as an Order of Preachers, and Innocent approved, so long as the community agreed to adopt one of the existing rules for religious community life. Dominic's group adopted the Rule of St. Augustine*, and was recognized by Pope Honorius III in 1216. Honorius approved the name, Order of Preachers, in 1217. The order spread rapidly through western and central Europe and, by the time of Dominic's death, had five provinces.

From the beginning, Dominic valued theological study in the service of preaching. Dominican houses were established at Paris, Oxford, Bologna, and other university towns, and the order obtained a chair of theology at Paris in 1229. Many Dominicans were among the intellectual leaders of the Middle Ages, for instance, Albert the Great*, Thomas Aquinas*, and Meister Eckhart*. Dominicans also carried on a ministry of itinerant preaching in Europe and expanded into missionary work in the Holy Land and on the fringes of Christian Europe. They were the primary agents of the Inquisition*. The order underwent a decline in the fourteenth century, offset somewhat by a reform movement inspired by St. Catherine of Siena*. In the Protestant* Reformation it lost its northern European provinces, but it recovered during the Counter-Reformation* in the Catholic countries. The Dominicans Vitoria and Cajetan led a sixteenth-century revival of Thomism*. The order expanded greatly overseas, especially in the Spanish possessions, where Dominicans were among the leaders in the missions*. Bartolomé de las Casas* is the best known of the Dominican missionaries. In the eighteenth century, the order was suppressed in many places, but it revived again in the mid-nineteenth century. The Dominicans Yves Congar* (1904-1995) and Edward Schillebeeckx (b. 1914) have been among the leading theologians of the twentieth century. Today, there are more than 6,500 Dominican friars in forty-eight provinces worldwide. They are led by a Master of the Order, who is elected for a term and lives in Rome.

Dominic's companion Diego founded a convent of nuns at Prouille in 1206, and Dominic founded one at Rome in 1219. Today there are more than four thousand contemplative Dominican nuns and about thirty-six thousand Dominican sisters (including the Maryknoll* Sisters) in a large number of congregations, engaging in apostolic work. All look back to Diego's and Dominic's foundations as their origin. In addition, there are around seventy thousand Dominican Laity in "third order" associations. Together with the friars and the nuns and sisters, they form a "Dominican family," led by the Master of the Order.

Dominic's feast is celebrated on August 8.

DONATISM. A schismatic (*see* SCHISM) movement in the North African church. It began when, in 311 or 312, Caecilian was consecrated bishop of Carthage. It was widely (though probably falsely) believed that one of the bishops who consecrated him had been a *traditor*, that is, someone who handed the Scriptures over to the secular authorities during the persecutions* under Diocletian (d. 305). Therefore, a synod of Numidian bishops declared Caecilian's consecration invalid and selected a rival, who was succeeded in 313 by Donatus. The Church throughout the rest of the world remained in communion with Caecilian, but the "party of Donatus" became dominant for a time in North Africa and long held influence there in the rural population and the lower social strata. The Donatists held that all sacraments conferred by *traditores* and those ordained in succession from them were invalid; hence they rebaptized converts to their sect from the Catholic Church. In the fifth century, the Catholics' attack against the Donatists was led by St. Augustine*. He emphasized the importance of communion with the apostolic churches, Rome in particular, and, in an argument that marked a decisive step in Catholic theology of the sacraments*, held that the sacraments were a work of Christ through the Church, dependent for validity* not on the character of the minister of the sacrament (or those who ordained him) but only on the proper intention and performance of the ritual. He also persuaded the secular authorities to impose legal penalties (though not the death penalty) on the Donatists. Nevertheless, Donatism, which combined traditional elements in the North African theology of the Church with currents of social unrest in the late Roman Empire in North Africa, survived until the Muslims conquered the area in the seventh and eighth centuries.

DUNS SCOTUS, JOHN (ca. 1265-1308). Medieval philosopher and theologian, known as "Doctor subtilis," for the subtlety of the distinctions he made. Born in Scotland (hence called "Scotus," "the Scot"), he entered the Franciscan* order around 1280, studied at Oxford and Paris, and taught at Paris. In philosophy, he carried on the Franciscan tradition of Bonaventure* but was more strongly influenced by Aristotle* than was Bonaventure. In comparison with Thomas Aquinas*, he narrowed the scope of reason in the knowledge of God and of the moral law. He emphasized the priority of love (or will) over knowledge (or intellect) in our relation with God. He was also known for his teaching that each thing had its own individual nature (*haecceitas*), and for his defense of the immaculate conception* of Mary. After his death, his system became the standard teaching within the Franciscan order. In a curious twist of language, the Protestant Reformers, ridiculing the excessive subtlety of scholastic thought, derived from his name the word "dunce."

E

EASTER (from a Germanic root meaning "dawn," perhaps by way of the name of an Anglo-Saxon spring goddess). The annual celebration of the resurrection* of Jesus; the principal and most ancient feast of the liturgical year. It appears that initially the celebration of the resurrection was weekly—Sunday*—rather than annual, but some parts of the Church celebrated the Passover* on the Jewish date of the fourteenth day of the lunar month of Nisan, commemorating both the Passover and the death and resurrection of Jesus, which had occurred at that time. Elsewhere, including at Rome when the feast was adopted there in the second half of the second century, the resurrection was celebrated on the Sunday following 14 Nisan. This custom prevailed, but disagreements continued over the determination of 14 Nisan, until the Council of Nicaea* in 325 called on the churches to celebrate Easter on the Sunday after the first full moon after the spring equinox. Easter thus comes between March 22 and April 25. Because some of the Eastern Orthodox Churches* calculate Easter by means of the Julian calendar rather than the Gregorian calendar (reformed in 1582), there is still sometimes a discrepancy between their date for Easter and that observed in the rest of the churches.

The primary celebration of Easter is the **Easter Vigil**, which dates at least from the second century. In the Middle Ages it became a daytime service on Holy Saturday, but in 1951 it was restored as an evening celebration. It comprises a ceremony for the lighting of the new fire and the Easter candle, followed by a long service of readings, recapitulating major events in the OT, especially the Exodus, and culminating in a gospel resurrection narrative. There follows a baptismal liturgy; from the third century, the Easter Vigil was the principal time for baptism*, and this has been restored in the Rite of Christian Initiation for Adults (RCIA) (*see* INITIATION). If there are no baptisms, there is at least a blessing of the baptismal font or water. The Vigil concludes with a eucharistic liturgy.

The Easter season continues until Pentecost* Sunday, seven weeks after Easter. A fifty-day celebration of Easter is noted in third-century sources, but it was broken somewhat by the development of Pentecost as a distinct feast and by the insertion of the feast of the Ascension* (fourth century). The Easter octave (first week after Easter) began as a time for post-baptismal catechesis* and developed into a period of special solemnity. The reforms of the liturgical year promulgated in 1969 in response to Vatican Council II* reemphasize the unity of the seven-week Easter celebration, suppressing the Octave of Pentecost and other observances that disrupted that unity. The RCIA (1972) establishes the entire season as a period of catechesis, called "mystagogy," for the newly baptized.

The Easter season is a time of celebration, marked by the use of "Alleluia" in the liturgy, the lighting of the Easter candle, and the wearing of white vestments. Scripture readings are drawn principally from the Gospel and First Epistle of John, the Acts of the Apostles, the First Letter of Peter, and the Book of Revelation.

The Easter cycle in the liturgy extends backward for a forty-day period, or Lent*, which is both the final period of the catechumenate* in preparation for Baptism and a penitential period in preparation for Easter. Initially a three-day fast, it had become forty days by the fourth century. Technically, Lent concludes before the Mass of the Lord's Supper on Holy Thursday. The period from this mass through Evening Prayer on Easter Sunday is called the Easter Triduum*. All together, the Easter cycle is the liturgical year's central celebration of the saving events of Jesus' passion, death, and resurrection. (*See also* CALENDAR, LITURGICAL.)

EASTER DUTY. The obligation of Catholics to receive the eucharist* during the Easter season, which in the United States is defined as the period from Ash Wednesday through Trinity Sunday (the Sunday after Pentecost). This obligation was instituted by Lateran Council IV* in 1215.

EASTER TRIDUUM (Lt "three-day period"), or **PASCHAL TRIDUUM** or **SACRED TRIDUUM**. The three-day solemn celebration of the mysteries of Jesus' passion, death, and resurrection, beginning with the Mass of the Lord's Supper on Holy Thursday (*see*

HOLY WEEK) evening and concluding with Evening Prayer on Easter Sunday. The liturgies of these days were restored to something like their ancient form in 1955; they were modified slightly in 1970.

The **Holy Thursday** evening mass commemorates Jesus' Last Supper with his disciples, and the institution of the eucharist* at that time; this is described in the second reading for the feast, 1 Cor 11.23-26. It also commemorates the parallel in John 13.1-15, read as the gospel at this mass, of Jesus' institution of a ritual of washing the feet of his disciples. A foot-washing ritual is part of this service, though it may be omitted. (This day is often called **Maundy Thursday**, because Jn 13.34, in which Jesus gives the commandment [Lt *mandatum*, hence "Maundy"] to love one another, is sung in the foot-washing ritual.) The mass concludes with a procession carrying the eucharist from the main altar to an altar of reservation, and prayer before the reserved eucharist till midnight. The celebration of a special Holy Thursday mass in commemoration of the Last Supper is first recorded in the fourth century in Jerusalem.

The Celebration of the Lord's Passion is held on the afternoon of **Good Friday**. It begins with a liturgy of the word, in which are read Is 52.13-53.12 (the fourth Suffering Servant song), Heb 4.14-16, 5.7-9 (Jesus as suffering high priest), and the passion narrative in John's gospel; it concludes with extended prayers of petition, dating from the fourth century, although revised. There follows a veneration of the cross and a communion service, but no mass. The service of readings and veneration of the cross were observed in fourth-century Jerusalem; the communion service was added in the West by the seventh century. From the thirteenth century to 1955, only the priest received communion.

Holy Saturday commemorates Jesus' burial in the tomb and his "descent into hell"*. There is no liturgical service except the daily liturgy of the hours*. The Easter* Vigil is celebrated in the evening. The Vigil is the central celebration of Easter, but daytime masses date from at least the fifth century. (*See also* PASCHAL MYSTERY.)

EASTERN CATHOLIC CHURCHES. Catholic churches that recognize the primacy of the pope* but that follow traditions of the Eastern churches. "Eastern" in reference to Christianity designates the churches that originated in the eastern part of the Roman Empire, particularly the patriarchates of Constantinople*, Alexandria*, Antioch*, and Jerusalem*. Most of the Eastern churches are not in communion with the Catholic Church; *see* ASSYRIAN CHURCH OF THE EAST, EASTERN ORTHODOX CHURCHES, and ORIENTAL ORTHODOX CHURCHES. Twenty-one Eastern churches, however, are in full communion with Rome. In most cases these represent groups from formerly separated churches that came into union with Rome; hence, these churches have been called **Uniate**, a term that is now rejected as a pejorative. These churches belong to seven *rites**. They have their own code of canon law*, the *Code of Canons of the Oriental Churches (Codex Canonum Ecclesiarum Orientalium)*, promulgated in 1990 and effective in 1991.

The Eastern Catholic Churches (principal locations in brackets) are: (1) in the Armenian Rite: the Armenian Church; (2) in the Byzantine Rite: the Albanian, Bulgarian, Byelorussian, Greek, Hungarian, Italo-Albanian, Melkite, Romanian, Russian, Ruthenian, Slovak, Ukrainian, and Yugoslav (Serbian and Croatian) Churches; (3) in the Coptic Rite: the Coptic Church [Egypt]; (4) In the East Syrian Rite: the Chaldean [Iraq] and Syro-Malabarese [India] Churches; (5) in the Ethiopian Rite: the Ethiopian Church; (6) in the Maronite Rite: the Maronite Church [Lebanon and worldwide]; (7) in the West Syrian Rite: the Syrian and Syro-Malankara [India] Churches. The churches of the Armenian, Coptic, Ethiopian, and West Syrian Rites correspond to Oriental Orthodox churches; those of the Byzantine Rite (except the Italo-Albanian), to Eastern Orthodox churches; those of the East Syrian Rite, to the Assyrian Church of the East. The Maronite and Italo-Albanian churches do not directly correspond to any church separated from Rome. The Coptic and Ethiopic Rites are sometimes referred to jointly as the Alexandrian Rite, the West Syrian and Maronite Rites as the Antiochene. There are about twelve million Eastern Catholics in all.

The liturgical rituals of the Eastern Catholic Churches follow traditions common to the Eastern churches and differ in some respects from the Roman Rite. Their liturgical calendars likewise differ somewhat from that of the Roman Rite, as do some aspects of sacramental practice. Confirmation* and communion normally follow immediately upon baptism. Married men may be ordained priests, although men may not marry after ordination. Bishops must be unmarried. The Coptic, Maronite, Syrian, Armenian, Melkite, and Chaldean Churches are headed by patriarchs*, whose rank is immediately beneath that of the pope; the other Eastern Catholic churches are headed by major archbishops* or metropolitans.

EASTERN ORTHODOX CHURCHES. A communion of Christian churches that accept the authority of the first seven ecumenical councils*, through Nicaea II* (787), as well as the Scripture, tradition, and creeds*. They include churches that derive from the ancient patriarchal sees of Constantinople*, Alexandria*, Antioch*, and Jerusalem*. There are thirteen (or fifteen) autocephalous (independent) Eastern Orthodox churches (most notably the Greek, Russian, Romanian, Serbian, and Bulgarian Orthodox), and about the same number of other Eastern Orthodox churches of various statuses. Eastern Orthodox churches are mostly divided on national or linguistic lines. These churches have the same sacraments* as does the Catholic Church, and the Catholic Church recognizes the validity* of their ministry and sacraments. The Patriarch of Constantinople is the spiritual leader of these churches but does not have jurisdiction over the other patriarchs; he is "first among equals." The Eastern Orthodox see themselves as a communion of sister churches, which form one Church in doctrine and practice. They are united by a common Byzantine heritage in liturgy and theology, as well as by the role of icons* in worship and spirituality.

The separation between the Eastern Orthodox and the Roman Catholic churches was a long and gradual process. The principal factor was the division of the Roman Empire and subsequent fall of the Empire in the West (fifth century), and, afterward, the inability of the Latin and Greek churches to understand each other's languages and customs. Stages in the division included the West's establishment of a separate empire under Charlemagne* (A.D. 800) and a schism* in connection with Photius* (858). The traditional date for the separation is 1054. Then, following a dispute over church customs, the pope's legates and the Patriarch of Constantinople solemnly excommunicated one another in Constantinople. The separation was sealed by the Fourth Crusade (1204), in which Western Crusaders sacked Constantinople and established a Latin kingdom there (*see* CRUSADES). Attempts at reunion were made at the Councils of Lyons* (1274) and Florence* (1439). In both cases the Byzantine emperor sought reunification for political and religious reasons and reunion formulas were drawn up on Western terms, but the Eastern Church at large rejected them.

The Eastern Orthodox have been involved in ecumenism* since the early twentieth century and have been members of the World Council of Churches* since its inception in 1948. There have been active dialogues between the Eastern Orthodox and the Oriental Orthodox* as

well as with the Anglican Communion* and some Protestant*
Churches. In 1965, Pope Paul VI* and Athenagoras I, Patriarch of
Constantinople, nullified the excommunications of 1054. An official
dialogue between the Eastern Orthodox and the Catholic Church has
been in progress on the international level since 1980 (subjects have
included the Trinity, the sacraments, and the Church) and in the United
States since 1965. The most important theological issues separating the
two are the jurisdiction and infallibility* of the pope* and the Western
addition of *filioque** (the Holy Spirit proceeds from the Father *and the
Son*) to the Nicene Creed. In practice, more immediate issues, such as
the status of the Eastern Catholic Churches*, the ownership of church
property confiscated by Communist regimes in Eastern Europe, and
accusations of "proselytism" (attempts to pressure others into
conversion) can be more divisive. According to Vatican Council II*,
"These Churches, though separated from us, yet possess true
sacraments, above all, by apostolic succession, the priesthood and the
eucharist, whereby they are still linked with us in closest intimacy.
Therefore some worship in common (*communicatio in sacris*) ... is not
merely possible but to be encouraged" (UR 15). The Eastern Orthodox
reject intercommunion*, however, in nearly all circumstances.

ECCLESIASTICAL UNIVERSITIES AND FACULTIES. Institutes
of higher learning founded by the authority of the Holy See* and
supervised by it (Canon 816). "Faculty" here refers to a division within
a larger institution, like an academic department. Chiefly, these
institutes instruct and do research in theology, canon law, and related
fields. They alone confer degrees that have canonical effects in the
Church. Ecclesiastical universities and faculties exist throughout the
world. In the United States, they include the Departments of Theology
and Canon Law and the School of Philosophy at The Catholic
University of America, as well as a number of seminaries* or divisions
of seminaries, schools of theology, or houses of study. They do not
include most Catholic universities* and colleges. Most ecclesiastical
universities are called **Pontifical Universities**, because their foundation
must be approved by the pope and they grant degrees in his name.
There are many pontifical universities in Rome, of which the most
prominent is the Pontifical Gregorian University, which developed from
the Roman College founded by St. Ignatius of Loyola* in 1551.

ECCLESIOLOGY (Gk *ekklēsia,* "assembly, church"). The branch of theology* that studies the Church*. Although NT writers, Church Fathers*, and medieval theologians spoke extensively about the Church, ecclesiology did not emerge as a distinct discipline until the fifteenth century, with Juan de Torquemada's *Summa de ecclesia.* Until the nineteenth century, Catholic ecclesiology focused almost exclusively on the authority of Church hierarchy*, especially that of the pope*. The nineteenth centuries saw the beginning of trends that led to Vatican Council II's* treatment of the Church as the whole "people of God"*. Topics dealt with in ecclesiology today include the foundation of the Church in Jesus' ministry and that of the apostles*, the role of the Holy Spirit* in the Church, authority* in the Church, the relation of the Catholic Church to other Christians (*see* ECUMENISM) and non-Christians (*see* SALVATION OUTSIDE THE CHURCH), the sacramental life of the Church, and the relation of the Church to the realms of culture and politics.

ECKHART, MEISTER (ca. 1260-1327/28). German theologian and mystic, one of the greatest medieval mystical theologians. Born in Thuringia, Eckhart entered the Dominican order ca. 1275. He studied at Cologne and at Paris, where he earned the title "Magister" (Ger *Meister,* Engl "Master") in 1302. Thereafter he taught at Paris and held administrative posts in his order in Germany. His writings include academic treatises in Latin and sermons in German. Both develop a mystical theology that is strongly Neo-Platonic (*see* PLATONISM), influenced by Pseudo-Dionysius* but also by Thomas Aquinas*. His theme is the soul's return to its origin in God. While God is utterly transcendent and next to God we are nothing, still, through God's grace, we can attain union with God, and in some sense are always in that union. Especially in his sermons, he indicates the transcendence of God by the use of paradoxical language, some of which suggests an identity between God and the creature (*see* CREATION). An often-quoted example is, "The eye with which I see God is the same eye with which God sees me." In 1326 he was accused of heresy*. He strenuously defended his orthodoxy, presenting his case at the papal court in Avignon* in 1327. After his death, twenty-eight propositions from his writings were condemned as heretical or dangerous. Scholars now see most, if not all, of these as capable of an orthodox interpretation.

ECOLOGY. The branch of science that studies the relations of organisms to their environment. It has become prominent in recent decades because of growing awareness of the damage done by human activity to the earth, its atmosphere, and the life it supports. Church authorities were slow to recognize the environmental crisis as a moral and religious problem. Vatican Council II* does not mention the environment. The first significant mention in church documents comes in Pope John Paul II's* *Sollicitudo rei socialis* (1987), which (in language echoing papal teaching on birth control*) recognizes "the need to respect the integrity and the cycles of nature and to take them into account when planning for development" (26). Pope John Paul's 1990 World Day of Peace Message, "Peace with All Creation," addressed the ecological crisis as a moral issue. The pope began from the OT creation story and its emphasis on the goodness of the created world (Gn 1.31). He described the destruction of the environment and acknowledged that "we cannot continue to use the goods of the earth as we have in the past." He traced the links of environmental destruction to such evils as war, poverty, social injustice, lack of respect for life, and a lifestyle of "instant gratification and consumerism." A 1991 U.S. Bishops' statement, "Renewing the Earth," amplifies these themes and focuses on the biblical notion of "stewardship," humans' responsibility to care for the earth as "stewards" of God (cf. Gn 2.15). Some theologians, notably Thomas Berry, reject this view as unduly "anthropocentric." They call for a new vision of the cosmos, in which the earth, or the universe, is the primary living subject, and the human being one of the principal modes in which it becomes aware of itself. Other theologians are skeptical of whether such a cosmology can preserve the ideas of human dignity, the centrality of revelation* in Christ rather than the universe, and the transcendence of God*. *See also* CREATION.

ECONOMIC JUSTICE FOR ALL. Subtitled *Pastoral Letter on Catholic Social Teaching and the U.S. Economy,* this document was issued by the National Conference of Catholic Bishops in 1986. The central moral principle of the letter is "Every economic decision and institution must be judged in light of whether it protects or undermines the dignity of the human person" (13). The document stresses the social nature of the human person and consequently the requirement that economic decisions preserve and enhance human community. It insists that persons have a right to participate in the decisions, including economic decisions, that affect them. It holds that society has a special obligation to the poor and vulnerable: "The poor have the single most urgent economic claim on the conscience of the nation" (86) (*see* OPTION FOR THE POOR). From the foundation of these and similar principles, the letter addresses specific problems, including unemployment, poverty, food and agriculture, and the relation of the United States economy to the developing nations.

ECUMENICAL DIALOGUES. Vatican Council II* called for theological dialogue with "separated brethren" (non-Catholic Christians), and subsequently the Catholic Church has been active in dialogue with most branches of Christianity. These dialogues have sometimes aimed simply at greater understanding, sometimes at "agreed statements" with an eye to eventual unity. Their content has been guided by specific points at issue between Catholics and other Christians, but also by essential points of Christian faith that can be assumed to be held in common. At the international level, "bilateral" dialogues (ordinarily supervised on the Catholic side by the Pontifical Council for Promoting Christian Unity) have taken place with representatives of the Oriental Orthodox*, Eastern Orthodox*, Anglicans*, Old Catholics*, Lutherans, Reformed, Methodists, Baptists, Disciples of Christ, Evangelicals, and Pentecostals (*see* PROTESTANT CHURCHES). The greatest progress has been made by the two Anglican-Roman Catholic International Commissions. Catholic representatives have also taken part in multilateral dialogues under the auspices of the World Council of Churches* and many national church councils. In the United States, there have been dialogues with most of the churches mentioned above and also with the Polish National Catholics (*see* OLD CATHOLICS). By far the most fruitful has been the Lutheran-Roman Catholic dialogue, which has produced statements indicating significant "convergence" on many issues, including those historically controverted between the two denominations. Topics of its statements have been: the Nicene Creed* (1965), baptism* (1966), the eucharist* as sacrifice* (1966), papal primacy (1974), teaching authority* and infallibility* (1979), justification* by faith* (1983), Mary* and the saints* (1992), and Scripture and tradition* (1995).

ECUMENISM, ECUMENICAL MOVEMENT (Gk *oikoumenē*, "inhabited world"). The movement to restore the unity of all Christians (*see* UNITY OF THE CHURCH). Concern for the unity of the Christian community is expressed in the NT, especially in Jn 17.21 and in the Pauline writings, e.g., 1 Cor 1.10-17. Yet over the centuries Christians divided into many separate churches. The modern ecumenical movement began in the early twentieth century among Protestant* Christians, especially in order to overcome conflict in mission fields. The first major ecumenical conference was the Edinburgh Missionary Conference in 1910. Eastern Orthodox* participation began in 1920 with an encyclical letter by the Patriarch of Constantinople. Catholic reaction was negative at first. The 1917 Code of Canon Law forbade "disputations or meetings, especially public ones, with non-Catholics." Pope Pius XI*, in his 1929 encyclical* *Mortalium Animos*, held that Catholic participation in ecumenical gatherings would promote the idea that one church was as good as another; he insisted that the only true way to Christian unity was the return of other Christians to the Catholic Church. By the 1950s, however, ecumenical contacts on the part of Catholics were increasingly common. The promotion of Christian unity was one of Pope John XXIII's* explicit objectives in calling Vatican Council II*. That council led to substantial official Catholic participation in ecumenism. Its *Decree on Ecumenism* (1964), while affirming that the "fullness of the means of salvation" (UR 3) was to be found only in the Catholic Church, held that genuine elements of Church life existed in the other Christian bodies, and that all sides shared in the responsibility for Christian division. It exhorted Catholics to take an active part in the movement for Church unity, through participation in theological dialogues, service in common, and, to a limited degree, common worship. Already in 1960, Pope John had founded the Secretariat for Promoting Christian Unity, to supervise Catholic participation in ecumenical relations on the international level. In 1988 it was renamed the Pontifical Council for Promoting Christian Unity. The corresponding body in the United States is the Bishops' Committee on Ecumenical and Interreligious Affairs. Both bodies have sponsored numerous theological dialogues and other activities with other Christians (*see* ECUMENICAL DIALOGUES). *See also* WORLD COUNCIL OF CHURCHES.

ENCYCLICAL (Gk, "circular"). An **encyclical letter** is a pastoral letter* addressed by the pope to the entire Church (or, in a few cases, to the whole world). An **encyclical epistle**, less common, is addressed to only part of the Church. Encyclicals normally concern matters of doctrine, morals, or Church discipline. The pope does not ordinarily invoke his supreme teaching authority in an encyclical, but his teaching is authoritative, belonging to the ordinary magisterium*, and an encyclical could contain material that is infallibly taught, in accordance with the "infallibility* of the ordinary magisterium." The first encyclical, in the present sense of the word, was issued by Pope Benedict XIV in 1740. Synopses of some major papal encyclicals can be found in Appendix IV.

ENLIGHTENMENT, THE (in German, *Die Aufklärung*). A movement in European thought in the seventeenth and eighteenth centuries ("The" is a twentieth-century addition to the movement's name). Important figures associated in various ways with it included John Locke (1632-1704) in England, David Hume (1711-1776) in Scotland, G. W. F. Leibniz (1646-1716), Immanuel Kant (1724-1804), and G. E. Lessing (1729-1781) in Germany, Voltaire (François Marie Arouet) (1694-1778), Jean-Jacques Rousseau (1712-1778), and Denis Diderot (1723-1784) in France. Its spirit was given classic expression in Kant's "What is Enlightenment?" (1784): "Enlightenment is man's release from his self-incurred tutelage." The tutelage in question was subservience to tradition and religious authority. In its place, Kant said, the Enlightenment motto was *Sapere aude!* ("Dare to think for yourself!"). Following René Descartes (1596-1650), Enlightenment thought applied a skeptical doubt to all truth-claims handed down by tradition. Truth was to be established by reason—in particular, "critical" reason modeled on the empirical sciences, especially the physics of Isaac Newton (1642-1727).

The Enlightenment thinkers tended to reject claims based on a revelation* that was transmitted by Church authority* in favor of those that could be established by philosophical reason. For some, this led to **deism**, a religious outlook that emphasized a creator God, knowable by reason through the creation but not directly involved in the world's course of events, and that therefore rejected revelation*, incarnation*, and miracles*. A famous deist image was Voltaire's comparison of God to a watchmaker who made a watch, wound it, and let it run by itself. When the arguments that supported deism were themselves subjected to skeptical doubt, atheism* was one result, as in the case of Baron d'Holbach (1723-1789). A different result of the Enlightenment was the critical study of the Bible (*see* BIBLICAL CRITICISM), which, despite its benefits, created conflict by calling the Bible's historical accuracy into doubt. Enlightenment religion subordinated ritual to ethical conduct. It was typical of Enlightenment worship services, even Catholic masses, that their ceremony was simple, the place of worship was ornamented austerely, and the center of the service was a sermon with ethical content.

Politically and economically, as well as intellectually, Enlightenment thought emphasized individual autonomy. Modern democratic and republican political theory and classical free-market economics are developments of Enlightenment thought. The Enlightenment tended toward a restriction of the political role of religious authorities and a (usually limited) "toleration" of religious diversity. The separation of church and state, first introduced in the United States, is one outgrowth of the Enlightenment, but so also were various degrees of state control of the Church (see GALLICANISM, FRENCH REVOLUTION, RELIGIOUS FREEDOM). The Enlightenment thinkers were highly critical of the pope and the institutional Church, one reason why the Enlightenment had more impact on Protestant* than Catholic religion. The Catholic response was defensive, and a serious intellectual engagement with the philosophical issues raised in the Enlightenment was postponed to the twentieth century (see LIBERALISM). While a rationalistic* neo-scholasticism* came to dominate Catholic thought, an affective devotionalism (see DEVOTIONS) was one reaction on the popular level to the Enlightenment's emphasis on reason.

EPHESUS. Port city in western Asia Minor, prominent site of the work of St. Paul (Acts 18-19), location of the church addressed in the Pauline Letter to the Ephesians and in one of the seven letters in the Book of Revelation (2.1-7). **COUNCIL OF EPHESUS** (431), called by the Emperor Theodosius II to settle the issue of Nestorianism*. Nestorius, bishop of Constantinople, held that Mary* should not be called *theotokos* ("God bearer," "Mother of God"), and this appeared to threaten the unity of Jesus as divine and human. The Council was dominated by Cyril of Alexandria, Nestorius's leading opponent, who engineered the condemnation and deposition of Nestorius before the arrival of the Syrian bishops (led by John of Antioch), who were more sympathetic to Nestorius. Upon arrival, John and his party met separately and excommunicated Cyril and his supporters. Cyril and John were eventually reconciled in 433, with a document called the Formula of Union. The Council, and the Formula of Union, reaffirmed the unity of Jesus as one person, divine and human, and declared Mary to be *theotokos*.

EPIPHANY (Gk *epiphaneia*, "manifestation"). The feast of the "manifestation" of Jesus. "Manifestation" has referred at different times to Jesus' birth, to his baptism, and to the manifestation of his divinity to the Magi (Mt 2.1-12) and in the miracle at the wedding feast at Cana (Jn 2.1-11). Traditionally January 6, the feast is now celebrated in the United States on the Sunday between January 2 and January 8. A celebration on January 6, commemorating the birth of Jesus, is first mentioned by Clement of Alexandria in the early third century. As with Christmas, there are two theories for the choice of this date. One explanation bases the date on that of an Egyptian solar new year festival, the other on Eastern traditions that situate the crucifixion and therefore the conception of Jesus on April 6, and thus his birth on January 6 (for further explanation, *see* CHRISTMAS). The Armenian Church still celebrates the nativity on January 6. When most of the East adopted the Western celebration of the nativity on December 25 (between the fourth and sixth centuries), January 6 became the celebration of the baptism of Jesus. In the West, the feast celebrated the "manifestations" of Jesus' divinity at his baptism, in the visit of the Magi and at Cana. The manifestation to the Gentiles, represented by the Magi, had become the main focus by the fifth century. Today, the readings for the feast still emphasize this theme; Mt 2.1-12 is the Gospel. In eighth-century Gaul, the feast of the **Baptism of Jesus** became the octave day (the day one week after) of the Epiphany, though it was not officially in the Roman Calendar till 1960. It is now celebrated on the Sunday after Epiphany.

EPISCOPAL CONFERENCES. Permanent institutions whereby bishops* in a nation or other territory jointly exercise pastoral functions in the Church. These conferences are to some extent successors of earlier regional councils* and synods*. They arose in Europe in the early nineteenth century and spread to other parts of the world by the end of the century. Vatican Council II* called for their establishment throughout the Church (CD 36-38), and the 1983 Code of Canon Law gives them official status (Canons 447-59). Their decrees require a two-thirds majority and must be reviewed by the Holy See*. Bishops meeting in conferences share in the Church's teaching authority or magisterium* (Canon 753), but the exact nature of the authority of episcopal conferences and their relation to episcopal collegiality* has been a matter of debate. Some of this debate was occasioned by the U.S. bishops' pastoral letters* *The Challenge of Peace** (1983) and *Economic Justice for All** (1986).

There are more than a hundred episcopal conferences in the world. In the United States, the episcopal conference is the **National Conference of Catholic Bishops (NCCB)**, established in 1966. Predecessor organizations to the NCCB and its operational agency, the United States Catholic Conference, were the National Catholic War Council (1917-1919) and the National Catholic Welfare Conference (1919-1967).

ESCHATOLOGY (Gk *eschaton*, "end"). Beliefs about, or the study of, the "last things." In much of theological tradition, the "four last things" were death*, judgment*, heaven*, and hell*. But this represents a narrowing and individualizing of biblical eschatology. Central to NT eschatology is the expectation of, or the experience of the presence of, the kingdom* (or reign) of God. This theme draws on the eschatology of the OT prophets, which calls for a hope in what God will do for Israel in the future in this world, and on the later apocalyptic* eschatology, which looks toward God's putting an end to the present order of the world. Only in later OT books (Daniel, Wisdom, Maccabees) is there a clear hope for an individual life after death, as distinct from belief in a shadowy underworld existence. In the NT, it is the resurrection* of Jesus that both inaugurates the last days and is the basis for eschatological hope in the future (see especially 1 Corinthians 15). This hope is collective more than individual, and in some passages it includes the whole earth (e.g., Rom 8.19-21, Rev 21).

A 1979 document of the Vatican Congregation for the Doctrine of the Faith, "On Certain Questions Pertaining to Eschatology," summarizes Church teaching on eschatology in seven points: (1) the general resurrection* (2) of the whole person*; (3) the survival of a spiritual element, called "soul"*, after death; (4) the value of prayer for the dead; (5) the second coming of Christ (*see* PAROUSIA); (6) the Assumption* of Mary; (7) heaven, hell, and purgatory*. The document expresses awareness of the limits of human language and imagination in regard to what lies beyond our experience, and also calls for a recognition both of the continuity and of the discontinuity between this life and the next. The affirmation of continuity responds to the common charge that eschatological hope distracts from care for this world; as

Vatican Council II* says: "The expectation of a new earth should not weaken, but rather stimulate, the resolve to cultivate this earth, where the body of the new human family is increasing and can even now constitute a foreshadowing of the new age" (GS 39). *See also* HOPE.

EUCHARIST (Gk *eucharistia*, "thanksgiving"). The central sacramental activity of the Church and indeed "the source and the culmination of all Christian life" (Vatican Council II, LG 11). In its primary meaning, "eucharist" refers to the liturgical activity, but secondly it refers to the eucharistic body and blood of Christ, received under the appearances of bread and wine.

First and foremost, the Church is the community that gathers to celebrate the eucharist "in remembrance of" Jesus. The sharing in the one bread and one cup makes Christians "one body" with Jesus and with one another (1 Cor 10.14-22). The NT has four accounts of Jesus' "institution" of the eucharist at the Last Supper (Mt 26.26-30, Mk 14.22-24, Lk 22.14-20, 1 Cor 11.23-26). In all of these accounts, Jesus takes bread and wine, identifies them with his body and blood, and tells the apostles to eat and drink them. In Luke and Paul, Jesus adds an injunction to "Do this in remembrance [*anamnēsis*] of me." John's gospel has no story of the institution of the eucharist, but includes a "eucharistic discourse" (6.22-59), in which Jesus calls himself the "bread from heaven" and tells the disciples to eat his flesh and drink his blood. The location of the Last Supper on "the night before he was handed over" associates the eucharist with Jesus passion. Paul speaks of each celebration as a remembrance of Jesus' death and also an anticipation of his coming (1 Cor 11.26).

Paul calls the eucharistic celebration "the Lord's Supper," while Acts speaks of it as "the breaking of the bread" (2.42,46; 20.7,11). The name "eucharist" is first found in the *Didachē** (late first century?) and Ignatius of Antioch* (early second century). Meaning "thanksgiving," it probably translates a Hebrew word for "blessing." The name "mass"* (*missa*) became standard only in the Middle Ages in the West. The *Didachē* provides some instructions for eucharistic celebration, and Justin Martyr*, writing around A.D. 155, provides the first full description. Justin's description includes all the main features that are familiar today: (in order) readings from the prophets and apostles, a discourse by the presider, prayers by the congregation, a greeting with a kiss, the bringing of bread and wine and water to the presider, a long prayer by the presider followed by "Amen" from the congregation, and the distribution of communion (*First Apology* 65-67).

Justin does not say who the "presider" is, but earlier Ignatius argued that it must be the bishop* or someone appointed by the bishop. There is no evidence in the NT as to who presided, while the *Didachē* speaks of "prophets" (and probably also bishops) as "giving thanks." From at least the second century to the present time, the presider or celebrant has had be a bishop or a priest* (presbyter). In Paul and the *Didachē*, the eucharistic celebration is accompanied by a meal (called an *agapē* or "love feast"); not so in later texts. Justin and Ignatius speak of Sunday* as the regular day to gather for eucharist (Acts 20.7-11 already spoke of a Sunday—perhaps Saturday evening—gathering for the breaking of the bread). Daily eucharistic liturgies did not begin until the fourth century.

The Fathers of the Church* speak of the eucharistic elements (bread and wine) as Jesus' body and blood or else as a symbol or figure of the body and blood, without clearly distinguishing these two understandings. Whether Jesus' eucharistic presence is real or symbolic became an issue in the West in the ninth century and again in the eleventh, with Church authorities endorsing a physical presence, sometimes in exaggerated terms. In the twelfth century, theologians began to use the term **transubstantiation** (change of substance) to indicate the type of change that occurs in the eucharist. This term was used by Lateran Council IV* (1215), but it was not until Thomas Aquinas* (d. 1274) that it received a systematic explanation: while the perceptible "accidents" of the bread and wine remained, the substance (the what-it-is, the essential nature) is changed into the body and blood of Christ.

In the East, the eucharistic liturgy retained its character as a communal celebration, but in the medieval West, the participation of the people declined. Communion became infrequent, to the point that IV Lateran had to mandate that Catholics receive communion at least annually. From the thirteenth century onward, laypeople received only the host, not the consecrated wine. Eucharistic piety centered not on receiving communion but on gazing on the consecrated host (eucharistic bread). Eucharistic devotions* outside of mass proliferated.

From NT times, the eucharist was understood as a *sacrifice*; in all the narratives of Jesus' institution of the eucharist, he speaks of his body as "given for you" and/or his blood as "shed for you" or "for many." While the earliest understanding of eucharistic sacrifice was that it was Christ's sacrifice, to which the Church joined itself sacramentally, increasingly the focus was on the presider, who, from the third century, began to be called a "priest," i.e., one who offers sacrifice. By medieval times, the mass was often regarded primarily as a sacrifice offered by the priest for the benefit of the living and especially of the dead in purgatory*. This led to the multiplication of "private masses" (only the priest present) in the late Middle Ages.

The Protestant* Reformers objected to the late medieval understanding of eucharistic sacrifice; they argued that Christ's one sacrifice on the cross was sufficient and unrepeatable, and so they purged most sacrifice language from the liturgy. They also sought to enhance the participation of the whole congregation, translating the liturgy into the languages of the people and calling for the laity to receive communion in both forms. The Reformers also objected to the idea of transubstantiation as a change effected by the priest, but they could not agree on a theology of the eucharistic presence of Christ. For Luther, Christ was physically present in the elements, but we should not try to say how. For Calvin, Christ was really, but only spiritually present. For Zwingli, the eucharist was a symbol or memorial of his presence.

The Council of Trent (1545-1563) declared that Jesus is really and substantially present in the eucharist, and that transubstantiation is an appropriate name for the change that the elements undergo. It declared that the mass is a true sacrifice, not an addition to that of Christ but a making-present of it, and that it is propitiatory for the living and the dead. It held that the full body and blood of Jesus is present in either of the eucharistic elements, and hence that it is not necessary to receive both. The council judged it not advisable to translate the mass from Latin into vernacular (commonly spoken) languages*. In the aftermath of Trent, the Roman Missal of 1570 prescribed a rigidly uniform order of mass to be celebrated everywhere (with a very few exceptions), thus curbing both abuses and local adaptations. An essentially medieval eucharistic piety remained dominant in Western Catholicism until Vatican Council II*, with some minor changes, e.g., Pope Pius X's* encouragement of frequent communion.

Beginning in the nineteenth century, however, the liturgical movement* recovered many aspects of the early Church's understanding of liturgy and promoted reforms in accordance with it. These efforts bore fruit at Vatican Council II* (1962-1965). The main themes of the Council's *Constitution on the Sacred Liturgy* (1963) were "intelligibility" and "participation," and the reformed eucharistic liturgy, in consequence, could be in the vernacular languages and allowed increased participation by the congregation. Communion under both forms was encouraged.

A renewed eucharistic theology, found both in Church documents and in the works of theologians, emphasizes the eucharist as the act of Christ and of the whole community led by the priest, not primarily of the priest. It locates the presence of Jesus first and foremost in the Church gathered to celebrate; the presence in the eucharistic elements is derivative from this. It emphasizes the uniqueness of the sacrifice of Christ, made present in the eucharist. Such an understanding has led to significant convergence on eucharistic issues, although not full agreement, in ecumenical dialogues* since Vatican II.

The liturgy familiar to most Western Catholics is the Mass of the Roman Rite, as set forth in the Roman Missal of 1969, revised in 1975. It is described in the article, MASS. Liturgies from the Byzantine, Syrian, Armenian, and Alexandrian traditions are approved for use in the Eastern Catholic Churches*.

EUCHARISTIC MINISTER. The ordinary minister for the celebration of the eucharist* is a bishop* or priest*. For the distribution of the eucharist, it is a bishop, priest, or deacon*. The term, "eucharistic minister," however, is most commonly used for "special" or "extraordinary" ministers of the eucharist. These are laypersons or religious sisters* or brothers* who are designated to distribute communion either in the liturgy or outside it, when distribution by an ordained person is impossible or inconvenient. This ministry* was instituted by Pope Paul VI in 1973. Its theological background is Vatican Council II's emphasis on the dignity of the laity* and the right and duty of all to participate in the eucharistic liturgy in accordance with their dignity. It is also linked to the practice of the reception of communion in the hand, common until the ninth century and revived after Vatican II. Eucharistic ministers are approved by the pastor and the bishop for a specified period of time. They may also be designated for particular occasions, such as a mass celebrated for a large gathering at a conference.

EUTHANASIA (Gk *eu*, "well"; *thanatos*, "death"). According to the 1980 "Declaration on Euthanasia" of the Congregation for the Doctrine of the Faith*, "By euthanasia is understood an action or an omission which of itself or by intention causes death, in order that all suffering may in this way be eliminated." Sometimes this is called **active euthanasia**. It is distinguished from murder in that its intention is the good of the person who is killed. The Church condemns euthanasia for the same reason it condemns murder, suicide*, and abortion*: it is wrong directly to kill an innocent human being. In his 1995 encyclical, *Evangelium vitae*, Pope John Paul II* uses language close to that of an infallible declaration to "confirm that euthanasia is a grave violation of the law of God" (65). These principles apply equally to **assisted suicide**. Church teaching on euthanasia as a distinct issue dates from the 1930s, when social movements for euthanasia became prominent in Europe and North America.

The Church does not always condemn the termination of life-support procedures when death is not directly intended. "When inevitable death is imminent in spite of the means used, it is permitted in conscience to take the decision to refuse forms of treatment that would only secure a precarious and burdensome prolongation of life, so long as the ordinary care due to the sick person in similar cases is not interrupted" ("Declaration"). The Church (especially Pope Pius XII*) distinguishes between "ordinary" and "extraordinary" means of treatment, and holds that one may forgo the latter. These terms do not refer primarily to what is and is not usual medical practice. Rather, "extraordinary" means are those that impose burdens on the patient or others, out of proportion to the benefits expected. The 1980 declaration suggests "disproportionate" as a synonym for "extraordinary" in these cases. (In popular language, but not Church documents, such termination of treatment is sometimes called "passive euthanasia.")

There is not a consensus among theologians and Church documents (in particular, statements by state bishops' conferences in the United States) as to the line between "ordinary" and "extraordinary" means of life support. In particular, there is disagreement about "artificial nutrition and hydration" (giving of food and water intravenously or by such means as nasogastric tubes) for patients in a "permanent vegetative state," for example, for whom there is no reasonable hope of return to consciousness. Those who see artificial nutrition and hydration as "ordinary" means liken their termination to starving a patient to death, while those who see them as "extraordinary" liken termination to discontinuing the use of a respirator for a permanently unconscious patient who otherwise could not breathe. According to the U.S. Bishops' "Ethical and Religious Directives for Catholic Health

Care Services" (1994), there should always be a presumption in favor of providing nutrition and hydration, "as long as this is of sufficient benefit to outweigh the burdens involved to the patient" and to others. Some theologians (e.g., Daniel Maguire and Charles Curran)—but no Church documents—challenge the moral relevance of the active/passive distinction and hold that active euthanasia may at times be morally acceptable. Rapid advances in life-support technology make discriminations of ordinary/extraordinary and active/passive difficult and in need of continued reassessment.

Theologians and Church documents raise additional questions about the social consequences of the legalization of active euthanasia or assisted suicide. Would they become means to contain medical costs? What would be the effects if doctors and patients understood that killing the patient was a legitimate option in the practice of medicine? Once the killing of terminally ill patients who wish to die was approved, how far would killing be likely to extend? A cautionary example is the fact that the killing of millions of Jews (*see* JUDAISM) and others in Nazi Germany began as a euthanasia program for patients considered "incurable."

EVANGELICAL COUNSELS. The ideals of poverty*, chastity, and obedience*. In one sense, these ideals obligate all Christians, who must observe the detachment from material possessions, the sexual norms, and the respect for authority that are appropriate to their state in life. As "counsels" rather than norms, these ideals are taken to a greater degree of asceticism and given a specific form in *religious life**; poverty, chastity, and obedience become, respectively, (1) renunciation of personal property, (2) celibacy*, and (3) obedience to a religious superior. Such observance of counsels is considered good but not obligatory. The counsels are "evangelical" in having some foundation in the gospels: poverty in Jesus' word to the rich young man to sell all he possessed (Mt 19.21), chastity in the praise of "eunuchs for the sake of the kingdom" (Mt 19.12), obedience in the passages that tell the disciples to be "servants" (e.g., Mk 9.35). They have been treated as a triad since the twelfth century. Members of religious orders and congregations take vows* or otherwise promise to observe the evangelical counsels. Vatican Council II presents the life of the counsels as one way in which Christians may be called by God to live "the fullness of the Christian life and the perfection of charity" (LG 39), to which all Christians are called (*see* HOLINESS). It is specially commended as a sign of total dedication to the kingdom* of God, a foretelling of the resurrected* state (LG 42-44), and a close imitation of the life of Jesus. It therefore "belong[s] unquestionably to [the] life and holiness" of the Church (LG 44).

EVANGELIZATION. The process of spreading the gospel*, the "good news" of Christian faith. The term, "evangelization," was seldom used in Catholicism before Vatican Council II*. "Missionary work" (*see* MISSIONS) or "propagation of the faith" were preferred. When "evangelization" began to be used, in the 1950s, the emphasis was narrowly on proclamation of the kerygma*, the Christian message, and the Council mainly used the term in that sense. Even now, to American Catholics, "evangelization" often chiefly connotes an aggressive form of Christian preaching. Pope Paul VI*, however, put forward a broader and deeper understanding of evangelization in the Apostolic Exhortation *Evangelii nuntiandi* (1975), and this understanding has been further developed by Pope John Paul II*. Pope Paul defined evangelization thus: "The Church may be truly said to evangelize when, solely in virtue of that news which she proclaims, she seeks to convert both the individual consciences of men and their collective conscience, all the activities in which they are engaged and finally their lives and the whole environment which surrounds them" (18). Evangelization, thus, is addressed not only to individuals but to cultures, and it reaches to all dimensions of personal and social life. It includes building the local church as well as preaching the gospel message (28). It incorporates, but cannot be reduced to, the promotion of justice and human liberation (31). It is carried out not only by proclamation but especially by the witness of Christian life (21). It is the responsibility not only of a special class of missionaries but of all Christian faithful. As defined above, evangelization is always needed by everyone; however, John Paul II's encyclical, *Redemptoris missio* (1990), makes a distinction between pastoral care and evangelization. Evangelization is addressed especially to those societies or sectors of society where Christian faith was never established or has largely been lost. In the second case, John Paul speaks of "re-evangelization." Both original evangelization and re-evangelization are part of the "new evangelization," for which John Paul has called in tones of urgency in light of the approaching end of the second millennium of Christianity. *See also* INCULTURATION.

EVIL. Physical or **material evil** refers to conditions that are bad, such as pain, suffering, damage, harm, ignorance. **Moral evil** is evil in the will, i.e., sin* or malice; often it leads to material evil. The classic "problem of evil" is the question of the origin of evil. If God creates evil things, then God intends evil, and thus God is not fully good. If something other than God causes evil, as in the dualistic systems of Gnosticism* and Manichaeism*, then God is not the creator of all things (*see* CREATION). Catholic tradition rejects both of these positions, holding that God creates all things and that all that God creates is good. Already in the OT, the Book of Job is a profound meditation on the suffering of the innocent; the final answer seems to be that the ways of God are too mysterious for the human mind to understand. In the Christian tradition, there have been many attempts at **theodicy**, the theological attempt to "justify God," to show how God is not to be held responsible for evil. Most influential has been that of Augustine*, who held that evil is not a "substance" but a "privation," the absence of some good. Thus it is not a *thing* created by God. Augustine's main concern was moral evil, and he located its cause in the will of the finite creature (human or angel), which had the freedom to turn away from God and did so. Human and angelic suffering is the result of sin or the just punishment for sin. Augustine's position has been standard in Catholic theodicy, but objections have been raised as to why God should allow this turning away, and why the innocent suffer. Contemporary process theology* holds that God's power is one of persuasion, not control. Evil is the result of other beings' independence of God, and God also suffers it. An objection to this position is that it does not make God absolute enough; God becomes one entity among many. Liberation theology* presents God as taking up the cause of the poor, whose suffering is the result of injustice. Three emphases are central to contemporary Catholic treatments of evil: (1) Evil is a mystery*, which we cannot fully comprehend. (2) The cross of Jesus is God's ultimate revelation in regard to evil; Jesus suffered as we do and more, yet Jesus' suffering is the route to God's victory over evil in the resurrection*. (3) Christians should regard evil not primarily as a theoretical problem but as an incentive for action, repenting of their own complicity in evil, and aligning themselves with God, who champions the victims of injustice. None of this is a full answer to the problem of evil; as the *Catechism of the Catholic Church* says, "Only Christian faith as a whole constitutes the answer to this question" (309). Since that too escapes full understanding, Christians cannot (in this world) escape the need to protest and to lament. *See also* DEMON, ORIGINAL SIN.

EVOLUTION. In *The Origin of Species* (1859), Charles Darwin (1809-1882) put forward the biological theory of evolution in its classic form. According to evolutionary theories (several were then in circulation), the various species of living being were not created directly by God, but evolved from other life forms. Darwin contended that evolution occurred by a process of **natural selection**: random variations produced new life forms, and those that were suited to survive and to reproduce in their environment established themselves as new species. (The genetic mechanism by which this process occurred was later discovered by Gregor Mendel [1822-1884].) Darwin extended his theory to the evolution of human beings in *The Descent of Man* (1871): humans evolved from apelike ancestors. Evolutionary theory, which is now almost universally accepted by biologists (though with much variation as to details), posed three challenges to Christian theology: (1) it conflicted with a literal reading of the creation narratives in Genesis 1 and 2; (2) it threatened the uniqueness of the human being; (3) it portrayed a random, purposeless process of the development of living beings, rather than the guidance of divine providence. Catholic reactions to Darwin's theory were at first guardedly negative. Because Catholic authors, such as St. Augustine*, had not read the Genesis narratives literally, the impact of evolutionary theory was not as explosive for Catholics as for some Protestants*. Nevertheless, *Evolution and Dogma* (1896), by John A. Zahm, C.S.C., which sought to harmonize evolutionary theory and Catholic faith, was prohibited by the Congregation for the Index of Forbidden Books*, and a Pontifical Biblical Commission decree of 1909 mandated a mainly literal reading of the Genesis narratives. In the encyclical *Divino afflante Spiritu* (1943), Pope Pius XII* removed one obstacle to Catholic acceptance of evolution by giving scholars freedom to employ modern historical criticism of biblical texts (*see* BIBLICAL CRITICISM), enabling them to profess the now commonplace view that the Genesis texts were never meant as history or science. In the encyclical *Humani generis* (1951), he stated that the Church did not forbid "evolutionism" as a theory of the development of the human body but did require belief in God's direct creation* of the human soul*. He expressed reservation about polygenism (the belief that there were more than two first humans), an issue still in conflict among biologists, saying, "It is not at all apparent how such a view can be reconciled with" the doctrine of original sin* (DS 3897). (Many contemporary theories of original sin are compatible with polygenism.) Today, Catholic theologians seldom challenge evolutionary theory, but they are concerned to show evolution as manifesting divine purpose. Many theologians are influenced by the synthesis of the scientist-theologian Pierre Teilhard de Chardin* (1881-1955), according to which the evolutionary process leads ultimately to Christ.

EXCOMMUNICATION. A penalty whereby a person is excluded from celebrating or receiving the sacraments or exercising any office or ministry in the Church. Excommunications *latae sententiae* ("by the sentence imposed") are incurred automatically in virtue of the offense committed, e.g., heresy*, schism*, abortion*, or desecration of the consecrated eucharistic elements. Excommunications *ferendae sententiae* ("by the sentence to be imposed") are imposed by judicial decision. Excommunications are usually imposed and lifted by the diocesan bishop*, but in some cases by the Holy See*. Excommunication, modeled on the practice of the Jewish synagogue, is found in the NT (e.g., Mt 18.17-18, 1 Cor 5.2). In the early Church, it was not clearly distinguished from the practice of sacramental penance and reconciliation*.

EXISTENTIALISM. A twentieth-century movement in philosophy and literature, with antecedents in the nineteenth century. Some trace existentialism to the Danish Lutheran theologian Søren Kierkegaard (1813-1855), who dwelled on the situation of the human being as an individual before God. Other forerunners to the movement were the Russian novelist Fyodor Dostoyevsky (1821-1881) and the German philosopher Friedrich Nietzsche (1844-1900). Important twentieth-century figures included the German philosophers Martin Heidegger (1889-1976) and Karl Jaspers (1883-1969), and the French philosophers, novelists, and playwrights Jean-Paul Sartre (1905-1980) and Albert Camus (1913-1960). The most prominent Catholic existentialist was the French philosopher and playwright Gabriel Marcel (1889-1973), whose philosophy centered on personal relationships and approached the question of God through human experience. The typical emphases of existentialism were human individuality, subjective experience, and freedom. The first two contrasted strongly with the neo-scholastic approach of objective analysis of human nature (*see*

SCHOLASTICISM). Many Catholic theologians saw existentialism as providing an important experiential dimension that was lacking in the scholastic tradition. The existentialist emphasis on human freedom and responsibility was also congenial to theologians, who strove to show, against the atheism* of such thinkers as Nietzsche and Sartre, that it was compatible with faith in God. Existentialism affected Catholic theology especially through Karl Rahner* (1904-1980), who studied under Heidegger. Edward Schillebeeckx drew on existentialism in developing a theory of the sacraments* as personal encounters. Catholic theologians were also influenced by existentialism by way of the three great Protestant theologians Karl Barth (1886-1968), Rudolf Bultmann (1884-1976), and Paul Tillich (1886-1965).

EXORCISM (Gk *exorkizein*, "to administer an oath"). A ritual for the expulsion of an evil spirit or demon*, especially from one who is possessed by the demon. **Possession** occurs when an evil spirit controls the thoughts and actions of a person, supplanting the person's ordinary voluntary control. It is not mentioned in the OT but appears frequently in the NT. Many of Jesus' healings are expulsions of demons (e.g., Mk 1.23-26, 34). In Luke 11.14-23, Jesus speaks of his exorcisms as manifesting the power of the kingdom* of God prevailing over the kingdom of Satan. Much of what would appear in a first-century world-view as demonic possession would today be understood as physical illness (e.g., Mk 9.14-29, which appears to be epilepsy) or mental illness; what is important is that in Jesus God prevails over the forces of evil that produce illness (*see* HEALING). The practice of exorcism in cases of possession (or demonic **obsession**—an attack that stops short of complete invasion) is found in the Church Fathers* and throughout Church history. The Church retains a ritual for exorcism, but it can only be performed by a priest who has special permission from the local bishop. It is used only rarely, in cases in which a person acts as if possessed and does not respond to conventional medical and psychotherapeutical treatment.

Exorcisms have also been part of the ritual for baptism* at least since the third century. The candidate for baptism was not understood as possessed or obsessed but as being saved from a world in which the powers of evil prevail. In the reforms of the baptismal ritual after Vatican Council II*, the exorcisms are not direct expulsions of demons but prayers to the Father and to Christ that the candidate be freed from all evil powers of whatever sort. For adult candidates, they appear most prominently in the stage of the catechumenate* called the "scrutinies," celebrated in Lent preceding baptism at the Easter Vigil.

EXTREME UNCTION. *See* ANOINTING OF THE SICK.

F

FAITH. The human response to God's revelation*. It combines *belief* in the truth of what God reveals and *trust* in the God who reveals. Catholic understandings of faith from the Middle Ages through Vatican Council I* tended to emphasize the element of belief, while Protestant* understandings, notably Martin Luther's, centered on the element of trust. Contemporary theology attempts to hold the two together, and this is reflected in the words of Vatican Council II , "In response to God's revelation our duty is 'the obedience of faith' (see Rom 16.26 ...). By this, a human being makes a total and free self-commitment to God, offering 'the full submission of intellect and will to God as he reveals' [Vatican Council I], and willingly assenting to the revelation he gives" (DV 5). This refers to the faith as an act of the believer (*fides quā creditur*, "faith by which it is believed"); "faith" may also refer to the content of what one believes (*fides quae creditur*, "faith which is believed"). In the latter sense, the "Catholic faith" is that which the Church believes, the normative faith for Catholics.

The act of genuine faith is not possible without the grace* of God. Considered as a habitual disposition rather than a distinct act, faith is one of the "theological virtues"*, which are special gifts of God.

Catholic teaching holds that faith is not contrary to reason, although what is believed in faith goes beyond what can be established by reason alone. *See* FIDEISM and RATIONALISM.

See also JUSTIFICATION.

FAST AND ABSTINENCE. To fast is deliberately to do without food. Abstinence is doing without meat. These practices are found in all religions. In Christianity, their purpose is usually penitential (*see* PENANCE) in a broad sense: to turn away from self-indulgence and to become more responsive to God. They may also be done in a spirit of solidarity with those who are suffering. Fasting may be a purification preparatory to some important event or decision. Thus, Jesus fasted forty days before beginning his ministry (Mt 4.2), and the apostles fasted before choosing elders in local churches (Acts 14.23). Later, Christians often fasted on the vigil (day before) of a great feast*. The *Didachē* (late first century) calls for fasting on Wednesdays (the day before Jesus' passion) and Fridays (the day of Jesus' death). By around A.D. 400, Saturday replaced Wednesday as a fast day in the West.

Seasons of fasting appeared early in Church history. One was Lent*. Another, dating from the third century, was the **Ember Days** ("Ember" from Lt *quattuor tempora*, "four seasons"): Wednesday, Friday, and Saturday in one week in each of the four seasons (these remained as fast days until 1966). Later, fasting was added in Advent, on the vigils of feasts, and at other times. Before 1917, the general law of the Western Church required fasting (including abstinence) on all weekdays of Lent, on the Ember Days, and on the vigils of Christmas*, Pentecost*, Assumption*, and All Saints*. Abstinence was required on all Fridays and Saturdays. There were many local dispensations and variations.

In the twentieth century, fast and abstinence days were reduced, but at a minimum, before 1966, abstinence was still required on all Fridays, and fast and abstinence on Ash Wednesday and Good Friday. Rules adopted by the U.S. bishops in 1951 enjoined, in addition, fast on the weekdays of Lent, the Ember Days, and several vigils, and partial abstinence on the Ember Wednesdays and Saturdays and the vigils of Pentecost and All Saints. **Partial abstinence** meant that meat was allowed at only the principal meal of a day. In 1966, Pope Paul VI* reduced the days of fast and abstinence and left much to the discretion of local episcopal conferences*. Since 1966, in the United States, fast and abstinence are to be observed on Ash Wednesday and Good Friday, abstinence on Fridays of Lent. Abstinence on other Fridays is recommended but no longer required.

The earliest Christian fasts involved abstaining from all food until sundown, but "fasting" later meant reducing consumption of food. Today, on a fast day, one may eat one full meal and two other meals that do not, together, equal a full meal. One may drink liquids between meals. On days of abstinence, one must not eat meat, but may eat fish, eggs, or milk products. The law of abstinence obliges all those fourteen or older, while the law of fast obliges those aged eighteen to fifty-nine; in both cases, those whose health or ability to work would be significantly impaired are not obliged.

The practice of fasting before receiving the eucharist* originated in the fourth century. For centuries, the fast extended from midnight until the reception of communion, but in 1964 it was reduced to one hour, during which no food or drink, except water, is allowed.

FATHERS OF THE CHURCH. Unlike "Doctor of the Church"*, which is formally conferred by Rome, the title "Father of the Church" arose in popular tradition. Thus, there is no definitive list of Church Fathers. Normally, the term refers to writers of the first eight centuries whose lives were saintly, whose works were orthodox*, and who are held in honor in the Church. Some writers are usually included among the Church fathers despite the fact that some of their assertions were regarded as unorthodox (e.g., Origen* and Tertullian*). A few women (e.g., Egeria, who wrote a journal of her pilgrimage to Jerusalem between A.D. 381 and 384) are sometimes included among the Church Fathers; at times they are called "Church Mothers." The term "Fathers of the Church" includes the Apostolic Fathers* and the Apologists* but refers especially to great writers of a slightly later period, noteworthy figures among whom included Augustine*, Jerome*, and Gregory the Great* in the West, and Origen*, the Cappadocian* Fathers, Athanasius*, and John Chrysostom* in the East. If a doctrine is commonly taught by the Fathers, this is taken as strong evidence that it is to be accepted by the Church as divinely revealed; if it is generally rejected by them, this is strong evidence that it is heresy*.

The study of the theology of the Fathers is **patristics**, while **patrology** is the historical and literary study of the Fathers.

FEAST. A day of special celebration in the liturgy*. The first Christian feast was Sunday*, but annual feasts, such as Easter* and Pentecost*, developed in early centuries. The latter two feasts, and others like them, are called **movable feasts**, in that they do not occur on the same calendar date every year. Feasts such as Christmas*, which always occur on the same date, are called **fixed observances** or **immovable feasts**. There are four categories of feast (listed in declining order of importance): (1) **solemnities**, which begin on the evening of the preceding day; (2) **feasts** (in a narrower sense), which are confined to one day but have special liturgical features, e.g., three Scripture readings in the day's eucharistic liturgy; (3) **memorials**, celebrated throughout the Church; (4) **optional memorials**. *See* CALENDAR, LITURGICAL and entries for specific feasts.

FEMINISM. A movement for the full and equal participation of women in all aspects of social and economic life, or the theoretical articulation of the rationale for this movement. In its "first wave," in North America and Europe in the late nineteenth and early twentieth centuries, the women's movement concentrated on women's participation in the institutions of society, especially on their right to vote. It was generally opposed by Church authorities and had little immediate impact on the Catholic Church. In its "second wave," which became prominent in the 1970s but drew on earlier thinkers, such as the French philosopher Simone de Beauvoir (1908-1986), it has put forward a deep challenge to all social and cultural institutions and has profoundly affected the life of the Church.

Feminist thought sees human institutions generally as corrupted by **patriarchy**, male domination over women, and **androcentrism**, taking men's perspectives as normative, to the exclusion or marginalization of women's perspectives. **Feminist theology** applies this approach to the Christian tradition. Feminist theologians note that Christian theology was shaped with minimal participation from women, who were excluded from positions of authority in the Church and, until recently, from higher education in theology. They argue that all of the standard topics of Christian theology need to be reconsidered from women's points of view. An important early effort in this direction was Rosemary Radford Ruether's *Sexism and God-Talk*; a more recent example is Elizabeth Johnson's book on God, *She Who Is*. Feminist historians have recovered neglected women's voices, such as Hildegard of Bingen*, in the theological tradition. Other feminist theologians have rejected the entire Christian tradition as irremediably patriarchal; Mary Daly, formerly a Catholic theologian, is the most prominent example. On the other hand, there are conservative women who argue that traditional roles for women are most in keeping with women's authentic nature, and that such a view is the true "feminism."

Feminist biblical hermeneutics*, of which Elisabeth Schüssler Fiorenza is the best-known advocate, calls for a "hermeneutics of suspicion," recognizing that biblical texts themselves are shaped by the patriarchal character of the societies from which they came. It draws upon the experience of women to identify liberating principles in the Bible, such as God's partisanship for the poor and outcast.

In practice, feminists work for greater participation of women at all levels of decision making in the Church. The impact of feminism has been especially strong among women religious (*see* RELIGIOUS

LIFE), since until recently their role in the Church had been defined, and their lives closely regulated, by male authorities. For some Catholic feminists, the ordination of women* is a key issue. For others, the entire hierarchical system, of which ordination is a part, is oppressive to women. Such feminists often form small egalitarian communities known as "Women-Church." These vary as to whether or not they (1) are associated with official Church structures and (2) admit men.

Feminism was initially a movement of well-educated middle class women in North America and Europe, and feminist theology has at times reflected an unconscious bias toward those societies and classes. Consequently, some African American women theologians prefer to call their thought **"womanist,"** while some Hispanic women call their approach *mujerista*. Recently, significant work, combining feminism with third-world liberation theology*, has been done by women theologians in Latin America, Asia, and Africa.

FIDEISM (Lt *fides*, "faith"). An excessive reliance on faith* instead of reason in matters pertaining to God. Its opposite is rationalism*. The word *fideism* was first used in the late eighteenth century. It could be applied to some forms of medieval nominalism* but was used especially in reference to nineteenth-century traditionalism*. The opinions of some fideist theologians, e.g., L. Bautin (1835), were condemned in the mid-nineteenth century. Vatican Council I's* declaration that God can "be known with certainty from the things which have been made, by the natural light of human reason" (DS 3026) is directed against fideism. The declaration does not specify the precise manner in which reason can know God, nor the exact relation of reason to faith.

FILIOQUE (Lt, "and [from] the Son"). Words added to the Nicene (Niceno-Constantinopolitan) Creed*, referring to the Holy Spirit* "who proceeds from the Father *and the Son*." The words reflect Augustine's* theology of the Trinity*, in which the Holy Spirit is the love joining the Father and the Son and hence "proceeds" from both. They were inserted into the creed in late sixth-century Gaul or Spain. Though the popes resisted their inclusion until the eleventh century, Charlemagne* in the late eighth century sought to impose them on the whole Church. This led to conflict between the Western and Eastern churches. In the ninth century, Photius*, patriarch of Constantinople, accused the Western church of heresy over this issue. The Eastern Orthodox* continue to criticize the *filioque* for two reasons: (1) the words were improperly added to the Creed, without the approval of an ecumenical council*; (2) they reflect a faulty theology of the Trinity, denying the Father his rightful status as sole source of the divine nature. Catholic and Protestant theologians and leaders today will often concede the first point, sometimes expressing willingness to omit the words from the Creed, but they resist the second. The issue remains an obstacle to reunion between the Catholic Church and the Eastern Orthodox.

FLORENCE (FERRARA-FLORENCE-ROME), COUNCIL OF. For the prior history of this council, *see* BASEL, COUNCIL OF. In 1437, Pope Eugenius IV decreed the removal of the Council of Basel to Ferrara, and in 1438, he and a minority of the Council convened there, joined later in 1438 by representatives of the Eastern (Greek) Church. Eugenius moved the council to Florence in 1439. (The Council at Basel continued until 1449, but decreased in numbers and influence.) The issue at hand in Florence was to resolve the schism* between the Eastern and Western Churches (*see* EASTERN ORTHODOX CHURCHES). The Eastern Emperor was interested in religious reunion in order to obtain Western aid for Constantinople, threatened by the Turks. The final agreement, *Laetentur caeli* (1439), reflected the principal issues discussed at the Council: Western doctrines of purgatory* and the primacy of the pope* were declared, the Greeks accepted the legitimacy of the Filioque* in the Creed but were not required to use it themselves, and both leavened and unleavened eucharistic bread were accepted. The reunion was not accepted in the East and came to a definitive end with the fall of Constantinople to the Turks in 1453. The Council also effected reunions with some members of non-Chalcedonian Eastern churches (*see* CHALCEDON; EASTERN CATHOLIC CHURCHES). Eugenius moved it to the Lateran in Rome in 1443, and its last recorded session was in 1445.

FORGIVENESS. God's forgiveness is a frequent theme in the OT (e.g., Ps 103.3). It is central to Jesus' proclamation of the kingdom of God*. Jesus portrays God's forgiveness especially in his parables, e.g., the Prodigal Son (Lk 15.11-32). He himself forgives sins by the power of God (Mk 2.5-11), and he tells his followers to forgive one another in consequence of God's forgiveness (e.g., Mt 18.21-35, the parable of the unforgiving servant). Christians' forgiveness of one another is to be unlimited (Mt 21.22). In the Lord's Prayer, Jesus' followers are to pray to be forgiven as they forgive one another (Mt 9.12). Jesus' death brings forgiveness (Mt 26.28, Heb 9.26). Jesus bestows on the apostles the power to forgive sins (Jn 20.21-23). The Church exercises this power in the sacraments of baptism* and reconciliation/penance* (*see also* ABSOLUTION). Both of these sacraments ritually combine forgiveness by God and acceptance by the community (either admission to it or reconciliation with it). Beyond sacramental ritual, Christian life requires both the seeking and acceptance of God's forgiveness, and mutual forgiveness and acceptance of forgiveness, without which we cannot live in love.

FORTY HOURS DEVOTION. A devotion consisting of the exposition of the Blessed Sacrament (consecrated eucharistic wafer), together with special masses and prayers. It lasts forty hours, probably in commemoration of Jesus' forty hours in the tomb between Good Friday and Easter morning. The forty-hour period may be continuous or interrupted at night. The ritual originated in Milan around 1534, drawing on older customs. It was formerly the custom for each parish to have Forty Hours once a year, but it is now celebrated less regularly.

FRANCIS DE SALES, ST. (1567-1622), **JANE FRANCES DE CHANTAL, ST.** (1572-1641). Francis de Sales, a native of Savoy, became bishop of Geneva in 1602. Because of Calvinist control of Geneva, he had to live in Annecy, where he carried on an extensive ministry of preaching and spiritual direction*. He wrote two classics of spiritual literature: *Introduction to the Devout Life* (1609) and *Treatise on the Love of God* (1616), as well as many letters of spiritual direction.

In 1604, Francis became spiritual director to Jane de Frémyot, Baroness de Chantal, a widow with four living children. The two developed a close spiritual and personal friendship and exchanged hundreds of letters. In 1610, they founded the Visitation of Holy Mary, a congregation of women devoted to prayer and to service to the needy, without the enclosure then typical of women's orders. In 1618, at the insistence of the archbishop of Lyons, the "Visitandines" became cloistered and took on the status of an order. Jane was the superior of the order until her death.

Salesian spirituality was at one time credited entirely to Francis, who was the theologian and senior partner of the pair. Today, Jane's contribution is acknowledged, but even more, the relationship between the two is seen as the source of their distinctive spirituality. Some typical emphases of Salesian spirituality are human freedom and responsibility, the possibility of holiness in almost any walk of life, lay as well as clerical or religious*, and the importance of human relationships in spiritual life. These and other Salesian ideals are developed in Francis's writings and in the life of the Visitation order.

Francis was canonized in 1655 and named a Doctor of the Church* in 1877. His feast is celebrated on January 24. Jane was canonized in 1767. Her feast is celebrated on December 12.

Francis founded no religious congregation of men, but several congregations, founded in the nineteenth century, took their inspiration from him. These include the Salesians of St. John Bosco, the Oblates of St. Francis de Sales, and the Missionaries of St. Francis de Sales.

FRANCIS OF ASSISI, ST. (1181/2-1226), **FRANCISCANS.** Francis of Assisi is one of the Church's best-known and best-loved saints*, called "another Christ" by Pope Pius XI*. Francis Bernardone was born in Assisi, Umbria, the son of a prosperous merchant, Pietro Bernardone, and his wife, Pica, from a distinguished French family. He fought in the chronic battles between Assisi and neighboring Perugia, but a series of spiritual events led him to turn away from business and the military life. An encounter with a leper and an identification of lepers with the crucified Christ (Is 53.3) led him to associate with lepers and to desire to live in poverty*. At San Damiano in 1205-1206 he heard Jesus speak from the crucifix* in the church, telling Francis to "repair my house." At first, he undertook to rebuild church buildings, but at the church called the Portiuncula at Assisi in 1208 he was profoundly struck by a reading of the gospel passage in which Jesus sends the disciples out without money or extra clothing (Mt 10.9). He resolved to live in complete poverty in imitation of Christ and to spend his life preaching penance and peace. He attracted a band of followers, who became a new form of religious community life. They lived under a rule, first approved by Pope Innocent III in 1209 (revised in 1221 and 1223), in complete poverty, but were not connected to a particular monastery, like monks (*see* MONASTICISM). They were the beginning of the Franciscans or Order of Friars Minor (O.F.M.), the first mendicant* order, so called because they gained sustenance by mendicancy (begging).

The preaching of Francis and his brothers became a powerful force for renewal in the medieval Church. In addition, Francis strongly desired to convert the Muslims. After two failed attempts to go to the Middle East, he traveled to Egypt in 1219 and preached unsuccessfully to the Sultan Malik al-Kamil at Damietta. In 1223, he built a crèche (Nativity scene) at Grecchio. This was the origin of what is now a standard Christmas* custom. While at prayer on Mount Alverna in 1224, he received the stigmata (the marks of the wounds of Jesus). He was canonized in 1228. His feast is celebrated on October 4.

The central theme of his spirituality was the imitation of Christ, especially of Christ's poverty. He also had a great love for God's creatures, especially animals, and an awareness of how God is seen through them. Another important theme was brotherhood and sisterhood, not only with the members of his orders but with all creatures, as strikingly shown in his "Canticle of Brother Sun" (1225), written when he was ailing and nearly blind. Despite his love for the physical world, however, he wore out his own body with harsh penances.

In 1210 or 1211, he attracted **St. Clare** (1194-1253) as a follower. In 1212 at San Damiano, he established a convent for her and several other women, who were the first of the Franciscan Second Order or Poor Clares. Unlike the Franciscan men, the women were to live in enclosure in the convent, but their way of life was otherwise patterned on the apostolic poverty of the men. Francis also attracted followers, married and single, who remained in their homes and their secular occupations, and wrote a rule of life for them. They became the Franciscan Third Order*, formally recognized in 1289.

After Francis's death, there was much conflict in the men's order over poverty and fidelity to Francis's vision. St. Bonaventure* united the order with new constitutions in 1260, but after Bonaventure's death, there was again great division between the Spirituals, who desired absolute poverty and adherence to Francis's rule, and the rest of the community, the Moderates. These conflicts were settled by the middle of the fourteenth century, but more conflicts broke out later in the century between the Observants, who desired a stricter observance of the Rule, and the Conventuals, who did not follow the Observants' reforms. In 1517, Pope Leo X established the Observants and the Conventuals as two orders of Franciscans, as they still remain. Today, the Observants are known simply as the Order of Friars Minor. A third major branch of the Franciscan men is the Capuchins (so called from an Italian word for the hoods they wore), established in 1528 as a result of a reform movement.

Many members of the Third Order began to live in community and take vows* of poverty, chastity, and obedience (*see* EVANGELICAL COUNSELS). These were constituted as a religious order, the Third Order Regular, in 1447. Most communities of Franciscan Brothers* and Sisters* are organized along the lines of the Third Order Regular. The 1994 *Catholic Almanac* listed eighty-four separate congregations of Franciscan women in the United States.

FRANCIS XAVIER, ST. *See* XAVIER, FRANCIS, ST.

FRENCH REVOLUTION (1789-1799). The precipitating cause of the French Revolution was a financial crisis that had brought the government of King Louis XVI near to bankruptcy. Louis was forced to call a session of the Estates General, consisting of representatives of the three "estates" (social orders) of clergy, nobility, and commoners. The privileges of the first two estates were one of the primary causes of the financial crisis; for instance, the Church owned about a tenth of the land in France and paid almost no taxes on it. The three Estates General voted to combine into a single National Assembly in June 1789 and took an oath to write a new constitution. The common people entered the revolutionary process with the storming of the Bastille prison in Paris on July 14, 1789, which was followed by uprisings throughout France. In August 1789, the National Assembly abolished all privileges, including those of the clergy. Church property began to be nationalized in November, though the Assembly agreed to pay salaries to clergy and to support institutions formerly run by the Church. In August the Assembly passed the "Declaration of the Rights of Man and of the Citizen," which proclaimed rights of liberty and equality, including freedom in expressing religious opinions.

In the spring of 1790, the Assembly began to suppress religious houses and confiscate their property. The Civil Constitution of the Clergy (July 1790) demanded that priests take an oath to support the government. Pope Pius VI condemned the Civil Constitution in 1791, adding that the rights declared in 1789 were contrary to nature and to divine law. The Church in France was divided into a Constitutional Church, which swore the oath, and a "nonjuring" Church, loyal to the pope. Measures against the Church continued under two successors of the National Assembly, the Legislative Assembly and the National

Convention, especially during the "Terror" under the latter in 1793 to 1794. All public and private worship was forbidden, priests were required to marry and give up the priesthood, and many priests were executed. A civic religion replaced Christian practice, with a Goddess of Reason enshrined in the Cathedral of Notre Dame. Places with saints' names were renamed, as were many children. The Gregorian calendar was abolished in October 1793, replaced by a revolutionary calendar without Sunday or feast days. (The revolution's campaign against Christianity was not equally successful in all parts of France, and many priests survived and continued their ministry.) After the Thermidorean reaction (July 1794) against the Terror and its perpetrators, France moved toward a separation of church and state, but persecution was renewed in 1797. Pius VI was captured and died in prison in France in 1799. Persecution ended with Napoleon's coup d'état in November 1799.

Pius VI and his successors in the nineteenth century were deeply shaken by these events. They came to see the Revolution as the necessary outgrowth of the Enlightenment*, or, further still, of the Protestant* Reformation. Influenced by the Ultramontane* thought of Joseph de Maistre and others, they came to see a restored medieval Christendom as the only alternative to the evils of the modern world, as manifested in the Revolution. The head of such a Christian civilization and the primary bulwark against chaos would be a strong pope. Such ideas underlay the Syllabus of Errors* (1864) of Pope Pius IX* and, to some degree, the declaration of papal infallibility* at Vatican Council I*. They play some role in the social teaching* of Pope Leo XIII*. The perception of a radical opposition between Catholicism and the modern world was clearly overcome in Vatican Council II* (especially its *Pastoral Constitution on the Church in the Modern World* [1965]), but resurfaced to some extent in Pope John Paul II's* conception of the role of the papacy.

FUNDAMENTAL OPTION. A term used in moral theology* to indicate either (1) the fundamental stance or orientation of one's life or (2) a particular choice in which such a stance is established. Based in the work of Karl Rahner*, this concept was made prominent by Joseph Fuchs, S.J., in the 1960s. At the most profound level, one's fundamental option is for openness to love of God and neighbor or for sin*—for the turning away from God and neighbor. Fundamental option theory has been used by theologians to explain the distinction between mortal and venial sins, that is, between sins that render one liable to damnation (*see* HELL) and sins that do not. A mortal sin enacts or expresses a fundamental decision against God. Most theologians who speak of fundamental option agree that a fundamental option may be expressed, enacted, or altered in particular, concrete moral actions; however, the moral seriousness of an action depends on whether it is "central" or "peripheral" to the agent's fundamental orientation. Church documents, for instance *Personae humanae*, the 1975 declaration of the Congregation for the Doctrine of the Faith* on sexual ethics, and Pope John Paul II's* 1993 encyclical *Veritatis splendor* (VS), accept the idea of a fundamental option but assert a stronger connection to particular acts. They hold that certain types of action, e.g., masturbation and contraception, are (if done in full knowledge and consent) in themselves mortally sinful, constituting a fundamental turning away from God (VS 70).

FUNDAMENTALISM. A late nineteenth- and twentieth-century American movement defined by George Marsden as "militantly anti-modern evangelical Protestantism." It takes its name from a series of twelve volumes published between 1905 and 1919 called *The Fundamentals*. A short list of the "five fundamentals" is: (1) the inspiration* and inerrancy* of Scripture; (2) the divinity and virgin birth* of Jesus; (3) the substitutionary atonement* of Jesus' death; (4) the bodily resurrection* of Jesus; (5) the literal return of Jesus in the Second Coming. The central doctrine of fundamentalism is the strict inerrancy of Scripture, read literally. These beliefs are combined with conservative positions in morality and politics. Major fundamentalist figures, past and present, include C. I. Scofield, William Jennings Bryan, Carl McIntyre, Jerry Falwell, and Pat Robertson. The Catholic response to fundamentalism is typified by the 1987 statement of a committee of the National Council of Catholic Bishops, "A Pastoral Response to Biblical Fundamentalism." Its primary criticism of fundamentalism is that, in proclaiming the Bible* alone to be sufficient for Christian life, "it eliminates from Christianity the Church as the Lord Jesus founded it"; it leaves no role for Church doctrine*, authority*, and liturgy*. The statement also criticizes the fundamentalist view of biblical inerrancy.

By analogy, the label "fundamentalism" is sometimes used of militantly antimodern movements in other religions, notably the Islamic revivalism of Iran's Ayatollah Khomeini and others. Few if any

Catholics call themselves "fundamentalists," but the name has been used of some Catholics by others. For instance, Gabriel Daly speaks of a "papal fundamentalism" among conservative Catholics who "treat the ecclesiastical magisterium in the same manner as the Protestant fundamentalists treat the Bible," while William Dinges finds in contemporary Catholic traditionalism* the same religious and social attitudes as are characteristic of Protestant fundamentalism.

FUNERAL. A liturgical celebration for taking leave of a deceased Christian and commending him or her to God's mercy. The present funeral rituals for the Roman Rite are set forth in the *Order of Christian Funerals* (1969, rev. and Engl. trans. 1985). Normally a "Funeral Mass" should be celebrated, but there is also a "Funeral Liturgy outside Mass," identical with the Funeral Mass except for the omission of the liturgy of the eucharist; a deacon or layperson may preside at this liturgy. The readings and prayers emphasize hope* for eternal life through the death and resurrection of Jesus. This replaces a focus on the final judgment*, characteristic of funeral liturgies in the Middle Ages and later. Both forms of funeral liturgy conclude with a "Rite of Committal," committing the body to its final resting place.

G

GALILEO GALILEI (1564-1642). Florentine astronomer, physicist, mathematician; one of the founders of modern science, especially in his insistence on experimental method and on a mathematical understanding of the laws of nature. He defended the theory of Nicholas Copernicus (1473-1543) that the earth moved around the sun and, using telescopes he himself had built, produced evidence to support it. Galileo's claims challenged the astronomy of Aristotle*, whose opinions, held rigidly, dominated the philosophy faculties of the Italian universities. Galileo's critics held that the Copernican theory contradicted the Scripture (e.g., Jos 10.12-13). In 1616, the Inquisition* (Holy Office) ordered Galileo not to hold or defend the Copernican theory. Galileo and his opponents later differed as to whether he had also been ordered not to teach about it. Galileo's *Dialogue Concerning the Two Chief World Systems* (1632) caused him to be called once again before the Inquisition in 1633. He was accused of having "taught" the Copernican theory in the dialogue, thus violating the order of 1616, was found to be under "vehement suspicion of heresy," and was condemned to indefinite imprisonment. Arrangements were made to have him placed under house arrest at his villa, where he remained until his death. The Holy Office gave an imprimatur* to Galileo's works in 1741, but not till 1846 were all restrictions removed on the publication of works asserting the Copernican theory. In 1981, Pope John Paul II* appointed a commission to restudy the Galileo case. The commission's final report, issued in 1992, admitting that the condemnation of Galileo had been in error, was officially accepted and endorsed by the pope.

GALLICANISM (Lt *Gallicanus*, "French"). Theories and practices, common in the French Church beginning in the fifteenth century, that sought to restrict the power of the pope in relation to the French king and local bishops. It is summarized in the four "Gallican Articles" adopted by the Assembly of the French Clergy in 1682, the first stating that the pope did not have power in temporal matters, the second asserting the validity of the decrees of the Council of Constance* that held that a council is superior to a pope (*see* CONCILIARISM), the third affirming the historic rights and privileges of the French Church, the fourth holding that the judgment of a pope is not irreformable without the consent of the Church. These were condemned by Pope Alexander VIII in 1690, but Gallicanism remained influential in France into the nineteenth century. It was definitively rejected in Vatican I's* definition of papal primacy and infallibility*.

GIBBONS, JAMES CARDINAL (1834-1921). Born in Baltimore of Irish parents, Gibbons studied at St. Mary's Seminary in Baltimore and was ordained priest in 1861. He was appointed bishop of the Vicariate Apostolic of North Carolina in 1868, bishop of Richmond in 1872, coadjutor bishop and then archbishop of Baltimore in 1877. In 1886 he was named a cardinal*. As the archbishop of the first see in the United States, he became the leading public figure in the American Church. His period of leadership coincided with many conflicts in the Church, for example, conflicts between German and Irish immigrant Catholics and theological conflicts over Americanism* and Modernism*. It also spanned the Spanish-American War, World War I, and a rise of anti-Catholic movements in the United States. His leadership was moderate and conciliatory, both within the Church and in relations between the Church and state. He was often called upon to explain the policies of the United States government to the Holy See, and vice versa, and he won the respect of several presidents. He presided over the Third Plenary Council of Baltimore in 1884 and oversaw the subsequent establishment of The Catholic University of America. Late in life, as dean of the American hierarchy, he presided over the creation of the National Catholic War Council (1917) and the National Catholic Welfare Council [later Conference] (1919), forerunners of the present National Conference of Catholic Bishops (*see* EPISCOPAL CONFERENCES). His popular apologetic* work, *The Faith of Our Fathers* (1876), was widely read inside and outside the Church.

GLOSSOLALIA (Gk *glōssē,* "tongue, language"; *lalein,* "to speak"). "Speaking in tongues"; a form of nonconceptual prayer, expressed vocally in languagelike utterance. Paul discusses glossolalia at length in 1 Cor 12-14, affirming both that speaking in tongues is a gift from God and that it should not be overemphasized and ought ideally to be followed by interpretation. In Acts 2.1-13, Luke may be describing glossolalia in the form of speech in a genuine language unknown to the speaker (though the gift may be being given to the hearers in this case). Glossolalia (chiefly in the Pauline sense) has been revived in twentieth-century Pentecostalism and the charismatic renewal*. Like other spiritual phenomena, it must be subjected to criteria of discernment*.

GNOSTICISM (Gk *gnōsis,* "knowledge"). A range of religious movements, pagan, Jewish, and Christian, in the early A.D. centuries. More narrowly, the term refers to movements within Christianity that were especially prominent in the second century. Gnostic thought is characterized by a belief that the material world, and the human body in particular, are evil. The world was created not by the supreme God but by a lesser divinity, acting out of ignorance or malice or both. Gnostics offered various elaborate mythological accounts of the creation of this world. The human spirit was said to be trapped in this world, to which it was alien, but could be liberated by secret knowledge (*gnōsis*) of God and of its own origin and destiny. Christian Gnostics portrayed Christ as the bearer of this knowledge. Their Christology was docetic*, holding that Christ did not have a material body and did not truly suffer. Many contemporary scholars locate the origin of Gnosticism within Judaism, though it had affinities with Greek philosophy and Persian thought as well. Some tendencies toward Gnosticism are reflected in the NT in positions combatted by the authors of some of the letters attributed to Paul (e.g., the letters to

Timothy and Titus) and John (e.g., 1 Jn 4.2-3). In the second century, Gnosticism flourished especially at Alexandria*, where major teachers included Valentinus and Basilides.

After the second century, Gnostic ideas continued to have influence through such later movements as Manichaeism* and the medieval Cathars*. One early Gnostic group, the **Mandaeans** (the name means "Gnostics"), survives today in Iraq; they reject Jesus as a false prophet. For centuries, scholars had to rely for their knowledge of Gnosticism on the works of the Gnostics' opponents, notably Irenaeus*, Tertullian*, and Hippolytus of Rome (ca. 170-ca. 236). In 1945 to 1946, however, a large store of Gnostic manuscripts, dating from the fourth century, was discovered at Nag Hammadi (Chenoboskion) in Egypt. These texts are basic to contemporary scholars' understanding of Gnosticism. *See also* MARCION.

GOD. Catholicism's central affirmation about God is that God is Trinity*, God is one, yet three. This in turn is based in the fundamental Christian revelation* of God in Jesus Christ*: God is encountered in Jesus, God is the Father to whom Jesus prays, God is the Holy Spirit* in whom the Christian community prays to the Father in union with Jesus, and these are all one and the same God.

Catholic belief in God arises from Jewish faith in Yahweh, the One God of Israel, and holds it to be the same God spoken of and to in both the Old and New Testaments (*see* BIBLE, JUDAISM, MARCION). Catholicism also holds that God can be known outside of any explicit relation to Israel or to Jesus. God is known, in some measure, in the other religions and by "natural reason." According to Vatican Council I* (1870), "If anyone says that the one, true God, our creator and Lord, cannot be known with certainty from the things that have been made, by the natural light of human reason—let him be anathema" (DS 3026). Thus, Catholic theology, in reflecting on God, draws considerably on philosophical discussions of God as the ultimate source of the world around us, or, in Karl Rahner's* words, "the transcendental source and horizon of all that exists." Vatican I's statement is not usually interpreted as asserting that there is strict philosophical proof of the existence of God, but the Catholic tradition has been favorable to the possibility of philosophical argument to the existence of God, for instance (in Thomas Aquinas's* "Five Ways") as the first mover, first cause, first necessary being, supremely perfect being, and source of order in the world. Other arguments begin not from the external world but from human consciousness (e.g., the "ontological argument" of St. Anselm*). Yet it is always affirmed that philosophical knowledge of God is radically incomplete, needing to be supplemented by God's revelation.

Catholic doctrine and theology seek to defend the **transcendence** of God, God's essential difference from the world and everything in it (*see* CREATION), while also maintaining God's **immanence**, presence in and involvement with the world.

See also ATHEISM, GRACE.

GOSPEL (Old Engl, "good news"; equivalent to Gk *euangelion*). Initially, the message of salvation proclaimed by Jesus and the early disciples. By the second century, the word also referred to written narratives of the life and teaching of Jesus. These narratives are not biographies in our sense, but attempts to convey the message of Jesus and evoke or sustain faith in him. Four such narratives, written in the late first century, are in the New Testament and thus called "canonical gospels" (*see* BIBLE). These do not bear authors' names but have, since at least the second century, been ascribed to the **evangelists** (gospel writers) Matthew, Mark, Luke, and John (these attributions are often questioned by scholars). The gospels of Matthew, Mark, and Luke are called **synoptic gospels** (from Gk "view together") because of their similarity; the explanation of the similarity favored by most scholars is that Matthew and Luke both drew on Mark and on another lost source, which has been labeled "Q" (an abbreviation for the German word for "source"). From the second to the fourth century other "gospels" were written, often by Gnostics*. Called "apocryphal gospels," these lack the length and historical value of the canonical gospels (*see* APOCRYPHA).

The Church, at Vatican Council II, affirmed the historical character of the four gospels, but, following the important *Instruction on the Historical Truth of the Gospels* (1964) of the Pontifical Biblical Commission, acknowledged that the gospels' account of the words and deeds of Jesus is shaped by the evangelists' purposes and by the decades of oral instruction that came between the life of Jesus and the writing down of the gospels (DV 19). They are thus not literal accounts of Jesus' words and deeds. Scholars may distinguish between what in the gospels derives directly from Jesus' own teaching and action, and what derives from the early Church's or the evangelists' reflection upon Jesus' teaching and action. *See* BIBLICAL CRITICISM.

GRACE (Lt *gratia*, "favor"). As used in the NT, especially by Paul, this term (Gk *charis*) expresses the quality of God's action toward us as free and favorable, treating us with a generosity we did not deserve. For Paul, the grace of God is primarily God's will to save us in Jesus Christ, or else the salvation we have received in Christ (e.g., Rom 3.24). It is contrasted with works (e.g., Rom 11.5) and with the law (e.g., Gal 2.21): salvation is given us by God's "favor," not given as something owed us for our works.

Grace did not become a specific topic for theological reflection until the conflict between Augustine* and Pelagius* in the fifth century. Pelagius held that humans could merit salvation, through exercising their natural free will and following the guidance given by the law and by the example of Jesus. Augustine argued in response that, as a consequence of original sin*, human beings lost all ability to do acts that would make them worthy of salvation. God, however, chose some persons from the human "mass of perdition," without regard to merit, and gave them the grace that would lead to salvation. The regional Council of Orange (529) followed Augustine on the necessity of grace for any meritorious act but not on the more extreme points of his theory of predestination*.

Augustine tended to speak of grace as the inner presence of God, specifically the Holy Spirit (see Rom 5.5). This is now called **uncreated grace**. Thomas Aquinas* (1226-1274) laid emphasis on grace as a "habit" or modification of the human spirit brought about by this indwelling of God. This came to be called **created grace**. Contrary to Aquinas's intention, later medieval practice seemed to imply that God's grace was measured out in accordance with human works, especially sacramental works. The Protestant* Reformers, notably Martin Luther, rebelled against this system, emphasizing salvation through God's grace alone (*sola gratia*). Catholic teaching on grace was restated at the Council of Trent* (1547), which asserted the absolute necessity of grace for salvation but also affirmed the inner transformation of the person as a result of grace and the importance of good works as cooperation with grace.

The scholastic textbooks that dominated Catholic theology from the eighteenth to the mid-twentieth century spoke of created grace almost exclusively. They developed the distinction between habitual or **sanctifying grace**, which made the person acceptable to God, and **actual grace**, which was given for particular actions, even to those not in a state of sanctifying grace.

Developments in Catholic theology of grace in the twentieth century, led by Karl Rahner*, restored the primary focus on grace as God's self-communication in the Holy Spirit*. Contemporary theology emphasizes the universality of God's grace, its presence throughout human life, but sees sacraments* as specially privileged events in the process of God's self-communication to humans. This understanding is reflected in the documents of Vatican Council II* and in developments in Catholic piety since the council, notably the fact that Catholics seldom any longer perform actions specifically to "gain grace."

GREAT (WESTERN) SCHISM. The division that occurred in the Western Church between 1378 and 1417, when there were first two, then three, claimants to the papacy. In 1377, Pope Gregory XI, who had been residing at Avignon*, as had his predecessors since 1309, returned the papacy to Rome. After his death in 1378, the cardinals, under pressure from the Roman authorities and populace to elect an Italian, elected Bartolomeo Prignani, who took the name Urban VI. Urban became increasingly autocratic and abusive (some observers, then and now, have suspected mental illness), and before the end of 1378, the cardinals reassembled, declared his election invalid due to duress, and elected Clement VII as his successor. Failing to establish himself in Rome, Clement moved to Avignon in 1379. There were now two lines of papal succession, and for thirty years efforts to resolve the schism by force or negotiation failed. The Avignon line had the support of France and the Spanish kingdoms, while the Roman line was supported by England, most of the Holy Roman Empire, and Italy. Each pope anathematized his rival and his rival's followers. In 1409, cardinals of both allegiances met in a council at Pisa, deposed both popes, Gregory XII of Rome and Benedict XIII of Avignon, and elected Alexander V. This action gained the support of most European rulers and an apparent majority of the Church, but the other popes refused to resign, and the authority of the Pisan line was weakened by the election of John XXIII (Baldassare Cossa), a man of notoriously bad character, as Alexander's successor in 1410. Under pressure from the Emperor Sigismund, John called a council to meet at Constance* in 1414. This council deposed John and accepted Gregory's resignation in 1415, deposed Benedict in 1417, and, also in 1417, elected Martin V. Though Benedict refused to resign, most of his party joined the others in supporting Martin, effectively ending the schism. This outcome was sealed by Benedict's death without a successor in 1423.

The Catholic Church has unofficially recognized the validity of the Roman line, in that the later popes Clement VII and John XXIII* chose the names and numbering of Avignon and Pisan popes, but it has made no official declaration, and scholars are still divided on the issue.

GREGORIAN CHANT. The most important type of Western church music* in the early Middle Ages, and a classic form of church music ever since. Gregorian chant is based on Latin liturgical texts, with the length of the line in the text determining the length of the musical line. It is not metrical, but rather in free rhythm, like prose. It is **monophonic**—one musical line at a time is sung. It combines **syllabic** (one note per syllable) and **melismatic** (more than one note per syllable) passages. There are eight modes in standard medieval chant theory, which predates the notion of major and minor keys; often called "church modes," they are distinguished by the placement of tones and semitones in the octave. Gregorian chant is probably named for Pope Gregory I* (pope 590-604), who ordered and codified liturgical texts and church music. Any direct connection with Gregory is uncertain, however, and it may even be named for Gregory II (pope 715-731). It may have originated in Rome but more probably resulted from the fusion of Roman and Gallican traditions in the Frankish kingdom and Carolingian empire in the eighth and ninth centuries. The earliest extant written texts of Gregorian chant date from the late ninth century; these are the earliest substantial written texts of Western music. Gregorian chant proper was largely replaced by polyphony (*see* MUSIC, CHURCH) in the later Middle Ages, though it continued to serve as a source for composers of polyphony. The Council of Trent* (1545-1563) called for a reform of chant, but scholarly critical texts did not become available until the nineteenth century. These were the work of the Abbey of Solesmes (*see* LITURGICAL MOVEMENT), and they sparked a great revival of chant in the Church. Twentieth-century Church documents have encouraged the use of Gregorian chant in worship, including Vatican Council II's *Constitution on the Sacred Liturgy*, which accords it "a place of primacy" (SC 116). Some composers have adapted it to languages other than Latin.

GREGORY I (THE GREAT), ST. (ca. 540-604). Pope 590-604 and Doctor of the Church*. One of the greatest of the popes, especially important for his role in establishing papal authority in the West after the decline of the power of the Empire. While pope, he became de facto temporal ruler of Italy, providing food and protection for the people and concluding an unofficial peace with the Lombards. He promoted missionary efforts in the rest of Western Europe, achieving his greatest success in the mission of St. Augustine, first bishop of Canterbury, in 596, to reestablish the Church in England. A monk and abbot before becoming pope, he did much to promote monasticism* in the West. Though he was not an original thinker, his writings were highly influential in the Middle Ages in the West. They include the *Book of Pastoral Care* (ca. 591), on the work of bishops, the *Dialogues* (ca. 593), which tell of the lives and miracles of the Italian saints, especially Benedict*, the *Moralia in Iob* (595), offering an allegorical moral and mystical interpretation of the Book of Job, and collections of homilies and letters. His feast is celebrated on September 3.

GREGORY VII, ST. (HILDEBRAND) (ca. 1020-1085). Pope 1073-1085. Born in Tuscany, he was the leader of the eleventh-century reform movement in the Western Church even before becoming pope. As pope, he campaigned especially against simony*, clerical marriage, and lay investiture*, which was a symbol of the Church's dependence on secular rulers. His *Dictatus Papae* (1075) set out a theory of absolute papal power over the Church and a papal right to depose secular rulers; this was in large measure made a reality by later medieval popes. His prohibition of lay investiture led to a long struggle with the Emperor Henry IV. In 1076, Henry convoked a synod that declared Gregory deposed. Gregory in turn deposed and excommunicated Henry. They were reconciled after Henry did public penance at Canossa in 1077, but, when Henry failed to carry out promises made at Canossa, Gregory again excommunicated and deposed him in 1080. Henry successfully set siege to Rome, and Gregory died in exile in Salerno. His feast is celebrated on May 25.

H

HABIT (Lt *habitus*, "mode, condition," hence "dress," from *habēo*, "have, hold"). The distinctive dress of those in religious life*. Distinctive dress for monks appeared in the fourth century. The traditional habit consisted of a tunic, belt, scapular*, and hood, with a veil for women. It was adapted from the ordinary clothing of ancient and medieval times. The color and style of clothing varied according to the religious community. Later communities patterned their habits on existing religious habits, the ordinary clothing of the time of their founding, or both. Some congregations of men, e.g., the Jesuits*, had no distinctive habit but dressed as did the diocesan clergy. After Vatican Council II, many communities simplified their habits, particularly apostolic congregations, who engaged in active ministries such as education and health care.

HEALING. Healing was an important part of Jesus' ministry. His healings were a sign of the presence of the kingdom* of God (Lk 7.21-22, 11.20). There was no sharp line drawn in Jesus' ministry between forgiveness* and healing, nor between healing and exorcism*. All are manifestations of the kingdom of God overcoming the power of sin* and Satan (*see* DEMON). Jesus sent the disciples out to heal (e.g., Mk 6.13). The Church has continued to exercise a ministry of healing, which takes three main forms. One is the **health care apostolate**, which includes especially the long tradition of Catholic hospitals*, as well as an array of clinics, pastoral counseling centers, and other facilities, and much work that is done outside of places specially designated for healing. The second is **sacramental healing**. The sacraments of reconciliation/penance* and anointing of the sick* are primarily for spiritual healing, but the latter may have physical effects as well. The eucharist* may also have healing effects. Thirdly, there is healing, which may be physical or spiritual, through (non-sacramental) **prayer on behalf of the sick**, either by the sick person or by others. An important form of this today is **charismatic healing**, which occurs in an assembly gathered for a service of healing and/or through the prayer of an individual who has a special gift, or "charism", of healing (1 Cor 12.9) (*see* CHARISMATIC RENEWAL). Just as in Jesus' ministry, Christian healers should avoid a sharp division between physical, mental, and spiritual healing, since the human being, as created by God and redeemed by Christ, is fundamentally a unity of all these levels. Moreover, since human beings are essentially social, the healing of individuals cannot entirely be separated from the healing of personal relationships (for instance in families) nor from the pursuit of justice* in larger social structures.

HEAVEN. The "dwelling place" of God (Ps 11.4, Mt 6.9) and those united with God: the good angels* and humans who have attained final salvation*. It is where Jesus comes from (Jn 3.13) and returns (Acts

1.11) and where those who believe in Jesus will have their home (2 Cor 5.1-5). The Bible (1 Cor 2.9) and Church tradition recognize that this state transcends human understanding and hence must be expressed in images, of which "heaven" (the sky) is one. NT images for this state include eternal life, the vision of God, the Kingdom* of God, mansions in God's house, the heavenly Jerusalem, and a wedding feast. Medieval theology emphasized the vision of God or beatific vision*. It is enjoyed immediately after death or the cessation of purgatory* (DS 1000), but the fullness of eternal life involves the body too and hence awaits the final resurrection*. In contrast to the medieval emphasis on the individual's vision of God, contemporary theology and Church teaching tend to speak of heaven in communal and Christological terms: heaven is a "communion with God and all who are in Christ" (CCC 1027). It involves not only personal beings but the whole of creation. Revelation 21.1 calls it a "new heaven and a new earth," and Vatican Council II says, "Along with the human race the whole universe, which is intimately related to humanity and through it attains its goal, will be established perfectly in Christ" (LG 48). *See also* ESCHATOLOGY.

HELL. This English word translates two Hebrew words, *Sheol* and *Gehenna*, whose meanings are distinct. In earlier OT passages, Sheol (Gk *Hades*) is a shadowy abode of the dead, where there is no remembrance of God (Ps 6.6) (*see* DESCENT INTO HELL). As the concept of rewards and punishments after death develops in later OT Judaism, the place of punishment is called Gehenna, the name of a valley outside Jerusalem where humans had been burned as sacrifices to Molech (2 Kgs 23.10). Jesus uses the image of Gehenna repeatedly in the synoptic gospels. It is a place of unquenchable fire (Mt 5.22, 18.8-9), where there is "wailing and grinding of teeth" (Mt 13.42). The concept of punishment for sinners after death also appears in the NT without the image of Gehenna, sometimes in positive language (darkness, destruction, God's anger), sometimes negative (exclusion from God's kingdom). While most Fathers of the Church* affirmed the existence of everlasting punishment, some, notably Origen* and Gregory of Nyssa, envisioned a final *apocatastasis* (restoration) (1 Cor 15.25-28) in which Christ's victory over evil would extend to everyone, and all would be saved. It is not clear to what extent these Fathers *asserted*, as distinct from *hoped for*, universal salvation. The doctrine of universal salvation, as hardened into a system by followers of Origen, was condemned by a synod at Constantinople in 543, and this condemnation was repeated in 553 by the bishops who were about to open the Second Council of Constantinople*. In the West, Augustine* argued not only that hell was eternal but that the majority of humanity would go there. The eternity of hell was stated by Lateran Council IV* (1215). A letter of Pope Innocent III* in 1201 distinguished two aspects of hell: the loss of the vision of God and eternal pain (DS 780). According to the 1979 Vatican statement on eschatology*, the Church "believes that there will be eternal punishment for the sinner, who will be deprived of the sight of God, and that this punishment will have a repercussion on the whole being of the sinner." The *Catechism of the Catholic Church* (1992) defines hell as "the state of definitive self-exclusion from communion with God and the blessed" (1033). Here the emphasis is on hell as a consequence of human free choice. For damnation, "a willful turning away from God (a mortal sin) is required, and persistence in it until the end" (1037). Not wanting to compromise the moral decisiveness of our free choices in this life, most contemporary theologians affirm the *possibility* of hell, while noting that the Church has not declared that any human person has actualized that possibility. But theologians increasingly emphasize God's will to save all (1 Tim 2.4) and the completeness of Christ's victory over sin. Hence, most are willing to hope, and some to assert, that no member of the human community will ultimately be excluded from the final union of love with God.

HERESY (Gk *hairēsis*, "choice, preference," whence "sect, party"). *Hairēsis* in Greek is a neutral term for "philosophical school," but in late OT Judaism it develops a pejorative sense of "deviant opinion." It is used in this negative sense in the NT (1 Cor 11.19, Gal 5.20, 2 Pt 2.1) and becomes the standard term in the Fathers of the Church* for an opinion opposed to the normative teaching of the Church. Canon law defines heresy as an obstinate denial or doubt, on the part of a baptized person, of some truth of faith that must be believed (Canon 751). Here, with the added element of willfulness, is the sin of **formal heresy**. **Material heresy** is the denial or doubt without the culpability. Often what appears to be heresy is merely a poorly worded version of orthodox* doctrine* or a development of doctrine that will at some point be recognized as orthodox. Heresy is to be distinguished from *apostasy** and *schism**.

HERMENEUTICS (Gk *hermēneuein*, "to interpret"). The theory of the interpretation of texts. The term initially referred mainly to the interpretation of the Bible but in the nineteenth century was expanded to refer to the understanding of all texts. The idea of hermeneutics became increasingly important with the growing awareness in nineteenth-century thought, after G. W. F. Hegel (1770-1831), of the role of history in human existence. As Wilhelm Dilthey (1833-1911), in particular, argued, the meaning and truth of a text from the past could not simply be assessed in terms of timeless structures of thought or of being. A text could be understood only in its historical context, into which the contemporary interpreter had somehow to transport himself or herself. Martin Heidegger (1889-1976) generalized the notion of hermeneutics to all of human understanding. Any act of knowledge takes place against a background of pre-reflective involvements with the world, which give us a "pre-understanding" of whatever we may be inquiring about. New understanding can occur only when new experience is related to our already-existing pre-understandings. Our pre-understandings, however, are changed by the new understanding. This reciprocal process is known as the **hermeneutical circle**. Hans-Georg Gadamer (1900-) emphasizes the importance of tradition in shaping the pre-understandings without which knowledge is impossible. To understand a text from the past, one must situate it in the traditions from which it came, while being aware of how one's own situatedness in tradition shapes the concerns of one's inquiry into the past. The desired result is a "fusion of horizons" between past and present. Since the enterprise of theology* depends on the interpretation of authoritative texts, whether of scripture or of dogma*, theologians have drawn considerably on hermeneutic philosophy. Against the skepticism of the Enlightenment*, it rehabilitates the sort of knowledge from tradition, accepted in faith*, on which theology must draw. Its emphasis on the relation of truth to historical circumstances, however, creates theological difficulties in explaining how a truth revealed by God can remain the same as it is handed down through different historical contexts in different human formulations.

HERMIT. *See* ANCHORITE.

HIERARCHY (Gk *hiera*, "sacred," *archē*, "order"). This term was introduced by Pseudo-Dionysius* (sixth century) to refer to a created order, arranged by ranks, imaging God's perfection. "Hierarchy causes its members to be ... clear and spotless mirrors reflecting the glow of primordial light and indeed of God himself. It ensures that when its members have received this full and divine splendor they can then pass on this light generously and in accordance with God's will to beings further down the scale" (*The Celestial Hierarchy* 3.2). Dionysius used the term chiefly of the orders of angelic* beings and of the sacred rituals of the Church and those who participate in them. The term later came to be used mainly of officeholders in the Church, in two ways. "Hierarchy of orders" refers to the orders of bishop*, priest*, and deacon*. "Hierarchy of jurisdiction" refers to the bishops with the pope* as their supreme head or to the authority that they exercise.

HIERARCHY OF TRUTHS. According to the *Decree on Ecumenism* (1964) of Vatican Council II, "When comparing doctrines with one another" in ecumenical dialogues, Catholic theologians "should remember that in Catholic doctrine there exists an order or 'hierarchy' of truths, since they vary in their connection with the foundation of the Christian faith" (UR 11). Theological discussion since the council has not fully clarified the meaning of the "hierarchy of truths," but it is clear that the "foundation of the Christian faith" is the revelation of God and the salvation of human beings in Jesus Christ*, and that some revealed truths refer more directly to this than do others. The more peripheral truths, however, are not any less true or less revealed. The concept of a hierarchy of truths marks a change from the Catholic theology of the Counter-Reformation period and later, when revealed truths were ranked chiefly in terms of the strength of the authority with which they were declared (*see* THEOLOGICAL NOTES) rather than in terms of their content. The hierarchy of truths is especially important in ecumenism*, whenever there is a question of whether a difference in doctrine is significant enough to prevent churches from entering into union or sharing in the eucharist. It can also be important as an ordering principle in systematic theology and catechesis*.

HILDEGARD OF BINGEN, ST. (1098-1179). Abbess of Regensburg, near Bingen on the Rhine; visionary, preacher, theologian, and composer; the first prominent woman theological writer of the Middle Ages. Her best-known work is *Scivias* (1151) (from *Scito vias Domini* [*Know the Ways of the Lord*]), organized as a series of twenty-six visions, each described and interpreted. Other major visionary works are the *Book of Life's Merits* and the *Book of Divine Works*. She also wrote important works in medicine and natural science. She composed hymns and the *Ordo Virtutum (Play of Virtues)*, the earliest morality play we possess; the musical notation for these works was preserved, and they have been recorded and performed in recent times. With the approval of church authorities, she went on three major tours to preach monastic and clerical reform. She carried on an extensive correspondence, including exchanges with the Emperor Frederick Barbarossa, St. Bernard of Clairvaux*, and other major figures of the twelfth century. Her feast is observed in some German dioceses on November 17.

HINDUISM (Persian, "Indian," from Indus River). The dominant religious tradition or traditions in India. The great diversity of Hinduism is united in a common acknowledgement of the *Vedas*, a body of hymns and other texts dating from 1500-400 B.C., as scripture. The different forms of Hinduism are more concerned with practice, aiming to liberate the human spirit from the limitations of the temporal world and join it to the divine, than with doctrine or theological theory. Hinduism encompasses monistic traditions, which deny any distinction between the human spirit and the divine, drawing on the *Upanishads* (the last of the Vedas; treatises written in the sixth century B.C. and later), as well as theistic traditions, which emphasize devotion (*bhakti*) to a personal God. Hindu theism may be monotheistic or polytheistic; there are also atheistic forms of Hinduism. According to the Second Vatican Council, "In Hinduism the divine mystery is explored and propounded with an inexhaustible wealth of myths and penetrating philosophical investigations, and liberation is sought from the distresses of our state either through various forms of ascetical life or deep meditation or taking refuge in God with loving confidence" (NA 2).

There have been numerous organized dialogues between Catholics and Hindus, especially in India. In the West, Mohandas Gandhi (1869-1948), a Hindu much influenced by Christianity, has in turn had great influence on Christians developing a theology of nonviolence. Hindu meditation* techniques are often used by Christians in prayer. While in 1989 Rome issued cautions about such techniques, it did not forbid them (*see* BUDDHISM). Some theologians, notably Raimon Panikkar, have combined Christian and Hindu ways of thinking about the divine. As with Buddhism, it is within monasticism* that the dialogue has progressed farthest. Two noteworthy figures are the Benedictines Abhishiktananda (Henri le Saux) (1910-1973) and Bede Griffiths (1906-1993), both of whom established monastic centers combining Christian and Hindu spirituality.

HOLINESS OF THE CHURCH. One of the four "marks" of the Church*, along with unity*, catholicity*, and apostolicity*, as stated in the Nicene Creed*. The holiness of the church is the holiness of Christ, who "handed himself over for her to sanctify her, cleansing her by the bath of water with the word, that he might present to himself the church in splendor, without spot or wrinkle or any such thing, that she might be holy and without blemish" (Eph 5.25-27). Whatever belongs to the essence of the Church as united with Jesus Christ in his Holy Spirit* must be holy. But the Church as it concretely exists is weakened by the sinfulness of its members, nor is it free from structural or social sin*. It thus is "at one and the same time holy and always in need of purification" (Vatican Council II, LG 8). For all individual Christians, holiness is a gift, first given in baptism*, but it is also something to which they are continually called (see 1 Pt 1.15-16). The call to holiness is not reserved for a special few; rather, "All the faithful, whatever their condition or rank, are called to the fullness of the Christian life and the perfection of charity" (LG 40). *See also* SAINTS.

HOLY DAY OF OBLIGATION. A feast*, other than a Sunday*, on which Catholics are obliged to attend mass*. As much as possible, they should also observe rest, as on Sundays. The universal Church law requiring attendance at mass on holy days dates from the twelfth century, but local laws preceded it. Between the thirteenth and seventeenth centuries, there were more than a hundred holy days of obligation in some dioceses, but their number has been steadily reduced. Today, canon law designates ten holy days of obligation: Christmas* (December 25), the feast of Mary, Mother of God (January 1), Epiphany* (January 6), Saint Joseph (March 19), the Ascension*, the feast of the Body and Blood of Christ (Corpus Christi, the Thursday following Trinity Sunday, which is the Sunday after Pentecost*), Saints Peter and Paul (June 29), the Assumption* (August 15), All Saints* (November 1), and the Immaculate Conception* (December 8). Episcopal conferences* may abolish certain holy days of obligation or transfer them to Sunday, with the approval of the Holy See*. In the United States, the feasts of Saint Joseph and Saints Peter and Paul are not observed as days of obligation, and Epiphany and Corpus Christi are transferred to Sunday, thus leaving six days of obligation; moreover, since 1993, attendance at mass is no longer required on January 1, the Assumption, or All Saints, if they fall on Saturday or Monday.

HOLY SEE or **APOSTOLIC SEE** (Lt *sedes*, "seat," i.e., of a bishop). The pope* considered as ruler of the Church (as distinct from his status as head of state of Vatican City* or as an individual), together with the offices of the Roman Curia*.

HOLY SPIRIT, THE. God the Third Person of the Trinity*, present in the lives of God's people, joining them to the Father through Jesus Christ*. The OT, though it has no theology of the Trinity, speaks of the spirit of God at work in creation (e.g., Ps 104.30), in extraordinary deeds (e.g., Jgs 15.14), and especially in prophecy (e.g., Is 61.1). The Spirit plays a more central role in the NT. The Spirit enables the virginal conception of Jesus (Lk 1.35), comes upon Jesus at his baptism (Mk 1.10), acts through him in his ministry (e.g., Mt 12.28), and is given by him to his followers after his resurrection (Jn 20.22). The Spirit empowers the disciples to proclaim salvation in Jesus (Acts 2), and enables them to acknowledge Jesus as Lord (1 Cor 12.3) and to stand in Jesus' intimacy with the Father, calling him "Abba" (Rom 8.14-17, Gal 4.6). The Spirit binds all Christians together into the one body of Christ (1 Cor 12.13) and is the basis of their communal life. The **fruits of the Spirit** are "love, joy, peace, patience, kindness, generosity, faithfulness, gentleness, self-control" (Gal 5.22-23). The NT still lacks a developed trinitarian theology but contains trinitarian formulas including the Spirit, notably the formula for baptism "in the name of the Father, and of the Son, and of the holy Spirit" (Mt 28.19).

There was little theological treatment of the Holy Spirit until the fourth century, when the crisis over Arianism* led the Church, at Nicaea* (325), to identify the Son as "one in being" (*homoousios*) with the Father. Of the Holy Spirit, Nicaea's creed said only, "and [we believe] in the Holy Spirit." Thereafter a party called "Macedonians" (after Macedonius, bishop of Constantinople) or *pneumatomachoi* ("those who fight against the Spirit") denied the divinity of the Spirit while accepting that of the Son. In response, Athanasius* and the Cappadocian Fathers* worked out a theology of the divinity of the Holy Spirit, which is expressed in the creed* of the First Council of

Constantinople* (381) (the "Nicene Creed"): "We believe in the Holy Spirit, the Lord, the giver of life, who proceeds from the Father [on the added words, 'and the Son,' *see* FILIOQUE]. With the Father and the Son he is worshipped and glorified."

The Second Vatican Council placed a renewed emphasis on the role of the Holy Spirit in forming and giving life to the Church, empowering it with spiritual gifts (see LG 4, UR 2). Contemporary theology speaks of grace* primarily as the indwelling of the Holy Spirit. These developments, together with the charismatic renewal*, have led to a greater focus on the Spirit in recent Catholic theology, prayer, and devotion. Vatican II also states that the Holy Spirit is, in some mysterious way, available to all persons, whether or not they are Christians (GS 22).

See also CONFIRMATION.

HOLY WEEK. The week before Easter. Also called "Great Week" in the Eastern Churches, this includes the last days of Lent* and the first days of the Easter Triduum*. From at least the second century it has been a period of prayer and fasting in preparation for the Easter Vigil. It begins with the sixth and last Sunday of Lent, called **Passion Sunday** because it includes a reading of the passion narrative (the story of Jesus' arrest, trial, suffering, death, and burial) from one of the Synoptic Gospels*. This Sunday is also called **Palm Sunday** because it contains a procession with palms to commemorate Jesus' entry into Jerusalem (Mt 21.1-11 and parallels). This ritual, which originated in Jerusalem in the fourth century, became part of the Roman liturgy in the twelfth century. It now precedes the Passion Sunday mass, which focuses on the passion of Jesus. The liturgies of Monday, Tuesday, and Wednesday of Holy Week do not differ significantly from those of other lenten weekdays. On the morning of Holy Thursday, the **Chrism Mass** is celebrated by the bishop (though it may be moved to another day). The priests of the diocese* gather with the bishop* to concelebrate the mass, showing their unity around the bishop. The liturgy may include a renewal of priestly commitment. At this mass, the bishop blesses the three holy oils: chrism*, the oil for the anointing of the sick*, and the oil for anointing catechumens*. The custom of having the bishop bless the chrism on Holy Thursday, the day of the last mass before the Easter Vigil, dates from the fourth century. Liturgically, Lent ends with the Mass of the Lord's Supper on Holy Thursday evening, but Holy Week continues through the Celebration of the Lord's Passion on Good Friday and concludes with the Easter Vigil. *See* EASTER TRIDUUM and EASTER.

HOMILY (Gk *homilia*, "conversation"). A form of preaching that is based in the text of the bible and integrated into a liturgical service. In the mass* and other services (e.g., baptismal or penitential services, communion services), the homily is part of the liturgy of the word. It follows the readings and leads into the sacramental celebration. Initially it was distinguished from other forms of **sermon** or preached discourse by its style—popular rather than formal—but now it is distinguished primarily by its scriptural basis and liturgical context. The homily was the typical form of Christian liturgical preaching from antiquity into the Middle Ages. By the late Middle Ages and especially the Counter-Reformation* period, it had generally been replaced by sermons that were doctrinal in emphasis and not based in the Scripture readings for the liturgy. Vatican Council II restored the term *homily*, stressed the importance of the homily in the liturgy, and stated that it should draw its content mainly from the scripture and the liturgy itself (SC 35, 52).

HOMOSEXUALITY. Consideration of Church teaching on homosexuality must begin with the distinction between homosexuality as an orientation and homosexual sexual acts. As an orientation, homosexuality is an erotic inclination toward persons of one's own gender. The 1975 "Declaration on Certain Questions of Sexual Ethics" (*Personae humanae*) by the Congregation for the Doctrine of the Faith* (CDF) recognized that for some people such an orientation was permanent, perhaps based in a "constitutional defect." According to the CDF's 1986 document, "On the Pastoral Care of Homosexual Persons": "Although the particular inclination of the homosexual person is not a sin, it is a more or less strong tendency ordered toward an intrinsic moral evil; and thus the inclination itself must be seen as an objective disorder." It might be likened to alcoholism as a morally neutral inclination to do something morally wrong (drink to excess). The Church condemns homosexual acts on the basis of the same principles that govern its evaluation of heterosexual sexual acts: they do not occur in the context of marriage* and they are not naturally ordered toward procreation (this principle would rule out homosexual marriages) (*see* SEXUAL ETHICS).

Homosexual activity is condemned in both the Old and New Testaments. Some classic texts are Lv 18.22 ("You shall not lie with a male as with a woman; such a thing is an abomination"), Lv 20.13, Rom 1.26-27, 1 Tm 1.10. The normative force of all of these texts is debated today. Some, e.g., John McNeill, have argued that the OT prohibitions refer to ritual impurity and that the NT texts are speaking of homosexual behavior by heterosexual persons. It is clear that the Bible does not have a concept of "constitutionally" homosexual persons, but there is no comparable agreement as to whether, if it had such a concept, its prohibitions would have changed.

The Fathers of the Church* and Catholic writers until recent times have condemned homosexual activity, though John Boswell has argued that in the early Middle Ages there was relative social toleration of it (Boswell's further argument that the Church had ceremonies for same-sex marriages has not won the general agreement of scholars). In the natural law* theory of St. Thomas Aquinas*, which dominated modern moral theology*, homosexual acts are among the worst sexual offenses (surpassed only by bestiality), as "sins against nature."

Several factors have caused the question of the morality of homosexual activity to be reopened in recent times. The discovery that homosexual tendencies may be "constitutional," perhaps genetically based, has led to questions as to what is "natural" for such persons. Another factor is the development among moralists of an understanding of sexuality primarily in terms of interpersonal love rather than procreation. A third is a willingness to listen to gay and lesbian Catholics on the subject of their sexual experience. These and similar considerations have led some writers (e.g., McNeill, Margaret Farley) to argue that homosexual acts are morally no different from heterosexual ones. Such a position is held by Dignity, an organization of Catholic gays and lesbians. Others, e.g., Charles Curran, have argued that homosexual activity, while less than ideal, may be the best available choice for some "constitutional" homosexuals. Still others (e.g., James Hanigan, John Harvey), unwilling to approve a severance of sexual activity from procreation, defend the Church's traditional position. The organization Courage is for homosexuals who wish support in living in accordance with the official teaching of the Church.

While condemning homosexual acts, the Church affirms the dignity of homosexuals as persons and condemns discrimination and violence against them (though an unfortunate sentence in the 1986 document finds violence understandable as a response to the public condoning of homosexual activity). Some bishops and state bishops' conferences in the United States have supported "gay rights" ordinances, while others have opposed them (this has partly depended on the wording of the ordinances). A 1992 document of the CDF declared that sexual orientation is not parallel to race, etc., in regard to discrimination, and that sexual orientation may legitimately be taken into account in such areas as the hiring of teachers and military recruitment. It is fair to surmise, in light of the prominence and contested nature of questions about it in contemporary culture, that homosexuality will remain a disputed issue in the Church for some time to come.

HOPE. Hope, along with faith* and love*, is one of the three theological virtues*, which are gifts of divine grace*. The word *hope* can refer not only to a virtue but to a state of mind and to the object of hope—that which is hoped for. The entire OT is a story of Israel's hope in God, a hope that took different shapes at different stages of Israel's history. The gospels present Jesus as proclaiming the kingdom of God, which fulfills Israel's hopes. For Paul, hope is focused on the final resurrection*, when the kingdom will be complete (Rom 8.23-25; 1 Cor 15.20-28). NT eschatology* maintains a tension between the this-worldly and the otherworldly: the kingdom of God* is coming about here and now but will not be complete until the end. In later patristic and medieval thought, the focus of treatments of hope shifted entirely to the life after death, but more recently the this-worldly side of the virtue of hope has been recovered. This is partly due to a rediscovery of biblical eschatology, partly due to the encounter with secular movements of hope, especially Marxism*. Thus, Vatican Council II says, "The expectation of a new earth should not weaken, but rather stimulate, the resolve to cultivate this earth where the body of the new human family is increasing and can even now constitute a foreshadowing of the new age" (GS 39). These principles have been developed in political theology* and liberation theology* since the council. It is important, however, not to reduce Christian hope to something entirely this-worldly (1 Cor 15.19).

Sins against hope are **presumption** and **despair**. Presumption can be an excessive trust in one's own powers or an assumption that God will save one without any need for conversion* on one's own part. Despair can be either an explicit giving up of hope for salvation or (more likely) a vague sense that life is irremediably meaningless.

HOSPITALITY (Lt *hospes*, "guest, host"). Both a necessity and a virtue in the ancient world, hospitality was central to the life of the early Church. The gospels portray Jesus as a guest in many people's houses and as a host at the Last Supper and in the stories of the multiplication of loaves and fishes. Jesus teaches that people will be judged (*see* JUDGMENT) on the basis of their hospitality to others, which was unwitting hospitality to Jesus himself ("I was ... a stranger and you welcomed me" [Mt 25.35]). In the early Church, Christian travelers who could present letters of presentation from their bishops could be assured of hospitality from all Christian communities along their route. Tertullian*, writing around 200, spoke of "the mutual bond of hospitality" as evidence of the unity* of the Church in the one apostolic tradition. The second-century pagan writer Lucian of Samosata ridiculed the gullibility of Christians in taking in strangers; this is evidence of how noteworthy the practice was in the eyes of outsiders. After Constantine*, in the fourth century, churches began to establish special buildings for the lodging of pilgrims, the sick, orphans, and others. These were the origin of hospitals*. In the Middle Ages, responsibility for Christian hospitality passed especially to the monasteries. It is featured prominently in the Rule of St. Benedict* (chapter 53), with an explicit connection to Mt 25.35. In recent times the term "hospitality" has come into frequent use in the Church. For example, the Catholic Worker* calls its soup kitchens and lodging houses "houses of hospitality." The U.S. Bishops have spoken of liturgy* as flourishing in a "climate of hospitality," which is created both by the worshiping community and the space in which they worship (*Environment and Art in Christian Worship* 11). Most broadly, spiritual writer Henri Nouwen treats hospitality, defined as "the creation of a free space where the stranger can enter and become a friend," as a general term for the attitude that a Christian should have toward others.

HOSPITALLERS. *See* KNIGHTS OF MALTA.

HOSPITALS. Care of the sick has been part of Christian hospitality* from the beginning. Fourth-century documents depict it as especially the responsibility of bishops, who were at that time beginning to construct buildings dedicated to the care of the needy. Initially these were inns (called *xenodochia,* from Gk *xenos,* "stranger") for travelers and pilgrims. Because they had to serve sick travelers, they came to serve the local sick as well. One of the most noteworthy *xenodochia* was built by Basil (*see* CAPPADOCIANS) at Caesarea around 372; it included a building specifically for invalids. On through medieval times, there was not a clear, universal distinction between what we would call hospitals, nursing homes, hospices, and other facilities for short- and long-term care. *Xenodochion*, latinized into *xenodochium*, was the common term into the twelfth century, when *hospitale* replaced it. In the early medieval West, hospitals often developed from monastery* infirmaries and might be situated immediately outside the monastery. In the twelfth century, there was a great proliferation of community hospitals in western Europe, to the point where most towns had a hospital. These were often very small (twelve patients was a standard size) and not very specialized. Some were operated by hospital guilds, which might include the patients. They had statutes that paralleled monastic rules, and some of them developed into religious orders. An unusual case was the Order of the Hospital of St. John of Jerusalem, which operated a huge facility (perhaps two thousand patients) in Jerusalem and later became the military order known as Knights of Malta*. Consonant with the Christian understanding of healing*, pre-modern hospitals combined physical care with spiritual care or pastoral ministry.

In late medieval times, the small hospitals were not equal to the tasks posed by the Black Death, the Hundred Years' War, the enclosure movement, and other social disruptions. Many disappeared, while others were absorbed into larger institutions. These remained under Church control at first, but by the sixteenth century many had become secularized. New religious congregations and associations sprang up in the sixteenth and seventeenth centuries, however, to found charitable institutions, including hospitals, in Europe. The Daughters of Charity, founded by St. Vincent de Paul* in 1633, is an outstanding example. New and older communities founded many hospitals in the mission lands. After another wave of secularization, culminating in the French Revolution*, the nineteenth century saw the rise of new religious congregations, particularly of women, specifically dedicated to nursing. They established many new Catholic hospitals in Europe and America. The first hospital in the United States to be staffed by religious was Baltimore Infirmary in 1823; the Sisters (now Daughters) of Charity of Emmitsburg managed it for a group of doctors who owned it. The Sisters of Charity opened a hospital of their own in St. Louis, Missouri, in 1828. In 1991, there were 5,617 Catholic hospitals in the world, and in 1993 there were 621 in the United States. In the United States, the Catholic Health Association (founded in 1915 as the Catholic

Hospital Association) is the national organization of leaders of Catholic health care institutions.

The complexity of modern health care systems and the decline in the number of members of religious communities have lessened the distinctiveness of Catholic hospitals. Health care has become a huge industry, and Catholic hospitals have become part of large systems that are comparable to large private business corporations in revenues and total employment. The proportion of Catholics on the staff and in the patient population often approximates that in the general public. The sponsoring religious orders often have little to do with the day-to-day operation of the hospitals. Services and facilities may be consolidated into systems with secular organizations. Yet the CHA and the religious communities that sponsor hospitals and health care systems have continued to strive for a distinctively Catholic identity in health care and to maintain the traditional integration of physical and spiritual care. A 1981 pastoral letter* by the U.S. bishops identified four areas in which Catholic hospitals could manifest such an identity: (1) providing care of the whole person, not focusing entirely on the body; (2) observing Catholic moral values, in matters such as abortion* and sterilization; (3) exercising a prophetic role, by promoting the cause of the poor and neglected and developing alternative health care methods; (4) observing justice in their own internal affairs, including recognition of the right of employees to organize and bargain collectively.

HOURS, LITURGY OF THE. Liturgical prayer of the Church, consisting mainly of psalms, biblical canticles, hymns, and readings, adapted to particular times of day, as described below. It is also known as the **Divine Office** (from Lt *officium*, "duty") and sometimes as the **breviary**, from the name for a book containing a shortened version (Lt *breviarium*) of the office. It seems likely that early Christian daily prayer drew on the model of Jewish morning and evening prayers, although direct evidence of this is lacking. Apostolic injunctions to "pray without ceasing" (e.g., 1 Thes 5.17) also contributed to the development of set times of prayer. Such times are recorded in third-century writings, but the Liturgy of the Hours as we know it dates mainly from the fourth century. It combines the public prayer of local churches (called the "cathedral office" in modern accounts) with the "monastic office" of the early monks. From the former it takes over prayer related to the time of day, while from the latter it takes over the effort to cover a broad range of the psalter, even all of it.

The ancient prayer of the Church has developed variously in the different rites of the Church, though always with a strong emphasis on the psalms. In the West, the Roman Office, which forms the basis for the present Liturgy of the Hours in the Roman Rite, became overloaded in medieval times with psalms and prayers and appended devotions. It became for the most part a preserve of clergy and monks, who prayed it in choir or privately; its character as communal prayer was largely lost, and often so was its connection to particular hours of the day. Several efforts at reform were made in modern times, culminating in a thorough overhaul of the Liturgy of the Hours published in 1971 after the Second Vatican Council.

The present form of the Liturgy in the Roman Rite, following ancient tradition, includes seven "hours." Primary among them are **Morning Prayer** (Lauds) and **Evening Prayer** (Vespers), which Vatican II called "the twofold hinge of the daily office" (SC 89). The chief parts of Morning Prayer are a hymn (in public celebration), a psalm, an Old Testament canticle, another psalm, a brief scripture reading with response (after which a homily is optional), the Canticle of Zechariah or *Benedictus* (Lk 1.68-79), intercessions, the Lord's Prayer, a prayer of the day, and a concluding blessing. Evening Prayer has a similar structure, except that two psalms and a New Testament canticle are recited between the opening hymn and the reading, and the Canticle of Mary or *Magnificat* (Lk 1.46-55) precedes the intercessions. The **Office of Readings** (formerly called "Matins" or "Vigil" and said during the night or before Morning Prayer) may now be prayed at any hour, though when recited in choir it remains a night office. Its chief parts are three psalms or sections of psalms and one reading each, of some length, from the Scripture and the Fathers of the Church* or, on a saint's feast, the life of the saint. There are shorter offices of **Terce, Sext**, and **None** (named from the Latin words for Third, Sixth, and Ninth hours). One of these may be selected and prayed as "Midday Prayer" or "Daytime Prayer." **Compline**, or Night Prayer, concludes the day.

Canon Law* obliges priests and deacons aspiring to the priesthood to perform the Liturgy of the Hours. Religious are bound as specified in the constitutions of their congregations, permanent deacons as specified by their episcopal conferences*. Vatican II's desire for public celebrations of the Liturgy of the Hours in parishes has not generally been realized.

HUMAN RIGHTS. A right is a kind of claim that some persons have upon others. Rights may be based in contracts or in civil laws (e.g., the Bill of Rights). But *human* rights appertain to human beings simply in virtue of their being human; they cannot be overridden by contracts or legal systems. The concept of human rights developed out of the natural law* tradition in the seventeenth and eighteenth centuries. Two important doctrines of "natural rights" were those of Hugo Grotius (1583-1648) and John Locke (1632-1704). Ideas of human rights were enshrined in the Declaration of Independence of the United States (1776) ("all men ... are endowed by their Creator with certain unalienable rights") and the French "Declaration of the Rights of Man and of the Citizen" (1789). For more than a century, the Church was generally hostile to the Enlightenment* thought upon which these declarations drew. Nonetheless, rights language entered Catholic social teaching* with the encyclical* *Rerum novarum* of Pope Leo XIII* in 1891. Leo was concerned with economic rights, such as rights to private property* and just compensation for labor*. A turning point in Catholic teaching came in the encyclical *Pacem in terris* of Pope John XXIII* (1963). This encyclical proclaimed a wide range of human rights, including rights to food, clothing, shelter, medical care, education, freedom of expression, religious freedom*, family, work, meeting and association, emigration and immigration, and political participation. The 1971 document of the Synod* of Bishops, *Justice in the World* incorporated all these rights in a "right to development," described as "the dynamic interpenetration of all those fundamental human rights upon which the aspirations of individuals and nations are based" (15). To this it added a "right to participation," politically and economically. The basis of Catholic teaching on human rights, as set out by Vatican Council II in its *Pastoral Constitution on the Church in the Modern World* (1965), is **human dignity**, the unique status of the human being as rational and free, created in the image of God and redeemed in Christ. Catholic teaching on human rights advocates both the political freedoms characteristic of Western liberal democracies and the "economic rights" to food, shelter, work, health care, etc., which have often been better acknowledged in socialist political and economic orders.

HUMANISM. Initially, a movement of thought associated with the Renaissance*. The term derives from *studia humanitatis*, an educational curriculum that stressed linguistic and literary studies based in texts from classical antiquity, rather than emphasizing logic, as did the scholastic liberal arts curriculum. The poet Francesco Petrarch (1304-1374) is often called the "father of humanism" because of his enthusiasm for ancient Roman literature, which he thought showed an appreciation for the natural goods of life that was lacking in scholasticism*. The most prominent Renaissance philosopher, Marsilio Ficino (1433-1499) of Florence, led a revival of Platonism* after two centuries in which Aristotelianism* had dominated the West. For many, Renaissance humanism is epitomized in the oration, *On the Dignity of Man* (1492), by Ficino's pupil, Giovanni Pico della Mirandola (1463-1494), which presented freedom as the distinctive feature of humanity. In the North, the leading humanist was Desiderius Erasmus (ca. 1469-1536) of Rotterdam, who prepared scholarly editions of the New Testament and works of classical authors and Church Fathers. The leading English humanist was Thomas More* (1478-1535).

All the men thus far named were devout Catholics, but they were critical of the reigning scholasticism and favored reform in the Church and a return to biblical and patristic sources. They thus had much in common with the Protestant* Reformers. Many of the Reformers, such as Luther's colleague Philipp Melanchthon (1497-1560), were also humanists. In Catholic thought, humanism continued to have an influence through the Ratio Studiorum of the Jesuits* and the spirituality of St. Francis* de Sales and St. Jane Frances de Chantal, among other ways.

Renaissance humanism influenced the Enlightenment's* exaltation of the autonomy of human reason, which in turn is the principal ancestor of contemporary **secular humanism**. This outlook promotes human fulfillment and rejects belief in God or any supernatural power either as contrary to reason or as an obstacle to the pursuit of the human good (*see* ATHEISM). In contrast, some authors claim the title "Christian humanism" for an understanding of the human being as created in God's image, damaged by sin, and redeemed through the incarnation* of God in Jesus. Jacques Maritain's* *Integral Humanism* (1936) is a classic of recent Christian humanism. In *Populorum progressio* (1967), Pope Paul VI* said, "There is no true humanism but that which is open to the Absolute and is conscious of a vocation which gives human life its true meaning. Far from being the ultimate measure of all things, man can only realize himself by reaching beyond himself" (42).

I

ICON (Gk *eikōn*). Originally referring to any image, this term later more narrowly designated a sacred image, painted on wood, or, less often, in mosaic. After the iconoclasm* controversy, icons have come to play a central part in the life of the Eastern Orthodox* and the corresponding Eastern Catholic churches*. The icon is seen as like a sacrament*, an earthly representation and embodiment (sometimes even called an "exact portrait") of heavenly reality. Icons, however, are not venerated in their own right; veneration is paid through them to what they represent. In Eastern Orthodox and Eastern Catholic churches, the **iconostasis** is a screen or wall covered with icons and separating the sanctuary of the church from the nave.

ICONOCLASM (Gk, "image breaking"). A movement of the eighth and ninth centuries in the East, opposing the use of sacred images. The movement was initially led by the Emperor Leo I (717-740) (inaccurately called "the Isaurian"), who, probably drawing on OT condemnations of images (see Ex 20.4), denounced the use of images as idolatry. Iconoclasm had affinities with monophysite* Christology, which de-emphasized the humanity of Christ. In turn, the iconoclasts accused their opponents of Nestorianism*, that is, of splitting Christ into two, since only his humanity could be represented in a picture. There was also apparent Islamic influence on iconoclasm, at least in its later stages. Under the sway of Leo's iconoclast son Constantine V, a synod at Hieria in 754 condemned the use of images. This synod was reversed at the Second Council of Nicaea* in 787, however. A series of iconoclast emperors in the early ninth century reopened the conflict, which was finally settled in favor of images by the patriarch Methodius in 843. The long controversy over images played a role in the growing estrangement of the West—particularly the Frankish court of Charlemagne—from the East.

The iconoclast spirit appeared again in many Protestant reformers (notably John Calvin and Ulrich Zwingli), who objected to abuses in the veneration of images in the late medieval Church. From this follows the relative lack of ornament in many Protestant churches.

Theologically, the controversy over images concerns the incarnation*. The use of holy images reflects the capacity of matter to represent and even to embody the divine, without becoming identified with it, as in idolatry. Thus, the Council of Trent* in 1563 reaffirmed the use of images, while emphasizing that the veneration given them is in virtue of the realities they represent and not of any divinity present in them.

IGNATIUS OF ANTIOCH, ST. Bishop of Antioch* in Syria, martyred near the end of the reign of the Roman Emperor Trajan (98-117). While en route to Rome to be martyred, he wrote seven letters: five to churches in the area of his journey, one to the church at Rome, and one to Polycarp. These letters insist on the true humanity and divinity of Jesus, against Judaizing and docetist* tendencies within the churches addressed. Ignatius is also noteworthy for his emphasis on the authority of a single bishop* within the local church. The following passage (the oldest extant use of the phrase, "the Catholic Church") illustrates his theology of the episcopacy: "Where the bishop is present, there let the congregation gather, just as where Jesus Christ is, there is the Catholic Church" (*Smyrnaeans* 8.2). His feast is celebrated on October 17.

IGNATIUS (OF) LOYOLA, ST. (1491-1556). Spanish mystic and founder of the Society of Jesus (*see* JESUITS). Born into a noble family in northern Spain, Iñigo (later Ignatius) trained for the life of a courtier and soldier. While recovering from a severe cannonball wound in 1521, Ignatius underwent a spiritual conversion and resolved thenceforward to be a knight in the service of Christ. In a year of meditation at Manresa, not far from Loyola, from 1522 to 1523, Ignatius developed his distinctive spirituality and made notes that eventually became the *Spiritual Exercises* (published 1548). After a pilgrimage to the Holy Land, Ignatius spent the years 1524 to 1535 mainly in university study in Spain and at Paris. At Paris, he gathered the group of companions, including St. Francis Xavier*, who would become the Society of Jesus. The Society was formally approved as a religious order in 1540, and Ignatius became its superior. He spent the rest of his life supervising the work of the society in spiritual direction*, preaching, missionary work, and education. Besides the *Exercises*, his principal writings were an incomplete *Autobiography*, the *Constitutions of the Society of Jesus*, and numerous letters. He was canonized in 1622; his feast is celebrated on July 31.

Ignatian spirituality is strongly trinitarian and centered in Christ, makes extensive use of the imagination, and is oriented toward a life of service within the Church. Its most characteristic expression is the thirty-day directed retreat* based on the *Exercises*. In it the retreatant, assisted by the director, seeks through prayer and meditation* to discern the will of God for his or her individual life.

IMMACULATE CONCEPTION. Mary's* freedom, through God's grace, from original sin*. Belief in the immaculate conception is a dogma* of Catholic faith, defined by Pope Pius IX* in 1854. In the words of the dogmatic definition, "The Most Blessed Virgin Mary from the first moment of her conception was, by the singular grace and privilege of Almighty God, in view of the merits of Christ Jesus the Savior of the human race, preserved immune from all stain of original sin" (DS 2803). The immaculate conception is not explicitly revealed in Scripture but is believed as a result of a long process of reflection on what is implied in Mary's being "Mother of God" (*theotokos*) (*see* EPHESUS, COUNCIL OF; DOCTRINE). Mary's sinlessness, in the sense of freedom from personal or actual sin, is affirmed in fourth-century writers, but the question of her freedom from original sin could not be raised until the doctrine of original sin had received clear formulation by Augustine*. Augustine's argument that original sin is transmitted through sexual intercourse implied that Mary, who was conceived through intercourse by her parents, contracted original sin. In the East, where the Augustinian theory was not dominant, the seventh-century writers Andrew of Crete and Germanus of Constantinople strongly asserted Mary's sinlessness, without explicitly speaking of original sin. The first Western writer to defend the immaculate conception was Eadmer (ca. 1060-ca. 1128), but other Western writers rejected it, at first because of the Augustinian theory of the transmission of original sin. When this theory was abandoned in the thirteenth century, there remained the objection, raised especially by Thomas Aquinas*, that had she been immaculately conceived, Mary would not have needed salvation through Christ, who thus would not be the savior of everyone. Duns Scotus* held that Mary's immaculate conception was itself effected through the grace of Christ, and this argument eventually prevailed. The issue was fought, however, into the seventeenth century, with Dominicans* supporting the position of Thomas Aquinas, a Dominican, and Franciscans* supporting the Franciscan Duns Scotus. In the seventeenth through nineteenth centuries, the popes received many requests, notably from the Spanish monarchy, for a definition of the doctrine. Pope Alexander VII expressed official support for the doctrine in 1661 but did not declare it. Before declaring the doctrine, Pius IX surveyed the bishops and ascertained that there was widespread support throughout the Church for a definition of the doctrine (see SENSUS FIDELIUM).

The principal driving force toward acceptance of the doctrine of the immaculate conception was the celebration of the feast of Mary's conception (see LEX ORANDI, LEX CREDENDI). This feast originated in the East in the seventh century. It reached England in the eleventh century and spread from there to continental Europe. It was given official approval by Pope Sixtus IV in 1477 and extended to the universal Church by Pope Innocent XII in 1693. The word "immaculate" was not officially added to the name of the feast till 1854. The feast is celebrated on December 8.

IMMORTALITY. The condition of not being subject to death. The concept of the immortality of the human soul* enters the Catholic tradition not from the Bible but from Greek philosophy. It appears in the Bible only in Wisdom (3.1-12; 8.13,17), itself heavily influenced by Greek thought. Elsewhere in the OT, there is a conception of a shadowy afterlife in the underworld (*Sheol*). Most of the works of the OT and NT do not divide the human being into body and soul; hence, the conception of the afterlife that develops in the Bible is that of a resurrection* of the whole person. In the Greek tradition, a dualistic anthropology was influential and achieved a classic statement in Plato's *Phaedo*, which argues for a soul (*psychē*) that, as knower of eternal truth, must be immortal, preexisting its body and surviving bodily death. The Fathers of the Church* generally did not accept preexistence (Origen* is an exception), but most embraced the Platonic conception of the soul and immortality. A few, such as Irenaeus* and Tertullian*, resisted the idea of natural immortality. The revival of Aristotelianism* in the Middle Ages introduced a new problem, since the Aristotelian soul, the "form" of the living body, is not immortal (only the intellect, *nous*, is immortal, and that is not individual). Thomas Aquinas* blended Platonic and Aristotelian arguments to defend a soul that, though naturally united with its body, was immortal and could endure between bodily death and resurrection. Lateran Council V* in 1513 declared the soul's individuality and immortality. A 1979 Vatican document on eschatology* stated in cautious terms that a spiritual element, with consciousness and will, survives after death, and that "soul" is an appropriate word for it (*see* text at SOUL).

IMPRIMATUR (Lt, "let it be printed"). An expression that indicates official permission to publish. Such permission is required for editions of the Bible, liturgical texts and prayer books, catechisms, textbooks on religious subjects (in the United States ordinarily excepting college texts), and books to be sold or distributed in churches. It may be given to other works. Approval is normally to be given by the bishop of the place where the book is published or the author lives. It indicates that the work is free of doctrinal error, not necessarily that the bishop agrees with its contents. It is preceded by a declaration *Nihil obstat* (Lt, "Nothing stands in the way") issued by a censor appointed by the bishop.

INCARNATION (Lt *incarnatio*, "becoming flesh"). The "becoming flesh" of the Word of God (*see* LOGOS, TRINITY) in Jesus Christ*. Based in John 1.14 ("And the Word became flesh and made his dwelling among us"), this is the standard term for the joining of divine and human in Jesus. *See also* CHRISTOLOGY.

INCULTURATION. This term, which came into common use in the 1970s, combines the theological concept of incarnation* (the Word of God becoming flesh in Jesus) with the anthropological concepts of *enculturation* (or socialization, the process whereby a person becomes part of a culture) and *acculturation* (the encounter between cultures). In the words of Vatican Council II, "The Church, so that it may be able to offer to all the mystery of salvation and the life brought by God, ought to insert itself into all these groups [peoples in mission lands] with the same thrust with which Christ himself, by his incarnation, bound himself to the particular social and cultural conditions of the people among whom he lived" (AG 10). Christian faith was encountering various cultures from the beginning and both transforming and being transformed by them. This was especially (although not exclusively) true of Greek and Roman culture, which, together with Christian faith, formed the "Western" or European tradition. The use of the word "inculturation" reflects a new stage in Christian thought: a recognition of the irreducible plurality of human cultures, rather than an unquestioned assumption of the superiority of

European culture over all others. There are two moments to inculturation. One is adaptation: the Church should express its message as much as possible in terms of the concepts and practices of the culture in question. The other is transformation: adaptation must leave room for Christian faith to challenge the standard assumptions and practices of the culture and thus to transform it from within, in the light of the gospel of Christ. Pope John Paul II* has made frequent use of "inculturation," although his emphasis on Church unity has made him suspicious of the pluralism* in theology and practice that results from inculturation; his model for the process is the work of Cyril and Methodius* in creating Slavic Christianity.

INDEX OF FORBIDDEN BOOKS (*INDEX LIBRORUM PROHIBITORUM*) (Lt *index*, "list"). An alphabetical list of books that Catholics were forbidden to read without permission from Church authorities. The Index was established in 1559 by the Congregation for the Inquisition* under Pope Paul IV in the context of the Protestant* Reformation and the great proliferation of printed books that it sparked. It was revised many times down to 1948 before being abolished in 1966. It was never intended as a complete list of forbidden books (there was a general rule against reading morally or spiritually harmful books) but only of harmful books that had been brought to Rome's attention. It included more than four thousand books, mostly theological treatises in Latin but also Machiavelli's *The Prince* and some other well-known works. Books on the Index included: (1) editions of the Bible* and books of Catholic religion that lacked proper ecclesiastical permission (*see* IMPRIMATUR), (2) books that attacked religion or the Church, (3) books that defended heresy* or immorality, (4) books judged obscene.

INDULGENCE. A remission of temporal punishment due to sins* already forgiven. Such punishment is not an arbitrary imposition by God but the consequences of sin itself. This temporal punishment is to be undergone on earth or in purgatory*. Indulgences draw on the solidarity of the Church or communion of saints*: just as one person's sin affects others, so does one person's holiness. This leads to the notion of the Church's "treasury" of merits* or satisfactions. Medieval theology unfortunately cast discussion of this treasury in the language of financial transactions, but the principle is that the prayers and good works of Jesus Christ*, Mary*, the saints*, and all good Christians benefit the whole Church or Body of Christ and can be applied to others. The Church exercises its authority in establishing specific "ways of applying the fruits of Christ's redemption to the individual faithful" (Pope Paul VI, *Indulgentiarum Doctrina*, 1967).

Indulgences may be **plenary** (remitting all temporal punishment) or **partial**. Partial indulgences formerly had time periods (e.g., three hundred days, seven years) attached. Originally indicating the remission of an amount of time of canonically imposed penance, they came, in popular understanding, to specify an amount of time reduced from one's stay in purgatory. Indulgences can be gained only by baptized persons in a state of grace. They may be applied to oneself or to the dead, but not to other living persons. All indulgences require sorrow for sin, freedom from serious sin, performance of the required work (prayer, pilgrimage, etc.), and intention to gain the indulgence. For plenary indulgences, in addition, one must "be free of all attachment to any sin at all" (*ibid.*), receive sacramental confession* and the eucharist*, and pray for the intention of the pope.

Indulgences originated in the eleventh century as remissions of canonically imposed penances for sin. They became prominent in connection with the Crusades*; crusaders who confessed their sins were granted a remission of all penance. The first official application of indulgences to the souls in purgatory was by Pope Sixtus V in 1476. Since indulgences could be given for good works, including almsgiving, they became a major source of revenue for the Church in the fifteenth and sixteenth centuries. This practice, which appeared to be a "sale" of indulgences and which occasioned some disedifying hucksterism, was the immediate context of Martin Luther's protest in 1517, the beginning of the Protestant* Reformation. In belated response, the Council of Trent* in 1563 attacked the abuse of indulgences, and in 1567 Pope Pius V abolished indulgences for financial contributions. Indulgences continued to proliferate, however, attached to a broad variety of practices, religious objects, places, and times. In 1967, Pope Paul VI* issued a document, *Indulgentiarum Doctrina*, which regulated them, among other ways by reducing the number of and strengthening the conditions for plenary indulgences and removing the time periods attached to partial indulgences. Probably because they seemed to introduce an element of manipulation and calculation into one's relation to God's forgiving grace*, indulgences have fallen into relative disuse.

INERRANCY. Freedom from error. The term is normally used of the Bible* and denotes a consequence of the inspiration* of the Bible. If, and to the extent that, God is the author of the Bible, it must speak the truth. Many Protestants*, especially Fundamentalists*, hold this to imply "plenary verbal inerrancy": every statement in the Bible is literally true. The Catholic Church holds for a "limited inerrancy," expressed as follows by the *Dogmatic Constitution on Divine Revelation* of Vatican Council II: "[Since] we should hold that whatever the inspired authors or 'sacred writers' affirm [*asserunt*], is affirmed by the Holy Spirit; [therefore] we must acknowledge that the books of Scripture teach firmly, faithfully, and without error such truth as God, for the sake of our salvation, wished the biblical text to contain" (DV 11). Inerrancy (and the meaning of "affirm") is confined to what pertains to our salvation; the biblical text may well contain material, incidental to its message of salvation, that can be judged historically or scientifically inaccurate from a modern standpoint.

INFALLIBILITY. A guarantee of freedom from error, through the gift of the Holy Spirit*. Infallibility is granted first and foremost to the whole Church. Jesus promised to be with the Church to the end of time (Mt 28.20), and he gave his Spirit to the Church (Jn 14.16). As a result, the Church is **indefectible**, that is, it can never completely fall away from Jesus. Infallibility follows from indefectibility: the Church cannot be unfaithful to Jesus in its fundamental beliefs. "The universal body of the faithful who have received the anointing of the holy one cannot be mistaken in belief. It displays this particular quality through a supernatural sense of the faith (*sensus fidei**) in the whole people, when ... it expresses the consent of all in matters of faith and morals" (Vatican Council II, LG 12).

The infallibility given to the Church is exercised especially by the bishops and the pope (*see* MAGISTERIUM). Bishops* do not have the gift of infallibility as individuals but may speak infallibly in the solemn declarations of an ecumenical council* (LG 25), provided the pope consents. The bishops also "even though dispersed throughout the world, but maintaining the bond of communion among themselves and with the successor of Peter, when in teaching authentically [authoritatively] matters concerning faith and morals, they agree about a judgment as one that has to be definitively held, ... infallibly proclaim the teaching of Christ" (LG 25). This is called the **infallibility of the ordinary magisterium**.

The pope* may proclaim a dogma* of the faith infallibly. The conditions for this exercise of infallibility were set out by Vatican Council I* in 1870: "When the Roman Pontiff speaks *ex cathedra*, that is, when in the exercise of his office as shepherd and teacher of all Christians, in virtue of his supreme apostolic authority, he defines a doctrine concerning faith or morals to be held by the whole Church, he possesses, by the divine assistance promised to him in blessed Peter, that infallibility which the divine Redeemer willed his Church to enjoy in defining doctrine concerning faith or morals. Therefore, such definitions of the Roman pontiff are of themselves, and not by the consent of the Church, irreformable" (DS 3074). Vatican I's definition is carefully limited. The pope must be speaking as head of the universal Church, not as an individual, or even as Bishop of Rome or Patriarch of the West. He must be defining "a doctrine concerning faith or morals," that is, a revealed truth regarding Christian belief or practice. In proclaiming such a doctrine, the pope must consult the faith of the Church somehow, but (against Gallicanism*) Vatican I explicitly ruled out any need for an *ex cathedra* papal declaration to be subsequently ratified by the Church. The pope has only once since Vatican I proclaimed a dogma *ex cathedra*: the Assumption* of the Blessed Virgin Mary, proclaimed in 1950.

While Vatican I dealt only with papal definitions of revealed truth, the Church holds that infallibility extends also to that which is necessary in order for revealed truth to be "guarded as sacred and faithfully expounded" (LG 25). This is called the **secondary object of infallibility**. The Church has not defined how far this infallibility extends, and it is debated by theologians, particularly as to whether it includes specific moral norms of the natural law*, such as the condemnation of contraception (*see* BIRTH CONTROL).

The fact that a truth is infallibly declared does not imply that the specific words in which it is expressed are entirely adequate. Such words are subject to the limitations of human language in speaking of God and also reflect the linguistic and conceptual frameworks of their historical period. An infallible declaration does not preclude further development of doctrine in regard to what is declared, but such development cannot contradict the proposition that was infallibly defined.

Belief in the infallibility of ecumenical councils developed from the authority that councils held in the early Church but was not explicitly stated until the ninth century. No explicit statement of the infallibility of the pope is found until the late thirteenth century; this doctrine, however, developed from earlier doctrine about the authority of the church of Rome* and its bishop.

INITIATION, CHRISTIAN. The process of becoming a full member of the Christian community. The full process of initiation is set forth in the *Rite of Christian Initiation of Adults* (RCIA) (1972) as comprising four stages: (1) a period of inquiry and evangelization* called the "precatechumenate"; (2) the catechumenate*; (3) the reception of the **sacraments of initiation**, in order, baptism*, confirmation*, and the eucharist* (for those baptized in infancy, the present sequence in the Roman rite is baptism, first eucharist, confirmation); (4) a period of further instruction and growth in the life of the community—this is called **mystagogy**, "leading into the mysteries." For adults, ideally, the catechumenate ends with Lent*, the sacraments are received at the Easter Vigil, and mystagogy extends through the Easter* Season till Pentecost*.

INNOCENT III, POPE (1198-1216) (Lotario dei Segni, b. 1160). The most powerful of the medieval popes. He made a reality the "plenitude of power" within the Church and secular society claimed by popes since Gregory VII*, achieving a status close to king of Europe. The first pope to claim the title "Vicar of Christ," he considered his position to be "set midway between God and man, below God but above man." He reestablished papal control over the Papal States* and claimed and exercised a right to approve the elected German Emperor. In 1213 he received England as a fief from King John, after placing it under interdict* for the king's refusal to accept Stephen Langton as Archbishop of Canterbury. He also exercised the power of interdict over King Philip Augustus of France, compelling him not to divorce his queen, Ingeborg of Denmark. Within the Church, he drew on his training in canon law to issue a large number of decretals (letters having the force of law), to provide for orderly administration of the Church, and to enact reforms. He gave approval to the new order of Francis of Assisi* and encouraged the Dominicans*. He was effective in reconciling heretics without the use of force but also initiated the crusade against the Albigensians in 1209 (*see* CATHARS). Lateran Council IV*, held near the end of his life in 1215, summed up his reforms within the Church.

INQUISITION (Lt *inquisitio*, "inquiry"). A term for a procedure to investigate heresy* (and later witchcraft* and other offenses) in the Middle Ages and early modern period, and for the tribunals that conducted these investigations. One must understand the Inquisition in the context of a time when heresy was seen as a threat to all the institutions of society. The principal threats at first were the Cathars* and the Waldensians*. Both Church and secular legislation requiring the prosecution of heretics had been in effect since the twelfth century. The Inquisition was first established in 1231 by Pope Gregory IX when he authorized the appointment of inquisitors, who held their power directly from the pope, not the local bishop. Inquisitors were chosen mainly from the Dominican* and Franciscan* orders. The Inquisition was active mainly in Germany, Italy, and France, especially in the south of France.

Inquisitors would establish themselves in an area and summon suspected heretics or sometimes the entire population of the region, urging those guilty of heresy to confess. Usually there was a "period of grace," during which those who confessed were given relatively light penances. Suspected heretics were then brought to trial. They were not told the names of the witnesses against them. Nor, in practice, could they be defended by lawyers, because their lawyers would then become liable for abetting a heretic. The torture of defendants (a feature of Roman law, then being revived in Europe) was authorized in 1252; it is not clear how often it was used. Penalties ranged from light penances, such as pilgrimages, floggings, and the wearing of the "cross of shame," through life imprisonment, to surrender to the secular authorities for burning at the stake. Confiscation of the defendant's goods accompanied sentences of life imprisonment or death.

The Inquisition was most active in the latter half of the thirteenth century, after which it gradually lost its function due both to the elimination of the Cathar movement and to the rise of secular power, though it existed into the sixteenth century. In 1542, Pope Paul III centralized the Inquisition in the Congregation of the Inquisition or Holy Office (*see* CONGREGATION FOR THE DOCTRINE OF THE FAITH). The work of the Holy Office was initially directed mainly against Protestantism, later (ca. 1580-1620) often against supposed witches.

The **Spanish Inquisition** differed from the papal Inquisition in that it was under the control of the kings of Spain rather than directly under Church authorities. Pope Sixtus IV authorized the kings to appoint inquisitors in 1478. The Inquisition was initially directed against Jews who were thought to have feigned conversion to Christianity. In its early years, it condemned perhaps two thousand people to death, almost all of them converted Jews. It also prosecuted converted Muslims and suspected heretics. It had a second period of activity in the late sixteenth century, against those suspected of Protestant sympathies and heretical forms of mysticism. In 1570, it was extended to Spanish possessions in the New World, where it was used mainly to establish *limpieza de sangre* ("purity of blood"), that is, freedom from Indian and African ancestry—such purity was (in theory) required for ordination. The Spanish Inquisition was officially abolished only in 1834.

While the Inquisition in its various forms embodied some of the most deplorable features of Church history, one should take care to distinguish its actual history from the exaggerations that became prevalent in later polemics and imaginative literature.

INSPIRATION of the Bible. The special assistance given by God to the authors and/or compilers of the texts of the Bible*, so that God is in some sense the author of the Bible—it is the "word of God." The term comes from 2 Timothy 3.16, "All scripture is inspired by God." The Catholic understanding of inspiration is stated in the *Dogmatic Constitution on Divine Revelation* of Vatican Council II as follows: "[H]oly Mother Church accepts as sacred and canonical all the books of both the Old Testament and the New, in their entirety ..., in the conviction that they were written under the inspiration of the Holy Spirit ... and therefore have God as their originator: on this basis they were handed on to the Church. In the process of composition of the sacred books God chose and employed human agents, using their own powers and faculties, in such a way that they wrote as authors in the true sense, and yet God acted in and through them, directing the content entirely and solely as he willed" (DV 11). This asserts both divine and human authorship of the biblical texts. In regard to the latter, the document goes on to note that a biblical text is affected by its literary form, its author's personal style, and the customs of thought and speech prevailing at the time of its writing. The Catholic Church has made no pronouncement on *how* God inspires the Scripture. Some Catholic theologians (e.g., P. Benoit) emphasize God's working on the individual author, while others (e.g., Karl Rahner*) locate inspiration primarily in God's working in the community of Israel and the Church, guiding it in compiling, preserving, and canonizing texts. (*See also* INERRANCY.)

INTEGRALISM (INTEGRISM). Broadly, integralism can refer to tendencies in nineteenth-century Catholicism that, in reaction to the Enlightenment* and the French Revolution*, favored strong papal authority and restoration of monarchy. More narrowly, it designates a movement that flourished in the wake of the papal condemnation of Modernism* in 1907. It opposed all liberalism* and sought to impose a uniform, neo-scholastic interpretation of Catholic teaching. Integralists generally were opposed to democratic and reformist trends in politics. The most influential integralist organization was the Sodalitium Pianum, or Sapinière, organized in 1909 by Umberto Benigni, an undersecretary of state at the Vatican. Operating often in secret, using pseudonyms and codes, the Sodalitium denounced bishops, scholars, and other figures in the Church as tainted by Modernism. Pope Benedict XV* suppressed the Sodalitium in 1921, but integralist attitudes and tactics are evident in some contemporary conservative and traditionalist* Catholic groups.

INTERCOMMUNION ("eucharistic sharing," "eucharistic hospitality"). The sharing in the eucharist* by Christians whose churches are not in union with one another. The basic principles governing intercommunion are set out by Vatican Council II*: "Witness to the unity of the Church generally forbids common worship, but the grace to be had from it sometimes commends this practice" (UR 8). The eucharist is both a sign and a cause of unity. Because it would be a sign of a unity that does not exist, it is generally forbidden by the Catholic Church. In cases of necessity or difficulty, however, when ministers of their own church are unavailable, Eastern* and Oriental Orthodox* Christians may receive communion from a Catholic minister and Catholics from an Orthodox minister. The Catholic Church acknowledges that the Eastern Orthodox are less willing to allow intercommunion than is the Catholic Church. Protestant* churches will usually admit Catholics to communion, but the Catholic Church generally forbids eucharistic sharing with Protestants, because Protestant churches, lacking apostolic succession*, lack a ministry that is sacramentally valid* in Catholic eyes and in many cases also do not have a theology of the eucharist that is compatible with Catholic belief. Protestants who share Catholic eucharistic faith and lack access to a minister of their own church may request communion from a Catholic minister, but Catholics are not to request communion from a minister whose ordination is not valid according to Catholic teaching. The principles set forth here also apply to the sacraments of reconciliation* and anointing*. Local bishops may issue more specific norms.

INTERDICT. A canonical penalty that consists in exclusion from the sacraments* (except in danger of death) but not exclusion from the communion of the Church (which would be excommunication*). In most respects, interdicts are treated in canon law similarly to excommunications. As with excommunications, some interdicts are automatically imposed (*latae sententiae*) for certain offenses, such as attempting to celebrate the eucharist* or give sacramental absolution* when one is not a priest*, while others are imposed by judicial decision. The 1983 Code of Canon Law speaks only of interdicts imposed on individuals, but previous canon law had provision for interdicts imposed on places or groups of people, even an entire country. Interdicts have existed at least since the sixth century.

INVESTITURE (LAY INVESTITURE) (Lt *investire*, "to clothe"). A medieval ceremony in which a man appointed to be bishop* or abbot* rendered homage to the king or other secular ruler, and the ruler in turn gave him the staff and ring and conferred on him the lands and jurisdiction pertaining to his position. Because it was symbolic of the power of secular rulers over the Church, it was condemned by Pope Nicholas II in 1059 and forbidden by Pope Gregory VII* in 1075. This led to much conflict, especially between the popes and the Holy Roman Emperors. In the Empire, it was resolved by the Concordat of Worms in 1122, which specified that the bishop or abbot would no longer be invested with the ring and staff (symbolic of his spiritual authority) by the temporal ruler, but would be invested with the symbols of temporal authority and do homage to the ruler.

IRENAEUS, ST. (ca. 130-ca. 200). Bishop of Lyons in Gaul. He was born in Smyrna in Asia Minor and studied in Rome before becoming a presbyter and later bishop in Lyons. He is noteworthy chiefly for giving expression to the normative apostolic tradition of Catholic faith, against Gnosticism*, especially in his large work, *The Refutation and Overthrow of the False Gnosis* (ca. 180), written in Greek but extant only in a Latin translation and usually known as *Adversus Haereses*

(Against Heresies). His other extant work is the *Demonstration of the Apostolic Preaching*, which survived in Armenian. In his defense of the Catholic tradition, he argues for the authority of the canonical Scriptures (he is the first to argue for the four gospels we possess) and for the tradition* of the churches founded by the apostles; these are interlinked, since the Scriptures are those books read as normative in the apostolic churches. He is the first to defend the principle of the apostolic succession (*see* APOSTOLICITY) of bishops*, and he argues for the especial authority of the church of Rome*, in light of its origin in Peter and Paul. (In 190, however, he defended the churches of Asia Minor against the intervention of bishop Victor I of Rome in a controversy over the date of Easter*.) Against the Gnostics, his theology emphasizes the unity and goodness of God. He is also noteworthy for his doctrine of the recapitulation (*anakephalaiōsis*) (Eph 1.10) of all things in Christ: Christ, as the new creation, both sums up and restores the old creation, canceling out all faults due to sin. His feast is celebrated on June 28.

ISLAM (Arabic, "submission" [to God]). The second largest (in number of adherents) of the world religions, after Christianity. Adherents of Islam are called **Muslims** (Moslems), "those who submit." Islam derives from the teaching of the Prophet Muhammad (Mohammed) (A.D. 570-632), or, as Muslims would say (and some Catholic theologians will in some sense accept), from the revelation of God through Muhammad. This revelation is recorded in the sacred book, the *Qur'an (Koran)* ("recitation"), which Muslims regard as the literal word of God. Muhammad did not see himself as the founder of a new religion but as restoring the original religion of submission to God, which was the religion of Abraham. Muslims regard the Old and New Testaments as containing the word of God, but distorted through human transmission. They reverence Moses and Jesus, among others, as prophets. Muhammad, as the Messenger of God, is the completion of the prophets. Islam's profession of faith is, "There is no God but Allah [The God], and Muhammad is the Messenger of God." Islam strongly emphasizes the unity of God. It therefore rejects the notion of the Trinity* and regards it as blasphemous to speak of God as having a son. It also rejects the Incarnation* as an unacceptable "association" (*shirk*) of God and a creature. As "Peoples of the Book," Jews and Christians were allowed to practice their religion in Muslim lands during most of their history, but were denied full citizenship. Christians usually were not so tolerant of Muslims (*see* CRUSADES).

The Second Vatican Council, after noting many points of common faith and practice between Catholics and Muslims, urged both "that, forgetting past things, they train themselves towards sincere mutual understanding" (NA 3). Since Vatican II, there have been many Catholic-Muslim dialogues under the auspices of the Pontifical Council for Interreligious Dialogue (formerly Secretariat for Non-Christians). The first officially sponsored national Catholic-Muslim dialogue meeting in the United States took place in 1991.

J

JANSENISM. A religious movement, chiefly in France and the Low Countries, in the seventeenth and eighteenth centuries. Its initial basis was in the work of Cornelius Jansen (Jansenius) (1585-1638), bishop of Ypres. His *Augustinus*, published posthumously in 1640, defended a strict Augustinian theology of grace* and predestination* and attacked the teaching of the Jesuits* on these subjects. The argument of this work in many ways resembled that of John Calvin (*see* PROTESTANT CHURCHES). Five propositions attributed to this work were condemned by Pope Innocent X in 1653. The thrust of these propositions was that Jesus Christ did not die for all persons and that those who were saved were given an irresistible gift of grace, which enabled them to obey God's commandments. The Jansenist cause was promoted by Jansenius's friend Jean Duvergier de Hauranne, later appointed as Abbé de Saint-Cyran and known as Saint-Cyran (1581-1643). He was spiritual director of the convent of Port-Royal, near Paris, and under his influence it became the center of Jansenism in France. Following Saint-Cyran, the most important Jansenist writers were Antoine Arnauld (1612-1694) and Blaise Pascal* (1623-1662), whose *Pensées* is the one spiritual classic of the movement. In 1713, Pope Clement XI, in the bull *Unigenitus*, condemned 101 propositions from the work of Pasquier Quesnel, a Jansenist leader whose thought was also strongly influenced by Gallicanism*. This led, in 1723, to a schism in Utrecht, Holland; the (Jansenist) Church of Utrecht survives as a branch of the Old Catholics*. The Jansenists were persecuted in eighteenth-century France but survived as a distinct party into the nineteenth century. Their influence lasted well into the twentieth century. Jansenist spirituality was marked by a pessimism about human nature, a strong sense of God's transcendence, and a morally rigorous view of Christian life. One characteristic and influential Jansenist tenet, originating in Arnauld, is that one should not receive communion frequently and should do so only after sacramental confession*.

JEROME, ST. (Eusebius Hieronymus) (ca. 347-419/20). Scholar, exegete, Doctor of the Church*. Born in Dalmatia, he studied in Rome and went to the Near East in 374, where he learned Hebrew. From 382 to 384 he was secretary to Pope Damasus. From 386 on, he lived in Bethlehem in a monastery that he founded. Under Damasus he began his translation of the Bible from the original languages into Latin, a task that occupied the rest of his life. This work formed the major part (though not the whole) of what came to be called the Latin Vulgate (*see* BIBLE). He left many works of biblical commentary and an extensive and important correspondence. A highly contentious man, he engaged in much controversial writing, notably over Origen* and Pelagianism*. His feast is celebrated on September 30.

JERUSALEM. City in the mountains of southeastern Palestine; the religious and political capital of the Jews in OT times and the place where Jesus died and rose from the dead; now a holy city for Jews, Christians, and Muslims. The earliest Christian community formed there (Acts 2.42-47) after Jesus' resurrection and Pentecost*, headed by the apostles*, Peter in particular. After Peter, James "the brother of the Lord" led the Jerusalem community (Acts 12.17). From Jerusalem, Christian missionaries went out to preach in surrounding areas. Acts 11.22 shows that the mother church in Jerusalem had some supervision over newer churches, in this case that of Antioch*. A meeting around A.D. 50, called the "Council of Jerusalem," approved Antioch's practice of baptizing Gentiles without requiring their observance of the Jewish law. This was an important event in the separation of Christianity from Judaism*.

After a Jewish revolt that began in A.D. 66, the Romans destroyed Jerusalem, from which the Christians had already fled, in A.D. 70. Some Jews and Christians returned, and a second Jewish rebellion broke out in 132. After crushing it in 135, the Romans destroyed the city again, banished all Jews from it, and built a pagan city, called Aelia Capitolina, on its location. A Gentile Christian community survived there. When Constantine* began to Christianize the Roman

Empire in the fourth century, basilicas* were built on sites commemorating events in Christ's life and monasteries flourished in the area. Jerusalem became an important destination for Christian pilgrimages*. Until 451, the see of Jerusalem was subordinate to the metropolitan at Caesarea. In 451, the Council of Chalcedon* raised it to the rank of a patriarchate*. The city was sacked by the Persians in 614, with most of its holy buildings destroyed, and it fell to the Arabs in 638. The Arabs were generally tolerant of the Christians. The patriarchate, vacant since 644, was restored in 705. It remained in communion with Constantinople when the Eastern and Western churches divided (*see* EASTERN ORTHODOX CHURCHES). In 1072, the Seljuks took the city and closed it to Christian pilgrims. This was an inciting cause of the Crusades*. The First Crusade captured Jerusalem in 1099 and set up a Latin kingdom and patriarchate there. In 1187, the city fell to the Muslims again, although the kingdom of Jerusalem lasted till 1291 at the fortress of Acre (Accho), where the patriarchs also took refuge. Thereafter, the Latin patriarchate was titular (*see* BISHOP) only, until 1847, when Pope Pius IX* restored it. In 1838, the Melkite (*see* EASTERN CATHOLIC CHURCHES) patriarch of Antioch added Jerusalem to his title.

Since the Six-Day War of 1967, Israel has ruled all of Jerusalem. The Vatican has pressed for a "special status" for Jerusalem, with international guarantees of free access to the holy places for all pilgrims. The primary Christian pilgrimage spots in Jerusalem are the Church of the Holy Sepulchre (Church of the Resurrection), at the traditional site of the tomb of Christ, and the Via Dolorosa, the traditional Way of the Cross, followed by Jesus from his trial to his crucifixion on Mount Calvary.

JESUITS. The Society of Jesus, a religious order of men founded by St. Ignatius of Loyola*. They originated in a group of seven men, including Ignatius, who in 1534 vowed poverty, chastity, and apostolic work in the Holy Land or, failing that, to do whatever work the pope would assign them. In 1540, since the Holy Land project had become impossible, they added a vow of obedience and were approved as a religious congregation by Pope Paul III. The Society quickly became a leader in Catholic life in the Counter-Reformation* period. By 1626, it had more than 15,000 members, and by 1749, more than 22,000. The principal work of the order was and is education. By 1749, the order had founded 669 colleges (most of which were more like preparatory schools today, but some of which were universities). Their plan of education, the *Ratio Studiorum*, drawn up in 1599, called for extensive formation in the humanities, with drama playing an especially important part. The Jesuits also carried on important ministries of spiritual direction* and retreats, based on Ignatius's *Spiritual Exercises*. Jesuits often served as confessors to European royalty. They distinguished themselves in theology, astronomy, and other areas of scholarship, producing two Doctors of the Church, Peter Canisius (1521-1597) and Robert Bellarmine* (1542-1621). Jesuits took the lead in the struggles against Jansenism* and Protestantism*.

From the beginning, they were very active in foreign missions. By 1552, Francis Xavier*, one of the original Jesuits, had preached in India, Malaya, the East Indies, and Japan. Francis died before entering China, but Matteo Ricci (1552-1610) and other Jesuits worked extensively in China in the following century. The Jesuit practice in missions was to adapt their manner and language as much as possible to the native culture where they were preaching. This gave rise to the Chinese Rites controversy* in the seventeenth and eighteenth centuries. Jesuits were important in mission work in North and South America (*see* NATIVE AMERICANS). Among the native populations of Spanish America, they established more than a hundred "reductions," political and economic communities under Jesuit direction.

Their power and influence gained them many enemies, including Enlightenment* figures outside the Church and Jansenists and Gallicans* within. These combined to cause the suppression of the order in many Catholic countries, including Portugal in 1759, France in 1764, and Spain in 1767. The rulers of these countries, joined by the Jesuits' enemies at Rome, prevailed on Pope Clement XIV to suppress the Society altogether in 1773. Because the Empress Catherine II of Russia refused to allow the suppression in her dominions, the Jesuits survived there. In 1804, Pope Pius VII partially restored the order, and in 1814 he revoked the suppression completely. The order resumed its ministries and grew to more than 35,000 members in 1964. It included some of the most important religious thinkers and theologians of the twentieth century, for instance, Pierre Teilhard de Chardin*, Bernard Lonergan*, John Courtney Murray*, and Karl Rahner*.

Like other religious communities, the Jesuits have been losing membership and reexamining their work in the years since Vatican Council II. Under the leadership of Pedro Arrupe, the Superior General, the Society's Thirty-Second General Congregation in 1974 to

1975 oriented the order toward the promotion of justice in all its ministries. This caused conflict both within the Church and with governments, especially in Latin America, where Jesuits have been active in formulating and implementing liberation theology*. On November 16, 1989, six Jesuit priests, their cook, and her daughter were murdered by soldiers in El Salvador because of the Jesuits' advocacy of the poor in that country.

There are about 23,000 Jesuits today. Most are priests; the rest are lay brothers* and "scholastics" studying for priesthood. They are governed by a Superior General, who is elected for life by a General Congregation. The order is divided into provinces, each headed by a provincial. Most Jesuit priests take solemn vows* of poverty*, chastity, and obedience*, as well as a fourth vow of obedience to the pope in the acceptance of missions. Some priests, called "spiritual coadjutors," take simple vows of poverty, chastity, and obedience and do not take the fourth vow.

JESUS CHRIST (Gk *Iēsous*, from Heb *Yeshua*, proper name; Gk *Christos*, "anointed one," translation of Heb *Messiah*) (ca. 6 B.C.-ca. A.D. 30 [the "Before Christ" birth date results from an error in the B.C./A.D. chronology, devised in the sixth century by Dionysius Exiguus]). At once a Palestinian Jewish teacher and healer of the first century *and* the incarnate Son/Word of God, the second person of the holy Trinity*. The challenge to Christian theology and piety has always been to hold both of these together, maintaining their link in the experience of Jesus as savior or bringer of salvation*.

Although minimal historical information about Jesus may be extracted from other sources—enough to affirm at least that he was executed by the Romans during the time when Pontius Pilate was prefect of Judea (A.D. 26-36)—the principal historical sources about Jesus are the four Gospels* of the NT. The Gospels are not histories in our sense and reflect much theological development, both on the part of their authors and on the part of the oral tradition that preceded their writing. They must be used carefully as historical sources, but contemporary historical scholarship concludes that they are reliable in, among other things, showing that Jesus taught the nearness of the kingdom (reign) of God*, was perceived as a healer and wonder-worker, and was crucified by the Romans as a political threat, with the connivance of Jewish religious leaders who saw him as a menace to their authority. After his death, his followers reported that he had risen from the dead and appeared to them. Although the resurrection* cannot be established or disestablished by critical history, it was the foundation of NT belief in Jesus as the Christ (Acts 2.36) and savior. The NT uses many terms, reflecting a variety of "christologies," to bring out the significance of Jesus' person and action. The most prominent such term, to the point of becoming regarded as part of Jesus' name, was "Messiah" or "Christ," God's "anointed one"; at one time applied to the king, this term had come by Jesus' time to designate a figure who would restore Israel. NT writings show, from a very early time, the use of language indicating his divinity, e.g., "Lord" (e.g., Phil 2.11) and even "God" (e.g., Jn 1.1 and 20.28).

Among the Fathers of the Church*, the principal concerns in theological reflection about Jesus were (1) affirming his divinity without denying the unity of God (*see* TRINITY; ARIANISM); (2) affirming his true humanity, against various theologies that appeared to deny it (*see* DOCETISM, ARIANISM, APOLLINARIANISM, MONOPHYSITISM, MONOTHELITISM); (3) maintaining his unity as divine and human (*see* NESTORIANISM). Crucial moments in the process of reflection were the doctrinal statements of the First Council of Nicaea* (325) that the Word of God, incarnate in Jesus, is *homoousios* ("one in being") with the Father, and of the Council of Chalcedon* (451) that Jesus was "one person in two natures," human and divine. (*See also* CONSTANTINOPLE and EPHESUS, COUNCILS OF.)

There were no major developments in Christology* during the medieval period. Medieval theologians dwelled on the implications of the Chalcedon formula, but showed an unfortunate tendency to separate Christology (the study of the person of Jesus Christ) from soteriology* (the study of Christ as savior). The Enlightenment*, with its ideal of critical history, led to skepticism about the reliability of the Gospels, and, with its suspicion of the supernatural, led to doubts or denials of the divinity of Jesus. This had a decisive impact upon Protestant Christology in the nineteenth and twentieth centuries, but did not affect Catholic Christology until the middle of the twentieth century. Since then, the greater openness of the Catholic Church to biblical criticism*, historical scholarship, and Protestant and secular thought has led to much creative work in Christology among Catholic theologians. The outstanding figures in late twentieth-century Catholic Christology are Karl Rahner* and Edward Schillebeeckx; their Christologies, though quite different from each other, have in common an effort to find grounding in historical-critical biblical scholarship, to rejoin Christology and soteriology, and to tie Christology to Christian practice. The link to practice is even more pronounced in Christologies that reflect the perspectives of liberation theology*, e.g., Jon Sobrino, or feminist theology*, e.g., Rosemary Radford Ruether.

JOHN XXIII, POPE (1958-1963) (Angelo Roncalli, b. 1881). Born to a peasant family at Sotto il Monte, near Bergamo, Roncalli was ordained and earned a doctorate in theology in 1904. He taught theology and Church history at the diocesan seminary in Bergamo, publishing several historical monographs. In 1921, he was made director of the Society for the Propagation of the Faith* in Italy. In 1925, he entered the papal diplomatic service, in which he served as apostolic visitor (later delegate) to Bulgaria (1925-1934), apostolic delegate to Turkey and Greece (1934-1944), and nuncio to France (1944-1953). In 1953 he was named Patriarch of Venice and cardinal*. He was nearly seventy-seven when elected pope, and many thought of him as a short-term, "caretaker" pope. Instead, his papacy revolutionized the Church. John had a notably more optimistic attitude toward the modern Western world than had his predecessors or successors, and he believed that the Church was much in need of *aggiornamento** ("updating"). For this purpose, he announced in 1959 that he would call an ecumenical council*, a decision that he attributed to a sudden inspiration by the Holy Spirit*. At the same time, he announced he would call a diocesan synod* for Rome, the first in Rome's history, which was held in 1960, and would initiate a revision of canon law* (completed only in 1990). Pope John solemnly opened the Second Vatican Council* on October 11, 1962. He lived to see only its first session, at which his intervention in favor of redrafting the schema on revelation* was a turning point in favor of progressive forces. He also issued two important encyclicals on social issues, *Mater et magistra* (1961) and *Pacem in terris* (1963), which expanded Church teaching on social justice (*see* JUSTICE, SOCIAL TEACHING, and Appendix IV) to the international sphere and set forth a doctrine of human rights*. He was instrumental in calming the Cuban missile crisis of 1962. He gave much support to ecumenism*, not only through the council but also in establishing the Secretariat for Christian Unity (1960) and fostering Catholic participation in activities of the World Council of Churches*. A highly cultured yet humble and simple man, he was greatly beloved throughout the Church.

JOHN CHRYSOSTOM, ST. (ca. 349-407), Doctor of the Church*. Born in Antioch*, John became a monk in the Syrian desert but returned to Antioch to be a presbyter. His brilliant oratory won him a large popular following. In 397, the imperial court decided to kidnap him and make him the bishop of Constantinople*. There his reforming spirit, his denunciation of luxury and abuse, and his aloof, austere personality earned him many enemies, including the emperor's powerful wife Eudoxia. When he gave a favorable reception to several followers of Origen*, known as the Tall Brothers, who had been exiled from Alexandria*, bishop Theophilus of Alexandria summoned a synod (known as the Synod of the Oak from the palace where it took place) in Chalcedon, which illegally deposed John in 403. The synod had the support of the emperor, so John was exiled, but his popular following led to his recall in 404. He proceeded to denounce the empress and was promptly exiled again. He died in exile in Pontus. In later years, his sermons were regarded as classics of Christian rhetoric, and he was given the title Chrysostom ("Golden Mouth"). While his denunciations were at times extravagant, his sermons also show a great understanding of the lives of ordinary Christians, including a more favorable attitude toward marriage and sexuality than that of most Fathers of the Church*. His name was eventually attached to the liturgy of the Byzantine Church, though it was not his composition. His feast is celebrated on September 13.

JOHN OF THE CROSS, ST. (1542-1591). Spanish mystic, poet, and theologian. John was born Juan de Yepes, at Fontiveros near Avila. He became a Carmelite in 1563 and studied at Salamanca from 1564 to 1568. In 1567 he met Teresa of Avila*, and he soon became her spiritual director and a leader in her "Discalced" Carmelite reform movement. Strife over the reform movement led to his imprisonment for nine months in 1577 to 1578 by other members of his order. He was kept in a damp cell, six feet by ten feet, fed little, and often brought out for public floggings. During this time he wrote some of his finest poetry. His mystical treatises take the form of commentaries on his poems. They are *The Spiritual Canticle* (1584), *The Ascent of Mount Carmel* (1579-1585), *The Dark Night of the Soul* (1582-1585), and *The Living Flame of Love* (1585-1587). The mystical theology of the commentaries is strongly apophatic*. John is best known for the concept of the "dark night of the soul"; in its most intense phase, which John calls the "passive night of the spirit," God "leaves the intellect in darkness, the will in aridity, the memory in emptiness, and the affections in supreme affliction, bitterness, and anguish, by depriving the soul of the feeling and satisfaction it previously obtained from spiritual blessings" (*Dark Night* 2.3.3). God's purpose in this is to free the soul of finite limitations in order to unite it with God's own understanding and love. Accordingly, a more affirmative (kataphatic) view of creatures appears in John's poems (which are regarded as classics of the Spanish language), in which creatures assume great value as objects and expressions of God's love. John was canonized in 1726 and named a Doctor of the Church* in 1926. His feast is celebrated on December 14.

JOHN PAUL I, POPE (1978) (Albino Luciani, b. 1912). Luciani was born in Forno di Canale, near Belluno, to working-class parents who were socialists. After ordination in 1935, he taught in the seminary at Belluno from 1937 to 1947. In 1947 he became pro-chancellor and then vicar-general of the diocese of Belluno. In 1958, he was made bishop of Vittoria Veneto and in 1969, Patriarch of Venice. While at Venice, he published *Illustrissimi*, a series of letters to historical and fictional characters (e.g., Goethe and Mr. Pickwick). Upon election as pope on August 26, 1978, he chose the names of his two immediate predecessors, becoming John Paul. Simple and unpretentious, he dispensed with the papal coronation ceremony and other ceremonial trappings. His ready smile won him popular affection. After thirty-three days in office, he died of an apparent heart attack on September 28, 1978. As pope, he issued no major documents and enacted no significant changes in policy.

JOHN PAUL II, POPE (1978-) (Karol Wojtyla, b. 1920). The first pope since the sixteenth century to come from outside of Italy, Wojtyla was born at Wadowice in the archdiocese of Krakow, Poland. He studied literature at the Jagiellonian University at Krakow and was active in the theater. During the Nazi occupation of Poland, he worked in a quarry and a chemical factory. In 1942, he began to study for priesthood. He was ordained in 1946, the year his first volume of poetry was published. He earned two doctorates, one at the Pontifical Angelicum University in Rome in Thomistic theology in 1948, the other at the Jagiellonian University in moral theology, where his habilitation thesis (1953) was on the phenomenologist Max Scheler (1874-1928). The combination of Thomism* and phenomenology characterizes his approach in philosophy. In 1954 he was appointed to the faculty of Christian philosophy at the Catholic University of Lublin, Poland. His major academic works include *Love and Responsibility* (1960), on sexual morality, and *The Acting Person* (1969, revised ET 1979). He also published several volumes of poetry and drama. He was named auxiliary bishop of Krakow in 1958, Archbishop of Krakow in 1963, and cardinal in 1967. As bishop, he worked to defend the rights of the Church against the communist government. He was an influential presence at Vatican Council II (1962-1965) and took part in four of the first five meetings of the Synod* of Bishops afterward.

John Paul's wide range of vigorous activity inside and outside the Church serves a vision of a united and disciplined Church, under strong central authority, evangelizing the world and thereby bringing justice and peace through human solidarity in Christ.

His pontificate has been characterized by a great expansion of the role of the pope as world leader. He has made more than sixty trips ("pilgrimages*") abroad, to every part of the world except Russia and China. These trips are highly publicized and usually include meetings with heads of state and Church leaders and public speeches to large audiences. Beginning with a speech at Gniezno in 1979, he was instrumental in the foundation and support of the Solidarity movement in Poland, which began the process that led to the downfall of communism in Poland and eventually in all of Eastern Europe. According to Mikhail Gorbachev, the last President of the Soviet Union, speaking in 1992, "Everything that happened in Eastern Europe in these last few years would have been impossible without the presence of this Pope." In 1981, John Paul was seriously wounded by a Turkish assassin, Mehmet Ali Agca, who may have been working in consort with agents of communist governments.

Pope John Paul has issued three major encyclicals on social issues: *Laborem exercens* (1981) (*see* WORK), *Sollicitudo rei socialis* (1987), and *Centesimus annus* (1991) (*see* Appendix IV). These documents make a strong call for international justice* and endorse the option* for the poor. A key theme is human solidarity* in the pursuit of justice. John Paul often uses language similar to that of liberation theology*, but his experience of communism has led him to recoil from liberation theology's use of Marxism*. In countries where liberation theology has been influential, he has tended to appoint bishops who were unfriendly to it. In 1985, the Congregation for the Doctrine of the Faith (CDF)* silenced Brazilian liberation theologian Leonardo Boff for a year. John

Paul has been critical not only of communism but also of the materialism and "consumerism" (life centered on acquisition and consumption) of Western capitalist society. He has repeatedly denounced modern war*, particularly the Gulf War of 1991, stopping just short of pacifism* in his call for humanity to "proceed resolutely towards the absolute banning of war."

John Paul has sought to strengthen the Church's internal discipline. His writings influenced Pope Paul VI's* encyclical *Humanae vitae* (1968), condemning artificial birth control*, and as pope himself he has repeatedly defended that teaching. His encyclical *Veritatis splendor* (1993) attacked the trends in moral theology* that have tended to underlie dissent* from Church teaching on birth control and related topics. In 1986, the CDF declared Charles E. Curran, a prominent dissident on birth control, ineligible to teach as a Catholic theologian, an action that led to his dismissal from the faculty of The Catholic University of America. Under John Paul, the Vatican has also taken action against Swiss theologian Hans Küng for his criticism of papal infallibility* and Dutch theologian Edward Schillebeeckx for his theology of ministry. He has sought to impose controls on theologians through an expanded Profession of Faith* and a requirement for approval by Church authorities of those appointed to teach theology in universities*. Publication of the *Catechism of the Catholic Church* in 1992 was another step toward doctrinal uniformity. John Paul has defended the requirement of celibacy* for priests and made it more difficult for men to leave the priesthood. He has very strongly rejected the ordination of women*, declaring in 1994 that the judgment that the church may not ordain women "is to be definitively held by all the Church's faithful." He has shown favor to conservative groups within the Church, such as Opus Dei* and the Italian movement Comunione e Liberazione.

John Paul has spoken in favor of Christian ecumenism*, especially with the Eastern Orthodox*, and made several important gestures toward it, such as his visit to the Lutheran Church in Rome in 1983. But under him the CDF has tended to evaluate specific ecumenical proposals negatively, particularly on the question of papal authority (*see* ANGLICAN COMMUNION and WORLD COUNCIL OF CHURCHES). John Paul's 1995 encyclical, *Ut unum sint*, however, renewed the call for ecumenism and in particular for a "patient and fraternal dialogue" on papal primacy. He made a striking gesture toward interfaith cooperation in gathering leaders of all the world's religions for a day of prayer for peace, at Assisi in 1986. Another important step that year was his visit to the Jewish synagogue at Rome.

JUDAISM. Jesus Christ* was an observant Jew, and the earliest Christians saw themselves as a movement within Judaism (Acts 2.46). The separation of Christians and Jews came about when some Christian communities (especially the churches associated with the ministry of St. Paul) began to accept Gentile converts without requiring them to keep the Jewish Law (Acts 15). The estrangement was worsened when the Romans destroyed Jerusalem* in A.D. 70 and 135, both because these events weakened the Jews and because Christians tended to see them as representing God's judgment on the Jews for rejecting Jesus. Although some communities of Jewish Christians remained into the fourth century at least, the main lines of developing Christianity tended to ignore Judaism as a continuing reality. Jews were accused of having misunderstood their own Scriptures in failing to see that they prophesied Jesus. Judaism (the Old Law) was regarded as superseded in Christianity (the New Law).

St. Augustine* argued for a limited tolerance for Jews in Christian society because they had given the world the Old Testament and because their conversion would precede the second coming of Christ. Augustine's position was in general followed in Christian Europe until the time of the Crusades*, when religious energy such as was devoted to the Crusades was also channeled into persecutions of European Jews. In the late Middle Ages, Church authorities tended to protect Jews from murderous mobs but imposed restrictions on the Jews, e.g., to wear distinctive clothing (Lateran Council IV*, 1215) or to live in special districts (called *ghettos*, from the name of the neighborhood to which they were restricted in Venice). Persecutions of Jews increased in late medieval and early modern times and were unabated by the Protestant Reformation. The bloody culmination of European anti-semitism (anti-Judaism) was the **Holocaust**, or *Shoah* (Heb "annihilation"): the execution of six million Jews under the German National Socialist regime from 1942 to 1945. Though the Nazis were not Christians, they drew on the legacy of Christian anti-Semitism and could rely on the silence, if not the cooperation, of most Christians.

A sense of responsibility for the Holocaust led many Christians to reassess the preceding nineteen centuries of Christian attitudes toward Jews and Judaism. In the Catholic Church—and indeed in Christianity as a whole—a key step was the document *Nostra Aetate (Declaration* *on the Relation of the Church to the Non-Christian Religions)* of Vatican Council II (1965). This document, acknowledging the church's "spiritual bond" with the Jews, drew on Romans 9-11 to affirm that "the Jews still remain very dear to God, whose gift and call are without regret" (4). It called for mutual understanding and respect, stated that the death of Christ cannot be blamed on all Jews then living nor on later Jews, and deplored all anti-Semitism (NA 5). The message of *Nostra Aetate* was amplified in later Church documents, especially *Notes on the Correct Way to Present the Jews and Judaism in Preaching and Catechesis in the Roman Catholic Church* (1985). This document recognizes the difference of Jewish and Christian readings of the OT and the value of both. It highlights the Jewishness of Jesus and notes that some of the anti-Jewish passages in the Gospels* reflect the situation of the Church long after the time of Jesus.

Since Vatican II, the Vatican has established a Commission for Religious Relations with the Jews, and extensive Jewish-Catholic dialogue has taken place, both officially sponsored and unofficial. Catholic theologians participating in this dialogue are unanimous in affirming that (1) God's covenant with the Jews is unbroken and the Jews are still somehow the chosen people, (2) Christianity does not merely supersede Judaism, and (3) Christian theology cannot be carried on without reference to the continuing reality of Judaism. They differ on the relation of the Sinai covenant to the covenant in Christ, and on whether and how the affirmation of a continuing validity to Judaism can be reconciled with the claim that all salvation is in and through Christ. Other points at issue are the appropriateness of any Christian mission toward the Jews, the centrality of the Holocaust for subsequent Christian theology, and the proper Christian attitude toward the state of Israel.

JUDGMENT (LAST JUDGMENT). The judgment of all by Christ at his Second Coming (*parousia**). "In the presence of Christ, who is Truth itself, the truth of each person's relationship with God will be laid bare" (CCC 1039). As described figuratively by Jesus in Mt 25.31-46, the "nations" will be judged on the basis of "whatever you did for one of these least brothers of mine" (a phrase that may have originally referred to Christians but is generalized in context to refer to all those in need). Thereafter, those judged will enter heaven* or hell*. The NT image of judgment draws on the OT concept of the Day of the Lord, when God comes to establish justice (e.g., Is 2), and on the notion of

Jesus as the "Son of Man," whose coming inaugurates the messianic kingdom (Dn 7.13) Medieval theology distinguished between the **particular judgment** of the individual immediately after death and the **general judgment** at the end of time, at the *parousia*; the particular judgment was affirmed by the Council of Florence* (DS 1304-06). A 1979 Vatican declaration on eschatology* holds that the *parousia* is "distinct and deferred with respect to the situation of people immediately after death." Any attempt to establish a precise relation between the particular and general judgments encounters the obstacle of our ignorance of the nature of time in the next life.

JULIAN OF NORWICH (1342-after 1416). English visionary and anchoress* at the Church of St. Julian in Norwich. Her fame rests on her *Showings*, which gives an account of a series of visions received by Julian during a serious illness on May 13, 1373. The *Showings* exists in two versions, a Short Text, written not long after the event and describing the visions, and a Long Text, written twenty years later, combining description with an elaboration of the visions' theological meaning. Her most prominent theme is the love of God for humanity. Recent scholarship acknowledges the originality of Julian's theology, especially on the themes of sin* and atonement*. A noteworthy feature of her writing is her extensive use of images of God and Jesus as mother.

JUSTICE. In the Bible, "justice" and its cognates translate the Hebrew *sedeq* and the Greek *dikaiosynē* and their cognates. These words are also often translated by "righteousness" and related words. Both of these English words (and others) are needed to render the rich family of meanings—all associated in one way or another with "rightness"—of the Hebrew and Greek words. In the OT, God's "justice" is both a legal quality (as a just judge, etc.) and his will to save, that is, to vindicate, to "make righteous" (e.g., Ps 36.7, Is 51.5-8). It is not separated from his love. It has particular concern with the needy and oppressed (e.g., Dt 10.18, Ps 103.6). In turn, for God's people, justice is a right relationship with God and with others. God demands justice of his people, which especially entails the right treatment of the poor and oppressed (e.g., Dt 16.20, Jer 22.3-4).

Jesus rarely speaks of "justice" in the gospels, but the "kingdom of God"*, as he proclaims it, incorporates "justice" in the OT sense. His advocacy of the poor and dispossessed is clear both in his preaching and in his association with such people in his ministry. In the NT, it is Paul who chiefly speaks of *dikaiosunē*. God's justice, for Paul, is first and foremost his saving will, made effective in Jesus Christ (Rom 1.16-17, 3.21-22). It is through the grace* of God in Jesus that humans are justified, made righteous, set in right relationship with God (Rom 3.24) (*see* JUSTIFICATION). This grace in turn enables them to live a new life (Rom 6.4) with one another in Christ (e.g., Rom 12).

Subsequent Catholic reflection on justice drew heavily on Greek philosophy, and, from the thirteenth century onward, especially on Thomas Aquinas's* development of Aristotle's* theory of justice. Aquinas defined justice as "a habit whereby one renders to each one his due by a constant and perpetual will" (ST 2-2.58.1). He followed Aristotle in distinguishing "general" or "legal justice," which directs the acts of all the virtues toward the common good, from particular justice, which has two forms: **commutative justice**, or equity between partners in a relationship or transaction, and **distributive justice**, right order between the community and the individual.

The Aristotelian-Thomistic view of justice underlay the first documents of modern Catholic social teaching*, e.g., Pope Leo XIII's* *Rerum novarum* (1891). In Pope Pius XI's *Quadragesimo anno* (1931), the term *social justice* replaced *legal justice*. It designates a just ordering of the whole of society toward the common good, and thus it incorporates commutative and distributive justice. An important theme in recent Catholic teaching about social justice is that of participation. Thus, according to the 1986 pastoral letter* of the U.S. bishops, *Economic Justice for All* (EJA)*, "Social justice implies that persons have a duty to be active and productive participants in the life of society and that society has a duty to enable them to participate in this way" (71).

Recent Church documents draw more on the biblical than the philosophical senses of "justice," but sometimes combine the two. EJA, for instance, incorporates a biblical "option for the poor"* into its conception of distributive justice. "Distributive justice requires that the allocation of income, wealth, and power in society be evaluated in light of its effects on persons whose basic material needs are unmet" (70). According to the 1971 Synod* of Bishops document *Justice in the World*, because God revealed himself as "the liberator of the oppressed and the defender of the poor" (30), and Jesus "identified himself with his 'least brethren,'" Christian faith is inseparable from "an absolute demand for justice" (34). Accordingly, a famous statement in the document makes the pursuit of justice central and indispensable to Catholicism: "Action on behalf of justice and participation in the transformation of the world fully appear to us as a constitutive dimension of the preaching of the gospel or, in other words, of the Church's mission for the redemption of the human race and its liberation from every oppressive situation" (6).

JUSTIFICATION. The act by which God makes human beings "just," "righteous," acceptable to God. The biblical context for the use of this term is discussed in the preceding article, on justice*. In the NT, justification is mentioned chiefly in Paul, especially in the letter to the Romans. Paul insisted that "a person is not justified by works of the law but through faith in Jesus Christ" (Gal 2.16). This justification is a work of God's grace* (Rom 3.24). Paul's treatment of justification was central to the conflict between Augustine* and the Pelagians* in the fifth century. Augustine held that human nature, damaged by original sin*, could do nothing to make itself just in God's sight. Only God's own free gift of grace could justify some sinners; otherwise, all would be damned. Medieval theologians worked within an Augustinian framework, but some allowed a greater role for human freedom in co-operating with God's grace than Augustine did. Late medieval piety lent itself to a view of salvation as something that could be earned through sacramental works, penances, pilgrimages*, monastic vows*, and the like.

Against this, Martin Luther (1483-1546) rebelled, drawing on Paul for a doctrine of "justification by faith" (*see* PROTESTANT CHURCHES). One is justified not by any work one does but only by God's grace in Jesus, which one accepts in faith*, which is itself a grace. Luther spoke of justification as an immediate act rather than a process of transformation; one was "simultaneously righteous and a sinner." For Luther, justification by faith was the "article by which the Church stands or falls." Responding to the Reformers, the Council of Trent* issued a "Decree on Justification" in 1547. It agreed with Luther that justification is only through the grace of Christ and that nothing of our own, prior to justification, merits it for us. Humans, however, must cooperate with the grace of justification, at least in not refusing it. Trent insisted that justification is not simply a declaration on God's part that one is acceptable to God but a transformation and sanctification of the one who is justified. It rejected the idea of "justification by faith alone," holding that faith must be accompanied by hope and love and issue in good works. Such works are at once gifts of God and meritorious of eternal life for the justified person (DS 1582). In 1983, the Lutheran-Roman Catholic dialogue group in the United States issued a major statement holding that there is no substantial disagreement between Lutherans and Catholics on the issue of justification, although there are significant differences of emphasis and conceptualization.

JUSTIN MARTYR, ST. (ca. A.D. 100-165). Early Apologist*, martyred under Marcus Aurelius. A Gentile from Samaria, he relates in his *Dialogue with Trypho* how he tried the various schools of philosophy* before being introduced to Christianity as the true philosophy. He wore the robe of a philosopher and set up a school in Rome. His thought reflects the influence of Platonism* and Stoicism* but is mainly based in Christian sources. Three of his works have come down to us, all in a single fourteenth-century manuscript. In the *Dialogue with Trypho* (ca. 160), he defends a Christian interpretation of Old Testament prophecies against a Jewish interlocutor. In the *First Apology* (ca. 155) he presents Jesus as the incarnation of the *logos** ("word," "reason"), which the philosophers sought and partially understood. He pleads for freedom for Christians and incidentally furnishes one of the earliest descriptions of Christian baptismal and eucharistic liturgies. The so-called *Second Apology* is a supplement to the first. His feast is celebrated on June 1.

JUSTINIAN (483-565). Byzantine emperor from 527 to 565, noteworthy for his efforts to restore political and religious unity to the Empire. He reconquered North Africa from the Vandals and Italy from the Ostrogoths. His efforts to reconcile the Catholics and monophysites* led to his calling of the Second Council of Constantinople (553)* but were unsuccessful. He was responsible for the building of many churches throughout the Empire, most notably Hagia Sophia in Constantinople. His codification of Roman law, the Code of Justinian (529), had considerable influence on the development of canon law* in the Middle Ages.

K

KERYGMA (Gk *kērygma*, "proclamation"). The central proclamation of Christian faith—that God offers salvation* through the risen Jesus—or the act of proclaiming it. This is continuous with Jesus' proclamation of the kingdom* of God, but it focuses on Jesus as the one through whom the kingdom is realized. Short kerygmatic formulas are frequent in Paul and Acts. Examples are 1 Cor 15.3-5, which proclaims that Christ died for our sins, was buried, was raised, and appeared, and Acts 10:36-43, which adds Jesus' ministry and his return in judgment*. In a broader sense, the four gospels* could be seen as kerygma. Kerygma may be contrasted with more detailed instruction in Christian faith.

KINGDOM OF GOD, REIGN OF GOD. The central theme of the preaching of Jesus, at least according to the synoptic gospels. "Kingdom" and "reign" translate the Gk *basileia*. "Reign" better captures the notion that it is a relationship with God rather than a place or static condition. (Matthew, desiring not to mention the name of God, uses "kingdom of heaven.") "Kingdom of God," though it appears only once in the OT (Wis 10.10), builds on the OT experience of God's saving power and on later OT hopes of a restoration of God's rule over Israel (*see* APOCALYPTIC, ESCHATOLOGY). Jesus' first words, keynoting Mark's gospel, are, "This is the time of fulfillment. The kingdom of God is at hand. Repent, and believe in the gospel" (Mk 1.14-15). The kingdom of God is something God is bringing about; it is characterized by God's forgiveness* and love*, illustrated especially in the parables in Matthew and Luke. On the part of humans, it is characterized by obedience to God and love of God, and reconciliation and justice* in our relations with one another; this is shown not only in the parables but in Jesus' own relationships with outsiders (Lk 15.1). Another characteristic is healing* and the overcoming of evil, sin, and the demonic powers that cause them; this is the significance of Jesus' miracles* (Lk 11.20, 7.22). Some gospel texts, including those just cited, indicate that the kingdom is present in Jesus, but others speak of it as still to come (e.g., Mt 6.10). Exegetes, drawing on such texts as the parable of the mustard seed (Mt 13.31-32), speak of the kingdom as "already but not yet"—here but not complete. This present-future tension is present in other NT writings, for instance, Paul's letters

(Rom 14.17, 1 Cor 15.24). The kingdom is begun in the risen Christ but will not be complete till the end of time; Christ is "the firstfruits of those who have fallen asleep" (1 Cor 15.20). Later Church tradition has not always retained the richness of the biblical view, so that the kingdom has at times been identified with the Church, with some this-worldly political arrangement, or only with the life after death. Vatican Council II* holds the present and future dimensions together: "For the values of human dignity, of fellowship and of freedom, those valuable fruits of nature and of our own energy which we shall have produced here on earth in the Spirit of the Lord and in obedience to God's command, will all be cleansed from all disfigurement and be shining and transformed, to be regained by us when Christ hands over to the Father an eternal and universal kingdom .... Here on earth that kingdom is already mysteriously present; at the Lord's coming it will be consummated" (GS 39).

KNIGHTS OF COLUMBUS. A fraternal and charitable organization of Catholic men. It was founded in 1882 in New Haven, Connecticut, by Fr. Michael McGivney. It now has more than one and a half million members in the United States and several foreign countries. One of its initial purposes was to make life insurance available to its members, and the society now includes a large insurance division with about $20 billion of insurance-in-force. Since 1948, the Knights have carried out an extensive Catholic Advertising Program, now integrated into a broader Catholic Information Service. The organization conducts numerous other educational, charitable, and social projects. It is governed by a Supreme Council headed by a Supreme Knight. It is subdivided into State Councils and Subordinate Councils. Membership is open to practicing Catholic men eighteen years old or older.

KNIGHTS OF MALTA (HOSPITALLERS). Full name: Sovereign Military Hospitaller Order of St. John of Jerusalem of Rhodes and of Malta. This order began with the Benedictine administrators of a pilgrim hospice in Jerusalem in the late eleventh century. It became a separate order in 1113, and the hospice became the first large hospital* in Catholic history. The Hospitallers became a military order (*see* TEMPLARS) in the middle of the twelfth century, and fighting superseded care of the sick as their primary task. After the fall of the Kingdom of Jerusalem* in 1291 they took refuge in Cyprus, then conquered the island of Rhodes, near Asia Minor, in 1309. There they became a prominent naval power in the Aegean Sea. After they were driven from Rhodes by the Turks in 1523, the Emperor Charles V granted them the island of Malta as a fiefdom in 1530. They ruled Malta until 1798, when they were driven out by Napoleon. In 1834, they established headquarters near Rome. Today their sovereignty is recognized by the Holy See and forty-eight other nations. In addition to members who take religious vows*, the order includes many laymen awarded membership as an honor. It includes some of the most prominent figures in business and politics in Europe and North America. It continues hospital and charitable work and has also been associated with conservative or right-wing politics.

L

LABOR. On labor considered as productive activity, *see* WORK. "Labor" also means workers in general, especially those who work for others who own the means of production (capital). The development of separate classes of owners and workers is a result of modern industrial organization, beginning in the eighteenth century. The major document of Church teaching on this subject is the encyclical *Rerum novarum* (1891) of Pope Leo XIII*, which addressed the problem of the exploitation and degradation of workers in late nineteenth-century capitalism*. In this encyclical, which was partly a response to the rise of socialism* among workers, Pope Leo attacked the idea that human labor was simply a commodity to be bought and sold. Rather, it has an inherent dignity based in the dignity of the worker. A "just wage" should be paid—not merely that which was agreed by on contract but enough to support the wage earner and his (only male workers were envisioned) family in "reasonable and frugal comfort" (34). Hours should not be excessive. Workers should be allowed to form associations (unions). The document implies a limited right to strike. It called for the state to intervene on behalf of workers when necessary. All these principles have been upheld and sometimes amplified in later documents of Catholic social teaching*. Vatican Council II added that workers have a right to participate in the control of the institutions that determine their working conditions (GS 68). Beginning with Pope John XXIII's* *Mater et magistra* (1961) and especially in Pope John Paul II's* *Laborem exercens* (1981), labor is treated first and foremost as the

234   Laity

worker's self-expression, not merely a means to earn a living (*see* WORK).

LAITY (Gk *laos*, "people"). Members of the Church who are not clerics*, that is, who have not received the sacrament of order*. Religious (those in religious life*) may be clerics or laity, but often—including in Vatican Council II's treatment of laity—"laity" is understood as excluding them. "Laity" first appears in Clement of Rome's *Epistle to the Corinthians* 40.6 (ca. A.D. 96), where it refers to the Christian people in contrast to their leaders. The notion of distinct orders of clerics and laity did not emerge until the third century, however. By the fifth century, and still more in the early Middle Ages, the Church had become stratified, with laity subordinate to clerics (and lay monks and nuns in a sort of middle position). Medieval theology and canon law treat the lay state as inferior to the clerical and the religious. An exception must be made for emperors and kings and other lay rulers, who exercised considerable power in the Church. The first eight ecumenical councils* were called not by the pope but by the emperor, and rulers long had the power to nominate candidates for bishop as well as to invest them with the emblems of their office (*see* INVESTITURE). At times imperial approval was required for consecration to the papacy, and as late as 1904 certain Catholic rulers could veto the election of a candidate as pope.

From the eleventh century, the Church saw the rise of influential lay movements, from the poverty* movements of the eleventh century, through the early Franciscans*, the Beguines* and Beghards, to the *devotio moderna* of the fourteenth century. The Protestant* Reformers, with the doctrine of the "priesthood of all believers" (*see* PRIEST) enhanced the status of the layperson in their churches. Catholic ecclesiology* in the Counter-Reformation* period, however, came close to identifying the Church with the clergy. Even so, the existence of an increasingly educated laity led to many movements for greater lay participation in the life of the Church and eventually, at Vatican Council II, to a rethinking of the status of laity in the Church.

Vatican II does not speak of laity as occupying an inferior status in the Church. Rather, all Christians have a "common dignity" (LG 32) and are equally called to holiness (LG 32,39), though in different ways. Through the ministries based in baptism and confirmation, laity share in Christ's work as priest, prophet, and king (LG 10-13). The laity have a "special vocation"*, which is "to seek the kingdom of God by engaging in temporal affairs and ordering these in accordance with the will of God" (LG 31). Laity's work in the world is an essential part of the building of God's kingdom (LG 36, GS 34,43). Laity also have an important role within the Church (LG 11,33, AA 10), both in the family, which is the "domestic Church" (LG 11), and in the parish, diocese, and wider levels of organization (AA 10). They have a right and sometimes a duty to express their opinion on matters in the Church that relate to their fields of expertise (LG 37). Since Vatican II, there has been a great expansion of lay ministries* in the Church. This is due not only to the Council's own intentions but to the decline, unforeseen by the Council, in the number of priests and religious, especially in the West.

LANGUAGES, LITURGICAL. The earliest Christian worship was probably in Aramaic, but *koinē* Greek, the vernacular (common speech) of the cities in the Roman Empire, soon replaced it. Other early liturgical languages included Syriac, Coptic, and Armenian. In the East, Christian worship has remained in the vernacular or language closely related to it, but some archaic languages, such as Ge'ez in Ethiopia and Old Slavonic in Russia, remained in liturgical use. The preservation of languages no longer spoken reflects the sacredness of liturgy*, as does the preservation of archaic forms, as in the usual English version of the Lord's Prayer or "Our Father" (see Appendix V). Latin supplanted Greek in Rome in the second half of the fourth century and soon became the standard liturgical language in the West, remaining so even after Latin was commonly spoken. The Protestant* Reformers, in order to encourage popular understanding and participation in worship, translated the liturgy into vernacular languages. In 1562, the Council of Trent* judged it not "advantageous that [the mass] should everywhere be celebrated in the vernacular" and condemned those who said that mass should only be celebrated in the vernacular (DS 1749,1759). After Trent, advocacy of vernacular liturgy was associated with Protestantism in the minds of Catholic authorities. Nevertheless, limited permission to make use of vernacular languages was granted here and there, and such permissions increased in the twentieth century. In its *Constitution on the Sacred Liturgy* (1963), Vatican Council II, while holding that Latin was to be retained in the Latin Rites, unless a particular law indicated otherwise (SC 36), indicated otherwise itself by giving broad (but vague) authorization of use of vernacular languages in the mass*, sacraments*, sacramentals*, and liturgy of the hours* (SC 39,54,63,101). In the reforms enacted after the council, full permission to use vernacular languages was granted. The general principle guiding these changes was that "the Christian people ... [should] be able to understand these things easily, and to enter into them through a celebration that is expressive of their full meaning, is effective, involving, and the community's own" (SC 21). Options remain for the use of Latin and other ancient languages (e.g., Greek in the *Kyrie eleison*) in the Roman Rite today.

LA SALLE, JOHN BAPTIST DE, ST. (1651-1719). Born at Rheims of a noble family, La Salle was ordained priest in 1678. Counter to his original intentions, he found himself engaged in a ministry of education of the poor. In 1684, he and twelve of the teachers in his schools decided to form a religious community, which they called the Brothers of the Christian Schools (**Christian Brothers**, FSC). Because the demand for their schools outran the number of brothers, La Salle recruited laymen as teachers. For them, he founded the first training schools for teachers, at Rheims in 1687, Paris in 1699, and Saint-Denis in 1709. In the early 1700s, he founded a boarding school for middle-class children at Rouen, the first of many such schools established by the Brothers in the eighteenth century. In 1705, he founded a school for delinquent boys at Rouen. His *Conduct of Schools* sets forth his educational innovations, notably a classroom rather than individual method of instruction, an insistence on pupil silence during lessons, and instruction in the vernacular rather than Latin. These set the style for subsequent Catholic education. He was canonized in 1900, and his feast is celebrated on April 7.

The Christian Brothers congregation grew throughout the eighteenth century until devastated by the French Revolution*. Restored in the nineteenth century, it expanded to more than thirteen thousand members in 1965, then declined to around eight thousand in 1992. The Brothers operate schools on all levels from elementary to graduate.

LAS CASAS, BARTOLOMÉ DE (1484-1566). Spanish "Protector of the Indians." Las Casas was born in Seville. His father and three uncles accompanied Christopher Columbus on his second voyage to the New World in 1493. Las Casas himself went to the New World in 1502 to manage his father's farm on Hispaniola. He made friends with local Indians and deplored Spanish violence against them. In 1506 he returned to Europe, and in 1507 he was ordained a priest at Rome. In

1510 he returned to Hispaniola, celebrating the first "new mass" (solemn high mass of a recently ordained priest) in the Western Hemisphere. In 1512, he went to Cuba, converting many natives in peace; again he was appalled by the violence of the Spanish colonists. There in 1514, he preached a sermon against the entire *encomienda* system, whereby a tract of land was entrusted to a colonist, who gained the right to the forced labor of the natives in return for a promise to instruct them in Christian faith. He returned to Spain and in 1519 persuaded the new king, Charles I (Charles V of the Holy Roman Empire), to grant him territory in Venezuela, where he would peacefully convert the Indians and establish them in free villages under Spanish supervision. The venture collapsed in 1521 due to Indian uprisings resulting from slaving and violence by nearby Spanish settlers. Discouraged, Las Casas entered the Dominicans in 1522 and devoted himself to study. He began his massive *History of the Indies* in 1527, and in 1534 wrote the first version of his influential *The Only Way to Draw All People to a Living Faith*, i.e., nonviolently. The tenets of this book were adopted in the bull *Sublimis Deus* of Pope Paul III in 1537. In 1539, he began his *The Destruction of the Indies,* of which he later wrote a widely read abridgement, published in 1552. He extolled the gentleness of the Indians while shocking his audience with accounts of the ferocity and cruelty of the Spanish. In 1542 and 1543, the "New Laws" incorporated many of his principles. In 1544, he became bishop of Chiapas in Mexico, where he encountered great opposition from the *encomenderos* (landholders). In response, his *Rules for Confessors* mandated the denial of absolution* to *encomenderos* unless they freed their Indians and made restitution. He was recalled to Spain, where in 1550 in Valladolid before the court he had a famous "debate" (not face-to-face) with the humanist Juan Ginés de Sepúlveda. Sepúlveda, drawing on Aristotle*, argued that the Indians were inferior by nature and suited for slavery*. Las Casas argued that the Indians were not inferior and that conquest was not an acceptable means of conversion. He spent the remainder of his life defending Indians' interests at court and in his writings. In 1552, he also denounced African slavery, repenting of his previous approval of it; he was among the first in Europe to do so.

LATERAN. The Basilica* of St. John Lateran is the cathedral* church of Rome*. The Lateran Palace was the residence of the popes in the Middle Ages. The Basilica and Palace stand on the Celian Hill in Rome on land that once belonged to the Roman family of the Laterani and was given to the Church by Constantine I* in the fourth century. Five councils regarded by the Catholic Church as ecumenical* were held at the Lateran Palace:

I (1123): Affirmed the Concordat of Worms (1122) as a resolution of the investiture* controversy, and dealt with numerous disciplinary matters.

II (1139): Ended a schism provoked by the election of the antipope Anacletus II in 1130. Declared marriage of clergy and religious invalid and addressed numerous other disciplinary matters.

III (1179): Ended a schism that extended from 1159 to 1178, in which three antipopes had opposed Pope Alexander III. Required a two-thirds majority of cardinals* for the election of a pope.

IV (1215): Called by Pope Innocent III*. Defined the doctrine of the eucharist*, using the word *transubstantiation* for the first time in an official document. Required Christians to receive the sacraments of penance* and the eucharist annually. Made preparations for a new crusade*, set for 1217. Condemned the doctrines of the Cathars* and the Waldenses* and set up rules for the suppression of heresy (these underlay the later inquisition*). Addressed many other disciplinary issues.

V (1512-1517): Called by Pope Julius II to condemn the work of a council held by some conciliarist* cardinals and bishops in Pisa in 1511 to 1512. Revoked Pragmatic Sanction of Bourges (1438), which had curbed papal power over the French church. Passed some reforming measures, but did little to deal with the abuses that led to the Protestant* Reformation, which began seven months afterward with the circulation of Martin Luther's *Ninety-Five Theses*.

LECTIONARY. A book containing the Scripture readings for mass*. The first lectionaries appeared in the early Middle Ages. By the thirteenth century they were absorbed into the missal*. The *Roman Missal* promulgated in 1570 and normative in the West until after Vatican Council II required two Scripture readings in each mass. The second was always from one of the gospels*, while the first was usually from the letters of Paul. The Old Testament was almost never read at mass. Vatican II called for a greater amount and range of Scripture reading in the liturgy (SC 35) (1963), and this was realized in the revised lectionary issued in 1969. Each Sunday* and feast day* mass now has three Scripture readings. The first is usually from the

Old Testament, otherwise from the Acts of the Apostles or the Book of Revelation. It is followed by a psalm to be recited or sung. The second is from one of the New Testament letters or the Book of Revelation. The third is from a gospel. The Sunday readings are on a three-year cycle, so that readings are drawn from a substantial part of the Bible. The gospel and second reading usually read through a biblical book in a "semicontinuous" way (sequential, with gaps), while the Old Testament reading is chosen to fit thematically with the gospel. Weekday masses have two readings: the second from the gospel, the first from any other part of Scripture. In "ordinary time," the first readings are on a two-year cycle, the gospels on a one-year cycle. Readings are semicontinuous in both cases. Weekday readings for Advent*, Lent*, and the Easter* season are on a one-year cycle. There are special readings (with various options) for the celebrations of saints and for other masses not mentioned above.

LECTOR (Lt "reader"). A minister whose primary responsibility is to read from the Scripture at liturgical celebrations. The title existed by the third century. By the fifth century, if not earlier, it was a "minor order" (*see* ORDER, SACRAMENT OF), to which men were ordained and which made them clerics*. In the Middle Ages, it became only a stage on the way to ordination as a priest*. In 1972, Pope Paul VI* made it a "ministry"* into which laymen were "installed," rather than an "order." The lector's duties include reading the scriptural selections other than the gospel at mass and leading the recitation of the responsorial psalm (*see* LECTIONARY). While only men may be officially installed as lectors, women may serve as lectors at mass.

LEGATE, PAPAL. The chief official representative of the pope in a country or other region. There are two principal kinds of papal legate: (1) an **apostolic delegate** represents the Holy See* to the local Church; (2) an **apostolic** (or **papal**) **nuncio**, in addition, serves as the chief diplomatic representative, or ambassador, of the Holy See (or Vatican City*) to the civil government of a country. According to a custom confirmed by the Congress of Vienna (1815), he is ordinarily the dean of the diplomatic corps in the country where he is accredited. An **apostolic pro-nuncio** to a country holds the title of ambassador but is not regarded in the country's civil law as the dean of the diplomatic corps. Papal legates were employed for various purposes throughout the Middle Ages. Nuncios in something like the modern sense date from the late fifteenth century. An apostolic delegate to the United States was appointed, against the initial opposition of the U.S. bishops, by Pope Leo XIII* in 1893. In 1984, the apostolic delegate was upgraded to an apostolic pro-nuncio.

LEGION OF MARY. An organization of laity dedicated to apostolic works. The Legion was founded by Frank Duff (1889-1980) in Dublin, Ireland, in 1921. It spread to the United States in 1931 and now exists throughout the world. Duff's inspirations included the spirituality of St. Louis de Montfort (1673-1716), who understood devotion to Mary to be the best route to union with Christ, and the work of the Society of Saint Vincent de Paul*. For the structure of the organization, he drew on the model of the ancient Roman Legion. A local group is a *praesidium*, and several praesidia in an area form a *curia*. Curiae are governed by a *comitium* and comitia by a *senatus*. The chief governing body is the international *concilium* in Dublin. Active members must be Catholics at least eighteen years old. They are obliged to attend weekly meetings and to do at least two hours of apostolic work a week. There are also junior members (ages ten through seventeen) and auxiliary members, who assist the Legion through reciting daily the prayers said at the weekly meetings. Legionaries perform a wide range of apostolic work, excluding only direct material assistance. Typical Legion activities include visitation of the sick and the unchurched, catechetical and informational work, transportation assistance, and any other work encouraged by the local pastor and approved by the bishop. Members take a special interest in fostering devotion to Mary, especially through praying the rosary*. There are more than a million active Legionaries throughout the world.

LENT (Middle Engl, "springtime"). The forty-day period of preparation for Easter*. The earliest records indicate only a two- to six-day period of fasting before the Easter Vigil. This may have combined with a tradition of a forty-day fast, observed in Egypt immediately after the Epiphany* in commemoration of Jesus' fast in the desert. By the middle of the fourth century, a forty-day fast starting with the sixth Sunday before Easter was in place in Rome. In the sixth century, the Wednesday through Saturday preceding the First Sunday of Lent were added to the fast, making forty days, excluding Sundays but including Holy Thursday, Good Friday, and Holy Saturday. Rites for the imposition of ashes on the first day of Lent as a penitential sign appeared by the tenth century; the practice was made general by Pope Urban II in 1091. Hence the day came to be known as **Ash Wednesday**.

When the catechumenate* developed in the third and fourth centuries, Lent became chiefly the period of final preparation for Easter baptism. The association of Lent with the catechumenate has been revived in the Rite of Christian Initiation of Adults (1972); its lenten liturgical stages are described in the article, CATECHUMENATE. With the rise of infant baptism and the decline of the catechumenate, Lent became primarily a penitential season. At Rome by the end of the fourth century, there was a ritual reconciliation of penitents* on Holy Thursday. In the fifth century, penitents may well have been publicly enrolled at the beginning of Lent.

Lent may be understood as a time of conversion* and preparation: catechumens for baptism, penitents for reconciliation* (though there is no longer a formal rite of lenten reconciliation), all Christians for renewal of life in Christ through the celebration of the Easter mysteries. Abstinence from meat is required on Ash Wednesday and the Fridays of Lent, while Ash Wednesday and Good Friday are days of fasting (*see* FAST AND ABSTINENCE). In the three-year cycle of the Sunday lectionary*, Year A contains gospel readings associated with the catechumenate, readings that may be used in other years when there are catechumens present. Gospels in Years B and C are addressed to the baptized, emphasizing the exaltation of Christ and the call to conversion, respectively.

Liturgically, Lent ends before the Mass of the Lord's Supper on Holy Thursday, which begins the Easter Triduum*. The last days of Lent, after the sixth Sunday, called Passion or Palm Sunday, are discussed in the entry, HOLY WEEK.

LEO I (THE GREAT), ST. Pope 440-461, Doctor of the Church*. Pope* at a time of political and religious disarray, he greatly augmented the authority of the papacy. He strongly asserted that supreme authority in the Church, given by Christ to Peter, was passed on through Peter to later bishops of Rome (popes), so that the pope should be seen as a personification of Peter. His authority was strengthened when his *Tome*, declaring Jesus Christ* to be "one person" in "two natures," human and divine, was accepted by the Council of Chalcedon* in 451 and used as the basis of its formula of orthodox faith against the monophysites*. "Peter has spoken through

Leo," the bishops at the council declared. Even so, Chalcedon's Canon 28 sought to establish Constantinople* as nearly the equal of Rome*; this Leo rejected. When the Empire in the West was near collapse, Leo's authority in the secular realm was shown when in 452 he dissuaded Attila the Hun from attacking Rome and in 455 he induced Gaiseric the Vandal to mitigate his sack of the city, sparing the Romans from fire, killing, and torture. His feast is celebrated on November 10.

LEO XIII, POPE (1878-1903) (Gioacchino Vincenzo Pecci, b. 1810). Pecci was born in Carpineto, south of Rome. After ordination in 1837, he entered the papal diplomatic service and served as governor of Benevento (1838-1841) and of Perugia (1841-1843) and as nuncio to Belgium (1843-1846). From 1846 to 1878 he was bishop of Perugia. As pope, he is best known for his encyclical, *Rerum novarum* (1891), which was the origin of modern Catholic social teaching*. *Rerum novarum* attacked both socialism* and capitalism* ("liberalism*"), as it then existed. He defended private property* but also the rights of workers to organize and to be paid a just wage (*see* LABOR) and the right of the state to intervene on workers' behalf. Leo was socially and politically conservative and fearful of revolution, but, unlike his predecessor Pius IX*, he believed the times called for an authoritative intervention of the Church on the side of the workers. Leo is also important for his promotion of Thomism*, especially in his encyclical, *Aeterni Patris* (1879). He gave cautious encouragement to Catholic use of new methods of biblical criticism* in *Providentissimus Deus* (1893), but then restricted biblical scholarship in 1902 by creating the Pontifical Biblical Commission. In 1899, his *Testem benevolentiae* censured "Americanism"*. He had a number of successes in international diplomacy but was disappointed in his attempts to reach a satisfactory resolution of the "Roman question" (the pope's loss of civil authority over Rome and the surrounding area).

LEX ORANDI, LEX CREDENDI (Lt "The law of praying is the law of believing"). This phrase perhaps originated in Prosper of Aquitaine's (ca. 390-ca. 463) *Legem credendi lex statuat supplicandi* ("Let the law of praying establish the law of believing"). Prosper's immediate context was an argument that the prayers in the Good Friday liturgy that those who lack faith be given it are evidence, against the "Semi-Pelagians" (*see* PELAGIUS), that God's grace* is necessary for faith* to begin to exist. Generalized, the point is that Christian liturgy* and prayer* are a "theological source," in that one can ascertain, from Christian practice in prayer, what it is that the Church believes but perhaps has not articulated clearly in doctrine* or theology*. For example, Christians were praying to Jesus* as to God before a clear theology of the divinity of Jesus was developed. Another example is Augustine's* theology of original sin*, which is based in the already-existing practice of infant baptism*.

LIBERAL ARTS (Lt *artes liberales*, "subjects of study proper to free persons"). An educational tradition growing out of ancient rhetoric and central to Christian education from antiquity to the present time. The term *liberal arts* is found as early as Cicero (106-43 B.C.). Varro (116-27 B.C.) codified and described nine liberal arts, but it was the listing of seven liberal arts by Martianus Capella (early fifth century) that governed medieval education. The seven arts were grammar, rhetoric, and dialectic (later called the *trivium* [three ways]); and arithmetic, geometry, astronomy, music [theory] (later called the *quadrivium* [four ways]). The tradition was Christianized in the works of Cassiodorus (ca. 485-580), Isidore of Seville (ca. 560-636), and Alcuin (ca. 735-804). In the early Middle Ages, grammar and rhetoric were most of what survived, but there was a revival of the study of the seven arts in the eleventh and twelfth centuries. In the medieval universities*, completion of the arts curriculum preceded entry into the higher faculties of theology, law, or medicine. The rediscovery of Aristotle* in the twelfth and thirteenth centuries led to the domination of the arts curriculum by Aristotelian philosophy, logic in particular, driving out literary studies. The conflicts over Aristotelianism (*see under* ARISTOTLE) that flared in the late thirteenth century were largely battles between the arts faculties and the theology faculties.

The humanists* of the Italian Renaissance*, beginning with Petrarch (1304-1374), reacted against scholasticism* and its domination by logic. They revived literary studies of the Greek and Roman classics and made them central to the curriculum. The liberal arts program of the humanists gradually spread throughout most of Europe, where it gained the support of both Protestants and Catholics. Within Catholicism, Jesuits*, who founded large numbers of schools, were particularly important in spreading it, through the influence of their *Ratio studiorum* (1599), which called for a program of humanistic literary studies leading up to the study of scholastic philosophy. The curriculum of most of the older Catholic liberal arts colleges in the United States, many of which were founded by Jesuits, was initially patterned upon the Jesuit ideal.

Since the Enlightenment*, there has been a tension within Western education between two ideals, both called "liberal [arts] education." One, deriving from the humanists, emphasizes a study of a normative body of classics and aims to inculcate virtues appropriate for citizenship. The other, deriving from the Enlightenment, instead exalts the freedom of individual reason and calls for critical scrutiny of supposedly normative traditions. John Henry Newman's* *The Idea of a University* (1858), a major statement within the Catholic liberal arts tradition, attempts something of a synthesis between them. Newman envisioned the goal of a liberal education as the cultivation of the powers of the intellect, which equips it for any specialized field of study. To Newman the study of classic texts is central to liberal education, but not the whole of it. Catholic liberal arts institutions in the United States tend to look to Newman in efforts to formulate their mission. Still, the humanist and Enlightenment ideals of liberal education sit together somewhat uneasily in most contemporary conceptions of liberal arts education, Catholic and otherwise.

LIBERALISM. A term, first used in the early nineteenth century, which has a broad range of meanings in politics, economics, theology, and elsewhere. Generally speaking, liberalism places a higher value on individual freedom and a lower value on tradition and authority than whatever position it is opposing. Today, in informal speech, one might call a Catholic a "liberal" if, for instance, he or she is inclined to dissent* from traditional positions on controversial issues, such as sexual morality*, or to favor changes in long-standing practices in the Church.

Nineteenth-century political liberalism promoted the ideals of the Enlightenment*, such as republican or democratic government, rights to life, liberty, and property, an expanded right to vote, freedom of speech and religion, and movement toward social equality. Economic liberalism favored a "laissez-faire" free-market economy, with minimal regulation. In the twentieth century, political liberalism has placed more emphasis on equality of opportunity and on positive human rights* to food, shelter, education, etc., and thus to favor a stronger role for government than did nineteenth-century liberalism (whose twentieth-century proponents are sometimes called "conservatives"). In the early and middle nineteenth century, a group of "liberal Catholics," led by Felicité de Lammenais and Charles de Montalembert, urged the compatibility of Catholicism and liberal institutions such as parliamentary government and religious freedom*. Their ideas were censured by Pope Gregory XVI in 1832 and condemned in general terms in the *Syllabus of Errors** of Pope Pius IX* in 1864, which declared that the pope should never reconcile himself to "liberalism." These popes, like many others in the Church, could see in liberalism only the excesses of the French Revolution*. The social encyclicals *Rerum novarum* (1891) of Pope Leo XIII* and *Quadragesimo anno* (1931) of Pope Pius XI* continued to condemn economic liberalism, in the sense of an unrestrained free market economy that impoverished the working classes (*see* CAPITALISM). Twentieth-century Catholic social thought has aligned itself with twentieth-century political liberalism in many respects, as is evident from the list of human rights* with which the encyclical *Pacem in terris* (1963) of Pope John XXIII* opens. In 1965, Vatican Council II endorsed one of the central tenets that the Church had opposed in nineteenth-century liberalism, namely religious freedom.

LIBERATION THEOLOGY. A theological movement that began in Latin America in the 1960s. Its starting point is the poverty and suffering of the great majority of people in Latin America, while wealth is concentrated in the hands of a few. Leading figures have been Gustavo Gutiérrez (1928-) of Peru, Juan Luis Segundo (1925-1996) of Uruguay, Jon Sobrino (1938-) of El Salvador, and Leonardo Boff (1938-) of Brazil.

Gutiérrez defined the method of liberation theology as "critical reflection on Christian praxis in the light of the Word." *Praxis*, a Greek word meaning "action," comes to liberation theology from Aristotle* via Karl Marx. It refers to the mutual influence of action and reflection. The "action" in question is all efforts to live out Christian faith, but chiefly action toward transforming social structures in favor of the poor and dispossessed. Liberation theologians reflect especially on the activities of the base Christian communities* in Latin America. In reflection on the causes of poverty and oppression, liberation theologians often use Marxist* social analysis, but they do not accept Marxist atheism and materialism. Reading the Bible through the lens of the struggle for justice, they have rediscovered God's advocacy of justice* and his partisanship of the poor and outcast in the Old

Testament (*see* OPTION FOR THE POOR). They lay particular stress on the role of God in the Exodus as liberator of the oppressed Hebrew people (Ex 3.7-8). Likewise, they emphasize Jesus' solidarity with the poor and outcast in the Gospels. These biblical images then guide their practice as disciples* of Jesus. "Liberation" is for them a very broad theme, including not only the establishment of political and social justice and freedom from oppression but also liberation from sin*. In speaking of sin, they tend to emphasize "social sin," embodied in unjust social structures and engendering further individual sin. Following Vatican Council II, the liberation theologians see continuity between justice and liberation in this world and the fullness of the kingdom of God* in the next (*see* ESCHATOLOGY).

The prehistory of liberation theology includes Vatican II's identification with the aspirations of humanity, especially of the poor (GS 1), as well as the papal social encyclicals* of the 1960s. Liberation theology also drew on Catholic involvement in movements for social change in Latin America in the 1950s and 1960s. In meetings of theologians preparing for the Second General Conference of Latin American Bishops (CELAM) at Medellín, Colombia, in 1968, Gutiérrez first used the term "theology of liberation." The documents of that conference put the Church, formerly closely allied with the dominant classes, on the side of social change and justice for the poor, saying, "The church—the people of God—will lend its support to the downtrodden of every social class so that they might come to know their rights and how to make use of them." The major works that shaped liberation theology appeared in the 1970s, especially Gutiérrez's *A Theology of Liberation* (1971).

Official Church reaction to liberation theology has been mixed. Some Church documents, for instance, the 1971 Synod of Bishops document *Justice in the World* (*see* JUSTICE), have used the language and endorsed the emphases of liberation theology. Pope John Paul II* has employed some themes of liberation theology in his social encyclicals. But two Instructions from the Vatican Congregation for the Doctrine of the Faith* have been cautious and somewhat critical. The first, "Instruction on Certain Aspects of the Theology of Liberation" (1984) confirmed the general aims of liberation theology and the legitimacy of the concept of "liberation," but criticized unnamed liberation theologians for reduction of faith to politics, excessive use of Marxist analysis (particularly the concept of "class struggle"), and disdain for the hierarchical structure of the Church. The second,

"Instruction on Christian Freedom and Liberation" (1986), took a more affirmative tone, asserting the need to change unjust structures while insisting on the primacy of spiritual over political liberation. CELAM's Third General Conference, at Puebla, Mexico, in 1979, confirmed the teaching of Medellín but elected Bishop Alfonso López Trujillo, a determined opponent of liberation theology, as President of CELAM. And in the two cases in which liberation theology has actually had direct influence in the government of a Latin American country, namely, Nicaragua under the Sandinista regime (1979-1990) and Haiti under President Jean-Bertrand Aristide (1991-1996) (a former Catholic priest), Rome has sided with the opposition.

Liberation theology has spread from Latin America to Asia and Africa. In North America, black theology and feminist* theology originated independently from Latin American liberation theology but have been influenced by it, and it by them.

LIGUORI, ALPHONSUS DE, ST. (1696-1787). The most influential Catholic theologian of the eighteenth century. Born near Naples, he became a lawyer but left the law for the priesthood in 1726. In 1732, he founded the Redemptorist order. From 1762 to 1775 he was bishop of Sant' Agata dei Goti. He wrote extensively, especially in moral theology* and spirituality*. His systematic *Moral Theology,* first published 1753 to 1755, sought a middle course between the rigorism of the Jansenists* and the excessive laxity ("laxism") of some teachers of the seventeenth century. It dominated the tradition of moral theology into the middle of the twentieth century. His spiritual writings, of which the best known is *The Glories of Mary* (1750), emphasized devotion to Mary (he held her to be the "mediatress of grace," though Jesus is the sole "mediator of justice") and to the eucharist. They had a major impact on the piety of the nineteenth century. He was canonized in 1839 and declared a Doctor of the Church* in 1871. His feast is celebrated on August 1.

LIMBO (Lt *limbus,* "border of a garment"). In medieval theology, a state without suffering but also without the beatific vision* experienced by children who died unbaptized (the *limbus puerorum,* "limbo of children") and by virtuous pagans of antiquity (the *limbus patrum,* "limbo of the fathers"). Against some associated with the Pelagian* movement, who held that infants who died unbaptized went to a "middle place" of happiness, Augustine* insisted that all who died

unbaptized were damned due to original sin* and suffered in hell*.
Abelard* and Peter Lombard* reduced the suffering of the unbaptized
to the "darkness" of separation from God, and Thomas Aquinas*
mitigated it still further into a natural happiness. Limbo was standard
Catholic teaching into the twentieth century, but never defined as
doctrine nor universally accepted. It has disappeared from
contemporary theology and Church teaching because of an increased
emphasis on God's will to save all people. A variety of explanations for
the salvation of the unbaptized have been proposed, for instance, a
moment of final choice at death (K. Rahner*), but none has won
general acceptance. An attitude of trust in God's mercy for the
unbaptized now prevails, however. *See also* BAPTISM, SALVATION
OUTSIDE THE CHURCH.

LITANY (Gk *litaneia*, "supplication"). A form of prayer in which a
leader says or sings a series of petitions, to which there is a set form
of response. Examples in the mass* are the *Kyrie eleison* ("Lord, have
mercy") in the opening penitential rite, the Prayer of the Faithful, and
the "Lamb of God" (Agnus Dei) before communion. Litanies first
appeared in Christian worship in the East in the fourth century,
spreading from Antioch* to Constantinople* and thence to Rome*.
They became the principal form of congregational participation in the
Greek liturgy. The Litany of the Saints is the oldest litany, with
antecedents back to the fourth century, and the most important in the
Roman Rite today. It is part of the liturgies for the Easter Vigil and for
ordinations, as well as of the Commendation of the Dying (*see*
DEATH) and the Forty Hours Devotion*. From the fifth century until
1969, the Litany of the Saints was said along with a procession on the
Feast of St. Mark (April 25) and on the Rogation Days (from Lt
rogare, "to pray"; the three days before the Feast of the Ascension*).
These were called the "Greater Litany" and the "Lesser Litanies,"
respectively. The Litany of Loreto, or Marian Litany, invokes Mary*
under many titles, with the response, "Pray for us." It is first attested
at Loreto in 1588 but draws on much older traditions, back to the
eighth century. Other litanies include those of the Holy Name, the
Sacred Heart, St. Joseph, and the Precious Blood.

LITURGICAL MOVEMENT. A movement, lasting from 1833 to
Vatican Council II*, that led to the complete reform of the liturgy* in
the Catholic Church (there was a parallel movement among

Protestants). The movement began in 1833, when Dom Prosper Guéranger (1805-1875) reestablished Benedictine monasticism* in France after its suppression during the French Revolution*, founding the monastery of St. Peter at Solesmes. Guéranger believed that monastic life should center in the mass* and the major feasts of the liturgical calendar* and that the monks should use Gregorian chant* in worship. Solesmes became a center of scholarship in liturgy and chant, and the movement spread to other Benedictine houses in Europe and then to a wider public. Liturgical scholarship continued into the twentieth century, carried on by Odo Casel (1886-1948), Josef Jungmann (1889-1956), and others. Once purified from Guéranger's romantic medievalism, it provided solid foundations for a claim that the contemporary liturgy—too often reduced to a clerical performance before a passive lay audience—was an aberration from the great traditions of the Church. A second stage of the movement began in 1909, when Lambert Beauduin (1873-1960), a monk of Mont-César, Belgium, joined liturgical scholarship with pastoral ministry, expressing the themes of the liturgical movement in popular language and using mass media. Virgil Michel (1890-1948), a monk of St. John's Abbey, Collegeville, Minnesota, brought Beauduin's ideas to the United States, where he founded the journal *Orate Fratres*, now *Worship*, and strove to join liturgical renewal with social reform. The liturgical movement spread by means of national and international conferences, especially International Liturgical Study Weeks in Europe and Liturgical Weeks, held annually in the United States from 1940 to 1968. Rome responded slowly to the movement, making a number of small changes and gradually accepting congregational participation in liturgy. A watershed was the approval of a revised Easter Vigil liturgy in 1951, followed by a reform of Holy Week* in 1955. In 1958, John XXIII*, who sympathized with the movement, became pope. Most of the leading figures in the liturgical movement at the time were involved in the Second Vatican Council or in the commissions that implemented its reforms. The Council's *Constitution on the Sacred Liturgy* (1963) and the resulting reforms realized nearly all of the immediate aims of the liturgical movement, which thus ended as movement. There remains, however, the task of embodying in the actual liturgy, as prayed in local churches, the aims that are reflected in the new liturgical texts, and there is a new challenge of inculturation* of the liturgy outside the liturgical movement's context of Western Europe and North America.

LITURGY (Gk *leitourgia*, "public work," from *laos*, "people," and *ergon*, "work"). The official, public prayer* of the Church. It is official in that it takes place under the supervision of the local bishop*, who is understood to be the principal liturgical celebrant in the diocese*, and in forms that are approved by Rome, representing the whole Church. It is public in that it normally takes place in an assembly of the faithful, though there are limit cases, such as private recitation of the liturgy of the hours*. According to Vatican Council II*, it is the "high point towards which the activity of the Church is directed and ... the source from which all its power flows out" (SC 10), though it is not the whole of the Church's activity (SC 9). Liturgical action is Christ's own act as well as the Church's: "Every liturgical celebration ... is the act of Christ the priest and his body which is the Church" and therefore surpasses all other activities of the Church (SC 7).

In ancient Greek, any public work, such as a festival or the erection of a building, could be called a *leitourgia*. The term is used in the Septuagint (*see* BIBLE) to designate Israel's ritual worship of God. Hebrews 8.6 uses the term to mean Jesus' sacrifice as high priest. The early Christians used it to mean public worship generally, but by the fourth century its meaning was limited to the eucharistic liturgy. In the East it still has this restricted meaning, while in the West it fell out of use altogether until revived in the sixteenth century in a general sense.

The eucharistic liturgy (*see* EUCHARIST, MASS) is the central act of the Church. Other liturgical rituals are the rites for the other six sacraments* (see articles for individual sacraments), the installation of acolytes* and lectors*, religious profession (*see* RELIGIOUS LIFE), the consecration of a virgin*, the dedication of a church, viaticum*, the commendation of the dead (*see* FUNERAL), the liturgy of the hours*, and the blessings in the Book of Blessings. Many of these events sanctify particular events in the life of the Church or its members, while others give a sacred ordering to time in general. There is a weekly cycle, centered in the celebration of the eucharist on Sunday*, and an annual cycle, centered on the celebration of the Church's great mysteries at Christmas* and Easter*. *See* LITURGICAL CALENDAR.

Different liturgical traditions developed in the various centers of Christian activity. In the East, there are the East and West Syrian traditions, the Byzantine, the Armenian, and the Alexandrian, which is divided into the Coptic and the Ethiopic. These traditions are preserved in the Eastern Catholic Churches*, the Assyrian Church of the East*, and the Eastern* and Oriental Orthodox* churches. The Roman tradition has predominated in the West, but there were early distinct traditions in North Africa, Gaul (the "Gallican Rite"), Spain (the "Mozarabic Rite"), Milan (the "Ambrosian Rite"), and the Celtic lands. After the Council of Trent* (1545-1563), a form of the Roman rite was adopted as the standard to be followed everywhere in the Western Church (with a few variations for ancient local usages). The Protestant churches*, beginning from the Roman rite, developed their own distinctive traditions, for instance, the Lutheran and Anglican. In 1963, Vatican Council II called for a reform of the liturgy in order to foster the "full, conscious and active" participation that "is demanded by the nature of the liturgy itself" (SC 14). It departed from the uniformity of the period after Trent by calling for adaptation of the liturgy to the traditions of different peoples (SC 37-40). After the Council, these principles governed a thorough reform of Catholic liturgy, completed in 1978.

LOGOS (Gk, "word, speech, reason"). The Word of God, second person of the Trinity*, God incarnate in Jesus Christ*. The classic biblical source for this term is the Prologue to the Gospel of John (Jn 1.1-18). The background of the term *logos* in John's prologue is chiefly the OT concepts of the word of God, given to the prophets (e.g., Hos 1.1), and of the personified Wisdom of God (e.g., Proverbs 8-9). *Logos* was also prominent in Greek philosophy, beginning with Heraclitus (sixth century B.C.), who saw it as the principle of order in the flux of the world. It was very important in Stoicism* as the divine cosmic Reason. Biblical and philosophical uses of the term were conjoined by the Jewish thinker Philo (ca. 20 B.C.-A.D. 50), then by the Christian apologists* of the second century, especially Justin Martyr*, finally by the Alexandrian theologians of the third century, Clement and Origen*. This combined heritage was the background of the fourth-century debates over the status of the *logos* (*see* ARIANISM, TRINITY). The common meaning is well expressed by J. D. G. Dunn, "Christ reveals the character of the power behind the world."

LONERGAN, BERNARD J. F. (1904-1984). Canadian philosopher and theologian. Lonergan was born in Buckingham, Quebec, and entered the Jesuits* in 1922. He was ordained a priest in 1936 and afterward studied at the Gregorian University in Rome, where he earned a licentiate in 1937 and completed work for a doctorate in 1940 (though he was not awarded the degree until 1946). He taught in Jesuit seminaries in Canada from 1940 to 1953, at the Gregorian from 1953 to 1965, and at Regis College, Ontario, from 1965 to 1971. After a year as Stillman Professor at Harvard, he concluded his academic career at Boston College. His first significant published writings were studies of Thomas Aquinas*. He also published textbooks on the Trinity* and Christology*. But he is best known for *Insight* (1957) and *Method in Theology* (1972). *Insight* put forward a theory of knowledge based in the implications of the four "transcendental precepts": "Be attentive," "Be intelligent," "Be reasonable," and "Be responsible," corresponding to the four levels of experiencing, understanding, judging, and deciding. From there Lonergan developed a metaphysics that argued to the existence of God* as the "unrestricted act of understanding" that makes possible the intelligibility of the world.

In *Method*, Lonergan understood theology as the mediation between a religious tradition and a culture. It comprises eight "functional specialties," corresponding to the four levels of consciousness mentioned above, once applied to the retrieval of the tradition, and once to the reflection on its significance and value in a culture. These eight are: research, interpretation, history, dialectic; foundations, doctrines, systematics, communications. Lonergan distinguished the "classical" notion of culture, which presupposed a single unchanging, universal, normative culture, from the "empirical" or "historically conscious" notion, wherein there are many cultures, changing over the course of time, so that new mediations of religious tradition are always needed (*see* HERMENEUTICS).

In his last years, Lonergan returned to a project that he had begun in the 1930s, a work of economic theory analyzing the circulation of money, goods, and services as a result of human understanding and free choices. This work, which exists in numerous incomplete recensions, has never been published in full.

LOVE. Love is at the very center of the meaning and message of Jesus. The greatest commandments, according to Jesus in the synoptic gospels, those on which the whole law and prophets depend and which are the way to eternal life, are to love God with one's whole heart, soul, mind, and strength and to love one's neighbor as oneself (Mt 22.34-40, Mk 12.28-34, Lk 10.25-28). In John's gospel, Jesus' commandment is for his disciples to love one another as Jesus has loved them, which in turn is how the Father has loved him (Jn 13.34,

15.9). The gospels' emphasis on love focuses rather than contradicts the OT. Both of the "great commandments" are from the OT (Dt 6.5, Lv 19.18), which portrays God as a faithful lover to his people (Hos 1-3). In the synoptics, especially Luke, Jesus' parables show what the character of the Father's love is (Lk 15.11-32) and what the extent of our love of neighbor ought to be (Lk 10.29-37). Love of neighbor must extend to those whom we would normally exclude (e.g., the Samaritan of Lk 10.29-37) and even, in imitation of the Father's love, to our enemies (Mt 5.43-48). Jesus' own actions model such a love, especially in his personal availability to the outcasts and outsiders of his society. Ultimately, as John's gospel brings out, it is his death on the cross that shows the extent of his love (Jn 15.13) and of the Father's (Jn 3.15).

God's love for us, our love for God, our love for one another all form a unity, as the Johannine writings urge, and the basis of it is that love is what God is: "God is love and whoever remains in love remains in God and God in him" (1 Jn 4.16). John links remaining in God's love with the Holy Spirit* (1 Jn 4.13). For Paul also, "The love of God has been poured out into our hearts through the holy Spirit that has been given to us" (Rom 5.5). Paul describes what our love should be in 1 Corinthians 13; without love, he says, all the other spiritual gifts are of no value.

The theology of the Trinity* understands God* as a community of love. On the basis of Romans 5.5, Augustine* and Thomas Aquinas* speak of the Holy Spirit as the love whereby the Father and the Son love each other. While Augustine and Peter Lombard* identify the love (*caritas,* **charity**) that dwells in us through God's grace* with the Holy Spirit, Aquinas holds that charity is a created virtue* in us, though one that surpasses our natural powers. Thus it, along with faith* and hope*, is a theological virtue*. By supernatural charity, which is a "friendship with God," we love God for God's own sake, without any reference to ourselves. This very act, says Thomas, includes love of our neighbor, for God's sake (ST 1.23-25).

The word regularly used in the Septuagint and the NT for "love" is *agapē* (verb *agapaō*). In Greek, it can be contrasted with *philia,* a term also used in the Bible, meaning the love that is characteristic of human friendship, and with *erōs,* the love of desire, especially sexual desire. Some, notably the Lutheran theologian Anders Nygren, have argued for a sharp contrast between Christian *agapē* (or *caritas*), understood as pure and other-regarding, and *erōs,* love that involves desire. If, however, as most contemporary theologians argue, God's grace* is somehow universally present, including in our ordinary willings and desirings, there may be more continuity among the different kinds of love. A special challenge in recent times for the Catholic tradition has been to integrate human sexual desire into a spirituality of love (*see* MARRIAGE, SEXUAL MORALITY).

LYONS. City in France on the Rhône River. It was the site of two ecumenical councils*. The **FIRST COUNCIL OF LYONS** (1245) was called by Pope Innocent IV to deal with the Emperor Frederick II, who had seized much territory belonging to the Papal States. The council excommunicated and deposed Frederick, but he continued to wage war in Italy until his death in 1250. The **SECOND COUNCIL OF LYONS** (1274), called by Pope Gregory X, effected a short-lived reunion of the Greek and Latin churches. The Greek Emperor Michael VIII Paleologus, fearing that Charles of Anjou would reestablish the Latin Empire in Constantinople (*see* CRUSADES), sought protection by way of religious union with the West. The Greek legates proclaimed acceptance of the Roman faith, including the primacy of the pope* and the *filioque*, but requested the continued use of their own liturgy. The union was not widely accepted in the East and did not outlast Michael's death in 1282 (*see* EASTERN ORTHODOX CHURCHES).

M

MAGISTERIUM (Lt *magister*, "master, teacher"). Authority to teach. Medieval theologians, Thomas Aquinas* for instance, spoke of a magisterium, or teaching authority, belonging to teachers of theology in the universities* and a magisterium belonging to bishops*. This usage persisted into the twentieth century in theological textbooks, but elsewhere "magisterium" came to be limited to the teaching authority of bishops and especially of the pope*. Sometimes, particularly with the definite article, "the," "magisterium" refers not to this authority but to the bishops and pope as its bearers. The magisterium of the bishops and pope is based in the authority Jesus gave the apostles to teach in his name (e.g., Lk 10.16) and in the status of the bishops as successors of the apostles (*see* APOSTOLICITY). According to Vatican Council II, "The task of authentically [authoritatively] interpreting the word of God, whether in its written form or in that of tradition, has been entrusted only to those charged with the Church's ongoing teaching function [magisterium], whose authority is exercised in the name of Jesus Christ. This teaching function is not above the Word of God, but stands at its service ..." (DV 10). Under some circumstances, the bishops and especially the pope, in their authoritative teaching, exercise the gift of infallibility*, which is bestowed on the Church by the Holy Spirit*. When a bishop is teaching in communion with the pope, even though not infallibly, "the faithful ought to concur with their bishop's judgment concerning faith and morals which he delivers in the name of Christ, and they are to adhere to this with a religious assent of the mind," and this applies especially to the teaching of the pope (LG 25) (*see* DISSENT). *See also* AUTHORITY IN THE CHURCH.

MANICHAEISM. A religion founded by the Persian prophet Mani (216-277). Raised in a Jewish-Christian sect known as the Elkasaites, Mani, at the age of twenty-four, received a call to preach his own religion, which combined elements of Gnostic* Christianity, Zoroastrianism, and Buddhism*. He won influential followers in the Persian court but was eventually executed by the emperor. From Persia, his religion spread east to China, where adherents were encountered as late as the seventeenth century, and west into the Roman Empire, where it presented itself as a form of Christianity. Manichaeism was especially influential in North Africa; there its most famous adherent was Augustine*, who was a "Hearer" (see below) of the sect from 373 to 382.

Mani posited two eternal principles, Light and Darkness. The realm of Darkness invaded the kingdom of Light and entrapped part of it. The universe as we see it is a mechanism for freeing the particles of Light trapped in Darkness. Christ was incarnate in the whole universe as the bringer of Light and liberator from Darkness; as the "suffering Jesus," he was crucified throughout creation. The Manichaean ethical code, to be practiced in full by the "Elect" of the sect, was based on the freeing of Light from Darkness. The Elect were to avoid sexual relations and procreation, which trapped Light in Darkness, were to avoid the killing and eating of animals (which contained light), and were to eat the most light-bearing, brightly colored vegetables. Upon death, the Elect would return to the kingdom of Light. A lower grade of Manichaeans were the "Hearers," who were obliged to keep part of the Manichaean code and to support the Elect; these could hope to be reborn as Elect.

Manichaeism died out in the west in the sixth or seventh century, but its ideas (or similar ideas) gained fresh currency in such medieval heresies as those of the Bogomils and Cathars*.

MARCION (d. ca. 160). Native of Sinope on the Black Sea, a prosperous shipowner and son of a bishop, he came to Rome around 140 and gained influence in the local church. Excommunicated in 144, he founded his own church, which remained influential for more than a century. He taught a radical distinction between Christian faith and Scriptures, on the one hand, and Judaism and the Old Testament on the other. According to Marcion, the God of the OT is an inferior demiurge, not the supreme God, and the OT shows him to be ignorant and malicious. The material world, which he created, is evil. In contrast, Jesus came to reveal the supreme God, a God of love rather than the OT's God of law, and to free his people from the power of the creator. Marcion's Christology was a form of docetism*: Jesus was not born of a woman and did not truly have a material body; his passion and death were brought about by the creator. Marcion's thought had much affinity with that of Gnosticism* but differed from the latter in that he had no elaborate speculations on the creation of the world and the fall of the soul nor a doctrine of secret, saving knowledge. Marcion was the first to draw a list of the canon of Scripture (*see* BIBLE). He excluded the entire OT as well as those parts of the NT that showed excessive influence of the OT; this left him with the Gospel of Luke and ten of the letters of Paul, but even these he felt obliged to purge of Judaizing passages, which he claimed were interpolated. Marcion's canon was a primary impetus toward the establishment of a canon of scripture on the part of the catholic churches.

MARITAIN, JACQUES (1882-1973). French philosopher, one of the leading Catholic intellectuals of the twentieth century. Maritain was born in Paris and baptized Protestant. He studied at the Sorbonne, where he met Raïssa Oumansoff (1883-1960), a Russian Jewish émigrée whom he married in 1904 and who was his intellectual and spiritual partner for the rest of her life. In 1906, influenced by the novelist Léon Bloy, Jacques and Raïssa became Catholics. Around 1908, Maritain began to study Thomas Aquinas*, whose thought was to guide his intellectual life from then on. Maritain taught at the Institut Catholique de Paris from 1914 to 1939. He spent the years of World War II in New York. From 1945 to 1948 he was French ambassador to the Vatican. Maritain then taught at Princeton, retiring in 1952 but remaining in Princeton till 1960. The Maritains then returned to Paris, where Raïssa soon died. Jacques spent the rest of his life with the Little Brothers of Jesus in Toulouse, formally joining them in 1971.

Maritain believed that only Thomism* could remedy the "anthropocentric humanism" of the modern world, the result of the ideas of Luther, Descartes, Rousseau, and Kant. In *The Degrees of Knowledge* (1932), Maritain distinguished scientific knowledge, metaphysical knowledge, and suprarational knowledge, which leads to God. A true or *Integral Humanism* (1936) must be open to the transcendent. Besides religion, art is for Maritain a means of such openness. Maritain is best known for his work in political philosophy, where he developed a theory of human rights*, based on an understanding of human beings as persons in community, not as isolated individuals. He was one of the architects of the 1948 United Nations Declaration of Human Rights, and his thought also influenced the social teaching* of the popes and Vatican Council II. Nevertheless, he believed that Catholic thought in the period of the council failed adequately to preserve the distinction between the world and the transcendent kingdom of God*, and his last major work, *The Peasant of the Garonne* (1967), was an impassioned attack on the trends he perceived in contemporary Catholic thinking.

MARRIAGE. Two texts in the initial pages of the Bible have been central to the Catholic understanding of marriage: the command to the first humans to "be fruitful and multiply" (Gn 1.28) and the statement that a husband and wife become "one flesh" (Gn 2.24). No OT passage rejects marriage, and most treat it favorably, especially where it is presented as an image of God's relationship with Israel (e.g., Is 54, 62.1-5). The clearest teaching of Jesus on marriage is his prohibition of divorce*. He cites Gn 2.24 in support of this teaching (Mk 10.7-8, Mt 19.5). Some NT texts express a preference for celibacy (e.g., 1 Cor 7.7-8) or depict marriage as an obstacle to the demands of discipleship* (e.g., Lk 18.29). Other NT texts, directed toward a more settled Christian Church rather than wandering missionaries, Christianize the "household codes" of ancient society and thus express a favorable view of marriage and family life. The most extensive of these is Eph 5.21-33, which has the added importance of viewing the relation of husband to wife as an image of the relation of Jesus to the Church.

This passage later became foundational to the conception of marriage as a sacrament*, but marriage was long considered essentially a civil affair, and there were no required ecclesiastical rites for it. The Fathers of the Church* wrote relatively little about marriage but defended it against Gnostic* and Manichaean* rejections of it. Augustine*, writing around A.D. 401, identified the goods of marriage as faithfulness between husband and wife, offspring, and *sacramentum* or symbolic value, signifying "the unity of us all made subject to God, which shall be hereafter in one heavenly city" (*The Good of Marriage* 18.21).

Liturgical wedding ceremonies developed in the sixth and seventh centuries. In the East, this led to the position that a priest's blessing was necessary for a valid marriage. In the West, marriage continued to be a matter between families. It was disputed in medieval times whether the marriage came into being through consent or sexual intercourse. The eventual conclusion of medieval scholastics was that marriage was initiated by the consent of the couple but "consummated" by sexual intercourse. Church wedding ceremonies became widespread in the eleventh century. In the twelfth century, marriage was included in the list of the Church's sacraments. Sacraments were said to be instituted by Christ, but as Christ clearly did not institute marriage, the scholastics argued that he instituted it as sacrament by elevating it to be a sign of his union with the Church. Duns Scotus* was the first to contend that the ministers of this sacrament were the couple themselves. This remains the official position in the Roman Rite, while in the Eastern Rites the priest is the minister of the sacrament. To curb secret marriages, the Council of Trent* mandated that marriages be contracted in the presence of a priest (as official witness of the Church) and two other witnesses. Against some of the Protestant* Reformers, it strongly affirmed the sacramentality and indissolubility of marriage.

Although Catholic treatments of marriage did not completely overlook the importance of affection between the partners, the primary good of marriage was understood as the procreation and education of offspring. This was stated in the 1917 Code of Canon Law. Yet in the West from the eighteenth century onward, the ideal of affection and romantic love in marriage became more prominent, and in the early twentieth century it entered Catholic theology, especially through the work of Herbert Doms. The most important recent treatment of marriage in Church documents is in Vatican Council II's *Pastoral Constitution on the Church in the Modern World* (1965). The Council understands marriage primarily as a "covenant ... in which spouses give themselves to each other and accept each other" (GS 48). Married couples "help and serve each other in their intimate union of persons and activities" (GS 48). "Of their nature marriage and married love are directed towards the begetting and bringing up of children" (GS 50). In the 1983 Code of Canon Law, covenant language replaces the treatment of marriage as a "contract."

The "Rite of Marriage" was revised in 1969 to reflect the Council's emphasis on increased participation in the liturgy*. It contains an entrance rite, a liturgy of the word, which provides many options for readings and encourages the couple to make the choice, a rite of marriage proper (including declaration of consent and blessing and exchange of rings), general intercessions, a nuptial blessing, and a conclusion rite. It may be done in the context of a mass (a **nuptial mass**), in which case a liturgy of the eucharist, including the nuptial blessing, follows the general intercessions. The officiating witness to a marriage does not need to be a priest but may be a deacon* or a designated layperson. Permission may be granted for a non-Catholic minister to serve as the officiating witness in cases of marriage between a Catholic and a non-Catholic Christian.

A marriage is considered sacramentally valid if it is contracted by a baptized person, if there is genuine consent on the part of both partners, if there is no impediment (canon law lists many impediments; examples include close blood relation between the partners and already-existing valid marriage on the part of one or both partners), and if the proper form of marriage ceremony is followed. Where one or more of these factors is lacking, a decree of nullity may be issued (*see* ANNULMENT).

MARRIAGE ENCOUNTER. A movement that aims to strengthen Christian marriages by bringing couples together for a weekend program focused on developing their ability to communicate with one another. Marriage Encounter grew out of the work of Father Gabriel Calvo in Spain, who began a series of conferences for married couples in 1952. It came to the United States in 1967, under the auspices of the Christian Family Movement, and has spread to all six inhabited continents. In 1971, the American movement split into what are now National Marriage Encounter and Worldwide Marriage Encounter. Differences include Worldwide Marriage Encounter's emphasis on "daily dialogue," a communication technique taught during the weekend, and on the formation of Marriage Encounter support communities. Both groups are predominantly Catholic in membership and inspiration, but Worldwide Marriage Encounter weekends are presented solely by Catholic couples and priests, while National Marriage Encounter weekends may be presented by couples and ministers of other faiths. Worldwide Marriage Encounter, however, has developed separate "expressions" for a number of Protestant churches. Marriage Encounter exists not only to improve couples' relations with each other but to strengthen their service to others. In some areas it has been an agency of renewal within parishes and in the Church at large.

MARTYR (Gk *martyros*, "witness"). One who is put to death for the sake of his or her Christian faith. *Martyros*, a common Greek word for "witness," acquired this technical Christian sense in the second century. To be a martyr, one's death must be voluntarily accepted, but it may not be directly sought. Death need not be for the sake of Christian faith as such; it may be for some consequence of it, as Thomas Becket was martyred in 1170 for his defense of the Church against King Henry II of England.

The model for Christian martyrs is the death of Jesus. The first recorded Christian martyrdom is that of Stephen (Acts 7.54). The great era of martyrs was during the Roman persecutions* of Christianity, which occurred intermittently until the legalization of Christianity in the early fourth century. Beginning with the *Martyrdom of Polycarp* (A.D. 168), "passions" (accounts of the trial and execution) of martyrs became a common genre of Christian literature. Martyrdom was venerated as the closest imitation of Christ, even union with Christ. It brought immediate entry into heaven and even counted as baptism* for martyrs who were unbaptized. Martyrdom also benefited others besides the martyr. At times it was believed that those en route to martyrdom, or those imprisoned but then released, had the status of presbyters (priests*) and the power to forgive sins. Tombs of the martyrs were venerated, with liturgies celebrated there on the anniversary of the martyr's death. Later, small churches, called *martyria*, were sometimes built there. After the era of persecutions, the life of asceticism* was understood as a sort of martyrdom.

In Europe after the Protestant* Reformation, Catholics were martyred at the hands of Protestants (especially in England) and vice versa. Many Christians were martyred in the mission lands of Asia, Africa, and the Americas in modern times. Groups of martyrs canonized or beatified include 119 from China (martyred 1648-1900), forty-two canonized from Japan (martyred 1587-1639), 103 canonized from Korea (martyred 1839-1846), 117 canonized from Vietnam (martyred 1745-1883), twenty-two canonized from Uganda (martyred 1885-1887), and eight canonized from North America (martyred 1642-1649). The few canonized or beatified are representatives of many more who were killed for their faith in these lands. Christians have been martyred at the hands of modern secular governments, e.g., the revolutionary government in France and various Communist governments in the twentieth century. Today, as in the case of Becket, Catholics may be martyred by Catholics, for example (arguably), Archbishop Oscar Romero*, assassinated in 1980 for the advocacy of justice* to which his faith impelled him.

MARXISM. The philosophical, sociopolitical, and economic theories of Karl Marx (1818-1883) and his followers. Marx held that history moved through a dialectical process of class struggle. By Marx's time, this process had led to capitalism*, but an uprising of the working class would overthrow the capitalists and produce a classless, socialist* society. Marx rejected religion, regarding it as "the opium of the people," weakening people's resistance to oppression by redirecting their attention toward an otherworldly satisfaction. V. I. Lenin (1870-1923) led the Marxist Bolshevik revolution in Russia (1917), modifying Marx's theories especially through the idea of a necessary period of dictatorship by the Communist Party. The Marxist-Leninist regimes in Russia (the Soviet Union) and elsewhere were hostile to Christianity, sometimes actively persecuting the Church, sometimes affording it a limited toleration. Catholic social teaching*, from Pope Leo XIII's* *Rerum novarum* (1891) onward, rejected Marxism for reasons summarized by Pope Paul VI* in *Octogesima adveniens* (1971) as follows: "The Christian ... cannot adhere to the Marxist ideology, to its atheistic materialism, to its dialectic of violence and to the way it absorbs individual freedom in the collectivity, at the same time denying all transcendence to man ..." (26). The same document, however, noted that there had been "a certain splintering of Marxism," which some think might "authorize certain concrete rapprochements." While noting Marxism's "various levels of expression," from a method of social analysis to a concentration of power in a single party, it warned of the "intimate link" between all of these aspects (32-34).

In subsequent years, some liberation theologians* made significant use of Marxist analysis of Latin American social conditions, though none accepted Marxist ideology completely. In response, a 1984 instruction of the Congregation for the Doctrine of the Faith* stated in strong terms that Marxist analysis was inseparable from the rest of Marxist ideology. That Catholics could make some borrowings from Marxism, however, seemed to be established by Pope John Paul II's* use of the Marxist idea of the alienation of labor* in his encyclical *Laborem exercens* (1981). In the aftermath of the collapse of the Marxist regimes in the Soviet Union and Eastern Europe in 1989 to 1991, Marxist thought has come seriously into question; Pope John Paul noted, though, "The crisis of Marxism does not rid the world of the situations of injustice and oppression which Marxism itself exploited and on which it fed" (*Centesimus annus* [1991] 26).

MARY, VIRGIN, Mother of Jesus. The Second Vatican Council speaks of Mary as occupying in the Church "the place that is highest after Christ" and yet very close to us (LG 54). She is uniquely privileged, as the mother of the incarnate God, and first among the saints*, but also the first member of the Church*, saved by God's grace* in Christ as are all who are saved.

There are relatively few mentions of Mary in the NT. Chief among them is the infancy narrative of Luke 1-2, where Mary is the first disciple*, whose consent allows the savior to be born. Luke also places her at the first Pentecost* and John places her at the foot of the cross of Jesus, in both cases emphasizing her status as disciple. Mark negatively contrasts Jesus' natural family, apparently including Mary, with his family of disciples (3.20-35).

Both Matthew and Luke affirm Mary's virginal conception of Jesus (*see* VIRGIN BIRTH). The beliefs in her physical virginity during Jesus' birth and in her lifelong virginity are attested in the second and third century, respectively. Reflection on Mary among the early Fathers of the Church* also parallels her with Eve, with Mary's obedience seen as undoing Eve's disobedience. The conflict over Nestorianism* and the resulting proclamation by the Council of Ephesus* (431) that Mary is *theotokos* or "Mother of God" gave a great impetus to Marian theology among the later Fathers, particularly in the East. In the medieval West, Marian devotion gained strength, partly due to a tendency to see Mary as the primary intercessor to Jesus, who was often portrayed as distant and harsh. Such prominent Marian prayers as the Hail Mary, the Hail Holy Queen (*Salve regina*) (*see* Appendix V), the rosary*, and the Marian litany* developed in the late Middle Ages.

Although many Protestant* Reformers, Martin Luther among them, had a personal devotion to Mary, Marian doctrine and devotion tended to drop out of Protestant religion because they were seen as jeopardizing the status of Jesus as the sole mediator of salvation. In reaction, Marian devotion received greater emphasis in the Catholic Church. After a decline during the eighteenth century, Marian devotion reached a peak in the Catholic Church in the nineteenth and early twentieth centuries, encouraged by numerous apparitions* of Mary, especially those revealing the Miraculous Medal (1830) and those at Lourdes (1858) and Fatima (1917). During this period the dogmas* of Mary's immaculate conception* (1854) and assumption* (1950) were declared, though both declarations were the outcome of processes of development, through reflection and liturgical practice, dating back to the Fathers of the Church.

Vatican Council II* (1962-1965) sought to foster devotion to Mary while eliminating any excess that detracted from belief in Jesus as the only Mediator (LG 60). It also stressed the relation of Mary to the Church as mother and model. Marian theology and devotion declined somewhat after the council but have revived in recent times in several different contexts. The plethora of recent alleged Marian apparitions, especially at Medjugorje in Bosnia, has sparked devotion of a generally conservative cast, often connected with the charismatic renewal*. A strongly apocalyptic note is associated with some apparitions. Within ecumenical dialogues*, significant convergence has been achieved, especially in overcoming the obstacle of the supposed conflict between devotion to Mary and belief in Jesus as the sole Mediator and Savior. Liberation theologians* hold up the Mary of the *Magnificat* (Lk 1.46-55) as a model for, and a liberator of, the poor. Feminist theologians* are reconsidering traditional images of Mary and emphasizing her prominence as a disciple and an active participant in God's work of salvation. Some feminist theologians note that feminine images belonging properly to God have become attached to the figure of Mary. Reflection on Mary can therefore be a key to recovering feminine aspects of the deity.

MARYKNOLL. The Catholic Foreign Mission Society of America, commonly known as Maryknoll Missioners, is a society of priests, brothers, and seminarians, founded in 1911 by two diocesan priests, James A. Walsh and Thomas F. Price. Canonically, it is a "society of the apostolic life" (*see* RELIGIOUS LIFE), whose members do not take vows. The Maryknoll Sisters (of St. Dominic) (Maryknoll Missionaries) is a religious congregation of women founded in 1912 by Mary Josephine (Mollie) Rogers (Mother Mary Joseph). Both groups have headquarters at Maryknoll, Westchester County, New York, and both have the purpose of working in foreign missions*. While the sisters form indigenous religious communities in mission territories, the men's community does not. Maryknoll also has Associates (priests, brothers, and laity for the Society and sisters for the Congregation), who commit themselves to service in the missions for limited periods of time.

The first major Maryknoll mission field was China, where Maryknoll priests arrived in 1918 and sisters in 1921. Thereafter, Maryknoll activities spread to Korea, the Philippines, Manchuria, and Japan. Maryknollers were imprisoned and/or expelled by the Japanese from their possessions during World War II and later expelled from China by the Communist government, which took power in 1949. Bishop James E. Walsh, M.M. (1891-1981), was not initially expelled but was imprisoned by the Chinese from 1958 to 1970. The expulsions enabled Maryknoll to send missionaries to Latin America, beginning in 1942, and to Africa in 1946. Maryknollers have since returned to Taiwan, the Philippines, Japan, South Korea, and (in the 1980s) China.

Prior to Vatican Council II, the Maryknoll Sisters had worked chiefly in such institutions as schools, hospitals, and orphanages. Renewal chapters in 1964 and 1968 reoriented them toward direct social action with the poor. Likewise, the Maryknoll Society was putting into effect an "option for the poor"*, seeking to share their life and join them in eliminating the causes of poverty. In 1980 in El Salvador, Maryknoll sisters Ita Ford and Maura Clarke, who worked with poor peasants, were (along with Ursuline sister Dorothy Kazel and lay volunteer Jean Donovan) raped and murdered by government soldiers. Maryknoll Father Miguel D'Escoto served as foreign minister in the leftist Sandinista Government in Nicaragua (1979-1990). Orbis Books, sponsored by the Maryknoll Society, is the leading publisher in the United States of books in Catholic social thought and liberation theology*. It also publishes works in missiology and interreligious dialogue. In 1993, there were about 1,600 Maryknollers in all, of whom 865 were in foreign missions in thirty-two countries.

MASS (Lt *missa*, "dismissal"). The liturgical celebration of the eucharist*. It acquired the name "mass" (*missa*) in the fifth century from the final dismissal formula in the Latin liturgy, *Ite, missa est*, "Go, it has been sent forth," or, "Go, it is over." By that time, *missa* (as a noun) had the broader meaning of "blessing." The present article describes the Mass of the Roman Rite, as modified after Vatican Council II* and set forth in the Roman Missal of 1969 (revised 1975) and as celebrated in English in the United States.

The Mass consists of four parts: (1) Introductory Rites, (2) Liturgy of the Word, (3) Liturgy of the Eucharist, (4) Concluding Rite. The first two parts were formerly called the "Mass of the Catechumens," because catechumens* were (and are once again, in the Rite of Christian Initiation of Adults) dismissed after them. The remainder was called the "Mass of the Faithful." The general shape of the eucharistic liturgy is of great antiquity. It was described by Justin Martyr* in the mid-second century and has roots in earlier Jewish worship.

(1) The Introductory Rites begin with an entrance procession including the priest celebrant (presider) and others (these may include priest concelebrants, deacons*, altar servers*, lectors*, eucharistic ministers*, or others). The procession may be accompanied by an "Entrance Song" or hymn. The priest bows and kisses the altar. The priest and congregation make the sign of the cross*. The priest greets the congregation, "The Lord be with you," and the congregation replies, "And also with you." The priest may then say a few words to introduce the day's liturgy. A short penitential rite may follow. This rite may include or be followed by the *Kyrie eleison* (Gk, "Lord, have mercy"), in English or Greek, a remnant of an ancient litany*. In place of, or in addition to, the penitential rite, the *Gloria*, a hymn that begins, "Glory to God in the highest," may be said or sung on Sundays and major feasts (except in Lent and Advent). (This description incorporates changes approved by the U.S. bishops in 1995). The *Kyrie* and *Gloria* have been part of the Roman liturgy since the seventh century. The priest then says the "Opening Prayer" or "Prayer of the Day," which is specific to each day's mass. It was formerly called the *Collect*, as "gathering together" or summarizing the themes of the liturgy.

(2) The **Liturgy of the Word** begins with readings from the Scriptures, as specified in the lectionary*. Normally, there are three readings on Sundays and major feasts, two otherwise. When there are

three readings, the first is usually from the Old Testament (in the Easter Season it is usually from the Acts of the Apostles, and on a few feasts it is from the Book of Revelation), and the second is from one of the New Testament letters or the Book of Revelation. When there are two readings, the first may be from any part of the Bible except the Gospels. The last reading is always from the Gospels. Between the first and second readings, a "Responsorial Psalm" is spoken or sung; this consists of a series of verses from an OT Psalm, each followed by a one-verse response by the congregation (before Vatican II, the psalm had been reduced to a single verse, called the *Gradual*). Before the Gospel, a "Gospel Verse," which is a brief Gospel passage preceded and followed by "*Alleluia*" (from Heb, "Praise God"), is said or sung; in Lent*, a different formula replaces the "Alleluia." After the Gospel comes the homily*, which normally has to do with the readings, and which (except by special permission) is to be preached by a deacon, priest, or bishop. On Sundays and major feasts, the "Profession of Faith" follows; normally, it is the Nicene Creed, but the Apostles' Creed may be substituted, usually in liturgies for children (*see* CREED). On some feasts, especially Easter, a renewal of baptismal promises replaces the Creed. The Creed first entered the Latin liturgy in the sixth century. The Liturgy of the Word concludes with the "General Intercessions" or "Prayer of the Faithful," a series of petitions with responses by the congregation. These were described by Justin Martyr, but they disappeared from the Roman liturgy in the fifth century; they were restored after Vatican II.

(3) The **Liturgy of the Eucharist** begins with the "Preparation of the Gifts." In the early Church, the eucharistic bread and wine were supplied by members of the congregation. Justin Martyr records that these and other gifts were brought forward in a procession. The procession was dropped from the Latin liturgy in the early Middle Ages because by then few people were receiving communion, and the leavened bread that people ordinarily used was not employed in the eucharist. The procession was restored after Vatican II and is often accompanied by a hymn. If there is a monetary collection at the mass, it is taken up at this time, and the money is carried in the procession and placed near the altar. The priest places the bread and wine on the altar and says a blessing prayer over each. He mixes water with the wine—at one time a standard part of preparing wine, but early acquiring the symbolism of the joining of humanity and divinity in Christ and the Christian. The Preparation of the Gifts concludes with

the "Prayer over the Gifts," which is specific to the day's liturgy. This prayer was formerly called the "Secret," which was taken to mean "silent prayer," but was actually derived from *oratio super secreta*, "prayer over the gifts which have been set apart."

Following is the center of the liturgy, the "Eucharistic Prayer." It is based in Jewish Passover ritual, and early Christian forms are found in the *Didachē*** (first century?) and Hippolytus (early third century). In the Latin tradition, it was long known as the **Canon** of the Mass, while in Greek it is called the *Anaphora* ("offering"). It begins with a dialogue (of great antiquity) between celebrant and congregation, after which the priest prays the "Preface," an opening prayer of praise and thanks. As a response to the Preface, the *Sanctus* (Lt, "holy"), a hymn beginning, "Holy, holy, holy, Lord God of power and might" (Is 6.3), is said or sung. There follows the eucharistic prayer proper, of which four versions are in general use: the ancient Roman Canon and three others composed after Vatican II but based on ancient models. Other eucharistic prayers may be approved for special occasions. The center of the eucharistic prayer is the "consecration," in which the celebrant recites the narrative of Jesus' institution of the eucharist, including the proclamation that the bread and wine are now Jesus' body and blood. All eucharistic prayers have some form of *epiclesis*: invocation of the Holy Spirit upon the gifts and upon the congregation. The other parts of the eucharistic prayer are prayers of praise and petition. At the conclusion of the eucharistic prayer, the congregation replies "Amen," as Justin describes. This is called the "Great Amen."

The Liturgy of the Eucharist continues with the "Communion Rite." This begins with the Lord's Prayer ("Our Father"). Next comes the "Sign of Peace": the priest prays for peace and says "The peace of the Lord be with you always" to the congregation, who respond "And also with you" to the priest and exchange an appropriate greeting with one another, usually a handshake in the United States. In the Eastern Rites, some ancient liturgies, and Justin's description, the "Peace" is exchanged before the Preparation of the Gifts, and the U.S. bishops in 1995 voted to allow but not require its restoration to that place. The priest then breaks the bread—originally a single loaf for the assembly, now a host broken to symbolize the sharing by many in Christ, the one bread of life (see 1 Cor 10.16-17). He places a piece of the host in the chalice that holds the consecrated wine, a ritual that originated in the necessity of keeping bread moist but acquired other customary and symbolic meanings over time. The hymn, "Lamb of God" (*Agnus Dei*) is said or sung to accompany these rituals. The priest says a preparatory prayer, then invites the congregation to communion, using a formula, "This is the Lamb of God .... Happy are those who are called to his supper." The congregation responds, "Lord, I am not worthy to receive you, but only say the word, and I shall be healed." Usually, the communicants receive communion in a standing position (from the Middle Ages to the recent reforms, kneeling had been the usual position). The minister places the host (eucharistic wafer) in the communicant's hand or directly on the tongue. If the eucharistic wine is offered, it is usually drunk directly from a chalice. A hymn is often sung to accompany the communion procession. A period of silent thanksgiving follows. The "Prayer after Communion," specific to the day's liturgy, concludes the Liturgy of the Eucharist.

(4) The Concluding Rite may open with announcements. The priest pronounces a blessing, which may be a simple invocation of the Trinity or a more solemn "Prayer over the People." The congregation responds, "Amen." The priest or deacon then dismisses the assembly with "Go, the Mass is ended" or a similar formula, and the congregation responds, "Thanks be to God." The priest kisses the altar and departs in a procession corresponding to the entrance procession. A "Closing Hymn" or "Recessional" may be sung.

MEDITATION (Lt *meditari*, "to consider, reflect"). Traditionally, a form or forms of mental prayer*, in which the mind is more active than in contemplation*. In the spirituality of early monasticism*, e.g., the *Rule of St. Benedict**, to "meditate" a text of the Bible is to study and learn it—to commit it to memory, to understand its meaning, to endeavor to live by it. In the modern period, from the sixteenth to the early twentieth century, the meaning of "meditation" was narrowed to the activity of using one's imagination and reason to develop an event or idea from Scripture or religious tradition, with a view toward enhancing one's affective devotion* and sanctifying one's life. Various systems of meditation were developed, often based in the spirituality of St. Ignatius Loyola*.

The term "meditation", however, often translates the Sanskrit *dhyana* and similar terms from Hindu* and Buddhist* traditions. This has given rise to Christian uses of "meditation" to refer to forms of prayer that are much less conceptual than those previously mentioned and that do not consist in a deliberate succession of mental acts. Here the line between "meditation" and "contemplation" is not sharp. For example, a common Hindu and Buddhist meditative practice is the repetition of a *mantra*, a brief prayer formula. It is intended that one will pass beyond awareness of the mantra into a state of pure, nonconceptual awareness. This practice has inspired the recovery of neglected Christian traditions of repetitive prayer, especially the repetition of the name of Jesus or a short "Jesus prayer," a practice which originated among the monks of the Christian East not later than the fourth century. In such prayer, sometimes known as "Centering Prayer," one repeats a prayer word or formula until, perhaps, one ceases to be aware of it. The practice is intended to foster an attitude of quiet receptivity to God. Should one become conscious of distracting thoughts, one returns to the repeated prayer. Thus, one may pass back and forth between active meditation and silent contemplation. The case is similar with Christian use of breathing meditation exercises adapted from Zen (a word derived from *dhyana*) Buddhism.

MENDICANT ORDERS (Lt *mendicare*, "to beg"). Religious orders that, when first founded, owned no communal property. Their members also owned no individual property and begged or worked for their support. Mendicant orders developed in the thirteenth century in the context of an increasingly urban population and widespread dissatisfaction with clerical wealth, conditions that earlier produced the poverty* movements of the eleventh and the twelfth centuries, such as the Waldensians*. The first mendicant orders were the Franciscans (*see* FRANCIS OF ASSISI), founded in 1209, and the Dominicans (*see* DOMINIC), who became a separate order in 1216. Later came the Carmelites (1245), Augustinians (1256), Servites (1424), and several others. The mendicant orders were a new form of religious life*, different from monasticism*. Unlike monks, the mendicants, called **friars** (Lt *fratres*, "brothers"), were not bound to a single monastery but to the entire order. Their novelty, together with their exemption from the jurisdiction of local bishops, aroused much opposition in the thirteenth century. Conflict was centered in the university* towns, where the mendicants established a strong presence. St. Bonaventure* and St. Thomas Aquinas*, both mendicants who were university professors, wrote in rebuttal to these attacks. In 1300, Pope Boniface VIII* limited mendicants' privileges, requiring episcopal approval for them to preach and hear confessions. Modifications were later made (for instance at the Council of Trent* in 1563), allowing nearly all of the mendicants to hold communal property. They may still beg, but only with the permission of their superiors and bishops.

MERIT (Lt *meritum*, "that which is deserved"). The worthiness of human conduct to be rewarded by God. Innumerable biblical passages speak of God as rewarding good deeds and punishing bad ones; Matthew 25:31-46 is a notable example. Beside them stand passages about how God's standards are different from human ones (e.g., Mt 20.1-16) and how human works are unprofitable (Lk 17.7-10) and Paul's arguments in Romans and Galatians that we are justified by God's grace* in Christ and not by our own works (*see* JUSTIFICATION). Against the Pelagians*, Augustine* held that without grace we can do nothing worthy of reward from God: "When God crowns our merits, he crowns nothing else but his own gifts" (Letter 194). Twelfth-century theologians, looking for some greater role for human nature than Augustine had allowed, distinguished merit as what is deserved in strict justice (*meritum de condigno*) from merit as suitability but not strict desert (*meritum de congruo*). In the latter sense, Thomas Aquinas* suggested that "God does not deny grace to those who do what is in them." Some later medieval theologians (e.g., Gabriel Biel) held that God had bound himself to be gracious to those who did what they could to seek him. Such a position was criticized by the Protestant* Reformers as leading to a futile effort to prove oneself worthy of God. Instead, Martin Luther proclaimed that we are justified by God's grace alone in Jesus Christ, without merit of our own. We acknowledge this grace in faith. The Council of Trent* in 1547 agreed that "nothing that precedes justification, neither faith nor works, would merit the grace of justification" (DS 1532) and that perseverance in faith is also by grace (DS 1541). It added, however, "To those who work well right to the end and keep their trust in God, eternal life should be held out, both as a grace promised in his mercy through Jesus Christ to the children of God, and as a reward to be faithfully bestowed, on the promise of God himself, for their good works and merits" (DS 1545). These good works are "fruits of justification," done through the strength infused by Christ, as from the vine into the branches (Jn 15.5) (DS 1546). A 1983 statement of the U.S. Lutheran-Roman Catholic Dialogue, which affirmed substantial agreement on justification, admitted that differences remain between Lutherans and Catholics in regard to the language of merit.

MERTON, THOMAS (LOUIS) (1915-1968). American monk and writer. Merton was born in Prades, France, the son of artists. Orphaned in his teens, he lived an unsettled life until moving permanently to the United States, his mother's native country, in 1935. He studied literature at Columbia University and there became acquainted with Catholicism, entering the Church in 1938. After several years spent teaching at Columbia and Saint Bonaventure University and writing poetry and fiction, he entered the Trappist Abbey of Our Lady of Gethsemani, Kentucky, in 1941. He took the monastic name Brother Louis, then Father Louis after ordination to priesthood in 1949. His abbot encouraged him to continue writing in the monastery. His spiritual autobiography, *The Seven-Storey Mountain* (1948), became a best-seller, and for the rest of his life, Merton lived in uneasy tension between his desire for solitude as a monk and his celebrity status as a writer. He published prolifically after 1949 and also maintained an extensive correspondence, including exchanges with world figures and with people otherwise almost unknown. The central theme of his writing was contemplation*, the simple awareness of God. To encounter God most intimately, he held, it is necessary to escape the "prison" of false, egocentric selfhood and to attain to a true selfhood that is complete openness to God. Merton came to see that contemplation was not the privilege of monks but was compatible with an active life in the world. A near-pacifist from early adulthood, as a monk he became a leader of, and something of a spiritual adviser to, the Catholic antiwar movement of the 1960s. His interest in contemplation led him to explore common ground with non-Christian religions. He included Buddhists, Hindus, and Muslims among his closest spiritual friends and was a pioneer in the movement of dialogue among religions. Late in 1968, he journeyed to India to visit religious sites and figures and attend an interreligious conference in Calcutta. From there he traveled to an international conference on monasticism*, in Bangkok, Thailand, where he was accidentally electrocuted on December 10, 1968.

MINISTRY (Lt *minister*, "servant"). This word commonly translates the NT Greek word *diakonia,* "service." Jesus characterizes his own work as "service" and calls on his followers to do the same (Mk 10.43-45). In this sense, all Christians are called to ministry. Already in the NT, many specific ministries are named (including *diakonos*, which sometimes means "helper" in general but at other times designates "deacon"*, as a specific sort of minister). Paul associated these diverse ministries with a diversity of gifts (charisms) of the Holy Spirit (1 Cor 12.4-11). By the second century, the chief ministers in all Christian churches were the bishop*, presbyters (*see* PRIEST), and deacons. Men were ordained to these offices by the laying on of hands (*see* ORDER, SACRAMENT OF). Other named ministries, sometimes associated with ordination rituals, included those of acolyte*, lector*, deaconess*, widow*, and virgin*. From late antiquity until Vatican Council II (1962-1965), Catholic understandings of ministry focused almost exclusively on the ordained ministry, especially the priesthood, although the ministry of unordained monks and other religious was important in the life of the Church (*see* RELIGIOUS LIFE). The words "ministry" and "minister" were seldom used in a Catholic context (the only article on ministry in the 1967 *New Catholic Encyclopedia* is "Ministry, Protestant"). But Vatican II revived the idea of ministry as belonging to the whole Church. Through baptism*, all Christians share in Christ's ministry as priest, prophet, and king (LG 10-13). The Council also envisioned more laity holding office in the Church (LG 33). In the 1972 document *Ministeria quaedam*, Pope Paul VI* suppressed the former minor orders (*see* ORDER, SACRAMENT OF) and created the lay ministries (*ministeria*) of acolyte and lector. He allowed for other ministries to be created at the request of episcopal conferences*. Since the Council, many laypersons have begun to exercise ministries formerly limited to clergy or perhaps to religious. These include liturgical ministries (e.g., eucharistic ministers*), offices in Church administration (e.g., pastoral administrators [*see* PARISH]), and service ministries (e.g., youth minister, campus minister, hospital chaplain). In areas where priests are few, laypersons may preside at liturgies of the word or communion services in place of Sunday eucharist. It is still quite unclear where to draw the lines between (1) the ministry that belongs to all Christians in virtue of baptism, (2) the ministry that belongs properly to those who receive the sacrament of order, (3) the ministries that belong to laypersons who appropriately bear the title "minister." Probably this last should be reserved for those in a designated public role that has explicit religious reference, whether in the context of liturgy (e.g., eucharistic minister) or the general ministry of the Church (e.g., youth minister).

MIRACLE (from Lt *mirari*, "to wonder at"). An extraordinary event that manifests the power of God. The gospels* record about thirty-five miracles performed by Jesus, chiefly healings*. Even Jesus' enemies did not challenge the fact that he worked wonders; they impugned the power by which he worked them, claiming it was that of demons* (Lk 11.14-23). Josephus, the Jewish-Roman historian, testified to Jesus' reputation as a wonder-worker. The gospels prefer the terms *power* (*dynamis*) and *sign* (*sēmeion*) over the standard term for *wonder* (*thauma*) in labeling Jesus' miracles. They are signs of the power of God's kingdom* at work in Jesus, dramatic manifestations of the power that is also at work in Jesus' preaching and relationships with others (cf. Mt 11.2-6). Modern scholastic theology treated miracles chiefly as proofs of Jesus' divinity, but this is contrary to the attitude of Jesus, who often asked for an expression of faith prior to working a miracle and on occasion would not perform them when faith was lacking (Mt 13.58).

In modern times, the NT miracle stories have functioned more as an obstacle to faith than as an incentive to it, because of their apparent incompatibility with a scientific view of the world. To remove this obstacle was a major motive of Rudolf Bultmann's program of demythologization of the NT (*see* MYTH). The philosopher David Hume (1711-1776) in particular argued that miracle stories could never be credible, in that they testified to violations of the laws of nature, which Hume, following Newton, pictured as strict, mechanistic patterns of causal necessity.

Contemporary views of the laws of nature as statistical generalizations allow somewhat more room for the extraordinary. Moreover, in light of the Christian belief that God is the creator of the world, miracles should not be understood as violations of the order of nature but as special manifestations of the power that underlies the working of nature. Still, Catholics, like everyone else, are less inclined to believe in miracles than were their ancestors a millennium or two ago, and the Church does not forbid historical-critical approaches that question the historicity of specific NT miracle stories, so long as God's power in Jesus to work miracles is not denied. The Church also counsels caution in regard to contemporary miracle stories, but it holds that God continues to work miracles in the world. The normal process of canonization* of a saint* requires attestation of two miracles performed through the intercession of the candidate for sainthood. And, after careful scientific scrutiny, some claims of miraculous healings at shrines*, e.g., Lourdes, France, have been admitted. For such healings to be accepted as miracles, they not only must not be explicable by normal scientific principles but also must manifest positive evidence of special divine activity.

MISSAL. A liturgical book containing the prayers, readings, and chants for mass*. The missal arose in the thirteenth century from the combination of the earlier sacramentary*, lectionary*, and *Graduale* (chant book). The word *missal* was first used of the sacramentary (book of priest's prayers) in the eighth century. The missal developed over the centuries as more and more was added to the sacramentary. In 1563, the Council of Trent* directed the reform of the missal, and this was completed as the *Roman Missal* under Pope Pius V in 1570. It curbed abuses and local variations and imposed a standard order to be observed throughout the Roman Rite. The missal was revised after Vatican Council II and was published in separate sacramentary, lectionary, and chant book in 1969 to 1971. A decree of Pope Alexander VII in 1661 was interpreted as prohibiting the translation of the missal from Latin into popular languages for the use of the laity. After Pope Leo XIII* lifted this prohibition in 1897, such missals became common. Today in the United States they have largely been replaced by **"missalettes"** (a trademark often used generically), booklets containing the mass prayers, readings, and hymns for a particular time period or liturgical season.

MISSIONS (Lt *missio*, "a sending," from *mittere*, "to send"). In the very broadest sense, the mission of the Church is to bring salvation* in Jesus Christ to the world. "Missions" is normally used more narrowly to mean "special undertakings of ... preaching the gospel and establishing the Church among peoples or groups who do not yet believe in Christ" (Vatican Council II, *Decree on the Missionary Activity of the Church* 6). During his ministry, Jesus sent his disciples out to preach and heal (e.g., Mt 10.1-15), and after his resurrection he gave them a mandate to "Go and make disciples of all nations" (Mt 28.19, cf. Mk 16.15, Lk 24.47, Jn 20.21). "Apostle"* means "one who is sent forth," and the Acts of the Apostles, by St. Luke, depicts the Church's earliest missionary efforts in Palestine and the northeastern Mediterranean world, concluding with Paul in Rome, the capital of the empire. Paul's own letters mostly address churches founded in his missionary journeys and contain much detail about his missionary work. Legend has the other apostles traveling as missionaries to various parts of the world, but there is little clear evidence. The Church spread rapidly along travel routes in the Roman Empire and, to a limited degree, outside it (e.g., in Ethiopia, India, and Ireland). In the empire, the example of the martyrs* and the hospitality* of Christian communities may have contributed more to the spread of Christianity than did direct missions of preaching. Once the empire was Christian, social suasion and sometimes direct coercion swelled its numbers. Monks and bishops went out as missionaries to the Germanic tribes that surrounded and eventually conquered the Empire in the West. The Frankish kingdom, especially under Charlemagne*, spread Christianity by forced conversions but also was the starting point for individual missionaries who won converts by persuasion of the leaders of surrounding tribes. The work of St. Boniface (ca. 675-754) among the Germanic tribes is a noteworthy example. In the ninth century, Saints Cyril* and Methodius led the efforts to spread the Christian faith to the Slavic peoples. Medieval Franciscan* and Dominican* friars made repeated efforts to evangelize in Muslim lands but had little success. Some fourteenth-century friars went as far as China, where a diocese was established at what is now Beijing in 1307. The Black Death, the disarray of the fourteenth-century Church in the West, and political changes in Asia brought an end to this effort.

The greatest expansion of the Church came with the "age of discovery" in the sixteenth century. Missionaries were under the "patronage" (Sp *patronato*, Port *padroado*) of the kings of Spain and Portugal, who supported their work but also could control it. With the Spanish and Portuguese exploration and imperial expansion, missionaries established the Church in Central and South America, southern North America (*see* NATIVE AMERICANS), Africa, India, Southeast Asia, the East Indies, the Philippines, China, and Japan. These missionaries were mostly Franciscans, Dominicans, and, increasingly, Jesuits*.

Although some rights of patronage lasted into the twentieth century, by the late sixteenth century there was much sentiment in Rome that patronage made missionary work excessively subservient to Spanish and Portuguese colonial interests. This led, in 1622, to the establishment of the Congregation for the Propagation of the Faith (known as "Propaganda" from its Latin name) by Pope Gregory XV for the supervision of all of the Church's missionary efforts. Jesuits were the leading missionaries in the seventeenth and eighteenth centuries, but the Chinese Rites controversy* set back their efforts to adapt the forms of Catholicism to native cultures, and the events leading to their suppression in 1773 dealt a severe blow to Catholic missions. The missions regained momentum in the nineteenth century. Irish clergy led missionary efforts in the British Empire, while French, Belgian, Dutch, and German clergy were prominent elsewhere. Propaganda's stated aim of creating indigenous churches with indigenous hierarchy was not realized to any great degree until the twentieth century.

In 1967, Propaganda was renamed Congregation for the Evangelization of Peoples. The name change reflects changes in the Church's understanding of mission work since Vatican Council II (*see* EVANGELIZATION). The recognition of the plurality of human cultures and the end of the assumption that Western European culture is the norm for all others has led to a more careful distinction between the spread of Catholic faith and the spread of Western culture. Missionaries must aim for a true inculturation* of the gospel into native cultures, which includes challenging cultures in the respects in which they fall short of gospel ideals. Increased recognition of the universal presence of God's grace, including God's work in the non-Christian religions*, has led in turn to an acknowledgment of the importance of interreligious dialogue in the Church's missionary efforts. The Church must listen as well as speak, but it still has a duty to proclaim Christ. As Pope John Paul II* states in his encyclical on the missions, *Redemptoris missio* (1990), "The fact that the followers of other religions can receive God's grace and be saved by Christ apart from the ordinary means which he has established does not thereby cancel the call to faith and baptism which God wills for all people" (55) (*see* SALVATION OUTSIDE THE CHURCH). Moreover, missionaries acknowledge a need to work for full human liberation and development, especially for the establishment of justice* and the removal of poverty* and oppression. The aim of missions must not be reduced to a this-worldly liberation, but neither should the continuity between justice and human development in this world and ultimate human fulfillment in the next be ignored (*see* ESCHATOLOGY, HOPE).

A **parish mission** is a program of sermons, devotional services, and (usually) increased availability of the sacrament of reconciliation*, all with the purpose of strengthening Christian life in a parish. It is usually conducted by a visiting priest or priests and lasts about a week. Parish missions date from the seventeenth century and were very popular in the United States in the nineteenth and early twentieth centuries. *See also* MARYKNOLL.

MODERNISM. A tendency in late nineteenth- and early twentieth-century Catholic thought, condemned by Rome in 1907 in the decree of the Holy Office *Lamentabili sane exitu* and the encyclical of Pope Pius X* *Pascendi dominici gregis*. *Pascendi* "gave the impression that [the Modernists] were a coordinated group of people with a coherent body of ideas, whereas ... they were in fact a highly diversified collection of individuals with inchoate and inconsistent ideas" (Alec Vidler). They had in common a desire to adapt Catholic thought and practice to the contemporary world, as against the intransigent opposition to the world expressed by Pope Pius IX*. In particular, they wished to restate Catholic teaching in a way more sensitive to history than was possible in the then-dominant neo-scholasticism (*see* SCHOLASTICISM).

The leading figure in Modernism was Alfred Loisy (1857-1940), a French biblical scholar. Loisy held that Jesus expected an imminent end of the world and arrival of the kingdom of God* and did not envision a church to come. It was necessary that there be a church in order to proclaim the gospel. Its statements of dogma* were true, however, not for all time but only within the thought framework of the age in which they were stated (*see* DOCTRINE). He was excommunicated in 1908 and rejected Catholicism thereafter. French Modernism was also influenced by the philosophy of Maurice Blondel (1861-1949), who opposed the dominant neo-scholastic apologetics* and took an Augustinian approach, seeing the movement of the human will as leading to a receptivity to divine revelation. Blondel distanced himself from Modernism, but his collaborator, the Oratorian priest Lucien Laberthonnière (1860-1932), was silenced from 1913 until his death. The other main figure in French philosophical Modernism was Edouard Le Roy (1870-1954), who sought to relate dogma primarily to practice rather than to speculative knowledge; his works were placed on the Index*.

The "chief engineer" (Vidler's term) of the movement was Baron Friedrich von Hügel (1852-1925), an Austro-Scot who lived in England and kept the Modernists in touch with one another and with kindred thinkers. He published significant work in the philosophy of religious experience. He escaped condemnation and died a Catholic. The most prominent Modernist in England, however, the Irish-born Jesuit George Tyrrell (1861-1909), who argued that dogmas were symbolic expressions of experience, was excommunicated in 1907. The principal Italian Modernist was Ernesto Buonaiuti (1881-1946), a priest and professor who popularized the ideas of Loisy and Tyrrell. He was excommunicated in 1925.

The term "social Modernism" is sometimes applied to social and political groups that sought to reconcile Catholicism and contemporary society, especially democracy, though they took no positions in dogmatic theology. Such groups existed in Italy and Germany, and one group in France, the Sillon, led by Marc Sangnier, was condemned by Pius X in 1910.

Lamentabili condemned sixty-five propositions associated with Modernism, while *Pascendi* presented Modernism as a system of thought, the "synthesis of all heresies," based on a fundamental agnosticism or skepticism about the human intellect's ability to know truth about God. In 1910, an oath* against Modernism was imposed on all candidates for holy orders and Church office. It was not revoked until 1967. Networks were set up through the Sodalitium Pianum (Sapinière) to report suspected Modernists to Rome (*see under* INTEGRALISM). The suppression of Modernism created a climate of suspicion and fear, which retarded the development of Catholic intellectual life for two generations. While Modernist skepticism about dogma was excessive, many of the Modernist concerns about the need for a historical perspective in biblical criticism* and theology and for greater attentiveness in theology to human experience have become part of the Catholic mainstream, given expression in the documents of Vatican Council II*.

MONASTICISM (from Gk *monachos*, "monk, one who lives alone," from *monos*, "one, alone"). A form of religious life* that involves withdrawal from ordinary life and cultivation of a relation with God in solitude, either alone or in community with others pursuing similar lives. Those who pursue monastic life are called **monks** or **nuns**. Monasticism is found in many religions (e.g., Hinduism* and Buddhism*), and the Jewish Essenes may have been an antecedent to Christian monasticism (*see* DEAD SEA SCROLLS). Christian monks looked back to Jesus' own prayer in solitude (e.g., Lk 6.12) and to the communal life of the earliest Christians. Christian monasticism as such began, however, with the movement into the desert in the third century, led by St. Antony (*see* DESERT FATHERS AND MOTHERS). The desert monks at first lived alone as hermits or anchorites*. Eventually some formed loose groupings around a spiritual leader, called *abba* ("father") or, more rarely, *amma*, "mother." Such a grouping was called a *lavra*.

The first cenobite* communities of monks living together under a rule and a superior were founded by Pachomius (ca. 286-346) in Egypt. Such communities are called **monasteries**. The writings of St. Basil (ca. 330-379) (*see* CAPPADOCIAN FATHERS) form the basis of Greek monasticism to this day. In the East, monasticism remains the only organized form of religious life. St. Athanasius* (ca. 297-373) brought the Eastern style of monasticism to the West, where it flourished in Gaul and, later, in Ireland. St. Augustine* (354-430) devised a form of monastic life for the priests of his diocese; together with St. Ambrose*, he founded "clerical monasticism" in the West. The form of monasticism that came to be dominant in the West, however, was that of St. Benedict* (ca. 480-ca. 547). Benedict's moderate, flexible rule set out a life of prayer and work for monks, who were mostly laymen. It became the standard pattern for religious life in Western Europe until the thirteenth century. Adaptations for communities of women (nuns) were developed for all of the types of cenobite monasticism mentioned here.

Through their absorption into the feudal system, western **Benedictine** monasteries developed into large complexes with extensive landholdings. They were the social and educational (and sometimes political) centers of the regions in which they stood. A reform movement began at Cluny in the tenth century reducing manual labor and centering monastic life in the liturgy, wherein the Cluniacs saw themselves as intercessors for the whole society. Another reform, based on a stricter observance of the Benedictine Rule and greater austerity of life, began at Cîteaux (Latin, "Cistercium") in 1098, near Dijon in Burgundy. This led to the **Cistercian** Order, whose principal early spokesman was St. Bernard of Clairvaux* (1090-1153). The first houses for Cistercian nuns began in 1147. A further reform in the direction of austerity began in 1678 under Armand de Rancé, abbot* of La Trappe, whose followers were called **Trappists**. The **Camaldolese**, founded ca. 1012, and the **Carthusians**, founded in 1084, combine the life of hermits with liturgy in common, somewhat as in the ancient *lavras*.

Monasticism declined in the later Middle Ages in the West, as the population became more urban, and other forms of religious life, especially the mendicant* orders, became prominent. Monasticism decayed internally, particularly in that, often, abbots were appointed by secular rulers and did not live in their monasteries but only drew the revenues accruing to their positions. The Protestant* Reformers rejected monasticism as a way of earning salvation through works rather than grace* (and see JUSTIFICATION), while secular rulers coveted monastic lands. Many monasteries were suppressed at the time of the Reformation. In the countries that remained Catholic, the French Revolution* and other secularizing movements had suppressed most monasteries by the early nineteenth century. A recovery began around 1890 under Pope Leo XIII*, who grouped formerly independent monasteries into worldwide orders. The number of monks and nuns increased considerably until after Vatican Council II*, when the monastic orders underwent the same strains as other religious communities (see under RELIGIOUS LIFE).

Benedictines vow **stability** (that is, to stay in the same monastery permanently), *conversatio morum* (monastic way of life [which includes poverty* and chastity]), and obedience*. Most other monks and nuns take vows* of poverty, chastity, and obedience. Monks' and nuns' lives center on prayer, both the Liturgy of the Hours* and private meditation*. Some continue the traditional monastic work of farming, while others have sought different forms of labor (computer work is popular). Some do "extern" work, for instance in education or missions. Most have a ministry of hospitality*, in which they share their lives with guests and those making retreats*.

MONOPHYSITISM (Gk *monos*, "one," *physis*, "nature"). An extreme form of the Christology* of the school of Alexandria*. It held that Christ did not have two natures, divine and human, but only one nature, that of the Word of God. It did not intend to deny the humanity of Jesus in the manner of Docetism* or Apollinarianism* but objected to "two natures" language as dividing Christ into two, as in Nestorianism*. Monophysitism arose among followers of Cyril of Alexandria, the leading opponent of Nestorianism, who held to Cyril's formula, "one incarnate nature of the Divine Word." Controversy broke out in 447 over the monophysite teaching of Eutyches, monk of Constantinople, who held that Christ was of two natures before the incarnation* but only one nature, a divine nature, afterward. Eutyches was condemned by Flavian, patriarch of Constantinople, but supported by Dioscorus, patriarch of Alexandria, who arranged Eutyches's rehabilitation and the deposition of Flavian at the Council of Ephesus in 449, later called the "Robber Synod." The ecumenical Council of Chalcedon* in 451 condemned Eutyches, however, deposed Dioscorus, and, following Pope Leo I*, proclaimed Christ to be "one person" in "two natures," human and divine.

Though they did not accept the extreme theology of Eutyches, one party at Alexandria, loyal to Dioscorus and to Cyril's language, rejected Chalcedon. Opposition to Chalcedon also grew at Antioch and eventually at Constantinople, leading to a schism between Rome and Constantinople from 484 to 519. Controversy continued in the East throughout the sixth century, by the end of which Chalcedon was generally accepted in the Roman Empire, and there was clear division between the Catholic Church and three non-Chalcedonian or Monophysite churches: one in Egypt, which came to be called "Coptic" (from the Greek word for "Egyptian" by way of Arabic); one in Syria, often called "Jacobite," after its leader, Jacob Bar'adai; and the church of Armenia. Descendants of these churches are the Oriental Orthodox Churches* of today.

MONOTHELITISM (MONOTHELETISM) (Gk *monos*, "one," *thelein*, "to will"). A heresy that held that Jesus Christ* had only one will, rather than distinct human and divine wills. It arose from efforts to reconcile the Monophysite* churches with the Catholic Church, which accepted the formula of the Council of Chalcedon* that Christ had two natures, divine and human. It was put forward by Sergius, patriarch of Constantinople (patriarch 610-638), with the support of the Emperor Heraclius. Sergius first proposed that in Christ there was only one activity or operation ("energy," hence "monoenergism"), then modified this to "one will." This latter formula won the endorsement of Pope Honorius (pope 625-638) but evoked opposition in the West and East as depriving Jesus of true humanity. Monothelitism was condemned at the Third Council of Constantinople* (680-81).

MONSIGNOR (Ital "my lord"). An honorific title granted by the pope to certain priests. These priests are known as **domestic prelates**. In Europe and Latin America, the title is often applied to bishops* and archbishops* as well.

MONTANISM. A charismatic, apocalyptic* sect of the second century, founded by Montanus, a presbyter from Phrygia in Asia Minor; known in its time as the "New Prophecy." Around 172, Montanus and two women followers, Maximilla and Prisca, prophesied in an ecstatic state, proclaiming the imminent Parousia*. Ecstatic prophecy characterized the movement, which eventually organized itself into a rival church, until its disappearance in the third century. The Montanists claimed that the gifts of the Holy Spirit* were absent from the mainstream Church because of moral laxity, and upheld a rigorous asceticism, condemning remarriage of widows and widowers and emphasizing strict fasting. Around 207, Tertullian* became an adherent, and it strongly influenced his subsequent writings.

MORAL THEOLOGY. Although biblical, patristic, and medieval Christian authors had much to say about morality, moral theology as a distinct discipline did not emerge until the sixteenth century. Its characteristic shape resulted from two decrees of the Council of Trent*. One (1563) called for the establishment of seminaries* in every diocese*. The other (1551) reiterated the requirement that one must confess to a priest all mortal sins (*see* SIN) according to number, kind, and circumstances. While the Council of Trent was still in progress, "manuals" of moral theology began to be developed. These manuals drew on the moral teaching of St. Thomas Aquinas* and on earlier *Summae confessorum* (summas* for confessors). They were intended for use in seminaries, to train priests for hearing confessions by correlating specific sins with particular penances. Because of this purpose, they focused on individual acts and had little to say about the broader themes of ethics, such as character and virtue*. They were also concerned to give a precise account of the seriousness of particular sins. This was done by applying the relevant law (divine, natural*, or ecclesiastical) to the act in question. Accordingly, the manuals blended ethics and canon law*. But they paid little attention to Scripture, systematic theology, and spirituality. The resulting systems, taught to generations of priests and (by way of catechisms) laity, were "individualistic, act-centered, law-oriented, and sin-conscious" (R. Gula).

Vatican Council II* called in 1965 for a renewal of moral theology: "Special care is to be taken for the improvement of moral theology. Its scientific presentation should be more based on the teaching of scripture, throwing light on the exalted vocation of the faithful in Christ and their obligation to bear fruit in charity for the life of the world" (OpT 16). Some renewal of this sort began in Germany in the nineteenth century and reached Rome before the Council in the teaching of Bernard Häring (1912-) and Josef Fuchs (1912-). The Council gave great impetus to the renewal, which is still in progress. Contemporary moral theology aims to take a broader view of moral life than the manuals did, incorporating theories of virtue and appreciation of circumstances. It seeks to pay careful attention to human moral experience, which is far more complex than the application of laws to cases. Moreover, Vatican II's ecclesiology* makes the experience of the whole people of God*, lay as well as clerical, relevant to the discernment of the standards of Christian morality. In recent years, special attention has been given to the experience of women and the dispossessed. Moral theology also seeks to take a genuinely theological, rather than philosophical and legal, approach, based in Scripture and integrated with systematic theology and spirituality. Finally, moral theologians have had to take greater account of history and its influence on moral standards. While they affirm some permanent elements in human nature, moralists can no longer draw with confidence on the timeless "natural law" of the manuals.

These developments and other changes in Church and society have made moral theology one of the areas of greatest conflict in the Church since Vatican II. The conflicts have taken place on several interlocking levels: specific issues, especially of sexual morality*, general approaches to moral questions, and the authoritativeness of church pronouncements on moral issues (*see* DISSENT). Pope John Paul II's* 1993 encyclical *Veritatis splendor* opposes some of the dominant trends in moral theology in recent decades and reflects the concerns of the manualist tradition in its defense of absolute, exceptionless moral norms proscribing certain kinds of act (particularly some sexual acts) as mortally sinful in themselves.

MORE, THOMAS, SIR, ST. (1478-1535). English humanist and martyr*. The son of a London lawyer, More studied at Oxford from 1492 to 1494, where he became acquainted with the leading figures of English humanism*. Subsequently he studied law at the Inns of Court. He lived with the Carthusian monks for four years, probably from 1500 to 1504. Deciding not to pursue religious life*, in 1504 he married Jane Colt, who bore him four children. After her death in 1509, he married Alice Middleton. His talent and reputation for fairness caused his career to advance rapidly. He became undersheriff of London in 1510 and entered the king's service in 1518. He was knighted in 1521 and became the speaker of Parliament in 1523, chancellor of the Duchy of Lancaster in 1525, and finally Lord Chancellor of England in 1529.

Meanwhile, he had become England's leading humanist and a close friend of the Dutch humanist Erasmus. More wrote a classic biography of Richard III, later drawn on by Shakespeare. In 1516, he published *Utopia* (a Greek coinage meaning "nowhere"), which portrays an ideal social and political order, in which all material goods are held in common, and indirectly indicts the pride, greed, and injustice of his own society. As the Protestant* Reformation gained momentum, he published many polemical tracts against Protestantism.

In 1527, King Henry VIII sought a decree of nullity of his marriage to his queen, Catherine of Aragon, in order to marry Anne Boleyn. When the pope refused to grant it, Henry took measures to place the Church in England under royal control (*see* ANGLICAN COMMUNION). More resigned as Chancellor in 1532. In 1534, he refused to swear the Oath of Supremacy, declaring the King the head of the Church in England, and for this he was imprisoned in the Tower of London until he was beheaded for treason, July 6, 1535. He was canonized in 1935, and his feast is celebrated on June 22.

MURRAY, JOHN COURTNEY (1904-1967). American theologian. Murray was born in New York City and entered the Jesuits* in 1920. He was ordained a priest in 1933 and received a doctorate at the Gregorian University in Rome in 1937. Thereafter he taught at the Jesuits' Woodstock College, Maryland, until his death. From 1941 until his death, he was editor of *Theological Studies*, a major Catholic theological journal founded by the Jesuits in 1940. Murray's work centered on questions of American pluralism* and religious freedom*. During and after World War II he saw the need for Catholics to work with Protestants and Jews on issues concerning the public good. He was disturbed by the trend toward a complete secularization of American public life and wanted to make it possible for religious voices to be heard in public debate. He argued, chiefly in *We Hold These Truths* (1965), that American political disagreements take place against the background of an "American consensus" based fundamentally in belief in natural law*. Murray held that the First Amendment to the U.S. Constitution, guaranteeing the separation of church and state, was beneficial to the Church, protecting its freedom and allowing it to cooperate with others, while preserving social harmony, which would be threatened by an effort to establish a religion. Religious freedom* was in fact an implication of the developing Catholic doctrine of human dignity. This view ran counter to the prevailing Catholic theological opinion and the statements of recent popes (e.g., Pius IX in the *Syllabus of Errors**), which held that the ideal relation of church and state was that the state should officially espouse Catholicism and give the Church special treatment (perhaps restricting the freedoms of adherents of other religious persuasions). From 1955 to 1963, Murray was forbidden to speak or to publish on the subject of church and state relations. In 1963, however, he was invited to Vatican Council II*. He was appointed head of the commission that revised the Council's *Declaration on Religious Liberty* (1965), in which a position essentially the same as Murray's became the official teaching of the Church.

MUSIC, CHURCH (SACRED MUSIC). Following recent Church documents, this may be divided into **liturgical music**, which is integrated with the Church's public worship, and other forms of religious music. Liturgical music is the main focus in this article.

The NT says little about Christian use of music, although it mentions the singing of hymns (e.g., Eph 5.19) and quotes a few hymns (e.g., Phil 2.6-11). Probably the first Christian use of music in worship was modeled on Jewish synagogue worship, where prayers were sung by the assembly without instrumental accompaniment. Some of the early Fathers of the Church* strongly objected to instrumental music as associated with immorality; use of instrumentation did not become common until the later Middle Ages. The first clear evidence of Christian singing of biblical psalms dates from the late second or early third century.

With the legalization and expansion of the Church in the fourth century, Christian liturgies became large public gatherings, which caused a change in styles of music. Specialized cantors and choirs began to appear. A body of Christian hymns developed, associated with such figures as Ambrose*; these were used especially in the liturgy of the hours*. Several different styles of liturgical **plainsong** (texts sung in free rhythm, like prose, rather than metrical rhythm; usually in unison, without accompaniment) developed by the end of antiquity. By the seventh century, there was a clear distinction between spoken and sung worship.

In the eighth century, the Frankish kings Pepin and Charlemagne* directed that the Roman liturgy and its chants be observed throughout their kingdoms. Gregorian chant* may have arisen from the fusion of Roman plainsong with Gallican traditions. In the ninth and tenth centuries there was an increasing tendency to expand chant elaborations of secondary parts of the liturgy, especially tropes (melodic extensions of texts) and sequences (rhymed verses sung before the gospel). As Latin ceased to be the common language (or where it never was), vernacular religious songs began to appear in the eighth and ninth centuries, but they were not integrated into the liturgy.

Polyphony, in which two or more lines of music are developed simultaneously, first appeared in the ninth century. It was initially simple, but developed by the end of the Middle Ages into elaborate forms, which often obscured the liturgical text. A great separation developed between liturgical polyphony, written and performed by professional musicians, and popular hymns in vernacular languages. (The majority of masses, however, were simply read by the priest and had no music at all.)

Martin Luther sought to integrate vernacular hymns and the liturgy, writing many new hymns himself (some of them now in use in Catholic churches). Some of the other Protestant* Reformers were more suspicious of music; Zwingli banned it from worship entirely. The Council of Trent* (1545-1563) retained the Latin liturgy, thus allowing little room for the vernacular, but called for intelligibility and restraint in liturgical music. The Council implicitly affirmed the polyphony of the day, best represented by Giovanni Palestrina (ca. 1525-1594), by having music of that kind performed before it. In subsequent centuries, Palestrina's polyphony stood alongside Gregorian chant as the classic forms of Catholic religious music.

In the Counter-Reformation* period, vernacular singing found a place especially in non-liturgical devotions* but only occasionally was allowed in the mass. In the baroque period of the seventeenth and eighteenth centuries, music that was at the artistic forefront was heavily influenced by opera. In a liturgical context, the choral and orchestral performances tended to overwhelm the liturgy; Joseph Jungmann called them "church concerts with liturgical accompaniment." Similarly, the masses written by the great classical composers of the eighteenth and nineteenth centuries, e.g., Mozart and Beethoven, were better suited to the concert hall than the church. In the late nineteenth and early twentieth centuries, there was a recovery of chant and polyphony associated with the beginnings of the liturgical movement*. At first this set back the use of vernacular music in worship. But as the momentum grew for participation of the people in worship and song, more vernacular music was permitted.

The Second Vatican Council commended sacred music as "expressing prayer more eloquently, ... building unity of heart and mind, [and] enriching the rites of worship with greater solemnity" (SC 112). It continued to give special prominence to chant and polyphony, but encouraged vernacular music and the use of indigenous musical traditions. In keeping with its emphasis for liturgy generally, it called for active participation of all the people in liturgical music, though not to the exclusion of choirs. As the liturgy was rendered into vernacular languages in the aftermath of the Council, there has been much variety and experimentation in Catholic liturgical music. Sources drawn on have included not only the Catholic tradition but the music of other Christian traditions and popular traditions in many cultures. In the United States, guidelines were provided in the National Conference of Catholic Bishops' document, *Music in Catholic Worship* (1972, revised 1982). It no longer upheld a priority of chant and polyphony, and stated that the grounds for evaluation of liturgical music should be musical quality, liturgical appropriateness, and pastoral suitability for the worshiping community.

MYSTERY (Gk *mystērion*, "that about which one must be silent," from *myein*, "to be silent"). Something pertaining to God, which is hidden from humans until revealed by God. In Mk 4.11 and parallels, Jesus speaks of the "mystery of the kingdom* of God" revealed to the disciples but shown to others only in parables. In the Pauline writings, the mystery is God's hidden plan of salvation*, revealed in Jesus (1 Cor 2.7, Eph 1.9, Col 1.26). Among the Fathers of the Church*, "mystery" refers especially to the rituals of the Church, especially the ritual of baptism* and the eucharist* at the Easter Vigil. The Latin word *sacramentum*, root of the English "sacrament," was a translation of *mystērion*; awareness of this connection enables better understanding of both "mystery" and "sacrament." (Though the sources of Christian rituals are Jewish rather than pagan, the language of the Christian "mysteries" may have been influenced by the pagan **mystery religions**. These were cults in which participants sought renewal of life by the power of a god through secret initiations in which they reenacted a myth involving the god.) The Fathers also use "mystery" to refer to the hidden senses of Scripture and other hidden or obscure truths of God.

In later scholastic theology, "mystery" came to mean revealed truths that exceed human capacities to demonstrate or understand. It is used in this sense by Vatican Council I* against rationalism*: "Besides those things to which natural reason can attain, there are proposed for our belief mysteries hidden in God, which, unless they are divinely revealed, are incapable of being known" (DS 3015). When such truths are accepted in faith, they may be understood partially, but they "so far surpass the created understanding" that reason "is never rendered capable of penetrating these mysteries in the way in which it penetrates those truths which form its proper object" (DS 3016). Such theology fostered a tendency to understand mysteries as incomprehensible propositions. In the twentieth century, Karl Rahner* developed a more profound theology of mystery in which the fundamental mystery is the incomprehensible God himself and God's communication of himself to human beings in grace. All other theological mysteries are aspects of this fundamental mystery.

See also PASCHAL MYSTERY, ROSARY.

MYSTICAL PHENOMENA. Various secondary spiritual and physical phenomena that may accompany mysticism* or contemplative prayer. Spiritual phenomena include **visions** and **locutions** (voices or words). These are classed as **corporeal** (bodily): those that appear to be exterior (*see* APPARITION); **imaginary**: those that have sensory form but are recognized as interior; and **intellectual**: those that lack sensory form, e.g., a profound sense of presence or an infusion of intuitive knowledge. There are also spiritual experiences related to the other senses or to music. Physical phenomena include **stigmata** (receiving the marks of the wounds of Jesus), **levitation** (the raising of the body in defiance of gravity), **bilocation** (simultaneous appearance in more than one place), **incorruption** (absence of decomposition of the dead body), and many others. All of these are well attested in the lives of Christian mystics, as examined, e.g., in canonization* hearings; they are also found in mystics in other traditions. None of these phenomena are proof of sanctity or of authentic experience of God. Christian spiritual tradition recognizes that they may have three sources: God, oneself (perhaps through paranormal but natural powers), or the devil* or diabolic powers. So criteria of discernment*, especially an examination of the effects of the experiences on the person who has them, must be employed. Secondary mystical phenomena are not ends in their own right; at most they are signs of how unity (or contact) with God transforms the whole person, body and soul.

MYSTICISM (Gk *myein*, "to be silent"). A **mystical experience** is a state of consciousness in which a human subject overcomes the limits of ordinary experience through an experienced union with a transcendent reality—in Christian terms, union with God. "Mysticism" can refer to such experiences or to theories or practices that grow out of them or are intended to lead into them. Mysticism is found in all the major world religions and is particularly prominent in Hinduism* and Buddhism*. It may be seen in the NT, especially in Paul's sense of oneness with Christ and in the oneness with the Father in Christ for which the Johannine Jesus prays for his followers. The term *mysticism* and its cognates, however, were not used till later. *Mystikos* (adjective) was first used to refer to the spiritual meaning of the Scriptures and the liturgy. In the *Mystical Theology* of Pseudo-Dionysius* (sixth century) it came to refer to spiritual awareness more generally, but it is only in modern times that it refers primarily to a state of consciousness.

As the Christian mystical tradition developed, beginning in the second century, it drew on the Platonic and neo-Platonic traditions in philosophy, developing a theology of the soul's return to the divine original of which it is an image, and which is centrally present within it. Prominent mystical theologians who drew on Platonism* and neo-Platonism include Origen*, Augustine*, Pseudo-Dionysius, and Eckhart*. In the twelfth century, in such figures as Bernard of Clairvaux*, mystical union began to be expressed in terms of interpersonal love rather than of the return of an image to its original. The mysticism of love had the advantage that the notion of interpersonal love better preserves the ultimate distinction of creator and creature than does neo-Platonism (*see* CREATION). Perhaps the most outstanding Catholic love mystics were the great Spanish mystics of the sixteenth century: Ignatius of Loyola*, Teresa of Avila*, John of the Cross*.

In the twentieth century, there has been a resurgence within Catholicism of the study of mysticism. This is a result both of the desire to recover the experiential dimension of Catholic religion and of the increasing dialogue with other religions, notably those of the Orient. In both these respects, the figure of Thomas Merton* (1915-1968) may be considered representative.

In Catholic mystical theology, genuine mystical states are always seen as gifts of God, rather than accomplishments of the mystic himself or herself; a mark of this is that the mystic perceives himself or herself as passive within the experience. Christian mysticism may thus be seen as the fullest experience of the life of grace* in which all Christians share.

MYTH (Gk *mythos*, "story"). A traditional story that presents in symbolic form some fundamental reality of human existence or some paradigmatic example for human beings. "Myth" is used in many senses, and there is no sharp line between myths and other folktales. The sense in which "myth" is used determines whether one may say there is myth in the Bible. In the popular sense in which "myth" is a story that is not true, or in the more sophisticated sense in which it is a story about the gods, there is no myth in the Bible. In this sense, Pope Pius XII* cautioned in *Humani generis* (1950) against likening biblical stories to the myths of other cultures, and the NT itself uses *mythos* pejoratively (e.g., 1 Tm 1.4). Still, there is much in the OT that resembles and may be drawn from ancient Near Eastern mythical patterns, and in the broader sense used at the beginning of this article, one may say that the literary form of much of Genesis 1-11 is that of "myth," and that mythic (or mythopoeic) elements are present elsewhere in the OT. Such myth is not scientific or historical error, because it is not intended to be science or history. The question of myth in the NT has been dominated by the Lutheran theologian and exegete Rudolf Bultmann (1884-1976). Bultmann held that to communicate to a modern audience the NT's essential message of salvation through Jesus Christ (*see* KERYGMA) requires an extensive **demythologization**, clearing away all the elements of an ancient mythical worldview that block its reception. Such elements include all that is supernatural or miraculous, heaven* and hell*, angels* and demons*, and the preexistence, resurrection*, and ascension* of Jesus. Catholic scholarship has admitted the legitimacy of some demythologization, while rejecting the full scope of Bultmann's application of it. Moreover, recent thought (e.g., narrative theology) acknowledges (as Plato knew) that we can sometimes penetrate further into fundamental truth by way of stories than by way of theoretical statements.

N

NATIVE AMERICANS. Peoples who inhabited the American continents and nearby islands at the time of the arrival of the Europeans in 1492 and afterward, and their descendants. For much of the period under discussion, most of them were known as American Indians, and many of them still prefer this designation (Eskimo and Aleut peoples are not considered in this article).

Catholic missionaries often accompanied the early Spanish, Portuguese, and French explorers of the Americas. Sometimes, the projects of conquest and Christianization were clearly separated, as with the Dominican Bartolomé de las Casas*, but often there was no clear line between them. Franciscans were in Santo Domingo in 1493 and on the mainland in 1513. They were the principal missionaries to the native populations in Spanish and Portuguese America until the arrival of the Jesuits* in Brazil in 1549 and in the Spanish territories in 1568. The "missions," which were established from the 1570s onward, were economic and political as well as religious institutions. They were like Spanish towns, in which the previously nomadic Indians were governed by the priests and soldiers and often were not free to leave the compounds. At times, as in the Jesuit "reductions" (from Sp *reducir*, "reduce" [organize] into townships) of Paraguay, these communities were quite prosperous and relatively independent of the colonial authorities.

The first Spanish missionary efforts in what later became the United States were made by Juan de Padilla, a Franciscan who arrived in what is now New Mexico in an expedition led by Francisco Vázquez de Coronado in 1540 and remained to preach in the Southwest until killed by Indians in Kansas around 1544. Indian missions were undertaken from St. Augustine, Florida, especially by Franciscans, from 1566 to the early eighteenth century. In 1598 a permanent Christian presence was established in New Mexico, and many Pueblo and Hopi were converted, but Christianity was almost wiped out there by a Pueblo uprising in 1680. A determined Spanish military and religious drive up the California coast was led by Junipero Serra (1713-1784), a Franciscan priest, who established a chain of missions, beginning with San Diego de Alcalá in 1769. Franciscans continued to build missions in California until 1823.

In French America, mission efforts were hindered by continual conflict between France and England, as well as by the overriding importance accorded by the French to the fur trade. The most successful missionary work was conducted by the Jesuits among the Hurons from 1632 to 1649. It was terminated by the bloody conquest of the Hurons by the Iroquois, who were allied with the English. Missions among the Iroquois included the conversion of Blessed Kateri Tekakwitha (1656-1680), a Mohawk, in 1680. French Jesuits also evangelized the native populations in the Great Lakes regions, the Mississippi valley, and the areas of Illinois and Indiana. French missions effectively ended with France's defeat by England in the French and Indian War in 1763 and the expulsion of the Jesuits from French territories in 1764.

Missions to Native American populations, chiefly in the Midwest, Southwest and Northwest, continued in the United States after independence. Among the most successful were those to the Potawatomi, in Michigan, Indiana, and then Kansas, and Jesuit missions to the Flatheads in Montana and Idaho, initiated by Peter DeSmet in 1840. President Grant's "peace policy" of 1870 put many Catholic Indians under the control of Protestant missionaries. Partly to combat this policy, the Bureau of Catholic Indian Missions was formed in 1874; it continues to represent the Church in its apostolate to Native Americans. Fifty-six Catholic Indian schools were in operation by 1900 and many still exist. There have been relatively few Catholic programs directed to Indians who live in cities rather than on reservations.

As of 1994, there were about 350,000 Native American Catholics in the United States, including two bishops. Translations of the liturgy into Navajo, Choctaw, and Lakota have been approved. The leading organization for Catholic Native Americans is the **Tekakwitha** **.Conference**, begun in 1939 as an organization of priests who served Native American populations but increasingly, especially after 1977, an organization of Native Americans themselves. It encourages the formation of local "Kateri Circles" for the cultivation of Native American Catholic spirituality. There has been conflict within the group regarding how far to incorporate traditional Native American rituals into Catholic liturgies.

NATURAL LAW. Moral principles knowable through human reason, without necessary reliance on God's revelation*. The key Scripture passage in the development of natural law theory is Romans 2.14-16, where Paul says of the Gentiles that "the demands of the law are written in their hearts, while their conscience also bears witness." The specific concept of natural law came into Christian thought from Stoicism* and Roman law. The most influential theory of natural law, that of Thomas Aquinas*, is integrated into a worldview that is Aristotelian* rather than Stoic. For Aquinas, the "eternal law" is the divine providence guiding all things to the fulfillment of their ends. Natural law is the participation of the rational creature in the eternal law, so that the creature is aware of the ends of its nature and can choose to act toward them. The first precept of natural law is, "Good is to be done and promoted, and evil is to be avoided" (ST 1-2.94.2), and "good" for humans is specified in terms of the tendencies ("inclinations") of human nature toward its own proper fulfillment. Thomas mentions tendencies toward preservation of life, propagation and education of the young, knowledge of truth and life in society, not meaning this to be an exhaustive list. From these and similar goods, more specific moral norms may be derived (for an example, *see* SUICIDE), though Thomas does not do this in a rigidly systematic manner. He often draws on the theory of the virtues* rather than natural law reasoning to reach particular conclusions, and he acknowledges that particular situations are complex and involve many exceptions to general rules. While deriving from Thomas, the natural law tradition in the manuals of moral theology* from the seventeenth to the twentieth centuries tended to be rationalistic and legalistic. The manuals overlooked the teleological character of "nature" in Aristotle and Thomas, its inherent directedness toward ends (that is, toward the fulfillments specific to each particular nature), and spoke as if one could derive moral principles from human nature as one observed it. One important theory today, that of Germain Grisez, John Finnis, and Joseph Boyle, reformulates natural law in terms of goods basic to human fulfillment. A fundamental principle in this theory is that one should never act directly against a basic good. Proportionalism* is another reformulation of natural law theory. Most moral theologians regard natural law theories as important in order to preserve some recognition of human goods that is common between Christians and non-Christians and thus to serve as a basis for cooperation in pursuit of those goods.

NESTORIANISM. A heresy* taught by, or ascribed to, Nestorius (d. after 436), patriarch of Constantinople. It represents a form of the

Christology* of the school of Antioch*. Nestorius expressed reservations about the title *theotokos* ("God-bearer," "Mother of God"), used of Mary*. This title was already long in use, but Nestorius would accept it only with many qualifications and preferred *christotokos*, "Christ-bearer," that is, mother of the human Jesus. This position was attacked by Cyril of Alexandria and others as splitting Christ into two persons, one human, one divine. It was condemned, and Nestorius deposed, at the Council of Ephesus* in 431. The East Syrian church, centered in Edessa, rejected the Council of Ephesus. Its descendant, the Assyrian Church of the East*, remains in separation from Rome and Constantinople but does not wish to be called "Nestorian."

NEWMAN, JOHN HENRY (1801-1890). English theologian and philosopher. Raised in the Church of England and ordained an Anglican priest in 1825, Newman was appointed vicar of St. Mary's at Oxford in 1828. There he became a major figure in the "Oxford Movement," which sought to restore Catholic elements in the Church of England. The six volumes of *Parochial and Plain Sermons* preached at St. Mary's (1834-1842) have remained among his most influential works. Work on his book, *An Essay on the Development of Christian Doctrine* (1845), originally conceived as a defense of his stance within the Anglican Church, led to his conviction that the Christian Church of the early centuries was continued in the Roman Catholic Church. He became a Roman Catholic in 1845 and was ordained a priest in 1847. He told the story of his conversion in *Apologia pro Vita Sua* (1864). From 1854 to 1858, he was Rector of a new Catholic university in Dublin, Ireland, an endeavor that occasioned *The Idea of a University* (1858), which set out an ideal of the university* as an environment for the development of the mind. This work has been highly influential in England, the United States, and elsewhere. It and the *Apologia* are considered to rank among the classics of nineteenth-century English prose. His major theological works were the book on the development of doctrine and *An Essay in Aid of a Grammar of Assent* (1870), which studied the relation of the act of faith to reason. He is noteworthy for his efforts to introduce the emerging historical consciousness of the nineteenth century into Catholic theology. He was named a Cardinal by Pope Leo XIII* in 1878.

NICAEA (NICEA). Town in Asia Minor (now Iznik in Turkey), site of two ecumenical councils* of the early Church.

NICAEA I (325): The first ecumenical council, called by the Emperor Constantine I* in order to settle the conflict over Arianism*. Between two and three hundred bishops, almost all of them from the East, were present. The council adopted a creed*, shorter than the present "Nicene Creed," including the statement that the Son of God is *homoousios*, "one in being," with the Father, and not a creature as the Arians claimed. Four anathemas against the Arians were appended to the creed. Twenty canons governing church discipline were also adopted. There was much opposition within the Church to the neologism, *homoousios*, and the Arian conflict raged for another half century.

NICAEA II (787): The seventh ecumenical council, the last of those recognized by the Eastern Orthodox* as ecumenical, called by the regent Empress Irene, with the approval of Pope Hadrian I, to resolve the controversy over iconoclasm*. It first met in Constantinople in 786 but was broken up by soldiers immediately upon convening. Around three hundred bishops reconvened in Nicaea in September 787. The council repudiated the iconoclast council of Hieria (754) and defended images, emphasizing their usefulness in showing the true humanity of Christ. In the West, a faulty translation of the council's decrees was attacked in the *Libri Carolini*, written by Theodulf of Orleans under the auspices of Charlemagne, but Pope Hadrian eventually wrote in approval of the council. In the East, several ninth-century emperors revived iconoclasm, and the authority of the council was not definitively accepted until 843.

NICHOLAS OF CUSA (CUSANUS) (1401-1464). Leading philosopher, theologian, and churchman of the fifteenth century. Born Nicholas Cryfftz (Krebs) at Kues (Cusa), on the Moselle River near Trier, Nicholas studied canon law at Padua and philosophy and theology at Cologne. At the Council of Basel*, he became prominent as a defender of conciliarism*, which received its most systematic exposition in his *De concordantia catholica (The Catholic Concordance)* (1433). Dissatisfied with the discord of Basel and desiring to promote unity with the Greek Church, he shifted his allegiance to the papal party in 1436 and helped to prepare for the short-lived reunification enacted at the Council of Florence* in 1439. In 1449 he was named a cardinal* and in 1450 became bishop of Brixen in the Tyrol, where his efforts at reform involved him in considerable strife. After 1439, he turned increasingly to speculative thought in mathematics, philosophy, and theology. His best-known speculative works are *De docta ignorantia (On Learned Ignorance)* (1440) and *De visione Dei (The Vision of God)* (1453), which develops a distinctive approach to mystical theology. Cusanus's thought stands in the tradition of medieval neo-Platonism (*see* PLATONISM), with Pseudo-Dionysius* a particularly strong influence, but in its emphasis on human knowledge and symbolism it has been seen—by the philosophers Ernst Cassirer and Karl Jaspers, among others—as a precursor of modern philosophy. In theology, Cusanus's *De pace fidei (The Peace of Faith)* (1453) is an early classic of interreligious dialogue, expressing a vision of concord or harmony of all the religions in the one truth that underlies them. His *Cribratio Alcorani (A Scrutiny of the Qur'an)* (1461) takes a notably more sympathetic attitude toward Islam* than was common in Catholicism until fairly recently.

NOMINALISM (Lt *nomen*, "name"). In philosophy, the denial that general or universal terms, e.g., *horse* in "Secretariat was a horse," correspond to anything in reality. All that really exist are individual things, such as Secretariat and Mister Ed; the universal term *horse* is merely a "name" designating a group of individuals. Nominalism flourished at two different periods in the Middle Ages. In the eleventh century it was championed by Roscelin of Compiègne (d. ca. 1125) against a "Platonist"* conception of universals as existing separately from particulars. In the fourteenth century, it was promoted in a different form by William of Ockham* against an Aristotelian* conception of universals as existing within particulars. Philosophers and theologians in the tradition of Ockham formed the school of Nominalism, the most important school of thought in the fourteenth and fifteenth centuries. In theology its tendency was to restrict the role of reason and expand that of faith in matters pertaining to God.

NOVENA (Lt *novem*, "nine"). A nine-day period of prayer, often including public devotions*, usually done to seek some special grace or favor, such as healing. Novenas may have originated from the ancient Greek and Roman custom of a nine-day mourning period, but they did not become prominent in the Church until the seventeenth century. The Church has approved novenas and attached indulgences* to some of them in the nineteenth century. It has sought, however, to curb the superstitions sometimes associated with novenas—for instance, the belief that they unfailingly bring about the favor that is being sought.

NUCLEAR WEAPONS. Modern weapons, especially nuclear weapons, have raised new questions regarding the morality of war*. In particular, it is doubtful whether their use can satisfy the just-war criteria of discrimination (immunity of noncombatants from direct attack) and proportionality (sufficient balance of good achieved over harm done). Vatican Council II issued a strong condemnation of counter-population warfare: acts of war directed against whole cities or large areas together with their populations (GS 81 [1965]; *see under* WAR). This apparently applied to the use of large, strategic nuclear weapons. In *The Challenge of Peace* (CP)* (1983), the U.S. Bishops rejected the initiation of nuclear war with smaller, tactical nuclear weapons, because of the danger of escalation to mass destruction. For the same reason, they expressed skepticism even about the retaliatory use of nuclear weapons in a "limited exchange" (150-161). The only reason left for possession of nuclear weapons was **nuclear deterrence**, whereby one side deters another from attacking by means of a threat of inflicting "unacceptable retaliatory damage" (163). Deterrence had been called unstable, but not condemned, by Vatican Council II (GS 81). Some theologians argue that it is strictly immoral in that it involves a willingness, if attacked, to attack population centers, killing millions of innocent people. If counter-population warfare is immoral, so is the willingness to engage in it in response to attack. Nonetheless, Pope John Paul II* in 1982 judged deterrence morally acceptable as "a step on the way toward a progressive disarmament" (CP 173), and the U.S. Bishops followed this judgment, arguing that deterrence did not necessarily involve a conditional intention to kill the innocent. Like the pope, however, they called for steps toward nuclear disarmament.

NUN. *See* SISTER.

NUNCIO. *See* LEGATE, PAPAL.

O

OATH. The invocation of God as witness to the truth of what one is saying (**declaratory oath**) or the reliability of what one is promising (**promissory oath**). Oaths are common in the OT, but in Mt 5.33-37 Jesus forbids his disciples to take them. This teaching is echoed in Jas 5.12, but Paul uses oath formulas repeatedly (e.g., 2 Cor 1.23, Gal 1.20). Some Fathers of the Church* objected to oaths: Chrysostom* thought they should be avoided entirely, while Augustine* thought they should generally be avoided because of the risk of false swearing. But others, citing the authority of Paul, approved them within limits. The Catholic tradition has followed the latter course. Thomas Aquinas* considered an oath, taken in the proper circumstances, to be in fact an act of the virtue of religion (ST 2-2.81.2).

According to canon law*, oaths should be taken in "truth, judgment, and justice" (Canon 1199). This excludes, respectively, false oaths, rash oaths, and oaths attesting what one ought not to say (even though true) or promising what one ought not to do. To lie under oath is **perjury**. Canon law requires oaths of various people, e.g., members of tribunals, participants in trials, and administrators of church property. Newly ordained bishops* must take an oath of fidelity to the Holy See* (Canon 380). In 1910, Pope Pius X* imposed on those who wished to receive a Doctorate of Sacred Scriptures the obligation to take an oath to uphold the decrees of the Pontifical Biblical Commission (*see* BIBLICAL CRITICISM). That same year, he imposed an oath against Modernism* on all who assumed ecclesiastical offices; this oath was not abolished until 1967. In 1989, the obligation to take an oath of fidelity was extended to vicars of a bishop, parish priests, rectors of seminaries* and ecclesiastical* or Catholic universities (having canonical charters), professors of theology and philosophy in seminaries, deacons*, religious superiors, and "teachers of subjects which deal with faith and morals at whatever universities." Most canonists think this last phrase does not include teachers at most Catholic universities*, which do not have canonical charters. *See also* PROFESSION OF FAITH.

OBEDIENCE (Lt *oboedire*, "to listen to," from *audire*, "to hear"). The core of Christian obedience is not passive submission to rules and commands but an attitude of listening and responsiveness to God. In the OT, God requires obedience to his will, as expressed through his commandments (e.g., Dt 1-4). The essence of sin is disobedience to God (Gn 3). In the NT, Jesus' obedience to God, "to death, even death on a cross" (Phil 2.8) is the model for Christians (Phil 2.5). Christians are to "obey God rather than men" (Acts 5.29), but human authority is from God (Rom 13.1). Obedience is therefore due to civil authorities, parents, masters (Rom 13.1-7, Eph 6.1,5). For Thomas Aquinas*, obedience to human authority is a moral virtue, in the general category of justice* (ST 2-2.104). Human authority may be disobeyed when it is unjustly held or commands unjustly, and must be disobeyed when it commands contrary to divine authority. Catholic tradition in general requires obedience to civil authority—even speed limits (GS 30)—for the common good, while allowing or requiring disobedience when authority is unjust (CCC 1897-1904, 2242). Obedience is more strongly due to those who hold authority* in the Church, even though they may err when not exercising the gift of infallibility*, for "By divine institution the bishops have succeeded to the place of the apostles as shepherds of the Church, and the one who hears them hears Christ, but whoever rejects them rejects Christ and him who sent Christ" (LG 20).

Obedience, as one of the three evangelical counsels*, is central to religious life*. The religious makes a vow* or other pledge of obedience to his or her religious superiors. Among the monks of the desert (see DESERT FATHERS AND MOTHERS), submission to a holy authority was an act of curbing self-will and maintaining openness to God's will. In the Rule of St. Benedict* (sixth century), the monk is to obey the abbot, who "is believed to hold the place of Christ in the monastery" (RB 2). The monk is to obey without hesitation, as if the command came from God himself (5). Obedience is understood similarly in most classic treatments of religious life.

Such obedience is at odds with modern culture's emphasis on individual autonomy and responsibility, and contemporary society is especially alert to the dangers of blind obedience, whether to secular (e.g., Nazi Germany) or religious authority (e.g., the mass suicide at Jonestown, Guyana, in 1978). Some religious, e.g., Sandra Schneiders, are attempting to reformulate obedience for a world in which equality and participation have replaced the principle of hierarchy. Here, Benedict's counsel to monks to obey one another (RB 71-72) (and thus obey God in one another) provides some guidance. In all events, in a culture in which the pursuit of individual autonomy tends to be identified with a drive toward *control* of one's life and circumstances, there is a need for some institutionalized witness to obedience in the sense of attentiveness to the word of God and willingness to let go of control in response to it.

OBLATE (Lt *oblatus*, "one who is offered up"). (1) A child dedicated by his or her parents to a monastery (*see* MONASTICISM) and given to the monastery to be raised. The oblate was bound perpetually to the monastic state. The practice is attested in the Rule of St. Benedict* (sixth century) and lasted until around the twelfth century. In 1563, the Council of Trent* set sixteen as the minimum age for monastic profession. (2) In medieval monasteries, a "lay brother", or *conversus*, who looked after the temporal affairs of the monastery and was not regarded as fully a monk. (3) An adult who remained in the world but donated his or her possessions to a monastery and lived according to the monastic rule under the direction of the abbot. (4) Today, a layperson formally affiliated with a monastery in some way, who strives to live according to the spirit of the monastic rule. The Oblates of Saint Benedict are the chief instance. (5) Certain religious congregations (*see* RELIGIOUS LIFE) who have "Oblate" in their name, e.g., Oblates of Mary Immaculate (O.M.I.) and Oblates of Saint Francis de Sales (O.S.F.S.).

OBLIGATION, HOLY DAY OF. *See* HOLY DAY OF OBLIGATION.

OLD CATHOLICS. A group of churches, mostly in Europe, that are in a state of schism* in relation to the Roman Catholic Church. The schism originated with the deposition by Rome in 1702 of the archbishop of Utrecht, Holland, for sympathies with Jansenism*. It became formally a schism when a French Canadian bishop consecrated a successor to the deposed bishop in 1724. The Church of Utrecht was joined by groups of Catholics who left the Roman Catholic Church in the 1870s in protest against Vatican Council I's* definitions of the infallibility* and universal ordinary jurisdiction of the pope*. It is among these groups that the name "Old Catholic" ("old" meaning "opposed to the innovations of Vatican I") originated. The Old Catholics were later joined by schismatic Polish churches in the United States, which joined to become the Polish National Catholic Church.

The Old Catholics are united doctrinally around the Declaration of Utrecht (1889), which accepts (as do the Eastern Orthodox*) the decisions of the first seven ecumenical councils* (though the Polish National Catholics deviate from this somewhat). Their practice resembles that of the Roman Catholic Church, although their priests and bishops may be married. The Old Catholics have been in full communion with the churches of the Anglican Communion* since the 1930s. They are members of the World Council of Churches* and are active in ecumenical dialogue* with the Eastern Orthodox. The Roman Catholic Church acknowledges the validity* of Old Catholic orders; i.e., it recognizes that Old Catholic bishops are in apostolic succession*. In the United States the Old Catholics have fragmented into numerous tiny sects, centered on the orders and the agenda of individual bishops. The European Old Catholics are not in communion with many of these small churches.

ONTOLOGISM. A philosophical and theological theory that was prominent in Italy, France, and Belgium in the mid-nineteenth century. It drew on St. Augustine's* idea of divine illumination and held that the guarantee of true knowledge was the immediate presence of God, as Infinite Being, to the mind. The chief proponent of ontologism was the Italian philosopher Vincenzo Gioberti (1801-1852). Ontologism was also important at the Catholic University of Louvain in Belgium, where the main figure was Gérard Casimir Ubaghs (1800-1875). The philosophy of Antonio Rosmini (1799-1855), though not exactly an ontologism, bore significant resemblance to it. Chiefly because it seemed to blur the distinction between nature and grace*, ontologism was condemned by the Holy Office in 1861 and 1866. Its central tenet, that finite knowledge depends on some prior knowledge of God, was revived in a different form by later transcendental Thomism*.

OPTION FOR THE POOR. A commitment "to evaluate social and economic activity from the viewpoint of the poor and powerless" (U.S. Bishops, *Economic Justice for All** [1986], 87) and to resist injustice and oppression. It is an *option* in the sense that those who are not poor are free to make such a commitment, but recent Church documents present it as a moral obligation. The term, *option for the poor*, often preceded by the adjective *preferential*, arose within liberation theology* and first appeared in Church documents in the final document of the Third General Conference of Latin American Bishops (1979) at Puebla,

Mexico: "We affirm the need for conversion on the part of the whole church to a preferential option for the poor, an option aimed at their integral liberation." This stance reflects the standpoint of God in the Old Testament, who hears the cry of his oppressed people and delivers them from Egypt (Ex 3.7-9), and who protects the poor and dispossessed (e.g., Ex 22.24-26). The prophets proclaim that God takes up the cause of the poor against their oppressors (e.g., Is 3.14-15, 10:1-4; Amos 2.6). Jesus announces "glad tidings for the poor" (Lk 4.18-21) and declares that they are "blessed" (Lk 6.20-21). He associates with the poor of his society and warns of the danger of riches (e.g., Lk 18.18-30). Pope John Paul II* has repeatedly called for a "preferential option for the poor," although he is concerned to distinguish it from a Marxist "class struggle" and to affirm that it does not exclude anyone. As the U.S. bishops say, "The 'option for the poor' ... is not an adversarial slogan that pits one group or class against another. Rather it states that the deprivation and powerlessness of the poor wounds the whole community." They emphasize that the purpose of this commitment is to enable the poor "to become active participants in the life of society" (EJA 88). It is not a matter of doing something *for* the poor but of acting in solidarity* with them and assisting them toward becoming the agents of their own liberation.

OPUS DEI (Lt, "Work of God"). Full name: Prelature of the Holy Cross and Opus Dei. Opus Dei was founded in 1928 by José María Escrivá de Balaguer (1902-1975), a Spanish priest, who was beatified in 1992. It was originally conceived as an organization of laypeople, the purpose of which was to live a life of holiness in the ordinary professions and circumstances of secular life. Priests were admitted in 1943. Opus Dei was recognized as a "pious union" in 1941 and a secular institute* in 1950, before being raised to the status of a **personal prelature** in 1982. A personal prelature (Canons 294-297) consists of diocesan priests and deacons*, under the authority of a prelate who has powers similar (though not identical) to a bishop in his diocese*. Laypeople may be associated with it. Opus Dei is the only personal prelature in the Church.

Full members, male and female, are called "numeraries." They are celibate and live in Opus Dei houses. Oblates* (*aggregati*) take on the same obligations as the numeraries but do not live in Opus Dei centers. "Supernumeraries" live with their families and may be married. Priests may be incardinated into (canonically affiliated to) Opus Dei or incardinated into a diocese and affiliated to Opus Dei as oblate or supernumerary priests through the Holy Cross Society of Priests. "Prelature priests," incardinated to Opus Dei, hold all top leadership posts. Laymen, but not women, may hold leadership posts below the top level. Opus Dei conducts universities and schools, sponsors publications, and engages in other apostolic works. It maintains considerable secrecy about its membership and activities. A member may reveal his or her own membership but not that of another. The 1993 *Annuario Pontifico* reported that Opus Dei had 76,394 lay members and 1,459 priests.

Opus Dei has been regarded favorably by Pope John Paul II* but, elsewhere in the Church, has met with much criticism for its secretiveness, its methods of recruiting and retaining members, its religious conservatism, and its involvement with right-wing governments.

ORDER, RELIGIOUS. *See* RELIGIOUS LIFE.

ORDER, SACRAMENT OF. The sacrament* by which people are ordained to the ministries of bishop*, priest*, and deacon*. The sacrament is also called **ORDERS** or **HOLY ORDER(S)**. Some ceremonies for installing designated ministers in the Church are mentioned in the NT. In Acts 6.6 and 13.3, 1 Tm 4.14, and 2 Tm 6, laying on of hands is mentioned in this context. Acts 14.23 mentions prayer and fasting but not laying on of hands. The variety of ministries mentioned in the NT coalesced into the threefold pattern of bishop, presbyter (priest), deacon by the middle of the second century. Hippolytus (ca. A.D. 215) gives the first full description of the ordination of bishops, presbyters, and deacons. The ritual involves a liturgical setting, prayer, and the laying on of hands, which is understood as conferring a charism of the Holy Spirit*. The terms *order* and *ordination* were first used by Tertullian* (early third century); they are legal terms meaning a distinct class of person and incorporation into such a class.

The third century saw the beginning of the understanding of Christian leaders as *priests* (Latin *sacerdotes*), persons whose role was primarily cultic, to offer sacrifice*. This was applied first to bishops, who were considered to have the fullness of the priesthood. By the eleventh century, in the West, but not the East, the presbyter (now appropriately called "priest") was understood to possess the fullness of the sacrament of order. Medieval sacramental theology tended to locate the essence of the priesthood in the power to consecrate the eucharistic body and blood of Christ. The difference between a bishop and a priest was only a matter of the bishop's jurisdiction, not of the sacrament. The Protestant* Reformers rejected the idea of a specific ordained class in the Church, set apart by their sacramental powers. In response, the Council of Trent* declared that order is a true sacrament instituted by Christ, that with it Christ instituted a true priesthood, and that there are several other orders of ministers in the Church. Vatican Council II* (1962-1965), influenced by a recovery of the early Church's theology of orders, stated that the fullness of the sacrament of order belongs to the bishop (LG 21). It understood the sacrament more broadly than the medievals and Trent had, as conferring a special share in Christ's powers of teaching and governing as well as of sanctifying. It stated that there is an essential difference between the ordained priesthood and the common priesthood of all the faithful (LG 10) but did not go far in specifying what constitutes that difference. Some further reflection on that distinction has occurred in ecumenical dialogues* on ministry.

Only a bishop may ordain. Normally, at least three bishops should take part in the ordination (also called **consecration**) of a bishop. Ordinations take place at mass*, after the gospel. The central ritual act is the laying of the bishop's hands on the person being ordained, followed by a consecratory prayer. The newly ordained person is then given objects symbolic of his new role: gospels, ring, miter, and episcopal staff for a bishop; paten and chalice (*see* VESSELS) with bread and wine for the priest; gospels for the deacon.

The **minor orders** of porter, lector*, exorcist, and acolyte*, and the order of subdeacon were suppressed in 1972. These orders probably date from the third century. In the twelfth century, they were standardized, in the order stated here, as steps on the way to the diaconate and then the priesthood. Theologians disagreed on whether ordination to these offices was sacramental. The 1972 document of Pope Paul VI*, *Ministeria quaedam*, replaced them with the ministries (not orders) of lector and acolyte, to which laypeople can be appointed.

In the Western Church, only celibates* may be ordained priests or bishops. In some of the Eastern rites, married men may be ordained priests but not bishops. Married men may be ordained deacons. No one, however, may marry after ordination. Ordination is restricted to males; *see* ORDINATION OF WOMEN. Some fourth- and fifth-century sources speak of an ordination of women as deaconesses*. It is in dispute whether this was the diaconate or something like the minor orders.

ORDINATION OF WOMEN. The ordination of women to the priesthood and episcopate did not become a live issue in the Catholic Church until the 1970s. Church tradition* has been uniform (or virtually uniform) against women priests. The question at issue is whether this tradition is normative for the Church or whether it merely reflects the influence of cultures that, by and large, excluded women from positions of authority. If the latter, it can be changed as cultural circumstances change. What has called the tradition into question is the movement for women's equality and full participation in social institutions (*see* FEMINISM), a movement that has been very strong in Western Europe and North America for decades and is gaining strength in the rest of the world. The Church itself forbids discrimination against women (GS 29), but the exclusion of women from the priesthood is not unjust discrimination if gender is relevant to the nature of the priesthood (just as it is not unfair to exclude non-Catholics from the Catholic priesthood). Most major Protestant* churches began ordaining women in the twentieth century, but the Eastern Orthodox* do not ordain women.

On May 22, 1994, Pope John Paul II* issued an apostolic letter, *Ordinatio sacerdotalis*, in which—in language that stopped just short of an infallible declaration—he sought to close the question of the ordination of women: "In order that all doubt may be removed regarding a matter of great importance, a matter which pertains to the Church's divine constitution itself, in virtue of my ministry of confirming the brethren (cf. Lk 22.32) I declare that the Church has no authority whatsoever to confer priestly ordination on women, and that this judgment is to be definitively held by all the Church's faithful." In a document dated October 28, 1995, the Congregation for the Doctrine of the Faith* (with explicit papal approval) declared that the teaching of *Ordinatio sacerdotalis* is infallible*. This declaration, though authoritative, is not itself infallible.

Ordinatio sacerdotalis relies on arguments that were previously developed in the declaration, *Inter insigniores* (I.I.) ("Declaration on the Admission of Women to the Ministerial Priesthood"), issued by the Congregation for the Doctrine of the Faith in 1976. I.I. argues principally from the unbroken tradition of the Church. It contends that this tradition reflects the will of Jesus, arguing that Jesus, despite his willingness to break customs regarding men's relations with women, chose no women among the Twelve apostles*. Neither did the early apostles ordain women. St. Paul, in 1 Cor 14.34-35, forbids women to speak in the assembly, while, in 1 Tim 2.12, the Pauline author forbids them to teach. I.I. interprets these as excluding women from "the official function of teaching in the Christian assembly," not from spontaneous prophecy, which other NT texts show was done by women (e.g., 1 Cor 11.5). In defense of the "normative character" of the practice of Jesus and the apostles, I.I. argues that, in celebrating the Eucharist, the priest "acts not only through the effective power conferred on him by Christ, but *in persona Christi*, taking the role of Christ, to the point of being in his very image, when he pronounces the words of consecration." Only a male can suitably be the image of the male Christ. Against the objection that Christ's maleness was incidental to his role as savior (as his height, for instance, would have been), I.I. cites biblical texts in which God's relation to his people (e.g., Hos 1-3) and Christ's relation to his Church (e.g., Eph 5.22-23) are likened to a bridegroom's relation to his bride.

Theologians who favor the ordination of women have sought to rebut all of these arguments since (absent considerations of infallibility) if they are refuted the basic argument from justice, cited above, would prevail. The unbrokenness of tradition, for instance, is challenged by E. Schüssler Fiorenza's argument that women would probably have presided at the eucharist in first-century house-churches when they were the heads of households. Proponents of women's ordination also argue that the ordination of women would resolve the shortage of priests and would enable women to exercise their special gifts in priestly ministry. An organization in the United States that advocates the ordination of women is the Women's Ordination Conference, founded in 1976. Opponents of the ordination of women often rely on theological anthropologies that emphasize the distinction (frequently understood as complementarity) between men and women, contending that the priesthood is appropriate only for the male. In practice, neither *Ordinatio sacerdotalis* nor the 1995 declaration has ended the debate.

The arguments of *Inter insigniores* do not exclude women from ordination to the diaconate, since deacons* do not celebrate the eucharist, and since there is evidence in Scripture and tradition for the existence of women deacons (*see* DEACONESS). The principal objection to women deacons is that the diaconate is a step toward priesthood. It is also debated whether deaconesses were ordained sacramentally and to what extent they were comparable to male deacons.

ORIENTAL ORTHODOX CHURCHES. The most common name for the churches that did not accept the declaration of the Council of Chalcedon* (451) that Jesus Christ* is one person in two natures. They are also sometimes called Ancient Oriental Churches or Non-Chalcedonian Churches, but the term monophysite* churches is now considered inappropriate. These churches did not accept the monophysite theology of Eutyches, but, seeing "two natures" language as Nestorian*, preferred Cyril of Alexandria's formula, "one incarnate nature of God's Word." Today there are six such churches: the Armenian Church, the Coptic Church, the Ethiopic Church (which separated from the Coptic Church in 1950 to become autocephalous [self-governing]), the Syrian Church (sometimes called "Syro-Jacobite"), and the Syrian Church of India (Malankara), which became autocephalous in 1912, and (since 1993) the Eritrean Church. These churches are in communion with one another, but have no center of unity such as the Patriarch of Constantinople for the Eastern Orthodox*. Today it is recognized that their differences with Roman Catholics and Eastern Orthodox over Christology are largely verbal. In 1973, Pope Paul VI* and Coptic Pope Shenouda III declared a common faith, and in 1984 Pope John Paul II* and Syrian Patriarch Ignatius Zakka I made a similar declaration. Differences remain over the authority of councils from Chalcedon onward, over papal primacy (*see* POPE), and over the Eastern Catholic Churches*. Official ecumenical dialogues are under way with the Coptic and Indian churches. Ecumenical relations between the Oriental Orthodox and Eastern Orthodox have progressed still further. The Catholic Church recognizes the validity of the sacraments of the Oriental Orthodox Churches.

ORIGEN (185/6-ca. 254). The greatest theologian among the Greek Fathers of the Church*. Born and raised in Alexandria*, he became the head of the catechetical school there. While at Alexandria, he learned Platonic philosophy, studying for a time with Ammonius Saccas, the teacher of Plotinus (*see* PLATONISM). He spent several sojourns in Caesarea in Palestine, where he settled permanently in 231 after a dispute with Demetrius, bishop of Alexandria. In Caesarea he wrote, preached, and conducted a school. His literary production was enormous, but most has not survived. His best-known works were the

Hexapla (an arrangement of six versions of the OT in parallel columns), commentaries on most of the books of the Bible, *On Prayer, Exhortation to Martyrdom, Contra Celsum* (a reply to an attack on Christianity by Celsus, a philosopher), and *On First Principles (Peri Archōn)*, a systematic and speculative work. Origen's scriptural commentaries made extensive use of allegory; he was the chief influence on subsequent patristic and medieval use of this method. His trinitarian theology, which tended toward subordinationism*, underlay all views in the subsequent controversies over Arianism*. In *On First Principles* (imperfectly preserved, mostly in a defective Latin translation by Rufinus of Aquileia), he speculates on a creation (eternal?) of rational souls, which fall into bodies, but can return to God. Some texts suggest that this process of fall and return may be carried out more than once (*see* REINCARNATION). He holds out hope for a restoration (*apocatastasis*) of all things to God, including the salvation of the damned, demons*, and the devil. Such speculations, especially as hardened into doctrines by some of Origen's followers, led to serious controversies in the fourth and sixth centuries and to suspicion regarding Origen's orthodoxy. Several Origenist propositions were condemned at the Second Council of Constantinople* in 553, but the inclusion of Origen's name among a list of heretics in the council's official acts is probably a later interpolation.

ORIGINAL SIN. (1) The first sin* committed by the first human beings; (2) the guilt or loss of grace* inherited by their descendants, all subsequent human beings, in consequence of the first sin. These two senses are distinguished in theology as *peccatum originale originans* (originating original sin) and *peccatum originale originatum* (originated original sin).

The story of the first sin of Adam (Heb, "the human") and Eve is narrated in Genesis 3. As a result of their disobedience, they are expelled from the Garden of Eden and condemned to a life of pain and toil, ending in death (Gn 3.16-24). Gn 3 is a prelude to Gn 4-11, showing how this first sin leads to a history of increasing sin, up through Noah's flood and the Tower of Babel. The story, however, does not contain any specific notion of an inherited sin or guilt. The other crucial biblical text for the theology of original sin is Romans 5.12-21. "Just as through one person [Adam] sin entered the world, and through sin, death, and thus death came to all, inasmuch as all sinned" (Rom 5.12), so the grace of justification* for eternal life has entered the world "for the many" (i.e., for all) through the one Jesus Christ (Rom 5.15).

The doctrine of original sin was given its classic form by Augustine* (354-430). Drawing on the Pauline text, on his own experience of sin, and on the practice of infant baptism*, Augustine argued that the sin of Adam made the whole human race a "mass of sin" worthy of damnation, from which God chooses to save some people through grace. He held that the whole race sinned in Adam, supporting this claim from a mistranslation of Romans 5.12 that construed as "*in whom* all sinned" the words rendered above as "inasmuch as all sinned." Augustine later speculated that original sin was transmitted from the first humans to their descendants through a disorder inherent in the act of sexual intercourse. In the conflict with the Pelagians*, the Church largely adopted Augustine's theology of original sin (without committing itself as to the means whereby it is transmitted) in provincial councils at Carthage in 418 and Orange (in Gaul) in 529. Echoing Carthage and Orange, the Council of Trent* in 1546 declared that the sin of Adam is passed on "by propagation not by imitation" to all humans (except Jesus and possibly Mary [*see* IMMACULATE CONCEPTION]) and can be removed only by the grace of Christ, which is communicated through baptism. It added that original sin is fully removed by baptism and that the concupiscence (tendency toward sin) that remains after baptism is not original sin itself but only an effect of it (DS 1510-16). Medieval and modern theologians provided several accounts of the "propagation" of original sin that were alternative to Augustine's.

A challenge to the traditional theory of original sin came when, as a result jointly of modern paleontology and biblical criticism, the narrative about the first humans in Genesis 2 and 3 came no longer to be taken literally by many Christians. Most traditional theology of original sin had assumed its literal truth at least in regard to the origin of sin. Today, however, it is generally understood as a narrative depicting fundamental truths about human sin at all times in the imagery of ancient near-Eastern myth*. The encyclical *Humani generis* of Pope Pius XII* (1950) upheld a cautious literalism about the sin of a first couple. Pius stated, "It is in no way apparent how" **polygenism** (the theory, then as now held by some but not all scientific authorities, that the human race originated in more than one original couple) could be reconciled with the doctrine of original sin, "which proceeds from a sin actually committed by an individual Adam and which through generation is passed on to all" (DS 3897). Most theologians today believe polygenism (whether or not it is true) is compatible with original sin (*see* EVOLUTION). Some hold nonetheless that there must have been one single original sinful act, which is the source of all subsequent sin. Others, e.g., P. Schoonenberg, identify original sin with the "sin of the world," whereby each of us is shaped into moral personhood in a social environment that is corrupted by past sins, so that sin becomes a part of our being. Still others, e.g., A. Vanneste, hold that "original sin" is nothing more than the fact that personal sin ("actual sin") is universal. Both of the latter theories have been criticized as inadequate to account for the attraction to evil* in the depth of the human heart and therefore insufficiently attentive to the magnitude of Christ's victory over evil.

ORTHODOXY (Gk *orthē*, "right," *doxa*, "opinion, glory"). "Right opinion" or "right belief," that is, the normative beliefs of the Church (*see* DOCTRINE, DOGMA), or personal belief in accordance with them. When not capitalized, "orthodoxy" is opposed to "heresy"* or else to "heterodoxy" ("different belief") as its opposite. Concern for right belief is as old as Christianity; for NT evidence, see, e.g., 1 Cor 11.2, 1 Tm 1.10. The words *orthodoxy* and *heterodoxy* are first found in Eusebius of Caesarea (ca. 260-340). *Orthodoxy* later came to mean adherence to the doctrine of the early ecumenical councils*, especially Ephesus* (431) and Chalcedon* (451) against Nestorianism* and monophysitism*. It was thus that it became (capitalized) part of the name of the eastern churches in communion with Constantinople* (*see* EASTERN ORTHODOX CHURCHES). In modern times, the churches that do not accept Chalcedon but accept the councils up through Ephesus have come to be called Oriental Orthodox*.

In 842, after the resolution of the controversy over iconoclasm*, the **Feast of Orthodoxy** was established, celebrated on the First Sunday of Lent in both the Eastern Orthodox and Eastern Catholic Churches*. In its liturgy, a litany* called the *Synodicon* is read, contrasting orthodox teachers and saints with heretics. In later Eastern Orthodox tradition, "orthodoxy" has sometimes been interpreted as "right worship," as if derived from *doxa* in its meaning of "glory."

Neo-orthodoxy was a twentieth-century theological movement, led by Karl Barth (1886-1968). It was chiefly Protestant but had some impact upon Catholic theology. A reaction against liberal Protestantism, it stressed the transcendence of God, God's judgment of a sinful world, and the need for grace*.

ORTHOPRAXIS (ORTHOPRAXY) (Gk *orthē*, "right," *praxis*, "action"). "Right action." A term that has been introduced in recent political* and liberation theology* to contrast with and to complement "orthodoxy"* ("right belief") and to restore right action to a primary place as a criterion of authentic Christianity. "Orthopraxis" usually means, first of all, action in solidarity* with the poor and oppressed in a spirit of discipleship* of Christ (*see* OPTION FOR THE POOR). When it is generalized to include all actions of discipleship, its kinship with the ancient principle of *Lex orandi, lex credendi** becomes evident. Theologians who stress orthopraxis do not wish to discard orthodoxy. Rather, they are concerned that an emphasis on orthodoxy leads to a narrow concentration on intellectual belief and verbal formulas of faith. In emphasizing praxis instead, they are not exalting action without belief, for the concept of praxis involves a mutual interplay of action and reflection (*see under* LIBERATION THEOLOGY). Their point is that right action, submitted to adequate reflection, leads to right understanding (or right belief), which in turn is a guide to further action.

P

PACIFISM. Opposition, on moral or religious grounds, to: (1) the use of violence against others, or (2) the use of lethal force against others, or (3) war*. Some sayings of Jesus (e.g., Mt 5.39: "Offer no resistance to one who is evil. When someone strikes you on your right cheek, turn the other one to him as well") and the example of Jesus in suffering crucifixion rather than resorting to violence have provided inspiration to Christian pacifists. The earliest Christian writers who addressed the question of the legitimacy of warfare, for instance, Tertullian* and Origen*, took a pacifist position. Christian pacifism was not universal, however, as some Christians served in the Roman army. After the Christianization of the empire, Christian pacifism mostly disappeared in favor of some form of just-war theory (*see* WAR). In a sense, a partial pacifism remained in the division of the Church into laity*, on the one hand, and clergy* and monks on the other, whose pursuit of Christian perfection usually excluded participation in warfare. Pacifism reappeared in the eleventh- and twelfth-century poverty movements, such as the Humiliati and Waldenses*. St. Francis of Assisi* (1182-1226), while not condemning those who took part in war, rejected military service for a life of nonviolence and preaching of peace. He required his "Third Order"* "not to take up lethal weapons, or bear them about, against anybody." Some Protestant* groups, particularly the Mennonites, Quakers, and Church of the Brethren, espoused pacifism, but the Catholic Church accepted the just-war theory as it was worked out by medieval and early modern theologians. The Catholic Worker* movement, led by Dorothy Day (1897-1980), revived Catholic pacifism in the United States in the 1930s. The first official document allowing room for pacifism was Vatican Council II's *Pastoral Constitution on the Church in the Modern World* (1965), which praised those who renounced the use of violence (78). It called for the law to make provision for conscientious objection* to war (78-79). The U.S. Bishops' pastoral letter, *The Challenge of Peace** (1983), expressed admiration of the witness of Christian pacifists but restricted pacifism to individuals as an option; governments are required to employ armed defense if necessary (73-75). The bishops saw "the just-war teaching and non-violence as distinct but interdependent methods of evaluating warfare. They diverge on some specific conclusions, but they share a common presumption against the use of force as a means of settling disputes" (120). They noted, as have many theologians, that in the case of many of the methods of modern warfare, pacifism and just-war theory agree in a negative judgment (121).

PANENTHEISM (Gk *pan*, "all," *en*, "in," *theos*, "God"). A theological position that holds that all things are in God*, but that God surpasses them. The term was probably coined by Karl C. F. Krause (1781-1832) but is chiefly associated with the theology of Charles Hartshorne (1897-). Hartshorne sought a middle position between pantheism*, which holds that God is identical with the sum of all things, and "classical theism," which he thought severed God from the world. For Hartshorne, God and the world are interdependent: God is cause of the world, but God changes in response to the world. God's perfection is perfect relationality: only God both affects and is affected by all other beings. Hartshorne's thought has influenced some

American Catholic theologians, for instance David Tracy. *See* PROCESS THEOLOGY.

PANTHEISM (Gk *pan*, "all," *theos*, "God"). The identification of God with all that is. No serious thinker makes this identification in a flat, unqualified way, as if this page were a small piece of God. Rather, pantheism is a tendency; thus, many systems of Hindu*, Buddhist*, Stoic*, and Platonic* thought have been labeled pantheistic, in that for them the ultimate reality of all that is is divine. But all these systems preserve some distinction between reality as we encounter it and reality as it ultimately is. The same can be said for those thinkers in the Christian tradition who have been accused of pantheism, including John Scotus Erigena (ca. 810-877), Amalric (Amaury) of Bène (d. 1206), Meister Eckhart* (ca. 1260-1327/8), and G. W. F. Hegel (1770-1831). There is an affinity between pantheistic doctrines and mysticism*, with its experiences of the ultimate oneness of all things. The crucial question in each case is whether a theology has adequately preserved divine transcendence and the difference of the creature from the creator (*see* CREATION). Pantheism was condemned by Vatican Council I (1870) (DS 3023-3025).

PAPACY. *See* POPE.

PAPAL STATES (STATES OF THE CHURCH). Areas of central Italy over which the pope* exercised civil authority. The remote beginnings of the Papal States lay in the "Patrimony of Peter," large areas of land held by the Church, beginning in the fourth century. As a sovereign political entity, the Papal States began with the **Donation of Pepin** (756), whereby the Frankish king Pepin granted the pope sovereignty over an extensive area. The Papal States always included the area around Rome*. Otherwise, their extent varied with shifting political fortunes of the papacy; at their peak in the sixteenth through nineteenth centuries, they reached north to Ferrara and east to Ancona. For many periods, one must distinguish between the area over which the popes claimed sovereignty and that which they effectively ruled. In the middle nineteenth century, many of the papal lands were lost to the rising state of Italy, but French power protected Rome. After the Franco-Prussian War and the overthrow of Napoleon I, French support was withdrawn, and the Italian armies captured Rome in September 1870. The people of the territory confirmed Italian rule in a plebiscite the following month, but the popes refused to accept the loss of temporal power. The issue, called the **Roman Question**, was finally resolved by the Lateran Pacts in 1929, creating the state of Vatican City*.

PARISH (Gk *paroikia*, from *paroikos*, "dwelling near"). "A parish is a definite community of the Christian faithful established on a stable basis within a particular church" (Canon 515). It is a division of a diocese*, usually but not always a unit of territory. It is supervised by a priest who is called the **pastor** (Lt, "shepherd"), under the authority of the diocesan bishop*. Due to a shortage of priests, care of a parish may be entrusted to a deacon* or layperson, but in this case some priest is assigned the powers of pastor to supervise the pastoral care (Canon 517).

PAROCHIAL SCHOOLS. *See* SCHOOLS, CATHOLIC, IN THE UNITED STATES.

PAROUSIA (Gk, "presence"; an official visit of a ruler). The Second Coming of Jesus; the return of Jesus at the end of time (e.g., Mt 24.3,27,37,39 (*see* ESCHATOLOGY). The term *parousia* and the imagery associated with it are connected with the "Son of Man," a figure prominent in apocalyptic* literature (e.g. Dn 7.13 and the apocryphal* books of Enoch and 4 Esdras), who will come in judgment at the end of the present order of the world and receive everlasting dominion from God. Jesus often speaks of himself in the synoptics as the "Son of Man"; scholars do not agree whether this derives from Jesus' actual usage, and if so, whether, as he used it, it had apocalyptic overtones. In any event, Jesus will come to judge the nations (Mt 25.31-46), and at his coming the dead will rise (1 Thes 4.16) (*see* JUDGMENT, RESURRECTION). It seems clear that the earliest Church expected the parousia to come quite soon (1 Thes 4.17), but the exact time was said to be unknown (Mk 13.32). Subsequent Church tradition has resisted attempts to predict the time of the parousia. That Jesus "will come again in glory to judge the living and the dead" is an article of faith, however, affirmed in the Nicene Creed*. Contemporary theology emphasizes that this "Second Coming" is not a return of one who was absent but a manifestation of one who was present in history all along.

PASCAL, BLAISE (1623-1662). French mathematician, scientist, and religious thinker. At the age of nineteen, he invented the first calculating machine. He later founded probability theory and contributed importantly to the development of differential calculus. He did significant research on barometric pressure and hydraulics and invented the syringe. But increasingly his concern was religion. He was attracted to Jansenism* and associated with the community of Port-Royal, where his sister was a nun. On November 23, 1654, he had a powerful religious experience of the "God of Abraham, Isaac, and Jacob, not the God of philosophers and scholars." Until his death he carried, sewn into his clothing, a brief written "Memorial" of this experience. Between 1655 and 1657, he wrote the *Provincial Letters*, in defense of the Jansenist Antoine Arnauld against the Jesuits*, a masterpiece of irony and polemic that is regarded as one of the classics of French literature. At the time of his death, he was working on a long treatise of Christian apologetics*, the fragments of which were later published as the *Pensées (Thoughts)*. His keynote was, "The heart has its reasons, which reason does not know," that is, rational, philosophical arguments can yield inadequate knowledge of God at best, but love can lead the soul to a more satisfying knowledge of the true God, whose love for us is revealed to "Abraham, Isaac, and Jacob," and ultimately in Christ.

PASCHAL MYSTERY (Gk *Pascha*, "Passover"). The saving work of Jesus' passion, death, and resurrection*. These events took place at the time of Passover*, and Passover themes early entered into Christian interpretation. Thus, the NT speaks of Jesus as the Paschal lamb (1 Cor 5.7; cf. Jn 1.29, 19.36) who is sacrificed. Passover readings are included in the liturgy of the Easter Triduum*; Ex 12.1-8,11-14, the story of the institution of the feast, is read at the Mass of the Lord's Supper on Holy Thursday, while Ex 14.15-15.1, the story of the deliverance from Egypt, is read at the Easter Vigil. Jesus is understood to have "passed over" from death to life, and with him all Christians "pass over." Through his death and resurrection, they are delivered from bondage to sin and death as the Israelites were delivered from Egypt.

PASSOVER. A principal festival of the Jewish year, first described in Ex 12.1-28. It commemorates the Exodus, the deliverance of Israel from Egypt. Its levels of meaning include the Angel of Death "passing over" the houses of the Israelites (Ex 12.27) and the Israelites "passing over" the Red Sea (Ex 14.10-22). The Paschal (Passover) lamb is slaughtered on the afternoon of the 14th day of the lunar month of Nisan, and the Passover meal, including the lamb and unleavened bread, is eaten that evening. Unleavened bread is to be eaten for a week afterward. The passion of Jesus occurred at Passover. The Synoptic* gospels portray Jesus' Last Supper, the night before his death, as a Passover meal; John instead places Jesus' death on the afternoon of the Passover, hence before the Passover meal. The earliest Christian celebration of Easter* was at the time of Passover, 14 Nisan. (*See* PASCHAL MYSTERY.)

PASTOR. *See* PARISH.

PASTORAL LETTER. (1) A formal teaching document addressed by a bishop* to his diocese*, by several bishops to their dioceses, or by an episcopal conference* to the dioceses in its region. Pastoral letters are authoritative documents of the ordinary magisterium* but have a relatively low degree of binding force. (2) Any of the two NT letters to Timothy and the letter to Titus, all ascribed to St. Paul; these are more commonly called the "Pastoral Epistles."

PATRIARCH (Gk, "father-ruler"). In the Bible, this term refers to the first males enumerated in the early chapters of Genesis, and then to Abraham, Isaac, Jacob, and Jacob's twelve sons. In the Church, it designates the pope* and bishops who rank immediately beneath the pope in jurisdiction. Without using the term *patriarch*, the Council of Nicaea* (325) accorded patriarchal status to the bishops of Rome*, Alexandria*, and Antioch*, in that order. The First Council of Constantinople* (381) added Constantinople*, and the Council of Chalcedon* (451) added Jerusalem*. By the sixth century, all and only the bishops of these sees ("patriarchates") were "patriarchs." Today, in the Eastern Catholic Churches*, there are six patriarchs, each of whom is the head (under the pope) of those who belong to his rite*: one of Alexandria (Coptic), three of Antioch (Syrian, Maronite, Melkite), one of Babylonia (Chaldaean), and one of Sis or Cilicia (Armenian). All of the Eastern-rite patriarchs are made cardinals*. In the Roman Rite, the pope is Patriarch of the West. During the Crusades, Latin patriarchates were established in Constantinople,

Alexandria, Antioch, and Jerusalem. They became titular (in name only) patriarchates and were abolished altogether in 1964, except for that of Jerusalem, which had been reestablished as a true patriarchate in 1847. The Latin-rite bishops of Lisbon, Venice, and Goa-Damao (India) also have the title but not the power of patriarchs.

PATRICK, ST. (Patricius) (ca. 390-ca. 460). British missionary to Ireland. Many traditional stories about St. Patrick are legendary, but he left behind two authentic works: a brief *Confession* describing his life and defending his ministry, and a *Letter to Coroticus*, rebuking a military leader for the massacre and kidnapping of a number of newly converted Irish Christians. From these and other sources, some facts and approximate dates may be established. Patrick's father, Calpornius, was a Romano-British municipal councilor and deacon, his grandfather Potitus a priest. At age sixteen, Patrick was captured by Irish raiders and taken in slavery to Ireland. While there, he underwent a personal religious conversion. After six years, he escaped. He studied for priesthood, possibly in Gaul, otherwise in Britain, and experienced a call to return to Ireland. He was sent to Ireland as bishop around 432, probably by the British church rather than by Pope Celestine I. There was already a small Christian community there, but Patrick is chiefly responsible for spreading Christianity around Ireland, especially to the north and west. He baptized many, ordained native priests, and established monasteries for men and women. He established his see at Armagh, in the north. His feast is celebrated on March 17.

PATRON SAINT. A saint*, or occasionally an angel*, named as a special protector of and intercessor for a person, group, place, activity, institution, or circumstance. The custom of choosing a saint's name at baptism* dates from the fourth century and was later followed by similar practices at confirmation* and profession as a monk or religious. The dedication of churches to saints began in the fourth or fifth century. In the Middle Ages, patron saints were designated for towns and many types of activity, as well as for patients suffering from specific illnesses. Today, most countries have patron saints, e.g., for the United States, Mary* under the title of the Immaculate Conception*, and patrons have been assigned for groups of people ranging from accountants (St. Matthew) to youth (St. Aloysius Gonzaga). The Church officially names some patron saints, but most are designated through popular devotion.

PAUL VI, POPE (1963-1978) (Giovanni Battista Montini, b. 1897). Montini was born into a wealthy family at Concesio, near Brescia. His father was a prominent landowner, newspaper publisher, and politician. Ordained in 1920, Montini entered the papal Secretariat of State in 1922. From 1924 to 1933, he was involved with Italian Catholic student movements, then in conflict with fascism. He became assistant to Eugenio Pacelli, the Secretary of State, in 1937. Pacelli became Pope Pius XII* in 1939, and after 1944 Montini reported directly to him, with Pius serving in effect as his own Secretary of State. Montini was much involved in relief efforts after World War II. In 1952 he was made Archbishop of Milan, where he made special efforts to address workers. In 1958, he was made a cardinal*.

Once elected pope, he immediately expressed his intention to continue the Second Vatican Council* and the other initiatives of his predecessor, John XXIII*. He presided over the remaining three sessions of the Council, in which all of its documents were produced, and then over the process of revising the liturgy* and Church structures in consequence of the Council's decisions. He actively pursued ecumenical contacts with the Eastern* and Oriental Orthodox*, Anglicans*, and Protestants*. A high point of his ecumenical work came when he and Patriarch Athenagoras of Constantinople in 1965 solemnly lifted the mutual excommunications imposed by Rome and Constantinople in 1054. Relations with Protestants were hindered by his reiteration in 1976 of the prohibition of the ordination of women*.

Breaking with papal precedent, he traveled to all parts of the non-communist world, including a pilgrimage to the Holy Land in 1964 and a journey to address the United Nations in New York in 1965. He paid far more attention to the Third World than had his predecessors, visiting Asia, Africa, and Latin America, and appointing numerous cardinals from those areas. He issued three important social documents (*see* SOCIAL TEACHING), the encyclical *Populorum progressio* (1965), the apostolic letter *Octogesima adveniens* (1971), and the apostolic exhortation *Evangelium nuntiandi* (1975), all of them making strong calls for justice* in the international order.

At a cost of considerable personal pain, he attempted to set a course of moderation during the years of turmoil following the Council, when large numbers left the priesthood and religious life, and many Catholics demanded more radical changes in the Church, while others actively resisted the changes that had been introduced. He oversaw the establishment, and the first five meetings, of the Synod* of Bishops, as an exercise of episcopal collegiality*, but restricted them to a largely consultative role in order not to encroach on papal authority. He defended priestly celibacy* and the indissolubility of marriage*, while allowing the establishment of relatively easy processes for laicization of priests who wished to marry and for annulment* of failed marriages. The great crisis of his papacy came in 1968, when in his encyclical *Humanae vitae* he reiterated the condemnation of artificial birth control*, amid widespread expectations that the teaching would be changed in light of the fact that a large majority of the pontifical commission appointed to study the subject favored a qualified approval of contraception. It appears that his chief concern was that to overturn prior papal teaching would undermine papal authority, but the result was the opposite, as theologians engaged in widespread dissent* on contraception and related issues, and laity departed from Church teaching on them in practice. His entire papacy was marked by a tension between a genuine desire for renewal in the Church and a cautious temperament, which made him fearful of what might be lost in radical change.

PAULISTS (Congregation of the Missionary Society of St. Paul the Apostle [C.S.P.]). A religious community founded by Isaac T. Hecker (1819-1888) and dedicated to evangelization* within the United States. Hecker, who had been an associate of the New England transcendentalists, including Ralph Waldo Emerson and Henry David Thoreau, converted to Catholicism in 1844. In 1845, he joined the Redemptorists, then primarily a German congregation. He desired to establish an English-speaking Redemptorist foundation for the purpose of bringing the Catholic message to non-Catholic Americans. After a dispute with his superiors that led to his expulsion from the order, he and several associates founded the Paulists in 1858, with the approval of Pope Pius IX*. They took solemn promises, rather than vows*, of poverty, chastity, and obedience (*see* EVANGELICAL COUNSELS). The Paulists' mission began as one of public speaking and writing. They have published the magazine, *The Catholic World*, since Hecker founded it in 1865 (from 1972 to 1988 it was *New Catholic World*). The Catholic Publishing Society, begun by Hecker in 1866, has developed into Paulist Press, the largest Catholic publishing house in the United States. The Paulist National Catholic Evangelization Association publishes *Share the Word*, a bimonthly commentary on the lectionary* readings, and assists parishes and dioceses in evangelization efforts. The Paulists also produce films and videotapes, including television series and even full-length features. Current Paulist priorities are reconciliation of alienated Catholics, bringing the gospel to American institutions and culture, and ecumenical relations. There were 237 Paulists in 1993.

PAX CHRISTI (Lt, "Peace of Christ"). An international Catholic peace* organization, founded in France in 1945 to promote reconciliation between French and German Catholics after World War II and later broadening into a movement for worldwide peace. Its headquarters are in Antwerp, Belgium. It has twenty-two national sections, including **Pax Christi USA**, founded in 1972 and headquartered in Erie, Pennsylvania. Pax Christi USA rejects war*, violence, and domination, and seeks to promote Christian nonviolence, peacemaking, disarmament, economic and interracial justice, human rights*, and respect for creation. Although the organization is Catholic, membership is open to non-Catholics. Members need not be strict pacifists*, though many are. Pax Christi USA has about 12,000 members (including several hundred collective memberships for religious communities and parishes), among them more than one hundred bishops.

PEACE. According to Vatican Council II, "Peace is not merely the absence of war" (GS 78). In the OT, peace (Heb *shalom*) connotes wholeness, prosperity, justice, and right order (Lv 26.3-13). It is a result of the community's maintaining covenant fidelity to God (e.g., Ez 37.26). The fullness of peace is a fruit of the Messianic time (Is 2.2-5, 9.5, 32.15-20). In the NT, Jesus brings a peace that the world cannot bring (Jn 14.27, 16.33). The kingdom* of God, which he proclaims, is characterized by peace and forgiveness. Jesus blesses the peacemakers (Mt 5.9) and calls for love of enemies (Mt 5.43-48). The peace of the kingdom is brought about through Jesus' death (Col 1.19-20) and resurrection (Jn 20.19-23).

Though for some time Church leaders promoted "holy wars" (*see* CRUSADES), the Christian tradition has generally seen war* as counter to the spirit of Jesus. Aside from a minority tradition of pacifism*, however, theologians and Church leaders, at least since the time of Constantine* (fourth century), have held that in this world, in which the kingdom of God is not fully realized, wars may regrettably be necessary. The long tradition of just-war thinking has had the intention—if not the effect—of curbing wars as much as possible. Vatican II has reiterated the connection of peace with justice, saying that peace "is rightly and properly called 'the work of justice' (Is 32.17). It is the fruit of the order which has been planted in human society by its divine founder and which is to be brought about by humanity in its thirst for ever more perfect justice." It is a gift from God, "an expression and result of the peace of Christ which follows from God our Father," but its achievement and preservation require continual human effort (GS 78).

PEACE OF GOD, TRUCE OF GOD. The Peace of God was a movement in reaction to the feudal anarchy that broke out with the decay of the Carolingian empire. It originated in several local councils of bishops in central and southern France in the late tenth century. The bishops called for protection of churches, clergy, peasants, and the poor. The councils became the scenes of popular demonstrations for peace, and at these ceremonies the bishops imposed oaths upon the knights in attendance to uphold the Peace. In the eleventh and twelfth centuries, the enforcement of the Peace was absorbed into the mechanism of secular government and used to further the ends of rulers. In the Truce of God, an outgrowth of the Peace of God, knights swore not to fight at certain times. The Truce first appeared in France in 1027, with a prohibition on fighting from Saturday evening to Monday morning. At a synod at Arles around 1043, it was expanded to include the period from Thursday to Monday morning, the seasons of Advent and Lent, and the major feast days. Lateran Council III* (1139) expanded it still further. The Truce embodied the idea that Christian knights should not be fighting one another; one effect was to divert military energy to the Crusades*.

PELAGIUS, PELAGIANISM. Pelagius (ca. 350-after 418) was a British lay ascetic who preached in Rome in the 390s. He sought to improve Christians' standard of behavior, arguing that people had it in their power to achieve Christian perfection. He thus minimized the damage done to human nature by sin* and appeared to deny the need for divine grace* to do works that would merit salvation. "Grace," for him, appears to have reduced to the sum of the powers of our nature, the law of Moses and of Christ, the forgiveness of sins, and the example of Christ. One of his followers, Caelestius, denied the necessity of infant baptism*. Pelagius and his followers evoked the opposition of Jerome* and especially Augustine*, and it was against the Pelagians that Augustine developed his doctrines of original sin* and predestination*. According to Augustine, all humans are worthy of damnation due to original sin, and any meritorious work they do is done through grace. Pelagius was judged orthodox by a synod of Palestinian bishops in 416, but was condemned in 417 by Pope Innocent I and in 418 by a council in Carthage and, after some vacillation, by Innocent's successor Zosimus.

In the late 420s a group centered in Marseille in Gaul, influenced by John Cassian, held that, while all other good acts require a prior infusion of grace, the initial act of conversion* (the "beginning of faith") was in humans' own power. Though its proponents were not defenders of Pelagius, this position came (in the sixteenth century) to be called **Semi-Pelagianism**. It was opposed by Augustine and was eventually condemned at the Second Council of Orange in 529, which did not, however, support the more extreme statements of Augustine on predestination.

PENANCE (Lt *paenitentia*). (1) An attitude of repentance. (2) One of the sacraments* of the Church, treated in this book under its alternate name, RECONCILIATION. The Latin word *paenitentia* often translates the biblical Greek *metanoia*, a term used to indicate the proper response to Jesus' proclamation of the Kingdom* of God (e.g., Mk 1.14). *Metanoia* means to turn away from one's former way of life and to take on a new way of thinking and living. It is not far in meaning from "conversion"*. This is the meaning that *penance* bears in the name of the sacrament. It includes turning away from one's sins and being sorry for them, but it also includes turning toward God in a reformation of one's life through grace. Unfortunately, the English word *penance* has come primarily to mean a penalty or punishment for sin. In that sense, it refers to only part of the sacrament, the penalty or satisfaction imposed by the confessor (usually prayers or other good works).

PENTECOST (Gk, "fiftieth"). A feast celebrated on the seventh Sunday after Easter*. It takes its name from the Jewish "feast of weeks," celebrated on the fiftieth day (seven weeks, a week of weeks) after Passover*. In Acts 2.1-13, Luke locates the descent of the Holy Spirit* on the disciples of Jesus on the Pentecost after the Passover when Jesus' passion occurred, though Jn 20.19-23 places it on the evening of the day of the resurrection. In Luke's narrative, the signs of the Holy Spirit are a wind, tongues of flame, and the disciples' speaking in different languages. According to second-century sources, the celebration of Easter lasted fifty days, and "Pentecost" was the name for all of the period. By the end of the third century, the feast of Pentecost celebrated the fiftieth day, the end of the Easter period, and by the fourth century it celebrated the descent of the Holy Spirit in particular. In the West, Pentecost became an alternate day for baptism*, for those unable to be baptized at Easter, and as such it acquired a vigil and an octave. Liturgical reforms after Vatican Council II sought to restore the unity of the Easter season, seeing Pentecost both as the closing of a fifty-day celebration of the Easter mysteries, including the coming of the Holy Spirit, and as especially a celebration of the latter. The octave was suppressed, the vigil retained.

PEOPLE OF GOD. One of Vatican Council II's* most prominent images of the Church*. This image is based in OT language about Israel as God's people (e.g., Ex 19.3-6) and NT language about the Christian community as a new People of God (e.g., 1 Pt 2.9-10). As developed in chapter two of the *Dogmatic Constitution on the Church (Lumen Gentium)*, this image highlights how all members of the Church, in virtue of their baptism, participate in Christ's threefold priestly, prophetic, and royal mission. The fact that Vatican II considers the Church as People of God before turning in chapter three to the Church's hierarchical structure represented a significant shift in official Catholic ecclesiology*. Chapter two of LG goes on to explain how all human beings have some relation to the Church as People of God. A limitation of this image is that it does not make clear the distinction and relation between the Church and the Jewish people, who in some sense remain the People of God (Romans 11.1-2; *see* JUDAISM).

PERSECUTION. Restriction of liberty, usually through violence, on account of religion, race, and the like. The earliest Christians were persecuted at times by Jewish and civil authorities. Such persecutions led to the executions of Stephen (Acts 6.8-8.1) (ca. A.D. 35) and James the brother of John (Acts 12.3) (A.D. 44). Christians were persecuted sporadically by Roman authorities, with the persecutions gaining in intensity in the third century. The first persecution recorded was under Nero in Rome in A.D. 64. It probably resulted from Nero's need to find a scapegoat for a fire that burned large parts of Rome and for which many people held him responsible. Persecutions occurred under Trajan (emperor 98-117), Marcus Aurelius (161-180), Septimius Severus (193-211), Maximinus Thrax (235-238), Decius (249-251) (with great severity), and Valerian (253-260). Their scope always varied from one region to another, and even when the emperor was not disposed to persecute Christians, there were sometimes local persecutions. The last and greatest persecutions took place under Diocletian (284-305) and his fellow rulers and successors, especially Galerius, from 303 to 312. They resulted from Diocletian's effort to reorganize and strengthen the empire, a program that included strict religious uniformity. Persecutions ended in 313 with the rise of Constantine* and official toleration of Christianity. Reasons for Roman persecution of Christians varied, but the most fundamental was probably Roman belief that the favor of the gods was essential for the well-being of the Empire, and that Christian refusal to worship the Roman gods would likely provoke their displeasure.

Once the Empire accepted Christianity, persecution of Christians began in the neighboring Persian Empire, lasting off and on into the seventh century. Christians were persecuted at times by Germanic peoples in the West. In turn, Catholics themselves often persecuted Jews and heretics during the Middle Ages (see INQUISITION, JUDAISM, RELIGIOUS LIBERTY). Catholics and Protestants* persecuted each other in the religious struggles between the Protestant Reformation and the Peace of Westphalia (1648). The French Revolution* led to more persecution of the Church after a century and a half of relative calm. Persecutions sometimes occurred in mission lands (see MARTYR); the most severe was in Japan from 1587 to 1638, which virtually wiped out the Church there. In the twentieth century, persecutions of the Church have taken place under Communist regimes, especially in Russia and China, as well as under the Nazis in Germany, secularist governments in Mexico between 1917 and 1940, and the Spanish Republicans in 1936 to 1939. In some places, for example, the southern Sudan, they continue to the present time.

In John 15.20, Jesus tells his disciples, "If they persecuted me, they will also persecute you." Christians can expect persecutions at least occasionally as long as they challenge the practices of those who hold power in society. For all the evils they inflict, persecutions have had the good effect of strengthening the faith in many who persevere through them, so that a nostalgia for times of persecution is sometimes felt. Some such feeling was one of the motivations of early monasticism*, as ascetics went to the desert to pursue spiritually the sort of struggle that was no longer possible on the physical level.

PERSON (Lt *persona*). This term, originally meaning an actor's mask, then a role or status, has undergone different histories regarding human and divine persons. (1) The classic definition of "person" is by Boethius (480-524): "an individual substance of a rational nature." This indicates reasonably well the sense of "person" that is at stake in moral theology in disputes over whether human fetuses (or certain animals or computers) are "persons." Boethius's definition was modified by Thomas Aquinas*, replacing "individual" with "complete, subsistent by itself, and separate from others"; thus he could include angels* as persons, while excluding the separated human soul* and the human nature of Jesus. In modern times, "person" is especially associated with consciousness and freedom or self-determination. (2) The term is first used of the Father, Son, and Holy Spirit in the Holy Trinity* by Tertullian* (early third century). It is a word for what in God is three, but has no clear conceptual content. Aquinas, following Augustine, spoke of the trinitarian persons as "subsistent relations"; they are constituted as persons by the relations of begetting, being begotten, and proceeding (*see* TRINITY). The modern sense of "person" as primarily a center of consciousness would, if applied to the Trinity, lead to tritheism*. Hence, some theologians propose different language (e.g., Karl Rahner* speaks of three "distinct manners of subsisting"), but this has not been generally accepted. (3) The two senses of "person" come together somewhat in Christology. According to the Council of Chalcedon*, Jesus Christ* is "one person in two natures," human and divine. He is a single individual, the second person of the Trinity possessing divine and human natures, which remain distinct; his divine and human consciousness must therefore remain distinct, without his being two persons.

PETER LOMBARD (ca. 1095-1160). Medieval theologian. Born in Lombardy, educated in Italy and at Rheims and Paris, he taught in the school of Notre Dame at Paris. In 1159 he became bishop of Paris. His *Sentences (Four Books of Sentences)*, written between 1155 and 1158, became the standard textbook (after the Bible) for theology and earned Peter the title "Master of the Sentences." The divisions of the work provided a model for later medieval theology. They were: Book I: God, Trinity and divine essence; Book II: Creation and Fall; Book III: Incarnation, redemption, virtues of Christ, Christian virtues; Book IV: Sacraments and eschatology. On each question treated, Peter assembled opinions (*sententiae*, hence "sentences") from the Fathers of the Church*, especially Augustine*, from canon law*, and from other contemporary sources, seeking to harmonize apparent conflicts. Peter's work was primarily one of compilation, but he did advance some influential arguments of his own (for instance, that there are exactly seven sacraments). Those studying to be masters of theology in the medieval universities were required to comment on at least part of the *Sentences*. Important commentaries on the *Sentences* were written by Albert the Great*, Bonaventure*, Thomas Aquinas*, Duns Scotus*, William of Ockham*, and Martin Luther, among others. The work retained its position in the theology curriculum into the seventeenth century.

PETRINE FUNCTION, PETRINE MINISTRY. *See* POPE.

PHILOSOPHY (Gk *philosophia*, "love of wisdom"). It is traditional to distinguish philosophy from theology* by saying that philosophy relies on natural human reason only, while theology draws also on divine revelation (see, for instance, Thomas Aquinas, ST 1.1.1). Theology then, as "faith seeking understanding," uses philosophy to interpret or explain the data of revelation* and strives to integrate revelation and philosophical knowledge into a Christian view of the world. (Philosophy is further distinguished from the empirical sciences in that it deals with fundamental or ultimate questions; the physicist may ask, "What do we know about matter?" but the philosopher asks, "What is matter?" and "What is it to know?")

The traditional philosophy/theology distinction is useful, but it neglects the historical peculiarity of the Western tradition. Other wisdom traditions, for example, the Hindu* and Buddhist*, do not make such a distinction. That the West does make it reflects the fact that "reason" has a history—what have been understood as the methods and conclusions of reason have varied over the course of time and from one culture to another. In Western antiquity, to speak loosely, reason was the methods and conclusions of Greek philosophy. Greek philosophy formed one of the two primary wisdom traditions that flowed into what is now Western culture; the biblical tradition was the other. Greek philosophy was more than an academic discipline; it was, or could be, a quasi-religious way of life—Plato called it "preparation for dying" (*Phaedo* 64a). The Fathers of the Church* worked to synthesize the biblical and Greek wisdom traditions, in the latter especially Platonism* but also Stoicism*. They judged the Greek heritage in terms of biblical revelation, but they also interpreted biblical revelation in Greek philosophical terms—varying in their assessments of the philosophical heritage from the receptivity of Justin Martyr* to the hostility of Tertullian*. Medieval theologians, led by Thomas Aquinas*, attempted the same sort of synthesis with the recovered heritage of Aristotelianism*. Aquinas gave the classic warrant for the use of philosophy in theology, to which the Catholic tradition is much more receptive than are some Protestant traditions: Christian revelation is not discontinuous with what natural reason can know, but rather builds upon it. "Since ... grace does not destroy nature, but perfects it, natural reason should minister to faith" (ST 1.1.8).

Modern philosophy, usually said to have originated with René Descartes (1596-1650), developed in a culture that was permeated by Christianity. It focused on questions of human knowledge, taking its models of knowledge from mathematics and the new physical sciences, and challenged many traditional religious claims, in order either to reject them or to reconstruct them on a more solid basis. Catholic theologians, feeling themselves under siege, responded, by and large, with a defensive reassertion of premodern philosophical stances (*see* ENLIGHTENMENT, THOMISM). Not until the twentieth century, in such figures as Karl Rahner*, did they make a serious effort of intellectual engagement with modern philosophy, and by then modern philosophy was fragmenting under the influence of its own discoveries regarding the historical conditionedness of all thought (*see* HERMENEUTICS). The project of "faith seeking understanding" in the West today necessarily leads to a pluralism* of theologies, reflecting the pluralism of contemporary Western philosophies. In the East, it is carried on especially in interreligious dialogue, which in many ways resembles the activities of Justin Martyr and the other early Church Fathers.

PHOTIUS (ca. 810-ca. 891). Patriarch of Constantinople 858-867 and 878-886. Photius was a layman when first made patriarch, after the Emperor Michael III deposed the previous patriarch, Ignatius. In 863, Pope Nicholas I declared Photius deposed and Ignatius restored. The issue became entwined with a conflict over the evangelization of Bulgaria, and in 867 Photius issued an encyclical* letter denouncing Latin missionaries in Bulgaria and accusing the West of heresy over the *filioque*. A council at Constantinople in 867 declared the pope deposed, thus creating schism* between the eastern and western churches. The Fourth Council of Constantinople* (869-870) ended the schism, anathematizing Photius and restoring Ignatius. After Ignatius died in 877, the Emperor Michael appointed Photius patriarch, and a council at Constantinople in 879 to 880 overturned the decisions of the council of 869-870, with the apparent approval of the papal legates. Photius was deposed in 886 by the Emperor Leo VI and died around 891. He is responsible for aggravating the estrangement of the western and eastern churches and for elevating the conflict over the *filioque* to the status of a dogmatic disagreement. He is regarded as a saint by the Eastern Orthodox.

PILGRIMAGE (Lt *peregrinatio*, from *peregrinus*, "foreigner"). A journey for religious reasons to a shrine* or other sacred place. Pilgrimages are found throughout the world's religions. Probably the distance to be traveled is symbolic of the transcendence of the divine, the journey a sort of sacramental overcoming of the estrangement between humans and God or the gods. In the OT, there were three pilgrim feasts, Passover, Pentecost, and the Feast of Tabernacles, when male Israelites were supposed to appear before God (Ex 23.14-17, Dt 16.1-16). Christians began making pilgrimages to the holy sites in Palestine in the second century, and these proliferated greatly once the Church was politically favored in the fourth century. Other pilgrimage spots were Rome*, especially the tombs of Peter and Paul and the martyrs' tombs in the catacombs, and monastic sites in the desert of Egypt. Pilgrimages were an important part of medieval religious life. To the ancient destinations were added many more shrines commemorating saints or celestial apparitions*. Medieval pilgrims were subject to great hardships of travel, but they also had special protections, somewhat like those of clerics*. To obtain these, they were required to carry a letter from their bishop or abbot, identifying them as genuine pilgrims and not mere adventurers. Pilgrimages might be imposed as penances, but more often they were undertaken for purposes of petition or thanksgiving, especially in matters of bodily health. Pilgrimages remain common, though no longer so difficult, in modern times. The Holy Land and Rome remain favorite destinations, as also are the Marian shrine at Czestochowa, Poland, and the shrines commemorating Marian apparitions at Lourdes (France), Fatima (Portugal), and Medjugorje (Bosnia). Ordinarily pilgrims receive the sacraments of reconciliation* and the eucharist*, and there are often distinctive devotional practices associated with a shrine. Frequently special indulgences* are attached to pilgrimage sites. Medieval theology customarily referred to earthly life as the "pilgrim" state, and Vatican Council II* applied the term to the life of the Church as a whole (LG 8).

PIUS IX, POPE (1846-1878) (Giovanni Maria Mastai-Ferretti, b. 1792). Born at Senigallia in Ancona, he became archbishop of Spoleto in 1827 and bishop of Imola in 1832. He was named a cardinal* in 1840. Elected to the papacy as a moderate liberal, he soon showed the limits of his liberalism when he refused to establish a constitutional monarchy in the Papal States* or to join the battle to drive Austria from Italy. In 1848, his prime minister, Rossi, was assassinated by Italian independence forces, and he himself had to flee Rome for Gaeta in the kingdom of Naples. Supported by French troops, he returned to Rome in 1850. Thereafter he steadfastly opposed all liberalizing trends in European politics and culture. His *Syllabus of Errors** (1864) summed up his unyielding stand. Even so, by 1860 he had lost control of all his territory except Rome, and in 1870 Rome itself fell. From then on, he remained a "prisoner in the Vatican." Within the Church, however, he strengthened his authority. Against bishops, who were often under the influence of civil rulers, he promoted centralization of authority in Rome. He founded many new dioceses, especially in the United States. In 1854, without explicit consultation of the bishops, he proclaimed the dogma* of the Immaculate Conception* of Mary*. He reached a high point of influence within the Church when Vatican Council I* in 1870 proclaimed the doctrine of papal infallibility*. He was the first pope to foster personal devotion to the pope, which has ever since been an important factor in Catholic piety.

PIUS X, ST. Pope 1903-1914 (Giuseppe Sarto, b. 1835). A native of Riese, Upper Venetia, he became bishop of Mantua in 1884 and Patriarch of Venice and cardinal in 1893. Taking the motto, "Restore all things in Christ" (Eph 1.10), he focused his attention more on internal Church affairs than on external politics. His papacy was marked especially by the conflict over Modernism*, a loose association of ideas (and individuals) related to the introduction of modern historical perspectives into the study of the Bible and Catholic doctrines. A 1907 decree of the Holy Office, *Lamentabili sane exitu*, condemned a list of sixty-five Modernist propositions. Later that year, Pius's encyclical *Pascendi dominici gregis* condemned Modernism as a "synthesis of all heresies." In 1910, Pius imposed an oath* against Modernism on all clerics and officeholders in the Church. With the support of Pius, the organization Sodalitium Pianum (Sapinière), led by Monsignor Umberto Benigni, an undersecretary to Secretary of State Cardinal Merry del Val, conducted a campaign of spying, harassment, and denunciation against suspected Modernists (*see* INTEGRALISM). Pius reformed the Roman Curia*, revised and codified canon law* (though the new code was not published until 1917), and reformed Church music*. He tended to oppose Catholic involvement in political movements that were not under the direct supervision of the hierarchy, especially those in which Catholics worked together with those of other faiths. Pius is also noted for his advocacy of frequent, even daily, communion, and for his reduction of the age of first communion to seven (*see* EUCHARIST). He was canonized in 1954, and his feast is celebrated on August 21.

PIUS XI, POPE (1922-1939) (Achille Ratti, b. 1857). Born at Desio, near Milan, he became a professor at the seminary in Milan in 1882. From 1888 to 1911, he worked at the Ambrosian Library in Milan. In 1911 he moved to the Vatican Library, becoming prefect in 1914. In 1918 he was made apostolic visitor, later nuncio, to Poland, and in 1921 he became Archbishop of Milan and cardinal. His papacy was shaped by world political events: the aftermath of World War I, the Great Depression, and the rise of totalitarian governments in Europe. In 1929, he settled the "Roman question" by concluding the Lateran Treaty with the Italian government, establishing the Vatican City* as an independent state, governed by the pope, while according recognition by the Holy See* to the Italian government, with its capital in Rome. His encyclical *Quadragesimo anno* (1931) repeated and extended the teaching of Leo XIII* on the rights of workers. He introduced the term *social justice* (*see* JUSTICE) into Catholic teaching and developed the principle of subsidiarity*. He challenged capitalism* and spoke favorably of a corporatist social order, as in fascism. He turned against Italian fascism, however, because of its restrictions on the Church and, later, its racism. He negotiated a concordat with

National Socialist Germany in 1933, but after it was repeatedly violated by the Nazis, he condemned National Socialism in the encyclical *Mit brennender Sorge* (1937). Other encyclicals that same year condemned atheistic communism and sharply attacked persecution of the Church in Mexico. His policies on internal Church matters were conservative. In *Mortalium animos* (1928), he forbade Catholic participation in ecumenical gatherings (*see* ECUMENISM). *Casti connubii* (1930) condemned contraception (*see* BIRTH CONTROL). He strongly promoted the foreign missions* and consecrated forty native bishops in mission lands. He canonized numerous saints, including Albert the Great*, Thomas More*, Robert Bellarmine*, and Thérèse of Lisieux*.

PIUS XII, POPE (1939-1958) (Eugenio Pacelli, b. 1876). Born in Rome, Pacelli entered the papal Secretariat of State in 1901. In 1917, he became nuncio to Bavaria and in 1920, to Germany. In 1930, he became Secretary of State. World War II was threatening as he became pope in March 1939, and Pius sought first to avoid war, then to discourage Italian participation in it. During the war, he unofficially supported the Allies (with some reservations owing to Russian participation), but his failure to speak out strongly against Nazi persecution of the Jews provoked much criticism, especially in Rolf Hochhuth's bitter 1963 play, *Der Stellvertreter (The Deputy)*. He did assist many individual Jews in gaining asylum, and he spoke in broad terms against racial genocide. Historians remain divided as to whether a more pointed condemnation would have been effective or even counterproductive. He strongly opposed communism and therefore was more favorable to capitalism* (since after the war it was the only apparent alternative) than Pius XI* had been. More clearly than any predecessor, he put the Church on the side of democracy.

His *Divino afflante Spiritu* (1943) authorized Catholic biblical scholars to make full use of modern methods of biblical criticism. *Humani generis* (1951) was critical of recent trends in the theology of grace* and original sin* but allowed qualified accommodation to the theory of evolution*. *Mystici corporis Christi* (1943) developed the idea of the Church* as the Mystical Body of Christ. In 1950, he solemnly proclaimed the dogma* of the bodily Assumption* of the Blessed Virgin Mary*. This has been the only time since papal infallibility* was defined at Vatican Council I* in 1870 that a pope formally invoked it.

He took the first steps in the renewal of the liturgy*, authorizing a completely revised ritual for Holy Week (1951, 1955).

PLATONISM. The philosophy of Plato (428/7-348/7 B.C.) and his followers. Plato's philosophy is contained in about twenty-eight dialogues (a few are of doubtful authenticity), in most of which the main speaker is **Socrates**, the philosopher (executed by Athens in 399 B.C.) who had been Plato's teacher. It is difficult to determine when the dialogues are expressing the ideas of Socrates and when the ideas put into Socrates' mouth are Plato's own. A central doctrine, probably original to Plato, is the "Theory of the Forms," which holds that the primary reality consists of timeless, perfect Ideas or Forms (such as Justice and Beauty), of which the things of the material world are only imperfect images. In the *Republic*, which portrays a sort of ideal political state, the Good is presented as the source of all the Forms; thus, all that is is in some way a reflection of goodness. The *Phaedo* presents the human person as an immortal soul* temporarily lodged in a body, and philosophy* as the purification of the soul from the body's influence.

Plato's ideas about God remained somewhat obscure, but later Platonic tradition developed them in a monotheistic direction and combined all the Forms into a single *logos** or divine word or mind. Platonism along these lines was given its most systematic and penetrating exposition by **Plotinus** (ca. 204-270), an Egyptian who taught at Rome. The philosophy of Plotinus and his followers was called **Neo-Platonism**. Plotinus spoke of three divine principles, or *hypostases*: a supreme and ineffable One, a Mind or Intellect (*Nous*) deriving from the One and containing all the Forms, and Soul, a third principle deriving from the One through the Nous and including time. Individual souls somehow take part in Soul. Plotinus's metaphysics was combined with an intellectual mysticism*, the point of which was for the individual soul to return to the One in timeless contemplative union.

Platonism had a significant impact on Jewish tradition, especially in the philosopher and theologian Philo of Alexandria (ca. 20 B.C.-ca. A.D. 50), and it may well be reflected in the biblical Book of Wisdom. It had major influence on the Fathers of the Church*, both directly and through Jewish tradition. Especially important in the development of Christian Platonism were Origen*, who studied under the same teacher as Plotinus, and Augustine*, whose thinking was revolutionized by his study of Plotinus. Platonism remained the dominant philosophical outlook of Christian theologians, both Greek and Latin, until in the Latin West Plato was eclipsed by the rediscovered Aristotle* in the thirteenth century. Even then, much of the neo-Platonic Augustinian heritage remained in such thinkers as Thomas Aquinas*. Platonism was attractive to Christian theologians because of its emphases on the supremacy of a transcendent reality, the goodness of all being, and the immortality* of the soul, as well as because of its ascetic ethic. Negative factors included its devaluing of the temporal and material order; thus, the Incarnation* of the Word of God and the resurrection* of the body do not cohere well with a Platonic vision of reality.

The study of Plato was revived in the Renaissance* by such thinkers as Marsilio Ficino. Since then, Plato has continued to play a major role in Western philosophy, as indicated in the epigram of Alfred North Whitehead, a modern Platonist (*see* PROCESS THEOLOGY), "The European philosophical tradition ... consists of a series of footnotes to Plato."

PLURALISM. (1) Acceptance of the legitimacy of diversity. Contemporary Western society, for instance, is pluralistic in accepting a diversity of religions, beliefs about the human good, and ways of life. **Theological pluralism** is the acknowledgment of an irreducible variety in the methods of theological inquiry and forms of theological expression within the one Christian faith as it is embodied in different individuals and cultures. It is ultimately based in a recognition of the transcendence of God over any human understanding or expression. **Doctrinal pluralism** allows for a diversity of doctrinal formulations; it is an important principle in ecumenism*. In the **theology of religions***, pluralism is the position that holds that Jesus is one of many savior figures, not the one and only savior.

(2) The holding of more than one benefice by the same person. A **benefice** is a permanent ecclesiastical office, such as those of bishop* or abbot*, which provides a right to an income. Pluralism was a serious abuse in the late medieval Church. It was curbed by the Council of Trent*.

POLITICAL THEOLOGY. A movement in twentieth-century European theology, led by Johann Baptist Metz (1928-). It opposes the individualism of the Enlightenment*, insisting that the human being is essentially social, and it rejects the "privatization" of religion in post-Enlightenment society, that is, the restriction of religion to a realm of private beliefs and moral virtues. It seeks to recover the potential of Christian faith to transform society. To this end, Metz speaks of the Church as the community that carries on the "dangerous memory" of Jesus, who took the side of the oppressed and was executed as a rebel by the civil authorities. Discipleship* of Jesus requires solidarity* with those who have been the victims of sinful structures of domination. Yet political theologians also emphasize the eschatological dimension of the Kingdom* of God and warn against the identification of any human political order with the realization of Christian hope*. Contemporary political theologians see the latter as the error of the "political theology" of the era of Constantine* and the Byzantine Empire.

Political theology preceded and influenced liberation theology*, but it is directed more to an academic audience in the "first world" of Western Europe and North America. Like liberation theology, it makes use of Marxist* thought, in this case the "sociology of knowledge" of the twentieth-century Frankfurt School. These theorists reject the idea of an ahistorical "pure reason"; rather, what humans take to be true will always by influenced by their commitments and interests. Accordingly, the political theologians affirm a qualified priority of Christian practice (*see* ORTHOPRAXIS) over Christian theory: good Christian theology will emerge from the practice of discipleship to Christ in solidarity with the poor and the outcast.

POLYGAMY (Gk *poly*, "many," *gamia*, "marriage"). The state of having more than one spouse at a time. **Polygyny**, in which a man has several wives, is far more common than **polyandry**, in which a woman has several husbands. Gn 2.18-25, in its portrait of Adam and Eve, presents a monogamous ideal, but the patriarchs and kings of the OT are depicted as having a plurality of wives. No OT text expressly forbids polygamy, but post-Exilic OT literature (sixth century B.C. onward) clearly presupposes monogamy as the norm and contains some passages in praise of monogamous unions (e.g., Prv 31.10-31). A standard of monogamy is presupposed in what the NT says about marriage*, though it nowhere explicitly condemns polygamy, which was not practiced in the Mediterranean world of its time. Augustine*, needing to justify the practice of the OT patriarchs, held that polygyny was not contrary to nature but was now forbidden by divine and human laws. Thomas Aquinas* held that it violated "secondary precepts" of natural law*, to which exceptions could be made. Against the views of some Protestant* Reformers, the Council of Trent* declared, "If anyone says that Christians may have more than one wife at once and that it is forbidden by no divine law, let him be anathema" (DS 1802). Vatican Council II* lists polygamy among practices that obscure the dignity of marriage (GS 47). Pope John Paul II* calls it contrary to the equal dignity of men and women and to conjugal love (*Familiaris consortio* 19). Polygamy is one of the important issues in the inculturation* of Catholicism into sub-Saharan African societies where polygyny is traditional. Canon law requires a newly baptized Christian who has more than one spouse to dismiss all but one, while mandating just provision for wives who are dismissed (Canon 1148). The impracticality—and, in the eyes of many Africans, the immorality—of such dismissal has led some (in particular the former missionary Eugene Hillman) to argue that the Catholic Church should tolerate continued polygamy in such cases, as the Anglican churches now do.

PONTIFICAL UNIVERSITIES AND FACULTIES. *See* ECCLESIASTICAL UNIVERSITIES AND FACULTIES.

POPE (Lt *papa*, "father" [informal]). The bishop* of Rome*, head of the college of bishops (*see* COLLEGIALITY), successor of St. Peter. The office of the pope is called the **PAPACY**. The papacy is the distinguishing—although not the central—feature of (Roman) Catholicism.

The term "pope" (*papa*), formerly used of other bishops, has been restricted to the bishop of Rome since the sixth century. Among his other titles are Supreme Pontiff (Lt *pontifex*, "priest"), Successor of Peter, and Vicar of Christ. He is also the head of state of the Vatican City*. "In virtue of his office he enjoys supreme, full, immediate and universal ordinary power in the Church" (Canon 331) (to say that his power is "ordinary" means that it is his in virtue of his office itself). He appoints, or confirms the election of, all bishops. He convokes an ecumenical council* and must confirm its decrees. "There is neither appeal nor recourse against a decision or decree of the Roman Pontiff" (Canon 333.3). Under certain circumstances, when speaking as supreme pastor and teacher of the Church, he has the gift of infallibility*: his declarations are guaranteed to be true, and they oblige the assent of all the members of the Church. Catholic teaching about the power of the pope is set out in the constitution *Pastor Aeternus* of

Vatican Council I* (1870) and situated in the broader context of the
college of bishops in *Lumen Gentium* of Vatican Council II* (1964).
The papacy developed gradually. It originates in the role of St.
Peter among the apostles*. He is the first to acknowledge Jesus as the
Messiah (Mk 8.29) and the first apostle to witness the risen Jesus (1
Cor 15.5); he is first when the Twelve are listed (Mk 3.16). Jesus
chooses him as the rock (*petra*) on which the Church is to be built and
gives him the power of the keys (Mt 16.17-19). He is given the charge
of strengthening his brothers in faith (Lk 22.32) and of feeding Jesus'
sheep (Jn 21.15-17). After the resurrection, he is the leader and
spokesman of the apostles (Acts 2.14). From these texts and others,
contemporary theologians have derived the idea of a **Petrine ministry**
or **Petrine function**, a ministry of promoting the unity* of the Church
and assisting communication and collaboration among the local
churches. This ministry was exercised by Peter and now belongs to the
bishop of Rome.

Though the NT does not mention it, a strong early tradition
(supported by archaeological evidence) holds that Peter went to Rome
and was martyred there. Rome* became preeminent among the early
churches because Peter and Paul were martyred there, as well as
because Rome was the capital city of the Empire. These reasons were
cited by Irenaeus* (ca. A.D. 180) in support of the claim that "all
churches must agree" with Rome. Earlier, the First Letter of Clement
(late first century) showed Rome exercising supervision over the church
at Corinth, and Ignatius of Antioch* (early second century) spoke of
the church of Rome as the church that "presides in love" over the
whole Church. The prestige of the Church of Rome naturally attached
to its bishop, and Cyprian (d. 258) was the first to argue for the bishop
of Rome's authority on the basis of Jesus' mandates to Peter. Pope
Siricius (384-399) was the first to claim that Peter still speaks through
the bishop of Rome, a position later strongly upheld by Pope Leo I*
(440-461). Important claims for papal authority were made by Gregory
VII* (1073-1085) and, in many cases, made effective by reforms
initiated by him. The title, "Vicar of Christ," was first claimed by
Innocent III* (1198-1216).

The decay of the Roman Empire in the West led to a situation in
which at times the papacy was a leading political power in the West.
Papal political power peaked in the early thirteenth century; afterward,
it receded as the emerging nation states of Europe gained strength. In
756, the Frankish king Pepin gave the pope power to rule the lands of

central Italy (*see* PAPAL STATES), and into modern times the popes were secular monarchs as well as leaders of the Church; often the former role predominated in the mind of the pope. Both religiously and politically, the papacy was weakened by the Avignon* residency (1309-1377), the Great Western Schism* (1378-1417), the rise of conciliarism*, and the Protestant* Reformation. The authority of the pope within the Church was strengthened, however, during the Counter-Reformation* period and especially at Vatican Council I. Papal power has been an important issue in ecumenical dialogues* since Vatican Council II. Eastern Orthodox*, Anglican* and some Lutheran dialogue partners would accept some form of papal primacy, but not infallibility and universal jurisdiction as defined at Vatican I.

The pope is elected by the College of Cardinals* in a closed meeting called a "conclave." Cardinals over eighty years of age may not vote. A two-thirds majority of those present is normally necessary for election; the cardinals may make an exception to this rule. Any baptized male Catholic may be elected pope, but if he is not a bishop he is ordained bishop before being proclaimed pope. The pope serves until death or resignation (only one pope has resigned); there is no provision to remove a pope from office involuntarily during his lifetime. It is customary, but not necessary, for a pope upon election to choose a new name, normally the name of one of his predecessors; thus, for instance, Karol Wojtyla became Pope John Paul II*.

A list of popes appears below as Appendix I, and it is there indicated which individual popes are the subjects of articles in this book.

POVERTY. Catholic teaching values poverty quite differently when it is voluntarily chosen for religious purposes than when it is imposed involuntarily due to unjust social conditions.

Religious poverty is a component of asceticism* in the imitation of Christ and his disciples (e.g., Mt 10.9-10). From Jesus' words to the rich young man (Mt 19.21), poverty is regarded as an evangelical counsel*. Early Christians often looked to Luke's idealized picture of the primitive church at Jerusalem, where "No one claimed that any of his possessions was his own, but they had everything in common" (Acts 4.32). Personal property was forbidden in the monastic* communities founded by Pachomius (fourth century) and Benedict*. In the eleventh century, there was a rise of movements for "apostolic life" among laity, including "apostolic poverty," giving up private property* and holding all things in common. These met with much opposition, as there was no clear precedent for such a state in life, and some, for example, the Waldensians*, separated from the Church. The same sort of motivation inspired the mendicant orders* of the thirteenth century, especially the Franciscans*. Until the middle of the fourteenth century, and recurrently afterward, there was much strife within the Franciscans as to the degree of poverty to be practiced. Today, poverty in imitation of Christ is an essential part of religious life*, but the specific way it is lived out depends on the laws of each religious community (Canon 600). Moreover, all Christians are obliged to justice, moderation, and a proper detachment in their use of material goods.

In regard to the involuntary poverty that afflicts many nations and large sections of the population even of rich nations, Church documents emphasize the need for justice*, in recent times adopting a "preferential option* for the poor" in imitation of God in the Old Testament and of Jesus. While not denying that individuals and nations may in some measure be responsible for their own poverty, the Church attacks the "economic, financial, and social mechanisms which ... [accentuate] the situation of wealth for some and poverty for the rest" (Pope John Paul II, *Sollicitudo rei socialis* 16). For instance, the pope criticizes the international trade and monetary systems in this context. Church documents call for "solutions to poverty that enable the poor to help themselves" and for the avoidance of "programs which do too much *for* and too little *with* the poor" (U.S. Bishops, *Economic Justice for All**188).

PRAYER (from Lt *precari*, "to ask, to beg"). "Prayer is the raising of one's mind and heart to God," according to the classic definition by St. John Damascene (ca. 675-ca. 749). It is not mere abstract thought about God but involves awareness of a personal relationship with God—one speaks and listens to God or dwells in communion with God.

The Gospels portray Jesus as frequently in prayer (e.g., Lk 6.12), and he is the model for Christians in their prayer. The earliest Christians used the prevailing Jewish forms of prayer, and to this day the Psalms of the Old Testament have a prominent place in Christian prayer. But still more central is the Lord's Prayer or "Our Father" (Mt 6.9-13, Lk 11.2-4), which Jesus himself taught. Catholic treatises on prayer often treat it as "the most perfect prayer" (Thomas Aquinas, ST 2-2.83.9) and the summary of all Christian prayer. The Lord's Prayer makes no explicit reference to the Trinity, but St. Paul makes clear the trinitarian shape of Christian prayer, including the Lord's Prayer, in saying, "God sent the spirit of his Son into our hearts, crying out, 'Abba, Father'" (Gal 4.6). Christians pray in the Spirit through the Son to the Father, and in the Lord's Prayer they take up Jesus' own stance toward the Father. They also very early began to address prayers directly to Jesus (e.g., Acts 7.59), and somewhat later to address God or Jesus through the intercession of Mary* or the saints*.

A traditional classification of the purposes of prayer is as follows: (1) **adoration**, or acknowledgment of God's transcendence and greatness, (2) **thanksgiving** for what God has given, (3) **petition**, asking that God grant something to us or to others, and (4) **reparation**, or expression of sorrow for sin and desire for forgiveness. Encompassing all of them is the simple desire for communion with God.

Prayer may be **public** or **private**. Central to the Church's public prayer is the liturgy*, especially the eucharist*. Public prayer also includes various kinds of devotion*. Private prayer may be **vocal** or **mental**. Vocal prayer includes not only prayers said aloud but also silent prayer according to established verbal formulas, e.g., the Our Father, Hail Mary, etc. Mental prayer may use words and images; a standard term for many kinds of such prayer is meditation*. A wordless dwelling in the presence of God is contemplation*. A state or form of prayer in which the normal awareness of the distinction between subject and object is transcended into an all-embracing sense of oneness with God is called mysticism*. Prayer may be not only an act or state but an attitude of awareness or mindfulness of God; in this sense, Christians are admonished to "pray without ceasing" (1 Thes 5.17).

Texts of some standard Catholic prayers are given in Appendix V.

PREDESTINATION. The eternal divine decree that orders certain people to eternal salvation*. It is to be distinguished from God's *foreknowledge* of future events. In predestination, God is not just the knower but the agent; Augustine* said, "This and nothing else is the predestination of the saints, namely, the foreknowledge and the preparation of God's favors, by which those who are delivered [saved] are most certainly delivered" (*The Gift of Perseverance* 14.35). Paul speaks of God as having "predestined to be conformed to the image of his Son" those whom he foreknew he would call (Rom 8.28-30) and as having "chosen before the foundation of the world" those whom he was to save in Christ (Eph 1.3-14). But those chosen retain freedom and the possibility of falling (e.g., Rom 11.22). In his conflict with the Pelagians*, Augustine hardened the Pauline teaching into a doctrine that, due to original sin*, the whole human race is a "mass of perdition," from which God chooses to save some people by grace*, without regard to actual or foreseen merits*. In some passages, Augustine indicated that God predestined others to eternal damnation; elsewhere he spoke of God as not intervening to prevent the damnation that was a consequence of original sin. Augustine thus rejected the idea that God wills to save all (1 Tm 2.4) and effectively excluded human freedom in the acceptance or rejection of divine grace. There was conflict in Gaul over Augustine's doctrine of grace for about a century after his death, ending with a declaration by the Second Council of Orange (529) that the faith* that brings salvation is purely a gift of grace, not the result of prior merit, but that no one is predestined to damnation (DS 396-397). Controversy broke out again in the ninth century and especially in the sixteenth, when the Protestant* Reformers Martin Luther and especially John Calvin put forward strong doctrines of predestination. Calvin unambiguously argued for "double predestination": that God predestines some to salvation and others to damnation. The Council of Trent* declared in 1547 that, while salvation is by grace, God offers saving grace to all, and those who are not saved have refused this offer (DS 1525, 1567). It is necessary to affirm (1) that only God—and not human effort—saves, (2) that God wills to save everyone, and (3) that God respects human freedom in his offer of saving grace. Exactly how these are compatible is a theological mystery*, an aspect of the fundamental mystery of the coexistence of God and the finite creature.

PRIEST (Gk *presbyteros*, "elder"). One who receives the second grade of the sacrament of order*, ranking between bishop* and deacon*. "By virtue of the sacrament of order, they are consecrated ..., as true priests of the new testament, to preach the gospel and nourish the faithful and celebrate divine worship" (Vatican Council II, LG 28). The history of the word shows two different biblical sources for Christian priesthood: elders and priests. A **presbyter** (source of the word "priest") was not a priest but an *elder*. In the OT, elders are mentioned frequently as religious and political leaders in the community. At the time of Jesus, the lay members of the ruling council, or Sanhedrin, were called "elders," as also were dignitaries in the synagogue. Elders did not have a liturgical role. The NT mentions elders in some Christian communities; in Jerusalem, they seem to form a governing council with the apostles (e.g., Acts 15). Elders preach, teach (1 Tm 5.17-19), lay on hands (1 Tm 4.14), and anoint the sick (Jas 5.14-15). In the NT, the distinction between elder and bishop (*episkopos*) is not clear (e.g., Ti 1.5-9). By the middle of the second century, a threefold ministry of bishops, then presbyters, then deacons was in place throughout the Church. The presbyters initially formed a council to advise the bishop.

No Christian leader is specifically identified as a "priest" in the NT. Besides referring to Jewish and pagan priests, the NT uses *priest* (Gk *hiereus*, Lt *sacerdos*) in two ways: the Letter to the Hebrews identifies Jesus as the new high priest (4.14 ff.), and 1 Peter and Revelation speak of the whole Christian community as a priestly people (e.g., 1 Pt 2.5,9, Rv 1.6). In the third century it began to become customary to speak of Christian bishops as "priests," understanding them as succeeding to the priesthood of the OT. By the time of Jesus, the primary role of Jewish priests was to offer sacrifice* and lead worship in the Temple. The NT portrays the death of Jesus as a sacrifice, and the words of the institution of the Eucharist* attach the meaning of sacrifice to that ritual as well. This is the foundation of the understanding of Christian ministers as priests. With the expansion of the Church in the fourth and fifth centuries, the presbyter rather than the bishop became the usual celebrant of the eucharist outside of the cities, and by the end of the fifth century presbyters were being called "priests" also.

Medieval western theology understood the priest rather than the bishop to possess the fullness of the sacrament of order and located the essence of the priesthood in the power to transform bread and wine into the body and blood of Christ. The Protestant* Reformers challenged the idea of the priest as a person set apart. Luther instead promoted the idea of a "priesthood of all believers," without essential distinction. The Council of Trent* in 1563 declared in response that Christ had established a "new, visible and external priesthood," centered in the powers to consecrate the eucharist and to forgive sins. Vatican Council II* recovered the NT and Reformation ideal of the entire Church as a priestly community, offering sacrifice to God in their rituals and Christian lives (LG 9-10). Unlike Luther, however, it held the "common priesthood of the faithful and the ministerial or hierarchical priesthood" to "differ in essence and not simply in degree" (LG 10).

Vatican II clearly subordinated priests to bishops sacramentally and in their ministry and revived the idea of the **presbytery** as a corporate body assisting the bishop. As the quotation at the beginning of this article illustrates, the Council construed the ministry of the priest more broadly than had Trent, emphasizing the priest's role in preaching and pastoral care along with his sacramental role.

PRIVATE PROPERTY. Catholic teaching defends a right to private ownership of property but also holds that the common good requires limits to the possession and use of property. According to St. Thomas Aquinas*, the private ownership of possessions is not a requirement of natural law* but a human specification of humans' natural dominion over the earth's goods. Pope Leo XIII*, in *Rerum novarum* (1891), went further in defending private property against socialism*, saying, "Every man has by nature the right to possess property of his own" (5). This right, he said, is connected to the human power of reason, which enables provision for the future. It is also tied to a man's obligation to provide for his family (10). Pope Leo argued that the law should enable as many people as possible to own property (35). In *Quadragesimo anno* (1931), Pope Pius XI*, while reaffirming a right to private property, emphasized "the social and public aspect of ownership." The misuse or nonuse of property may forfeit the right to it (47). Vatican Council II, in its *Pastoral Constitution on the Church in the Modern World* (1965), stated, "We ought to regard the exterior things we lawfully possess not just as our own but also as common, in the sense that they can profit not only the owners but others also," adding, "Everyone has the right to have a part of these goods that is sufficient for each and his or her dependents" (69). The common good may therefore require the expropriation of large estates when the majority of people are landless (71). Similarly, Pope John Paul II* spoke of private property as having a "social mortgage." In his encyclical, *Centesimus annus* (1991), he generalized Church teaching about property to apply to the possession of knowledge or technical skill as well (32).

PROCESS THEOLOGY. A family of theologies that view all reality, including God*, as essentially temporal and continually changing. They draw on modern science, especially Einsteinian physics and evolutionary biology, both of which conceive their objects of study as constituted more by temporal processes than by static entities. The leading school of process theology derives from the thought of Alfred North Whitehead (1861-1947), an English mathematician and philosopher who moved to the United States in 1924. Whitehead held that God is "dipolar": he has a "primordial" and a "consequent" nature. God's primordial nature contains all possibilities but is not conscious. The existing world is composed of "actual entities," which are more like events than things. They actualize themselves freely under the influence of an initial aim that God gives them. God's power over them is persuasive rather than coercive. God's consequent nature is his response to the concrete entities of the world. "God is the great companion—the fellow-sufferer who understands." As experienced by God, entities both complete God's nature and gain an "objective immortality" in God's experience of them, though they themselves perish. Whitehead's thought was developed by the American philosopher Charles Hartshorne (1897-), who refers to his position as "panentheism"*. The world is in God, but in some ways God exceeds the world. God's power is not unlimited but is the greatest power possible, surpassable only by God himself. Most American process theologians have come from Protestant backgrounds, but the movement has influenced some Catholics, such as David Tracy and Joseph Bracken. The theology of Pierre Teilhard de Chardin* is sometimes classed with the process theologies, though it is significantly different from American process theology.

The chief theological advantage of process theology is that it clearly allows room for creaturely freedom and can account for evil* in terms of it, without making God responsible for evil. It is questionable, however, whether it adequately preserves divine transcendence, in that it makes God one of the powers in the world process, although the supreme one. In Christology*, the doctrine of the unique incarnation* of God in Jesus is problematic for process theology, since God is "incarnate" in the entire world process. Moreover, the concept of "objective immortality" falls short of the richness of Christian eschatology*.

PROFESSION OF FAITH. All Catholics are obliged to witness to their faith and forbidden to deny it, even under threat of death. On some occasions, a formal, public profession of faith is made. In the rite of baptism* in the West, this profession is the Apostles' Creed. In baptism in the East, and in the liturgies for most Sundays and major feasts in the whole Church, it is the Nicene (Niceno-Constantinopolitan) Creed. *See* CREED.

From about the seventh century, a public profession of faith, using a trinitarian credal formula, has been required of those about to be consecrated bishops*. In 1564, after the Council of Trent*, Pope Pius IV issued the "Profession of Tridentine Faith," which was to be taken by nearly all who held office in the Church. To the Nicene Creed it added affirmations of belief in Trent's teachings concerning the Bible*, the sacraments*, original sin*, justification*, the mass*, purgatory*, the saints*, indulgences*, and papal authority*. To this, Pope Pius IX* in 1877 added statements about papal primacy and infallibility*, as declared at Vatican Council I*. In 1967, Pope Paul VI* simplified the profession to the Nicene Creed and a general profession of adherence to all dogmas* of Catholic faith.

The 1983 Code of Canon Law requires a profession of faith for voting members of a council* or synod*, cardinals*, bishops*, administrators of vacant dioceses*, vicars of the bishop, parish priests, rectors of seminaries* and Catholic universities* with canonical charter, deacons*, professors of theology and philosophy in seminaries, "teachers of subjects which deal with faith and morals at whatever universities," and religious superiors, all before assuming their offices (Canon 833). The text of the profession was promulgated in 1989. After (1) the Nicene Creed, one professes (2) to believe in all dogmas put forward by the Church, (3) to embrace all that the Church puts forward "definitively" concerning faith and morals, and (4) to adhere with religious *obsequium* ("submission, respect") to other teachings of the authoritative magisterium* (*see* DISSENT). There are several disputed areas regarding this profession. One is whether it is appropriate to include matter that is not strictly "of faith" (*de fide*, that is, dogmas) in a profession of faith; this applies to parts (3) and (4) of the profession. Another is what is meant by teaching that is put forward "definitively"; this is a new category, recently instantiated by a 1994 declaration by Pope John Paul II* against the ordination of women*. A third is whether teachers of theology at Catholic universities that do not have canonical charters must make the profession. *See also* OATH.

PROPORTIONALISM. A position in moral theology* about how to determine the moral rightness or wrongness of actions. Prominent theorists associated with this position include Peter Knauer, Bruno Schüller, and Richard McCormick. According to proportionalism, one must weigh the "pre-moral" or "ontic" goods or evils (values or disvalues, benefits or harms) in the available alternative courses of action. (Such "weighing" is not a quasi-mathematical calculation but a prudent judgment made by a virtuous person.) The morally right or good choice is that which realizes the greatest "proportion" of good in the circumstances. Proportionalism should not be confused with a strict consequentialism, which considers only the goodness and badness of the likely results of various courses of action. The proportionalist considers not only consequences but also goods and evils inherent in the action. (Thus, the morality of breaking a promise is not simply a matter of whether the *results* of breaking the promise are, over all, better than those of keeping it; it also involves the inherent evil of breaking a promise—an evil that may be overridden in some cases.) Proportionalists prefer not to speak of particular types of action as always *morally* evil (wrong to choose) in themselves, independently of circumstances, although they may say that some types of action are seemingly always, or nearly always, morally evil or wrong to choose, because of the ontic evil they involve. Pope John Paul II* attacks this aspect of proportionalism in the encyclical *Veritatis splendor* (1993), which holds that there are exceptionless moral norms, forbidding certain types of action as morally evil in themselves, irrespective of circumstances (VS 71-83, especially 75). Some critics of proportionalism also contend that it is impossible to carry out the weighing of goods and evils that proportionalism requires.

PROTESTANT CHURCHES. One of the three principal divisions of Christian churches (the others are the Catholic Church and the Eastern Orthodox* churches). The many Protestant churches originate in—or bear some relationship to—important reforming movements in the sixteenth-century Church. A few that predate these movements, for example, the Waldensians* and Moravians, were influenced by them in their later development.

By the sixteenth century, there was a widespread sense of a need for thorough reform in the Western Church. The papacy had not recovered from the effects of the Avignon* residency and the Great Western Schism*, and the popes of the Renaissance* were often more concerned with personal and familial wealth and power than with spiritual leadership. Clergy were often uneducated, and laity were excluded from significant participation in worship and Church life. The specific case that sparked the Reformation—the use of indulgences* as fund-raisers, both for the papacy and for the local prince-bishop—is typical of the abuses that existed.

The **Protestant Reformation** is usually dated from October 31, 1517, when **Martin Luther** (1483-1546), an Augustinian monk and professor at Wittenberg, Germany, circulated the *Ninety-Five Theses* against the abuse of indulgences. Luther's central theological tenet was justification* by faith*: one is made acceptable to God not by any works that one does but by God's free grace* in Jesus Christ*, which one accepts in faith. This theology, though in essence acceptable in Catholicism, stood in apparent opposition to the sacramental system as it existed in Luther's day. Luther soon was asserting the authority of Scripture alone (*sola scriptura*) above Church tradition*, including the teachings of councils* and popes*. He also reformed the liturgy* in order to increase the participation of the laity. His excommunication in 1521 led eventually to the formation of the Lutheran Church, which became the primary Christian body in Germany and the Scandinavian countries.

Shortly afterward, **Ulrich Zwingli** (1484-1531) began a reform movement in Switzerland. Zwingli agreed with Luther on many points but broke with Luther's retention of a Catholic theology of the real presence of Christ in the eucharist*; for Zwingli, the eucharist was only a symbol or memorial of Christ. After Zwingli's death, reform in Switzerland was led by **John Calvin** (1509-1564), who developed a systematic theology that strongly emphasized the sovereignty and grace of God. Calvin sought to revive what he saw as the NT church order, with pastors, teachers, elders, and deacons as officers, and without pope, bishops, and priests. Calvin's reform movement became dominant in Switzerland, the Low Countries, and Scotland and led to the Reformed and Presbyterian churches of today.

A third and more radical wing of the Reformation, which completely rejected Catholic doctrine regarding the sacraments*, also arose shortly after Luther's protest. Its adherents were often called **Anabaptists** (rebaptizers) because they believed that only adult baptisms were valid. They held that the Church should separate itself from secular society, and thus often espoused pacifism*. A leading theologian of the movement was Menno Simons (1496-1561), from whom today's Mennonite churches descend.

Finally, in England, the Reformation began not over issues of doctrine but with the effort of King /Henry VIII in 1534 to assert jurisdiction over the Church. Influences of European Protantism, especially Calvinism, were soon felt in the English Church, but it retained most of the Catholic forms of worship and church structure. *See* ANGLICAN COMMUNION. Anglicans often regard themselves as Catholic rather than Protestant. The **Methodist Church** grew out of a reform movement, led by John Wesley (1703-1791), in the Church of England; it became a separate church in 1784 in a dispute over the ordination of clergy in North America.

All the major branches of the Reformation in Europe spread to the colonies that became the United States, where numerous other Protestant bodies also settled or arose. Especially prominent were the **Baptists**, who, like the Anabaptists and somewhat influenced by them, emphasized the importance of adult baptism. Many Baptists and members of other churches, large and small, call themselves **Evangelical** Protestants. This term designates a strong emphasis on the authority of the Bible and on the importance of a life-changing or "born again" experience upon acceptance of Jesus as one's savior. Evangelicals are generally conservative in matters of belief and practice. Fundamentalism* is a militant movement within evangelical Protestantism.

Catholic responses to the Protestant Reformation have had two phases. (1) In the Counter-Reformation* period, particularly at the Council of Trent* (1545-1563), the Catholic Church curbed some of the abuses that had triggered the Reformation but strongly reasserted other elements of Catholic belief and practice, for example, the authority of tradition and of the pope, the seven sacraments, and the mass in Latin without congregational participation. In the centuries that followed, Protestants were regarded as rebels, or the descendants of rebels, whose appropriate course should be to "return to Rome," that is, to the Catholic Church. (2) Vatican Council II* (1962-1965), in contrast, acknowledged that many elements of the true life of the Church, for example, Scripture and baptism, and thus of God's grace, are found in the Protestant churches, and that the blame for the division lies on both sides (UR 3,7,19-24). Some reforms were enacted that addressed Protestant concerns, for example, for lay participation in liturgy. Since Vatican II, the Catholic Church has taken an active part in ecumenical relations with Protestants (*see* ECUMENICAL DIALOGUES, ECUMENISM, WORLD COUNCIL OF CHURCHES). Theological dialogues (sometimes envisioning full unity, sometimes only better understanding), common action on matters of mutual concern, and limited worship in common have become frequent.

Church authority* and sacraments remain important areas of division, however.

PSEUDO-DIONYSIUS (THE AREOPAGITE). Around the beginning of the sixth century, probably in Syria and probably in monophysite* circles, a body of writings was put forward under the name of Dionysius the Areopagite, who had been converted by St. Paul in Athens (Acts 17.34). Their true author has never been identified. The Dionysian corpus contains four treatises and ten letters. It presents Christian theology and mysticism in a strongly neo-Platonic form (*see* PLATONISM). The treatises comprise, first in logical sequence, *The Divine Names*, on the applicability of language to God, then *The Mystical Theology*, on God's transcendence of all human words and thoughts. This work is the classic expression of Christian apophatic* theology. *The Celestial Hierarchy* and *The Ecclesiastical Hierarchy* introduce the concept of a hierarchy* as a sacred order reflecting the perfection of God. *The Celestial Hierarchy* treats angelic beings (the origin of the "nine choirs of angels"), while *The Ecclesiastical Hierarchy* has to do chiefly with the liturgy rather than with office in the Church. Because these works were taken to be by a disciple of Paul, they were very influential in the Middle Ages, especially in the twelfth and thirteenth centuries. Thomas Aquinas* cites them some 1,700 times. Their authenticity as first-century writings was first challenged by the humanist Lorenzo Valla in 1457, then later by Erasmus, but not conclusively disproved till 1895. Even so, they have retained the status of classic works of Christian spirituality.

PURGATORY (Lt *purgatorium*, "means of purification"). A state or place of purification between death and ultimate salvation (heaven*). Those undergoing purification are assured of salvation (hence, purgatory is essentially different from hell*) but must be purified from sin* or the effects of sin. Belief in purgatory is tied to belief in the value of prayer for the dead, which is praised in 2 Mc 12.38-46. Though earlier Church Fathers mention purification after death, Augustine* gives the first real argument for it; he relies on 1 Cor 3.12-15, which speaks of a purifying fire. The two texts just mentioned are the principal scriptural support of the doctrine of purgatory, though neither states it directly. The imagery of purgatory as a distinct place intermediate between hell and heaven, given its classic expression in

Dante's* *Divine Comedy*, dates from the twelfth century. The Councils of Lyons II* (1274) and Florence* (1439) affirmed the existence of purgatory. On the basis of their doctrine of salvation by grace* alone, the Protestant* Reformers rejected the idea of purgatory, along with prayers for the dead and indulgences*. In response, the Council of Trent* (1563) declared "that [1] purgatory exists, and that [2] the souls detained there are helped by the prayers of the faithful." These two points are all that the Church officially declares on the subject. Trent goes on to discourage excessive speculation on purgatory. One limit to speculation (not mentioned by Trent) is our ignorance of the nature of temporality "after" death. Today, some theologians see purgation as occurring in the moment of death. At any rate, as the 1979 Vatican declaration on eschatology* says, "The Church excludes every way of thinking or speaking that would render meaningless or unintelligible her prayers, her funeral rites and the religious acts offered for the dead."

Q

QUIETISM. A spiritual movement of the seventeenth century, which emphasized purely passive mental prayer* and tended to minimize active meditation*. It held that one must let go of all effort and desire, and open oneself completely to God. Principal figures of Quietism were Miguel de Molinos (1628-1697), a Spaniard, and Madame Jeanne Guyon (1648-1717) and Archbishop François Fénelon (1651-1715), both French. Sixty-eight propositions purportedly expressing teachings of Molinos were condemned by the Holy Office in 1687. For instance, Molinos was accused of having counseled nonresistance to temptation (though we do not know the context in which he might have said this). Though Molinos recanted, he was accused of immorality and was imprisoned for the rest of his life. Twenty-three propositions of Fénelon were condemned in 1699. Despite these condemnations, most of the teaching of the Quietists was quite similar to what can be found in such orthodox spiritual writers as St. John of the Cross*. The errors of the Quietists consisted mainly in a few extreme statements and in a one-sided emphasis on the passive aspects of spiritual life.

R

RACISM. Though human beings have always been inclined to value their own social groups over others, racism, in the sense of a belief in the biologically based superiority of some races or ethnic groups over others, originated only with the expansion of European exploration and colonization in the fifteenth century. Europeans, encountering the native peoples of Africa, Asia, and the Americas, greatly different in culture and appearance from Europeans, sought to justify conquest and sometimes enslavement of these peoples by means of arguments that they were inferior, sometimes claiming they were no more than animals. In a stricter sense, racism dates from the late eighteenth century (when the term *race* was introduced) and especially the nineteenth century, when scientific-sounding theories of the inferiority of non-European races were developed by authors such as Count Arthur de Gobineau (1816-1882) and H. S. Chamberlain (1855-1927). These theories were direct ancestors of the racial beliefs of German National Socialism, which led to the killing of millions of Jews and others during World War II.

At high levels, the Catholic Church has long condemned racism. In 1537, Pope Paul III, drawing on the work of Bartolomé de las Casas*, denounced the opinion that "the inhabitants of the West Indies and the southern continents ... should be treated like irrational animals and used exclusively for our profit and our service." Popes repeatedly condemned the slave trade. Nevertheless, the Church's witness against racism was weakened by its acceptance of slavery*, an acceptance based in Greek philosophy, Roman law, and biblical and Christian tradition and voiced as late as 1866. Moreover, Catholics have tended to cooperate with social practices and institutions based in racism, for instance, segregation in parts of the United States and apartheid in South Africa. (Catholic schools in the American South were not fully integrated until the 1960s.)

Twentieth-century Church documents have strengthened the Church's stand. The encyclical *Mit brennender Sorge* of Pope Pius XI* in 1937 denounced the racist doctrines of the Nazis. Vatican Council II declared in 1965: "Every type of discrimination affecting the fundamental rights of the person, whether social or cultural, on grounds of sex, race, color, class, language or religion, should be overcome and done away with, as contrary to the purpose of God" (GS 29). A 1979 pastoral letter by the U.S. bishops, *Brothers and Sisters to Us*, labeled racism a sin*—not only overt racism but the subtle racism of acceptance of social structures based on discrimination. The Pontifical Justice and Peace Commission's *The Church and Racism: Toward a More Fraternal Society* (1989), the first Vatican document exclusively on racism, reviewed the many forms of racism throughout the world and condemned them all as "contrary to Christian faith and love" (33).

RAHNER, KARL (1904-1984). The most influential Catholic theologian of the twentieth century. Rahner was born in Freiburg-im-Breisgau, Germany, and entered the Jesuits* in 1922. His brother Hugo (1900-1968) was also a Jesuit and theologian. Karl Rahner was sent to study philosophy at Freiburg, where he attended the lectures of Martin Heidegger (*see* EXISTENTIALISM). After his director at Freiburg rejected his doctoral dissertation, later published as *Spirit in the World*, he took a doctorate in theology at the University of Innsbruck, Austria, in 1936. From 1937 to 1964, he was a professor of theology at Innsbruck. He later taught at Munich and Münster. His thought had great influence on Vatican Council II*, at which he was present. Rahner published an enormous amount, favoring short essays, meditations, and collaborative reference works over long, systematic treatises. His major essays have been published as *Theological Investigations* (twenty-three volumes in English). The nearest to a systematic expression of his theology is *Foundations of Christian Faith* (1978). No single influence was decisive for Rahner's thought. The strongest influence was the neo-scholastic tradition (*see* SCHOLASTICISM), but Heidegger, German idealism, Joseph Maréchal (*see* THOMISM), and the early twentieth-century "return to the sources" of theology (*ressourcement*) in the Fathers of the Church* were also important, and Rahner's Jesuit spirituality was pervasive in his work. Moreover, there is no one specific concept or thesis that is the necessary starting point for an exposition of Rahner's thought. A central theme, however, is that all human knowing and acting take place within the encompassing horizon of the mystery* of God. We are not directly aware of God as an object of experience, but we are indirectly aware of God as a precondition of all our experience. (In the language of Immanuel Kant, this is a "transcendental" approach, an approach by way of specifying the conditions of the possibility of the experience we actually have; thus, Rahner's theology is sometimes classified as "transcendental Thomism*".) Yet God freely chooses not to remain only incomprehensible mystery but rather to reveal himself and to share his life with human beings. This "self-communication" of God is grace*, and it is available to all human beings, but it is oriented toward and fully accomplished in Jesus Christ*, who is both the fullness of God's revelation* (the Word of God) and the fullness of the human response to God. Within this perspective, Rahner wrote on the whole range of Catholic doctrine, of which he was the most widely read expositor in his time, and spirituality. He was honored for his ability to make sense of these topics for a modern audience but, correspondingly, was criticized for too uncritically embracing modern philosophy (especially a Kantian approach to what is knowable by way of an analysis of the knowing human subject).

RATIONALISM. In theology, this term refers to excessive reliance on reason in matters of religious truth. Rationalism either denies or gives too little a place to the role of divine revelation* and faith*. The opposite of rationalism is fideism*. Vatican Council I*, while affirming that reason can have knowledge of God, condemns rationalism, insisting that the divine mysteries* surpass the capacity of human reason and can be known only if God reveals them (DS 3015, 3016, 3041).

In philosophy, rationalism was a movement in the seventeenth and eighteenth centuries, emphasizing knowledge through reason rather than sense experience. Its ideal of knowledge was mathematics. Prominent rationalists were René Descartes (1596-1650), Benedict (Baruch) Spinoza (1632-1677), and G. W. F. Leibniz (1646-1716).

RECEPTION. The process by which a particular teaching, decision, or practice comes to be accepted into the life of the Church. It is a test of the validity of the teaching, decision, or practice that is to be received; failure of reception suggests that it is not in accord with the "sense of the faithful"*. Reception, however, does not confer validity. Important teachings or actions that have not been received include the Council of Florence's* uniting of the Eastern and Western churches and the conciliarism* of the Council of Constance*. Sometimes, as with the Council of Nicaea*, reception is uncertain for a long time. Today, reception is especially important in ecumenism*, when there are questions of churches' reception of ecumenical agreements or of one church's reception of the faith and practice of another.

RECONCILIATION. In a very broad sense, the overcoming of estrangement between human beings and God, or among human beings. This is one way to characterize the work of God in Jesus (2 Cor 5.19). More narrowly, reconciliation is a name for one of the sacraments* of the Church, a sacrament by which sins are forgiven and sinners are reconciled with God and the Church. There is much terminological confusion about this sacrament. Its official name in canon law is **The Sacrament of Penance**. The Church's ritual for it is titled "Rite of Penance," but its three liturgical forms are each titled "Rite of Reconciliation." Catholics often call the sacrament **confession**, singling out one of its most important parts. PENANCE and CONFESSION are both subjects of other articles in this book. Here, "reconciliation" is chosen as the most comprehensive term for the sacrament and the one in most common use. Sin* effects an estrangement between the sinner and God, and between the sinner and God's people, the Church*; reconciliation overcomes both of these estrangements.

Jesus entrusted the disciples with the power to forgive sins (Jn 20.23) and to "bind and loose" (Mt 16.19, 18.18). These texts show the two facets of the sacrament, reconciliation with God and with the community ("bind and loose" probably has to do with excommunication*). Baptism* was the preeminent sacrament of forgiveness* of sin, but these texts show that a need for post-baptismal reconciliation was recognized. The NT does not describe any ritual for this reconciliation, however.

The practice that developed in the second and third centuries involved enrolling the repentant sinner in an **order of penitents**. The penitents undertook acts of repentance, for example, fasting and the wearing of sackcloth and ashes, and they were reconciled with the Church in a liturgy with the bishop presiding. The process was closely modeled on the catechumenate*. It was to be done only once in a lifetime. In the fourth century and later, this process was called "canonical penance." It became increasingly elaborate and difficult (e.g., requiring lifelong celibacy*) and so fell into disuse by the sixth century. By then, the most common penance ritual was deathbed reconciliation, which previously had been for emergencies.

In the West in the sixth century, the space left empty by canonical penance began to be filled by a quite different practice. Irish monks, doing missionary work in Gaul, took from eastern monasticism the practice of going to a spiritual father for direction (*see* SPIRITUAL DIRECTION). They extended this practice to the laity and adapted it through a conception of sin and satisfaction derived from Celtic law. The penitent gave the confessor (not necessarily a priest) a detailed list of sins, and to each sin a precise penalty was assigned. Lists of these penalties were contained in books called **penitentials**. The practice came to be known as "tariff" or "tax penance." Church authorities initially resisted it, but eventually worked out compromises, so that the standard medieval practice included private confession of sins and absolution* by a priest. Increasingly, confession was made to priests, though confession to laity existed as late as the sixteenth century. The Fourth Lateran Council* (1215) required annual confession before the required Easter communion (Catholics are still required to make annual confession of any serious sins). The classic medieval theology of the sacrament of penance was worked out by Thomas Aquinas*: the "matter" of the sacrament was the penitent's contrition (sorrow), confession, and satisfaction (payment of the penalty), while its "form" was the priest's absolution. While the priest served as a representative of the Church, the communal aspect of the sacrament (reconciliation with the Church), so prominent in the early Church, was neglected, and the sacrament privatized.

After most of the Protestant* Reformers rejected private confession, the Council of Trent* (1551) reiterated the medieval theology of penance, and insisted on the sacramentality of confession and the necessity of "integral" confession (of all mortal sins [*see* SIN]) to a priest. The ritual for penance that resulted after Trent (promulgated 1614) was simple and private. The penitent spoke to the confessor through a screen, for privacy. The penitent was to say how long it had been since his/her last confession, to make a general statement of contrition, to state all his/her mortal sins by kind and number, and other sins as seemed fitting. The priest was to ask questions discreetly, give counsel, impose a penance (e.g., prayers or good works) for the penitent to carry out, and pronounce the words of absolution. The ritual was in essence reduced to the four elements of contrition, confession, satisfaction, and absolution.

After twentieth-century liturgical scholars recovered the early history of reconciliation, Vatican Council II in 1963 directed the reform of the sacrament but gave no specific guidelines. The reformed Rite of Penance was approved in 1973 (the English version went into effect in the United States in 1977). In keeping with the Council's emphases for liturgical reform, the revised rites are more communal or ecclesial (showing the role of the Church) and more biblical. There are three forms: "Rite for Reconciliation of Individual Penitents," "Rite for Reconciliation of Several Penitents with Individual Confession and Absolution," and "Rite of Reconciliation of Several Penitents with General Confession and Absolution" (known as Rites I, II, and III, respectively). All three rites begin with a liturgy of the word, though the reading of Scripture is optional in Rite I. Canon law restricts Rite III, which does not involve individual confession, to cases of serious necessity, and obliges those absolved of serious sin by it to make individual confession as soon as possible. The reformed rite also makes provisions for non-sacramental penitential services.

Despite Church law, there has been a precipitous decline in individual confession, especially in the West, in the years since Vatican II. The reasons are various and not fully understood. Pope John Paul II* stresses the decline in the sense of sin. But this must be balanced with evidence of a felt need for spiritual healing*, for instance, increased recourse to pastoral counseling. For one reason or another, though, this need is not being met by the sacrament of reconciliation in its present form.

REDEMPTION (from Lt *redemere*, "to buy back"). The work of Jesus Christ* in delivering human beings from sin* and evil*. The image is that of "buying back" a person from slavery. Both in the NT and in the theological tradition, it exists alongside other images and concepts for the work of Christ, for example, justification*, reconciliation*, and atonement*. There are two Hebrew terms for redemption in the OT. One, *padah*, "to redeem," is used in Exodus to characterize God's work of delivering Israel from slavery in Egypt. The other, *go'el*, "redeemer, savior," someone who redeems an individual from slavery, is used in the prophets, especially the latter parts of Isaiah, to designate God's deliverance of Israel from captivity in Babylon. Both terms stand in the background of the NT's understanding of the work of Christ, who, as the early formula cited in 1 Cor 15.3 says, "died for our sins." The gospels—perhaps Jesus himself—draw on the Suffering Servant songs in Isaiah (especially 52.13-53.12) for an understanding of Jesus' death as a shedding of blood that is an expiation for others (e.g., Mk 10.45, 14.24). The Letter to the Hebrews develops an understanding of Jesus as both the high priest and the victim in the ultimate and complete sacrifice* for sins (Heb 1.1-4).

The Church has not defined doctrines explaining how Jesus redeems humankind. Theological theories have abounded, some (labeled "objective") focusing on the change wrought by Jesus in the situation of human beings before God, others (called "subjective") emphasizing the change within human beings brought about by Jesus. The most influential objective theory is that of St. Anselm* (1033-1109), according to which the death of Jesus is both necessary and sufficient to make the satisfaction that God requires for human sin. An important subjective theory is that of Abelard* (1079-ca. 1142), according to which the incarnation, life, and death of Jesus reveal God's love* for humankind and arouse a human response of love for God. Some theories, such as Anselm's, concentrate narrowly on Jesus' death as the redeeming act, while others take his life and resurrection* into account or see the incarnation* as itself the redeeming act. *See also* SALVATION.

REGULA FIDEI (Lt, "rule of faith"). The norm that is to guide the church in its statements of belief, interpretation of Scripture, and practice. This term probably originated in the second century. It (or "rule of truth") was used by Irenaeus* to designate the faith of the apostolic churches, as against the Gnostics'* claims to special revelations. Tertullian* uses the term to introduce a creedlike statement (*De praescriptione haereticorum* 13; ca. A.D. 200). The *regula fidei* was more comprehensive than a creed*, however, in that it included the normative practices of the Church.

REIGN OF GOD. *See* KINGDOM OF GOD.

REINCARNATION (REBIRTH). Also called **metempsychosis** (Gk *meta*, "after," *empsychōsis*, "animation"). Belief that the human soul* animates a succession of bodies. Such a belief is central to most forms of Hinduism*, which hold that the soul's re-embodiment is determined by the *karma* ("effects of action") accrued in previous lives. The cycle of reincarnation is regarded as undesirable, and Hindu practice aims at liberation (*moksha*) from it. Some forms of Buddhism*, which reject a substantial self or soul, hold for rebirth in the sense that one life gives rise to another; *nirvāna* is the cessation of this sequence of births.

Reincarnation was a belief in some ancient philosophies, especially Pythagoreanism and Platonism (e.g., Plato, *Phaedo* 80d-84b). In addition, reincarnation is a popular belief in many parts of the world, including Europe and North America (a 1989 survey revealed that 31 percent of practicing European Catholics believed in it). The Fathers of the Church*, for instance, Irenaeus* and Tertullian*, rejected it as incompatible with the final judgment* and the resurrection* of the body. Both doctrines imply that one life is decisive for one's salvation. Origen*, who held that one's embodiment was a consequence of a fall of a preexistent soul, was often accused in antiquity of believing in reincarnation, on the strength of a passage (*On First Principles* 1.8.4) where he speculates about it without affirming it; elsewhere, however, he squarely denies it. In Thomism*, reincarnation is impossible, because the soul, as the "form of the body," is made individual by its body and therefore cannot ensoul more than one body. Recent dialogues between Christians and Hindus and Buddhists have led to some convergence and mutual illumination. Some theologians note similarities between beliefs in reincarnation and in purgatory*. Reincarnation and resurrection seem to imply radically different attitudes toward selfhood, embodiment, and history, however.

RELICS (Lt *reliquiae*, "remains"). The remains of a saint's body or objects closely associated with him or her, such as clothing. These are called first-class relics, while **secondary relics** are objects touched to first-class relics. The cult of relics derives from the veneration of the bodies of martyrs*, of which our earliest evidence is in the *Martyrdom of Polycarp* 17.2 (ca. A.D. 156). The practice of dividing the bodies of martyrs and dispersing the pieces to many places originated in the East in the fourth century. The cult of relics was approved by the Second Council of Nicaea* in 787 in the context of settling the iconoclasm* controversy. In the East, however, the prominence of icons* later reduced relics to a minor role. In contrast, in the medieval West, relics became more and more prominent, especially due to the belief in their miraculous powers. Each altar* was required to contain relics, and shrines* containing relics were important sites for pilgrimages*. A large commerce in relics (not all of them authentic) developed, especially after the armies of the Fourth Crusade (1204) sacked Constantinople and other leading cities of the East. Martin Luther (echoed by other Protestant* Reformers) denounced the cult of relics, especially the association of relics with indulgences*. In response, the Council of Trent* in 1563 defended relics, in that they are the bodies of those who, while living, were "members of Christ and a temple of the Holy Spirit" and who will be raised by Christ in the final resurrection* (DS 1822). The council called for an end to superstition, abuse, and profiteering in regard to relics and required bishops to examine and approve any alleged new relics. Canon law* calls for preservation of the tradition of keeping saints' relics under a fixed altar*, that is, an altar attached to the floor of a church.

RELIGIONS. There is no consensus on exactly how to define a "religion." At a plausible minimum, a religion includes (1) an outlook on the world and human life, and in particular on their ultimate meaning—an outlook that relates them somehow to a transcendent reality, a reality that is more fundamental and more important than that which is ordinarily present to the senses; and (2) practices consistent with such an outlook. Ninian Smart lists seven "dimensions" of religion: practical-ritual, experiential-emotional, narrative-mythic, doctrinal-philosophical, ethical-legal, social-institutional, material (artifacts). Religious traditions vary as to which of these dimensions are more prominent. Usually, Hinduism*, Buddhism*, Judaism*, Christianity, and Islam* are classified as "world religions." There are other religions that have fewer adherents or less wide geographical distribution (e.g., the traditional religions of indigenous peoples), and there are many systems of belief (e.g., Stoicism*) and/or practice (e.g., Shinto) that have enough resemblance to the world religions that they are sometimes classified as "religions."

OT texts tend to take a negative view of the alien religious practices encountered by Israel as it first established the worship of Yahweh in the land and later felt the continuing attraction of various local cults. The OT, however, also includes a tradition of the "righteous pagan," for example, Job. The NT is concerned with Christian self-definition in relation to Judaism and to the syncretism that was prevalent in the Hellenistic world, but otherwise does not address the question of other religions. Some of the Fathers of the Church*, notably Justin Martyr*, believed that God's saving revelation was present to non-Christians; Justin, however, drew on Greek philosophy (which he saw as based on Christ the *logos**) to make a strong critique of pagan religion (which he saw as the work of demons*). The history of the Church's attitude to the possible salvation* of non-Christians is detailed in the article SALVATION OUTSIDE THE CHURCH. Non-Christians' specifically religious beliefs and practices tended to be seen not as the work of God but at best that of humans (responding to a general divine revelation*), at worst that of the devil. According to Vatican Council II, however, the non-Christian religions "frequently reflect a ray of that truth which enlightens everyone" and include "spiritual and moral good things" (NA 2). Vatican II clearly affirms that adherents of these religions may be saved (LG 16) but stops short of saying that they are saved through their practice of their religions.

Since Vatican II, the central issue in the Catholic theology of religions is that of the relation of other religions to the salvation that is made available in Jesus Christ* and his church. Three main positions have been put forward: (1) **Exclusivism** holds that salvation is only through explicit acceptance of Christ. This view is common among evangelical and fundamentalist* Protestants* and was the standard position of medieval theologians. (2) **Inclusivism** holds that adherents of non-Christian religions can be saved, but that their salvation is through Christ, present in them but unknown (Karl Rahner's* "anonymous Christianity"), or that Jesus is the fulfillment of these religions (earlier writings of Hans Küng). (3) **Pluralism** holds that Jesus is one of God's revelations and one mediator of the salvation that God offers, but not the only one (Paul Knitter). While exclusivism seems incompatible with the teaching of Vatican II, pluralism is in apparent conflict with the doctrine that Jesus is the one incarnate Son of God and savior. Inclusivism seems closest to the teaching of the Church, but it is criticized for imposing an alien, Christian framework on other religions. Accordingly, some theologians (e.g., Gavin D'Costa, J. A. DiNoia), who uphold the uniqueness of salvation in Jesus but are not satisfied with inclusivism, maintain that the precise relation of Christian revelation and salvation to the truth and salvific value of other religions can only emerge through dialogue with those religions.

RELIGIOUS FREEDOM. According to Vatican Council II's *Declaration on Religious Freedom (Dignitatis humanae)* (1965), "The human person has a right to religious freedom. Such freedom consists in this, that all should have such immunity from coercion by individuals, or by groups, or by any human power, that no one should be forced to act against his conscience in religious matters, nor prevented from acting according to his conscience, whether in private or in public, whether alone or in association with others, within due limits" (2). It is related to **toleration**, but the latter is a negative term, suggesting the permission of something that is undesirable, while the Council presents religious freedom positively, as a right based in human dignity.

The early Christian apologists* argued for Christians' freedom to practice their religion in the Roman Empire. But when the Empire became Christian, it seemed a matter of good civic order to suppress religious dissension. Augustine* was the first to justify persecution* of deviant Christians, in this case Donatists*. Through the Middle Ages, some toleration of Jews and pagans was practiced, but Christian heretics* were allowed no freedom. Thomas Aquinas* argued that Jews and pagans ought not to be compelled to become Christians, "because to believe depends on the will," but heretics and apostates* may be compelled, because their promise at baptism created an enforceable obligation (ST 2-2.10.8). An obstinate heretic is not to be tolerated; rather, "The Church, no longer hoping for his conversion, looks to the salvation of others ... and delivers him to the secular tribunal to be exterminated from the world by death" (ST 2-2.11.3). Church practices against heretics became increasingly harsh in the later Middle Ages (*see* INQUISITION).

After the Protestant* Reformation, there were some experiments in religious toleration, for example, in William Penn's Pennsylvania. The United States officially adopted a principle of religious freedom in the First Amendment to the Constitution (1791). Some American Catholic leaders, such as John Carroll* and Isaac Hecker, defended religious freedom as advantageous to the Church. The prevailing opinion among Church authorities, however, was negative, as religious liberty was seen as tied to indifferentism (the belief that all religions were equally true or untrue) or anticlericalism. In the *Syllabus of Errors** (1864), Pope Pius IX* condemned as an error the proposition: "Everyone is free to embrace and profess that religion which he, led by the light of reason, thinks to be the true religion" (15). A standard theological position prior to Vatican II was that ideally the state should officially espouse Catholicism and repress other religions, but when that is not practicable, the Church may accept the toleration of other religions.

Several factors caused a changed climate of opinion at Vatican II. One was the growth of religious freedom in the West, a second was the experience of the denial of religious freedom in communist countries, and a third was theological defenses of religious freedom by John Courtney Murray* and others. The *Declaration* grounds its endorsement of religious freedom in human dignity, as known through reason and revelation (DH 2). Human reason and free will require that the search for and acceptance of truth be free from coercion. Especially in their relation with God, humans should not be forced to act against their consciences* or prevented from acting in accordance with their consciences (3). Moreover, the social nature of human beings requires that they should be allowed to express their religion in external acts and to form and maintain religious communities (4). Freedom from religious coercion finds support in the traditional teaching that the act of faith must be free and in the practice of Jesus and the apostles, who did not coerce anyone. At times in the history of the Church, though, "There have been ways of acting hardly in tune with the spirit of the gospel, indeed contrary to it" (12).

The *Declaration on Religious Freedom* was the most controversial document at the Council because it was most clearly a departure from past teaching. The document itself acknowledges its intention to "develop" (*evolvere*) Church teaching on the topic (DH 1). Religious freedom is perhaps the outstanding case of a reversal of long-standing high-level teaching by Church authorities; it can be understood as development of doctrine* if it is seen as a gospel value of which changed circumstances have enabled new awareness.

RELIGIOUS LIFE. Forms of discipleship* of Christ, characterized by commitment to the evangelical counsels* of poverty*, chastity, and obedience*, and having the approval of Church authorities. Vatican Council II treats it as a special witness to Christ in the living out of the call to holiness* that is addressed to all Christians. Religious life is not a third state of life in addition to the clerical and lay; rather, religious themselves are either clerics* or laity*.

Most religious belong to communities, which are called "religious institutes" in canon law. Religious institutes are one kind of **institute of consecrated life**. Members of religious institutes pronounce public vows* to observe the evangelical counsels, and they "live a life in common as brothers and sisters" (Canon 607.2). Their witness requires a "separation from the world" (distinctive life of prayer and solitude) "proper to the character and purpose of each institute." Technically, religious institutes are **orders** if members take solemn vows, **congregations** if they take simple vows (*see under* VOW), but both terms are often used indiscriminately for all religious communities. Other forms of "institute of consecrated life" recognized in canon law are those of a hermit or anchorite* and of a consecrated virgin*, and secular institutes*. Besides institutes of consecrated life, there are **societies of apostolic life**, whose members live in common and have an apostolate or religious mission but do not take public vows (though in some societies the members commit themselves in some other way to the observance of the evangelical counsels). The Paulists* and Maryknoll Missioners* are examples of such societies.

Religious life has taken many concrete forms. The first recorded instance of a group set apart for prayer and celibacy* are the widows* (1 Tm 5.3-16) and virgins*. The late third and early fourth centuries saw a great movement toward the practice of the solitary life in the desert (*see* DESERT FATHERS AND MOTHERS). Pachomius (ca. 286-346) is credited with the establishment of monastic life in community. Such monasticism* remains the standard form of religious life in the East, but in the West, new forms have arisen. In the mendicant* orders, such as the Franciscans* and Dominicans*, which originated in the thirteenth century, members belonged to the order as a whole rather than to individual monasteries. **Canons regular**, who originated in the eighth century, were clerics who lived together under a rule. Eventually, the Rule of St. Augustine* became standard for them. The hospitaller and military orders (*see* TEMPLARS and KNIGHTS OF MALTA) grew out of the canons regular. The beguines* and beghards in the late Middle Ages developed a form of religious life without official recognition and regulation by Church authorities. Since the sixteenth century, many "apostolic congregations" of men and women have been founded, dedicated to missionary work or education, health care, and the like. Of these, the Jesuits*, an order of "clerics regular" who broke with monasticism in not having common prayer of the Liturgy of the Hours*, were pioneers. Secular institutes were approved in 1947.

In 1965, Vatican Council II called for renewal of religious life, based in (1) return to the sources of Christian life in general and to the original inspiration of each community and (2) adaptation to new circumstances, both in the work of the communities and in the surrounding cultural environment. In 1966, every religious institute was required to convoke, within three years, an extraordinary general chapter for renewal. Moreover, Vatican II's themes that (1) the call to holiness is addressed equally to all Christians, and (2) the Church's stance toward the world is one of dialogue and service forced religious to reexamine the traditional idea that they were pursuing a life of

Christian perfection in separation from the world. As religious communities were reexamining their ministries and undertaking experimental and permanent changes in their ways of life, and the rationale for religious life was being challenged, and partly because of these factors, the number of people entering religious life dropped and the number leaving it increased. The decline in the number of religious was often balanced by an expanded and newly appreciated ministry* of laity in general. Some "non-canonical" communities have been formed (e.g., Sisters for a Christian Community), which, like the beguines, do not seek official approval. Still, in 1991, there were more than two hundred thousand men religious and eight hundred thousand women religious in the world, and they were engaged in a much broader range of ministries than had been the case prior to Vatican II.

RENAISSANCE (Fr, "rebirth"). A period of European cultural history that began in the fourteenth century and lasted into the seventeenth. The name *renaissance* (*rinascita* in Italian), appears to have been coined by the art historian Giorgio Vasari (1511-1574). The beginnings of the Renaissance are usually traced to fourteenth-century Italy, whose various city-states were gaining economic and political strength. It was characterized by—and derived its name from—a revival and development of the styles of ancient Greece and Rome in literature and the arts (*see* ARCHITECTURE, ART, HUMANISM). From Italy it spread, beginning in the late fifteenth century, to Spain, France, Germany, and England. While many of the major figures of the Renaissance were devoutly Catholic, there was some tendency among Renaissance thinkers to revive and to extol not only the styles but also the mores of ancient pagan civilization, as against those of the Christian "Middle Ages" (a concept that may derive from Petrarch [1304-1374]).

The popes from Nicholas V (1447-1455) through Leo X (1513-1521) or slightly later are known as the **Renaissance popes**. They sought to enhance the standing of the papacy (weakened by the Great Western Schism* and by conciliarism*) through extensive patronage of the arts. Among their achievements are the establishment of the Vatican Library by Nicholas V and the construction of the new St. Peter's Basilica*. For the most part, however, they devoted more attention to the promotion of the political fortunes of the Papal States and of their own families than to the spiritual leadership of the church. The personal morals of several—especially Alexander VI (Borgia) (1492-1503), who fathered at least seven illegitimate children—caused great scandal. Their

failure to reform the Church was one of the causes of the Protestant*
Reformation.

RESURRECTION. (1) **The Resurrection of Jesus.** Jesus' passage
from death* to a new mode of life, his overcoming of death. It must
be distinguished from the revival of a dead person to ordinary life, as
in the cases of the widow's son (Lk 7.11-17) and Lazarus (Jn 11.1-44).
That Jesus is risen was the center of the earliest Christian proclamation
(Acts 2.22-24; 1 Cor 15.3-5) (*see* KERYGMA). The NT does not
describe the Resurrection, however. What it describes are (1) the
appearances of the risen Jesus and (2) the discovery that Jesus' tomb
is empty. There are seven different accounts of the appearances of the
risen Jesus (Mt 28, Mk 16:1-8, Mk 16:9-20, Lk 24, Jn 20, Jn 21, 1
Cor 15). The details of who saw Jesus and where cannot easily be
harmonized, but the very diversity of traditions attests to the
importance of the original events. In these stories, Jesus appears only
to those who have believed in him (an exception is the later appearance
to Paul, Acts 9, 1 Cor 15.8). The stories emphasize that it is truly
Jesus, in his body, not a phantasm or ghost (e.g., Lk 24.36-43), but
also present him as not immediately recognizable (e.g., Lk 24.31). We
have no evidence that anyone at the time denied that the tomb of Jesus
was empty, however the fact might be explained (see Mt 28.11-15); in
the NT, this story supports the belief in Jesus' bodily resurrection.

In the tradition of the Church, the centrality of the belief in Jesus'
resurrection is indicated in the facts that Sunday*, the day of the
Resurrection, is the principal feast, and that Easter* is the chief
liturgical celebration of the year. In doctrine and theology, the
resurrection has sometimes held a subordinate place to the incarnation*
and the crucifixion of Jesus. In Catholic theology of the eighteenth to
early twentieth centuries, the resurrection was often treated mainly as
proof of the divinity of Jesus, but more recent theology has restored it
to its central place as the culminating point in God's work of revelation
and salvation in Jesus (see Vatican Council II, DV 4). *See also* JESUS
CHRIST.

(2) **The general resurrection.** A resurrection of the dead is
affirmed in some late OT passages, for example, Dn 12.2, 2 Mac 7.9,
Is 26.19. At the time of Jesus, the resurrection of the dead was upheld
by the Pharisee party but denied by the Sadducees. Jesus (Mk 12.18-
27; Acts 23.6-8) and Paul align themselves with the Pharisees on this
question. But what is distinctive of NT belief in the resurrection is its

connection to the resurrection of Jesus. It is through the resurrection of Jesus that Christians are born to new life in this world (e.g., Rom 7.4-6) and after death. The resurrection of Jesus is the evidence for and the "first fruits" of the resurrection of all Christians (1 Cor 15). Jesus is "the resurrection and the life"; those who believe in him will "never die" (Jn 11.25-26). The NT is concerned mainly with the resurrection of Christians, but some texts speak of a resurrection of all persons (e.g., Jn 5.28-29, 2 Co 5.10). That our resurrection will be bodily is assumed in NT thought, which does not divide the human person into body and soul. The important point is that it will be the whole person that is resurrected. In 1 Cor 15, Paul argues that our risen bodies will be changed into "incorruptible, spiritual" bodies. Though Paul does not explicitly say so, presumably the risen body of Jesus is our model.

Church tradition has emphasized the bodiliness of the resurrection against the Gnostics* and others who reject the goodness of the body. Hence, the Apostles' Creed affirms "the resurrection of the body," clearly meaning the resurrection of the whole person. The 1979 Vatican document "Reflections on Certain Questions Pertaining to Eschatology" calls on Christians to believe in both the "fundamental continuity" and the "radical break" between this life and the next. Some Scripture passages (e.g., Rom 8.19-21, Rev 21) suggest that there is to be a resurrection of the whole physical world as the environment for our risen bodies; so also Vatican Council II (GS 39).

See also ESCHATOLOGY, HEAVEN, IMMORTALITY.

RETREAT. A period of withdrawal from one's usual activities and of concentration on spiritual life. Antecedents of modern retreats include Jesus' practice of withdrawal for solitary prayer (e.g. Lk 6.12), the intensification of spiritual practice in monasteries at certain seasons, especially Lent*, and, for laity, the practice of pilgrimages*. Modern retreats originate in the *Spiritual Exercises* (1548) of St. Ignatius Loyola* and in the work of the Jesuit and other orders in Counter-Reformation* times. Retreats exist in many different shapes and may run from less than a day to more than a month. A **private retreat** is made by an individual in solitude. In a **directed retreat** the retreatant meets regularly with a spiritual director* to discuss the retreatant's meditation* and issues of discernment*. A **preached retreat** centers on "conferences" (lectures or sermons) given by a retreat director. In a **closed retreat** (as distinguished from an **open retreat**) one spends the entire time at a retreat center away from one's usual home and work.

Retreats may be oriented toward specific groups or specific spiritual issues. Clergy and religious are required to make an annual retreat, while laypersons are strongly encouraged to make retreats. There are well over three hundred retreat centers in the United States.

REVELATION (Lt *revelatio*, "unveiling," equivalent to Gk *apokalypsis*). God's self-disclosure to human beings. While it has always been assumed in the Bible and Christian tradition that God makes himself known, "revelation" became a specific theological category only in the Middle Ages and especially after the Enlightenment*. At the time, a "propositional" theory of revelation was prevalent, focusing on revelation as the communication of truths inaccessible (or accessible only with difficulty) to human reason. Vatican Council II, in its *Dogmatic Constitution on Divine Revelation (Dei Verbum)*, offers a broader, relational understanding of revelation in deed and word: "It has pleased God ... to reveal himself and to make known the secret purpose of his will ... so as to invite and receive [human beings] into relationship with himself. The pattern of this revelation unfolds through deeds and words bound together by an inner dynamism, in such a way that God's works, effected during the course of the history of salvation, show forth and confirm the doctrine and the realities signified by the words, while the words in turn proclaim the works and throw light on the meaning hidden in them" (DV 2). The human response to God's revelation is faith* (DV 5).

Catholic theology distinguishes between **general** or natural **revelation**, made available to all human beings (distinct but not separate from the knowledge of God available to reason), and **special** or historical **revelation**, which is centered in Jesus Christ*, "the mediator and the fullness of all revelation" (DV 2). This revelation in Christ is entrusted by God to the Church (DV 7) and is transmitted in the Scriptures (*see* BIBLE) and the tradition* of the Church. "Tradition and scripture together form a single sacred deposit of the word of God, entrusted to the Church" (DV 10). This revelation entrusted to the Church is called **public revelation**. **Private revelations** are special gifts of knowledge given by God to individuals for their own benefit or that of others; this term applies, for instance, to revelations given to mystics (*see* MYSTICISM) or in apparitions*. The Church may approve such revelations but does not require belief in them.

(The **Book of Revelation** or Apocalypse is the last book of the New Testament; most of it describes a series of symbolic visions.)

RITE (Lt *ritus*, "ceremony, usage"). (1) A ritual or ceremony. (2) A distinct tradition of liturgy*, church discipline, and religious heritage. Most Catholics in the West belong to the Roman Rite (sometimes called the Latin Rite). Previously there were non-Roman rites in the West, notably the African, Ambrosian (Milanese), Gallican (France), and Mozarabic (Spain), some vestiges of which remain. There are seven rites among the Eastern Catholic Churches*: the Armenian, Byzantine, Coptic, East Syrian, Ethiopian, Maronite, and West Syrian.

ROME. Situated in central Italy on hills surrounding the Tiber River, Rome was the capital of the Empire and the leading city of the world at the time of Jesus, who was crucified by Roman authorities. Both the Roman historian Suetonius and Acts 18 obscurely indicate a Christian presence in Rome as early as A.D. 49; clearly a Christian community flourished there when Paul wrote his Letter to the Romans around A.D. 57. Acts ends with Paul in Rome, and strong early traditions hold that he and Peter were martyred there. The association with Peter and Paul, plus the prestige of the capital city, led to the church at Rome becoming, by the second century, the preeminent church in the Christian communion, and this led in turn to the authority of the Bishop of Rome over the whole Church (*see* POPE). From 756 to 1870, the pope was the civil ruler of Rome and its surrounding territory (*see* PAPAL STATES). By the Lateran Pacts of 1929, the pope is civil ruler of Vatican City*, a tiny sovereign state entirely surrounded by Rome; the Vatican also has control of numerous church and other buildings in Italian territory in and near Rome. The pope governs the Church from offices in the Vatican, but as Bishop of Rome his cathedral* church is the Basilica* of St. John Lateran. Rome is the location of several important Pontifical Universities and Institutes, which make it a principal center of Catholic intellectual life.

ROMERO, OSCAR ARNULFO (1917-1980). Archbishop of San Salvador, El Salvador. Romero was born in Ciudad Barrios, El Salvador, and studied in seminaries in El Salvador and at the Gregorian University, Rome, before ordination as a priest in 1942. He became an auxiliary bishop of San Salvador in 1970 and bishop of Santiago de Maria in 1974. Romero's opinions had been conservative on religious and political issues, but his experience at Santiago de Maria made him sensitive to the poverty and powerlessness of the peasants in a country in which a few wealthy families owned most of the land. In 1977, he was named Archbishop of San Salvador, around the same time as attacks increased by government supporters against church representatives. Six priests were killed during his tenure as archbishop. In his Sunday homilies, broadcast over the archdiocesan radio station, he denounced human rights abuses in El Salvador. They became the most popular program in the country, but they provoked the enmity of the military and the ruling oligarchy. While saying mass on March 24, 1980, Archbishop Romero was shot to death by an assassin.

ROSARY (Lt *rosarium*, "rose garden"). One of the most popular non-liturgical devotions* of Catholics in the modern period. As currently prayed, its essential parts are fifteen sets of ten Hail Marys, each set (called a "decade") preceded by the Lord's Prayer and followed by the doxology, "Glory [be] to the Father, ...". The fifteen decades are divided into three sets of five, and to each decade is attached the name of a "mystery"*, an event in the life of Jesus or Mary. The five "Joyful Mysteries" are the Annunciation of the conception of Jesus, the Visitation of Mary to her relative Elizabeth, the birth of Jesus, the presentation of Jesus in the Temple at Jerusalem, and the finding of Jesus in the Temple. The five "Sorrowful Mysteries" are Jesus' agony in the garden, scourging, crowning with thorns, carrying of the cross, and crucifixion. The five "Glorious Mysteries" are the Resurrection* of Jesus, his Ascension* to heaven, the descent of the Holy Spirit at Pentecost*, the Assumption* of Mary into heaven, and her crowning as queen of heaven. Typically, one of these three sets of five mysteries is prayed at a given time. It is usually preceded by the Apostles' Creed, the Lord's Prayer, three Hail Marys, and the Glory to the Father. After the five decades, the Hail Holy Queen is usually said. (See Appendix V for texts of prayers.)

The term *rosary* also designates the chain or string of beads (the word *bead* originally meant "prayer") used in this form of prayer. As most commonly found, it is circular, with five sets of ten beads, and a larger bead between sets. Attached to the circle is a string or chain ending in a crucifix*; between the crucifix and the circle are one large bead and three smaller ones. At the point where this string joins the circle, there is often a medallion.

Repetitive prayers date from the early centuries of Christianity. The present rosary originated in the twelfth century, when 150 Lord's Prayers or Marian prayers (the Hail Mary did not assume its present form till the sixteenth century) were said by the laity in place of the 150 Psalms. From then it developed gradually till it attained more or less its present form, including the fifteen mysteries, in the sixteenth century.

ROTA, ROMAN. *See* TRIBUNAL.

S

SACRAMENT (Lt *sacramentum*, "oath"). One of the central rituals of the Church, an act that incorporates participants into the life of Christ's saving grace* in the Church in a special way. Since the twelfth century, the name "sacrament" has been reserved for seven rituals: baptism*, confirmation*, the eucharist*, marriage*, order*, reconciliation*/penance, anointing of the sick*. The word *sacrament*, first introduced by Tertullian* around A.D. 200, translates the Greek *mystērion* ("something sacred which is hidden"; *see* MYSTERY). Among early Christian writers, both *mystērion* and *sacramentum* are used much more broadly than was later the norm, referring to any sort of sacred symbol or ritual. Theologians of the twelfth century sought to define "sacrament" more clearly in order to specify which rituals were sacraments. Lists ranged from five to thirty. Peter Lombard* argued for seven sacraments, chiefly on the basis of the significance of the number seven. This argument would not have prevailed were it not that the seven acts he enumerated really were central to the life of the medieval Church in the West. Lombard was the first to present the sacraments as causes of the grace that they signify.

Thirteenth-century theologians, led by Thomas Aquinas*, refined the theory of the sacraments. They analyzed the sacrament in Aristotelian* terms as composed of matter (the ritual actions and elements) and form (the ritual words). The sacrament is a genuine sacrament *ex opere operato*, "by virtue of the work done"; that is, so long as the proper action (matter and form) is carried out with the proper intention, there is a sacrament and sacramental grace is available, irrespective of the moral or religious worthiness of the minister or the participant. For example, an unbelieving, sinful priest saying mass genuinely consecrates and administers the eucharistic body and blood of Christ, though he gains no sacramental grace in doing so. A sacrament is a public act of Christ through his Church, and it cannot be dependent for its reality on the invisible disposition of the minister (*see* DONATISM). Later at times this principle led to a mechanical understanding of the sacraments, as if the care, faith, and understanding of those participating were of no consequence for the sacrament's effectiveness.

Such misunderstanding was one of the causes of the Protestant* Reformation. Moreover, the Reformers rejected much Catholic sacramental practice as contrary to the doctrine of justification* by faith or as not adequately based in Scripture. Martin Luther held that only baptism and the eucharist were clearly sacraments instituted by Christ. In response, the Council of Trent* (1545-1563) reaffirmed the number of sacraments as seven, held that they were all "instituted by Christ," and defended their validity* *ex opere operato*. Such polemical points dominated Catholic sacramental theology for centuries, until the liturgical movement* in the nineteenth and twentieth centuries re-opened a wider view, understanding the sacraments as liturgy* and liturgy as central to Christian life.

In 1952, Edward Schillebeeckx's *Christ the Sacrament of the Encounter with God* presented an understanding of Christ as the primary sacrament, manifesting God to the world. The sacraments are privileged occasions for personal encounters with God in Christ. Karl Rahner, in *The Church and the Sacraments* (1961), argued that the Church is the fundamental sacrament and that the traditional seven sacraments are key moments in the life of the Church. It was in founding the Church that Christ instituted the seven sacraments; therefore, it is not necessary to find clear texts in Scripture showing direct acts of institution by Jesus. These theories reintegrated sacramental theology with Christology* and ecclesiology* and had much influence on Vatican Council II*, the revision of sacramental rituals after the Council, and subsequent sacramental theology. Vatican II's reforms enhanced the participation of the whole community in sacramental liturgies and also gave a greater role to the Scriptures in the rituals. Important issues in sacramental theology today include the relation of sacraments to Christian moral life and social action (a theme stressed especially in liberation theology*), the sacraments in ecumenical relations (*see* ECUMENISM), and the role of the Holy Spirit* in the sacraments.

SACRAMENTAL. A sign that is related in some way to a sacrament*. It signifies and provides an occasion for grace*, but, unlike a sacrament, does not bring about that which it signifies. Sacramentals are not instituted by Christ but by the Church, and they may appear and disappear over the course of time. Some sacramentals are rituals, for example, exorcism*, the dedication of a church, and the distribution of ashes on Ash Wednesday. Others are objects, for example, holy water and wedding rings. Some sacramentals may be administered only by a cleric*, others by laity. The distinction between sacraments and sacramentals was not clearly made until the standardization of the number of the sacraments at seven in the thirteenth century.

SACRAMENTARY. A book that contains the celebrant's prayers ("presidential prayers") for mass*. Sacramentaries originated around the end of the fourth century. They often contained additional prayers used by priests and bishops, for example, ordination formularies and various blessings. In the thirteenth century, the sacramentary was combined with the lectionary* and the *Graduale* (book of chants) to form the missal*. Since 1970, the sacramentary for mass has again been published separately.

SACRED HEART OF JESUS. In biblical and patristic language, "heart" refers to the center of a person's subjectivity. It includes not only emotions and feelings, but also will and thought. The heart of Jesus is thus the center of his human subjectivity. It is a symbol of his human and divine love. Devotion to the heart of Jesus was common in the Middle Ages, chiefly in connection with devotion to Jesus' five wounds. It became prominent in the seventeenth century, especially as a result of private revelations* received by St. Margaret Mary Alacoque (1647-1690). She urged devotion to the Sacred Heart of Jesus, frequent communion, communion on the first Friday of each month, Holy Hours of reparation on Thursdays, and the institution of a feast of the Sacred Heart. That feast was approved for Poland in 1765 and for the whole Church in 1856. It is celebrated on the Friday following the second Sunday after Pentecost.

SACRIFICE (Lt *sacer*, "holy, sacred," *facere*, "to make"). In religion generally, a sacrifice is the giving of something to a deity by removing the thing from the realm of human activity, through consumption or destruction. It establishes, confirms, or repairs a bond between the human community and the divine realm. Sacrifice figures prominently in the OT, most importantly the **holocaust** or "whole burnt offering" of an animal (Lv 1), and the **sin offering** or atonement* sacrifice (Lv 4). The prophetic literature is often critical of emphasis on external acts rather than inward dispositions in sacrifice (e.g., Ps 50, Hos 6.4-6), but it does not reject the institution of sacrifice. This critique is continued in the NT (e.g., Mt 9.13).

The NT sees the death of Jesus as a sacrifice; this is especially true of the Letter to the Hebrews, where Jesus is portrayed as both the new high priest and the sacrificial victim (Heb 9-10). Jesus' sacrifice obviates any need for further sacrifices (Heb 9.25-28). Jesus' "words of institution" of the eucharist* portray his death as a sacrifice: his body is "given for you," his blood "shed for you" (Lk 22.19-20). This underlies the Christian understanding of the eucharist, the "memorial" of Jesus' death, as a sacrifice. Such an understanding is implicit in the NT and becomes explicit only in the third century, when bishops began to be referred to as "priests"*. By the late Middle Ages, the eucharist (mass) was often understood as a sacrifice performed by the priest, somehow repeating or adding to the sacrifice of Jesus. Concerned to defend the once-for-all character of Christ's sacrifice, the Protestant* Reformers purged sacrifice language from the liturgy. In response, the Council of Trent* declared in 1562 that the mass is a "true and proper sacrifice" (DS 1751). It spoke of the mass not as "repeating" but as "representing" (making present again) Christ's sacrifice (DS 1739). Recent Catholic theology and ecumenical dialogues* emphasize that the eucharist is a sacrifice in the sense that through it Christians join themselves in a special way with the one, unique sacrifice of Christ.

Some NT passages speak of Christian life as sacrifice (e.g., Rom 12.1, 1 Pt 2.1-10). St. Augustine* says that "the true sacrifice is every act which is designed to unite us to God in a holy fellowship," and singles out acts of compassion (*City of God* 10.6). Vatican Council II, drawing on 1 Peter, links the idea of the priesthood of all the faithful to that of Christian sacramental and moral life as sacrifice (LG 10-11). The emphasis is not (as sometimes in popular understandings of "sacrifice") on "giving something up" but on joining one's life to God in Christ.

SAINT PETER'S BASILICA. The principal church and central building of the Vatican*. Six hundred nineteen feet long, it is the second largest church in Christendom (after the Basilica of Our Lady

Queen of Peace in Yamoussoukro, Ivory Coast). It is built on the traditional site of the tomb of St. Peter, where, around A.D. 320, Constantine* had a basilica* constructed. This building lasted into the fifteenth century, when its disrepair led Pope Nicholas V (1447-1455) to undertake to rebuild it. Construction continued off and on into the seventeenth century. Around 1546, Michelangelo (1475-1564) was given charge of the project. He designed the basilica's great dome, which was completed in 1590. The exterior was completed in 1614, and the church was consecrated in 1626. The interior was finished in the seventeenth century under the supervision of G. L. Bernini (1598-1680) and others. St. Peter's was the site of Vatican Councils I and II*. It houses many treasures of art, notably Michelangelo's sculpture, the *Pietà*. One enters St. Peter's and the Vatican by way of **Saint Peter's Square**, an elliptical plaza more than six hundred feet across and surrounded by a colonnade designed by Bernini.

SAINTS (Lt *sancti,* "holy ones"). In the NT, the most common meaning of "saints" (Gk *hagioi*) is Christian believers (see, e.g., Rom 1.7). In contemporary use, the term refers primarily to those officially recognized by the Church as enjoying eternal life with God (*see* CANONIZATION). The Church, however, acknowledges that many who have not been officially canonized are enjoying eternal life; they are celebrated in the Feast of All Saints*. In addition, living persons who are models of holiness are sometimes called "saints."

In the life of the Church, saints (in the sense of those enjoying eternal life) serve as *models* of Christian virtue, for Christians to imitate (or at least to admire), and as *intercessors*, who pray for the Church on earth. Saints are not to be venerated in such a way as to detract from the uniqueness of Christ as savior and mediator. The saints' virtues are the result of the grace* of Christ, and in their prayer they are one with Christ's prayer. Thus, the Second Council of Nicaea* (787) distinguished between the veneration (Gk *douleia)* due to saints and the worship or adoration (*latreia*) due to God and therefore to Christ.

The veneration of saints began in the Christian tradition with the cult of the martyrs*. After the end of persecutions* in the Roman Empire, this veneration was extended to ascetics and great figures in the Church. The first lives of the saints date from the fourth century. These became an important genre of medieval literature, combining history and legend. In late medieval popular piety, the cult of the saints proliferated to such an extent as to appear to threaten the centrality of Christ. In reaction, the Protestant* Reformers curbed devotion to the saints and forbade their invocation in prayer. The Council of Trent* (1563), in response, affirmed that "it is a good and beneficial thing to invoke" the saints "to obtain blessings from God" through Jesus Christ "who is our sole redeemer and savior" (DS 1821). Still, in the proliferation of devotions* to the saints and to Mary* in the Catholic Church in the Counter-Reformation period and especially in the nineteenth century, awareness of the centrality of Christ was not always maintained in practice. It was clearly reaffirmed by Vatican Council II, "Our communion with the saints joins us to Christ, from whom as from the source and the head flows all grace and life of the people of God itself" (LG 50). With this in mind, contemporary ecumenical dialogues* have narrowed, but not eliminated, the division between Catholics and Protestants over the invocation of the saints.

See also COMMUNION OF SAINTS.

SALVATION (from Lt *salvus*, "safe, sound"). Most religions have some concept of salvation. Ordinary human life is subject to a threat from which we must be made *safe*, a peril from which we must be *saved*, a sickness from which we must be *healed*, a fragmented or fragmentary state from which we must be made *whole*—all the emphasized terms are etymologically related to the root of "salvation." In Christianity, it is Jesus Christ* who brings salvation, first and foremost from sin* (e.g., Mt 1.21) but also from suffering and injustice. "Salvation" is thus closely related to "redemption"*, with the latter more often indicating the work of Jesus and the former the result of the work; *see also* KINGDOM OF GOD. Salvation is the work of God in Jesus (1 Tm 2.3-6, Acts 4.12). It is already present in this world, e.g., in Jesus' healings (Mk 5.34), but achieves completion only in the next (1 Pt 1.5). Contemporary liberation theology* has emphasized the continuity between liberation from poverty* and oppression in this world and ultimate liberation and salvation. Salvation is communal rather than strictly individual; as Vatican Council II said, "It has pleased God ... to sanctify and save men and women not individually and without regard for what binds them together, but to set them up as a people who would acknowledge him in truth and serve him in holiness" (LG 9). Salvation extends, in fact, beyond the human community to include all of creation (Rom 8.19-23). *See also* ESCHATOLOGY, RESURRECTION.

SALVATION OUTSIDE THE CHURCH. This is the problem of whether non-Christians and non-Catholic Christians can be saved. It is distinct from, though related to, the question of the salvation of unbaptized persons (chiefly infants) within the Catholic community (*see* BAPTISM, LIMBO), and the question of the salvation of those who lived before Christ. Because Catholic doctrine affirms that Jesus Christ* is uniquely the savior, it holds that the Church, as the "body of Christ," his continuing presence on earth, has some role in the salvation of all who are saved.

The conclusions drawn from this principle have varied considerably over time. The earliest Fathers of the Church* tended to affirm the possibility of salvation for virtuous Jews and pagans. Justin Martyr* (d. 160) held that all who had lived according to reason (*logos*) were really Christians, since Christ was the *Logos**. St. Cyprian (third century) originated the maxim, "No salvation outside the Church" (*extra ecclesiam nulla salus*), in reference to those who separated themselves from the Church due to heresy* or schism*. Once the Roman Empire became Christian in the fourth century, this principle was applied to Jews and pagans as well. Augustine* in the fifth century held that those who died unbaptized were not among those God predestined to be saved. Most medieval theologians and Church leaders were unwilling to deny (as Augustine had) that God offers saving grace* to all but continued to affirm the damnation of pagans and Jews. The often tacit assumption was that the Christian message was known to all, and it was through their own fault that pagans and Jews did not accept it.

The discovery of the New World refuted this assumption, and some sixteenth-century theologians began to argue for the possibility of the salvation of New World natives who had not heard the Gospel or had not had it presented to them in a sufficiently persuasive way. The preferred solution, expressed by Robert Bellarmine* and others, was that those who believed in God and sought to do good were in the Church by implicit *desire* and thus could be saved. Pope Pius IX* declared in 1863 that those who without fault were ignorant of Christian faith and who lived "honest and upright lives" could be saved through divine grace.

The Second Vatican Council (1962-1965) makes a distinction between non-Catholic Christians, who have a saving relationship to the Church by means of their own "churches and ecclesial communities," and non-Christians. The latter, even those who are atheists, can be saved and "are ordered to [the Church] in various ways" (LG 13). The

Council seems to hold, but does not clearly say, that God's offer of saving grace necessarily implies a relation to the Church as the "universal sacrament of salvation" (LG 48 and elsewhere). Some conciliar and post-conciliar statements suggest that those who adhere to non-Christian religions* are saved precisely through those religions, as mediations of God's saving grace. There continues to be much theological discussion as to the relation of the Church to those non-Christians who are saved.

SATAN. *See* DEMON.

SAVONAROLA, GIROLAMO (1452-1498). Italian Dominican* preacher and religious reformer. At San Marco in Florence, he preached sermons, prophetic and apocalyptic* in tone, criticizing lax morals in the Church and society and calling for reform. He saw Florence as the spearhead for moral reform of all of Christendom and gained such influence that by the middle of 1495 he in effect ruled the city through his preaching. In 1494, when he spoke of the invading French king, Charles VIII, as God's instrument for the chastisement of Italy, he aroused the enmity of Pope Alexander VI. In late 1495, after refusing a summons to defend himself in Rome, he was forbidden to preach. He resumed preaching in 1496, apparently with papal approval, but his continued defiance of the pope led to his excommunication* in 1497. In early 1498, he appealed for a general council to depose the pope. Shortly afterward, he was arrested, tried, tortured, and convicted of heresy* and schism*. He was hanged on May 23, 1498, and his body was burned.

SCAPULAR (Lt *scapula*, "shoulder"). A garment hanging over the shoulders. Originally a sort of apron, it became a part of the religious habits* of some orders. In the thirteenth century, a reduced scapular, consisting of small pieces of cloth worn on the front and back of the body and connected by strings, was given to members of third orders* associated with religious communities. In the sixteenth century, the scapular was reduced still further, sometimes to only one small piece of cloth worn on a string or cord; the piece of cloth often contained a holy image. Since 1910, a **scapular medal**, having images of the Sacred Heart* of Jesus on one side and the Blessed Virgin Mary on the other, may be worn in place of a scapular. The scapular is a symbol of religious devotion and often of association with a religious order, and the Church has attached indulgences* to the wearing of scapulars. There are about twenty kinds of scapular in use. The best known is the brown Carmelite scapular. Carmelite legend has it that in 1251, Mary appeared to St. Simon Stock in Cambridge, England, and declared that whoever wore the brown scapular at death would be spared from hell* and would be taken to heaven* on the first Saturday after death. The Church has not pronounced on the accuracy of this legend, but the promise must be understood consistently with Church teaching: no object is spiritually efficacious in itself, without the proper interior disposition, and no one can in this life be absolutely certain of salvation.

SCHISM (Gk *schisma*, "division"). Schism is defined in canon law* as "the refusal of submission to the Roman Pontiff or of communion with the members of the Church subject to him" (Canon 751). More broadly it refers to any division in the Church where the issues are mainly of authority and communion. It is distinguished from heresy*, in which the issues are mainly doctrinal, though in practice the distinction is not always clear. The term *schism* is first used, in the broader sense, by Paul in 1 Cor 1.10, 11.18, 12.25. The most important schism in church history is that between the Catholic Church and the Eastern Orthodox Churches*. Second in importance was the Great Western Schism* (1378-1417).

SCHOLASTICISM (Lt *schola*, "school"). The style of thought and argumentation, particularly in philosophy* and theology*, characteristic of the medieval universities*. Its notable features include a close reading of texts, considerable reliance on the authority of texts in order to justify positions taken, use of Aristotelian* logic to advance from premises to conclusions, and a subordination of philosophy to theology. Typical literary forms of scholasticism grew out of the medieval classroom. From the *lectio* ("reading"), or text-based "lecture," grew the commentary, and from the *disputatio* or *quaestio* grew the written *quaestio* or "question." The form of the latter, reflecting classroom procedure, consisted in the posing of a question, the marshaling of arguments on both sides, the master's reply and argument in support of it, and responses to contrary opinions. It can be found in many medieval works, for instance, the *Summa theologiae* of St. Thomas Aquinas*. The word *scholasticism* is sometimes used more broadly to refer to all of medieval philosophy or at least to all that used

Aristotelian methods. In this latter sense, Anselm* and Abelard* are called the founders of scholasticism, though they predate the university context. "Scholasticism" is also used narrowly to mean Thomism*.

"Scholasticism" also refers to philosophy and theology done in continuity with medieval thought. The late sixteenth and early seventeenth century was a period of much creativity in scholasticism. Major schools were the Thomist, the Scotist (from Duns Scotus*), and the Suarezian, after the Spanish Jesuit Francisco Suarez (1548-1617). In the mid-seventeenth century, scholastic thought tended to adopt a deductive, quasi-mathematical format, reflecting the rationalism* of René Descartes. In this format, which characterized the textbooks used in Catholic institutions into the twentieth century, the *thesis* replaced the question and a highly deductive style of argument was employed to "prove" the thesis. **Neo-Scholasticism** designates this style of scholastic thought, or, more narrowly, efforts to revive scholasticism (chiefly Thomism) in the nineteenth and twentieth centuries.

SCHOOLS, CATHOLIC, IN THE UNITED STATES. The earliest Catholic schools in the territory that became the United States were mission schools in Spanish America in the sixteenth century. In the English colonies, the first Catholic school was operated by the Jesuits* at Newtown Manor in Maryland in 1653. The first **parochial schools** (school operated by a parish) appeared in Pennsylvania in the eighteenth century; one of them was founded in 1782 at St. Mary's Church in Philadelphia. The first school for girls was opened in 1727 by Ursulines in New Orleans, in French territory. An academy for girls, later known as Visitation Academy, was founded in Georgetown (now District of Columbia) in the 1790s. St. Elizabeth Anne Seton* founded a free parochial school, open to both sexes, at Emmitsburg, Maryland, in 1810.

Catholic schools increased significantly in number after 1830, largely due to Catholic immigration. Like other church-related schools, they often received public funds, a practice that lasted into the twentieth century in some places. The rise of the public school movement in the 1840s provoked Catholic bishops, led by John Hughes of New York, to endeavor to build a parochial school system, as the public schools were strongly Protestant in character. In 1884, the Third Plenary Council of Baltimore mandated that a school should be erected near each parish church and that all Catholic children should attend parochial schools. Some exceptions were permitted, and some opposition remained, so that these goals were never fully realized. Even so, a strong parochial school system arose as an alternative to the increasingly secularized public schools. The number of parochial elementary schools more than doubled between 1880 and 1910, to 4,845. Secondary schools were at first mostly operated by religious communities, but diocesan secondary schools became widespread by 1910. The National Catholic Educational Association, the chief organization of Catholic educators in the United States, was founded in 1904. The peak year for Catholic schools was 1965, in which there were 10,879 Catholic elementary schools and 2,413 secondary schools, together educating 5.6 million students, about 12 percent of all American elementary and secondary students. The schools were staffed chiefly by religious sisters*, who served for very low salaries.

Catholic schools were central to the transmission of Catholic faith and culture to the young and also to the socialization of Catholic immigrants into mainstream American society. These two purposes were somewhat at odds, and a decline in Catholic schools began in the 1960s, as Catholics became less an immigrant population and more native and middle class. Coinciding with this development were changes in the Church as a result of Vatican Council II* (1962-1965), which in general discouraged Catholic separatism and favored engagement in the modern world. There was a precipitous drop in the number of members of religious communities teaching in schools, from 94,000 in 1967 to 20,000 in 1990. The need to pay salaries of lay teachers caused a financial crisis, leading to the closing of many schools and much higher tuition in the others, at a time when increased taxation for public school support placed greater burdens on parents. Court rulings allowed the existence of religious schools but generally forbade government financial aid to them. Efforts by Catholic leaders to gain public funding for Catholic schools, or at least tax relief for parents of students, have been unsuccessful, though courts have upheld small public expenditures for transportation, textbooks, and special education for nonpublic school students. Many Catholics, echoing complaints already raised in the nineteenth century, objected to the limitations imposed on other ministries by the percentage of Church revenues dedicated to schools.

Still, repeated studies in the 1970s and 1980s showed Catholic schools to be relatively effective in providing education (at a time when public schools were drawing increasing criticism) and in transmitting Catholic belief and values. In addition, Catholic schools in inner cities reoriented themselves toward the mission of educating poor children of all religious backgrounds. They became an important agent in the effort to overcome the effects of pervasive poverty in the cities, especially among African Americans. Tension between the goals of educating the poor and educating young Catholics was often felt in the process of allocating diocesan funds for education. Catholic schools have remained an important part of the mission of the Church in the United States, in 1994 educating almost two million students in 7,136 elementary schools (almost all diocesan or parochial) and more than six hundred thousand students in 1,248 high schools (about 60 percent diocesan or parochial, the others private).

SECULAR INSTITUTE. A society of men or women that is an "institute of consecrated life" according to canon law* but is not a "religious institute" (religious community). *See* RELIGIOUS LIFE. Members take vows* or make some other form of commitment to observe the evangelical counsels* of poverty, chastity, and obedience. They do not, however, undertake life in common, in the manner of religious communities. Members may be laity* or clerics*. If they are laity, they live like ordinary single persons "in the world." If clerics, they live as diocesan priests* (or perhaps in rare cases as single permanent deacons*). The first secular institute was the Institute of the Daughters of the Sacred Heart of Mary, founded at Paris in 1790 and approved in 1857. The number of institutes grew, and various forms of approval were received, until Pope Pius XII* gave them official recognition in the apostolic constitution *Provida Mater Ecclesia* in 1947. The 1983 Code of Canon Law has statutes (Canons 710-730) governing secular institutes and distinguishing them more clearly from religious institutes than did the 1947 document. A secular institute begins as an association, called a "pious union." It may then become an "institute of diocesan right" and eventually an "institute of pontifical right." In 1994, there were twenty-seven secular institutes in the United States.

SEMINARY (Lt *seminarium*, "seed bed"). A school for training candidates for the priesthood. In the early Middle Ages, priests had been educated at cathedral* schools, but by the later Middle Ages, many clergy lacked sufficient education for their ministry. To address this problem, the Council of Trent* decreed in 1563 that each diocese should open a seminary, or, failing that, that dioceses join in constructing one. Seminaries exist on several levels: high school seminaries, college seminaries, and major seminaries or theologates. College seminaries offer a four-year program, concentrating in the liberal arts*, especially philosophy. Those who enter major seminaries, if they have not had sufficient academic preparation, especially in philosophy, may have to spend a year or two as "pre-theologians." The major seminary offers a four-year curriculum concentrating in theology. All seminaries provide an environment for spiritual formation, in addition to their academic programs. Seminaries may be primarily for diocesan priesthood or for members of religious communities. In the latter case, they may be called "theologates" or "houses of study" rather than "seminaries." In the United States, seminary training is governed by the *Program of Priestly Formation* (fourth edition, 1992) of the National Conference of Catholic Bishops.

The first seminary in the United States was St. Mary's Seminary, Baltimore, founded in 1790. By 1963, there were 444 seminaries in the United States. Since that time, there has been a sharp drop in the number of seminarians, especially on the high school and college level. Many smaller seminaries closed or merged with or into larger institutions. In very recent years, the decline in seminarians appears to have ended on the major seminary level. In 1994, there were 5,549 seminarians in 213 seminaries in the United States.

The model for seminaries in the period between Trent and Vatican Council II* envisioned seminaries as self-sufficient and having relatively little contact with the external world. Since Vatican II, there has been much greater emphasis on interaction with the outside world, including ecumenical contacts. Although the majority of major seminaries in the United States are freestanding or independent, increasingly they participate in consortia or other cooperative arrangements with other institutions, not all of them Catholic. Seminaries that are not freestanding are attached to a college or university, or have formed a collaborative body, such as the Washington Theological Union. Besides training for priesthood, seminaries now often offer programs for lay ministers or academic graduate programs in theology. In such cases, they are required to maintain a distinct program of spiritual formation specifically for priesthood.

SENSE OF FAITH (*SENSUS FIDEI*); SENSE OF THE FAITHFUL (*SENSUS FIDELIUM*). According to Vatican Council II, "The universal body of the faithful who have received the anointing of the holy one ... cannot be mistaken in belief. It displays this particular quality through a supernatural sense of faith [*sensus fidei*] in the whole people when ... it expresses the consent of all in matters of faith and morals" (LG 12) (*see* INFALLIBILITY). This "sense of faith" is not an articulated set of beliefs but an inarticulate or incompletely articulate "sense" or "instinct" as to what is in accordance with revelation*. *Sensus fidelium* is usually a synonym for *sensus fidei*, but sometimes it refers more narrowly to that which is believed by the faithful, while the *sensus fidei* is that by which they believe. *Consensus fidelium* ("consensus of the faithful") is their general agreement. According to Vatican II, the sense of faith "loyally defers" to the hierarchical teaching authority; it can, however, lead to new declarations of doctrine, as in the cases of the immaculate conception* and assumption* of Mary. The question of whether the sense of the faithful can be at odds with official teaching is currently being discussed in connection with disputes over birth control* and related issues. *See also* TRADITION.

SETON, ELIZABETH ANNE BAYLEY, ST. (1774-1821). The first American-born saint. Elizabeth Anne Bayley was born into a prominent Episcopalian family in New York. In 1794 she married William Seton. They had five children. William's business went bankrupt, and he died in Italy in December 1803, on a trip undertaken with his family for the sake of his failing health. Elizabeth, always devoutly religious, was introduced to Catholicism by her Italian hosts, the Filicchi family, and after returning to the United States she entered the Catholic Church in 1805. In 1808 she was invited to found a school in Baltimore, and while in Baltimore she and several other women founded a community of Sisters of Charity of St. Joseph, under the supervision of Bishop John Carroll*. Elizabeth began to be called "Mother Seton" at that time. In 1809, she moved her school and community to Emmitsburg, Maryland, where the school became St. Joseph Academy, a successor to which still exists as an elementary school. The community adopted a version of the rule of St. Vincent de Paul*, but formally became a branch of the Daughters of Charity of St. Vincent de Paul only in 1850. Their motherhouse remains in Emmitsburg. Mother Seton continued as superior of her community until her death. She was canonized in 1975, and her feast is celebrated on January 4.

SEXUAL ETHICS. In the tradition of recent centuries, Catholic sexual ethics may be derived from two basic principles. One is that genital sexual expression is to be reserved for marriage*. This principle draws on biblical prohibitions of adultery (Ex 20.14), fornication (Eph 5.5), and homosexual* activity (Lv 18.22). The other is that the procreative and unitive purposes of marriage should not be separated in particular actions. This principle, while not directly biblical, is linked to biblical injunctions of marital fecundity (Gn 1.28). Within marriage, it rules out contraception (*see* BIRTH CONTROL) and sexual actions of a sort that could not be procreative (oral sex, for instance). It has also been used recently to prohibit married couples' use of *in vitro* fertilization and artificial insemination with the husband's semen, since in these cases procreation occurs without an act of intercourse.

The Fathers of the Church* took a generally negative attitude toward sexuality, preferring virginity* to marriage. The source of this attitude is not entirely clear. The passages in the NT that praise celibacy* played a part, and so did a disparagement of the body in general and sexuality in particular, which is found in much ancient philosophy, especially Platonism*. Against the Gnostics*, though, the Fathers affirmed the goodness of the body and of procreation. They adopted from Stoicism* the principle that sexual intercourse was permissible only for procreation. Suspicion of sexuality was enhanced by Augustine's* argument that sexual intercourse was the means whereby original sin* was transmitted.

Thomas Aquinas* took over much from Augustine in his treatment of sexuality but also incorporated it into his theory of natural law*. Drawing on Roman law, Aquinas argued that the primary purpose of sexual intercourse is that which humans and animals have in common, namely the procreation and education of offspring. He distinguished "sins against nature," such as masturbation and homosexuality, from "sins according to nature," in which the natural biological structure of the act of intercourse is observed; these include rape, adultery, heterosexual incest, and fornication. This distinction was preserved into the twentieth century in the manuals of moral theology*, which developed the natural law approach and applied it to specific cases. The manuals followed Aquinas in seeing sexual offenses as always involving "grave matter," so that they were mortal sins (*see* SIN) if done with full knowledge and consent. All directly willed sexual pleasure outside of the context of marital intercourse was judged mortally sinful. Marital intercourse itself was primarily justified by its orientation to procreation, while writers differed on the extent to which it was justified for other purposes. The 1917 Code of Canon Law stated the traditional teaching on the ends of marriage: "The primary end of matrimony is the procreation and raising of offspring; the secondary, mutual help and the remedy for concupiscence" (Canon 1013.1).

A more "personalist" view entered Catholic sexual ethics in the twentieth century, especially through the work of Herbert Doms in the 1930s. Personalism treated sexual activity primarily in the context of the interpersonal relationship between spouses rather than the biological functions of sexuality. Vatican Council II, in its treatment of marriage in its *Pastoral Constitution on the Church in the Modern World* (1965) avoids ranking the "ends of marriage." It speaks of marriage, however, as "the human action in which spouses give themselves to each other and accept each other" (GS 48) and says of sexual acts that "they express and encourage a mutual giving in which a couple gladly and gratefully enrich each other" (49), before going on to say, "Of their nature marriage and married love are directed towards the begetting and bringing up of children" (50).

Vatican II explicitly avoided speaking about birth control*. During and after the Council many people expected that the Church would allow artificial contraception within marriage, so that spouses could have intercourse to foster mutual love in circumstances when procreation would be inadvisable. In 1968, however, Pope Paul VI* reiterated the traditional ban against contraception, on the grounds of "the inseparable connection ... between the unitive significance and the procreative significance ... [of] the marriage act" (*Humanae vitae* 12). Since 1968, there has been much controversy in the Church in the area of sexual ethics. Partly this is a result of conflicts over sexuality in Western culture as a whole, partly it results from theologians' greater attentiveness to work on sexuality in the natural and social sciences. In the context of Church tradition, however, the specific question is to what extent a primarily personalist understanding of sexual activity can preserve the traditional norms that were formulated within an understanding of sexuality as primarily procreative. Pope John Paul II*, working within a personalist framework, defends the traditional prohibitions and has acted to curb theological dissent* in this area. By contrast, the 1977 study, *Human Sexuality*, commissioned by the Catholic Theological Society of America, seemed to permit any sort of sexual activity, so long as it is "creative and integrative." The contemporary challenge to Catholic moralists is to incorporate into the tradition a fuller appreciation of human sexuality and its goodness, while drawing on the tradition to correct contemporary secular culture's neglect of the procreative dimension of sexuality.

SHRINE (Lt *scrinium*, "box for books or papers," whence "reliquary"). Defined in canon law as "a church or other sacred place to which the faithful make pilgrimages*" (Canon 1230). A shrine may mark the site of an apparition* or other holy event, or the presence of a saint's* tomb, relics*, or a sacred image, or simply be erected to honor God, Jesus, or a saint. "National shrines," for example, the National Shrine of the Immaculate Conception, Washington, D.C., may be designated by national episcopal conferences*. A "crowned shrine" is specially approved by the pope; such approval authorizes public devotion at the shrine and implies that at least one miracle* has resulted from such devotion. More loosely, "shrine" may refer to a place of prayer set up indoors or outdoors, whether or not officially approved.

SHROUD OF TURIN. A linen cloth thought by some to be the burial shroud of Jesus (Jn 20.5-6). It is about fourteen by three and a half feet, and it bears a life-size image of a man with wounds like those caused by crucifixion. The image is like a photographic negative, and the manner in which it was imprinted on the cloth is unknown—it is not painted, stained, or scorched onto it. The cloth was first reported at Troyes, France, in the fourteenth century. It was later given to the House of Savoy, who in 1578 had it stored at the Cathedral in Turin, Italy, where it remains. In 1988, laboratories in three different countries performed carbon-14 dating tests on small squares of the cloth, and all yielded a date of between A.D. 1260 and 1390. Ninety-five percent accuracy is claimed for these results.

SIGN OF THE CROSS. A gesture forming the shape of a cross*. Such gestures have been part of Christian prayer since at least the second century. Initially, the cross was marked on the forehead by the right hand. This sign is still part of the rituals for baptism* and confirmation*. A larger form, made by touching the forehead, breast, and shoulders, dates from the fifth century. It is customary in the West to touch first the left shoulder, then the right; in the East, right then left. In the West, a trinitarian verbal formula usually accompanies the sign: "In the name of the Father [touch forehead], and of the Son [touch below breast], and of the Holy [left shoulder] Spirit [right shoulder], Amen." The sign of the cross often marks the beginning and end of prayers or periods of prayer. In prayers of blessing, a sign of the cross is made over the person(s) or object(s) to be blessed.

SIGNATURA, APOSTOLIC. *See* TRIBUNAL.

SIMONY. The buying and selling of spiritual goods, for example, sacraments* and church offices. The name derives from Simon Magus, who sought to buy from Peter and John the power of conferring the Holy Spirit (Acts 8.9-24).

SIN. The wrongdoing of a rational creature (human or angelic), considered as offense against God or break in relationship with God. The OT has a wide range of terms for sin. Its central idea of sin is that of a breach in a covenant with God (Hos 8.1), though sin existed before God established a covenant. Connotations of the Hebrew words used include "missing the mark," "rebellion," "deviation," and "folly." The narrative of the sin of Adam and Eve in Genesis 3 is better understood as a model of all human sin than as an account of the historical origins of sin (*see* ORIGINAL SIN). Adam and Eve sin through disobedience to God because of their desire to "be like gods" (Gn 3.5), to put themselves in the place of God. As a result of sin, human beings are set at odds with God, with one another, within themselves, and with the material world, and, ultimately, they are subject to death* (Gn 3.16-19). The NT develops OT themes on sin but tends more to see sin as a unified power, overcome in the kingdom of God* established by Jesus. The most searching treatment of sin in the NT is in Romans 1-8, in which Paul depicts sin as having entered the world through Adam's sin and from there gaining sway over the whole world, Gentile as well as Jewish. The reign of sin is broken by the death and resurrection* of Christ, and Christ's victory is for all who are baptized in him.

The Western theological tradition about sin has been dominated by Augustine*. Against the Manichaeans*, Augustine insisted that sin enters the world through the free choice of rational beings. Against the Pelagians*, he argued that humans are so corrupted by original sin—the sin of Adam and Eve passed on to all their descendants—that they cannot do good works worthy of salvation without the assistance of God's grace*. Various Scripture passages indicate that sins have degrees of seriousness. Augustine drew on 1 Cor 3.10-15 in urging, against the Pelagians, that not all sins warrant eternal condemnation. Medieval theology developed this point into the distinction between **mortal sins** (Lt *mors*, "death") and **venial sins** (Lt *venia*, "pardon"). According to Thomas Aquinas*, "When the soul is so disordered by sin as to turn away from its last end, God, ... there is mortal sin; but when it is disordered without turning away from God, there is venial sin" (ST 1-2.72.5). A mortal sin, if not forgiven, merits eternal damnation, while a venial sin merits only temporal punishment, on earth or in purgatory*. For there to be a mortal sin, there must be "grave matter" (serious violation of love of God or neighbor), sufficient reflection, and full consent of the will (ST 1-2.88.2,6).

The Council of Trent* (1545-63) affirmed the mortal-venial distinction (DS 1537) and required the sacramental confession* of all mortal sins by species (kind) and number (DS 1679-1680). This requirement led to a preoccupation in subsequent moral theology* with identifying which specific actions are mortal sins. In an effort to shift the focus away from isolated acts to a person's entire moral life, some twentieth-century theologians introduced the idea of a fundamental option*. According to this theory, individual acts, even if seriously wrong, do not in isolation lead to eternal damnation. The true mortal sin is a fundamental option against God, a choice (which is expressed and may be enacted in particular actions) for self-centeredness rather than love of God and neighbor. While accepting the idea of a fundamental option, Pope John Paul II* declared in the encyclical *Veritatis splendor* (1993) that certain kinds of acts by their very nature constitute a fundamental option against God.

Sin is essentially a personal choice, but as human persons are not isolated from social relations, neither is sin. Recent theology and church documents have shown increasing awareness of **social sin** or **structures of sin**, sin embodied in social structures and patterns of thought and action, "which go far beyond the actions and brief life span of an individual" (Pope John Paul II, *Sollicitudo rei socialis* 36). Social sin is the result of personal sinful choices, but it is also a cause of them (see Vatican Council II, GS 25). Sinful social structures shape the persons who make choices and the conditions within which they choose. Social sin may be seen in situations in which people are aware of the evil intrinsic to the structures in which they live but do not see how they can extricate themselves from it. It also manifests itself in the "false consciousness" whereby people can feel justified in their complicity in oppression. (On the sin of angels, *see* DEMON.)

SISTER. A woman member of a religious congregation (*see* RELIGIOUS LIFE). Sisters take simple vows* of poverty, chastity, and obedience (*see* EVANGELICAL COUNSELS). In contrast, a **nun** (also usually addressed as "Sister") belongs to a religious order and has taken solemn vows (or simple vows in a religious house where others take or ought to take solemn vows).

Women's religious life began with the widows* and virgins* of the early Church. It developed in parallel with men's monasticism* into the Middle Ages, but diverged due to the growing tendency for monks to be ordained to the priesthood and due to the strictness of the requirement for **cloister** (Lt *claustrum*, "enclosed place") for women. Those in cloister are limited as to their ability to go outside of their religious house (or certain parts of it) and as to the entry of others into the house (or designated part). The requirement of cloister for religious men and women originated in the sixth century and became increasingly restrictive for women. It was made universal in 1298 by Pope Boniface VIII* and strengthened by the Council of Trent* in 1563. Thereafter it was gradually relaxed, but only in 1841 did a congregation of sisters (as distinct from nuns) receive official approval, and only in 1900 was a general official recognition accorded to apostolic congregations of women with simple vows.

SLAVERY. A social institution whereby some human beings are the property of others. Both the OT and the NT take the existence of slavery for granted, neither defending nor attacking the institution. The NT challenges its basis with the doctrine that in Christ there is no distinction between slave and free person (e.g., Gal 3.28), but its specific counsel is that slaves should obey their masters and masters should be kind to slaves (e.g., Eph 6.5-9). When the Roman Empire became Christian, the conditions of slavery were mitigated but not abolished. Slavery was slowly transformed into serfdom and eventually disappeared in Europe but was still justified in theory by medieval theologians. Slavery was revived with the great European explorations of Africa and the Americas in the fifteenth and following centuries. In the Americas, many religious communities owned Indian and African slaves. Church authorities and theologians alternated condemnations of slavery with statements of qualified approval. In 1839, Pope Gregory XVI condemned the slave trade, but his language was vague enough that bishops in the United States were able to argue that it did not apply to American slavery. Though some Catholic spokespersons condemned slavery in the United States before the civil war, most supported it, and no bishop spoke out against it. "Traditional moral theology gave them no warrant" to do so (J. Hennessey). Some, for example, John England of Charleston, South Carolina, and Augustin Verot of St. Augustine, Florida, publicly voiced justification of it. The campaign for the abolition of slavery was led by Protestant Christians. As late as 1866, the Holy Office ruled that the buying and selling of slaves was not contrary to the natural law*. In 1890, Pope Leo XIII* forthrightly condemned the entire institution of slavery (which by then had been abolished everywhere in the West), and Vatican Council II condemns it strongly as an offense against human dignity (GS 27). The development of Catholic teaching on this issue may be seen as an instance of the Church becoming aware of the implications of a gospel value in response to changes in secular society, which themselves were fundamentally motivated by Christian values.

SOCIAL JUSTICE. *See* JUSTICE.

SOCIAL TEACHING. At all times, Catholic teaching has had some bearing on social issues, but the term *Catholic social teaching* refers specifically to a body of official teaching that began with the encyclical* *Rerum novarum* of Pope Leo XIII* in 1891. This body of teaching applies principles of the Catholic tradition to specific social, economic, and political problems of modern industrial and post-industrial society. Until the 1960s, the term *social doctrine* was often used, but it was abandoned as suggesting an unchanging body of truths rather than an effort to apply principles to changing situations. Pope John Paul II* has revived the term but used it in a qualified way, together with other terms.

The basis of Catholic social teaching is the belief in the dignity of the human person, together with an understanding of the human person as essentially social. Social and economic policies must respect the freedom and dignity of the individual but also promote the common good of society. *Rerum novarum* responded to the condition of industrial labor* in nineteenth-century Europe and America. It defended workers' rights to private property* and a just wage and to organize into unions, and it asserted that the state may intervene in economic affairs to protect workers. It thus was critical of both capitalism* and socialism*. Pope Pius XI* restated and extended these principles in *Quadragesimo anno* ("Forty Years After" *Rerum novarum*) (1931).

The next major documents of social teaching were the encyclicals *Mater et magistra* (1961) and *Pacem in terris* (1963) of Pope John XXIII*. To the continuing critique of the social order of developed societies, these encyclicals added a treatment of the international order, calling for social justice among nations and an end to the international arms race. Vatican Council II*, in its *Pastoral Constitution on the Church in the Modern World (Gaudium et Spes)* (1965), summarized Catholic social teaching as it then stood, centering on the theme of human dignity and the centrality of justice* both to economic life and to peace* and cooperation among nations. The encyclical *Populorum progressio* (1965) of Pope Paul VI* addressed international poverty* and distanced the Church somewhat from the prevailing Western model of economic development.

Pope Paul's apostolic letter *Octagesima adveniens* and the Synod of Bishops'* *Justice in the World (Justitia in mundo)*, both 1971, dealt with the structural injustice that causes poverty. The latter document was important in stating that action on behalf of justice is an inseparable part of preaching the Gospel. These documents emphasized the right of the poor to participate in determining solutions to their poverty. Pope John Paul II* addressed social issues in three major encyclicals, *Laborem exercens* (1981), *Sollicitudo rei socialis* (1987), and *Centesimus annus* (1991). He again denounced unjust structures and called for solidarity* of the poor and oppressed with one another and of the Church with them. His writings have shown the influence of liberation theology*, although he has criticized its association with Marxism*. He has been concerned with the negative effects of technology, especially the technology of warfare, on human life and has addressed issues of ecology* for the first time in Catholic social teaching.

Catholic social teaching has also been advanced by the work of episcopal conferences*. Noteworthy are the documents of the Second and Third General Conferences of Latin American Bishops (CELAM) at Medellín, Colombia, in 1968, and Puebla, Mexico, in 1979 (*see* LIBERATION THEOLOGY and OPTION FOR THE POOR), and the pastoral letters* of the U.S. Bishops, *The Challenge of Peace** (1983) and *Economic Justice for All** (1986). *The Challenge of Peace* makes a clear statement about the authority* of its teaching, which may be applied to all the social documents: their general principles have a high degree of authority and may be "universally binding," while judgments they make about specific cases should be given serious attention but are not (perhaps it would be better to say, "not necessarily") binding in conscience (9-10).

See Appendix IV for summaries of the encyclicals mentioned here.

SOCIALISM. A family of movements and political systems that sought to place the means of production under collective rather than private ownership. Socialism first arose in the early nineteenth century, in response to the industrial revolution. After the middle of the nineteenth century, Marxism* became the dominant form of socialism in Europe. Pope Leo XIII* in *Rerum novarum* (1891) condemned socialism for denying the natural right of private property*, setting the state in the place of the parent, and leveling natural human inequalities; it thus injured those whom it was intended to benefit. In *Quadragesimo anno* (1931), Pope Pius XI* condemned the atheism* and violence of Marxist-Leninist communism, its reliance on class warfare, and its abolition of private property. He noted that a "more moderate socialism" had developed, whose "programs often strikingly approach the just demands of Christian social reformers" (113). Nonetheless, regarding it as essential to socialism that it subordinate all human dignity to the material abundance of the society, he concluded, "No one can be at the same time a sincere Catholic and a true socialist" (120). Popes Leo and Pius, while rejecting socialism, also opposed its opposite, economic "liberalism"*, and proposed limits on the economic freedom of capitalists that might themselves well have been labeled "socialistic." By 1971, Pope Paul VI*, in *Octogesima adveniens*, acknowledged that socialism had developed "many different forms" and called for careful "distinctions ... to guide concrete choices between the various levels of socialism" in order "to see the degree of commitment possible" for Christians (31). Pope John Paul II*, in *Centesimus annus* (1991), continued to reject socialism in that it "considers the individual person simply as an element ... within the social organism" (13). The extent and the limits of socialization* called for in the documents of Catholic social teaching, however, are quite compatible with the programs of moderate socialist parties such as have existed in Western Europe. *See also* CAPITALISM, LIBERATION THEOLOGY.

SOCIALIZATION. A process whereby people's lives have become more interdependent and increasingly subject to large institutions (59-60). This term was introduced into Catholic social teaching* in the working Italian version of the encyclical *Mater et magistra* (1961) of Pope John XXIII*. Though dropped from the official Latin version of the document, perhaps as too suggestive of socialism*, the term reappeared in the same sense in Vatican Council II's* *Pastoral Constitution on the Church in the Modern World* (GS 25,75). The process of socialization, according to *Mater et magistra,* requires increased state intervention into economic life, including some state ownership of "goods pertaining to production of wealth" (this is "socialization" in one of the more common senses of the term in English) and greater state involvement in dealing with social problems (116-121). *Mater et magistra,* however, with Catholic social teaching generally, calls for socialization to be balanced by subsidiarity*, so that social problems are dealt with on the lowest level of organization (the most local level) at which they can be effectively addressed.

SOCIETY FOR THE PROPAGATION OF THE FAITH. The Church's principal fund-raising body for worldwide missions*. The Society was founded as a lay organization in Lyons, France, in 1822. Pauline Jaricot, whose efforts beginning in 1818 laid the groundwork for the Society, is recognized as its foundress. The Society was officially authorized by Pope Pius VII in 1823 and soon spread outside of France, with increasing involvement of the clergy. The primary beneficiary of the Society during its first decade was the Church in the United States. A branch of the Society was organized in the United States in 1897. In 1922, the Society's international headquarters were transferred from Lyons to Rome, and the Society was placed under the direction of the Roman Curia's* Congregation for the Propagation of the Faith, now called the Congregation for the Evangelization of Peoples. The Society is subdivided along national and diocesan lines.

SOCIETY OF SAINT VINCENT DE PAUL. A leading lay Catholic charitable organization. It was founded in Paris in 1833 by Antoine Frédéric Ozanam as the Conference of Charity, becoming the Conference of St. Vincent de Paul in 1834. Ozanam's aim was to bear witness to Christian faith through direct service to the poor. In 1835, the society adopted a rule based in the writings of St. Vincent de Paul*. It spread rapidly through France, then the rest of Europe, and by 1853 had local groups, called "conferences," in Africa, Asia, and the Americas. The first conference in the United States was founded in 1845 in St. Louis, Missouri, where the society's national office is still located. The society engages in a broad variety of services to the needy, including home visitation, information programs, food centers, soup kitchens, shelters, prison ministries, youth programs, thrift shops, and rehabilitation workshops. It has always been a lay organization, but it works cooperatively with the Church hierarchy. It was instrumental, for instance, in the foundation of Catholic Charities USA* and still works closely with that organization. Membership was initially restricted to men, but women were admitted in 1973. There are around 4,700 local units, usually parish-based, in the United States, with a total of around sixty-one thousand members. Worldwide, there are more than forty-three thousand "conferences" in 112 countries, with around eight hundred fifty thousand members. Local conferences are coordinated by an ascending hierarchy of councils, led by a Council General, headquartered in Paris.

SOLIDARITY. In the social thought of Pope John Paul II*, a virtue that responds to human interdependence. "It is a firm and persevering determination to commit oneself to the common good; that is to say to the good of all and of each individual, because we are all really responsible for all" (*Sollicitudo rei socialis* 38). The term had appeared in previous Church social documents in more or less its ordinary sense of "community of purpose and sympathy," but it was developed and emphasized in the encyclicals *Laborem exercens* (LE) (1981) and *Sollicitudo rei socialis* (SRS) (1987). "Solidarity" was also the name of the labor union that led the movement to overthrow Communism in John Paul's native Poland, and this was not accidental, since the union may have been influenced in its choice of name by the thinking of then-Cardinal Wojtyla before he became pope, and the union in turn provided a concrete instance of what the pope had in mind. LE concentrated on the solidarity of workers as a reaction against degradation and exploitation (8) and as having led to greater worker control of production. In LE "solidarity" took somewhat the place occupied in Marxism* by "class struggle." For John Paul, however, the struggle "aims at the good of social justice," not at eliminating the opponent (LE 20). SRS broadened the sense of "solidarity" to make it the primary social virtue and the attitude that is directly opposed to structures of sin*. Solidarity applies not only to relationships within a society but also (by analogy) to relations among nations and even to human relations with the other creatures in the world. It is the "path to peace and ... development" (39). In its specifically Christian form, it is "love and service of neighbor" (46) and includes "total gratuity, forgiveness and reconciliation," seeking a communion of human beings that is an image of the communion of the three persons in the Trinity* (40).

SOUL. The center of personality in a human being, the locus of consciousness and freedom. Most parts of the Bible do not speak of a soul as an entity distinct from the body. The Hebrew word, *nephesh*, often translated "soul," more nearly means "life" or "living being" or "self." This is also true of the Greek *psychē* in the NT and in the Septuagint, where it is the usual translation of *nephesh*. For Plato* (428/7-348/7 B.C.), however, the soul *is* the person or self; his *Phaedo* develops the conception of the soul as immaterial and immortal, temporarily inhabiting a mortal body. In the *Phaedo*, the soul is virtually identified with the rational mind; in the *Republic*, Plato broadens his conception of the soul to include emotions and appetites. A conception of an immortal soul, separable from the body, appears in the OT Book of Wisdom (first century B.C.), which is influenced by Greek thought. The Fathers of the Church mostly adopted Plato's idea of the soul, though, with some exceptions (notably Origen*), they rejected the soul's preexistence. (Tertullian* is unusual in regarding the soul as material.)

Aristotle*, though once Plato's pupil, developed a very different conception of the soul as "form of the body," the principle of life and of the vital, sensory, and rational functions. Aristotle had no difficulty with plants and animals as having "souls"; that simply meant they were alive. The death of the organism was the end of its soul. This appears to be true (the texts are obscure) for the human soul as well; only an impersonal intellect survives. With the revival of Aristotelianism in the Middle Ages, an Aristotelian notion of the soul became standard in Western Christian thought. It cohered better with the doctrine of the resurrection* of the body but made immortality* problematic. Thomas Aquinas* argued that the form of the human body was at the same time the immortal intellectual power; its body made it individual. Against Peter John Olivi (who distinguished the spiritual soul from the sensory principle), the Council of Vienne* (1312) declared that the intellectual soul is the form of the human body (DS 902). Against Pietro Pomponazzi, the Fifth Lateran Council* (1513) declared that the soul, which is the form of the body, is individual and immortal (DS 1440). These declarations should not be interpreted as making Aristotelian philosophical psychology into official doctrine, but rather as affirming, within an Aristotelian framework common to Church authorities and their opponents, the unity, individuality, and immortality of the soul. Contemporary Church teaching continues to speak of a "soul," but in cautious language. According to the 1979 Vatican document on eschatology*, "The Church affirms that a spiritual element survives and subsists after death, an element endowed with consciousness and will, so that the 'human self' subsists. To designate this element, the Church uses the world 'soul,' the accepted term in the usage of Scripture and Tradition. Although not unaware that this term has various meanings in the Bible, the Church thinks that there is no valid reason for rejecting it; moreover, she considers that the use of some word as a vehicle is absolutely indispensable in order to support the faith of Christians." *See also* IMMORTALITY, REINCARNATION.

SPIRITUAL DIRECTION. A relationship in which one person (the director) assists another (the directee) in developing the latter's relationship with God. The specific emphasis on the relationship with God distinguishes spiritual direction from pastoral counseling. "Direction" normally implies a long-term, somewhat formal relationship, though short-term (as in a directed retreat*) and less formal varieties exist. While spiritual teaching and companionship have existed from the beginning of Christianity (as in all religions), the specific practice of spiritual direction arose among the Desert Fathers and Mothers*, when the advice of a spiritually experienced figure would be sought out, and continued in the monastic* communities. The term *direction* came into prominence with the Jesuits* of the sixteenth century, among whom the process achieved a classic form. Today *direction* may have authoritarian connotations, but these are misleading; the director's role is not to tell the directee what to do, but rather to listen together with the directee, to assist in the directee's own process of discerning the call of God in his or her life. When the director is a priest, spiritual direction may be connected with the sacrament of reconciliation*. Directors may also be sisters*, brothers*, deacons*, or laity*.

SPIRITUALITY. Broadly, one's fundamental orientation in regard to God, oneself, others, and the world; more narrowly, one's explicit relationship with God. One may speak of an individual's spirituality in either sense, or of the spirituality of a narrow or broad tradition, for example, Carmelite spirituality, Catholic spirituality, Western spirituality. "Spirituality" can also refer to the academic study of spirituality in individuals or traditions. The word *spirituality* (Latin, *spiritualitas*) first appeared in the fifth century, referring to life according to the Holy Spirit*, as spoken of by St. Paul. It acquired other meanings in medieval Latin (including that of "church property") before attaining something like its present sense in seventeenth-century French writing. It entered English (at first mainly in Catholic circles) from the French *spiritualité* and has become prominent especially since around 1970, when it began to appear in the names of academic courses, programs, and institutes. For about a century prior to that time, the concerns now dealt with in the academic study of spirituality were addressed in what was called "ascetic and mystical theology." In contrast with its immediate predecessor, contemporary Catholic spirituality addresses the life of all Christians, not simply those in religious life*, and all aspects of life, considered as affected by or affecting one's fundamental relationship with God. It is particularly sensitive to the link between individual spirituality and social relations and thus has strong links with contemporary social ethics.

See also ASCETICISM, LITURGY, MYSTICISM, PRAYER.

STATIONS OF THE CROSS (WAY OF THE CROSS) (Lt *statio*, "place to stand, stop"). A devotion* that consists in meditations* on the passion and death of Jesus. It is based in imitation of the custom whereby pilgrims to the Holy Land would retrace the way followed by Jesus to Calvary. Fostered by the Franciscans*, the devotion became widespread in the fifteenth century. The number of stations was standardized at fourteen by Pope Clement XII in 1731. The traditional stations are: (1) Jesus is condemned to death; (2) Jesus takes up his cross; (3) Jesus falls for the first time; (4) Jesus meets his Mother; (5) Simon of Cyrene assists Jesus; (6) Veronica wipes Jesus' face; (7) Jesus falls the second time; (8) Jesus speaks to the women of Jerusalem; (9) Jesus falls the third time; (10) Jesus is stripped of his garments; (11) Jesus is nailed to the cross; (12) Jesus dies; (13) Jesus is taken down from the cross; (14) Jesus is buried in the tomb. Some contemporary versions add a fifteenth station for the Resurrection*. Most of the stations are taken from the gospels. The three falls and the story of Veronica, in which Jesus is said to have left a picture of his face on Veronica's veil, are medieval legends. Most Catholic churches have paintings or statues representing the stations on their walls;

stations may be found in outdoor shrines* and other places as well. The devotion consists in passing through the sequence of stations, stopping for prayers and meditations at each.

STIPEND (Lt *stipendium*, "payment"). Also called **mass offering**. A sum of money given to a priest, obligating him to celebrate mass for the intention of the donor. The practice of offering a stipend dates from around the eighth century. It was a successor, to some extent, of the practice of the faithful's bringing the bread and wine to be offered at the mass. People might offer a stipend for an individual mass or establish an endowment, from the income of which stipends were to be paid for masses over a period of time. By the end of the Middle Ages, the practice led to abuses, particularly in that there came to be large numbers of priests who lived on mass stipends and whose only job (besides reciting the divine office or liturgy of the hours*) was to say mass at a particular altar. Consequently, the Church has regulated the practice closely. The present form of the regulations is found in Canons 945 to 958 of the 1983 Code of Canon Law. A priest is obligated to say one mass for each offering accepted (a 1991 document allowed occasional masses with multiple intentions and stipends, if the donors consent). He may entrust the obligation and the stipend to others. He may retain a stipend for only one mass per day (except on Christmas). The bishops of the local province are to determine the normal amount for a stipend, and the priest is not to request more, though he may accept a greater stipend. He may accept less, and he is encouraged to celebrate mass for people's intentions even if no offering is received. Accurate records are to be kept of all mass offerings.

The practices surrounding mass stipends make sense in a medieval theology of the eucharist*, in which the mass is understood to be offered by the priest, who controls its fruits (resulting graces), which are limited. It fits less comfortably into a contemporary theology in which the whole assembly offers the mass, and no attempt is made to measure the fruits (which are at the disposal of God alone). Offering masses for particular intentions is a form of petitionary prayer*, however, that is sanctioned by long tradition. Stipends should be regarded as gifts, like the gifts offered in the offertory of the mass, and not as fees for service.

STOICISM. A philosophical tradition founded by Zeno of Citium (336/5-264/3 B.C.), and named for the *Stoa poikilē* (Painted Porch) in

Athens, where he taught. Together with Platonism*, it formed part of the common mind-set of educated persons of the Roman Empire, and as such had much influence on many of the Fathers of the Church*, notably Justin*, Origen*, Tertullian*, and Augustine*. Besides Zeno, other prominent Greek Stoics were Cleanthes (331/0-233/2) and Chrysippus (ca. 280-ca. 207). Prominent Roman Stoics were Seneca (4 B.C.-A.D. 65), Epictetus (ca. 50-ca. 130), and the Emperor Marcus Aurelius (121-180). The central concept of Stoicism was that of a cosmic *logos**, or reason, usually construed materialistically as an all-pervasive energy ("fiery fire"), but seen as conscious and identical with God. Virtue and happiness consisted in living according to reason, that is, according to the *logos*. The "passions" (Gk *pathē*) (emotions, desires, feelings of pleasure and pain, etc.) were contrary to reason; hence, the Stoic aspired to a state of *apatheia*, not "apathy" in our sense but "freedom from passion," emotional calm and equilibrium. The ethics of natural law* is a Stoic legacy within Christianity.

SUBORDINATIONISM. Any theology of the Trinity* that makes the Son lesser than (subordinate to) the Father and/or the Holy Spirit lesser than both. Because it fits well into the hierarchical framework of Greek thought, especially Platonism*, a number of the early Fathers of the Church*, for instance Justin Martyr* and Origen*, tended toward subordinationism. The conflict over Arianism*, an extreme form of subordinationism, led to a clear rejection of subordinationism, especially at the Councils of Nicaea I* (325) and Constantinople I* (381).

SUBSIDIARITY. A principle in Catholic social teaching*, first articulated by Pope Pius XI* in the encyclical *Quadragesimo anno* (1931) as follows: "It is a fundamental principle of social philosophy … that one should not withdraw from individuals and commit to the community what they can accomplish by their own enterprise and industry. So, too, it is an injustice and at the same time a grave evil and a disturbance of right order to transfer to the larger and higher collectivity functions which can be performed and provided for by lesser and subordinate bodies" (79). The principle thus upholds the freedom of individuals and "mediating" communities (such as families, neighborhoods, and trade associations) relative to the state. It balances the need for state intervention in economic affairs, which is a consequence of the process of "socialization"*. In *Pacem in terris*

(1963), Pope John XXIII* applied the principle of subsidiarity to the relations of individual nation-states to international authorities.

SUICIDE. The intentional causing of one's own death. The Church condemns suicide as an offense against life (Vatican Council II, GS 27). The standard arguments against suicide are set forth by Thomas Aquinas* (ST 2-2.64.5): (1) Suicide is a violation of natural law*, as contradicting the natural tendency toward the preservation of life, and it is also an offense against the charity whereby one should love oneself. (2) Because one is a part of the human community, suicide is an injury to the community (i.e., to the various human communities to which one belongs). (3) Suicide is an offense against God, who alone has sovereignty over life. (These arguments are reiterated in CCC 2280-2281.) The Church realizes that there are mitigating factors in many suicides, which are often committed in a state of depression or other psychological disorder. It counsels prayer for those who have committed suicide and no longer ordinarily denies them Catholic funerals or burial in Catholic cemeteries. *See also* EUTHANASIA.

SUMMA (Lt, "main part, summary, synthesis"). A literary form in medieval scholasticism*, offering a systematic exposition of a field of inquiry. The most famous summa is the *Summa theologiae* of St. Thomas Aquinas*; "the Summa," without further qualification, refers to this work. Other important summas of theology were written by Albert the Great* and Alexander of Hales.

SUNDAY. The day of Jesus' resurrection*, as all four gospels testify (Mt 28.1, Mk 16.2,9, Lk 24.1, Jn 20.1)), and therefore the "original feast day" for the Church (Vatican Council II, SC 106). For Jews, the Sabbath, the seventh day of the week (Saturday), is a day of rest and religious assembly. The earliest Christians presumably continued to observe the Sabbath but also gathered on Sunday. Acts 20.7-11 records a Sunday assembly for preaching and "breaking of the bread" (*see* EUCHARIST). Justin Martyr* (ca. A.D. 155) describes regular Sunday eucharistic liturgies. The name, "the Lord's day," for Sunday appears in Revelation 1.10 and *Didachē* 14, both late first century (and still today in Romance languages, e.g., Sp *domingo*). "The Lord" means Jesus, and Sunday was the original Easter* celebration, before the annual Easter. The Letter of Barnabas (late first or early second century) speaks of Sunday as the "eighth day," the first day of the new creation. "Eighth day" imagery develops the eschatological* aspects of Sunday—its anticipation of the fullness of the kingdom of God*.

The eucharist is the center of Catholic Sunday observance, and Catholics are obliged to attend mass on Sunday. This "Sunday obligation" has been in canon law* since the twelfth century and was anticipated in decrees of regional councils back to the sixth century. Since 1970 (reviving the ancient custom of a Sunday vigil), Catholics may fulfill the Sunday mass obligation on the preceding Saturday evening. Sunday is also the most appropriate day for baptisms* and ordinations (*see* ORDER, SACRAMENT OF).

As early as Ignatius of Antioch* (early second century), Sunday was seen as replacing, not just supplementing, the Sabbath. The commandment to "keep holy the Sabbath" (Ex 20.8) was applied to the Lord's Day instead, and Jewish practices of abstaining from work on the Sabbath were Christianized. In 321, Constantine* forbade most kinds of work on Sunday. Medieval and especially early modern interpretations of Sunday rest emphasized abstention from "servile" work. Initially "servile work" was used metaphorically for sin*, but later—especially from the seventeenth through nineteenth centuries—it was interpreted literally as physical labor. Contemporary interpretations emphasize leaving time and energy for worship and joy in the Lord.

SYLLABUS OF ERRORS. A document issued together with the encyclical *Quanta cura* by Pope Pius IX* in 1864 and presented as a summary of the errors of the time. It consisted of eighty propositions condemned in earlier documents of Pius IX. The subjects of the propositions included pantheism*, rationalism*, socialism* and "condemned associations," the authority of the state over the Church; morals, marriage, the civil power of the pope*, and liberalism*. The last four propositions, on liberalism, attracted the most attention, especially in the United States. Condemned as errors were: "In this age of ours it is no longer expedient that the Catholic religion should be the only religion of the state, to the exclusion of all other cults whatever" (77), and "The Roman Pontiff can and should reconcile and adapt himself to progress, liberalism, and the modern civilization" (80). The propositions of the Syllabus were lifted out of their original contexts and are often difficult to understand without them. At times, in context, they say less than they appear to say. The Pope himself commended a mitigating interpretation published by Félix Dupanloup. Nevertheless, the document was a high mark of papal intransigence against modern culture.

SYNOD (Gk *synodos*, "meeting"). A meeting of Church leaders or representatives to determine Church doctrine or practice. Especially in the early centuries, there is no clear distinction between a synod and a council*, though meetings covering a smaller region tended to be called "synods," while "councils" were those covering a broader region. Today a council may also be called a "synod," but canon law* designates two sorts of assembly specifically as synods: (1) The **Synod of Bishops**. This body is composed of bishops* elected by the various episcopal conferences* as well as some *ex officio* members and some appointed by the pope. It meets periodically to advise the pope, who may give it deliberative power. It is convoked by the pope and chaired by him or his representatives. This body was created by Pope Paul VI* in 1965, and, as of 1994, has met in nine ordinary and two extraordinary assemblies. Subjects considered have included bishops' relations with the pope, priesthood, justice* in the world, evangelization*, catechetics, the family, penance and reconciliation*, a review of Vatican Council II*, the laity*, the formation of priests*, and religious life*. The Synod of Bishops is one of the primary expressions of episcopal collegiality*. (2) **Diocesan synods**. These are assemblies of priests, religious, and laity convoked by the diocesan bishop in order to advise him on the affairs of the diocese*.

T

TEILHARD DE CHARDIN, PIERRE (1881-1955). French Jesuit paleontologist and religious thinker. Born near Clermont-Ferrand, Teilhard entered the Society of Jesus in 1899. He was ordained priest in 1911 and in 1912 began graduate study in paleontology at the Museum of Paris. Drafted into the French army in 1914, he served, chiefly as a stretcher bearer, in some of the bloodiest battles of World War I. While in the service, he formed the main lines of his thought, which combined evolutionary biology and Christian theology. He received his doctorate in 1922 and spent most of the years from 1923 to 1946 doing research in China, where he was involved in the discovery of the Peking Man, one of the earliest human fossils, in 1928. As early as 1924, he fell under the suspicion of Church

402   Templars

authorities for his view of evolution* and his symbolic interpretation of the Adam and Eve story. Suspicion and restrictions remained throughout his life, and, while he published numerous scientific papers, his major religious works could not be published until after his death.

Teilhard's primary systematic work was *The Phenomenon of Man*, written between 1937 and 1940. In it he argued that consciousness is inherent, at least in rudimentary form, in all matter, and that matter is evolving toward ever-increasing degrees of complexity and thus of consciousness. From the "geosphere" (inert matter) evolves the "biosphere" of living beings, and thence, in human beings, the "nöosphere" (sphere of thought). The process will continue as individual consciousnesses converge into a "hyperpersonal" consciousness in which each consciousness will remain individual yet all will unite and interpenetrate in love. The final goal is the "Omega Point," in which all matter becomes the body of Christ and all persons are united with the risen Christ, so that Christ is "all in all" (Col 3.11). In *The Divine Milieu*, written in 1926, he developed a spirituality of human work* as advancing the completion of the world in Christ.

Criticisms of Teilhard's work by scientists have focused on his idea of evolution as a linear, goal-directed process, rather than a Darwinian, random process. Theological critiques have noted the affinity of his thought with pantheism* and, especially, the limited attention he paid to sin* and evil* in his optimistic portrait of the cosmic process. In 1962, the Holy Office issued a warning against an uncritical acceptance of his writings, though it did not condemn them. Even so, they had an apparent influence on Vatican Council II's* *Pastoral Constitution on the Church in the Modern World (Gaudium et Spes)*, with its positive attitude toward the modern world and the value of human work in the world. He also had much influence on theology and the arts in the mid-twentieth century.

TEMPLARS (KNIGHTS TEMPLAR). Full name: "Poor Knights of Christ and of the Temple of Solomon." The most prominent of the military orders formed during the time of the Crusades*. A **military order** combined monasticism* and knighthood; members took vows* of poverty*, chastity, and obedience* and also vowed to defend Christians in the Holy Land. The Templars were founded in 1118/19 by Hugh of Payns and eight companions. Their rule was drawn up by (or at the instigation of) St. Bernard of Clairvaux* in 1128 and formally approved by the pope in 1139. "The Church's recognition of a religious community dedicated to fighting as well as to prayer was a revolutionary step" (J. Riley-Smith). The Templars played a prominent part in the crusader states in the Holy Land until the fall of the Kingdom of Jerusalem in 1291. They acquired great wealth, which aroused the cupidity of King Philip IV (the Fair) of France. He brought charges of sodomy, blasphemy, and heresy against the Templars. Most of the Templars in France confessed under torture, though modern historians doubt their guilt. Under pressure from the king, Pope Clement V suppressed the Templars at the Council of Vienne* in 1312. Their possessions were given to the rival order of Hospitallers (see KNIGHTS OF MALTA).

TERESA OF AVILA (TERESA OF JESUS), ST. (1515-1582). Spanish mystic. Born Teresa de Ahumada at Avila, she entered the Carmelite order at the age of twenty. Around the age of thirty-nine she underwent a spiritual conversion, in which she experienced Christ calling her to an intensified life of interior prayer. Finding her crowded Carmelite convent uncongenial to silence and solitude, she set out to found a new house of Carmelites, observing a stricter rule. Teresa's reform movement, which came to be called Discalced ("shoeless," because its members wore Franciscan-style sandals) Carmelites, grew to fourteen houses between the first foundation in 1562 and the time of her death. She inspired a parallel reform of men's Carmelite houses, led by St. John of the Cross*. At the behest of her spiritual directors, she wrote of her spiritual experiences in her *Life* (1562) and especially in *The Interior Castle* (1577). There the soul is described as a castle containing many "dwelling places" ("mansions" [cf. Jn 14.2]) arranged in seven concentric rings, from the initial dwelling places of humility or self-knowledge to the central dwelling place of a life of complete union with God in Jesus. Teresa's other important writings are *The Way of Perfection* (1566) and the *Book of Foundations* (1573-1582). In her writings Teresa describes many mystical states (see MYSTICISM, MYSTICAL PHENOMENA) that she had herself experienced, but her emphasis is always on growth in love* of God and neighbor rather than pursuit of extraordinary experiences. She was canonized in 1622 and in 1970 was declared the first woman Doctor of the Church*. Her feast is celebrated on October 15.

TERTULLIAN, QUINTUS SEPTIMIUS FLORENS (160/170?-after 212). The first Father of the Church* who left writings in Latin. A resident of Carthage, he was probably trained as a pleader in law, but he is not identical with the Roman legal theorist Tertullianus. His surviving works, which date between 193 and 212, include apologetic, controversial, and moral treatises. His writings are marked by a sharp hostility toward classical philosophy (of which he nevertheless makes much use) and the idolatry of Roman society and a sense of their discontinuity with Christian revelation and life; "What has Athens to do with Jerusalem?" is one of his many memorable turns of phrase. He provided later Latin theology with much of its standard terminology, especially for the theology of the Trinity*. His ethical teaching is harshly ascetical, becoming increasingly rigorous in his later writings. By 207, he came under the influence of Montanism*, although it is unknown if he ever formally separated from the Catholic Church.

THEOLOGICAL NOTES. Brief qualifying phrases, formerly used in theological textbooks, indicating the degree of authority of a theological statement. Such degrees range from "of divine and Catholic faith" (applying to a dogma* of faith, whether solemnly proclaimed or proposed by the Church's ordinary, universal magisterium*) to "probable." Corresponding to theological notes are **theological censures**, of which the strongest is "heretical"* (applied to the denial of a dogma of faith) and the weakest, "rash" in one or another degree. The terminology of theological notes and censures began to develop in the thirteenth century. It was systematized, sometimes in great detail (one theologian listed sixty-three "notes") in the seventeenth and eighteenth centuries. Systems of theological notes have fallen somewhat into disuse since Vatican Council II but retain their usefulness in questions of ecumenism* and legitimate theological pluralism*. They should be used together with the concept of the hierarchy of truths*. The latter ranks doctrinal statements *materially* in terms of their centrality to Catholic faith, while theological notes represent a ranking *formally*, in terms of the degree of authority with which a doctrine is promulgated.

THEOLOGICAL VIRTUES. Virtues* that "dispose Christians to live in a relationship with the Holy Trinity" (CCC 1812). They are faith*, hope*, and love* (charity) (1 Cor 13.13). According to Thomas Aquinas*, they are distinguished from the intellectual and moral virtues in that they direct us to a supernatural happiness, given us by God in the beatific vision*, unattainable by our natural powers. Accordingly, these virtues themselves are not acquired through human practice but infused by God's grace*. Aquinas took the term "theological virtues" from William of Auxerre (d. 1231). These virtues "are so called, first, because their object is God ...; secondly, because they are infused in us by God alone; thirdly, because these virtues are not made known to us, save by divine revelation" (ST 1-2.62.2).

THEOLOGY (Gk *theos*, "God"; *logos*, "speech, reasoning"). The effort to understand and to give reasoned expression to what is believed in faith*. A book title by St. Anselm* (1033-1109) has served as the classic definition of theology: "faith seeking understanding." Theologies appear wherever there is religious faith, Christian or otherwise. Within Christianity, they vary in their conception of how to identify the truths of faith and, especially, in what is involved in understanding and giving expression to them, for these activities change from one cultural setting to another (*see* HERMENEUTICS). Theologies should be distinguished from doctrines*: doctrines state what (in some sense) the Church as a whole believes, while theologies are constructed by individuals or groups within the Church. Still, theologies provide the framework and often the impetus for the formulation of doctrines.

Christian theologies are already present in the New Testament, as different writers employ different categories from Jewish or Hellenistic culture to express the significance of Jesus Christ and his work. Among the Fathers of the Church*, theology was done in the efforts to defend Christian faith, to provide expositions of it that would appeal to educated people in the ancient world, and to address problems that arose in Christian thought and life. In the early medieval period in the West, the dominant style of theology was bound up with monastic life* and featured meditation on the Scriptures for the sake of prayer. In the later medieval universities*, theology became an academic discipline, interpreting Christian revelation in relation especially to the revived intellectual framework of Aristotelianism*. In the Counter-Reformation* and early modern period, Catholic theology was focused more on the defense of an achieved understanding of faith, against the challenges of the Reformation* and the Enlightenment*, than on the effort to understand and give expression to faith in the new cultural setting created by these events. Much creative theological work was done in the nineteenth and twentieth centuries, however, and this both led to and was further encouraged by Vatican Council II's* commitment to a full engagement with the modern world. Most of the outstanding figures of twentieth-century Catholic theology, for example, Karl Rahner* and Bernard Lonergan*, have worked in a university setting, but liberation theology* has opened a new approach, drawing on the experience of the poor and oppressed and reflecting on the implications of Christian action with and for them. Liberation theology marks the emergence of the continents of Latin America, Africa, and Asia as centers of Catholic theological reflection, previously mainly a European endeavor.

Theology as an academic discipline may be subdivided into **fundamental** or **foundational theology**, which explores the nature of theology and the conditions for meaning and truth in theological language; **systematic theology**, which seeks an orderly exposition of the truths of Christian revelation as a unified whole; and **practical theology**, which addresses the life of Christians, and includes moral theology*, pastoral theology, the study of liturgy*, and spirituality*. The disciplines of Biblical studies and Church history are sometimes incorporated within theology, sometimes understood as independent enterprises.

THERESE OF LISIEUX, ST. (1873-1897). Thérèse Martin was born in Alençon, France, the youngest of nine children. Very religious from an early age, she succeeded, through persistence, in being allowed to enter the Carmelites at the age of fifteen, following two of her older sisters. Under the religious name of Thérèse of the Child Jesus, she spent the rest of her life in the convent at Lisieux. There she developed a spirituality that she called the "little way of spiritual childhood," the center of which was a childlike trust in God's love and a desire to let that love work through her in the small events and relationships of life. She sometimes spoke of herself as a "little flower," which became a popular title for her. In her last years she suffered much from the tuberculosis that caused her death. This was accompanied by great spiritual distress, through which her faith carried her. In 1895, she was ordered to write a spiritual autobiography, which she completed shortly before her death on September 30, 1897. Published after her death as *The Story of a Soul*, it became extremely popular and sparked an intense devotion to Thérèse in the first half of the twentieth century. She was canonized in 1925. Her feast is celebrated on October 1.

THIRD ORDER. An association of laity whose members live in the world according to a rule in the spirit and under the direction of a religious institute (*see* RELIGIOUS LIFE). They are called "third" orders because they came into being after men's and women's religious orders (first and second). Members of third orders (called "tertiaries") are not in religious life; they do not take vows* nor live in community. They go through a period of preparation, however, make some sort of profession, live according to a rule adapted to their state in life, and may wear a habit*, normally not a full habit but a reduced form, such as a scapular* and cord or a medal. The first Third Order was founded by St. Francis of Assisi*, whose rule for it was approved in 1221. Other "third orders" appeared informally in the thirteenth century, but none were formally approved until the fourteenth century. Third Orders now exist for the Franciscans, Carmelites, Dominicans, and Servites, among others. The Oblates* of St. Benedict are like a third order. The number of tertiaries grew until the sixteenth century, then declined, but grew again in the nineteenth century. Beginning in the fifteenth century, some groups of tertiaries undertook vowed lives in common and were recognized as religious congregations, called Third Orders Regular.

THOMAS AQUINAS, ST. (1225/6-1274). Medieval theologian and philosopher, known as "The Angelic Doctor." In his combination of scope and depth, he was the greatest of the medieval theologians and one of the two or three greatest theologians of the entire Catholic tradition. Though his philosophy* was done in the service of theology*, he also stands in the very front rank of Western philosophers.

He was born near Naples, studied there, and joined the Dominican* order in 1242/3. His family, opposed to this choice, held him captive for two years. After escaping in 1246, he studied under Albert the Great* at Paris and Cologne. He returned to the University of Paris to complete his studies in 1251, and taught there from 1256 to 1259. From 1259 to 1268, he was in Italy. He taught at Paris again from 1268 to 1272, when he returned to Naples to start a house of studies for his order. He died en route to the Second Council of Lyons* on March 7, 1274.

A teacher and writer for his entire adult life, he left behind an enormous body of written work. His principal works were two summas* (systematic expositions of theology), the *Summa contra Gentiles* (full title: "The Truth of the Catholic Faith against the Errors of Unbelievers") (1259-1266), and the *Summa theologiae* (or *Summa* *theologica*) (1266-1273). His other works include commentaries on many biblical books and on works of Aristotle*, Pseudo-Dionysius*, and Boethius; an important *Commentary on the Sentences of Peter Lombard* (written in completion of his studies at Paris); many *Disputed Questions* and shorter works; and the Office for the Feast of Corpus Christi. More than anyone else, he was responsible for the incorporation of the newly rediscovered works of Aristotle into the tradition of Christian thought. He was, however, much influenced also by Platonism*, especially through Augustine* and Pseudo-Dionysius.

His Aristotelianism led to suspicion in the years immediately following his death (*see under* ARISTOTLE). In 1277, the bishop of Paris condemned 219 propositions, some of them associated with Thomas's teaching, and Thomas narrowly escaped direct censure. But he was partially rehabilitated at Paris in 1285, and in 1325 the condemnation of 1277 was revoked to the extent that it appeared to apply to Thomas. He was canonized in 1323 and made a Doctor of the Church* in 1567. His feast is celebrated on January 28.

In 1879, in the encyclical *Aeterni Patris*, Pope Leo XIII* called on the Church to revive and disseminate the wisdom of Thomas. This official endorsement of Thomas was strengthened by Pope Pius X* and included in the 1917 Code of Canon Law, which directed that priests should be trained in philosophy and theology "according to the method, doctrine, and principles of the Angelic Doctor." Thomistic thought has become somewhat less central in Catholicism in the second half of the twentieth century; Vatican Council II* implicitly endorsed this trend by itself drawing on other sources and using other modes of discourse. Still, the 1983 Code of Canon Law says that candidates for priesthood are to study dogmatic theology "with St. Thomas as their teacher in a special way" (Canon 252).

See also SCHOLASTICISM, THOMISM.

THOMISM. The philosophy and theology of Thomas Aquinas* and the tradition to which his thought gave rise. It is characterized by its distinction between the orders of grace* and nature, and therefore between faith* and reason, but also by a harmony between these orders. In its conception of reason and its analysis of the order of nature, it tends to follow the philosophy of Aristotle*, with some influence of Platonism* via the Augustinian tradition. There have been diverse forms of Thomism in the centuries since the death of Thomas in 1274.

Initially, Thomism was carried forward chiefly by members of Thomas's own order, the Dominicans*. It gained wider influence through the work of fifteenth-century commentators, of whom the most important was Tommaso de Vio Cajetan (1480-1547). Spain became an especial center of Thomistic thought; major figures there were Francisco de Vitoria (ca. 1485-1546) and John of St. Thomas (1589-1644). Thomism was the principal theological influence on the Council of Trent* (1545-1563), a fact that helped solidify its role in the Church. Thomism declined in the eighteenth century but was revived in the **Neo-Thomism** of the nineteenth century. The principal Neo-Thomists were Matteo Liberatore (1810-1892) and Joseph Kleutgen (1811-1883). They saw in Thomism a coherent system that could refute the errors of modern philosophy, resolve the issue of the relation of faith and reason, and provide a secure foundation for Catholic apologetics*. Kleutgen is thought to have been the chief author of Vatican Council I's* constitution *Dei Filius* (on faith and reason) and Leo XIII's* encyclical *Aeterni Patris*, which promoted the study of Thomas Aquinas in the Church (*see under* THOMAS AQUINAS).

The revival of the study of Thomas had the unforeseen consequence of uncovering differences between the thought of Thomas and that of his commentators and of the Neo-Thomists. As a result, several distinct schools of Thomistic thought developed. The most important Thomistic thinkers of the twentieth century were Jacques Maritain* (1882-1973), whose "traditional Thomism" continued and developed the thought of Thomas and his commentators, and Etienne Gilson (1884-1978), whose historical research led him to emphasize the differences between Thomas and the commentators. The **transcendental Thomism** of Joseph Maréchal (1878-1944) found a link between Thomas and the modern philosophies of Immanuel Kant and G. W. F. Hegel in the dynamic movement of the human intellect toward Infinite Being (God). Its starting point of the human subject unites it with the tradition of modern philosophy arising from René Descartes (1596-1650). This school has had great influence in twentieth-century Catholic theology, especially through the work of Karl Rahner* (1904-1984) and Bernard Lonergan* (1904-1984). *See also* SCHOLASTICISM.

TRADITION (Lt *traditio*, "handing over"). The "handing on" of Catholic faith and practice from the apostolic generation down to the present, or that which is handed on in this process. "The expression 'what has been handed down from the apostles' includes everything that helps the People of God to live a holy life and to grow in faith. In this way the Church, in its teaching, life, and worship, perpetuates and hands on to every generation all that it is and all that it believes" (Vatican Council II, *Dei Verbum* 8). It is thus the vehicle by which God's revelation* is brought to later generations. Important bearers of tradition are the liturgy*, the writings of the Fathers of the Church*, and the "sense of the faithful"*. But central to tradition are the written Scriptures. Though the tradition of the Church determined which writings belonged to the canon of the Bible*, the biblical writings are the norm by which other traditions are to be judged.

The Protestant* Reformers contrasted scripture to tradition and held that "Scripture alone" (*sola scriptura*) was normative for the Church. In response, the Council of Trent* in 1546 declared that Christ's saving truth and rules of conduct "are contained in written books and in unwritten traditions" (DS 1501). It was common between Trent and Vatican II to see Scripture and tradition as two distinct sources of revelation, but Vatican II (1965) emphasizes their unity: "Tradition and scripture together form a single sacred deposit of the word of God, entrusted to the Church" (DV 10).

Vatican II also understands tradition not as static but as including development "under the assistance of the Holy Spirit. There is growth in understanding of what is handed on, both the words and the realities they signify" (DV 8). Supervision of this process and of the interpretation of Scripture and tradition is entrusted to the bishops* as successors of the apostles*; it is their task to discern and declare what is to be the norm for Catholic belief and practice (*see* APOSTOLICITY, AUTHORITY, MAGISTERIUM). "It is clear that … tradition, scripture, and the Church's teaching function are so connected and associated that one does not stand without the others" (DV 10).

TRADITIONALISM. (1) A school of thought in early nineteenth-century theology that denied that human reason by itself could know the existence of God, the immortality* of the soul*, or the basic principles of morality. Rather, God made these truths known in a primitive revelation, after which they were handed down by tradition. Traditionalism developed in reaction to the rationalism* of the Enlightenment* and also objected to the seeming rationalism of the scholasticism* then dominant in Catholic theology. Important figures associated with traditionalism included Louis de Bonald, Joseph de

Maestre, Felicité de Lammenais, Augustin Bonnetty, and Louis Bautain. Many ecclesiastical condemnations of traditionalism were issued between 1832 and 1869, chiefly because it appeared to confuse revelation and reason and to give inadequate scope to reason. Vatican Council I's* affirmation that "God can be known with certainty from the consideration of created things, by the natural power of human reason" (DS 3004) rejects traditionalism along with other forms of fideism*.

(2) In contemporary use, *traditionalism* refers to rejection of reforms enacted by or in response to Vatican Council II* (1962-1965) and adherence to doctrinal formulas and liturgical and devotional patterns in effect prior to the Council. Traditionalists are best known for opposing the reforms of the mass* enacted after the council, including the use of the vernacular language; they insist on the Latin mass as reformed after the Council of Trent* (the "Tridentine mass"). Some traditionalist groups remain within the Catholic Church; the Catholic Traditionalist Movement, founded by Fr. Gommar de Pauw in 1965, is an example. Others have broken with the Church, notably the Society of Saint Pius X, founded by Archbishop Marcel Lefebvre (1905-1991). Lefebvre incurred automatic excommunication when he ordained bishops without papal approval in 1988.

TRENT, COUNCIL OF (1545-1563). The nineteenth ecumenical council*, which restated Church doctrine and reformed Church discipline in response to the Protestant* Reformation. The first important fact about this council is the delay in its occurrence: the Reformation had been in progress for twenty-eight years by the time the council met. This delay was caused by papal fears of conciliarism*, by tensions between the popes and Holy Roman Emperor Charles V, and by wars between France and the Empire. Finally the council was summoned by Pope Paul III in 1542 to meet in Trent (Trento), an Italian city under the rule of the Empire. Further war intervened, and the council did not meet until December 13, 1545. In all, the council met in twenty-five sessions in three periods. All sessions were at Trent, except for two at Bologna in 1547.

First period (1545-1548). The council's first major decrees were on revelation*. It listed the canonical books of the OT and NT and declared the authoritative status of the Latin Vulgate (see BIBLE). Against the Reformers' insistence on the normativity of "scripture alone," Trent accepted the authority of unwritten traditions* "with a like feeling of piety and reverence." A decree on original sin* followed, asserting that it is passed on to Adam's descendants "by propagation and not by imitation" and that it is fully removed by baptism*. The most important decree of the first period was on justification*, agreeing with Luther that justification is at all stages the work of God's grace* but holding that human cooperation with grace is necessary. Justification, the council said against Luther, "consists not only in the forgiveness of sins but also in the sanctification and renewal of the inward being" (DS 1528). A decree on the sacraments* set their number at seven and issued canons on baptism* and confirmation*. Several reforming decrees strengthened the requirement for bishops and pastors to live in the areas over which they had jurisdiction and curbed various exemptions that limited the power of bishops in their dioceses. The council was transferred to Bologna in March 1547, but strife between the emperor and the pope over the transfer led to its suspension on February 16, 1548.

Second period (1551-1552). The council resumed under Pope Julius III on May 1, 1552. This period's most important decree was on the eucharist*. It defined the real presence of Christ and stated that the change of the bread and wine into the body and blood of Christ is "suitably and properly called" transubstantiation. The council also issued a decree on the sacraments of penance (*see* RECONCILIATION) and last anointing (*see* ANOINTING OF THE SICK). Lutheran representatives arrived under safe conduct in 1552, but the council refused to meet their demand that its earlier resolutions be revoked, and the Lutherans did not participate further in the council's deliberations. The council was suspended on April 28, 1552, following a revolt of German princes against Charles V.

Third period (1562-1563). Political unrest and opposition to the council by Pope Paul IV (1555-1559) caused a ten-year hiatus until the council was re-convoked by Pope Pius IV (1559-1565) in 1560. It reopened on January 18, 1562. Its first major decree was on communion, holding that the body and blood of Christ are fully contained in either species of bread and wine, and hence that communion under both kinds is not required. Children below the age of reason were not required to receive communion. A decree on the sacrifice of the mass* declared that the mass is a true sacrifice*, but one that does not jeopardize the uniqueness of the sacrifice of Jesus on the cross. A decree on the sacrament of order* declared that priestly ordination is a true sacrament. It also stated that the hierarchy* of bishops*, priests*, and ministers* in the Church is of divine institution. Various reforms pertaining to holy orders were enacted, most importantly one requiring the establishment of seminaries* for the training of priests. A decree on marriage* declared that it is a sacrament instituted by Christ, while a further decree stated that secret marriages would henceforth be considered invalid. A lengthy reform decree dealt with the selection of bishops, strengthened bishops' authority, and required provincial and diocesan synods*. Reforms were enacted concerning monks and nuns. Brief decrees reasserted the doctrine of purgatory* and the legitimacy of indulgences* and of the veneration of saints* and their relics* and images, though directing that abuses and superstitions regarding them be curbed. Revision of the Index of Forbidden Books*, the missal*, and the breviary (*see* HOURS, LITURGY OF THE) and preparation of a catechism* were entrusted to the pope and accomplished under Pius IV and Pius V (1566-1572). The council closed on December 4, 1563.

TRIBUNAL. A court of canon law*. Normally, each diocese* is required to have a tribunal, although, with permission from Rome, several dioceses may form one jointly. The bishop* is the judge of the tribunal; he normally exercises his jurisdiction through a priest appointed as **judicial vicar** or **officialis**, however. The bishop may appoint assistants to the judicial vicar, who are called **adjutant judicial vicars** and must be priests. In addition, he may appoint **diocesan judges**, who may be clerics or laity (men or women). All of these various judges are expected to have advanced degrees (licentiate or doctorate) in canon law. Since most of the cases heard by a tribunal have to do with annulment* of marriages*, the courts are often called "marriage tribunals." Cases are normally heard by a panel of three judges, who decide by majority vote. Appeals are heard by an **appellate tribunal**, or "court of second instance," which is usually a tribunal in a neighboring diocese.

Two tribunals of the Roman Curia* judge canonical cases. The **Roman Rota** is the "court of third instance" for appeals, and certain cases are reserved to it. It originated in the twelfth century, when the increasing number of cases referred to the pope led to the appointment of clerics as **auditors** (from Lt *audire*, "to hear") for cases. The name *Rota* (Lt, "Wheel") originated in the fourteenth century and may derive from the bookcase that held the records of cases and was moved on wheels from one auditor to another. The **Apostolic Signatura** is the supreme tribunal of the Church. It hears appeals of decisions of the Rota and decides issues concerning the proper jurisdictions and procedures of lower courts. It is also the supreme court of the state of Vatican City*. It originated in and derives its name from the "referendaries" (reporters) of the early Middle Ages, who reported to the pope on cases submitted to him and presented documents to him for signature or signed them personally. It was established as a distinct body under Pope Eugenius IV (1431-1447). A third Roman tribunal, the **Apostolic Penitentiary**, deals with questions of conscience, absolutions*, dispensations, indulgences*, and related matters. Records of individual priests serving the pope as "penitentiary" date from the thirteenth century, while records of the Penitentiary as an organized body date from the fourteenth century.

TRIDUUM. *See* EASTER TRIDUUM.

TRINITY (Lt *trinitas*). One God in three persons*, Father, Son (*Logos** or Word), and Holy Spirit*. This, the central Christian affirmation about God*, should be understood not as a theological abstraction but as a summary of the basic Christian experience of God. Christians experienced God as the Father, the One whom Jesus addressed in prayer as *Abba*; they experienced God in Jesus; and they experienced God in the Spirit of God—who was also the Spirit of Jesus (Rom 8.9)—present among them and in whom they prayed. And all of this was experience of one and the same God. The doctrine of the Trinity was not formulated until the fourth century, but its chief elements are already present in the NT (with antecedents in the OT), especially in the doctrine of the Word of God in John's Gospel (Jn 1.1-3) and in Paul's teaching about the spirit, taken together with the Johannine teaching about the Paraclete (Jn 14-16). The NT contains several trinitarian formulas used in prayer and worship, notably the formula for baptism "in the name of the Father, and of the Son, and of the holy Spirit" (Mt 28.19).

In the second and third centuries, the trinitarian question focused on the divinity of Jesus and its consistency with monotheism*. **Monarchianism** asserted the oneness of God in such a way as to threaten the distinctness of the Word of God. A form of monarchianism was **modalism** or **Sabellianism** (after Sabellius, a third-century theologian, about whom little is known), which held that the Father, Son, and Holy Spirit were simply three different modes or manners in which God was manifest in history. Modalism was sometimes called "Patripassianism" (from the Latin words for "Father suffering"), because it seemed to its opponents to say that the Father had suffered on the cross. Positions that clearly upheld the distinctness of the Trinitarian persons were sometimes accused of tritheism*, or belief in three Gods. Theologians of these centuries did not clearly reject Subordinationism*, the belief that the Son and Spirit were less than the Father. Tertullian* (early third century) was the first known to have used the Latin word *trinitas* of God. The Greek *trias* is attested somewhat earlier. Neither word is at first used clearly to designate "three-in-oneness" as distinct from simple "threeness."

It was the crisis over Arianism* in the fourth century that evoked the classic formulations of the doctrine of the Trinity. Against Arius's claim that the Word of God was a creature, the First Council of Nicaea* in 325—the first ecumenical council* of the Church—declared that the Word of God (God incarnate in Jesus) was "one in being" (*homoousios*) with the Father. The Nicene position was defended and elaborated in the fourth century by St. Athanasius* and the Cappadocian Fathers*. The latter developed the theology of the Father, Son, and Holy Spirit as distinct *hypostases*, though one in being (*ousia*). They were distinct in their "processions" or "modes of coming to be": the Father unbegotten, the Son begotten of the Father, the Spirit proceeding from the Father through the Son (*see FILIOQUE*). This theology was taken up into the creed* of the First Council of Constantinople* (381), today known as the "Nicene Creed." Latin theology preferred the term *person* (*persona*, Gk *prosōpon*) for the trinitarian three. This term originally meant an actor's mask, then something like a role or status; it must mean more than that, if modalism is to be avoided, but—to avoid tritheism—cannot be taken to refer to a distinct consciousness or will.

Catholic faith affirms, then, the unity of the trinitarian persons in one God, the equality of the persons, the distinctness of the persons from one another, and the difference of the persons in their processions. Focus on these assertions in isolation led to a highly technical and abstract trinitarian theology in the medieval and modern periods. Within the limits of the dogmatic affirmations of the early councils, contemporary trinitarian theology has sought to recover its foundation in the Trinity as revealed in salvation history (this is known as the **economic Trinity**, from "economy [order] of salvation," in contrast to the **immanent Trinity**) and to develop the relation of the Trinity to Christian prayer and spiritual life.

TRITHEISM. Belief in three Gods; a label attached to positions in the theology of the Trinity* that are seen as making of each trinitarian person* a separate being, hence a God.

TRUSTEEISM (LAY TRUSTEEISM). A system of church organization, prominent in the Catholic Church in the early years of the United States, whereby a group of laymen established a corporation to purchase property for a church and to establish and administer the church. Power was vested in lay trustees elected by the congregation; trustees controlled church property and at times hired and fired the pastor. This system, based in American Protestant church organization, was favored in the civil law of a number of states. Its supporters also cited as a precedent the European custom of lay patronage, whereby lay benefactors of churches (ordinarily, the rulers who established them, and the heirs or legal successors of such rulers) gained rights over them. It led to frequent conflict between bishops and trustees. The first such conflict occurred in 1786 between John Carroll*, not yet a bishop but prefect apostolic of the United States, and the trustees of St. Peter's Church in New York. The most serious occurred at St. Mary's in Philadelphia in 1822, when trustees continued to support William Hogan, a pastor who had been excommunicated by Bishop Henry Conwell. The tide was turned against trusteeism by the First Provincial Council of Baltimore in 1829, which enacted canonical legislation to strengthen bishops' control of church property and reassert their right to appoint and remove pastors. Still, sporadic controversies continued throughout the nineteenth century and, in a few ethnic parishes, into the twentieth.

U

ULTRAMONTANISM (Lt *ultra montes*, "beyond the mountains," sc. the Alps). A movement, chiefly in the eighteenth and nineteenth centuries in France, Germany, and England, favoring a centralization of authority in the pope*. The movement arose in opposition, on the one hand, to Gallicanism*, Jansenism*, and other movements that supported greater autonomy of national churches, and on the other, to the secularizing trends growing out of the Enlightenment* and the French Revolution*. Its best-known representatives, such as Joseph de Maistre (1753-1821), sought to make the papacy the bulwark for European civilization against liberalizing forces that were causing it to disintegrate. Some early nineteenth-century French ultramontanists, however, saw the papacy as itself an agency of liberalization. Vatican Council I's* declaration of the pope's infallibility* and universal jurisdiction was a triumph for the ultramontanists, but the definition of infallibility was hedged with qualifications that many ultramontanists would have preferred to omit.

UNITY OF THE CHURCH. Along with holiness*, catholicity*, and apostolicity*, one of the four marks of the Church, as stated in the Nicene Creed (*see* CREED). The unity of the Church is grounded in the oneness of God and the uniqueness of Jesus as savior and Lord. The Pauline author of Ephesians calls his audience to unity in the name of "one Lord, one faith, one baptism, one God and Father of all" (Eph 4.5). Jesus prays that his followers may be one as he and the Father are one (Jn 17.20-23). For Paul, the Holy Spirit* is especially the source of the unity of Christians: "In one Spirit we were all baptized into one body" (1 Cor 12.13). Likewise the eucharist* is a source of unity: "We, though many, are one body, for we all partake of the one loaf" (1 Cor 10.17). Division and rivalry in the Church are contrary to the unity of Christ (1 Cor 1.10-13). But the image of the Church as the body of Christ calls for diversity within unity, like the difference among parts of the same body (1 Cor 12:12-27). Unity in the Church therefore does not mean uniformity.

Biblical admonitions toward unity have motivated modern ecumenism*. Vatican Council II, in its *Decree on Ecumenism*, while deploring divisions in the Church, upholds the principle of diversity in unity when it praises and calls for the preservation of the variety of customs, disciplines, and theological formulations in the eastern churches (UR 16-17). Within the Church, the "Petrine ministry" belonging to the pope* is a ministry of attending to the "unity of faith and communion" (LG 18) of the whole Church.

UNIVERSITIES AND COLLEGES. The word *university* (Lt *universitas*) initially referred not to an educational institution but to a medieval guild, in this case a guild of teachers or students at the urban schools of the twelfth century. The word is first attested at Paris in

1221. The medieval term more closely corresponding to our "university" was *studium* ("school") or *studium generale* (*generale* perhaps means "drawing students from a broad area"). By the end of the twelfth century, a mark of the *studium generale* was that it possessed one of the three higher faculties of law, medicine, or theology. Students went on to these faculties only after completing a course of study in the liberal arts*, which by the thirteenth century chiefly meant the philosophy of Aristotle*. The earliest university may have been Salerno, which concentrated on the study of medicine. The most important universities in the twelfth and thirteenth centuries were Bologna, which was distinguished in the study of Roman and canon law*, and Paris, which was the center of theological study. The major theologians of the thirteenth and fourteenth centuries, for example, Bonaventure*, Thomas Aquinas*, Duns Scotus*, all taught there. Oxford was founded in the late twelfth century, Cambridge in 1209, and Salamanca (Spain) around 1229. By the end of the thirteenth century, there were about twenty universities in Europe. The shape of the theology of the period was affected by the structure of the course of studies, with "arts" (philosophy) coming before theology, and by the standard classroom techniques, which led to the name, "scholasticism"*. The university faculties of theology, especially Paris, acquired an official or quasi-official role in the Church in matters such as the censure of heresy*. University theologians were given a deliberative vote in some late medieval councils, for example, Constance* and Basel*. At Paris, this role, which earned it the title of "consultant of Christendom" and "Permanent Council of the Gauls," lasted in some degree into the eighteenth century.

College (Lt *collegium*) originally meant a corporate body. It came to be a name for residence houses for students in the universities, and these in turn became houses of study. In some universities, the colleges became the locus of most instruction, while the university granted degrees. Today, in the United States, "college" and "university" are close to synonyms ("university" will be used in this article), with "university" normally connoting a wider range of subjects taught and more graduate degrees offered. A "college" may also be a subdivision of a university, such as the College of Arts and Sciences of Georgetown University.

The original universities were, in essence, ecclesiastical institutions. Beginning in the fifteenth century, some came under the control of secular authorities, while during the following century many went over into Protestant hands. The Jesuits* founded numerous colleges in the sixteenth and seventeenth centuries (444 by 1626)—most of these were something like today's preparatory schools, but some were universities. In the United States, the first Catholic college was Georgetown College (now University), founded in 1789. The Catholic University of America, founded in 1889, was the first Catholic university in the United States to offer graduate instruction. It was founded by the American hierarchy specifically for that purpose, acquiring undergraduate programs only in 1905. Today, there are more than two hundred Catholic colleges and universities in the United States; they constitute about one-fourth of such institutions in the world.

There are several kinds of Catholic college and university. First, there are ecclesiastical universities and faculties*, founded by the authority of the Holy See* and having special rights and responsibilities in canon law. There are also Catholic universities that have a canonical charter; The Catholic University of America is the only such institution in the United States. Thirdly, there are universities, in most cases founded by a religious community, which are committed by their own statutes to having a Catholic character but are governed by an independent board of trustees. These, which include most of the Catholic universities in the United States, are not strictly under the canonical jurisdiction of Church authorities. Finally, there are institutions that have some tie to the Catholic tradition, for instance foundation by a religious community, but are now officially secularized.

The Apostolic Constitution *Sapientia Christiana* (1979) governs ecclesiastical universities and faculties, while the Apostolic Constitution *Ex corde ecclesiae* (1990) applies to other sorts of Catholic university. *Ex corde ecclesiae* portrays the Catholic university as a setting for evangelization*, especially through dialogue between faith and culture. It also calls for a measure of juridical control by Church authorities over Catholic universities, and especially over theologians, invoking Canon 812 in the 1983 Code of Canon Law, which requires teachers of theology to obtain a mandate from ecclesiastical authorities. This sort of control does not cohere well with certain features of Catholic universities as they have developed in the United States, for example, governance by an independent board of trustees, hiring of faculty for professional competence without reference to religious commitment, academic freedom for theologians, acceptance of government funding, accreditation (hence, Canon 812 was not implemented in the United

States as of 1996). A contested issue is the extent to which Catholic universities in the United States can and ought to retain Catholic identity, within the limits of the American university system. Likewise contested is the degree to which Catholic identity requires control by Church authorities, especially over theologians. One promising approach is to conceive the relationship between Church authorities and universities not in legal terms but in terms of communion within the Church, considered as the whole people of God* (Ladislas Orsy). The hierarchy and the universities have different gifts and responsibilities, and they need to cooperate in order to advance the mission of the Church as a whole.

USURY. In ancient and medieval use, this term meant interest charged on a loan. Today it ordinarily means excessive interest charged. Ez 18.5-13 classes taking interest on a loan as something a just man does not do and an unjust man does. Ps 15.5 says that the just person "lends not his money at usury." Lv 25.35-37 and Dt 23.20-21 prohibit lending money at interest to one's own countryman. Luke 6.35, "Lend expecting nothing back," was often read as condemning the taking of interest. The Fathers of the Church* repeated and amplified the OT and (supposed) NT condemnations of usury. After Albert the Great*, the medievals were influenced by Aristotle's argument that taking interest is contrary to nature (*Politics* 1258b). Thomas Aquinas* argued that in the case of consumables, such as food and drink, the use *is* the consumption of the thing, so it is wrong to charge both for the use and for the consumption. Money is a consumable like food or drink. Therefore, a lender may ask for "the return of the thing [money] in equal measure" but not for "the price of the use, which is usury" (ST 2-2.78.1). Condemnations against the taking of usury were issued by several ecumenical councils*, including II Lateran* (1139), III Lateran* (1179), and Vienne* (1311-1312). According to Vienne, anyone who affirmed that usury was not sinful was to be punished as a heretic. Popes, at least from Alexander III (1159-1181) to Benedict XIV (1740-1758), also denounced usury. But, beginning in the sixteenth century, as European society moved from an agricultural to a commercial economy, some scholastics expanded the extrinsic grounds for taking interest, for example, profit forgone from the money lent out, risk of failure to repay. Others challenged the analysis of money which was a premise in the argument against interest. A number of opinions of the Holy Office in the nineteenth century approved lending at moderate rates of interest. A few Catholic voices, for example, writers connected with the *Catholic Worker**, still oppose all interest-taking, along with the capitalistic* economy that depends on it. But official teaching and most theological opinion now condemn only the *unjust* taking of interest, for which the name "usury" is reserved.

V

VALIDITY, SACRAMENTAL. A sacramental act is valid if it is genuinely performed or enacted as sacramental. In secular life, a vote in an election may be invalid if the voter is ineligible or if the vote is cast in the wrong place or time or manner; in such a case, the "voter" has not truly voted. Sacramental actions can fail in analogous ways. For validity, there must be a proper minister with proper intention, an eligible recipient with proper intention, and proper matter and form (normally, verbal formula and physical action). An ordination may fail, for instance, if the minister is not a bishop*, if the recipient is not baptized, or if the prescribed ritual for ordination is not followed, at least in its essential parts. An annulment* is a declaration that a marriage*, considered as sacrament, is invalid. A major obstacle to intercommunion* between Catholics and Protestants* is the judgment, on the part of the Catholic Church, that the Protestant churches lack a valid sacrament of order* and therefore a valid eucharist*.

The term *valid* was first used of sacraments* in the fourteenth century but did not become standard until the eighteenth. A judgment about validity is a matter of Church law and cannot set limits on how God may act, so a sacramentally invalid act may still be a means of grace*, but not in a strictly sacramental way. Conversely, a valid sacramental act may fail to communicate grace, due to some defect in the recipient (e.g., receiving communion while in a state of mortal sin*). Moreover, a valid sacramental act is not necessarily *licit*; it may violate Church laws other than those that are constitutive of it as a sacrament. An example is the ordination of a baptized man who has not received the sacrament of confirmation*. Church laws regarding validity may change, as the Church comes to a better understanding of what is essential to a particular sacrament.

VATICAN CITY. A sovereign state ruled by the pope*. It is situated west of the Tiber River in the city of Rome*, which entirely surrounds it. Occupying 108.7 acres, it is the smallest sovereign state in the world. It has its own currency and stamps, interchangeable with those of Italy, and its own flag, the papal flag. It includes the Church's central administrative offices (*see* CURIA, HOLY SEE), St. Peter's Basilica*, St. Peter's Square, and surrounding buildings and grounds. Its resident population is around a thousand. Vatican City was formed in 1929 by the Lateran Pacts between Italy and the Holy See, which resolved the "Roman question" left after the fall of the Papal States* in 1870. The pope is the absolute monarch of Vatican City, which he administers through the Pontifical Commission for the State of Vatican City. As of 1993, Vatican City had diplomatic relations with 146 nations, including the United States. It holds a seat in the United Nations.

VATICAN COUNCILS. Two ecumenical councils* that met at St. Peter's Basilica* in the Vatican.

I (1869-1870): Pope Pius IX* announced his intention to convoke this council in 1864 and formally convoked it in 1868. The council opened on December 8, 1869. About eight hundred church leaders attended. Though fifty-one preparatory documents (called "schemata") were presented to it, the council adopted only two documents, the doctrinal constitutions *Dei Filius,* on faith and reason, and *Pastor aeternus,* defining the primacy and infallibility* of the pope*. *Dei Filius* affirmed the possibility of knowledge of God by reason but also the insufficiency of such knowledge, thus condemning the opposite errors of fideism* and rationalism*. The infallibility of the pope was the most controversial issue at the council, and a substantial minority either opposed its definition or thought it "inopportune" to define at that time. In the end, *Pastor aeternus* declared the infallibility of the pope "when he speaks *ex cathedra*" (*see under* INFALLIBILITY). The outbreak of the Franco-Prussian War and the subsequent occupation of Rome by Italian troops led to the suspension of the council by Pius IX on October 20, 1870.

II (1962-1965): This was the best attended and farthest reaching of the ecumenical councils. On January 25, 1959, Pope John XXIII* announced his intention to convoke it, for the purpose of renewing the Church and better adapting it to contemporary conditions. Official convocation was on December 25, 1961. Between two thousand and 2,500 church leaders attended the four annual sessions, which began on October 13, 1962, and continued under Pope Paul VI* after John's death in May 1963. Eastern Orthodox* and Protestant* representatives, as well as numerous theological experts, also attended, though they could not vote or participate in council debates. Preparatory commissions dominated by the Roman Curia* drew up seventy schemata, quite traditional in tone and content. A turning point was reached, however, when, in its opening session, the Council decided to elect members of its own choosing to the commissions charged with preparation of its documents. These new commissions rejected all but one of the original schemata. Eventually, the council adopted sixteen documents, which effected a thorough restatement of the nature and mission of the Church. The most important documents were the *Dogmatic Constitution on the Church (Lumen Gentium)*, which identified the Church primarily as the "people of God"*, subordinating the hierarchical structure of the Church, which had been the main emphasis at Vatican I and in previous ecclesiology*, and the *Pastoral Constitution on the Church in the Modern World (Gaudium et Spes)*, which addressed modern Western society in a spirit of service and dialogue. Other influential documents were the *Dogmatic Constitution on the Liturgy,* which emphasized the increased participation of the laity* in worship, the *Dogmatic Constitution on Divine Revelation*, the *Decree on Ecumenism*, whereby the Church endorses and joins the ecumenical movement, the *Declaration on the Relation of the Church to Non-Christian Religions*, especially noteworthy for its reconsideration of the Church's attitude toward Judaism*, and the *Declaration on Religious Freedom.* "Vatican II" is often used as an adjective, denoting not only the council itself, but also actions and attitudes that promote the council's spirit of recognition of the importance of the laity in the Church and openness to other Christians, non-Christians, and modern culture.

See Appendix III for summaries of the documents of Vatican II.

VESSELS, SACRED. Containers for elements used in rituals. Most are derived from ordinary utensils employed in antiquity. Following are some of the more important among many vessels in use today. (1) **Chalice** (Lt *calix*, "cup"). A cup to hold the wine that becomes the blood of Christ at the eucharist*. (2) **Paten** (Gk *patanē*, "plate"). A dish for the eucharistic bread (body of Christ). (3) **Ciborium** (possibly from Gk *kiborion*, "drinking cup"). A lidded, usually cylindrical container (sometimes on a stem with a base) used for holding bread to be consecrated or already consecrated. (4) **Pyx** (Gk *pyxis*, "box"). A small, cylindrical container for the host (eucharistic wafer), used in carrying the eucharist to the sick. (5) **Monstrance** (from Lt *monstrare*, "to show"). An instrument for display of the host in ceremonies such as benediction*. At its center is a pyx or **luna** to hold the host. This is usually surrounded by ornate metalwork and attached to a stem (for elevation) and base. The monstrance originated in the late Middle Ages.

VESTMENTS. Liturgical vestments derive from men's ordinary clothing in the Roman Empire. Initially, Christian ministers did not wear distinctive clothing. When Christianity became legal in the fourth century, Constantine* accorded bishops the honors due to civil magistrates, and bishops began to wear the clothing characteristic of magistrates. After the Germanic invasions, when styles of men's clothing changed, liturgical clothing did not change.

Following are descriptions of the major liturgical vestments. (1) **Alb** (Lt *albus*, "white"): a full-length white robe, worn over ordinary clothing and under other vestments. (2) **Cincture** (from Lt *cingere*, "to gird"): a cord that serves as a belt for the alb. (3) **Stole**: a long, scarflike garment. A priest wears it around his neck, and it extends to near the knee. A deacon wears it over his left shoulder; it is crossed and fastened on his right side. (4) **Chasuble** (Lt *casula*, "little house"): a sleeveless outer garment, worn by the priest or bishop when celebrating mass. Concelebrants (priests who join with the principal celebrant in offering mass) need wear only an alb and stole. They sometimes wear a special alb, called a chasuble-alb, designed as an outer garment and worn without a cincture. (5) **Dalmatic**: a sleeved outer garment worn by a deacon.

The **colors** of outer vestments vary with the liturgical season and other circumstances. **White**, symbolizing purity and divine life, is worn in the Christmas* and Easter* seasons and on most major feasts*. **Green**, symbolizing hope, is worn in Ordinary Time. **Violet**, symbolizing penance, is worn in Advent* and Lent*. **Red**, symbolic of the pouring out of life's blood, is worn on Passion (Palm) Sunday, Good Friday (*see* HOLY WEEK), Pentecost*, and feasts of apostles*, Evangelists, and martyrs*. **Rose**, symbolic of anticipation, may be worn on the Third Sunday of Advent and the Fourth Sunday of Lent. **Black**, symbolic of mourning, may be worn at masses for the dead; other options are white and violet.

VIATICUM (Lt, "provision for a journey"). The eucharist* administered to a dying person. According to the ritual book, *Pastoral Care of the Sick: Rites of Anointing and Viaticum*, "Viaticum rather than anointing* is the sacrament for the dying." It is preferable that viaticum be received within mass*, but there is also a ritual for viaticum outside of mass. Distinctive features of the rituals are renewal of baptismal promises by the dying person, special words accompanying the administration of the eucharist, and the sign of peace involving the dying person. In the ritual for viaticum within mass, the sign of peace precedes communion and an Apostolic Pardon is given in the concluding rite. Outside of mass the Apostolic Pardon follows the penitential rite, and the sign of peace concludes the rite. Communion is normally to be under both kinds. There are simplified rituals for emergencies and other extraordinary circumstances. The practice of eucharistic viaticum dates from the early centuries of the Church. In medieval and modern times, anointing of the sick often followed viaticum. Vatican Council II, reestablishing anointing as a sacrament for the sick rather than the dying, called for a separate ritual for viaticum (SC 73-74). The new rituals were issued in 1972 and revised in 1982.

VIENNE, COUNCIL OF (1311-1312). Vienne is a city in France on the Rhône River. Pope Clement V, then residing in Avignon*, convoked an ecumenical council* at Vienne to deal with the Templars*, accused by the French King Philip IV (the Fair) of heresy and immorality. The council ruled initially in favor of the Templars, but, under pressure from Philip, Clement suppressed them in 1312, and his decree doing so was promulgated at the council. The council also censured the Beguines and Beghards*.

VINCENT DE PAUL, ST. (1581-1660). Born of a peasant family in Pouy, France, Vincent was ordained a priest in 1600. Around 1618 or 1619, he became friends with St. Francis de Sales* and St. Jane Frances de Chantal. Influenced by them, in 1625 he founded the Congregation of the Mission (now known as Vincentians). That same year, he befriended St. Louise de Marillac, and in 1633 he assisted her in forming the Daughters of Charity. He took an interest in the education of the clergy, offering retreats (which today might be called "mini-courses") for those about to be ordained and later founding two seminaries. He also undertook a variety of charitable works, founding hospitals and orphanages and providing relief for victims of the Wars of Religion. He was canonized in 1737, and his feast is celebrated on September 27.

VIRGIN. A person who has not had sexual intercourse and has made a commitment, for religious motives, to perpetual sexual abstinence. The term is used far more often of women than of men. Virginity is a sign of an all-encompassing love of God and, in some cases, of a complete availability to the service of others. It is also an eschatological sign, a sign of the kingdom* of God (Mt 19.12), a reminder that this world is passing away (1 Cor 7.31). The model for Christian virginity is the virginity of Jesus himself. Virginity as a chosen, perpetual state is unknown in the OT. The primary NT source is 1 Corinthians 7. Second- and third-century sources testify to a distinct category of (women) virgins within the Church, comparable to (and at times included among) "widows"*. Virgins had a special place in the liturgical assembly. They made a public profession or vow*, and the veil was their symbol. The first known liturgical ceremony of consecration of virgins is from fourth-century Rome. Later the status of virginity was for the most part absorbed into monastic life* and the life of religious institutes (*see* RELIGIOUS LIFE), but there is still provision in canon law for "the order of virgins, who ... are consecrated by the diocesan bishop ..., are betrothed mystically to Christ, and are dedicated to the service of the Church" (Canon 604.2), and there is a liturgical rite for such consecration.

VIRGIN BIRTH. Both the Apostles' and the Nicene Creeds* say that Jesus was "born of the Virgin Mary." But "virgin birth" designates three distinct, though related, aspects of the virginity of Mary*.

(1) Mary's **virginal conception** of Jesus (*virginitas ante partum*, "virginity before birth"). This is attested in the "infancy narratives" in the gospels of Matthew and Luke. Matthew 1.18-25 tells of how, before Mary and Joseph lived together, "she was found with child through the holy Spirit" (18), though she had had no sexual relations with Joseph (25). Matthew understands this as a fulfillment of Is 7.14, which in Greek reads, "Behold the virgin shall be with child and bear a son, and they shall name him Emmanuel" (23). In Luke 1.26-38, the angel Gabriel announces to Mary, "a virgin betrothed to a man named Joseph" (27), that she will conceive and bear a son. When she questions, "How can this be, since I have no relations with a man?"

(34), the angel replies that "The holy Spirit will come upon you" (35). This is a sign that Jesus is "the Son of God" (35), but the Holy Spirit is not Jesus' father; Jesus is not a demigod, half god and half man, as in Greek myths. Apparently, Luke's and Matthew's accounts were composed independently, giving two attestations to the virginal conception. Is the virginal conception a historical fact or a *theologoumenon*, or symbol, of the divine origin of Jesus as Son and savior? Many Catholic exegetes do not think this can be settled by scriptural exegesis alone. Most theologians, however (with some exceptions, such as Hans Küng), regard the virginal conception as a dogma* of faith, infallibly taught.

(2) Mary's *virginitas in partu* ("virginity in giving birth"), that is, her physical integrity and freedom from birth pangs in giving birth. This is attested in the second century apocryphal gospel, the *Protevangelium of James*. It was rejected by Tertullian* but generally affirmed throughout tradition. Some theologians (e.g., M. O'Carroll) regard it as a dogma of faith. Karl Rahner* understood it not as a matter of physiology but as a corollary of Mary's sinlessness: she was free from all aspects of ordinary childbirth that were a consequence of sin. A 1960 instruction of the Holy Office (now Congregation for the Doctrine of the Faith*) cautioned against an "unbecoming," overly biological approach to Mary's virginity *in partu*. Vatican Council II says that "her first-born ... did not diminish her virginal integrity but consecrated it" (LG 57).

(3) Mary's **perpetual virginity**, especially after the birth of Jesus (*virginitas post partum*, "virginity after giving birth"). Third century sources, for instance Origen*, affirmed this, and it became more prominent in the late fourth century, when the Marian title "ever-virgin" became popular. The obvious objection is the NT's frequent references to Jesus' "brothers" and sometimes "sisters" (e.g., Mk 3.31, 6.3). From the time of St. Jerome*, it has been argued that these "brothers and sisters" are really cousins, and it seems possible to read the Greek *adelphoi* and *adelphai* in some such sense, though that is not their normal meaning. One theory is that the "brothers and sisters" were children of Joseph's sister, reared in Joseph's home after their father's death. Most Protestant opinion now regards them as Jesus' true siblings, children of Mary and Joseph born after Jesus. Some Catholic theologians and exegetes (e.g., Rudolf Pesch) have recently taken that position, but most regard the perpetual virginity of Mary as a dogma of faith.

VIRTUE (Lt *virtus*, from *vir*, "man, male"). Aristotle*, who stands at the fountainhead of Western thought on virtue, spoke of virtue (*aretē*, often translated "excellence") as a "state of character which makes a human person good and enables that person to do his or her own work well" (*Nicomachean Ethics* 1106a22). ("State of character" renders the Greek *hexis*, which was translated into Latin as *habitus*. Hence, virtues are often classed as "habits," meaning not unthinking routines but settled tendencies of rational choice and action.) Aristotle understood human "goodness" and human "work" as contributing to the supreme good of *eudaimonia*, human well-being or flourishing (often rendered "happiness"). He classified virtues into **intellectual virtues**, various kinds of knowledge and understanding, and **moral virtues**, which concern the rational governance of the desires and passions. In contemporary philosophy and theology, "virtue" normally refers to the moral virtues.

Augustine* understood virtue as "rightly ordered love" (*City of God* 15.22), with God alone to be loved for his own sake and all other loves subordinated to love of God. Since only grace*, which comes through Christ, enables a human being to love God above all else, it follows that non-Christians cannot possess true virtue. Thomas Aquinas's* treatment of the virtues, which has been the primary influence on subsequent Catholic thought on the subject, harmonized Aristotle and Augustine. According to Aquinas, "Human virtue is a good habit, productive of good works" (S.T. 1-2.55.3). He followed Aristotle in distinguishing intellectual and moral virtues. He reduced the moral virtues to the four cardinal virtues* of prudence, temperance, fortitude, and justice. According to Aquinas, if we consider human nature in abstraction from sin* and grace*, the intellectual and moral virtues are sufficient for human happiness in the natural order, that is, for the perfection of human nature insofar as this can be attained through natural human powers. But God also offers the human being a happiness that surpasses human nature, a sharing in God's own life in the beatific vision*. To be directed to this end requires virtues beyond those attainable through our own powers. These virtues are faith*, hope*, and love* (charity) (1 Cor 13.13). Aquinas called them the theological virtues*.

From the fourteenth century through the beginning of the twentieth, moral theology* turned its focus from virtues to laws and to specific acts, considered as conforming to or violating moral laws. Virtues were understood as tendencies to obey moral laws. Recent moral theology (and moral philosophy as well) has revived the study of the virtues, emphasizing the moral importance of character and the limitations of law-based morality. Among the good effects of this revival has been a reuniting of moral theology and spirituality*. In such theology, the distinction between the moral and theological virtues is acknowledged, but the two are not treated as separately as had been customary, since in concrete life the orders of nature and grace are not separated.

VOCATION (Lt *vocatio*, "calling"). A calling from God, especially a calling to the clerical* or religious* state of life. The relation of God to humans in the Bible is often characterized in terms of call and response. God calls Abraham (Gn 12.1-3) and Moses (Ex 3.4). He calls the prophets (e.g., Is 6.1-13). Through the patriarchs and prophets he calls the whole people (Is 42.6, 43.1). Jesus calls his disciples* (e.g., Mk 1.17, 2.14), rather than wait for them to seek him out. Paul (Acts 9.1-9) and Barnabas (Acts 13.2) receive special calls to ministry. 1 Pt 2.9 says that God has called all Christians out of darkness into his light.

The classic account of a religious vocation is the story of St. Antony, the Desert Father*, who heard the call of God in a passage of Scripture (Mt 19.21) read in Church. John Cassian (ca. 360-ca. 435) speaks of three ways God can call a person to monastic* life: directly, through the words of holy people, or through the accidents of one's life. Medieval authors are concerned chiefly with vocation in the sense of a personal calling by God to the clerical or religious "state of life" (a term taken from Roman law). Consonant with the movement toward interiority and affectivity in early modern thought (*see under* MARRIAGE), the seventeenth-century school of Saint-Sulpice understood a religious vocation as an "inner attraction" implanted by God in the soul. The Roman Catechism (*Catechism of the Council of Trent*) (1566), however, said only, "They are called by God who are called by the lawful ministers of the Church." There was much debate in Catholic theology into the twentieth century as to the relation of the interior call and the exterior call by bishops and religious superiors. Prior to Vatican Council II (1962-1965), Catholic theologians rarely spoke of "vocations" for the laity, and then only in terms of the married or single "states of life."

The Protestant* Reformers, rejecting the idea of specially meritorious states of life, understood one's vocation or calling to be one's proper work in the world. "The homeliest service that we do in an honest calling, though it be but to plow or dig, if done in obedience and conscience of God's commandments, is crowned with an ample reward" (Joseph Hall, 1574-1656). Vatican II incorporated something of the Reformers' perspective into a broadened range of meanings for "vocation." Most generally, it spoke of the "total calling" of humans as the human fulfillment to which all actions should be directed (GS 35). In reference to Christians, "All the faithful of every state and condition are called by the Lord, each in their own way, to that perfect holiness whereby the Father is perfect" (LG 11). LG mentions priestly and religious vocations and then adds, "It is the special vocation of the laity to seek the kingdom of God by engaging in temporal affairs and ordering these in accordance with the will of God" (LG 31). Finally, the council uses "vocation" to refer to specific states, occupations, or dimensions of life such as marriage (GS 52), teaching (GE 5), and political activity (GS 75). Some theologians, for example, Germain Grisez, speak of each Christian as having a "personal vocation," a unique way to follow Jesus, in the light of personal gifts and circumstances.

VOW (Lt *votum*). A promise freely made before God to do something that is good but not otherwise required. By a vow, one imposes an obligation upon oneself, which may be enforceable by others. A vow is **public** if it is officially accepted by a superior in the Church; otherwise it is **private**. Since the thirteenth century, canon law has distinguished between **solemn** and **simple** vows. Formerly, acts contrary to solemn vows—for instance, marriage by one vowed to chastity (celibacy*)—were invalid (*see* VALIDITY), while those contrary to simple vows were merely illicit, but the 1983 Code of Canon Law does not make that distinction. At present, vows are "solemn" if the Church acknowledges them as such; otherwise they are "simple." A vow is **permanent** if it binds for life, otherwise **temporary**. Vows appear in both the OT and the NT (e.g., nazirite vows, Nm 6.1-21, Acts 21.22-26). Public vows or pledges of virginity appeared in the Church in the third century, but monastic vows in a strict, juridical sense are found only from the late eighth century. A clear notion of a vow as creating an enforceable obligation appeared in canon law only around 1095. Profession of the three vows of poverty, chastity, and obedience (*see* EVANGELICAL COUNSELS) dates from around 1200. While these religious vows have a special place in the Church (*see* RELIGIOUS LIFE), other vows, such as vows to go on a pilgrimage* or crusade*, have also been important. (The promises made in marriage ceremonies are not, technically, vows.)

W

WALDENSES (WALDENSIANS). A medieval reform movement that developed into a separate church. The Waldensian movement represented many of the same spiritual currents that gave rise, at about the same time, to the mendicant orders*, and later to the Protestant* Reformation. It was founded in 1173 by Valdes (Waldes, Waldo), a merchant of Lyons. Valdes called for a literal following of the Gospel, especially the injunction to "sell all you have" (Mt 19.21). His followers went about preaching and lived by begging. It was their insistence on preaching, without Church permission, that led to trouble with Church authorities. They were excommunicated by the bishop of Lyons in 1182, and the movement was condemned by Pope Lucius III in 1184. Neither action impeded the spread of the movement. Critical of the hierarchical Church for its attachment to wealth, they held (like the Donatists*) that unworthy priests could not celebrate valid sacraments. Accordingly, they chose their own clergy, who included women. They denied the doctrine of purgatory* and opposed oaths*, war*, capital punishment*, and prayer for the dead. In the thirteenth century, they were combatted by the Inquisition*, but they survived in and north of the Alps, where the Inquisition was not continuously active. At the time of the Reformation, the French Waldenses associated with the Genevan reform, while many German Waldenses became Lutherans. The Waldenses survived, however, in the Piedmont and Savoy regions of Italy. Today there are perhaps 30,000 Waldenses, mainly in Italy. They maintain a theological seminary in Rome.

WAR. The OT often portrays God as a warrior (e.g., Ex 15.3), who leads his people in battle. It also shows God as desiring peace* (e.g., Ps 85.9), however, and it looks forward to a time when universal peace will be established (e.g., Is 2.2-5). Jesus calls for nonresistance to violence and for love of enemies (Mt 5.38-48) (*see* PACIFISM). He accepts his own unjust execution without violent resistance, telling Peter to put away his sword (Mt 26.52). On the other hand, the NT seems to take the military profession for granted, as in Jesus' praise for the centurion (Mt 8.5-13) and Peter's baptism of the centurion

Cornelius (Acts 10). The earliest postbiblical Christian writers defend Christians' refusal to fight (e.g., Justin Martyr*, Athenagoras, Tertullian*, and Origen*). The *Acts of the Martyrs* include stories of Christians who were martyred because they refused to fight in the Roman army. The motives for Christian unwillingness to serve in the army were mixed: sometimes, as with Origen, strictly pacifist motives—the belief that it is wrong for a follower of Jesus to kill—predominated, but at other times the chief motive seems to have been to avoid the idolatry that was a normal part of military practice. Christian pacifism was not universal: Tertullian, Cyprian, Eusebius, and other sources speak of Christians who serve in the army.

With the rise of Constantine* in the fourth century, Christian pacifism abated. Soldiers were now defending a Christian, not a pagan, empire. Saints Ambrose* and Augustine*, in the fourth and fifth century, began to develop the theology of the **just war**. Augustine held that violence may be undertaken if commanded by a legitimate civil authority for defense or for punishment of crime. He opposed killing for self-defense but allowed killing in defense of others, for the sake of the common good.

In medieval times, the Church sought to curb warfare among Christians (*see* PEACE OF GOD, TRUCE OF GOD) but actively promoted it against Muslims and heretics (*see* CRUSADES). Medieval and early modern canonists and theologians, notably Thomas Aquinas* (1226-1274) and Francisco de Vitoria (ca. 1485-1546), developed the just-war theory into a standard form, which is still used within the Church. A war, to be morally licit, had to satisfy criteria of *jus ad bellum* (rightness in going to war) and *jus in bello* (rightness in conduct of war). As the tradition developed, criteria for *jus ad bellum* included: (1) just cause (in 1944, Pope Pius XII* restricted this to defense against aggression), (2) competent (legitimate and proper) authority, (3) right intention, (4) last resort, (5) probability of success, (6) proportionality (the goods to be attained by warfare must sufficiently outweigh the evils expected to be caused). Criteria for *jus in bello* included: (1) discrimination (immunity of noncombatants from direct attack) and (2) proportionality, this time referring to the benefits and harms expected from the means used in fighting.

The great destructiveness of modern war, particularly that caused by nuclear weapons*, has raised questions of whether any modern war can satisfy the *jus in bello* criteria, and thus has drawn the Church closer to pacifism in practice. Vatican Council II in 1965 declared that nations have a duty to defend their citizens by military means if necessary (GS 79). Yet it strongly condemned "total war": "Every operation of war which aims indiscriminately at the destruction of whole cities, or of widespread areas with their inhabitants, is a crime against God and humanity itself which is to be firmly and unhesitatingly condemned" (GS 80). Echoing statements of Popes Pius XII* and John XXIII*, the Council also condemned the modern arms race: "The arms race is a virulent plague affecting humanity and … it does intolerable harm to the poor" (GS 81). It called for steps toward disarmament and the establishment of an international authority to prevent war. The Council recognized that war can be prevented only if justice* is established within and among nations.

The Council expressed admiration for those who renounced violence (GS 78), and since the Council support for pacifism—especially in regard to modern warfare—has grown within the Church. Popes Paul VI* and John Paul II* have strongly denounced the violence of modern war but not excluded all resort to warfare. A still-underdeveloped area of Church teaching relates to wars of liberation of subject peoples. The standard just-war criterion of "legitimate authority" cannot neatly fit such cases, nor is it easy to maintain the combatant/noncombatant distinction. The supposition that liberation theology* supports violent revolution is one apparent reason for Vatican suspicion of it. Support for violence is very limited among liberation theologians, however, and some take a strict nonviolent stance. Church documents themselves have not excluded all possibility of revolutionary violence against an oppressor. Another unresolved issue is the use of military interventions for humanitarian purposes (e.g., the entry of United Nations forces into Somalia in 1992).

WIDOW. A ministry of women in the early Church. The earliest evidence of a distinct order of widows in the Church is 1 Timothy 5.3-16 (late first century?). This text specifies that widows who are "enrolled" are to be at least sixty years old and married only once. Such widows are supported by the Church. Their main duty is prayer, but later texts show them engaging in charitable work as well. Ignatius of Antioch* (second century)* and Tertullian* (third century) speak of virgins* enrolled among the widows. Some third-century sources include widows among the clergy*. After the third century, widows decline in relation to deaconesses*, but the widows, more than the deaconesses, are the forerunners of later monastic communities of women.

WILLIAM OF OCKHAM (OCCAM) (ca. 1285-1347). Late-medieval philosopher and theologian. Born at Ockham in Surrey in England, he entered the Franciscan* order and studied at Oxford. He never became a Master but was instead called to the papal court at Avignon* in 1324 to defend himself against charges of heresy. He was not formally condemned, but at Avignon he became embroiled in a conflict over Franciscan poverty between Michael of Cesena, the Franciscan minister general, and Pope John XXII. With Michael, he fled to the protection of the Emperor Louis of Bavaria. He died in Munich.

In philosophy, he is important for his nominalism*, which held that universal terms are merely names attached to concepts signifying similar individual things; there is no universal nature in particular things. This is one of many instances of his principle of simplicity, known as **Ockham's razor**: "What can be explained by assuming fewer terms is vainly explained by positing many." He de-emphasized reasoning based in the nature of things, in favor of reliance on empirical observation in matters of natural science and on divine revelation in matters of theology. He laid great stress on God's omnipotence, holding that by his "absolute power" God can do anything that does not involve a contradiction. God could have mandated any order of ethics and any means of salvation he pleased; that he established a moral order partly knowable by reason and that he established the Christian order of salvation are matters of contingent fact. The effect of Ockham's work was to increase skepticism about the use of reason in matters pertaining to God, and thus to promote a separation of philosophy from theology.

In the course of his conflict with John XXII, he produced important political writings, in which his principal concern was to curb abuses of papal power. These works influenced later conciliarism*.

WITCHCRAFT (Old Engl *wicca*, "male witch, wizard," *wicce*, "female witch"). In regard to most of biblical and Christian history, "witchcraft," "magic," and "sorcery" are synonyms for the effort to use occult natural or supernatural forces to produce effects in the world. Magic is found in all cultures and religious traditions. The OT condemns it (Ex 22.17) and displays its power as weak compared with that of Yahweh (e.g., Ex 7-9, Moses vs. Pharaoh's magicians). The

NT's view is similar; see, for example, Acts 13.6-11 and Gal 5.20. The Church Fathers* condemn sorcery as the work of demons*. In the early Middle Ages, sorcery was punished by excommunication. The Church continues to condemn all forms of magic and sorcery (CCC 2117).

From about 1450 to 1750, a "witch craze" swept Western Europe and extended into North America. About one hundred thousand people, mostly women, were put to death for witchcraft. The craze peaked between 1550 and 1650, after the Protestant* Reformation, and there were about as many Protestants as Catholics among the accusers and accused. The causes of the craze were social and political as well as religious, but developments within Catholicism were important in engendering it. First was the rise of heresy* in the twelfth century (*see* CATHARS), followed by the establishment of the Inquisition* to combat it. Second was the development in thirteenth- and fourteenth-century scholasticism of a systematic demonology, including the idea of a pact with the devil. According to J. Russell, the notion of a *pact* with the enemies of Christ enabled the assimilation of witchcraft to heresy, rather than sorcery, and thus the use of the Inquisition against it. The Inquisition itself had a relatively minor role in the persecution of suspected witches, but its methods, especially its use of torture, were adopted by secular and ecclesiastical courts. Accused witches were tortured until they confessed to the crimes their accusers expected to find, and each confession strengthened the accusers' expectations of what they would find in the next case. The standard story on the Continent included a secret nocturnal meeting, desecration of the eucharist and crucifix, orgies, sexual intercourse between the devil and humans (usually women, since the devil was seen as male), infanticide, and cannibalism. This story gained increased currency through the *Malleus Malleficarum (Hammer of Witches)* (1486), by the Dominicans Heinrich Institoris (Kramer) and Jacob Sprenger, a handbook for the investigation of witches. A bull of Pope Innocent VIII, *Summa desiderantes affectibus* (1484), gave full support to the use of the inquisition against witches and was published as a preface to the *Malleus*.

Wicca or "Neo-paganism" is a popular revival of witchcraft, derived from the teachings of Gerald Gardner (1884-1964). Its claims to continuity with ancient pagan religion are tenuous, and it has no connection whatever with what medieval and early modern witches were accused of doing; in fact, it disavows belief in the devil. In its devotion to the Goddess as chief deity, it converges somewhat with currents in Catholic feminism* that have sought to develop a view of the deity as feminine.

WOMEN, ORDINATION OF. *See* ORDINATION OF WOMEN.

WORK. Catholic tradition—and Jewish tradition before it—sees an ambiguity in human work. Genesis 1.28 understands human work as, in a sense, continuing God's creative work. Gn 3.17-19, on the contrary, depicts the toil of work as a consequence of sin*. In English, the word *work* tends to connote the creative or productive aspect of human activity, while *labor** connotes the toil. For the most part, the Bible takes work for granted as a component of human life and the well-ordering of the world (Ps 104.23). The Fathers of the Church* had little to say about work, beyond some ethical principles. This may show the influence of philosophies that disparaged involvement in the material world and thus favored contemplation* over action, or it may reflect the class structure of Greco-Roman society, in which physical labor was the province of slaves. Physical labor was integrated into the life of early medieval monks, but the Rule of St. Benedict* speaks of its spiritual value only in terms of the avoidance of a dangerous idleness. It remained for the Protestant* Reformers to begin to see ordinary human work as a medium for the encounter with God. The Reformers opposed the effort to earn one's salvation through works, and therefore opposed monasticism*, but conversely saw secular work in terms of divine calling or vocation*, so that it was the medium in which one served God. Vatican Council II treated the work of the laity* as their ordinary means of building the kingdom of God* and thus participating in Christ's kingship (LG 31,36). "Men and women … can rightly regard themselves as furthering the creator's work by their labor, as being concerned for the wellbeing of their fellows and as making a personal contribution to the achievement of the divine plan in history" (GS 34). The good work that we have done in this life, we will find again transfigured and purified in the next (GS 39; *see* KINGDOM OF GOD). To Vatican II's emphasis on the results of work, Pope John Paul II*, in the encyclical *Laborem exercens* (LE) (1981), added a treatment of work as the self-expression of workers, individually and collectively. By work, the human being, "in the image of God," shares in the work of the Creator (LE 26). In the inevitable toil and frustration of work in this life, the worker can join in the redemptive suffering of Christ (27).

WORLD COUNCIL OF CHURCHES. A fellowship of Christian churches, including almost all major Christian bodies except the Catholic Church. One of the principal expressions of the ecumenical movement, it was founded in 1948 with the merger of the Faith and Order (founded 1910) and Life and Work (founded 1920) movements. In 1972, the Catholic Church decided not to pursue membership. Obstacles to membership include its size (about twice the size of all other WCC member churches combined) and centralized structure (most members are national churches). The Catholic Church, however, is actively involved in WCC programs by means of a Joint Working Group of the Catholic Church and the WCC. The Catholic Church is a full member of the WCC's Faith and Order Commission, whose most important achievement to date is the Lima Document, "Baptism, Eucharist, Ministry" (1982). This document expressed a significant degree of agreement between all representatives, Catholic, Protestant, and Orthodox, on the three subjects mentioned in its title. In a 1987 Vatican response, by the Secretariat for Promoting Christian Unity and the Congregation for the Doctrine of the Faith*, the document was called a significant development, but reservations were expressed about its theology of sacrament*, apostolic tradition, and authority* in the Church.

X

XAVIER, FRANCIS, ST. (Francisco Javier) (1506-1552). Pioneer Jesuit* missionary to the Far East. Born in Navarre, he studied at the University of Paris*, where he was one of the original band of seven who, with Ignatius of Loyola*, formed the nucleus of what would become the Society of Jesus. He was ordained a priest in 1537. In 1540, King John III of Portugal requested members of the Society of Jesus to preach in the mission lands of his empire. Francis was chosen, and in 1541 he sailed for Goa, the capital of Portuguese India, arriving in May 1542. He stayed at Goa for four months, then preached among the poor pearl fishers on the Fishery Coast in southern India, where he learned enough Tamil to make thousands of converts and to teach many other natives who had been baptized but not catechized. Between 1544 and 1548, he preached in the Malay Peninsula and what is now Indonesia, reaching as far as the Moluccas. At Malacca (Melaka) on the Malay Peninsula, he met a young Japanese, who stirred him with the desire to go to Japan. In August 1549 he arrived at Kagoshima in Kyushu. He studied Japanese and taught in Kagoshima and Yamaguchi, where he made about five hundred converts. From the Japanese, he learned about the civilization of China, and he resolved to go there. After returning to India in 1551, he sailed for China on Easter 1552, but he was unable to gain entry. He became ill and died on the offshore island of San Chien (Changchuen) on December 3. He was canonized, along with Ignatius, in 1622. His feast is celebrated on December 3.

Appendix I

Popes[1]

1. St. Peter[2] (d. ca. A.D. 64)
2. St. Linus[3] (ca. 66-ca. 78)

---

[1]Sources for this list are J. N. D. Kelly, *The Oxford Dictionary of Popes* (New York: Oxford University Press, 1986), *Annuario Pontificio 1993* (Vatican City: Libreria Editrice Vaticana, 1993), and (to 1534) Bernhard Schimmelpfennig, *The Papacy* (New York: Columbia University Press, 1992). Dates and spellings in the *Oxford Dictionary* are usually preferred. Antipopes (claimants to the throne not recognized as legitimate) are listed in italics and are not numbered in the list. Traditional listings are followed uncritically here in regard to antipopes, though some of them had strong claims to legitimacy. In earlier times there were sometimes long interregna between popes, as the dates given here reflect.

[2]Technically, Peter was not a pope, that is, not *bishop** of Rome. Rather, he was an apostle*, to whom the popes are successors. Thus, the earliest lists of popes begin with Linus, but in the third century Peter is placed at the head of the list.

[3]The earliest extant lists of popes date from the late second century, one by Hegesippus (ca. 160), preserved in Eusebius (early fourth century), the other by Irenaeus* (ca. 180). There is considerable uncertainty about the dates and sometimes the names of the early popes, especially because it appears that the monepiscopacy (single bishop per local church) was not in effect at Rome until the mid-second century (*see* BISHOP). Thus, these names designate important leaders in the Church at Rome, but not exactly popes in our sense. See James F. McCue, "The Roman Primacy in the Patristic Era: I. The Beginnings through Nicaea," in *Papal Primacy and the Universal Church*, Lutherans and

3. St. Anacletus (Cletus)[4] (ca. 79-ca. 91)
4. St. Clement I (ca. 91-ca. 101)
5. St. Evaristus (ca. 100-ca. 109)
6. St. Alexander I (ca. 109-ca. 116)
7. St. Sixtus I (ca. 116-ca. 125)
8. St. Telesphorus (ca. 125-ca. 136)
9. St. Hyginus (ca. 138-ca. 142)
10. St. Pius I (ca. 142-ca. 155)
11. St. Anicetus (ca. 155-ca. 166)
12. St. Soter (ca. 166-ca. 174)
13. St. Eleutherius (ca. 174-189)
14. St. Victor I (189-198)
15. St. Zephyrinus (198/9-217)
16. St. Callistus I (Calixtus) (217-222)
    St. Hippolytus (217-235)
17. St. Urban I (222-230)
18. St. Pontian (230-235)
19. St. Anterus (235-236)
20. St. Fabian (236-250)
21. St. Cornelius (251-253)
    Novatian (251-258)
22. St. Lucius I (253-254)
23. St. Stephen I (254-257)
24. St. Sixtus II (Xystus) (257-258)
25. St. Dionysius (260-268)
26. St. Felix I (269-274)
27. St. Eutychian (275-283)
28. St. Gaius (Caius) (283-296)
29. St. Marcellinus (296-304)
30. St. Marcellus I (306-308)
31. St. Eusebius (309 or 310?)

Catholics in Dialogue V, ed. Paul C. Empie and T. Austin Murphy (Minneapolis: Augsburg, 1974): 44-72.

[4]Names in parentheses before dates indicate different spellings or versions of the pope's name; names in parentheses after dates indicate the pope's original name, when the pope took a new name upon assuming the papacy. The first pope to take a new name was John II in 533.

32. St. Miltiades (Melchiades) (311-314)
33. St. Silvester I (Sylvester) (314-335)
34. St. Mark (Marcus) (336)
35. St. Julius I (337-352)
36. Liberius (352-366)
    St. Felix II (355-365)
37. St. Damasus I (366-384)
    Ursinus (366-367)
38. St. Siricius (384-399)
39. St. Anastasius I (399-401)
40. St. Innocent I (401-417)
41. St. Zosimus (417-418)
    Eulalius (418-419)
42. St. Boniface I (418-422)
43. St. Celestine I (422-432)
44. St. Sixtus III (Xystus) (432-440)
45. St. Leo I* (440-461)
46. St. Hilarus (461-468)
47. St. Simplicius (468-483)
48. St. Felix III[5] (483-492)
49. St. Gelasius I (492-496)
50. Anastasius II (496-498)
51. St. Symmachus (498-514)
    Lawrence (498-499, 501-506)
52. St. Hormisdas (514-523)
53. St. John I (523-526)
54. St. Felix IV (526-530)
    Dioscorus (530)
55. Boniface II (530-532)
56. John II (533-535) (Mercury)
57. St. Agapitus I (535-536)
58. St. Silverius (536-537)
59. Vigilius (537-555)
60. Pelagius I (556-561)
61. John III (561-574) (Catelinus)
62. Benedict I (575-579)

---

[5]This and subsequent Felixes are misnumbered because of the mistaken inclusion of the antipope Felix II on the list of genuine popes.

63. Pelagius II (579-590)
64. St. Gregory I* (590-604)
65. Sabinian (604-606)
66. Boniface III (607)
67. St. Boniface IV (608-615)
68. St. Deusdedit (Adeodatus I) (615-618)
69. Boniface V (619-625)
70. Honorius I (625-638)
71. Severinus (640)
72. John IV (640-642)
73. Theodore I (642-649)
74. St. Martin I (649-653)
75. St. Eugene (Eugenius) I (654-657)
76. St. Vitalian (657-672)
77. Adeodatus II (672-676)
78. Donus (676-678)
79. St. Agatho (678-681)
80. St. Leo II (682-683)
81. St. Benedict II (684-685)
82. John V (685-686)
83. Conon (686-687)
    Theodore (687)
    Paschal (687)
84. St. Sergius I (687-701)
85. John VI (701-705)
86. John VII (705-707)
87. Sisinnus (708)
88. Constantine (708-715)
89. St. Gregory II (715-731)
90. St. Gregory III (731-741)
91. St. Zacharias (741-752)
    Stephen (II) (752)[6]
92. Stephen II (III) (752-757)

---

[6]Stephen died four days after his election, without being consecrated pope. Lists from the sixteenth century to the mid-twentieth regarded him as authentic; since then, in recognition that in the eighth century consecration was deemed necessary to be pope, he has been dropped from the list and subsequent Stephens renumbered.

93. St. Paul I (757-767)
      Constantine (767-768)
      Philip (768)
94. Stephen III (IV) (768-772)
95. Hadrian I (772-795)
96. St. Leo III (795-816)
97. Stephen IV (V) (816-817)
98. St. Paschal I (817-824)
99. Eugene II (824-827)
100. Valentine (827)
101. Gregory IV (827-844)
      John (844)
102. Sergius II (844-847)
103. St. Leo IV (847-855)
104. Benedict III (855-858)
      Anastasius Bibliothecarius (the Librarian) (855)
105. St. Nicholas I (858-867)
106. Hadrian II (867-872)
107. John VIII (872-882)
108. Marinus I (882-884)
109. St. Hadrian III (884-885)
110. Stephen V (VI) (885-891)
111. Formosus (891-896)
112. Boniface VI (896)
113. Stephen VI (VII) (896-897)
114. Romanus (897)
115. Theodore II (897)
116. John IX (898-900)
117. Benedict IV (900-903)
118. Leo V (903)
      Christopher (903-904)
119. Sergius III (904-911)
120. Anastasius III (911-913)
121. Lando (913-914)
122. John X (914-928)
123. Leo VI (928)
124. Stephen VII (VIII) (928-931)
125. John XI (931-935/6)
126. Leo VII (936-939)
127. Stephen VIII (IX) (939-942)

444   Appendix I

128. Marinus II (942-946)
129. Agapitus II (946-955)
130. John XII (955-964) (Octavian)
131. Leo VIII (963-965)[7]
       Benedict V (964)
132. John XIII (965-972)
133. Benedict VI (973-974)
       Boniface VII (974, 984-985)[8]
134. Benedict VII (974-983)
135. John XIV (983-984) (Peter Canepanova)
136. John XV (985-996)
137. Gregory V (996-999) (Bruno)
       John XVI (997-998)
138. Silvester II (999-1003) (Gerbert)
139. John XVII (1003)
140. John XVIII (1003-1009)
141. Sergius IV (1009-1012) (Peter)
142. Benedict VIII (1012-1024) (Theophylact)
       Gregory (1012)
143. John XIX (1024-1032) (Romanus)
144. Benedict IX (1032-1044; 1045; 1047-1048) (Theophylact)
145. Silvester III (1045) (John)
146. Gregory VI (1045-1046) (John Gratian)
147. Clement II (1046-1049) (Suidger)
148. Damasus II (1048) (Poppo)
149. St. Leo IX (1049-1054) (Bruno)
150. Victor II (1055-1057) (Gebhard)
151. Stephen IX (X) (1057-1059) (Frederick)
       Benedict X (1058-1059) (John Mincius)
152. Nicholas II (1058-1061) (Gerard)
153. Alexander II (1061-1073) (Anselm)

---

[7]The overlap between John XII and Leo VIII is due to the deposition of John by a synod at Rome in December 863, an act of questionable validity. John regained power in February 864. In turn, if Leo VIII was a valid pope, Benedict V was an antipope.

[8]He was regarded as a legitimate pope on ancient lists; hence the next Boniface was regarded as the eighth.

Honorius (II) (1061-1064)
154. St. Gregory VII* (1073-1085) (Hildebrand)
     Clement III (1080; 1084-1100) (Guibert)
155. Bl. Victor III (1086; 1087) (Desiderius)
156. Bl. Urban II (1088-1099) (Odo)
157. Paschal II (1099-1118) (Rainerius)
     Theoderic (1100-1101)
     Albert (Adalbert) (1101)
     Silvester IV (1105-1111) (Maginulf)
158. Gelasius II (1118-1119) (John)
     Gregory (VIII) (1118-1121) (Maurice Burdinus)
159. Callistus II (1119-1124) (Guido)
160. Honorius II (1124-1130) (Lamberto)
     Celestine (II) (1124-1125/6) (Teobaldo)
161. Innocent II (1130-1143) (Gregorio Papareschi)
     Anacletus II (1130-1138) (Pietro Pierleoni)
     Victor IV (1138) (Gregorio Conti)
162. Celestine II (1143-1144) (Guido)
163. Lucius II (1144-1145) (Gherardo Caccianemici)
164. Bl. Eugene (Eugenius) III (1145-1153) (Bernardo Pignatelli)
165. Anastasius IV (1153-1154) (Corrado)
166. Hadrian IV (1154-1159) (Nicholas Breakspear)
167. Alexander III (1159-1181) (Orlando Bandinelli)
     Victor IV (1159-1164) (Ottaviano)
     Paschal III (1164-1168) (Guido)
     Callistus (III) (1168-1178) (Giovanni)
     Innocent (III) (1179-1180) (Lando)
168. Lucius III (1181-1185) (Ubaldo Allucingoli)
169. Urban III (1185-1187) (Umberto Crivelli)
170. Gregory VIII (1187) (Alberto de Morra)
171. Clement III (1187-1191) (Paolo Scolari)
172. Celestine III (1191-1198) (Giacinto Bobo)
173. Innocent III* (1198-1216) (Lotario dei Segni)
174. Honorius III (1216-1227) (Cencio Savelli)
175. Gregory IX (1227-1241) (Ugolino dei Segni)
176. Celestine IV (1241) (Goffredo da Castiglione)
177. Innocent IV (1243-1254) (Sinibaldo Fieschi)
178. Alexander IV (1254-1261) (Rinaldo dei Segni)
179. Urban IV (1261-1264) (Jacques Pantaléon)
180. Clement IV (1265-1268) (Guy Foulques)

181. Bl. Gregory X (1271-1276) (Tedaldo Visconti)
182. Bl. Innocent V (1276) (Pierre of Tarentaise)
183. Hadrian V (1276) (Ottobono Fieschi)
184. John XXI (1276-1277) (Peter of Spain, Petrus Hispanus)
185. Nicholas III (1277-1280) (Giovanni Gaetano Orsini)
186. Martin IV⁹ (1281-1285) (Simon de Brie)
187. Honorius IV (1285-1287) (Giacomo Savelli)
188. Nicholas IV (1288-1294) (Girolamo Masci)
189. St. Celestine V (1294) (Pietro del Morrone)
190. Boniface VIII (1294-1303) (Benedetto Caetani)
191. Bl. Benedict XI (1301-1304) (Niccolo Boccasino)
192. Clement V (1305-1314) (Bertrand de Got)
193. John XXII (1316-1334) (Jacques Duèse)
    Nicholas V (1328-1330) (Pietro Rainalducci)
194. Benedict XII (1334-1342) (Jacques Fournier)
195. Clement VI (1342-1352) (Pierre Roger)
196. Innocent VI (1352-1362) (Etienne Aubert)
197. Bl. Urban V (1362-1370) (Guillaume de Grimoard)
198. Gregory XI (1370-1378) (Pierre Roger de Beaufort)
199. Urban VI (1378-1389) (Bartolomeo Prignano)¹⁰
    Clement (VII) (1378-1394) (Avignon) (Robert of Geneva)
200. Boniface IX (1389-1404) (Pietro Tomacelli)
    Benedict (XIII) (1394-1423) (Avignon) (Pedro de Luna)
201. Innocent VII (1404-1406) (Cosimo Migliorati)
202. Gregory XII (1406-1415) (Angelo Correr)
    Alexander V (1409-1410) (Pisa) (Pietro Philarghi)
    John (XXIII) (1410-1415) (Pisa) (Baldassare Cossa)
203. Martin V (1417-1431) (Oddo Colonna)
    Clement (VIII) (1423-1426) (Gil Sanchez Muñoz)

---

⁹Called Martin IV because Marinus I and II were erroneously listed as Martinus (Martin).

¹⁰The Great Western Schism* lasted from 1378 to 1415, with one line of popes in Rome, a second in Avignon, and after 1409 a third in Pisa. The list here follows the traditional reckoning of the Roman line as authentic. There was never a formal pronouncement by the Church to that effect, but it was tacitly acknowledged in subsequent popes' choices of numerical designations (Clement VII, Benedict XIII, John XXIII, but not Alexander VI).

Benedict (XIV) (1425-1430?) (Bernard Garnier)
204. Eugene (Eugenius) IV (1431-1447) (Gabriele Condulmaro)
    Felix V (1439-1449) (Amadeus of Savoy)
205. Nicholas V (1447-1455) (Tommaso Parentucelli)
206. Callistus III (1455-1458) (Alfonso de Borja [Borgia])
207. Pius II (1458-1464) (Enea Silvio Piccolomini)
208. Paul II (1464-1471) (Pietro Barbo)
209. Sixtus IV (1471-1484) (Francesco della Rovere)
210. Innocent VIII (1484-1492) (Giovanni Battista Cibo)
211. Alexander VI (1492-1503) (Rodrigo de Borja [Borgia])
212. Pius III (1503) (Francesco Todeschini)
213. Julius II (1503-1513) (Giuliano della Rovere)
214. Leo X (1513-1521) (Giovanni de' Medici)
215. Hadrian VI (1522-1523) (Adrian Florensz)
216. Clement VII (1523-1534) (Giulio de' Medici)
217. Paul III (1534-1549) (Alessandro Farnese)
218. Julius III (1550-1555) (Giovanni Maria Ciocchi del Monte)
219. Marcellus II (1555) (Marcello Cervini)
220. Paul IV (1555-1559) (Giampietro Carafa)
221. Pius IV (1559-1565) (Giovanni Angelo Medici)
222. St. Pius V (1566-1572) (Michele Ghisleri)
223. Gregory XIII (1572-1585) (Ugo Boncompagni)
224. Sixtus V (1585-1590) (Felice Peretti)
225. Urban VII (1590) (Giambattista Castagna)
226. Gregory XIV (1590-1591) (Niccolo Sfondrati)
227. Innocent IX (1591) (Giovanni Antonio Fachinetti)
228. Clement VIII (1592-1608) (Ippolito Aldobrandini)
229. Leo XI (1605) (Alessandro de' Medici)
230. Paul V (1605-1621) (Camillo Borghese)
231. Gregory XV (1621-1623) (Alessandro Ludovisi)
232. Urban VIII (1623-1644) (Maffeo Barberini)
233. Innocent X (1644-1655) (Giambattista Pamfili)
234. Alexander VII (1655-1667) (Fabio Chigi)
235. Clement IX (1667-1669) (Giulio Rospigliosi)
236. Clement X (1670-1676) (Emilio Altieri)
237. Bl. Innocent XI (1676-1689) (Benedetto Odescalchi)
238. Alexander VIII (1689-1691) (Pieto Ottoboni)
239. Innocent XII (1691-1700) (Antonio Pignatelli)
240. Clement XI (1700-1721) (Giovanni Francesco Albani)
241. Innocent XIII (1721-1724) (Michelangelo dei Conti)

242. Benedict XIII (1724-1730) (Pietro Francesco Orsini)
243. Clement XII (1730-1740) (Lorenzo Corsini)
244. Benedict XIV (1740-1758) (Prospero Lambertini)
245. Clement XIII (1758-1769) (Carlo Rezzonico)
246. Clement XIV (1769-1774) (Lorenzo Ganganelli)
247. Pius VI (1775-1799) (Giovanni Angelo Braschi)
248. Pius VII (1800-1823) (Luigi Barnaba Chiaramonte)
249. Leo XII (1823-1829) (Annibale della Genga)
250. Pius VIII (1829-1830) (Francesco Saverio Castiglione)
251. Gregory XVI (1830-1846) (Bartolomeo Alberto Cappellari)
252. Pius IX* (1846-1878) (Giovanni Maria Mastai-Ferretti)
253. Leo XIII* (1878-1903) (Gioacchino Vincenzo Pecci)
254. St. Pius X* (1903-1914) (Giuseppe Sarto)
255. Benedict XV* (1914-1922) (Giacomo della Chiesa)
256. Pius XI* (1922-1939) (Achille Ratti)
257. Pius XII* (1939-1958) (Eugenio Pacelli)
258. John XXIII* (1958-1963) (Angelo Roncalli)
259. Paul VI* (1963-1978) (Giovanni Battista Montini)
260. John Paul I* (1978) (Albino Luciani)
261. John Paul II* (1978-) (Karol Wojtyla)

Appendix II

Ecumenical Councils

Twenty-one councils are commonly reckoned as ecumenical by Catholics. There is no official list, however, and the ecumenicity of some (especially Constantinople IV) is questioned by some Catholic scholars. Only the first seven councils are recognized as ecumenical by the Eastern Orthodox.

For more information, see entry in Dictionary on each council as well as the entry, COUNCIL. (For the seventeenth council, see entries on BASEL, COUNCIL OF and FLORENCE, COUNCIL OF.)

1. Nicaea I (325)
2. Constantinople I (381)
3. Ephesus (431)
4. Chalcedon (451)
5. Constantinople II (553)
6. Constantinople III (680-681)
7. Nicaea II (787)
8. Constantinople IV (869-870)
9. Lateran I (1123)
10. Lateran II (1139)
11. Lateran III (1179)
12. Lateran IV (1215)
13. Lyons I (1245)
14. Lyons II (1274)
15. Vienne (1311-1312)
16. Constance (1414-1418)
17. Basel-Ferrara-Florence-Rome (1431-1445)
18. Lateran V (1512-1517)

19. Trent (1545-1563)
20. Vatican I (1869-1870)
21. Vatican II (1962-1965)

Appendix III

The Documents of Vatican Council II

The Second Vatican Council* (1962-1965) issued sixteen documents, by far the largest output of any ecumenical council in the history of the Church. Four of these documents are called "Constitutions," which set forth fundamental principles. Nine are "Decrees," which address questions that have practical significance. Three are "Declarations," which set forth positions on specific issues. The synopsis below deals with the Constitutions, Decrees, and Declarations in that order. Within each category, documents are summarized in chronological order of their acceptance by the Council and promulgation by the pope.

Constitutions

Constitution on the Sacred Liturgy (Sacrosanctum concilium). December 4, 1963. The liturgy*, especially the celebration of the eucharist*, is the central act of the Church, "the high point towards which the activity of the Church is directed, and ... the source from which all its power flows out" (10). Believers should "take a full, conscious and active part in liturgical celebration" (14). This requires that liturgy be intelligible to them. To promote participation and intelligibility, the rituals for the eucharist* and the other sacraments*, the sacramentals*, and the Liturgy of the Hours* should be reformed. The liturgical calendar* should be reformed in order to give priority to the central mysteries of Christian faith, celebrated in the different liturgical seasons.

Dogmatic Constitution on the Church (Lumen gentium). November 21, 1964. The Church, as a reality combining a divine and a human element, is a *mystery**. It is a *sacrament** or outward sign of the communion that God brings about in Christ. As a human reality it is affected by sin and is always in need of purification. It is the new "People of God"* made one in Christ. As such, all members share in Christ's threefold ministry as priest, prophet, and king. Only Catholics are "fully incorporated into the society of the Church" (14), but other Christians and devout non-Christians, even morally upright unbelievers, are joined to the People of God in some way. Within the people of God, ordained ministers are set apart for special forms of service. The document reaffirms what Vatican I* said about the pope* but concentrates on bishops*, who form a "college," headed by the pope, who together share supreme authority* in the Church. The laity* share in Christ's priestly, prophetic, and kingly functions chiefly in their activities in the secular world, but the institutional Church has need of their expertise, and they have the right and sometimes the duty to make their opinions known. All members of the Church are equally called to holiness*, but different categories of person in the Church have different ways toward holiness. The way of religious life*, following the evangelical counsels* of poverty, chastity, and obedience, has special dignity. The Church will attain its full perfection only at the end of time, but its members on earth are joined with those members who are united with God in Christ in heaven, namely, the saints*. The document concludes with a chapter on Mary*, which was formerly a separate document. As the Mother of the Son of God, Mary occupies the highest place in the Church after Christ, a role that does not diminish the uniqueness of Christ as redeemer. Most of the Council's "Decrees" provide more specific applications of principles contained in this document.

Dogmatic Constitution on Divine Revelation (Dei verbum). November 18, 1965. God has revealed himself definitively in Christ. This revelation* was committed to the apostles* and transmitted by them through the written Scriptures and oral tradition*. "Tradition and scripture together form a single sacred deposit of the word of God, entrusted to the Church" (10). The task of interpreting it has been given to the teaching authority (magisterium*) of the Church, which "is not above the word of God but stands at its service" (10). Sacred Scripture, Old and New Testaments, is inspired by God and teaches "without error such truth as God, for the sake of our salvation, wished the biblical text to contain" (11). Its human authors were true authors, however, writing in human fashion, and to understand their meaning it is necessary to use the methods of historical investigation and literary criticism. The council encourages the study of the Scripture by clergy, biblical scholars, theologians, and the church at large, as well as non-Christians. To aid in this study, translations are to be made from the original languages.

Pastoral Constitution on the Church in the Modern World (Gaudium et spes). December 7, 1965. This document provides a synthesis of Catholic social teaching* as it stood at the time of the Council. In an introduction, the Council Fathers take up a stance of dialogue and service toward the modern world, in which the rapid pace of social change has caused both great hope and great anguish. Part one, in four chapters, develops general principles. The document begins from the unique dignity of the human person, created in God's image, redeemed in Christ. It addresses the causes of modern atheism* and calls for solidarity between believers and unbelievers toward the betterment of the world. Chapter two considers the social nature of the human being and the need to pursue the common good while respecting the rights of individuals. The third chapter deals with the value of human action, the autonomy of secular affairs and disciplines, and the incompleteness of human activity, perfected only at the end of time. Chapter Four speaks of the interrelation of the Church and the world. To the world the Church can offer an awareness of God as the goal of human life and the ground of human dignity and community, but the Church can in turn learn from the disciplines and techniques of secular society. Part two of the document turns to specific issues: marriage and the family, the development of culture, economic development and justice, the political community, and the avoidance of war and the promotion of peace.

Decrees

Decree on the Instruments of Social Communication [Mass Media] (Inter mirifica). December 4, 1963. The Church may and must use contemporary media of communication. The use of mass media must be subject to moral norms. Human beings have a right to be informed about matters that affect them.

Decree on the Eastern Catholic Churches (Orientalium ecclesiarum). November 21, 1964. The Council expresses respect for the Eastern Catholic Churches*, whose rites* are of equal dignity with the Latin Rite. Their distinctive liturgical and spiritual heritages are to be preserved. The Eastern Catholic Churches can play a special role in promoting reunion with the separated Eastern churches.

Decree on Ecumenism (Unitatis redintegratio). November 21, 1964. The Council desires to promote the restoration of unity* among all Christians. It recognizes that many authentic elements of the life of the Church are present among the separated Christians of the East and the West (chiefly Orthodox and Protestants). It acknowledges that blame for Christian divisions often lies on both sides. A united Church can and should have a healthy diversity in spiritual life, discipline, ritual, and theology. The work of ecumenism* requires a repentance of past offenses against unity. It calls for some common prayer and worship, study of the traditions of others, and action together, but not a spirit of hasty compromise. In considering differences of doctrine, Catholics should be aware of the "hierarchy of truths"* (11).

Decree on the Pastoral Office of Bishops in the Church (Christus Dominus). October 28, 1965. After a preface on the primacy of the pope and the authority of the bishops as successors of the apostles, the document considers the role of bishops in (1) the universal Church, (2) their own dioceses*, and (3) episcopal regions, devoting one chapter to each. It calls for the establishment of the Synod* of Bishops, with delegates from throughout the world, to assist the pope. It also calls for a reform of the Roman Curia* to make it more representative of the universal Church. Within the diocese, the bishop's tasks are to teach and to preach, to oversee sacramental life, and to foster the holiness of the Church. He is assisted by coadjutor and auxiliary bishops, the diocesan curia* and councils, the diocesan clergy, and religious. Civil authorities are no longer to have any right to nominate or select bishops. Episcopal conferences* are to be established everywhere.

Decree on the Appropriate Renewal of Religious Life (Perfectae caritatis). October 28, 1965. The renewal of religious life* is to be governed by (a) a continual "return to the sources of Christian life in general" (2), that is, Jesus Christ and his gospel, and to the original inspiration of the particular religious community, and (b) the accommodation of the community to the particular circumstances of its time, place, and work. Such renewal is to be accomplished by religious communities themselves.

Decree on Priestly Formation (Optatam totius). October 28, 1965. Major seminaries* should aim to prepare priests for pastoral work. Doctrinal and pastoral training should be closely linked with spiritual formation. Candidates need special training for celibacy*. They should have opportunities to gain pastoral experience. Their academic program should build on a base of education in the humanities and sciences. In seminary studies, philosophy* and theology* should be integrated. Dogmatic and moral theology* should be clearly based in Scripture. Seminarians should learn about separated Christians and other religions. There is a need for continuing education of priests after ordination. Episcopal conferences are to develop specific "Programs of Priestly Formation" for their regions.

Decree on the Apostolate of the Laity (Apostolicam actuositatem). November 18, 1965. The apostolate of the laity* derives from their participation as members of the Church in Christ's ministry of teaching, sanctifying, and governing. The laity's distinctive ministry is exercised in the temporal (secular) order; they are to permeate it with the spirit of the gospel and thus perfect it (2,5). Some specific areas of lay apostolate in the world are the family, ministry to youth, the social environment, and national and international affairs (9). Laypeople also can and should play an active role in the life and work of the Church (10). Their apostolates can be exercised as individuals or through the formation of groups, such as those known as "Catholic Action" (20). Catholic institutions should see to the proper formation of laity for their apostolates.

Decree on the Missionary Activity of the Church (Ad gentes). December 7, 1965. This decree is about missions* in the sense of "evangelization and the establishing of the Church among peoples and groups in whom it has not yet taken root" (6). Missionary work is essential to the Church, based in God's call to all human beings to share his life through Christ in the Holy Spirit. Christian witness should be shown in efforts to educate people and to eliminate famine and disease. The gospel is to be proclaimed and a community of Christians formed. It is to be desired that the local church produce its own priests, deacons, lay catechists, and religious. The Church should be genuinely incarnated into the different human cultures. "From the customs and traditions of their own peoples, from their wisdom and learning, from their arts and sciences, these churches borrow everything which can contribute to praising the glory of the creator, to making manifest the grace of the Savior and to the due regulation of Christian life" (22).

Decree on the Ministry and Life of Priests (Presbyterorum ordinis). December 7, 1965. From the People of God*, all of whom share in Christ's priesthood, some are set apart by ordination for a special priestly ministry of proclamation of the Word of God, administration of the sacraments, and shepherding (pastoring) God's people in the name of their bishop*. The ministry of priests* is subordinate to and derivative of that of the bishop. Within a diocese*, all priests are united sacramentally in a collective body called a "presbytery." A council or senate of priests should be established in each diocese to represent the presbytery. The particular form of holiness to which priests are called is determined by their ministry. The Council praises celibacy* as particularly appropriate to this ministry but does not propose to change the practice of a married priesthood in the Eastern Churches.

Declarations

Declaration on Christian Education (Gravissimum educationis). October 28, 1965. The document sets forth basic principles that every human being has a right to an education, which should be a formation of the whole person, physical and moral as well as intellectual, and every Christian a right to a Christian education. It goes on to consider education in the family, religious education programs, Catholic schools, Catholic colleges and universities, and schools of theology.

Declaration on the Relation of the Church to Non-Christian Religions (Nostra aetate). October 28, 1965. All human beings have a common origin and destiny in God. People of all religions* experience the same mysteries of the human condition and have some perception of God.

"The Catholic Church rejects nothing of those things which are true and holy in" Hinduism* and Buddhism* and other religions. Their teachings and ways of life "frequently reflect a ray of that truth which enlightens everyone" (2). The Church holds Muslims in special esteem as fellow-worshipers of the one God who venerate Jesus and Mary. Catholics should engage in dialogue and common action with those of other religions. The Church is specially linked to the Jews, among whom was the origin of its own faith and who "remain very dear to God." Jews should not be blamed collectively for the death of Christ, nor should they be "represented as rejected by God or accursed" (4). The Church reproves all persecution and discrimination, as well as any displays of anti-Semitism (*see* JUDAISM).

Declaration on Religious Freedom (Dignitatis humanae). December 7, 1965. The Council consciously sets out to "develop" Church teaching on religious freedom*. The human person has a right to religious freedom. This right is founded in "the dignity of the human person as this is known from the revealed word of God and from reason itself" (2). People may not be coerced into violating their consciences* nor prevented from acting in accord with their consciences (within limits set by moral norms and the common welfare). Because human persons are social, religious freedom requires free public exercise and profession of religion for collective religious bodies (e.g., churches) as well as individuals. Jesus did not coerce, nor did the apostles, though at times in the history of the Church "there have been ways of acting hardly in tune with the spirit of the gospel, indeed contrary to it" (12).

Appendix IV

Papal Encyclicals

Two hundred and eighty-nine encyclicals* have appeared between the first, *Ubi primum*, by Benedict XIV in 1740 and early 1996. Some of the more important, including all those of Pope John Paul II*, are summarized below. English translations of all encyclicals up to 1981 may be found in Claudia Carlen, IHM, ed., *The Papal Encyclicals (1740-1981)*, 5 vols. (n.p.: McGrath, 1981). Volume and page references and subtitles up to 1981 are from Carlen.

1. Benedict XIV. *Ubi primum*. "On the duties of bishops." December 3, 1740. Carlen I: 5-8. Enjoins care in the ordination of priests, establishment of seminaries, residency in one's diocese, visitation of parishes, and similar responsibilities.

33. Gregory XVI. *Mirari vos*. "On liberalism and indifferentism." August 15, 1832. I: 235-242. Defends church discipline, papal authority, clerical celibacy, indissolubility of marriage. Attacks indifferentism (the view that one may gain salvation no matter what kind of religion one professes), liberty of conscience, freedom of publication, and rebellion against lawful civil authority.

63. Pius IX*. *Quanta cura*. "Condemning current errors." December 8, 1864. I: 381-386. Attacks the removal of religion from civil society and the notion that civil authorities should not punish offenses against the Catholic religion. Defends temporal power of the pope. The *Syllabus of Errors** was attached to this letter.

80. Leo XIII*. *Aeterni patris*. "On the restoration of Christian philosophy." August 4, 1879. II: 15-27. Praises the role of philosophy

in theology and the defense of Christian faith. Urges the restoration and dissemination of the philosophy of St. Thomas Aquinas*.

115. Leo XIII. *Rerum novarum.* "On capital and labor." May 15, 1891. II: 241-261. The first major document of modern Catholic social teaching*. Criticizes abuse of workers in industrial society. Defends right to private property. Sets forth duties of workers and employers and right of worker to a just wage. The state may intervene in the economic order to promote the interests of the poor or the common good. Workers have the right to form unions.

128. Leo XIII. *Providentissimus Deus.* "On the study of Holy Scripture." November 18, 1893. II: 325-339. The Church's first official response to modern biblical scholarship. Encourages study of Bible in seminaries and universities. Defends Bible's trustworthiness. There is no conflict between the Bible and natural science because biblical writers were not intending to teach science. Rejects view that inspiration* and inerrancy* are limited to passages that deal with faith and morals.

134. Leo XIII. *Longinqua (oceani).* "On Catholicism in the United States." January 6, 1895. II: 363-370. Praises American people and bishops. Acknowledges that American Constitution has allowed the Church to grow without impediment but denies that the American model offers the most desirable status for the Church. Praises the recent foundation of The Catholic University of America. Defends the appointment of an apostolic legate to the United States [an appointment opposed by most United States bishops]. Prefers all-Catholic labor organizations over those that combine Catholics and non-Catholics.

174. Pius X*. *Pascendi dominici gregis.* "On the doctrines of the Modernists." September 8, 1907. III: 71-98. Presents Modernism* as a "synthesis of all heresies," based in "agnosticism" and a denial of the supernatural. Rejects interpretation of dogma* as symbol rather than truth statement. Establishes procedures for vigilance against Modernism.

208. Pius XI*. *Casti connubii.* "On Christian marriage." December 31, 1930. III: 391-414. Praises Christian marriage*. Attacks divorce*, cohabitation, contraception (while leaving some room for the use of

natural methods of birth control*), abortion*, eugenic sterilization, and treatment of marriage as a purely human institution.

209. Pius XI. *Quadragesimo anno*. "On reconstruction of the social order." May 15, 1931. III: 415-443. Commemorates the fortieth anniversary of *Rerum novarum* and develops its thought to apply to the political and economic turmoil of Europe in the Depression. Criticizes capitalism* and socialism*, favoring an economy based in corporate entities based in vocations; appraises fascism noncommittally. Introduces concept of social justice and principle of subsidiarity*.

218. Pius XI. *Mit brennender Sorge*. "On the Church and the German Reich." March 14, 1937. III: 525-535. Attacks intimidation of the Church by the National Socialist regime in Germany. Condemns exaltation of state over church and Germanic paganism over traditional Christianity.

225. Pius XII*. *Mystici corporis Christi*. "On the Mystical Body of Christ." June 29, 1943. IV: 37-63. Develops a theology of the Church as the Mystical Body of Christ, with Christ as its head. Treats of the union of the faithful with Christ in his body. Identifies the Roman Catholic Church with the Mystical Body of Christ on earth.

226. Pius XII. *Divino afflante Spiritu*. "On promoting biblical studies, commemorating the fiftieth anniversary of *Providentissimus Deus*." September 30, 1943. IV: 64-79. Encourages Catholic scholars to make use of the methods of modern biblical criticism*, including biblical archaeology, textual criticism, and the study of the literary forms of biblical works. Encourages study of biblical texts in their original languages.

240. Pius XII. *Humani generis*. "Concerning some false opinions threatening to undermine the foundations of Catholic doctrine." August 12, 1950. IV: 175-184. Allows (without asserting) theory of evolution* as an explanation of the origin of the human body but insists on the direct divine creation of the human soul*. Expresses skepticism that polygenism (more than one pair of original human beings) can be reconciled with divine revelation. Criticizes various teachings associated with the "new theology," the revival of theology in France after World War II.

267. John XXIII*. *Mater et magistra.* "On Christianity and social progress." May 15, 1961. V: 59-90. Reviews prior Catholic social teaching and develops it to apply to current conditions. Affirms subsidiarity, but increasing socialization* calls for a greater role for the state in protection of workers and the poor. Calls for justice in relations between developed and less-developed nations and for increased international cooperation.

270. John XXIII. *Pacem in terris.* "On establishing universal peace in truth, justice, charity, and liberty." April 11, 1963. V: 107-129. Sets forth a broad range of human rights* and related duties. Considers rights and duties in the relation between individuals and public authorities, relations between states, and the relation of individuals and political communities with the whole world community.

273. Paul VI*. *Mysterium fidei.* "On the Holy Eucharist." September 3, 1965. V: 165-177. Defends (1) legitimacy of private masses (with only the priest present), (2) necessity of the term "transubstantiation" to characterize the change of bread and wine into Christ's body and blood, (3) Christ's continued presence in consecrated hosts that remain after the celebration of the mass.

275. Paul VI. *Populorum progressio.* "On the development of peoples." March 26, 1967. V:183-201. Asserts that development is not merely economic but must involve people's full humanity, including moral, cultural, and spiritual dimensions. It entails a willingness to cooperate peaceably with others in pursuit of the common good. Addresses the structural causes of the gap between rich and poor nations and calls for justice among nations.

276. Paul VI. *Sacerdotalis caelibatus.* "On the celibacy of the priest." June 24, 1967. V: 203-221. Defends requirement of celibacy* for priests in the Roman rite. Celibacy is an imitation of the celibate Christ and a sign of his universal love. It signifies the priest's total dedication to the service of the Church on earth and the Kingdom of God to come.

277. Paul VI. *Humanae vitae.* "On the regulation of birth." July 25, 1968. V: 223-236. Condemns artificial birth control* (contraception) as violating the proper orientation of sexual intercourse to the transmission of human life. Accepts natural methods of spacing births

through timing of sexual intercourse for infertile times in a woman's ovulatory cycle.

278. John Paul II*. *Redemptor hominis.* "On redemption and the dignity of the human race." March 4, 1979. V: 245-273. Considers the internal relation between redemption in Christ and human dignity. Christ has in a sense united himself with each person. Because Christ is the "way" for the Church, every human being is the "way" for the Church. Contemporary humans are increasingly threatened by their own products. The full development of persons is the criterion for assessing technological progress.

279. John Paul II. *Dives in misericordia.* "On the mercy of God." November 30, 1980. V: 275-298. Christ is the incarnation and revelation of the Father's mercy. In the contemporary world, in which people feel threatened by war, domination through technology, and economic injustice, solutions based on justice alone are not enough. Mercy is "the most profound source of justice" (145). The Church must proclaim God's mercy and put it into practice.

280. John Paul II. *Laborem exercens.* "On human work." September 14, 1981. V: 299-326. The dignity of work* lies in the worker, the "subject" of work, whose self-expression work is. Workers are encouraged to solidarity* in pursuit of social justice. Labor has a priority over capital, which results from labor. Workers should participate in the direction of their industries. Through work, humans share in God's creative activity and Christ's life, death, and resurrection.

281. John Paul II. *Slavorum apostoli.* "Commemorating Sts. Cyril and Methodius, on the eleventh centenary of the death of St. Methodius." June 2, 1985. *Origins* 15 (1985-1986): 113, 115-125. Extols Cyril and Methodius* as pioneers of ecumenism, in their concern for the whole Church, East and West, and their work as a model of inculturation*, in incarnating the Gospel in Slavic culture.

282. John Paul II. *Dominum et vivificantem.* "On the Holy Spirit in the Church and the world." May 18, 1986. *Origins* 16 (1986-1987): 77, 79-102. Completes a trilogy (with 278 and 279) on the trinitarian persons. Discusses the Holy Spirit in the Trinity and as gift to the

Church. Understands sin as the refusal to accept the love that is the Holy Spirit. Sees the Spirit as the "giver of life," overcoming our culture's materialism and its signs of death, for example, abortion, war, terrorism.

283. John Paul II. *Redemptoris mater*. "On the role of Mary in the mystery of Christ and her active and exemplary presence in the world." March 25, 1987. *Origins* 16 (1986-1987): 745, 747-766. Treats of Mary's relation to redemption in Christ and her position at the center of the Church. Discusses her importance in ecumenism, especially with the Eastern churches. Understands Mary's mediation (between God and humans) as a distinctively maternal sharing in the one mediation of Christ. Announces a Marian Year for 1987-1988.

284. John Paul II. *Sollicitudo rei socialis*. "On social concerns, on the twentieth anniversary of *Populorum Progressio*." December 30, 1987. *Origins* 17 (1987-1988): 641, 643-660. Sees deterioration in progress toward human development since 1967, shown especially in the widening gap between the few rich and the many poor, increased unemployment and underemployment, and growing international debt. Authentic human development includes human rights and concern for ecology*. Failures of true development show the power of "structures of sin." These are overcome by the "virtue" of solidarity*, which involves a recognition of interdependence and a collaboration to pursue the common good and is the path to peace and development.

285. John Paul II. *Redemptoris missio*. "On the permanent validity of the Church's missionary mandate." December 7, 1990. *Origins* 20 (1990-1991): 541, 543-568. Affirms uniqueness of Jesus as savior; salvation is offered in him to all persons. Missionary evangelization* is the primary service that the Church can render to the world. There is great need for missions* to non-Christians and for re-evangelization of formerly Christian people. Interreligious dialogue is not a replacement for evangelization but a part of it.

286. John Paul II. *Centesimus annus*. "Commemorating the centenary of *Rerum novarum* and addressing the social question in a contemporary perspective." May 1, 1991. *Origins* 21 (1991-1992): 1, 3-24. Looks back at *Rerum novarum* and affirms its basic principles. Examines

social questions in the light of recent events, chiefly the collapse of "real socialism" (Communism) in Europe. Gives qualified approval to capitalism* and democracy, but they must respect human rights and human dignity. Condemns "consumerist" possession-oriented lifestyle, ecological destruction, destruction of the family, marginalization of Third World people, and other social evils.

287. John Paul II. *Veritatis splendor.* "Regarding certain fundamental questions of the Church's moral teaching." August 6, 1993. *Origins* 23 (1993-1994): 297, 299-334. Blames false teachings in moral theology on an over-exaltation of human freedom, neglecting its dependence on truth. States that there are certain specific kinds of action that are intrinsically morally evil, regardless of intention, consequences, or circumstances.

288. John Paul II. *Evangelium vitae ["The Gospel of Life"].* March 25, 1995. *Origins* 24 (1994-1995): 689, 691-727. Sees a "culture of death" developing, against which Christianity proclaims a "gospel of life." Confirms "that the direct and voluntary killing of an innocent human being is always gravely immoral" (57). Declares "that direct abortion ... always constitutes a grave moral disorder" (62). Confirms "that euthanasia is a grave violation of the law of God" (65). States that civil laws permitting these evils do not bind and must be resisted. Also condemns assisted suicide*, infanticide, contraception, and artificial methods of reproduction and attacks capital punishment*. Exhorts the Church to protect life and promote a "culture of life."

289. John Paul II. *Ut unum sint.* "On commitment to ecumenism." May 25, 1995. *Origins* 25 (1995-1996): 49, 51-72. Presents ecumenism* as an organic part of the Church's activity. Reviews progress in ecumenism with separated churches of the East and West. Calls for further dialogue and reception of results already achieved. Speaks of the papacy as a ministry of unity and pledges to look for "a way of exercising the primacy" that is open to the new ecumenical situation (95).

Appendix V

Prayers

1. Our Father (The Lord's Prayer) (traditional wording). Our Father, who art in heaven, hallowed be thy name. Thy kingdom come, thy will be done on earth as it is in heaven. Give us this day our daily bread, and forgive us our trespasses as we forgive those who trespass against us. And lead us not into temptation, but deliver us from evil. (For thine is the kingdom, the power, and the glory, forever and ever.) Amen.

> This prayer is from Matthew 6.9-13 (see also Lk 11.2). The line in parentheses appears in some manuscripts of Matthew, though not the best ones, and in the *Didachē**. Catholics usually do not include it in the Lord's Prayer. In the mass, the line, in modern English, is used as a congregational response after the priest's prayer, "Deliver us, O Lord, from all evil ...," which follows the recitation of the Lord's Prayer up to "Deliver us from evil": "For the kingdom, the power, and the glory are yours, now and forever."

2. Hail Mary. Hail, Mary, full of grace, the Lord is with you. Blessed are you among women, and blessed is the fruit of your womb, Jesus. Holy Mary, mother of God, pray for us sinners now and at the hour of our death. Amen.

> The first two sentences are based on Lk 1.28 and Lk 1.42. The last sentence, in its present form, dates from the sixteenth century.

3. Doxology (Glory to the Father, Glory Be). Glory (be) to the Father, and to the Son, and to the Holy Spirit, as it was in the beginning, is now, and will be forever. Amen.

4. The Apostles' Creed.

I believe in God, the Father almighty, creator of heaven and earth.

I believe in Jesus Christ, his only Son, our Lord. He was conceived by the power of the Holy Spirit and born of the Virgin Mary. He suffered under Pontius Pilate, was crucified, died, and was buried. He descended to the dead. On the third day he rose again. He ascended into heaven and is seated at the right hand of the Father. He will come again to judge the living and the dead.

I believe in the Holy Spirit, the holy catholic Church, the communion of saints, the forgiveness of sins, the resurrection of the body, and the life everlasting. Amen.

On the origin of this and the following creed, see CREED. This version is that of the International Consultation on English Texts, approved for use in the liturgy and published in the Roman Sacramentary.

5. The Nicene Creed (Niceno-Constantinopolitan Creed).

We believe in one God, the Father, the Almighty, maker of heaven and earth, of all that is seen and unseen.

We believe in one Lord, Jesus Christ, the only Son of God, eternally begotten of the Father, God from God, Light from Light, true God from true God, begotten, not made, one in Being with the Father. Through him all things were made. *For us men and for our salvation he came down from heaven: by the power of the Holy Spirit he was born of the Virgin Mary, and became man.*[1] For our sake he was crucified under Pontius Pilate; he suffered, died, and was buried. On the third day he rose again in fulfillment of the Scriptures; he ascended into heaven and is seated at the right hand of the Father. He will come again in glory to judge the living and the dead, and his kingdom will have no end.

---

[1]In 1995, the U.S. bishops approved the replacement of the words between asterisks with: "For us and our salvation he came down from heaven, was incarnate of the Holy Spirit and the Virgin Mary and was made man."

We believe in the Holy Spirit, the Lord, the giver of life, who proceeds from the Father and the Son. With the Father and the Son he is worshiped and glorified. He has spoken through the Prophets. We believe in one holy catholic and apostolic Church. We acknowledge one baptism for the forgiveness of sins. We look for the resurrection of the dead, and the life of the world to come. Amen.

This translation is that approved by the International Commission on English in the Liturgy and published in the Roman Sacramentary.

6. Hail, Holy Queen (Salve Regina). Hail, Holy Queen, mother of mercy, our life, our sweetness and our hope. To you do we cry, poor banished children of Eve. To you do we send up our sighs, mourning and weeping in this valley of tears. Turn then, most gracious advocate, your eyes of mercy toward us, and after this exile show us the blessed fruit of your womb, Jesus. O clement, O loving, O sweet Virgin Mary.
Pray for us, O holy mother of God,
—that we may be made worthy of the promises of Christ. Amen.

This prayer dates from the eleventh or twelfth century.

7. Memorare. Remember, O most gracious Virgin Mary, that never was it known that anyone who fled to your protection, implored your help, or sought your intercession was left unaided. Inspired by this confidence, I fly unto you, O Virgin of virgins, my mother. To you do I come, before you I stand, sinful and sorrowful. O Mother of the Word incarnate, despise not my petitions, but in your mercy hear and answer me. Amen.

This prayer, whose earliest texts date from the fifteenth century, was later ascribed to St. Bernard of Clairvaux* (1090-1153).

Bibliography

Despite its length, this bibliography is highly selective. It concentrates mainly on books in English, especially ones published recently in the United States. Readers desiring further references are directed to the bibliographies of the books listed here.

Outline of Bibliography

I. Bibliographies
II. Reference Works
III. Periodicals
    A. Periodical Index
    B. Directory
    C. Newspapers
    D. Popular Magazines
    E. Semipopular Periodicals
    F. Scholarly/Academic Journals
    G. Trade, Professional, Special-Interest Publications
    H. Selected Periodicals Published Outside the United States
IV. Official Church Documents
V. Series of Primary Texts and Translations
VI. General Works on Catholicism
VII. History
    A. General
    B. Specific Periods and Places
        1. Ancient Church
        2. Byzantine Church
        3. Medieval and Renaissance Church in the West
        4. Counter-Reformation and Modern Church to Vatican II
        5. Contemporary Period: Vatican II and After
        6. Asia and Africa
        7. Latin America
        8. The United States
        9. Missions
        10. Monasticism and Religious Orders and Congregations
VIII. Bible
    A. Edition with Commentary

I. Bibliographies (listed alphabetically by title)

"American Catholic Bibliography 1970-1982." By James Hennessey. Charles and Margaret Hall Cushwa Center for the Study of American Catholicism, University of Notre Dame, Working Paper. Series 12, No. 1. Fall 1982.

The Church: A Bibliography. By Avery Dulles and Patrick Granfield. Wilmington, Del.: Michael Glazier, 1985.

Critical Guide to Catholic Reference Books. By James Patrick McCabe. 2d ed. Littleton, Colo.: Libraries Unlimited, 1980 (1971).

A Guide to American Catholic History. By John Tracy Ellis and Robert Trisco. 2d ed. Santa Barbara, Calif.: ABC-Clio, 1982.

The Laity: A Bibliography. By Leonard Doohan. Wilmington, Del.: Michael Glazier, 1987.

Liberation Theologies: A Research Guide. By Ronald G. Musto. New York: Garland, 1991.

Papal Pronouncements: A Guide: 1740-1978. By Claudia Carlen. 2 vols. Ann Arbor, Mich.: Pierian, 1990.

The Peace Tradition in the Catholic Church: An Annotated Bibliography. By Ronald G. Musto. New York: Garland, 1987.

"Supplement to American Catholic Bibliography 1970-1982." By James Hennessey. Charles and Margaret Hall Cushwa Center for the Study of American Catholicism, University of Notre Dame, Working Paper. Series 14, No. 1. Fall 1983.

Theological and Religious Reference Materials. By G. E. Gorman and Lyn Gorman, with the assistance of Donald N. Matthews. 3 vols. Westport, Conn.: Greenwood, 1984-86.

II. Reference Works (listed alphabetically by title; some more specific reference works are listed in the subject classifications below)

Annuario Pontificio. Vatican City: Libreria Editrice Vaticana, annual.

The Blackwell Encyclopedia of Modern Christian Thought. Alister E. McGrath, ed. Oxford: Blackwell, 1993.

Butler's Lives of the Saints. Complete edition, edited, revised, and supplemented by Herbert Thurston and Donald Attwater. 4 vols. New York: P. J. Kenedy, 1956.

The Catholic Almanac. Felician A. Foy, ed. Huntington, Ind.: Our Sunday Visitor, annual.

Catholic Customs and Traditions: A Popular Guide. By Greg Dues. Mystic, Conn.: Twenty-Third Publications, 1989.

The Catholic Encyclopedia. 16 vols. New York: Robert Appleton, 1907-12.

The Collegeville Pastoral Dictionary of Biblical Theology. Ed. Carroll Stuhlmueller. Collegeville, Minn.: Liturgical, 1996.

A Concise Dictionary of Theology. By Gerald O'Collins and Edward G. Farrugia. New York, Paulist, 1991.

Dictionary of American Catholic Biography. By John J. Delaney. Garden City, N.Y.: Doubleday, 1984.

Dictionary of the Bible. By John L. McKenzie. New York: Macmillan, 1965.

Dictionary of Catholic Devotions. By Michael Walsh. San Francisco: HarperSanFrancisco, 1995.

Dictionary of Christianity in America. Ed. Daniel G. Reid. Downers Grove, Ill.: InterVarsity, 1990.

Dictionary of the Ecumenical Movement. Ed. Nicholas Lossky, et al. Geneva: WCC Publications; Grand Rapids: William B. Eerdmans, 1991.

Dictionary of Fundamental Theology. Ed. René Latourelle and Rino Fisichella. New York: Crossroad, 1994.

Dictionary of the Middle Ages. Ed. Joseph R. Strayer. 13 vols. New York: Scribner, 1982-89.

Dictionary of Saints. By John J. Delaney. Garden City, N.Y.: Doubleday, 1980.

Dictionnaire d'Archéologie Chrétienne et de Liturgie. 15 vols. Paris: Letouzey et Ané, 1924-1953.

Dictionnaire d'Histoire et de Géographie Ecclésiastiques. 24 vols. through "H" (1993). Paris: Letouzey et Ané, 1912- .

Dictionnaire de Spiritualité, Ascétique et Mystique, Doctrine et Histoire. 16 vols. Paris: Beauchesne, 1936-1994.

Encyclopedia of American Religions. By J. Gordon Melton. Fourth ed. Detroit: Gale Research, 1993.

Encyclopedia of Early Christianity. Ed. Everett Ferguson. New York: Garland, 1990.

Encyclopedia of the Early Church. Ed. Angelo di Berardino. Foreword and Bibliographic amendments by W. H. C. Frend. Trans. Adrian Walford. 2 vols. New York: Oxford University Press, 1992.

The Encyclopedia of Religion. Ed. Mircea Eliade. 16 vols. New York: Macmillan, 1986.

Encyclopedia of Theology: The Concise Sacramentum Mundi. Ed. Karl Rahner. New York: Seabury, 1975.

Handbook of Catholic Theology. Ed. Wolfgang Beinert and Francis Schüssler Fiorenza. New York: Crossroad, 1995.

The HarperCollins Encyclopedia of Catholicism. Ed. Richard P. McBrien. San Francisco: HarperSanFrancisco, 1995.

Harper's Bible Dictionary. Paul J. Achtemeier, gen. ed. New York: Harper and Row, 1986.

Masterpieces of Catholic Literature in Summary Form. Ed. Frank N. Magill. New York: Harper and Row, 1965. [Summaries of 300 works.]

The Modern Catholic Dictionary. By John A. Hardon. Garden City: Doubleday, 1980.

The Modern Catholic Encyclopedia. Ed. Michael Glazier and Monika K. Hellwig. Collegeville, Minn.: Liturgical, 1994.

New Catholic Encyclopedia. 15 vols. New York: McGraw-Hill, 1967. Supplementary Volumes: Vol. 16: Washington, D.C.: Publishers Guild, 1974. Vol. 17: Washington, D.C.: The Catholic University of America Press, 1979. Vol. 18: Palatine, Ill.: Jack Heraty, 1988. Vol. 19: Palatine, Ill.: Jack Heraty, 1996.

The New Dictionary of Catholic Social Thought. Ed. Judith Dwyer. Collegeville, Minn.: Liturgical, 1994.

The New Dictionary of Catholic Spirituality. Ed. Michael Downey. Collegeville, Minn.: Liturgical, 1993.

The New Dictionary of Sacramental Worship. Ed. Peter E. Fink. Collegeville, Minn.: Liturgical, 1990.

The New Dictionary of Theology. Ed. Joseph A. Komonchak, Mary Collins, Dermot A. Lane. Wilmington, Del.: Michael Glazier, 1987.

The Official Catholic Directory. New Providence, N.J.: P. J. Kenedy in association with R. R. Bowker, annual. [Facts about the U.S. church, including complete lists of parishes and priests.]

The Oxford Dictionary of the Christian Church. Second edition. Ed. by F. L. Cross and E. A. Livingstone. New York: Oxford University Press, 1974.

The Oxford Dictionary of Popes. By J. N. D. Kelly. New York: Oxford University Press, 1986.

The Oxford Dictionary of Saints. By David Hugh Farmer. Third ed. New York: Oxford University Press, 1992.

The Oxford Encyclopedia of the Reformation. Ed. Hans J. Hillerbrand. 4 vols. New York: Oxford University Press, 1996.

III. Periodicals (selected Catholic periodicals published in the United States; most addresses are from *The Catholic Almanac 1995*)

A. Periodical Index

The Catholic Periodical and Literature Index. Haverford, Pa.: The Catholic Library Association. Published bimonthly with annual bound cumulation.

B. Directory

The Catholic Press Directory. Ronkonkoma, N.Y.: Catholic Press Association, annual.

C. Newspapers

Most Catholic dioceses publish official diocesan newspapers. The following nationally distributed newspapers do not have official standing.

Catholic Twin Circle. Weekly. 15760 Ventura Blvd., Suite 1201, Encino, Calif. 91436.

The Catholic Worker. 8 times a year. 36 E. First St., New York, N.Y. 10003. [See dictionary entry on Catholic Worker*.]

National Catholic Register. Weekly. 15760 Ventura Blvd., Suite 1201, Encino, Calif. 91436. [Conservative.]

National Catholic Reporter. Weekly. P.O. Box 419281. Kansas City, Mo. 64141. [Liberal.]

Our Sunday Visitor. Weekly. 200 Noll Plaza. Huntington, Ind. 46750.

The Wanderer. Weekly. 201 Ohio St., St. Paul, Minn. 55107. [Very conservative.]

D. Popular Magazines

The Bible Today. Bimonthly. Liturgical Press, Collegeville, Minn. 56321.

The Catholic Digest. Monthly. P.O. Box 64090, St. Paul, Minn. 55164.

New Covenant. Monthly. Our Sunday Visitor, Inc., 200 Noll Plaza, Huntington, Ind. 46750. [Charismatic Renewal* perspective.]

St. Anthony Messenger. Monthly. 1615 Republic St., Cincinnati, Ohio 45210. [Published by Franciscan friars.]

Salt. Monthly. 205 W. Monroe St., Chicago, Ill. 60606. [Published by Claretians; social action emphasis.]

Today's Parish. Monthly, September to May. P.O. Box 180, Mystic, Conn. 06355.

U.S. Catholic. Monthly. 205 W. Monroe St., Chicago, Ill. 60606. [Published by Claretians.]

E. Semipopular Periodicals

America. Weekly. 106 W. 56th St., New York, N.Y. 10019. [Opinion journal sponsored by U.S. and Canadian Jesuits*.]

Catholic World. Bimonthly. 997 Macarthur Blvd., Mahwah, N.J. 07430. [Published by Paulists*.]

Church. Quarterly. 299 Elizabeth St., New York, N.Y. 10012. [Published by National Pastoral Life Center.]

Commonweal. Biweekly. 15 Dutch St., Room 502. New York, N.Y. 10038. [Independent, lay-edited, liberal.]

Crisis. Monthly. 1511 K St., N.W., Suite 525, Washington, D.C. 20005. [Lay-edited, conservative.]

Homiletic and Pastoral Review. Monthly. 86 Riverside Dr., New York, N.Y. 10024. [Conservative.]

Modern Liturgy. 10 issues a year. 160 E. Virginia St., No. 290, San Jose, Calif. 95112.

The New Oxford Review. 10 issues a year. 1069 Kains Ave., Berkeley, Calif. 94706. [Independent, lay-edited.]

The Pope Speaks. Bi-monthly. Our Sunday Visitor, Inc., 200 Noll Plaza, Huntington, Ind. 46750. [Papal documents.]

F. Scholarly/Academic Journals

The American Catholic Philosophical Quarterly. Institute of Philosophical Studies, University of Dallas, Irving, Tex. 75062. [Journal of the American Catholic Philosophical Association. Formerly *The New Scholasticism.*]

Catholic Biblical Quarterly. Catholic University of America, Washington, D.C. 20064. [Journal of the Catholic Biblical Association.]

Catholic Historical Review. Quarterly. 620 Michigan Ave., N.E., Washington, D.C. 20064.

Communio: International Catholic Review. Quarterly. P.O. Box 4557, Washington, D.C. 20017.

Concilium. Bi-monthly. Orbis Press, P.O. Box 302, Maryknoll, N.Y. 10545. [Each issue published as a separate volume.]

Horizons. Semiannual. Villanova University, Villanova, Pa. 19085. [Journal of the College Theology Society.]

Journal of Hispanic-Latino Theology. Quarterly. St. John's Abbey, Collegeville, Minn. 56321.

Linacre Quarterly. 850 Elm Grove Rd., Elm Grove, Wisc. 53122. [Published by National Federation of Catholic Physicians Guilds.]

The Living Light. 3211 Fourth St., N.E., Washington, D.C. 20017. [Published by Department of Education, U.S. Catholic Conference.]

New Theology Review. Quarterly. Liturgical Press, Collegeville, Minn. 56321.

Theological Studies. Quarterly. 37th and O Sts., N.W., Washington, D.C. 20057. [Sponsored by U.S. Jesuits.]

Theology Digest. Quarterly. St. Louis University, 3634 Lindell Blvd., St. Louis, Mo. 63108.

The Thomist. Quarterly. 487 Michigan Ave., N.E., Washington, D.C. 20017. [Published by Dominican Fathers.]

U.S. Catholic Historian. Quarterly. 200 Noll Plaza, Huntington, Ind. 46750.

Worship. Bimonthly. Published by Liturgical Press, Collegeville, Minn. 56321. [Formerly *Orate Fratres.*]

G. Trade, Professional, Special-Interest Publications

The Catechist. 8 times a year. 330 Progress Rd., Dayton, Ohio 45449.

Catholic Library World. Quarterly. 461 W. Lancaster Ave., Haverford, Pa. 19041. [Published by Catholic Library Association.]

Health Progress. Monthly. 4455 Woodson Rd., St. Louis, Mo. 63134. [Published by Catholic Health Association.]

Religion Teacher's Journal. Monthly during school year. P.O. Box 180, Mystic, Conn. 06355.

Review for Religious. Bimonthly. Room 428, 3601 Lindell Blvd., St. Louis, Mo. 63108.

Sisters Today. Bimonthly. Liturgical Press, Collegeville, Minn. 56321.

H. Selected Periodicals Published Outside the United States

Downside Review. Downside Abbey, Stratton on Fosse, Bath, BA3 4RH, England.

Month. Monthly. 114 Mount St., London W1Y 6AH, England.

New Blackfriars. Blackfriars, Oxford, OX1 3LY, England. [Published by English Dominicans*.]

L'Osservatore Romano. Daily with weekly English edition. Via del Pellegrino. 00120 Vatican City. [The Vatican's official newspaper.]

Priests and People. Monthly. 1 King Street Cloisters, Clifton Walk, London W6 0QZ, England. [Formerly *The Clergy Review.*]

The Tablet. Weekly. 1 King Street Cloisters, Clifton Walk, London W6 0QZ, England.

The Way. Quarterly. 114 Mount St., London W1Y 6AN, England.

IV. Official Church Documents

Abbott, Walter M., general ed. *The Documents of Vatican II.* New York: America Press, 1966. [Translations with commentary.]

Acta Apostolicae Sedis. Vatican City: Libreria Editrice Vaticana, monthly. [The official publication of the Holy See.]

Carlen, Claudia, ed. *The Papal Encyclicals (1740-1981).* 5 vols. [Wilmington, N.C.]: McGrath, 1981.

Flannery, Austin, ed. *Vatican Council II: The Conciliar and Post-Conciliar Documents.* 2 vols. Collegeville, Minn.: Liturgical, 1975-1982. [Originally published by Costello Publishing Company. Volume 1 contains the 16 documents of the Council and 49 related post-conciliar documents. Volume 2 contains 57 more post-conciliar documents to 1982.]

Nolan, Hugh J., ed. *Pastoral Letters of the United States Catholic Bishops.* 5 vols. Washington, D.C.: National Conference of Catholic Bishops/United States Catholic Conference, 1989.

O'Brien, David J., and Thomas A. Shannon, eds. *Catholic Social Thought: The Documentary Heritage.* Maryknoll, N.Y.: Orbis, 1992. [Contains encyclicals numbered 115, 209, 267, 270, 275, 280, 284, 286 in Appendix IV above; also Vatican II, *Gaudium et Spes;* U.S. Bishops, *The Challenge of Peace** and *Economic Justice for All**; and other documents.]

Origins. Weekly publication of Catholic News Service. 3211 4th St., N.E., Washington, D.C., 20017. [Since 1972 has published official documents and other items, such as speeches by bishops, relevant to institutional Church in the United States.]

Rosales, Gaudencio B., and Catalino G. Arévalo, eds. *For All the Peoples of Asia: Federation of Asian Bishops' Conferences Documents from 1970 to 1991.* Maryknoll, N.Y.: Orbis, 1992.

Tanner, Norman P., ed. *Decrees of the Ecumenical Councils.* 2 vols. Washington, D.C.: Georgetown University Press, 1990. [Texts in original languages, usually Greek or Latin, with English translations.]

V. Series of Primary Texts and Translations

Ancient Christian Writers. 1946- . 56 volumes through 1996. English translations with notes and commentary. Now published by Paulist (New York). [Among authors discussed in this book, includes writings of

Athanasius, Augustine, the *Didachē*, Gregory of Nyssa, Gregory the
Great, Ignatius of Antioch, Irenaeus, Jerome, John Chrysostom, Justin
Martyr, Origen, Patrick, Tertullian.]

*The Ante-Nicene Fathers: Translations of the Writings of the Fathers down to
A.D. 325.* 1885-1896. 10 vols. Reprinted, Grand Rapids, Mich.:
Eerdmans, 1951. *The Classics of Western Spirituality.* New York:
Paulist, 1978- . 86 volumes through 1995. [In English. Not confined to
Catholic authors, but features them. Among authors discussed in this
book, includes volumes on Albert the Great and Thomas Aquinas,
Athanasius, Augustine, Robert Bellarmine, Bernard of Clairvaux,
Bonaventure, Catherine of Siena, Meister Eckhart, Francis and Clare of
Assisi, Francis de Sales and Jane de Chantal, Gregory of Nyssa,
Hildegard of Bingen, Ignatius of Loyola, John of the Cross, Julian of
Norwich, John Henry Newman, Origen, Pseudo-Dionysius, Teresa of
Avila, Vincent de Paul and Louise de Marillac.]

Corpus Christianorum Series Graeca. Turnhout: Brepols, 1977- . [Critical
Greek texts of patristic and medieval writers.]

Corpus Christianorum Series Latina. Turnhout: Brepols, 1953- . [Critical Latin
texts of patristic and medieval writers.]

Corpus Scriptorum Christianorum Orientalium. Louvain, 1903- . [Critical texts
in Arabic, Armenian, Coptic, Ethiopic, Syriac, and other languages, with
translations in Latin or modern languages.]

Corpus Scriptorum Ecclesiasticorum Latinorum. Vienna, 1866- . [Critical Latin
texts of patristic writings.]

The Fathers of the Church: A New Translation. 1947- . 93 volumes through
1995. Washington, D.C.: The Catholic University of America Press.

The Library of Christian Classics. Ed. John Baillie, John T. McNeill, and
Henry P. Van Dusen. 26 vols. Philadelphia: Westminster, 1953-1969.
[Translations of works from the second through the sixteenth centuries.]

Patrologia Orientalis. Paris, Turnhout, 1907-1986. 43 vols. [Patristic writings
in Arabic, Armenian, Coptic, and Ethiopic, with French, English, or
Italian translations.]

Patrologiae Cursus Completus Series Graeca [Patrologia Graeca]. Ed. J. P.
Migne. Paris, 1857-1866. 162 volumes. [Greek texts of patristic writings,
with Latin translations.]

Patrologiae Cursus Completus Series Latina [Patrologia Latina]. Ed. J. P.
Migne. Paris, 1844-1880. 221 volumes. Two Supplementary Volumes
published 1958-60. [Latin texts of patristic and medieval writings.]

*A Select Library of the Nicene and Post-Nicene Fathers of the Christian
Church.* Ed. Philip Schaff and Henry Wace. 1886-89. 28 vols. in two
series. Reprinted, Grand Rapids, Mich.: Eerdmans, 1956.

Sources Chrétiennes. Paris: Cerf, 1941- . 406 volumes through 1995. [Critical
Greek and Latin patristic texts with French translations.]

VI. General Works on Catholicism

Adam, Karl. *The Spirit of Catholicism*. Tr. Justin McCann. Garden City, N.Y.: Doubleday Image Books, 1954.

Bianchi, Eugene, and Rosemary Radford Ruether, eds. *A Democratic Catholic Church: The Reconstruction of Roman Catholicism*. New York: Crossroad, 1992.

Bokenkotter, Thomas. *Essential Catholicism*. Garden City, N.Y.: Doubleday Image Books, 1986.

Chilson, Richard. *Catholic Christianity: A Guide to the Way, the Truth, and the Life*. New York: Paulist, 1987.

Collinge, William J. "Handing on Tradition at Modernity's End" [review article]. *The Living Light* 28 (1992): 347-52.

———. "Recent Introductions to Catholic Christianity: A Review Article." *The Living Light* 24 (1988): 354-65.

Cunningham, Lawrence. *The Catholic Experience*. New York: Crossroad, 1985.

———. *The Catholic Faith: An Introduction*. New York: Paulist, 1987.

———. *The Catholic Heritage*. New York: Crossroad, 1983.

Greeley, Andrew M. *The Catholic Myth: The Behavior and Beliefs of American Catholics*. New York: Scribner, 1990.

Happel, Stephen, and David Tracy. *A Catholic Vision*. Philadelphia: Fortress, 1984.

Haughton, Rosemary. *The Catholic Thing*. Springfield, Ill.: Templegate, 1979.

Hellwig, Monika. *Understanding Catholicism*. New York: Paulist Press, 1981.

McBrien, Richard. *Catholicism*. New Edition. San Francisco: HarperSanFrancisco, 1994.

———. *Inside Catholicism: Rituals and Symbols Revealed*. San Francisco: HarperSanFrancisco, 1995.

Rausch, Thomas P. *The Roots of the Catholic Tradition*. Wilmington, Del.: Michael Glazier, 1986.

Wilhelm, Anthony J. *Christ Among Us: A Modern Presentation of the Catholic Faith for Adults*. Fifth revised edition. San Francisco: HarperSanFrancisco, 1990.

VII. History

A. General

Bausch, William J. *The Pilgrim Church: A Popular History of Catholic Christianity*. Mystic, Conn.: Twenty-Third, 1987.

Bihlmeyer, Karl, and Herman Tüchle. *Church History*. 3 vols. Tr. Victor E. Mills. Westminster, Md.: Newman, 1966.

Bokenkotter, Thomas. *A Concise History of the Catholic Church*. Revised and expanded edition. Garden City, N.Y.: Doubleday Image Books, 1990.

Dwyer, John. *Church History: Twenty Centuries of Catholic Christianity*. New York: Paulist, 1985.

Holmes, J. Derek, and Bernard W. Bickers. *A Short History of the Catholic Church*. New York: Paulist, 1984.

Jedin, Hubert, Konrad Repgen, and John Dolan, eds. *History of the Church*. 10 vols. [Translated from *Handbuch der Kirchengeschichte*.] New York: Seabury, 1980-81.

Küng, Hans. *Christianity: Essence, History, and Future*. Tr. John Bowden. New York: Continuum, 1995.

Lapple, Alfred. *The Catholic Church: A Brief History*. Tr. Peter Heinegg. New York: Paulist, 1982.

McManners, John, ed. *The Oxford Illustrated History of Christianity*. New York: Oxford University Press, 1990.

B. Specific Periods and Places

1. Ancient Church

Arnold, Duane W.-H. *The Early Episcopal Career of Athanasius of Alexandria AD 328-AD 335*. Notre Dame: University of Notre Dame Press, 1991.

Barnard, L. W. *Justin Martyr*. Cambridge: Cambridge University Press, 1967.

Barnes, T. D. *Athanasius and Constantius: Theology and Politics in the Constantinian Empire*. Cambridge, Mass.: Harvard University Press, 1993.

————. *Constantine and Eusebius*. Cambridge, Mass.: Harvard University Press, 1980.

————. *Tertullian: A Historical and Literary Study*. Oxford: Clarendon Press, 1971.

Bonner, Gerald R. *St. Augustine of Hippo: Life and Controversies*. Revised ed. Norwich: Canterbury Press, 1986 [1963].

Brown, Peter. *Augustine of Hippo: A Biography*. Berkeley and Los Angeles: University of California, 1969.

————. *The Body and Society: Men, Women, and Sexual Renunciation in Early Christianity*. New York: Columbia University Press, 1988.

Brown, Raymond E. *The Churches the Apostles Left Behind*. New York: Paulist, 1984.

Brown, Raymond E., and John P. Meier. *Antioch and Rome: New Testament Cradles of Catholic Christianity*. New York: Paulist, 1983.

Brown, Raymond E., et al. *Peter in the New Testament: A Collaborative Assessment by Protestant and Roman Catholic Scholars*. New York: Paulist, 1973.

Burton-Christie, Douglas. *The Word in the Desert: Scripture and the Quest for Holiness in Early Christian Monasticism*. New York: Oxford University Press, 1993.

Cameron, Averil. *Christianity and the Rhetoric of Empire: The Development of Christian Discourse*. Berkeley and Los Angeles: University of California Press, 1991.

Chadwick, Henry. *Augustine*. Past Masters. New York: Oxford University Press, 1986.

———. *The Early Church*. The Pelican History of the Church 1. Baltimore: Penguin, 1967.

Chitty, Derwas. *The Desert a City*. Oxford: Blackwell, 1966.

Clark, Elizabeth A. *The Origenist Controversy: The Cultural Construction of an Early Christian Debate*. Princeton, N.J.: Princeton University Press, 1992.

Crouzel, Henri. *Origen*. Tr. A. S. Worrall. San Francisco: Harper and Row, 1989.

Daniélou, Jean, and Henri Marrou. *The First Six Hundred Years*. Tr. Vincent Cronin. The Christian Centuries 1. New York: McGraw-Hill, 1964.

Davis, Leo Donald. *The First Seven Ecumenical Councils (325-787): Their History and Theology* (Wilmington, Del.: Michael Glazier, 1987).

Eno, Robert C. *Teaching Authority in the Early Church*. Wilmington, Del.: Michael Glazier, 1984.

Fox, Robin Lane. *Pagans and Christians*. New York: Knopf, 1986.

Frend, W. H. C. *The Donatist Church: A Movement of Protest in Roman North Africa*. 2d ed. Oxford: Clarendon Press, 1971.

———. *Martyrdom and Persecution in the Early Church: A Study of a Conflict from the Maccabees to Donatus*. Garden City, N.Y.: Anchor Books, 1967.

———. *The Rise of Christianity*. Philadelphia: Fortress, 1984.

———. *The Rise of the Monophysite Movement: Chapters in the History of the Church in the Fifth and Sixth Centuries*. Cambridge: Cambridge University Press, 1979.

———. *Saints and Sinners in the Early Church: Differing and Conflicting Traditions in the First Six Centuries*. Wilmington, Del.: Michael Glazier, 1985.

Grant, R. M. *Greek Apologists of the Second Century*. Philadelphia: Westminster, 1988.

———, ed. *The Apostolic Fathers: A New Translation and Commentary*. 6 vols. New York: Thomas Nelson, 1964-8.

Gryson, Roger. *The Ministry of Women in the Early Church.* Collegeville, Minn.: Liturgical, 1976.

Halton, Thomas, ed. *Message of the Fathers of the Church.* 22 vols. Wilmington, Del.: Michael Glazier, and Collegeville, Minn.: Liturgical, 1983- . [Selections from Church Fathers on various topics.]

Hanson, R. P. C. *Saint Patrick: His Origins and Career.* New York: Oxford University Press, 1968.

———*The Search for the Christian Doctrine of God: The Arian Controversy 318-381.* Edinburgh: T & T Clark, 1988.

Jonas, Hans. *The Gnostic Religion: The Message of the Alien God and the Beginnings of Christianity.* Second edition, revised. Boston: Beacon, 1963.

Jurgens, William A., ed. and trans. *The Faith of the Early Fathers.* 3 vols. Collegeville, Minn.: Liturgical, 1970-79.

Kelly, J. N. D. *Jerome: His Life, Writings, and Controversies.* New York: Harper and Row, 1975.

MacMullen, Ramsay. *Constantine the Great.* New York: Dial, 1969.

———. *Christianizing the Roman Empire (A.D. 100-400).* New Haven, Conn.: Yale University Press, 1984.

Markus, Robert A. *The End of Ancient Christianity.* New York: Cambridge University Press, 1990.

Martimort, A. G. *Deaconesses: An Historical Study.* San Francisco: Ignatius Press, 1986.

McLynn, Neil B. *Ambrose of Milan: Church and Court in a Christian Capital.* Berkeley and Los Angeles: University of California Press, 1994.

Minns, Denis. *Irenaeus.* Washington, D.C.: Georgetown University Press, 1994.

Osborn, Eric. *The Emergence of Christian Theology.* New York: Cambridge University Press, 1993.

Pelikan, Jaroslav. *Christianity and Classical Culture: The Metamorphosis of Natural Theology in the Christian Encounter with Hellenism.* Gifford Lectures 1992-1993. New Haven: Yale University Press, 1993.

Perkins, Pheme. *Gnosticism and the New Testament.* Minneapolis: Fortress, 1993.

Quasten, Johannes. *Patrology.* 4 vols. Vol. 1: *The Beginnings of Patristic Literature.* Vol. 2: *The Ante-Nicene Literature after Irenaeus.* Vol. 3: *The Golden Age of Greek Patristic Literature from the Council of Nicaea to the Council of Chalcedon.* Vol. 4: Ed. Angelo di Berardino. *The Golden Age of Latin Patristic Literature from the Council of Nicaea to the Council of Chalcedon.* Westminster, Md.: Newman/Christian Classics, 1950-1986.

Robinson, James M., general ed. *The Nag Hammadi Library in English.* Third revised edition. San Francisco: HarperSanFrancisco, 1990.

Rorem, Paul. *Pseudo-Dionysius: A Commentary on the Texts and an Introduction to Their Influence*. New York: Oxford University Press, 1993.

Rudolph, Kurt. *Gnosis*. Tr. P. W. Coxon and K. W. Kuhn. Ed. R. McL. Wilson. San Francisco: Harper and Row, 1983.

Schnackenburg, Rudolf. *The Church in the New Testament*. Tr. W. J. O'Hara. New York: Herder and Herder, 1965.

Schneemelcher, Wilhelm, ed. *New Testament Apocrypha*. Tr. R. McL. Wilson. 2 vols. Louisville: Westminster/John Knox, 1991-92.

Stead, Christopher. *Philosophy in Christian Antiquity*. Cambridge: Cambridge University Press, 1994.

Stevenson, J. *A New Eusebius*. New York: Macmillan, 1957.

Thurston, Bonnie Bowman. *The Widows: A Women's Ministry in the Early Church*. Minneapolis: Fortress, 1989.

Trigg, Joseph Wilson. *Origen: The Bible and Philosophy in the Third-Century Church*. Atlanta: John Knox, 1983.

van der Meer, F. *Augustine the Bishop: Religion and Society at the Dawn of the Middle Ages*. Tr. Brian Battershaw and G. R. Lamb. New York: Harper, 1965.

Wallace-Hadrill, D. S. *Christian Antioch: A Study of Early Christian Thought in the East*. Cambridge: Cambridge University Press, 1982.

Wilken, Robert L. *The Christians as the Romans Saw Them*. New Haven: Yale University Press, 1984.

Witherington III, Ben. *Women in the Earliest Churches*. New York: Cambridge University Press, 1984.

Young, Frances. M. *From Nicaea to Chalcedon: A Guide to the Literature and its Background*. Philadelphia: Fortress, 1983.

2. Byzantine Church

Hussey, J. M. *The Orthodox Church in the Byzantine Empire*. The Oxford History of the Christian Church. Oxford: Clarendon Press, 1986.

Kazhdan, Alexander P., ed. *The Oxford Dictionary of Byzantium*. 3 vols. New York: Oxford University Press, 1991.

Nicol, Donald M. *The Last Centuries of Byzantium, 1261-1453*. 2d ed. New York: Cambridge University Press, 1993.

Runciman, Steven. *The Byzantine Theocracy*. New York: Cambridge University Press, 1977.

3. Medieval and Renaissance Church in the West

Alberigo, Giuseppe, ed. *Christian Unity: The Council of Ferrara-Florence 1438/39-1989*. Proceedings of an International Symposium, Florence

1989. Bibliotheca Ephemeridum Theologicarum Lovaniensum. Louvain: Louvain University, 1991.

Barber, Malcolm. *The New Knighthood: A History of the Order of the Temple*. New York: Cambridge University Press, 1995.

Bredero, Adriaan H. *Christendom and Christianity in the Middle Ages: The Relations between Religion, Church, and Society*. Tr. Reinder Bruinsma. Grand Rapids, Mich.: Eerdmans, 1994.

Brundage, James A. *Law, Sex, and Christian Society in Medieval Europe*. Chicago: University of Chicago Press, 1987.

Carney, Margaret. *The First Franciscan Woman: Clare of Assisi and Her Form of Life*. Quincy, Ill.: Franciscan Press, 1993.

Chenu, Marie-Dominique, O.P. *Toward Understanding Saint Thomas*. Tr. A.-M. Landry and D. Hughes. Chicago: Henry Regnery, 1964.

Davies, Brian. *The Thought of Thomas Aquinas*. Oxford: Clarendon Press, 1992.

Duffy, Eamon. *The Stripping of the Altars: Traditional Religion in England c. 1400-c. 1580*. New Haven: Yale University Press, 1992.

Erdmann, Carl. *The Origin of the Idea of Crusade*. Translated by Marshall W. Baldwin and Walter Goffart. Foreword and additional notes by Marshall W. Baldwin. Princeton, N.J.: Princeton University Press, 1977.

Flanagan, Sabina. *Hildegard of Bingen 1098-1179: A Visionary Life*. New York: Routledge, 1989.

Fortini, Arnaldo. *Francis of Assisi*. Trans. Helen Moak. New York: Crossroad, 1981.

Frank, Isnard Wilhelm. *A Concise History of the Medieval Church*. Tr. John Bowden. New York: Continuum, 1995.

Gilson, Etienne. *The Christian Philosophy of Saint Thomas Aquinas*. New York: Random House, 1956.

———. *History of Christian Philosophy in the Middle Ages*. New York: Random House, 1955.

Habig, Marion A., ed. *St. Francis of Assisi: Writings and Early Biographies, English Omnibus of the Sources for the Life of St. Francis*. Chicago: Franciscan Herald Press, 1972.

Hamilton, Bernard. *The Medieval Inquisition*. New York: Holmes and Meier, 1981.

Head, Thomas, and Richard Landes. *The Peace of God: Social Violence and Religious Response in France around the Year 1000*. Ithaca, N.Y.: Cornell University Press, 1992.

Housley, Norman. *The Later Crusades, 1274-1580: From Lyons to Alcazar*. New York: Oxford University Press, 1992.

Kamen, Henry. *Inquisition and Society in Spain in the Sixteenth and Seventeenth Centuries*. Bloomington, Ind.: Indiana University Press, 1985.

Knowles, David. *The Evolution of Medieval Thought*. Second Edition. Ed. D.
    E. Luscombe and C. N. L. Brooke. London: Longman, 1988.
————, with Dimitri Obolensky. *The Middle Ages*. The Christian Centuries 2.
    New York: McGraw-Hill, 1968.
Leff, Gordon. *William of Ockham: the Metamorphosis of Scholastic Discourse*.
    Totowa, N.J.: Rowman and Littlefield. 1975.
Marius, Richard. *Thomas More: A Biography*. New York: Random House,
    1984.
Mayer, Hans Eberhard. *The Crusades*. Translated by John Gillingham. New
    York: Oxford University Press, 1990.
McGrade, Arthur Stephen. *The Political Thought of William of Ockham:
    Personal and Institutional Principles*. New York: Cambridge University
    Press, 1974.
McNeill, John T. *The Celtic Churches: A History A.D. 200 to 1200*. Chicago:
    University of Chicago Press, 1974.
More, Thomas, St. *The Complete Works of St. Thomas More*. New Haven:
    Yale University Press, 1963- . 14 volumes in 19 books to 1990.
Newman, Barbara. *Sister of Wisdom: St. Hildegard's Theology of the Feminine*.
    Berkeley: University of California Press, 1987.
Nuth, Joan M. *Wisdom's Daughter: The Theology of Julian of Norwich*. New
    York: Crossroad, 1991.
Partner, Peter. *The Murdered Magicians: The Templars and their Myth*. New
    York: Oxford University Press, 1982.
Peters, Edward. *Inquisition*. New York: The Free Press, 1988.
Peterson, Ingrid J. *Clare of Assisi: A Biographical Study*. Quincy, Ill.:
    Franciscan Press, 1993.
Powell, James M., ed. *Innocent III: Vicar of Christ or Lord of the World?*
    Second edition. Washington, D.C.: The Catholic University of America
    Press, 1994.
Richards, J. *Consul of God: The Life and Times of Gregory the Great*. Boston:
    Routledge and Kegan Paul, 1980.
Riley-Smith, Jonathan. *The Crusades: A Short History*. New Haven, Conn.:
    Yale University Press, 1987.
————. *What Were the Crusades?* Totowa, N.J.: Rowman and Littlefield,
    1977.
Runciman, Stephen. *A History of the Crusades*. 3 vols. Cambridge: Cambridge
    University Press, 1951-54.
Russell, Jeffrey Burton. *Dissent and Order in the Middle Ages: The Search for
    Legitimate Authority*. Twayne's Studies in Intellectual and Cultural
    History. New York: Twayne, 1992.
Shannon, Albert C. *The Medieval Inquisition*. Washington, D.C.: Augustinian
    College Press, 1983.

Southern, R. W. *Saint Anselm: A Portrait in a Landscape.* New York: Cambridge University Press, 1990.

———. *Western Society and the Church in the Middle Ages.* The Pelican History of the Church 2. Baltimore: Penguin, 1970.

Straw, Carole. *Gregory the Great: Perfection in Imperfection.* Berkeley and Los Angeles: University of California Press, 1988.

Thomas Aquinas, St. *Summa Theologiae.* Text and English translation. 60 vols. Oxford and Cambridge: Blackfriars, 1966-80.

———. *The Summa Theologica of St. Thomas Aquinas.* Translated by the Fathers of the English Dominican Province. 5 vols. Westminster, Md.: Christian Classics, 1994 [1920].

Tobin, Frank. *Meister Eckhart: Thought and Language.* Philadelphia: University of Pennsylvania Press, 1986.

Trinkaus, Charles E. *In Our Image and Likeness: Humanity and Divinity in Italian Humanist Thought.* 2 vols. Chicago: University of Chicago Press, 1970.

Vauchez, André. *The Laity in the Middle Ages: Religious Beliefs and Devotional Practices.* Tr. Margaret J. Schneider. Notre Dame: University of Notre Dame, 1993.

Weisheipl, James A. *Friar Thomas d'Aquino.* Revised ed. Washington, D.C.: The Catholic University of America Press, 1983.

Wolter, Allan B. *The Philosophical Theology of John Duns Scotus.* Ed. M. Adams. Ithaca, N.Y.: Cornell University Press, 1990.

4. Counter-Reformation and Modern Church to Vatican II

Aubert, Roger, et al. *The Church in a Secularized Society.* The Christian Centuries 5. New York: Paulist, 1978.

Barstow, Anne Llewellyn. *Witchcraze: A New History of the European Witch Hunts.* New York: HarperCollins, 1994.

Bossy, John. *The English Catholic Community 1570-1850.* Oxford: Oxford University Press, 1570.

Buckley, Michael. *At the Origins of Modern Atheism.* New Haven, Conn.: Yale University Press, 1987.

Caraman, Philip. *Ignatius Loyola: A Biography of the Founder of the Jesuits.* San Francisco: Harper and Row, 1990.

Chadwick, Owen. *Newman.* Past Masters. New York: Oxford University Press, 1983.

———. *The Popes and European Revolution.* The Oxford History of the Christian Church. New York: Oxford University Press, 1981.

———. *The Reformation.* The Pelican History of the Church 3. Baltimore: Penguin, 1964.

Cragg, Gerald R. *The Church and the Age of Reason 1648-1789*. The Pelican History of the Church 4. Baltimore: Penguin, 1960.

Drake, Stillman. *Galileo*. New York: Hill and Wang, 1980.

Dupré, Louis. *Passage to Modernity: An Essay in the Hermeneutics of Nature and Culture*. New Haven, Conn.: Yale University Press, 1993.

Fantoli, Annibale. *Galileo: For Copernicanism and for the Church*. Tr. George V. Coyne. Notre Dame, Ind.: University of Notre Dame Press, 1994.

Francis de Sales. *Introduction to the Devout Life*. Trans. John K. Ryan. New York: Doubleday, 1982.

———. *Treatise on the Love of God*. 2 vols. Trans. John K. Ryan. Rockford, Ill.: TAN Books, 1974.

Geffré, Claude, and Jean-Pierre Jossua, eds. *1789: The French Revolution and the Church*. Concilium 201. Edinburgh: T & T Clark, 1989.

Gibson, Ralph. *A Social History of French Catholicism, 1789-1914*. New York: Routledge, 1989.

Holmes, J. Derek. *The Papacy in the Modern World 1914-1978*. New York: Crossroad, 1981.

Jedin, Hubert. *Crisis and Closure of the Council of Trent*. Tr. Norman D. Smith. London: Sheed and Ward, 1967.

———. *Geschichte des Konzils von Trient*. 5 vols. Freiburg: Herder, 1949-75. Eng. trans. of first two volumes: *A History of the Council of Trent*. Tr. Ernest Graf. St. Louis: B. Herder, 1957, 1961.

Jones, Frederick M. *Alphonsus de Liguori: Saint of Bourbon Naples*. Westminster, Md.: Christian Classics, 1992.

Ker, Ian. *John Henry Newman: A Biography*. New York: Oxford University Press, 1988.

Kurtz, Lester R. *The Politics of Heresy: The Modernist Crisis in Roman Catholicism*. Berkeley: University of California Press, 1986.

Levack, Brian P. *The Witch-Hunt in Early Modern Europe*. New York: Longmans, 1987.

Livingston, James C. *Modern Christian Thought: From the Enlightenment to Vatican II*. New York: Macmillan, 1971.

Misner, Paul. *Social Catholicism in Europe: From the Onset of Industrialization to the First World War*. New York: Crossroad, 1991.

O'Connell, Marvin R. *Critics on Trial: An Introduction to the Catholic Modernist Crisis*. Washington, D.C.: The Catholic University of America Press, 1994.

Rhodes, Anthony. *The Vatican in the Age of the Dictators, 1922-1945*. London: Hodder and Stoughton, 1973.

Russell, Jeffrey B. *A History of Witchcraft: Sorcerers, Heretics, and Pagans*. London: Thames and Hudson, 1980.

Tellechea Idígoras, José Ignacio. *Ignatius of Loyola: the Pilgrim Saint*. Tr. Cornelius Buckley. Chicago: Loyola University Press, 1995.

Vidler, Alec R. *A Variety of Catholic Modernists*. Cambridge: Cambridge University Press, 1970.

——. *The Church in an Age of Revolution: 1789 to the Present Day*. The Pelican History of the Church 5. Baltimore: Penguin, 1961.

Wright, Wendy M. *Bond of Perfection: Jeanne de Chantal and François de Sales*. New York: Paulist, 1985.

5. *Contemporary Period: Vatican II and After*

Alberigo, Giuseppe, Jean-Pierre Jossua, and Joseph Komonchak, eds. *The Reception of Vatican II*. Washington, D.C.: The Catholic University of America Press, 1987.

Alberigo, Giuseppe, and Joseph Komonchak, eds. *The History of Vatican II: 1959-1965*. 5 vols. 1: *Announcement and Preparation*. Tr. Matthew J. O'Connell. Maryknoll, N.Y.: 1996.

Berry, Jason. *Lead Us Not into Temptation: Catholic Priests and the Sexual Abuse of Children*. New York: Doubleday, 1992.

Butler, Christopher. *The Theology of Vatican II*. Revised edition. Westminster, Md.: Christian Classics, 1981.

Cuneo, Michael W. *Catholics Against the Church: Anti-Abortion Protest in Toronto, 1969-1985*. Toronto: University of Toronto Press.

D'Antonio, William, et al. *Laity: American and Catholic: Transforming the Church*. Kansas City, Mo.: Sheed and Ward, 1996.

Estruch, Joan. *Saints and Schemers: Opus Dei and its Paradoxes*. New York: Oxford University Press, 1995.

Flynn, Eileen P. *Catholicism: Agenda for Renewal*. Lanham, Md.: University Press of America, 1994.

Hansen, Eric O. *The Catholic Church in World Politics*. Princeton, N.J.: Princeton University Press, 1987.

Hastings, Adrian, ed. *Modern Catholicism: Vatican II and After*. New York: Oxford University Press, 1991.

Hebblethwaite, Peter. *Paul VI: The First Modern Pope*. New York: Paulist, 1993.

——. *Pope John XXIII: Shepherd of the Modern World*. New York: Doubleday, 1985.

——. *The Year of the Three Popes*. Cleveland: Collins, 1979.

John XXIII, Pope. *Journal of a Soul*. Tr. Dorothy White. New York: McGraw-Hill, 1965.

John Paul II, Pope. *Crossing the Threshold of Hope*. Tr. Jenny McPhee and Martha McPhee. New York: Knopf, 1994.

Kelly, George A. *The Battle for the American Church*. Garden City, N.Y.: Doubleday, 1978.

Latourelle, René, ed. *Vatican II: Assessment and Perspectives, Twenty-five Years After (1962-87)*. 3 vols. New York: Paulist, 1988-89.

Lernoux, Penny. *People of God: The Struggle for World Catholicism*. New York: Viking, 1989.

Martin, James. "Opus Dei in the United States." *America* 25 Feb. 1995: 8-15, 26-27.

McCarthy, Timothy G. *The Catholic Tradition: Before and After Vatican II, 1878-1993*. Chicago: Loyola University Press, 1994.

O'Malley, John H. *Tradition and Transition: Historical Perspectives on Vatican II*. Wilmington, Del.: Michael Glazier, 1989.

Ratzinger, Joseph Cardinal, with Vittorio Messori. *The Ratzinger Report: An Exclusive Interview on the State of the Church*. Tr. Salvator Attanasio and Graham Harrison. San Francisco: Ignatius, 1985.

Ruether, Rosemary Radford. *Contemporary Roman Catholicism: Crises and Challenges*. Kansas City, Mo.: Sheed and Ward, 1987.

Szulc, Tad. *Pope John Paul II: The Biography*. New York: Scribner, 1995.

Vorgrimler, Herbert, ed. *Commentary on the Documents of Vatican II*. Various translators. 5 vols. New York: Herder and Herder, 1967-1969.

Walsh, Michael. *Opus Dei: An Investigation into the Secret Society Struggling for Power within the Roman Catholic Church*. San Francisco: HarperSanFrancisco, 1992.

Willey, David. *God's Politician: Pope John Paul II, the Catholic Church, and the New World Order*. New York: St. Martin's, 1993.

Williams, George Huntston. *The Mind of John Paul II: Origins of His Thought and Action*. New York: Seabury, 1981.

Wojtyla, Karol, Cardinal [Pope John Paul II]. *The Acting Person*. Tr. Andrzej Potocki. Dordrecht: Reidel, 1979.

――――. *Love and Responsibility*. Tr. H. T. Willetts. New York: Farrar, Straus, and Giroux, 1981.

6. Asia and Africa

Cragg, Kenneth. *The Arab Christian: A History in the Middle East*. Louisville: Westminster/John Knox, 1991.

Dunne, George H. *Generation of Giants*. Notre Dame: University of Notre Dame Press, 1962.

Fujita, Neil S. *Japan's Encounter with Christianity: The Catholic Mission in Pre-Modern Japan*. New York: Paulist, 1991.

Hastings, Adrian. *African Catholicism: Essays in Discovery*. Philadelphia: SCM/Trinity Press International, 1989.

――――. *The Church in Africa, 1450-1950*. The Oxford History of the Christian Church. New York: Oxford University Press, 1995.

Isichei, Elizabeth. *A History of Christianity in Africa: From Antiquity to the Present*. Grand Rapids, Mich.: Eerdmans, 1995.

Minamiki, George. *The Chinese Rites Controversy from Its Beginning to Modern Times*. Chicago: Loyola University Press, 1985.

Moffett, Samuel Hugh. *A History of Christianity in Asia. Vol. 1: Beginnings to 1500*. San Francisco: Harper San Francisco, 1992.

Neill, Stephen. *A History of Christianity in India*. Vol. 1: *The Beginning to A.D. 1707*. Cambridge: Cambridge University Press, 1984.

Ross, Andrew C. *A Vision Betrayed: The Jesuits in Japan and China 1542-1742*. Maryknoll, N.Y.: Orbis, 1994.

Spence, Jonathan D. *The Memory Palace of Matteo Ricci*. New York: Viking Penguin, 1984.

Tang, Edmond, and Jean-Paul Wiest, eds. *The Catholic Church in Modern China: Perspectives*. Maryknoll, N.Y.: Orbis, 1993.

7. Latin America

Brockman, James R. *Romero: A Life*. Maryknoll, N.Y.: Orbis, 1989.

Caraman, Philip. *The Lost Paradise: The Jesuit Republic in South America*. New York: Seabury, 1976.

Dussel, Enrique, ed. *The Church in Latin America, 1492-1992*. Maryknoll, N.Y.: Orbis, 1992.

Gutiérrez, Gustavo. *Las Casas: In Search of the Poor of Jesus Christ*. Tr. Robert R. Barr. Maryknoll, N.Y.: Orbis, 1993.

Klaiber, Jeffrey. *The Catholic Church in Peru 1821-1985: A Social History*. Washington, D.C.: The Catholic University of America Press, 1992.

Las Casas, Bartolomé de. *The Devastation of the Indies: A Brief Account*. Tr. Herma Briffault. Baltimore: Johns Hopkins University Press, 1992.

———. *Indian Freedom: The Cause of Bartolomé de Las Casas*. Tr. and ed. Francis P. Sullivan. Kansas City: Sheed and Ward, 1995.

———. *The Only Way*. Ed. Helen Rand Parish. Tr. Francis Patrick Sullivan. Sources of American Spirituality. New York: Paulist, 1992.

Lernoux, Penny. *Cry of the People: The Struggle for Human Rights in Latin America—The Catholic Church in Conflict with U.S. Policy*. New York: Penguin, 1982.

8. The United States

Appleby, R. Scott. *"Church and Age Unite!" The Modernist Impulse in American Catholicism*. Notre Dame, Ind.: University of Notre Dame Press, 1992.

Briggs, Kenneth A. *Holy Siege: The Year that Shook Catholic America*. San Francisco: HarperSanFrancisco, 1992.

Carey, Patrick W., ed. *American Catholic Religious Thought*. New York: Paulist, 1987.

———. *People, Priests, and Prelates: Ecclesiastical Democracy and the Tensions of Trusteeism*. Notre Dame, Ind.: University of Notre Dame Press, 1987.

———. *The Roman Catholics*. Denominations in America, 6. Westport, Conn.: Greenwood, 1993. [Bibliographic essay 353-61.]

Cenkner, William, ed. *The Multicultural Church: A New Landscape in U.S. Theologies*. New York: Paulist, 1995.

Coy, Patrick G., ed. *A Revolution of the Heart: Essays on the Catholic Worker*. Philadelphia: Temple University Press, 1988.

Davis, Cyprian. *The History of Black Catholics in the United States*. New York: Crossroad, 1991.

Day, Dorothy. *By Little and By Little: The Selected Writings of Dorothy Day*. Edited by Robert Ellsberg. New York: Alfred A. Knopf, 1983.

———. *The Long Loneliness*. New York: Harper, 1952.

Dolan, Jay P. *The American Catholic Experience: A History from Colonial Times to the Present*. Garden City, N.Y.: Doubleday, 1985.

———, ed. *The American Catholic Parish: A History from 1850 to the Present*. 2 vols. Vol. 1: *The Northeast, Southeast, and South Central States*. By Joseph J. Casino, Michael J. McNally, and Charles E. Nolan. Vol. 2: *The Pacific, Intermountain West, and Midwest States*. By Jeffrey M. Burns, Carol L. Jensen, and Stephen J. Shaw. New York: Paulist, 1987.

———. *Catholic Revivalism: The American Experience, 1830-1900*. Notre Dame, Ind.: University of Notre Dame Press, 1978.

Dolan, Jay P. and Gilberto M. Hinojosa, eds. *Mexican Americans and the Catholic Church, 1900-1965*. The Notre Dame History of Hispanic Catholics in the U.S. 1. Notre Dame, Ind.: University of Notre Dame Press, 1994.

Dolan, Jay P., and Jaime R. Vidal, eds. *Puerto Rican and Cuban Catholics in the U.S., 1900-1965*. The Notre Dame History of Hispanic Catholics in the U.S. 2. Notre Dame, Ind.: University of Notre Dame Press, 1994.

Dolan, Jay P., and Allan Figueroa Deck, eds. *Hispanic Catholic Culture in the U.S.: Issues and Concerns*. The Notre Dame History of Hispanic Catholics in the U.S. 3. Notre Dame, Ind.: University of Notre Dame Press, 1994.

Ellis, John T. *Documents of American Catholic History*. Wilmington, Del.: Michael Glazier, 1987.

———. *The Life of James Cardinal Gibbons*. 2 vols. Milwaukee: Bruce, 1952.

Enochs, Ross. *The Jesuit Mission to the Lakota Sioux: A Study of Pastoral Ministry, 1886-1945*. Kansas City, Mo.: Sheed and Ward, 1996.

Fisher, James Terence. *The Catholic Counterculture in America, 1933-1962.* Chapel Hill: University of North Carolina Press, 1989.

Fogarty, Gerald P. *The Vatican and the American Hierarchy from 1870 to 1965.* Wilmington: Michael Glazier, 1985.

Gleason, Philip. *Keeping the Faith: American Catholicism Past and Present.* Notre Dame, Ind.: University of Notre Dame Press, 1987.

Halsey, William M. *The Survival of American Innocence: Catholicism in an Era of Disillusionment.* Notre Dame, Ind.: University of Notre Dame Press, 1980.

Hennessey, James. *American Catholics: A History of the Roman Catholic Community in the United States.* New York: Oxford University Press, 1981.

Kauffman, Christopher J. *Faith and Fraternalism: The History of the Knights of Columbus 1882-1982.* New York: Harper and Row, 1982.

————. *Ministry and Meaning: A Religious History of Catholic Health Care in the United States.* New York: Crossroad, 1995.

————. *Tradition and Transformation in Catholic Culture: The Priests of Saint Sulpice in the United States from 1791 to the Present.* New York: Macmillan, 1988.

Kauffman, Christopher J., general ed. *Makers of the Catholic Community.* 6 vols. 1: Gerald P. Fogarty, ed., *Patterns of Episcopal Leadership.* 2: Joseph P. Chinnici, *Living Stones: The History and Structure of Catholic Spiritual Life in the United States.* 3: Margaret Mary Reher, *Catholic Intellectual Life in America: A Historical Study of Persons and Movements.* 4: Dolores Liptak, *Immigrants and their Church.* 5: David O'Brien, *Public Catholicism.* 6: Karen Kennelly, ed., *American Catholic Women: A Historical Exploration.* New York: Macmillan, 1989.

Kelly, Ellin, and Annabelle Melville, eds. *Elizabeth Seton: Selected Writings.* Sources of American Spirituality. New York: Paulist, 1987.

Kenneally, James K. *The History of American Catholic Women.* New York: Crossroad, 1990.

Killoren, John J. *Come, Blackrobe: DeSmet and the Indian Tragedy.* Norman, Okla.: University of Oklahoma Press, 1994.

Meconis, Charles. *With Clumsy Grace: The American Catholic Left, 1961-1975.* New York: Seabury, 1979.

Melville, Annabelle M. *Elizabeth Bayley Seton, 1774-1821.* New York: Charles Scribner, 1985 [1951].

Miller, William D. *Dorothy Day: A Biography.* San Francisco: Harper and Row, 1982.

Mott, Michael. *The Seven Mountains of Thomas Merton.* Boston: Houghton, Mifflin, 1984.

Oates, Mary J. *The Catholic Philanthropic Tradition in America.* Bloomington, Ind.: Indiana University Press, 1995.

O'Brien, David J. *Isaac Hecker: An American Catholic*. New York: Paulist, 1992.

O'Connell, Marvin R. *John Ireland and the American Catholic Church*. St. Paul, Minn.: Minnesota Historical Society, 1988.

Orsi, Robert Anthony. *The Madonna of 115th Street: Faith and Community in Italian Harlem, 1880-1950*. New Haven: Yale University Press, 1985.

Piehl, Mel. *Breaking Bread: The Catholic Worker and the Origin of Catholic Radicalism in America*. Philadelphia: Temple University Press, 1982.

Raboteau, Albert J. *Slave Religion*. New York: Oxford University Press, 1978.

Sandoval, Moises, ed. *Fronteras: A History of the Latin American Church in the USA since 1513*. San Antonio, Tex.: Mexican American Cultural Center, 1983.

———. *On the Move: A History of the Hispanic Church in the United States*. Maryknoll, N.Y.: Orbis, 1990.

Shannon, William A. *Silent Lamp: The Thomas Merton Story*. New York: Crossroad, 1992.

Shea, John Gilmary. *History of the Catholic Missions among the Indian Tribes of the United States, 1529-1854*. New York: P. J. Kenedy, 1882.

Spalding, Thomas W. *The Premier See: A History of the Archdiocese of Baltimore, 1789-1989*. Baltimore: The Johns Hopkins University Press, 1989.

Steltenkamp, Michael F. *Black Elk: Holy Man of the Oglala*. Norman, Okla.: University of Oklahoma Press, 1993.

Stewart, George C., Jr. *Marvels of Charity: History of American Sisters and Nuns*. Huntington, Ind.: Our Sunday Visitor, 1994.

Troester, Rosalie Riegle. *Voices from the Catholic Worker*. Philadelphia: Temple University Press, 1993. [Contains list of Catholic Worker houses and farms.]

Weaver, Mary Jo, and R. Scott Appleby, eds. *Being Right: Conservative Catholics in America*. Bloomington, Ind.: Indiana University Press, 1995.

"What We Have Seen and Heard;" Black Bishops' Pastoral on Evangelization. *Origins* 18 (1984): 273-87.

White, Joseph M. *The Diocesan Seminary in the United States*. Notre Dame, Ind.: University of Notre Dame Press, 1989.

Zanca, Kenneth A., ed. *American Catholics and Slavery, 1789-1866: An Anthology of Primary Documents*. Lanham, Md.: University Press of America, 1994.

9. Missions

Latourette, Kenneth Scott. *A History of the Expansion of Christianity*. 7 vols. New York: Harper and Brothers, 1937-1945.

Neill, Stephen. *A History of Christian Missions*. The Pelican History of the Church 6. Baltimore: Penguin, 1964.

Yates, Timothy. *Christian Mission in the Twentieth Century*. New York: Cambridge University Press, 1994.

10. Monasticism and Religious Orders and Congregations

Ashley, Benedict M. *The Dominicans*. Collegeville, Minn.: Liturgical, 1990.

Bangert, William V. *A History of the Society of Jesus*. St. Louis: Institute of Jesuit Sources, 1972.

Burton, Janet. *Monastic and Religious Orders in Britain 1000-1300*. Cambridge Medieval Textbooks. New York: Cambridge University Press, 1994.

Fry, Timothy, ed. *RB 1980: The Rule of St. Benedict in Latin and English with Notes*. Collegeville, Minn.: Liturgical, 1981.

Kardong, Terrence. *The Benedictines*. Wilmington, Del.: Michael Glazier, 1988.

Knowles, David. *Christian Monasticism*. World University Library. New York: McGraw-Hill, 1969.

Lawrence, C. H. *The Friars: The Impact of the Early Mendicant Movement on Western Society*. London: Longman, 1994.

———. *Medieval Monasticism: Forms of Religious Life in Western Europe in the Middle Ages*. Second edition. London: Longman, 1989.

Leclercq, Jean. *The Love of Learning and the Desire for God: A Study of Monastic Culture*. Tr. Catharine Misrahi. New York: Fordham University Press, 1982 [1957].

Lekai, Louis J. *The Cistercians: Ideals and Reality*. N.p.: The Kent State University Press, 1977.

Lernoux, Penny, with Arthur Jones and Robert Ellsberg. *Hearts on Fire: The Story of the Maryknoll Sisters*. Maryknoll, N.Y.: Orbis, 1993.

Moorman, John A. *A History of the Franciscan Order from its Origins to the Year 1517*. Chicago: Franciscan Herald, 1968.

O'Malley, John. *The First Jesuits*. Cambridge, Mass.: Harvard University Press, 1993.

Ranft, Patricia. *A History of Women's Religious Communities, 4th to 17th Century*. New York: St. Martin's, 1995.

Short, William J. *The Franciscans*. Wilmington, Del.: Michael Glazier, 1990.

VIII. Bible

A. Edition with Commentary

Senior, Donald, ed. *The Catholic Study Bible*. New York: Oxford University Press, 1990. [New American Bible translation and notes with additional commentary.]

B. Reference Tools (see also under II. Reference Works)

Aland, Kurt, ed. *Synopsis of the Four Gospels*. English ed. N.p.: United Bible Societies, 1982.
Brown, Raymond E., Joseph A. Fitzmyer, and Roland E. Murphy, eds. *The New Jerome Biblical Commentary*. Englewood Cliffs, N.J.: Prentice-Hall, 1990.
Hartdegen, Stephen J., gen. ed. *Nelson's Complete Concordance of the New American Bible*. Nashville, T. Nelson, 1977.

C. Commentary Series

The Anchor Bible. Gen. ed. William Foxwell Albright and David Noel Freedman. New York: Doubleday, 1965- . [This series includes works by prominent Catholic scholars, though it is not limited to Catholic authors.]
Collegeville Bible Commentary. Old Testament Series. Ed. Dianne Bergant. 36 booklets. New Testament Series. 11 booklets. Collegeville, Minn.: Liturgical, 1983-86.
New Testament Message: A Biblical-Theological Commentary. Ed. Wilfrid Harrington and Donald Senior. 22 vols. Wilmington, Del.: Michael Glazier, 1979-81.
Old Testament Message: A Biblical-Theological Commentary. Ed. Carroll Stuhlmueller and Martin McNamara. 23 vols. Wilmington, Del.: Michael Glazier, 1982-84.
Sacra Pagina. Ed. Daniel Harrington. 5 vols. published of 18. Collegeville, Minn.: Liturgical. 1991- . [Commentaries on New Testament.]

D. Books and Articles on Specific Topics

Barrett, C. K. *The New Testament Background: Selected Documents*. Revised ed. San Francisco: Harper and Row, 1989.
Boadt, Lawrence. *Reading the Old Testament: An Introduction*. New York: Paulist, 1984.

Brown, Raymond E. *Biblical Exegesis and Church Doctrine.* New York: Paulist, 1985.

Collins, Raymond. *Introduction to the New Testament.* Garden City, N.Y.: Doubleday, 1983.

Farmer, William R., and Denis M. Farkasfalvy. *The Formation of the New Testament Canon: An Ecumenical Approach.* New York: Paulist, 1983.

Fitzmyer, Joseph A. *Responses to 101 Questions on the Dead Sea Scrolls.* New York: Paulist, 1992.

Fogarty, Gerald P. *American Catholic Biblical Scholarship: A History from the Early Republic to Vatican II.* San Francisco: Harper and Row, 1989.

Kelly, Joseph F. *Why Is There a New Testament?* Wilmington, Del.: Michael Glazier, 1986.

Lienhard, Joseph T. *The Bible, the Church, and Authority: The Canon of the Christian Bible in History and Theology.* Collegeville, Minn.: Liturgical, 1995.

Perkins, Pheme. *Reading the New Testament: An Introduction.* Revised edition. New York: Paulist, 1988.

Pontifical Biblical Commission. "The Interpretation of the Bible in the Church." *Origins* 23 (1993-94): 497, 499-524.

Rome and the Study of Scripture: A Collection of Papal Enactments on the Study of Holy Scripture together with the Decisions of the Biblical Commission. 7th ed. St. Meinrad, Ind.: Grail, 1962.

Schneiders, Sandra M. *The Revelatory Text: Interpreting the New Testament as Sacred Scripture.* San Francisco: HarperCollins, 1991.

Vawter, Bruce. *Biblical Inspiration.* Philadelphia: Westminster, 1972.

Vermes, Geza, ed. *The Dead Sea Scrolls in English.* 4th ed. New York: Penguin, 1995.

IX. Doctrine and Theology

A. Catechisms

Catechism of the Catholic Church. English translation for the United States of America. Washington, D.C.: U.S. Catholic Conference, 1994.

The Church's Confession of Faith: A Catholic Catechism for Adults. Originally published by the German Bishops' Conference. Tr. George Wentworth Arndt. Ed. Mark Jordan. Communio Books. San Francisco: Ignatius, 1987.

The Common Catechism: A Book of Christian Faith. New York: Seabury, 1975.

Lawler, Ronald, Donald Wuerl, and Thomas Lawler, eds. *The Teaching of Christ.* Huntington, Ind.: Our Sunday Visitor Press, 1976.

A New Catechism: Catholic Faith for Adults [The "Dutch Catechism"]. Tr. Kevin Smyth. New York: Herder and Herder, 1967.

O'Malley, William, et al. *The People's Catechism: Catholic Faith for Adults.* New York: Crossroad, 1995.

Pennock, Michael Francis. *This Our Faith: A Catholic Catechism for Adults.* Notre Dame, Ind.: Ave Maria, 1989.

The Roman Catechism. Translated and annotated in accord with Vatican II and Post-Conciliar Documents and the New Code of Canon Law by Robert I. Bradley, S.J., and Eugene Kevane. Boston: St. Paul Editions, 1984.

B. Histories

Congar, Yves M.J. *A History of Theology.* Garden City, N.Y.: Doubleday, 1968.

Kelly, J. N. D. *Early Christian Doctrines.* 2d ed. New York: Harper and Row, 1960.

McCool, Gerald A. *Catholic Theology in the Nineteenth Century: The Quest for a Unitary Method.* New York: Seabury, 1977.

———. *From Unity to Pluralism: The Internal Evolution of Thomism.* New York: Fordham University Press, 1987.

Pelikan, Jaroslav. *The Christian Tradition: A History of the Development of Doctrine.* 5 vols. Chicago: University of Chicago Press, 1971-88.

Schoof, T. Mark. *A Survey of Catholic Theology, 1800-1970.* New York: Paulist Newman, 1970.

C. General Works of Doctrinal, Fundamental, and Systematic Theology

1. Creed

Kelly, J. N. D. *The Athanasian Creed.* New York: Harper & Row, 1964.

———. *Early Christian Creeds.* 3d ed. New York: McKay, 1972.

Leith, John H., ed. *Creeds of the Churches.* 3d ed., Louisville: John Knox Press, 1982.

Marthaler, Berard L. *The Creed: The Apostolic Faith in Contemporary Theology.* Revised edition. Mystic, Conn.: Twenty-Third, 1993.

Schaff, Philip. *The Creeds of Christendom.* 3 vols. 6th ed. reprinted. Grand Rapids: Baker Book House, 1983.

2. Revelation and Faith

Congar, Yves. *Tradition and Traditions: An Historical and Theological Essay.* Tr. M. Naseby and T. Rainborough. New York: Macmillan, 1967.

Dulles, Avery. *The Assurance of Things Hoped For: A Theology of Christian Faith*. New York: Oxford University Press, 1994.

————. *Models of Revelation*. Garden City, N.Y.: Doubleday, 1983.

————. *Revelation Theology*. New York: Herder and Herder, 1969.

International Theological Commission. "On the Interpretation of Dogmas." *Origins* 20 (1990): 1-14.

Latourelle, René. *Theology of Revelation*. Staten Island, N.Y.: Alba House, 1966.

Skillrud, Harold C., J. Francis Stafford, and Daniel F. Martensen, eds. *Scripture and Tradition*. Lutherans and Catholics in Dialogue IX. Minneapolis: Augsburg, 1995.

3. Doctrines

Dulles, Avery. *The Resilient Church*. New York: Doubleday, 1977.

Lindbeck, George. *The Nature of Doctrine: Religion and Theology in a Postliberal Age*. Philadelphia: Westminster, 1984.

Lonergan, Bernard. *Doctrinal Pluralism*. Milwaukee: Marquette University Press, 1971.

Newman, John Henry. *An Essay on the Development of Christian Doctrine*. Garden City, N.Y.: Doubleday, 1960 [1845].

Walgrave, Jan. *Unfolding Revelation*. Philadelphia: Westminster, 1972.

4. Fundamental Theology, Theological Methodology, Apologetics

Buckley, James J. *Seeking the Humanity of God: Practices, Doctrines, and Catholic Theology*. Collegeville, Minn.: Liturgical, 1992.

Cooke, Bernard J. *The Distancing of God: The Ambiguity of Symbol in History and Theology*. Minneapolis: Fortress, 1990.

Dulles, Avery. *The Craft of Theology: From Symbol to System*. Revised Edition. New York: Crossroad, 1995.

————. *A History of Apologetics*. New York: Corpus, 1971.

Fiorenza, Francis Schüssler. *Foundational Theology: Jesus and the Church*. New York: Crossroad, 1984.

Guarino, Thomas G. *Revelation and Truth: Unity and Plurality in Contemporary Theology*. Scranton: University of Scranton Press, 1993.

Lash, Nicholas. *Easter in Ordinary*. Charlottesville: University Press of Virginia, 1988.

Lonergan, Bernard. *Method in Theology*. New York: Crossroad, 1972.

Meynell, Hugo A. *Is Christianity True?* Washington, D.C.: The Catholic University of America Press, 1994.

Nichols, Aidan. *The Shape of Catholic Theology: An Introduction to Its Sources, Principles, and History*. Collegeville, Minn.: Liturgical, 1991.

O'Collins, Gerald. *Fundamental Theology*. New York: Paulist, 1981.

Portier, William L. *Tradition and Incarnation: Foundations of Christian Theology*. New York: Paulist, 1994.

Ratzinger, Joseph. *Principles of Catholic Theology: Building Stones for a Fundamental Theology*. San Francisco: Ignatius, 1987.

Tracy, David. *The Analogical Imagination: Christian Theology and the Culture of Pluralism*. New York: Crossroad, 1981.

—————. *Blessed Rage for Order*. New York: Seabury, 1975.

—————. *Plurality and Ambiguity: Hermeneutics, Religion, Hope*. New York: Harper and Row, 1987.

5. Systematic Theologies

Fiorenza, Francis Schüssler, and John P. Galvin, eds. *Systematic Theology: Roman Catholic Perspectives*. 2 vols. Minneapolis: Fortress, 1991.

Rahner, Karl. *Foundations of Christian Faith*. Tr. William V. Dych. New York: Seabury, 1978.

van Beeck, Frans Jozef. *God Encountered: A Contemporary Catholic Systematic Theology*. 1: *Understanding the Christian Faith*. San Francisco: Harper and Row, 1989. 2/1: *The Revelation of the Glory—Introduction and Part 1: Fundamental Theology*. 2/2: *The Revelation of the Glory—Part 2: One God, Creator of All That Is*. Collegeville, Minn.: Liturgical, 1995.

von Balthasar, Hans Urs. *The Glory of the Lord: A Theological Aesthetics* [translation of *Herrlichkeit*.] 7 vols. 1: *Seeing the Form*. Tr. Erasmo Leiva-Merikakis. Ed. Joseph Fessio and John Riches. 2: *Studies in Theological Style: Clerical Styles*. Tr. Andrew Louth, Francis McDonagh, Brian McNeil. Ed. John Riches. 3: *Studies in Theological Style: Lay Styles*. Tr. Andrew Louth et al. Ed. John Riches. 4: *The Realm of Metaphysics in Antiquity*. Tr. Brian McNeil et al. Ed. John Riches. 5: *The Realm of Metaphysics in the Modern Age*. Tr. Oliver Davies et al. Ed. Brian McNeil and John Riches. 6: *Theology: The Old Covenant*. Tr. Brian McNeil and Erasmo Leiva-Merikakis. Ed. John Riches. 7: *Theology: The New Covenant*. Tr. Brian McNeil. Ed. John Riches. San Francisco: Ignatius, 1982-91.

—————. *Theo-Drama: Theological Dramatic Theory* [translation of *Theodramatik*]. 4 vols. published of 5. Tr. Graham Harrison. 1: *Prolegomena*. 2: *The Dramatis Personae: Man in God*. 3: *The Dramatis Personae: The Person in Christ*. 4: *The Action*. San Francisco: Ignatius, 1988-94.

D. Specific Themes in Systematic Theology

1. God

Cousins, Ewert H., ed. *Process Theology: Basic Writings.* New York: Newman, 1971.

Dupré, Louis. *The Other Dimension: A Search for the Meaning of Religious Attitudes.* Garden City, N.Y.: Doubleday, 1972.

Johnson, Elizabeth A. *She Who Is: The Mystery of God in Feminist Theological Discourse.* New York: Crossroad, 1992

Küng, Hans. *Does God Exist? An Answer for Today.* Tr. Edward Quinn. Garden City, N.Y.: Doubleday, 1980.

Murray, John Courtney. *The Problem of God.* New Haven: Yale University Press, 1964.

Prestige, George Leonard. *God in Patristic Thought.* 2d ed. London: SPCK, 1962.

Shea, John. *Stories of God: An Unauthorized Biography.* Chicago: Thomas More, 1978.

2. The Trinity

Bracken, Joseph. *The Triune Symbol: Persons, Process and Community.* Lanham, Md.: University Press of America, 1985.

Hill, William. *The Three-Personed God.* Washington, D.C.: University Press of America, 1983.

Kasper, Walter. *The God of Jesus Christ.* Tr. Matthew J. O'Connell. New York: Crossroad, 1984.

LaCugna, Catherine M. *God for Us: The Trinity and Christian Life.* San Francisco: HarperSanFrancisco, 1991.

Marsh, Thomas. *The Triune God: A Biblical, Historical, and Theological Study.* Mystic, Conn.: Twenty-Third, 1994.

O'Carroll, Michael. *Trinitas: A Theological Encyclopedia of the Holy Trinity.* Wilmington, Del.: Michael Glazier, 1987.

Rahner, Karl. *The Trinity.* Tr. Joseph Donceel. New York: Herder and Herder, 1970.

Studer, Basil. *Trinity and Incarnation: The Faith of the Early Church.* Tr. Matthias Westerhoff. Collegeville, Minn.: Liturgical, 1993.

Weinandy, Thomas G. *The Father's Spirit of Sonship: Reconceiving the Trinity.* Edinburgh: T & T Clark, 1995.

3. Jesus Christ

Boff, Leonardo. *Jesus Christ Liberator: A Critical Christology for Our Time.* Tr. Patrick Hughes. Maryknoll, N.Y.: Orbis, 1978.

Brown, Raymond E. *The Birth of the Messiah: A Commentary on the Infancy Narratives in the Gospels of Matthew and Luke.* The Anchor Bible Reference Library. New Updated Edition. New York: Doubleday, 1993 (1977).

————. *The Death of the Messiah: A Commentary on the Passion Narratives in the Four Gospels.* 2 vols. New York: Doubleday, 1994

————. *The Virginal Conception and Bodily Resurrection of Jesus.* New York: Paulist, 1973.

Fitzmyer, Joseph A. *A Christological Catechism: New Testament Answers.* New York: Paulist, 1982.

————. *Scripture and Christology: A Statement of the Biblical Commission with a Commentary.* New York: Paulist, 1986.

Fuller, Reginald. *The Formation of the Resurrection Narratives.* New York: Macmillan, 1971.

Galot, Jean. *Who Is Christ? A Theology of the Incarnation.* Chicago: Franciscan Herald, 1981.

Goergen, Donald. *A Theology of Jesus.* 3 vols. to date. Vol. 1: *The Mission and Ministry of Jesus.* Wilmington, Del.: Michael Glazier, 1986. Vol. 2: *The Death and Resurrection of Jesus.* Wilmington, Del.: Michael Glazier, 1988. Vol. 3: *The Jesus of Christian History.* Collegeville, Minn.: Liturgical Press, 1992.

Grillmeier, Alois. *Christ in Christian Tradition.* Vol. 1: *From the Apostolic Age to Chalcedon (451).* 2d ed. Tr. John Bowden. Atlanta: John Knox, 1975. Vol. 2: *From the Council of Chalcedon (451) to Gregory the Great (590-604).* Part 1: *Reception and Contradiction. The Development of the Discussion about Chalcedon from 451 to the Beginning of the Reign of Justinian.* Tr. Pauline Allen and John Cawte. Part 2: (with Theresia Hainthaler) *The Church of Constantinople in the Sixth Century.* Part 4: (with Theresia Hainthaler) *The Church of Alexandria with Nubia and Ethiopia after 451.* Tr. O. C. Dean, Jr. Atlanta: John Knox, 1995.

Kasper, Walter. *Jesus the Christ.* Tr. V. Green. New York: Paulist, 1976.

Küng, Hans. *On Being a Christian.* Tr. Edward Quinn. Garden City, N.Y.: Doubleday, 1976.

Lane, Dermot. *The Reality of Jesus.* New York: Paulist, 1975.

McDermott, Brian O. *Dimensions of Christology.* Collegeville, Minn.: Liturgical, 1992.

Meier, John P. *A Marginal Jew: Rethinking the Human Jesus.* Vol. 1: *The Roots of the Problem and the Person.* New York: Doubleday, 1991. Vol. 2: *Mentor, Message, and Miracles.* New York: Doubleday, 1994.

Neyrey, Jerome H. *Christ Is Community: The Christologies of the New Testament*. Wilmington, Del.: Michael Glazier, 1985.

O'Carroll, Michael. *Verbum Caro: An Encyclopedia on Jesus, the Christ*. Wilmington, Del.: Michael Glazier, 1992.

O'Collins, Gerald. *Christology: A Biblical, Historical, and Systematic Study of Jesus Christ*. New York: Oxford University Press, 1995.

———. *Interpreting Jesus*. New York: Paulist, 1983.

———. *Interpreting the Resurrection: Examining the Major Problems in the Stories of Jesus' Resurrection*. New York: Paulist, 1988.

———. *Jesus Risen: An Historical, Fundamental and Systematic Examination of Christ's Resurrection*. New York: Paulist, 1987.

———. *What Are They Saying about the Resurrection?* New York: Paulist, 1978.

Pelikan, Jaroslav. *Jesus through the Centuries: His Place in the History of Culture*. New Haven: Yale University Press, 1985.

Perkins, Pheme. *Resurrection: New Testament Witness and Contemporary Reflection*. Garden City, N.Y.: Doubleday, 1984.

Rahner, Karl. "Current Problems in Christology." Tr. Cornelius Ernst. *Theological Investigations* I (Baltimore: Helicon, 1961): 149-200.

Schillebeeckx, Edward. *Christ: The Experience of Jesus as Lord*. Tr. John Bowden. New York: Seabury, 1980.

———. *Jesus: An Experiment in Christology*. Tr. Hubert Hoskins. New York: Seabury, 1975.

Schüssler Fiorenza, Elisabeth. *Jesus: Miriam's Child, Sophia's Prophet: Critical Issues in Feminist Christology*. New York: Continuum, 1994.

Senior, Donald. *Jesus: A Gospel Portrait*. Rev. ed. New York: Paulist, 1992.

Sloyan, Gerard S. *Jesus in Focus: A Life in its Setting*. Revised ed. Mystic, Conn.: Twenty-Third, 1994.

Sobrino, Jon. *Christology at the Crossroads*. Tr. John Drury. Maryknoll, N.Y.: Orbis, 1978.

———. *Jesus in Latin America*. Maryknoll, N.Y.: Orbis, 1987.

Thompson, William M. *The Jesus Debate: A Survey and Synthesis*. New York: Paulist, 1985.

4. The Holy Spirit

Congar, Yves. *I Believe in the Holy Spirit*. Tr. David Smith. 3 vols. New York: Seabury, 1983.

O'Carroll, Michael. *Veni Creator Spiritus: An Encyclopedia of the Holy Spirit*. Wilmington, Del.: Michael Glazier, 1990.

5. Creation, Evil

Binns, Emily. *The World as Creation: Creation in Christ in an Evolutionary World View.* Collegeville, Minn.: Liturgical, 1990.

Forsyth, Neil. *The Old Enemy: Satan and the Combat Myth.* Princeton: Princeton University Press, 1987.

Hayes, Zachary. *What Are They Saying about Creation?* New York: Paulist, 1980.

Kelly, Henry Ansgar. *The Devil, Demonology, and Witchcraft.* Rev. ed. Garden City, N.Y.: Doubleday, 1974.

Latourelle, René. *The Miracles of Jesus and the Theology of Miracles.* Tr. Matthew J. O'Connell. New York: Paulist, 1988.

McMullin, Ernan, ed. *Evolution and Creation.* Notre Dame, Ind.: University of Notre Dame Press, 1985.

Russell, Jeffrey Burton. *The Devil: Perceptions of Evil from Antiquity to Primitive Christianity.* Ithaca, N.Y.: Cornell University Press, 1981.

———. *Lucifer: The Devil in the Middle Ages.* Ithaca, N.Y.: Cornell University Press, 1984.

———. *Mephistopheles: The Devil in the Modern World.* Ithaca, N.Y.: Cornell University Press, 1986.

———. *The Prince of Darkness: Radical Evil and the Power of Good in History.* Ithaca, N.Y.: Cornell University Press, 1988.

———. *Satan: The Early Christian Tradition.* Ithaca, N.Y.: Cornell University Press, 1981.

Teilhard de Chardin, Pierre. *The Phenomenon of Man.* Tr. Bernard Wall. New York: Harper and Row, 1959.

Tilley, Terrence W. *The Evils of Theodicy.* Washington, D.C.: Georgetown University Press, 1991.

6. Theological Anthropology, Grace, Sin

Anderson, H. George, T. Austin Murphy, and Joseph A. Burgess, eds. *Justification by Faith.* Lutherans and Catholics in Dialogue VII. Minneapolis: Augsburg, 1985.

Boff, Leonardo. *Liberating Grace.* Tr. John Drury. Maryknoll, N.Y.: Orbis, 1979.

Duffy, Stephen J. *The Graced Horizon: Nature and Grace in Modern Catholic Thought.* Collegeville, Minn.: Liturgical, 1992.

———. "Our Hearts of Darkness: Original Sin Revisited." *Theological Studies* 49 (1988): 597-622.

Fox, Matthew. *Original Blessing.* Sante Fe, N.M.: Bear and Co., 1983.

Gaffney, James. *Sin Reconsidered.* New York: Paulist, 1983.

Haight, Roger. *The Experience and Language of Grace*. New York: Paulist, 1983.

John Paul II, Pope. Apostolic Letter, *Mulieris dignitatem*, "On the Dignity and Vocation of Women." *Origins* 18 (1988): 261, 263-83.

McDermott, Brian O. *What Are They Saying about the Grace of Christ?* New York: Paulist, 1984.

———. "The Theology of Original Sin: Recent Developments." *Theological Studies* 38 (1977): 478-512.

McGrath, Alister E. *Iustitia Dei: A History of the Christian Doctrine of Justification*. 2 vols. Cambridge: Cambridge University Press, 1986.

Reumann, John. *"Righteousness" in the New Testament*. With responses by Joseph A. Fitzmyer and Jerome D. Quinn. Philadelphia: Fortress, 1982.

Rondet, Henri. *The Grace of Christ: A Brief History of the Theology of Grace*. Westminster, Md.: Newman, 1966.

Schoonenberg, Piet. *Man and Sin: A Theological View*. Tr. Joseph Donceel. Notre Dame: University of Notre Dame Press, 1965.

Segundo, Juan Luis. *Evolution and Guilt*. Tr. John Drury. Maryknoll, N.Y.: Orbis, 1974.

Sullivan, Francis A. *Salvation Outside the Church? Tracing the History of the Catholic Response*. New York: Paulist, 1992.

Tavard, George. *Justification: An Ecumenical Study*. New York: Paulist, 1983.

Vandervelde, George. *Original Sin: Two Major Trends in Contemporary Roman Catholic Reinterpretation*. Washington, D.C.: University Press of America, 1981.

Vanneste, Alfred. *The Dogma of Original Sin*. Tr. Edward P. Callens. Brussels: Vander, 1971.

7. The Church

a. General Works

Boff, Leonardo. *Church: Charism and Power: Liberation Theology and the Institutional Church*. Tr. John W. Diercksmeier. New York: Crossroad, 1985.

———. *Ecclesiogenesis: The Base Communities Reinvent the Church*. Tr. Robert R. Barr. Maryknoll, N.Y.: Orbis, 1986.

Burtchaell, James Tunstead. *From Synagogue to Church: Public Services and Offices in the Earliest Christian Communities*. New York: Cambridge University Press, 1992.

Doyle, Dennis M. *The Church Emerging from Vatican II: A Popular Approach to Contemporary Catholicism*. Mystic, Conn.: Twenty-Third, 1992.

Dulles, Avery. *The Catholicity of the Church*. Oxford: Clarendon Press, 1985.

————. *A Church to Believe in: Discipleship and the Dynamics of Freedom.* New York: Crossroad, 1982.

————. *Models of the Church.* Expanded edition. New York: Doubleday, 1987.

————. *The Reshaping of Catholicism: Current Challenges in the Theology of the Church.* San Francisco: Harper and Row, 1988.

Evans, G. R. *The Church and the Churches: Towards an Ecumenical Ecclesiology.* New York: Cambridge University Press, 1994.

Hamer, Jerome. *The Church Is a Communion.* Tr. Ronald Matthews. New York: Sheed and Ward, 1964.

Jay, Eric. *The Church: Its Changing Image through Twenty Centuries.* Atlanta: John Knox, 1980.

Kasper, Walter. *Theology and Church.* Tr. Margaret Kohl. New York: Crossroad, 1989.

Küng, Hans. *The Church.* Tr. Ray and Rosaleen Ockenden. New York: Sheed and Ward, 1968.

Newman, John Henry. *On Consulting the Faithful in Matters of Doctrine.* 1859. Introd. by John Coulson. Kansas City: Sheed and Ward, 1985.

Oakley, Francis. *Council over Pope? Towards a Provisional Ecclesiology.* New York: Herder and Herder, 1969.

Sanks, T. Howland. *Salt, Leaven, and Light: The Community Called Church.* New York: Crossroad, 1994.

Schillebeeckx, Edward. *Church: The Human Story of God.* Tr. John Bowden. New York: Crossroad, 1990.

Schüssler Fiorenza, Elisabeth. *Discipleship of Equals: A Critical Feminist Ekklesia-logy of Liberation.* New York: Crossroad, 1993.

Sullivan, Francis. *The Church We Believe In: One, Holy, Catholic and Apostolic.* New York: Paulist, 1988.

Tavard, George H. *The Church, Community of Salvation: An Ecumenical Ecclesiology.* Collegeville, Minn.: Liturgical, 1992.

Tillard, Jean-Marie. *Church of Churches: The Ecclesiology of Communion.* Tr. R. C. DePeaux. Collegeville, Minn.: Liturgical, 1992.

b. Laity

Congar, Yves. *Lay People in the Church: A Study for a Theology of the Laity.* Tr. Donald Attwater. Revised edition. Westminster, Md.: Newman, 1965.

Faivre, Alexandre. *The Emergence of the Laity in the Early Church.* Tr. David Smith. New York: Paulist, 1990.

John Paul II, Pope. *The Lay Members of Christ's Faithful People.* Boston: Daughters of St. Paul, 1988.

c. Ministry

Bernier, Paul. *Ministry in the Church: A Historical and Pastoral Approach.* Mystic, Conn.: Twenty-Third, 1992.

Champlin, Joseph M. *An Important Office of Immense Love.* New York: Paulist, 1980. [On eucharistic ministers.]

Collins, John N. *Diakonia: Reinterpreting the Ancient Sources.* New York: Oxford University Press, 1990.

Cooke, Bernard. *Ministry to Word and Sacraments: History and Theology.* Philadelphia: Fortress, 1976.

O'Meara, Thomas Franklin, O.P. *Theology of Ministry.* New York: Paulist, 1983.

Osborne, Kenan. *Ministry: Lay Ministry in the Roman Catholic Church: Its History and Theology.* New York: Paulist, 1993.

Power, David N. *Gifts That Differ: Lay Ministries Established and Unestablished.* New York, Pueblo, 1980.

Rademacher, William J. *Lay Ministry: A Theological, Spiritual, and Pastoral Handbook.* New York: Crossroad, 1991.

Schillebeeckx, Edward. *The Church with a Human Face: A New and Expanded Theology of Ministry.* Tr. John Bowden. New York: Crossroad, 1985.

d. Bishops and Priests (see also X.C.5: Sacrament of Order)

Brown, Raymond E. *Priest and Bishop: Biblical Reflections.* Paramus, N.J.: Paulist, 1970.

Legrand, Hervé, Julio Manzanares, and Antonio García y García, eds. *The Nature and Future of Episcopal Conferences.* Washington, D.C.: The Catholic University of America Press, 1988.

Osborne, Kenan B. *Priesthood: A History of Ordained Ministry in the Roman Catholic Church.* New York: Paulist, 1988.

Reese, Thomas J. *Archbishop: Inside the Power Structure of the American Catholic Church.* San Francisco: Harper and Row, 1989.

————. *A Flock of Shepherds: The National Conference of Catholic Bishops.* Kansas City, Mo.: Sheed and Ward, 1992.

————, ed. *Episcopal Conferences: Historical, Canonical, and Theological Studies.* Washington, D.C.: Georgetown University Press, 1989.

e. The Papacy

Dionne, J. Robert. *The Papacy and the Church: A Study of Praxis and Reception in Ecumenical Perspective.* New York: Philosophical Library, 1987.

Empie, Paul C., and T. Austin Murphy, eds. *Papal Primacy and the Universal Church*. Lutherans and Catholics in Dialogue 5. Minneapolis: Augsburg, 1974.

Eno, Robert. *The Rise of the Papacy*. Wilmington, Del.: Michael Glazier, 1990.

Granfield, Patrick. *The Limits of the Papacy: Authority and Autonomy in the Church*. New York: Crossroad, 1987.

————. *The Papacy in Transition*. Garden City, N.Y.: Doubleday, 1980.

McCord, Peter J., ed. *A Pope for All Christians?* New York: Paulist, 1976.

Miller, J. Michael. *What Are They Saying about Papal Primacy?* New York: Paulist, 1983.

Schimmelpfennig, Bernard. *The Papacy*. Tr. James Sievert. New York: Columbia University Press, 1992 .

Tillard, J. M. R. *The Bishop of Rome*. Translated by John de Satgé. Wilmington, Del.: Michael Glazier, 1983.

f. Authority, Dissent

Boyle, John P. *Church Teaching Authority: Historical and Theological Studies*. Notre Dame, Ind.: University of Notre Dame Press, 1994.

Curran, Charles E. *Faithful Dissent*. Kansas City, Mo.: Sheed and Ward, 1986.

Curran, Charles E., Robert E. Hunt, et al. *Dissent In and For the Church*. New York: Sheed and Ward, 1969.

Curran, Charles E., and Richard A. McCormick, eds. *Readings in Moral Theology, No. 6: Dissent in the Church*. New York: Paulist, 1988.

Kaufman, Philip S. *Why You Can Disagree and Remain a Faithful Catholic*. Revised and expanded edition. New York: Crossroad, 1995.

Orsy, Ladislas. *The Church: Learning and Teaching*. Wilmington, Del.: Michael Glazier, 1987.

Prusak, Bernard P., ed. *Raising the Torch of Good News: Catholic Authority and Dialogue with the World*. The Annual Publication of the College Theology Society, volume 32, 1986. Lanham, Md.: University Press of America, 1988.

Rausch, Thomas P. *Authority and Leadership in the Church: Past Directions and Future Possibilities*. Wilmington, Del.: Michael Glazier, 1989.

Sullivan, Francis A. *Magisterium: Teaching Authority in the Catholic Church*. New York: Paulist, 1983.

g. Infallibility

Bermejo, Luis M. *Infallibility on Trial: Church, Conciliarity and Communion*. Westminster, Md.: Christian Classics, 1992.

Chirico, Peter. *Infallibility: The Crossroads of Doctrine*. Reprinted with new introduction. Wilmington, Del.: Michael Glazier, 1983 [1977].

Empie, Paul C., T. Austin Murphy, and Joseph A. Burgess, eds. *Teaching Authority and Infallibility in the Church*. Lutherans and Catholics in Dialogue 6. Minneapolis: Augsburg, 1980.

Gaillardetz, Richard R. *Witnesses to the Faith: Community, Infallibility, and the Ordinary Magisterium of Bishops*. New York: Paulist, 1992.

Küng, Hans. *Infallible? An Inquiry*. Trans. E. Quinn. Garden City: Doubleday, 1971.

————. *Infallible? An Unresolved Inquiry*. New expanded edition, with a preface by Herbert Haag. New York: Continuum, 1994.

O'Gara, Margaret. *Triumph in Defeat: Infallibility, Vatican I and the French Minority Bishops*. Washington, D.C.: The Catholic University of America Press, 1988.

Tekippe, Terry J., ed. *Papal Infallibility: An Application of Lonergan's Theological Method*. Washington, D.C.: University Press of America, 1983.

Tierney, Brian. *Origins of Papal Infallibility, 1150-1350: A Study on the Concepts of Infallibility, Sovereignty, and Tradition in the Middle Ages*. Leiden: Brill, 1972.

8. Mary and the Saints

Anderson, H. George, J. Francis Stafford, Joseph A. Burgess, eds. *The One Mediator, the Saints, and Mary*. Lutherans and Catholics in Dialogue VIII. Minneapolis: Augsburg Fortress, 1992.

Brown, Peter. *The Cult of the Saints: Its Rise and Function in Latin Christianity*. Chicago: University of Chicago Press, 1981.

Brown, Raymond, et al. *Mary in the New Testament*. Philadelphia: Fortress, and New York: Paulist, 1978.

Cunningham, Lawrence. *The Meaning of Saints*. New York: Harper and Row, 1980.

————. "A Decade of Research on the Saints." *Theological Studies* 53 (1992): 517-33.

Donnelly, Doris, ed. *Mary: Woman of Nazareth: Biblical and Theological Perspectives*. New York: Paulist, 1989.

Graef, Hilda. *Mary: A History of Doctrine and Devotion*. 2 vols. New York: Sheed and Ward, 1963-65.

Jelly, Frederick M. *Madonna: Mary in the Catholic Tradition*. Huntington, Ind.: Our Sunday Visitor, 1986.

O'Carroll, Michael. *Theotokos: A Theological Encyclopedia of the Blessed Virgin Mary*. Wilmington, Del.: Michael Glazier, 1982.

O'Connor, E. D., ed. *The Dogma of the Immaculate Conception—History and Significance.* Notre Dame, Ind.: University of Notre Dame Press, 1958.

Rahner, Karl. *"Virginitas in Partu." Theological Investigations.* Vol. 4: *More Recent Writings.* Tr. Kevin Smith. Baltimore: Helicon, 1966. 134-162.

Tambasco, Anthony J. *What Are They Saying about Mary?* New York: Paulist, 1984.

Thompson, William. *Fire and Light: The Saints and Theology.* New York: Paulist, 1987.

Woodward, Kenneth L. *Making Saints: How the Catholic Church Determines Who Becomes a Saint, Who Doesn't, and Why.* New York: Simon and Schuster, 1990.

Zimdars-Swartz, Sandra L. *Encountering Mary: From La Salette to Medjugorje.* Princeton, N.J.: Princeton University Press, 1991.

9. Eschatology

Bernstein, Alan E. *The Formation of Hell: Death and Retribution in the Ancient and Early Christian Worlds.* Ithaca, N.Y.: Cornell University Press, 1993.

Boros, Ladislas. *The Mystery of Death.* Tr. Gregory Bainbridge. New York: Herder and Herder, 1965.

Daley, Brian E. *The Hope of the Early Church: A Handbook of Patristic Eschatology.* New York: Cambridge University Press, 1991.

Dyer, George J. *Limbo: Unsettled Question.* New York: Sheed and Ward, 1964.

Häring, Hermann, and Johann-Baptist Metz, eds. *Reincarnation or Resurrection? Concilium* 1993/5. London, 1993.

Hayes, Zachary. *Visions of a Future: A Study of Christian Eschatology.* Wilmington, Del.: Michael Glazier, 1989.

————. *What Are They Saying about the End of the World?* New York: Paulist, 1983.

Hellwig, Monika K. *What Are They Saying about Christian Hope?* New York: Paulist, 1978.

International Theological Commission. "Some Current Questions in Eschatology." *The Irish Theological Quarterly* 58 (1992): 209-43.

Küng, Hans. *Eternal Life? Life after Death as a Medical, Philosophical, and Theological Problem.* Tr. Edward Quinn. Garden City, N.Y.: Doubleday, 1984.

Le Goff, Jacques. *The Birth of Purgatory.* Tr. Arthur Goldhammer. Chicago: University of Chicago Press, 1984.

Phan, Peter C. "Contemporary Context and Issues in Eschatology." *Theological Studies* 55 (1994): 507-536.

Rahner, Karl. *On the Theology of Death*. Tr. C. H. Henkey. New York: Herder and Herder, 1961.

Ratzinger, Joseph. *Eschatology: Death and Eternal Life*. Tr. Michael Waldstein. Washington, D.C.: The Catholic University of America Press, 1988.

Richards, Hubert J. *Death and After*. Mystic, Conn.: Twenty-Third, 1987.

Sachs, John R. "Apocatastasis in Patristic Theology." *Theological Studies* 54 (1993): 617-40.

————. "Current Eschatology: Universal Salvation and the Problem of Hell." *Theological Studies* 52 (1991): 227-54.

Sacred Congregation for the Doctrine of the Faith. "The Reality of Life after Death" ["On Certain Questions Pertaining to Eschatology"]. In Austin Flannery, ed., *Vatican Council II: More Postconciliar Documents* (Northport, N.Y.: Costello, 1982) 500-04.

Schillebeeckx, Edward, and Boniface Willems, eds. *The Problem of Eschatology. Concilium*, vol. 41. New York: Paulist, 1969.

Schnackenburg, Rudolf. *God's Rule and Kingdom*. 2d ed. Tr. John Murray. New York: Herder, 1968.

Tugwell, Simon G. *Human Immortality and the Redemption of Death*. London: Darton, Longman, and Todd, 1990.

Van de Walle, A. R. *From Darkness to the Dawn*. Mystic, Conn.: Twenty-Third, 1985.

Walls, Jerry L. *Hell: The Logic of Damnation*. Notre Dame, Ind.: University of Notre Dame Press, 1992.

E. Individual Contemporary Theologians

Crowe, Frederick E. *Lonergan*. Outstanding Christian Thinkers. Collegeville, Minn.: Liturgical, 1992.

Dych, William V. *Karl Rahner*. Outstanding Christian Thinkers. Collegeville, Minn.: Liturgical, 1992.

Gregson, Vernon, ed. *The Desires of the Human Heart: An Introduction to the Theology of Bernard Lonergan*. New York: Paulist, 1988.

Kennedy, Philip. *Schillebeeckx*. Outstanding Christian Thinkers. Collegeville, Minn.: Liturgical, 1993.

Meynell, Hugo A. *An Introduction to the Philosophy of Bernard Lonergan*. New York: Barnes and Noble, 1976.

————. *The Theology of Bernard Lonergan*. Atlanta: Scholars, 1986.

Nichols, Aidan. *Yves Congar*. Wilton, Conn.: Morehouse-Barlow, 1989.

Oakes, Edward T. *Pattern of Redemption: The Theology of Hans Urs von Balthasar*. New York: Continuum, 1994.

O'Donnell, John. *Hans Urs von Balthasar*. Outstanding Christian Thinkers. Collegeville, Minn.: Liturgical, 1992.

O'Donovan, Leo J., ed. *A World of Grace: An Introduction to the Themes and Foundations of Karl Rahner's Theology.* New York: Seabury, 1980.

Rahner, Karl. *A Rahner Reader.* Ed. Gerald McCool. New York: Seabury, 1975.

———. *Theological Investigations.* 23 volumes. Various translators and publishers. 1961-94.

Schreiter, Robert J., and Mary Catherine Hilkert, eds. *The Praxis of Christian Experience: An Introduction to the Theology of Edward Schillebeeckx.* San Francisco: Harper and Row, 1989.

Vorgrimler, Herbert. *Understanding Karl Rahner: An Introduction to his Life and Thought.* Tr. John Bowden. New York: Crossroad, 1986.

F. Moral Theology

1. General and Historical Works

Bernardin, Joseph Cardinal, et al. *Consistent Ethic of Life.* Kansas City, Mo.: Sheed and Ward, 1988.

Collins, Raymond F. *Christian Morality: Biblical Foundations.* Notre Dame, Ind.: University of Notre Dame Press, 1986.

Curran, Charles E. *Critical Concerns in Moral Theology.* Notre Dame, Ind.: University of Notre Dame Press, 1984.

Gallagher, John A. *Time Past, Time Future: An Historical Study of Catholic Moral Theology.* New York: Paulist, 1990.

Grisez, Germain. *The Way of the Lord Jesus.* Vol. 1: *Christian Moral Principles.* Chicago: Franciscan Herald, 1983. Vol. 2: *Living a Christian Life.* Chicago: Franciscan Herald, 1993.

Grisez, Germain, and Russell Shaw. *Fulfillment in Christ: A Summary of Christian Moral Principles.* Notre Dame, Ind.: University of Notre Dame Press, 1989.

Happel, Stephen, and James J. Walter. *Conversion and Discipleship: A Christian Foundation for Ethics and Doctrine.* Philadelphia: Fortress, 1986.

Häring, Bernard. *Free and Faithful in Christ: Moral Theology for Clergy and Laity.* 3 vols. New York: Seabury, 1978.

———. *The Law of Christ: Moral Theology for Priests and Laity.* Tr. Edwin G. Kaiser. Westminster, Md.: Newman, 1961-66.

Mahoney, John. *The Making of Moral Theology: A Study of the Roman Catholic Tradition.* Oxford: Clarendon, 1987.

McCormick, Richard A. *The Critical Calling: Reflections on Moral Dilemmas Since Vatican II.* Washington, D.C.: Georgetown University Press, 1989.

———. *Notes on Moral Theology 1965 through 1980.* Lanham, Md.: University Press of America, 1981.

————. *Notes on Moral Theology 1981 through 1984.* Lanham, Md.: University Press of America, 1984.

————. "Moral Theology 1940-1989: An Overview." *Theological Studies* 50 (1989): 3-24.

McDonagh, Enda. *The Making of Disciples: Tasks of Moral Theology.* Wilmington, Del.: Michael Glazier, 1982.

O'Connell, Timothy E. *Principles for a Catholic Morality.* Revised Edition. San Francisco: Harper and Row, 1990.

Pinckaers, Servais. *The Sources of Christian Ethics.* Tr. Sr. Mary Thomas Noble. Washington, D.C.: The Catholic University of America Press, 1995.

2. Fundamental Moral Theology

Curran, Charles E., and Richard A. McCormick, eds. *Readings in Moral Theology No. 1: Moral Norms and Catholic Tradition.* New York: Paulist, 1979.

Gula, Richard M. *Reason Informed by Faith: Foundations of Catholic Morality.* New York: Paulist, 1989.

————. *What Are They Saying about Moral Norms?* New York: Paulist, 1982.

Hoose, Bernard. *Proportionalism: The American Debate and its European Roots.* Washington, D.C.: Georgetown University Press, 1987.

McCormick, Richard, and Paul Ramsey, eds. *Doing Evil to Achieve Good.* Chicago: Loyola University Press, 1978.

3. Virtues

Cessario, Romanus, O.P. *The Moral Virtues and Theological Ethics.* Notre Dame, Ind.: University of Notre Dame Press, 1991.

Harak, G. Simon. *Virtuous Passions: The Formation of Christian Character.* New York: Paulist, 1993.

Porter, Jean. *The Recovery of Virtue: The Relevance of Aquinas for Christian Ethics.* Louisville: Westminster/John Knox Press, 1990.

Rahner, Karl. *The Love of Jesus and the Love of Neighbor.* Tr. Robert Barr. New York: Crossroad, 1983.

Spohn, William C. "The Return of Virtue Ethics." *Theological Studies* 53 (1992): 60-75.

Vacek, Edward Collins. *Love, Human and Divine: The Heart of Christian Ethics.* Washington, D.C.: Georgetown University Press, 1994.

Wadell, Paul J. *The Primacy of Love: An Introduction to the Ethics of Thomas Aquinas.* New York: Paulist, 1992.

4. Natural Law

Curran, Charles E. *Directions in Fundamental Moral Theology*. Notre Dame, Ind.: University of Notre Dame Press, 1986.
————, and Richard McCormick. *Readings in Moral Theology No. 7: Natural Law and Theology*. New York: Paulist, 1991.
Finnis, John. *Natural Law and Natural Rights*. New York: Oxford University Press, 1980.
Fuchs, Joseph. *Natural Law: A Theological Investigation*. New York: Sheed and Ward, 1965.

5. Specific Issues

a. Abortion

Burtchaell, James Tunstead. *Rachel Weeping and Other Essays on Abortion*. Kansas City, Kans.: Andrews and McMeel, 1982.
Connery, John. *Abortion, the Development of the Roman Catholic Perspective*. Chicago: Loyola University Press, 1977.
Gorman, Michael J. *Abortion and the Early Church: Christian, Jewish, and Pagan Attitudes in the Greco-Roman World*. New York: Paulist, 1982.
Grisez, Germain G. *Abortion: The Myths, the Realities, and the Arguments*. New York: Corpus Books, 1970.
Jung, Patricia Beattie, and Thomas A. Shannon, eds. *Abortion and Catholicism: the American Debate*. New York: Crossroad, 1988.
Maguire, Daniel C., James Tunstead Burtchaell, and the Editors. "The Catholic Legacy and Abortion: A Debate." *Commonweal* 114 (1987): 657-680.
Noonan, John T., Jr., ed. *The Morality of Abortion: Legal and Historical Perspectives*. Cambridge, Mass.: Harvard University Press, 1970.

b. Capital Punishment

Böckle, Franz and Jacques Pohier, eds. *The Death Penalty and Torture*. *Concilium* 120. New York, Seabury, 1979.
John Paul II, Pope. Encyclical *Evangelium Vitae*. *Origins* 24 (1995): 689, 691-730.
Langan, John. "Capital Punishment." *Theological Studies* 54 (1993): 111-24.
Melton, J. Gordon. *The Churches Speak on Capital Punishment*. Detroit: Gale Research, 1989.

c. Euthanasia

Cahill, Lisa Sowle. "Notes on Moral Theology 1990: Bioethical Decisions to End Life." *Theological Studies* 52 (1991): 107-27.
Congregation for the Doctrine of the Faith. "Declaration on Euthanasia" (May 5, 1980). In Austin Flannery, ed., *Vatican Council II: More Postconciliar Documents*. Northport, N.Y.: Costello, 1982. 510-17.
Grisez, Germain, and Joseph Boyle. *Life and Death with Liberty and Justice: A Contribution to the Euthanasia Debate*. Notre Dame, Ind.: University of Notre Dame Press, 1979.
Gula, Richard M. *What Are They Saying about Euthanasia?* New York: Paulist, 1986.
Maguire, Daniel. *Death by Choice*. Garden City, N.Y.: Doubleday, 1974.
Ohio Bishops. "Pastoral Considerations: Euthanasia, Assisted Suicide." *Origins* 23 (1993): 373-78.
Pennsylvania Bishops. "Nutrition and Hydration: Moral Considerations." *Origins* 21 (1992): 541, 543-53.

d. Health Care

Ashley, Benedict, and Kevin D. O'Rourke. *Ethics of Health Care: An Introductory Textbook*. Washington, D.C.: Georgetown University Press, 1994.
Griese, Orville N. *Catholic Identity in Health Care: Principles and Practice*. Braintree, Mass.: Pope John XXIII Center, 1987.
McCormick, Richard A. *Health and Medicine in the Catholic Tradition: Tradition in Transition*. New York: Crossroad, 1987.
National Conference of Catholic Bishops. "Ethical and Religious Directives for Catholic Health Care Services." *Origins* 24 (1994): 449-62.
O'Rourke, Kevin D., and Philip Boyle. *Medical Ethics: Sources of Catholic Teachings*. 2d ed. Washington, D.C.: Georgetown University Press, 1993.
"Special Catholic Healthcare Report." *The National Catholic Reporter* (June 16, 1995): 11-18.
U.S. Bishops. "Pastoral Letter on Health and Health Care." *Origins* 11 (1981): 396-402.

e. Sexual Ethics

Cahill, Lisa Sowle. *Between the Sexes: Foundations for a Christian Ethics of Sexuality*. Philadelphia: Fortress, 1985.
———. "Catholic Sexual Ethics and the Dignity of the Person: A Double Message." *Theological Studies* 50 (1989): 120-150.

Curran, Charles E., and Richard McCormick, eds. *Readings in Moral Theology No. 8: Dialogue about Catholic Sexual Teaching.* New York: Paulist, 1993.

Fox, Thomas C. *Sexuality and Catholicism.* New York: Braziller, 1995.

Genovesi, Vincent J. *In Pursuit of Love: Catholic Morality and Human Sexuality.* Wilmington, Del.: Michael Glazier, 1987.

Guindon, André. *The Sexual Creators: An Ethical Proposal for Concerned Christians.* Lanham, Md.: University Press of America, 1986.

John Paul II, Pope. *Original Unity of Man and Woman: Catechesis on the Book of Genesis.* Boston: Daughters of St. Paul, 1981.

Keane, Philip S., S.S. *Sexual Morality: A Catholic Perspective.* New York: Paulist, 1977.

Kosnik, Anthony, et al. *Human Sexuality: New Directions in American Catholic Thought.* A Study Commissioned by the Catholic Theological Society of America. New York: Paulist, 1977.

Lawler, Ronald, Joseph M. Boyle, Jr., and William E. May. *Catholic Sexual Ethics: A Summary, Exposition, and Defense.* Huntington, Ind.: Our Sunday Visitor Press, 1985.

Urbine, William, and William Seifert. *On Life and Love: A Guide to Catholic Teaching on Marriage and the Family.* Mystic, Conn.: Twenty-Third, 1993.

f. Birth Control

Curran, Charles E., ed. *Contraception: Authority and Dissent.* New York: Herder and Herder, 1969.

Grisez, Germain G. *Contraception and Natural Law.* Milwaukee: Bruce, 1964.

[Grisez, Germain G., John C. Ford, et al.]. *The Teaching of* Humanae vitae: *A Defense: Is its Teaching Infallible? Are its Norms Defeasible?* San Francisco: Ignatius, 1988.

John Paul II, Pope. *Reflections on* Humanae vitae: *Conjugal Morality and Spirituality.* Boston: Daughters of St. Paul, 1984.

Kaiser, Robert Blair. *The Politics of Sex and Religion: A Case History in the Development of Doctrine, 1962-1984.* Kansas City, Mo.: Leaven, 1985.

Kippley, John F. *Birth Control and the Marriage Covenant.* Collegeville, Minn.: Liturgical, 1976.

May, William E. *Contraception:* Humanae vitae *and Catholic Moral Thought.* Chicago: Franciscan Herald, 1984.

Noonan, John T., Jr. *Contraception: A History of its Treatment by the Catholic Theologians and Canonists.* Cambridge, Mass.: Harvard University Press, 1965.

Shannon, William H. *The Lively Debate: Responses to* Humanae Vitae. New York: Sheed and Ward, 1969.

Smith, Janet E. Humanae vitae: *A Generation Later*. Washington, D.C.: The
   Catholic University of America Press, 1991.

g. Homosexuality

Boswell, John. *Christianity, Social Tolerance, and Homosexuality: Gay People
   in Western Europe from the Beginning of the Christian Era to the
   Fourteenth Century*. Chicago: University of Chicago Press, 1980.
———. *Same-Sex Unions in Premodern Europe*. New York: Villard, 1994.
Coleman, Gerald D. *Homosexuality: Catholic Teaching and Pastoral Practice*.
   New York: Paulist, 1995.
Congregation for the Doctrine of the Faith. "Letter to the Bishops of the
   Catholic Church on the Pastoral Care of Homosexual Persons." *Origins*
   16 (1986): 377, 379-82.
———. "Responding to Legislative Proposals on Discrimination against
   Homosexual Persons." *Origins* 22 (1992): 173, 175-77.
Curran, Charles E. "Dialogue with the Homophile Movement." In *Catholic
   Moral Theology in Dialogue*. Notre Dame: University of Notre Dame
   Press, 1976.
Gramick, Jeannine, and Pat Furey, eds. *The Vatican and Homosexuality:
   Reactions to the "Letter to the Bishops of the Catholic Church on the
   Pastoral Care of Homosexual Persons."* New York: Crossroad, 1988.
Hanigan, James P. *Homosexuality: The Test Case for Christian Sexual Ethics*.
   New York: Paulist, 1988.
Harvey, John F. *The Homosexual Person: New Thinking in Pastoral Care*. San
   Francisco: Ignatius, 1987.
Holtz, Raymond C., ed. *Listen to Their Stories: Gay and Lesbian Catholics
   Talk About Their Lives and the Church*. New York: Garland, 1991.
Horner, Tom. *Homosexuality and the Judeo-Christian Tradition: An Annotated
   Bibliography*. Metuchen, N.J.: Scarecrow, 1981.
Malloy, Edward A. *Homosexuality and the Christian Way of Life*. Lanham,
   Md.: University Press of America, 1981.
McNeill, John J. *The Church and the Homosexual*. Updated edition. Boston:
   Beacon, 1988 [1976].
Nugent, Robert, ed. *A Challenge to Love: Gay and Lesbian Catholics in the
   Church*. New York: Crossroad, 1984.
Scroggs, Robin. *The New Testament and Homosexuality: Contextual
   Background for Contemporary Debate*. Philadelphia: Fortress, 1983.

h. Social Ethics (see also IX.G.1-2: Political and Liberation Theologies)

Curran, Charles E. *American Catholic Social Ethics: Twentieth-Century
   Approaches*. Notre Dame, Ind.: University of Notre Dame Press, 1982.

Curran, Charles E., and Richard A. McCormick, eds. *Official Catholic Social Teaching*. Readings in Moral Theology 5. New York: Paulist, 1986.

Coleman, John. *An American Strategic Theology*. New York: Paulist, 1982.

Coleman, John, and Gregory Baum, eds. Rerum Novarum: *One Hundred Years of Catholic Social Teaching. Concilium* 1991/5. Philadelphia: Trinity, 1991.

Dorr, Donal. *Option for the Poor: A Hundred Years of Catholic Social Teaching*. Revised edition. Maryknoll, N.Y.: Orbis, 1992.

Economic Justice for All: Pastoral Letter on Catholic Social Teaching and the U.S. Economy. Washington, D.C.: National Conference of Catholic Bishops, 1986.

Ferguson, Thomas P. *Catholic and American: The Political Theology of John Courtney Murray*. Kansas City: Sheed and Ward, 1993.

Gremillion, Joseph. *The Gospel of Peace and Justice: Catholic Social Teaching since Pope John*. Maryknoll, N.Y.: 1976.

Haughey, John C., ed., *The Faith that Does Justice: Examining the Christian Sources for Social Change*. Woodstock Studies 2. New York: Paulist, 1977.

Hollenbach, David. *Claims in Conflict: Retrieving and Renewing the Catholic Human Rights Tradition*. New York: Paulist, 1979.

————. *Justice, Peace, and Human Rights: American Catholic Social Ethics in a Pluralistic Context*. New York: Crossroad, 1988.

Kammer, Fred. *Doing Faithjustice: An Introduction to Catholic Social Thought*. New York: Paulist, 1991.

McElroy, Robert W. *The Search for an American Public Theology: The Contribution of John Courtney Murray*. New York: Paulist, 1989.

McGovern, Arthur F. *Marxism: An American Christian Perspective*. Maryknoll, N.Y.: Orbis, 1980.

Murray, John Courtney. *We Hold These Truths: Catholic Reflections on the American Proposition*. New York: Sheed and Ward, 1960.

Noonan, John T., Jr. *The Scholastic Analysis of Usury*. Cambridge, Mass.: Harvard University Press, 1957.

Novak, Michael. *The Catholic Ethic and the Spirit of Capitalism*. New York: Free Press, 1993.

Pelotte, Donald E. *John Courtney Murray: Theologian in Conflict*. New York: Paulist, 1975.

Schuck, Michael J. *That They Be One: The Social Teaching of the Papal Encyclicals 1740-1989*. Washington, D.C.: Georgetown University Press, 1991.

Walsh, Michael, and Brian Davies. *Proclaiming Justice and Peace: Documents from John XXIII-John Paul II*. Mystic, Conn.: Twenty-Third, 1985.

i. Racism

Baum, Gregory, and John Coleman, eds. *The Church and Racism. Concilium*
151. New York: Seabury, 1982.
National Conference of Catholic Bishops. *Brothers and Sisters to Us: U.S.
Bishops' Pastoral Letter on Racism in Our Day* [1979]. Bilingual edition.
Revised to include *For the Love of One Another* [Bishops' Committee on
Black Catholics, 1989]. Washington, D.C.: U.S. Catholic Conference,
n.d. [1990?].
Pontifical Justice and Peace Commission. "The Church and Racism: Toward
a More Fraternal Society." *Origins* 18 (1989): 613-26.

j. War and Peace

Au, William A. *The Cross, the Flag, and the Bomb: American Catholics
Debate War and Peace, 1960-1983.* Westport, Conn.: Greenwood, 1985.
Bainton, Roland H. *Christian Attitudes Toward War and Peace: A Historical
Survey and Critical Re-evaluation.* New York: Abingdon, 1960.
Cadoux, C. John. *The Early Christian Attitude to War: A Contribution to the
History of Christian Ethics.* New York: Seabury, 1982 [1919].
Cahill, Lisa Sowle. *Love Your Enemies: Discipleship, Pacifism, and Just War
Theory.* Minneapolis: Fortress, 1994.
Douglass, James W. *The Non-Violent Cross: A Theology of Revolution and
Peace.* New York: Macmillan, 1968.
Finnis, John, Joseph M. Boyle, Jr., and Germain Grisez. *Nuclear Deterrence,
Morality and Realism.* Oxford: Clarendon Press, 1987.
Helgeland, John, Robert J. Daly, and J. Patout Burns. *Christians and the
Military: The Early Experience.* Philadelphia: Fortress, 1985.
Hellwig, Monika K. *A Case for Peace in Reason and Faith.* Collegeville,
Minn.: Liturgical, 1992.
Hollenbach, David. *Nuclear Ethics: A Christian Moral Argument.* New York:
Paulist, 1983.
Hornus, Jean-Michel. *It Is Not Lawful for Me to Fight: Early Christian
Attitudes Toward War, Violence, and the State.* Revised Edition. Tr. Alan
Kreider and Oliver Coburn. Scottdale, Pa.: Herald, 1980.
Johnson, James Turner. *Just War Tradition and the Restraint of War: A Moral
and Historical Inquiry.* Princeton, N.J.: Princeton University Press,
1981.
McSorley, Richard. *New Testament Basis of Peacemaking.* Scottdale, Pa.:
Herald, 1985.
Miller, Richard B., ed. *War in the Twentieth Century: Sources in Theological
Ethics.* Louisville, Ky.: Westminster/John Knox, 1992.

Murnion, Philip J., ed. *Catholics and Nuclear War: A Commentary on* The Challenge of Peace, *the U.S. Catholic Bishops' Pastoral Letter on War and Peace*. New York: Crossroad, 1983.

Musto, Ronald G. *The Catholic Peace Tradition*. Maryknoll, N.Y.: Orbis, 1986.

————, ed. *Catholic Peacemakers: A Documentary History*. Vol. 1: *From the Bible to the Era of the Crusades*. New York: Garland, 1993. Vol. 2: *From the Renaissance to the Twentieth Century*. Two parts. New York: Garland, 1996.

Russell, Frederick H. *The Just War in the Middle Ages*. Cambridge: Cambridge University Press, 1975.

Shannon, Thomas A. *What Are They Saying about Peace and War?* New York: Paulist, 1983.

Swift, Louis J. *The Early Fathers on War and Military Service*. Message of the Fathers of the Church 19. Wilmington, Del.: Michael Glazier, 1983.

Weigel, George. *Tranquillitas Ordinis: The Present Failure and Future Promise of American Catholic Thought on War and Peace*. New York: Oxford University Press, 1987.

k. Work

Baum, Gregory. *The Priority of Labor: A Commentary on* Laborem exercens, *Encyclical Letter of Pope John Paul II*. New York: Paulist, 1982.

————, ed. *Work and Religion*. *Concilium* 131. Edinburgh: T & T Clark, 1980.

Chenu, Marie-Dominique. *The Theology of Work*. Tr. Lilian Soiron. Chicago: Regnery, 1963.

Fox, Matthew. *The Reinvention of Work: A New Vision of Livelihood for Our Time*. San Francisco: HarperSanFrancisco, 1994.

l. Ecology

Barnes, Michael, ed. *An Ecology of the Spirit: Religious Reflection and Environmental Consciousness*. The Annual Publication of the College Theology Society 1990 (vol. 36). Lanham, Md.: University Press of America, 1994.

Berry, Thomas. *The Dream of the Earth*. San Francisco: Sierra Club Books, 1988.

Boff, Leonardo. *Ecology and Liberation: A New Paradigm*. Tr. John Cumming. Maryknoll, N.Y.: Orbis, 1995

Haught, John F. *The Promise of Nature: Ecology and Cosmic Purpose*. New York: Paulist, 1993.

John Paul II, Pope. "Peace with All Creation." 1990 World Day of Peace
  Statement. *Origins* 19 (1989-90): 465-68.
McDonagh, Sean. *The Greening of the Church*. Maryknoll, N.Y.: Orbis, 1990.
Murphy, Charles. *At Home on Earth: Foundations for a Catholic Ethic of the
  Environment*. New York: Crossroad, 1989.
U.S. Bishops. "Renewing the Earth." *Origins* 21 (1991-92): 425-32.

G. Political, Liberation, and Feminist Theologies (see also IX.F.5.h: Social Ethics)

1. Political Theologies

Chopp, Rebecca. *The Praxis of Suffering: An Interpretation of Liberation and
  Political Theologies*. Maryknoll, N.Y.: Orbis, 1986.
Fiorenza, Francis Schüssler. "Political Theology as Foundational Theology."
  Proceedings of the Catholic Theological Society of America 32 (1977)
  142-77.
Lakeland, Paul. *Freedom in Christ: An Introduction to Political Theology*. New
  York: Fordham University Press, 1986.
Lamb, Matthew. *Solidarity with Victims: Toward a Theology of Social
  Transformation*. New York: Crossroad, 1982.
Metz, Johann Baptist. *The Emergent Church: The Future of Christianity in a
  Postbourgeois World*. Tr. Peter Mann. New York: Crossroad, 1981.
————. *Faith in History and Society: Toward a Practical Fundamental
  Theology*. Tr. David Smith. New York: Seabury, 1980.
————. *Theology of the World*. Tr. Wilhelm Glen-Doepel. New York: Herder,
  1969.

2. Liberation Theologies

Aristide, Jean-Bertrand. *In the Parish of the Poor: Writings from Haiti*. Tr. and
  ed. Amy Wilentz. Maryknoll, N.Y.: Orbis, 1991.
Aristide, Jean-Bertrand, with Christophe Wargny. *Aristide: An Autobiography*.
  Tr. Linda M. Maloney. Maryknoll, N.Y.: Orbis, 1993.
Azevedo, Marcello. *Basic Ecclesial Communities in Brazil: The Challenge of
  a New Way of Being Church*. Tr. John Drury. Washington, D.C.:
  Georgetown University Press, 1987.
Barbe, Dominique. *Grace and Power: Base Communities and Nonviolence in
  Brazil*. Maryknoll, N.Y.: Orbis, 1987.
Berryman, Phillip. *Liberation Theology: Essential Facts about the
  Revolutionary Movement in Latin America—and Beyond*. New York:
  Pantheon, 1987.

Boff, Leonardo. *Church: Charism and Power: Liberation Theology and the Institutional Church.* Tr. John W. Diercksmeier. New York: Crossroad, 1985.

———. *Ecclesiogenesis: The Base Communities Reinvent the Church.* Tr. Robert R. Barr. Maryknoll, N.Y.: Orbis, 1986.

Boff, Leonardo, and Clodovis Boff. *Introducing Liberation Theology.* Tr. Paul Burns. New York: Orbis, 1987.

Brown, Robert McAfee. *Liberation Theology: An Introductory Guide.* Louisville: Westminster/John Knox, 1993.

Dussel, Enrique. *History and the Theology of Liberation: A Latin American Perspective.* Tr. John Drury. Maryknoll, N.Y.: Orbis, 1976.

Ellacuría, Ignacio, and Jon Sobrino, eds. *Mysterium Liberationis: Fundamental Concepts of Liberation Theology.* Maryknoll, N.Y.: Orbis, 1993.

Ellis, Marc H., and Otto Maduro, eds. *The Future of Liberation Theology: Essays in Honor of Gustavo Gutiérrez.* Maryknoll, N.Y.: Orbis, 1989.

Ferm, Deane William. *Third World Liberation Theologies: A Reader.* Maryknoll, N.Y.: Orbis, 1986.

Gutiérrez, Gustavo. *On Job: God-Talk and the Suffering of the Innocent.* Tr. Matthew J. O'Connell. Maryknoll, N.Y.: Orbis, 1987.

———. *The Power of the Poor in History: Selected Writings.* Tr. Robert R. Barr. Maryknoll, N.Y.: Orbis, 1983.

———. *A Theology of Liberation: History, Politics, and Salvation.* Revised ed. Tr. and ed. Sister Caridad Inda and John Eagleson. Maryknoll, N.Y.: Orbis, 1988 [1971].

Haight, Roger. *An Alternative Vision: An Interpretation of Liberation Theology.* New York: Paulist, 1985.

Hennelly, Alfred T. ed. *Liberation Theology: A Documentary History.* Maryknoll, N.Y.: Orbis, 1990.

McGovern, Arthur F. *Liberation Theology and Its Critics: Toward an Assessment.* Maryknoll, N.Y.: Orbis, 1989.

Novak, Michael. *Will It Liberate? Questions about Liberation Theology.* New York: Paulist, 1986.

Pieris, Aloysius. *An Asian Theology of Liberation.* Maryknoll, N.Y.: Orbis, 1988.

Romero, Oscar. *Voice of the Voiceless: The Four Pastoral Letters and Other Statements.* Tr. Michael J. Walsh. Maryknoll, N.Y.: Orbis, 1985.

Segundo, Juan Luis. *The Liberation of Theology.* Tr. John Drury. Maryknoll, N.Y.: Orbis, 1976.

———. *A Theology for the Artisans of a New Humanity.* 5 vols. Tr. John Drury. Maryknoll, N.Y.: Orbis, 1973-75.

Sigmund, Paul E. *Liberation Theology at the Crossroads: Democracy or Revolution?* New York: Oxford University Press, 1990.

Sobrino, Jon. *Christology at the Crossroads: A Latin American Approach.* Tr. John Drury. Maryknoll, N.Y.: Orbis, 1978.

————. *Jesus the Liberator: A Historical-Theological View.* Tr. Paul Burns and Francis McDonagh. Maryknoll, N.Y.: Orbis, 1993.

Torres, Sergio and John Eagleson, eds. *The Challenge of Basic Christian Communities.* Maryknoll, N.Y.: Orbis, 1981.

3. Feminist Theologies

Aquino, María Pilar. *Our Cry for Life: Feminist Theology from Latin America.* Tr. Dinah Livingstone. Maryknoll, N.Y.: Orbis, 1993.

Carr, Anne E. *Transforming Grace: Christian Tradition and Women's Experience.* San Francisco: Harper and Row, 1988.

Coll, Regina A. *Christianity and Feminism in Conversation.* Mystic, Conn.: Twenty-Third, 1994.

Conn, Joann Wolski, ed. *Women's Spirituality: Resources for Christian Development.* New York: Paulist, 1986.

Daly, Mary. *Beyond God the Father: Toward a Philosophy of Women's Liberation.* Boston: Beacon, 1973.

————. *Gyn-Ecology: The Metaethics of Radical Feminism.* Boston: Beacon, 1978.

Fabella, Virginia, and Mercy Amba Oduyoye, eds. *With Passion and Compassion: Third World Women Doing Theology.* Maryknoll, N.Y.: Orbis, 1988.

Fiorenza, Elisabeth Schüssler. *But She Said: Feminist Practices of Biblical Interpretation.* Boston: Beacon, 1992.

————. *In Memory of Her: A Feminist Reconstruction of Christian Origins.* New York: Crossroad, 1983.

Isasi-Díaz, Ada María. *En la Lucha/In the Struggle: A Hispanic Women's Liberation Theology.* Minneapolis: Fortress, 1993.

Johnson, Elizabeth. *She Who Is: The Mystery of God in Feminist Theological Discourse.* New York: Crossroad, 1993.

Johnson, Elizabeth, Susan A. Ross, and Mary Catherine Hilkert. "Feminist Theology: A Review of the Literature." *Theological Studies* 56 (1995): 327-352.

LaCugna, Catherine M., ed. *Freeing Theology: The Essentials of Theology in Feminist Perspective.* San Francisco: HarperSanFrancisco, 1993.

Mannion, M. Francis. "The Church and the Voices of Feminism." *America* 165 (1991): 212-16, 228-30.

Martin, Francis. *The Feminist Question: Feminist Theology in the Light of Christian Tradition.* Grand Rapids, Mich.: Eerdmans, 1994.

Oduyoye, Mercy Amba, and Musimbi R. A. Kanyoro, eds. *The Will to Arise: Women, Tradition and the Church in Africa.* Maryknoll, N.Y.: Orbis, 1992.

Ruether, Rosemary Radford. *Sexism and God-Talk: Toward a Feminist Theology.* Boston: Beacon, 1983.

―――. *Women-Church: Theology and Practice of Feminist Liturgical Communities.* San Francisco: Harper and Row, 1985.

Schneiders, Sandra. *Beyond Patching: Faith and Feminism in the Catholic Church.* New York: Paulist, 1991.

Tamez, Elsa, ed. *Through Her Eyes: Women's Theology from Latin America.* Maryknoll, N.Y.: Orbis, 1989.

Weaver, Mary Jo. *New Catholic Women: A Contemporary Challenge to Traditional Religious Authority.* San Francisco: Harper and Row, 1985.

X. Liturgy and Sacraments

A. Liturgy

Adam, Adolf. *The Eucharistic Celebration: The Source and Summit of Faith.* Tr. Robert C. Schultz. Collegeville, Minn.: Liturgical, 1994.

―――. *Foundations of Liturgy: An Introduction to Its History and Practice.* Tr. Matthew J. O'Connell. Collegeville, Minn.: Liturgical, 1992.

―――. *The Liturgical Year: Its History and Its Meaning after the Reform of the Liturgy.* Tr. Matthew J. O'Connell. New York: Pueblo, 1981.

Bouley, Allan, ed. *Catholic Rites Today: Abridged Texts for Students.* Collegeville, Minn.: Liturgical, 1992.

Bradshaw, Paul F. *The Search for the Origins of Christian Worship: Sources and Methods for the Study of Early Liturgy.* New York: Oxford University Press, 1992.

Bugnini, Annibale. *The Reform of the Liturgy, 1948-1975.* Tr. Matthew J. O'Connell. Collegeville, Minn.: Liturgical, 1990.

Casel, Odo. *The Mystery of Christian Worship.* Westminster, Md.: Christian Classics, 1982 [1932].

Daly, Robert J. *The Origins of the Christian Doctrine of Sacrifice.* Philadelphia: Fortress, 1978.

Emminghaus, Johannes H. *The Eucharist: Essence, Form, Celebration.* Trans. Matthew J. O'Connell. Collegeville, Minn.: Liturgical, 1978.

Fisher, Eugene J., ed. *The Jewish Roots of Christian Liturgy.* New York: Paulist, 1990.

Irwin, Kevin W. *Advent Christmas: A Guide to the Eucharist and Hours.* The Liturgical Seasons. New York: Pueblo, 1986.

―――. *Context and Text: Method in Liturgical Theology.* Collegeville, Minn.: Liturgical, 1994.

————. *Easter: A Guide to the Eucharist and Hours.* The Liturgical Seasons. Collegeville, Liturgical, 1991.

————. *Lent: A Guide to the Eucharist and Hours.* The Liturgical Seasons. New York: Pueblo, 1985.

Jones, Cheslyn, et al. *The Study of Liturgy.* Revised ed. New York: Oxford University Press, 1992.

Jungmann, Joseph A. *The Mass: An Historical, Theological, and Pastoral Survey.* Trans. Julian Fernandes. Collegeville, Minn.: Liturgical, 1976.

————. *The Mass of the Roman Rite.* Trans. Francis A. Brummer. New York: Benziger Brothers, 1951, 1955.

Kavanagh, Aidan. *On Liturgical Theology.* New York: Pueblo, 1984.

Kilmartin, Edward J. *Christian Liturgy: Theology and Practice.* Vol. 1: *Systematic Theology of Liturgy.* Kansas City: Sheed and Ward, 1988.

Martimort, A. G., ed. *The Church at Prayer: An Introduction to the Liturgy,* New Edition. Tr. Matthew J. O'Connell. Volume I: *Principles of the Liturgy.* Volume II: *The Eucharist.* Volume III: *The Sacraments.* Volume IV: *The Liturgy and Time.* Collegeville, Minn.: Liturgical, 1985-88.

The Rites of the Catholic Church as Revised by Decree of the Second Vatican Ecumenical Council and Published by Authority of Pope Paul VI. English tr. prepared by the International Commission on English in the Liturgy. 2 vols. New York: Pueblo, 1980, 1983.

Taft, Robert. *The Liturgy of the Hours in East and West: The Origins of the Divine Office and Its Meaning for Today.* Collegeville, Minn.: Liturgical, 1986.

Talley, Thomas J. *The Origins of the Liturgical Year.* New York: Pueblo, 1986.

Vogel, Cyrille. *Medieval Liturgy: An Introduction to the Sources.* Rev. and tr. William G. Storey and Niels Krogh Rasmussen. Washington, D.C.: Pastoral, 1986.

Wegman, Herman. *Christian Worship in East and West: A Study Guide to Liturgical History.* Tr. G. W. Lathrop. New York: Pueblo, 1985.

White, James F. *Roman Catholic Worship: Trent to Today.* New York: Paulist, 1995.

B. Sacraments in General

Cooke, Bernard J. *Sacraments and Sacramentality.* Mystic, Conn.: Twenty-Third, 1983.

Duffy, Regis A. *Real Presence: Worship, Sacraments, and Commitment.* San Francisco: Harper and Row, 1982.

Ganoczy, Alexandre. *An Introduction to Catholic Sacramental Theology.* Tr. William Thomas. New York: Paulist, 1984.

Gelpi, Donald L. *Committed Worship: A Sacramental Theology for Converting Christians.* 2 vols. I: *Adult Conversion and Initiation.* II: *The Sacraments of Ongoing Conversion.* Collegeville, Minn.: Liturgical, 1993.

Guzie, Tad. *The Book of Sacramental Basics.* New York: Paulist, 1981.

Martos, Joseph. *The Catholic Sacraments.* Wilmington, Del.: Michael Glazier, 1983.

————. *Doors to the Sacred: An Historical Introduction to Sacraments in the Catholic Church.* Expanded ed. Tarrytown, N.Y.: Triumph Books, 1991.

————. "Sacraments in the 1980s: A Review of Books in Print." *Horizons* 18 (1991): 130-42.

Osborne, Kenan. *Sacramental Guidelines: A Companion to the New Catechism for Religious Educators.* New York: Paulist, 1995.

————. *Sacramental Theology: A General Introduction.* New York: Paulist, 1988.

Power, David N., Regis A. Duffy, and Kevin W. Irwin. "Sacramental Theology: A Review of Literature." *Theological Studies* 55 (1994): 657-706.

Rahner, Karl. *The Church and the Sacraments.* Tr. W. J. O'Hara. New York: Herder and Herder, 1963.

Schanz, John P. *Introduction to the Sacraments.* New York: Pueblo, 1983.

Schillebeeckx, Edward. *Christ the Sacrament of the Encounter with God.* Tr. Paul Barrett. New York: Sheed and Ward, 1963.

Vorgrimler, Herbert. *Sacramental Theology.* Tr. Linda M. Maloney. Collegeville, Minn.: Liturgical, 1992.

C. Particular Sacraments

1. Baptism, Confirmation, Christian Initiation

Austin, Gerald. *The Rite of Confirmation: Anointing with the Spirit.* New York: Pueblo, 1985.

Duffy, Regis A. *On Becoming Catholic: The Challenge of Christian Initiation.* San Francisco: Harper & Row, 1984.

Kavanagh, Aidan. *Confirmation: Origins and Reform.* New York: Pueblo, 1988.

————. *The Shape of Baptism: The Rite of Christian Initiation.* New York: Pueblo, 1978.

McDonnell, Kilian, and George Montague, eds. *Christian Initiation and Baptism in the Holy Spirit.* Second Revised Edition. Collegeville, Minn.: Liturgical, 1995.

Mick, Lawrence A. *RCIA: Renewing the Church as an Initiating Assembly.* Collegeville, Minn.: Liturgical, 1989.

Morris, Thomas H. *The RCIA: Transforming the Church*. New York: Paulist, 1989.

Osborne, Kenan B. *The Christian Sacraments of Initiation: Baptism, Confirmation, Eucharist*. New York: Paulist, 1987.

Searle, Mark, ed. *Baptism and Confirmation*. Vol. 2 of *Alternative Futures for Worship*. Collegeville, Minn.: Liturgical, 1987.

Walsh, Liam G. *The Sacraments of Initiation: Baptism, Confirmation, Eucharist*. London: Geoffrey Chapman, 1988.

2. *Eucharist* (see also under X.A.: Liturgy)

Bouyer, Louis. *Eucharist: The Theology and Spirituality of the Eucharistic Prayer*. Tr. Charles Underhill Quinn. Notre Dame, Ind.: University of Notre Dame Press, 1968.

Fitzpatrick, P. J. *In Breaking of Bread: The Eucharist and Ritual*. New York: Cambridge University Press, 1993.

Hellwig, Monika. *The Eucharist and the Hunger of the World*. New York: Paulist, 1976.

Kilmartin, Edward J. "The Catholic Tradition of Eucharistic Theology: Towards the Third Millennium." *Theological Studies* 55 (1994): 405-58.

Léon-Dufour, Xavier. *Sharing the Eucharistic Bread: The Witness of the New Testament*. Trans. Matthew O'Connell. New York: Paulist, 1987.

Macy, Gary. *The Banquet's Wisdom: A Short History of the Theologies of the Lord's Supper*. New York: Paulist, 1992.

Mazza, Enrico. *The Eucharistic Prayers of the Roman Rite*. Tr. Matthew O'Connell. New York: Pueblo, 1986.

Mitchell, Nathan. *Cult and Controversy: The Worship of the Eucharist Outside Mass*. New York: Pueblo, 1982.

Nichols, Aidan. *The Holy Eucharist: From the New Testament to Pope John Paul II*. Dublin: Veritas, 1991.

O'Carroll, Michael. *Corpus Christi: An Encyclopedia of the Eucharist*. Wilmington, Del.: Michael Glazier, 1988.

Power, David N. *The Eucharistic Mystery: Revitalizing the Tradition*. New York: Crossroad, 1992.

Powers, Joseph M. *Eucharistic Theology*. New York: Seabury, 1967.

Rubin, Miri. *Corpus Christi: The Eucharist in Late Medieval Culture*. Cambridge: Cambridge University Press, 1991.

Schillebeeckx, Edward. *The Eucharist*. Tr. N. D. Smith. New York: Sheed and Ward, 1968.

3. Penance/Reconciliation

Cuschieri, Andrew. *The Sacrament of Reconciliation: A Theological and Canonical Treatise*. Lanham, Md.: University Press of America, 1992.

Dallen, James. *The Reconciling Community: The Rite of Penance*. New York: Pueblo, 1986.

Favazza, Joseph. *The Order of Penitents*. Collegeville, Minn.: Liturgical, 1988.

Fink, Peter. *Reconciliation*. Alternative Futures for Worship 4. Collegeville, Minn.: Liturgical, 1987.

Gula, Richard M., S.S. *To Walk Together Again: The Sacrament of Reconciliation*. New York: Paulist, 1984.

Hellwig, Monika. *Sign of Reconciliation and Conversion*. Wilmington, Del.: Michael Glazier, 1982.

John Paul II, Pope. "Apostolic Exhortation on Penance and Reconciliation." *Origins* 14 (1984-85): 432, 434-57.

Kennedy, Robert, ed., *Reconciliation: The Continuing Agenda*. Collegeville, Minn.: Liturgical, 1987.

Orsy, Ladislas. *The Evolving Church and the Sacrament of Penance*. Denville, N.J.: Dimension, 1978.

Osborne, Kenan B. *Reconciliation and Justification: The Sacrament and its Theology*. New York: Paulist, 1990.

Poschmann, Bernhard. *Penance and Anointing of the Sick*. Tr. and revised by Francis Courtney. New York: Herder and Herder, 1964.

Rahner, Karl. *Theological Investigations*. Vol. 15: *Penance in the Early Church*. Tr. Lionel Swain. New York: Crossroad, 1982.

The Rite of Penance: Commentaries. 3 vols. Washington, D.C.: Liturgical Conference, 1975-78.

Schillebeeckx, Edward, ed. *Sacramental Reconciliation*. *Concilium* 61. New York: Herder and Herder, 1971.

4. Marriage (Divorce, Annulment)

Brooke, Christopher N. L. *The Medieval Idea of Marriage*. New York: Oxford University Press, 1989.

Hillman, Eugene. *Polygamy Reconsidered: African Plural Marriage and the Christian Churches*. Maryknoll, N.Y.: Orbis, 1975.

Kasper, Walter. *Theology of Christian Marriage*. Tr. David Smith. New York: Crossroad, 1981.

Kilcourse, George. *Double Belonging: Interchurch Families and Christian Unity*. New York: Paulist, 1989.

Lawler, Michael G. *Secular Marriage, Christian Sacrament*. New York: Paulist, 1987.

Mackin, Theodore. *Marriage in the Catholic Church.* Vol. 1, *What is Marriage?* New York: Paulist, 1982. Vol. 2, *Divorce and Remarriage.* New York: Paulist, 1984. Vol. 3, *The Marital Sacrament.* New York: Paulist, 1989.

Noonan, John T., Jr. *Power to Dissolve: Lawyers and Marriages in the Courts of the Roman Curia.* Cambridge, Mass.: Harvard University Press, 1972.

Orsy, Ladislas. *Marriage in Canon Law.* Wilmington, Del.: Michael Glazier, 1986.

Phillips, Roderick. *Putting Asunder: A History of Divorce in Western Society.* New York: Cambridge University Press, 1988.

Pospishil, Victor J. *Eastern Catholic Marriage Law.* Brooklyn: St. Maron, 1991.

Roberts, William P., ed. *Commitment to Partnership: Explorations of the Theology of Marriage.* New York: Paulist, 1987.

Schillebeeckx, Edward. *Marriage: Secular Reality and Saving Mystery.* Tr. N. D. Smith. New York: Sheed and Ward, 1965.

Stevenson, Kenneth W. *To Join Together: The Rite of Marriage.* New York: Pueblo, 1987.

Thomas, David M. *Christian Marriage: A Journey Together.* Wilmington, Del.: Michael Glazier, 1983.

Whitehead, James, and Evelyn Whitehead. *Marrying Well: Stages on the Journey of Christian Marriage.* New York: Doubleday, 1984.

Zwack, Joseph P. With C. Robert Nixon and Roger D. Conry. *Annulment: Your Chance to Remarry within the Catholic Church.* New York: Harper and Row, 1983.

5. *Sacrament of Order (Holy Orders)* (see also under IX.D.7.c.: Systematic Theology: Church: Bishops and Priests)

Cooke, Bernard. *Ministry to Word and Sacraments: History and Theology.* Philadelphia: Fortress, 1976.

Donovan, Daniel. *What Are They Saying about the Ministerial Priesthood?* New York: Paulist, 1992.

Dunn, Patrick. *Priesthood: A Re-Examination of the Roman Catholic Theology of the Presbyterate.* Staten Island, N.Y.: Alba House, 1990.

Eucharist and Ministry. Lutherans and Catholics in Dialogue 4. [New York and Washington, D.C.:] Representatives of the U.S.A. National Committee of the Lutheran World Federation and the Bishops' Committee for Ecumenical and Interreligious Affairs, 1970.

Galot, Jean. *Theology of the Priesthood.* San Francisco: Ignatius, 1984.

Mitchell, Nathan. *Mission and Ministry: History and Theology of the Sacrament of Order.* Wilmington, Del.: Michael Glazier, 1982.

Nichols, Aidan. *Holy Order: The Apostolic Ministry from the New Testament to the Second Vatican Council.* Dublin: Veritas, 1990.

Osborne, Kenan B. *Priesthood: A History of the Ordained Ministry in the Roman Catholic Church.* New York: Paulist, 1988.

a. Ordination of Women

Ashley, Benedict M. "Gender and the Priesthood of Christ: A Theological Reflection." *The Thomist* 57 (1993): 343-79.

Bouyer, Louis. *Woman in the Church.* Tr. Marilyn Techert. San Francisco: Ignatius, 1979.

Congregation for the Doctrine of the Faith. "Declaration on the Question of the Admission of Women to the Ministerial Priesthood" [*Inter insigniores*]. *Origins* 6 (1977): 517, 519-24.

————. "Response to 'Dubium': Inadmissibility of Women to Ministerial Priesthood." *Origins* 25 (1995): 401, 403-05.

Coriden, James A., ed. *Sexism and Church Law.* New York: Paulist, 1977.

Gardiner, Anne Marie, ed. *Women and Catholic Priesthood: An Expanded Vision.* New York: Paulist, 1976.

Hauke, Manfred. *Women in the Priesthood? A Systematic Analysis in the Light of the Order of Creation and Redemption.* Tr. David Kipp. San Francisco: Ignatius, 1988.

John Paul II, Pope. Apostolic Letter, *Ordinatio sacerdotalis. Origins* 24 (1994): 49, 51-52.

Meer, Haye van der. *Women Priests in the Catholic Church? A Theological-Historical Investigation.* Tr. Arlene and Leonard Swidler. Philadelphia: Temple University Press, 1973.

Moll, Helmut, ed. *The Church and Women: A Compendium.* San Francisco: Ignatius, 1988.

Raming, Ida. *The Exclusion of Women from the Priesthood: Divine Law or Sex Discrimination?* Tr. Norman R. Adams. Metuchen, N.J.: Scarecrow, 1976.

Rattigan, Virginia Kaib, and Arlene Anderson Swidler, eds. *A New Phoebe: Perspectives on Roman Catholic Women and the Permanent Diaconate.* Kansas City, Mo.: Sheed and Ward, 1990.

Rossi, Mary Ann. "Priesthood, Precedent, and Prejudice: On Recovering the Women Priests of Early Christianity." *Journal of Feminist Studies in Religion* 7 (1991): 73-93.

St. Pierre, Simone M. *The Struggle to Serve: The Ordination of Women in the Roman Catholic Church.* Jefferson, N.C.: McFarland, 1994. [Annotated bibliography pp. 177-198.]

Stuhlmueller, Carroll. *Women and Priesthood: Future Directions.* Collegeville, Minn.: Liturgical, 1978.

Swidler, Leonard, and Arlene Swidler, eds. *Women Priests: A Catholic Commentary on the Vatican Declaration.* New York: Paulist, 1977.

6. *Anointing of the Sick*

Cuschieri, Andrew. *Anointing of the Sick: A Theological and Canonical Study.* Lanham, Md.: University Press of America, 1993.

Empereur, James L. *Prophetic Anointing: God's Call to the Sick, the Elderly, and the Dying.* Wilmington, Del.: Michael Glazier, 1982.

Fink, Peter E., ed. *Anointing of the Sick.* Alternative Futures for Worship 7. Collegeville, Minn.: Liturgical, 1987.

Gusmer, Charles W. *And You Visited Me: Sacramental Ministry to the Sick and the Dying.* New York: Pueblo, 1984.

Ziegler, John J. *Let Them Anoint the Sick.* Collegeville, Minn.: Liturgical, 1987.

7. *Sacramentals*

Rutherford, Richard, with Tony Barr. *The Death of a Christian: the Order of Christian Funerals.* Revised ed. Collegeville, Minn.: Liturgical, 1990.

XI. Spirituality

Aumann, Jordan. *Christian Spirituality in the Catholic Tradition.* San Francisco: Ignatius, 1985.

Barry, William A., and William J. Connolly. *The Practice of Spiritual Direction.* San Francisco: Harper and Row, 1982.

Bouyer, Louis, Francois Vandenbroucke, and Jean Leclercq. *A History of Christian Spirituality.* 3 vols. Various translators. New York: Seabury, 1982.

Chinnici, Joseph. *Living Stones: The History and Structure of Catholic Spiritual Life in the United States.* New York: Macmillan, 1989.

de Mello, Anthony. *Sadhana: A Way to God. Christian Exercises in Eastern Form.* Garden City, N.Y.: Doubleday Image Books, 1984.

Dupré, Louis and Don Saliers, eds. *Christian Spirituality: Post-Reformation and Modern.* World Spirituality: An Encyclopedic History of the Religious Quest 18. New York: Crossroad, 1989.

Jones, Cheslyn, Geoffrey Wainwright, and Edward Yarnold. *The Study of Spirituality.* New York: Oxford University Press, 1986.

Laurentin, René. *Catholic Pentecostalism.* Garden City, N.Y.: Doubleday, 1977.

Linn, Dennis, and Matthew Linn. *Healing Life's Hurts: Healing Memories through the Five Stages of Forgiveness.* New York: Paulist, 1978.

MacNutt, Francis. *Healing*. Notre Dame, Ind.: Ave Maria Press, 1974.

Magill, Frank N., and Ian P. McGreal, eds. *Christian Spirituality: The Essential Guide to the Most Influential Spiritual Writings of the Christian Tradition*. San Francisco: Harper and Row, 1988.

McDonnell, Kilian, ed. *Presence, Power, Praise: Documents on the Charismatic Renewal*. Collegeville, Minn.: Liturgical, 1980.

McGinn, Bernard, John Meyendorff, and Jean Leclercq, eds. *Christian Spirituality: Origins to the Twelfth Century*. World Spirituality: An Encyclopedic History of the Religious Quest 16. New York: Crossroad, 1986.

Merton, Thomas. *Contemplative Prayer*. New York: Herder and Herder, 1969.

———. *New Seeds of Contemplation*. New York: New Directions, 1962.

———. *The Seven-Storey Mountain*. New York: Harcourt, Brace, 1948.

———. *Zen and the Birds of Appetite*. New York: New Directions, 1968.

———. *Thomas Merton, Spiritual Master: The Essential Writings*. Ed. Lawrence S. Cunningham. New York: Paulist, 1992.

Nolan, Mary Lee, and Sidney Nolan. *Christian Pilgrimage in Modern Western Europe*. Chapel Hill: University of North Carolina Press, 1989.

Nouwen, Henri. *Reaching Out: The Three Movements of the Spiritual Life*. Garden City, N.Y.: Doubleday, 1975.

Pennington, M. Basil, *Daily We Touch Him: Practical Religious Experiences*. Garden City, N.Y.: Doubleday Image Books, 1979.

Raitt, Jill, ed. *Christian Spirituality: High Middle Ages and Reformation*. World Spirituality: An Encyclopedic History of the Religious Quest 17. New York: Crossroad, 1988.

Schneiders, Sandra. "Spirituality in the Academy." *Theological Studies* 50 (1989): 676-97.

———. "Theology and Spirituality: Strangers, Rivals, or Partners." *Horizons* 13 (1986): 253-74.

Taves, Ann. *The Household of Faith: Roman Catholic Devotions in Mid-Nineteenth-Century America*. Notre Dame, Ind.: University of Notre Dame Press, 1986.

Thérèse of Lisieux, St. *Story of a Soul: The Autobiography of St. Thérèse of Lisieux*. Trans. John Clarke, O.C.D. 2d ed. Washington, D.C.: Institute of Carmelite Studies, 1976.

Teilhard de Chardin, Pierre. *The Divine Milieu*. New York: Harper and Row, 1960.

Williams, Rowan. *Christian Spirituality: A Theological History from the New Testament to Luther and St. John of the Cross*. Atlanta: John Knox, 1980.

Wright, John H. *A Theology of Christian Prayer*. 2d ed. New York: Pueblo, 1988.

A. Mysticism

Dupré, Louis. *The Other Dimension: A Search for the Meaning of Religious Attitudes.* New York: Doubleday, 1972.

Dupré, Louis, and James A. Wiseman, eds. *Light from Light: An Anthology of Christian Mysticism.* New York: Paulist, 1988.

Egan, Harvey. *An Anthology of Christian Mysticism.* Collegeville, Minn.: Liturgical, 1991.

———. *Christian Mysticism: The Future of a Tradition.* New York: Pueblo, 1984.

Johnston, William. *The Inner Eye of Love: Mysticism and Religion.* San Francisco: Harper and Row, 1978.

Lossky, Vladimir. *The Mystical Theology of the Eastern Church.* Tr. by members of the Fellowship of St. Alban and St. Sergius. London: J. Clarke, 1957.

Louth, Andrew. *The Origins of the Christian Mystical Tradition from Plato to Denys.* Oxford: Clarendon, 1981.

Maréchal, Joseph, S. J. *Studies in the Psychology of the Mystics.* Tr. Algar Thorold. Albany: Magi, 1964 [1927].

McGinn, Bernard. *The Presence of God: A History of Western Christian Mysticism.* Vol. 1: *The Foundations of Mysticism.* New York: Crossroad, 1991. Vol. 2: *The Growth of Mysticism: Gregory the Great through the Twelfth Century.* New York: Crossroad, 1994.

Thurston, Herbert. *The Physical Phenomena of Mysticism.* Chicago: Regnery, 1952.

Underhill, Evelyn. *Mysticism.* New York: Dutton, 1961 [1911].

XII. Religious Life, Evangelical Counsels (see also VII.B.10, History: Monasticism and Religious Orders and Congregations)

Dolan, Jay P., et al. *Transforming Parish Ministry: The Changing Roles of Catholic Clergy, Laity, and Women Religious.* New York: Crossroad, 1989.

Hite, Jordan, Sharon Holland, and Daniel Ward, *A Handbook on Canons 573-746: Religious Institutes, Secular Institutes, Societies of the Apostolic Life.* Collegeville, Minn.: Liturgical, 1985.

Leddy, Mary Jo. *Reweaving Religious Life: Beyond the Liberal Model.* Mystic, Conn.: Twenty-Third, 1991.

Moloney, Francis J. *A Life of Promise: Poverty, Chastity, Obedience.* Wilmington, Del.: Michael Glazier, 1984.

O'Connor, David F. *Witness and Service: Questions about Religious Life Today*. New York: Paulist, 1990.

Quiñonez, Lora Ann, and Mary Daniel Turner. *The Transformation of American Catholic Sisters*. Philadelphia: Temple University Press, 1992.

Schillebeeckx, Edward. *Celibacy*. Tr. C. A. L. Jarrott. New York: Sheed and Ward, 1968.

Schneiders, Sandra. *New Wineskins: Re-imaging Religious Life Today*. New York: Paulist, 1986.

Sipe, A. W. Richard. *A Secret World: Sexuality and the Search for Celibacy*. New York: Bruner/Mazel, 1990.

XIII. Education

A. General Works on Religious Education

Boys, Mary C. *Educating in Faith*. San Francisco: Harper and Row, 1989.

Groome, Thomas H. *Christian Religious Education: Sharing Our Story and Vision*. San Francisco: Harper and Row, 1980.

————. *Sharing Faith: A Comprehensive Approach to Religious Education and Pastoral Ministry*. San Francisco: HarperSanFrancisco, 1991.

B. Catechisms: Secondary Works

Bryce, Mary Charles. *Pride of Place: The Role of the Bishops in the Development of Catechesis in the United States*. Washington, D.C.: The Catholic University of America Press, 1984.

Marthaler, Berard L. *The Catechism Yesterday and Today: The Evolution of a Genre*. Collegeville, Minn.: Liturgical, 1995.

————, ed. *Introducing the Catechism of the Catholic Church: Traditional Themes and Contemporary Issues*. New York: Paulist, 1994.

Walsh, Michael J., ed. *Commentary on the* Catechism of the Catholic Church. Collegeville, Minn.: Liturgical, 1994.

C. Schools

Bryk, Anthony S., Valerie E. Lee, and Peter B. Holland. *Catholic Schools and the Common Good*. Cambridge, Mass.: Harvard University Press, 1993.

Buetow, Harold A. *The Catholic School: Its Roots, Identity, and Future*. New York: Crossroad, 1988.

————. *Of Singular Benefit: The Story of Catholic Education in the United States*. New York: Macmillan, 1970.

Gleason, Philip. *Keeping the Faith: American Catholicism Past and Present.* Notre Dame, Ind.: University of Notre Dame Press, 1987.

Greeley, Andrew M., William C. McCready, and Kathleen McCourt. *Catholic Schools in a Declining Church.* Kansas City: Sheed and Ward, 1976.

Ryan, Mary Perkins. *Are Parochial Schools the Answer? Catholic Education in the Light of the Council.* New York: Holt, Rinehart and Winston, 1964.

Walch, Timothy. *Parish School: A History of American Catholic Parochial Education from Colonial Times to the Present.* New York: Crossroad, 1995.

D. Seminaries

White, Joseph M. *The Diocesan Seminary in the United States: A History from the 1780s to the Present.* Notre Dame, Ind.: University of Notre Dame Press, 1989.

E. Universities and Colleges

Curran, Charles E. *Catholic Higher Education, Theology, and Academic Freedom.* Notre Dame, Ind.: University of Notre Dame Press, 1990.

Evans, G. R. *Old Arts and New Theology.* Oxford: Clarendon, 1980.

Gallin, Alice, ed. *American Catholic Higher Education: Essential Documents, 1967-1990.* Notre Dame: University of Notre Dame Press, 1992.

Ganss, George E. *Saint Ignatius' Idea of a Jesuit University.* Milwaukee: Marquette University Press, 1954.

Gleason, Philip. *Contending with Modernity: Catholic Higher Education in Twentieth-Century America.* New York: Oxford University Press, 1995.

Hassenger, Robert, ed. *The Shape of Catholic Higher Education.* Chicago: University of Chicago Press, 1967.

Hesburgh, Theodore M., ed. *The Challenge and Promise of a Catholic University.* Notre Dame, Ind.: University of Notre Dame Press, 1994.

Kimball, Bruce A. *Orators and Philosophers: A History of the Idea of Liberal Education.* New York: Teachers College Press, 1986.

Langan, John P., ed. *Catholic Universities in Church and Society: A Dialogue on Ex corde ecclesiae.* Washington, D.C.: Georgetown University Press, 1993.

O'Brien, David J. *From the Heart of the American Church: Catholic Higher Education and American Culture.* Maryknoll, N.Y.: Orbis, 1994.

Orsy, Ladislas. *The Church: Learning and Teaching.* Wilmington, Del.: Michael Glazier, 1987.

Rashdall, Hastings. *The Universities of Europe in the Middle Ages.* 3 vols. Ed. F. M. Powicke and A. B. Emden. Oxford: Clarendon, 1936.

538 Bibliography

XIV. Canon Law

Canon Law Society of Great Britain and Ireland. *The Canon Law: Letter and Spirit.* Collegeville, Minn.: Liturgical, 1995.
Code of Canons of the Eastern Churches. Latin/English ed. Washington, D.C.: Canon Law Society of America, 1992.
Coriden, James A. *An Introduction to Canon Law.* New York: Paulist, 1991.
Coriden, James A., Thomas J. Green, and Donald E. Heintschel, eds. *The Code of Canon Law: A Text and Commentary.* New York: Paulist, 1985.
Orsy, Ladislas. *The Profession of Faith and the Oath of Fidelity: A Theological and Canonical Analysis.* Wilmington, Del.: Michael Glazier, 1990.

XV. Mission, Evangelization, Inculturation

Bosch, David J. *Transforming Mission: Paradigm Shifts in Theology of Mission* Maryknoll, N.Y.: Orbis, 1991.
Boyack, Kenneth, ed. *The New Catholic Evangelization.* New York: Paulist, 1992.
Bühlmann, Walbert. *The Coming of the Third Church.* Maryknoll, N.Y.: Orbis, 1977.
Dulles, Avery. "John Paul II and the New Evangelization." *America* 166 (1992): 52-59, 69-72.
Schineller, Peter. *A Handbook of Inculturation.* New York: Paulist, 1990.
Schreiter, Robert. *Constructing Local Theologies.* Maryknoll, N.Y.: Orbis, 1985.
Shorter, Aylward. *Toward a Theology of Inculturation.* Maryknoll, N.Y.: Orbis, 1988.
Thomas, Norman E., ed. *Classic Texts in Mission and World Christianity.* Maryknoll, N.Y.: Orbis, 1995.

XVI. Ecumenical and Interfaith Relations

A. Christian Ecumenism

Anglican-Roman Catholic International Commission. *The Final Report.* Cincinnati: Forward Movement Publications and Washington, D.C.: U.S. Catholic Conference, 1982.
Bird, David, et al. *Receiving the Vision: The Anglican-Roman Catholic Reality Today.* Collegeville, Minn.: Liturgical, 1995.
Burgess, Joseph A., and Jeffrey Gros, eds. *Building Unity: Ecumenical Dialogues with Roman Catholic Participation in the United States.* Ecumenical Documents 4. New York: Paulist, 1989.

Congregation for the Doctrine of the Faith and Pontifical Council for Promoting Christian Unity, "Vatican Responds to ARCIC I Final Report." *Origins* 21 (1991): 441, 443-47.

Empie, Paul C., and T. Austin Murphy, eds. *Lutherans and Catholics in Dialogue I-III*. I: The Status of the Nicene Creed as Dogma of the Church. II: One Baptism for the Remission of Sins. III: The Eucharist as Sacrifice. Minneapolis: Augsburg, n.d. [1965-67].

Fries, Heinrich, and Karl Rahner. *Unity of the Churches: An Actual Possibility.* Tr. Eric and Ruth Gritsch. Philadelphia: Fortress, 1985.

Horgan, Thaddeus D., ed. *Walking Together: Roman Catholics and Ecumenism Twenty-Five Years after Vatican II.* Grand Rapids, Mich.: Eerdmans, 1991.

Hughes, John Jay. *Absolutely Null and Utterly Void: The Papal Condemnation of Anglican Orders, 1896.* Washington, D.C.: Corpus, 1968.

———. *Stewards of the Lord: A Reappraisal of Anglican Orders.* London: Sheed and Ward, 1970.

Lowery, Mark D. *Ecumenism: Striving for Unity amid Diversity.* Mystic, Conn.: Twenty-Third, 1985.

Nichols, Aidan. *The Panther and the Hind: A Theological History of Anglicanism.* Edinburgh: T & T Clark, 1993.

———. *Rome and the Eastern Churches: A Study in Schism.* Collegeville, Minn.: Liturgical, 1992.

Nilson, Jon. *Nothing Beyond the Necessary: Roman Catholicism and the Ecumenical Future.* New York: Paulist, 1995.

Pawley, Bernard, and Margaret Pawley. *Rome and Canterbury through Four Centuries: A Study of the Relations between the Church of Rome and the Anglican Churches, 1530-1973.* New York: Seabury, 1975.

Pontifical Council for Promoting Christian Unity. "Directory for the Application of Principles and Norms in Ecumenism." *Origins* 23 (1993): 129-60.

Roberson, Ronald G. *The Eastern Christian Churches: A Brief Survey.* 5th ed. Washington, D.C.: U.S. Catholic Conference, 1995.

Skillrud, Harold C., J. Francis Stafford, and Daniel Martensen, eds. *Scripture and Tradition.* Lutherans and Catholics in Dialogue 9. Minneapolis: Augsburg Fortress, 1995.

Stormon, E. J., ed. and tr. *Towards the Healing of Schism: The Sees of Rome and Constantinople: Public Statements and Correspondence between the Holy See and the Ecumenical Patriarchate, 1959-1984.* Ecumenical Documents 3. New York: Paulist, 1987.

Tavard, George H. *A Review of Anglican Orders: The Problem and the Solution.* Collegeville, Minn.: Liturgical, 1990.

Vischer, Lukas, and Andreas Karrer, eds. *Reformed and Roman Catholic in Dialogue.* Geneva: World Alliance of Reformed Churches, 1988.

Witmer, Joseph W., and J. Robert Wright, eds. *Called to Full Unity: Documents on Anglican-Roman Catholic Relations, 1966-1983.* Washington, D.C.: U.S. Catholic Conference, 1986.

World Council of Churches. *Baptism, Eucharist, Ministry.* Faith and Order Paper No. 111. Geneva: World Council of Churches, 1982.

B. Relations with Judaism

Callan, Terrance. *Forgetting the Root: The Emergence of Christianity from Judaism.* New York: Paulist, 1986.

Croner, Helga, ed. *Stepping Stones to Further Jewish-Christian Relations.* New York: Stimulus, 1977.

————, ed. *Further Stepping Stones.* New York: Paulist, 1985.

Fisher, Eugene J., and Leon Klenicki, eds. *In Our Time: The Flowering of Jewish-Catholic Dialogue.* With an annotated bibliography by Eugene J. Fisher. New York: Paulist, 1990.

Fisher, Eugene J., A. James Rudin, Marc H. Tanenbaum, eds. *Twenty Years of Jewish-Catholic Relations.* New York, Paulist, 1986.

Flannery, Edward. *The Anguish of the Jews.* Revised ed. New York: Paulist, 1985.

John Paul II, Pope. *Texts on Jews and Judaism, 1979-1995.* With Commentary and Introduction by Eugene J. Risher and Leon Klenicki. New York: Crossroad, 1995.

Klenicki, Leon, and Geoffrey Wigoder, eds. *A Dictionary of the Jewish Christian Dialogue.* Expanded edition. New York: Paulist, 1995.

Pawlikowski, John T. *What Are They Saying About Christian-Jewish Relations?* New York: Paulist 1980.

Rousmaniere, John. *A Bridge to Dialogue: The Story of Jewish-Christian Relations.* New York: Paulist, 1992.

Ruether, Rosemary. *Faith and Fratricide: The Theological Roots of Anti-Semitism.* New York: Seabury, 1974.

Shermis, Michael. *Jewish-Christian Relations: An Annotated Bibliography and Resource Guide.* Bloomington, Ind.: Indiana University Press, 1988.

C. Theology of Religions and Interreligious Dialogue

1. General Works

Braybrooke, Marcus. *Pilgrimage of Hope: One Hundred Years of Global Interfaith Dialogue.* New York: Crossroad, 1992.

D'Costa, Gavin. *Theology and Religious Pluralism: The Challenge of Other Religions.* Oxford: Blackwell, 1986.

———, ed. *Christian Uniqueness Reconsidered: The Myth of a Pluralistic Theology of Religions.* Maryknoll, N.Y.: Orbis, 1990.

DiNoia, J. A. *The Diversity of Religions: A Christian Perspective.* Washington, D.C.: The Catholic University of America Press, 1992.

Dunne, John S. *The Way of All the Earth: Experiments in Truth and Religion.* Notre Dame, Ind.: University of Notre Dame Press, 1978 [1972].

Dupuis, Jacques. *Jesus Christ at the Encounter of World Religions.* Tr. Robert R. Barr. Maryknoll, N.Y.: Orbis, 1991.

Griffiths, Paul J. *An Apology for Apologetics: A Study in the Logic of Interreligious Dialogue.* Maryknoll, N.Y.: Orbis, 1991.

———, ed. *Christianity through Non-Christian Eyes.* Maryknoll, N.Y.: Orbis, 1990.

Hick, John, and Knitter, Paul F. *The Myth of Christian Uniqueness.* Maryknoll, N.Y.: Orbis, 1987.

Idel, Moshe, and Bernard McGinn, eds. *Mystical Union and Monotheistic Faith: An Ecumenical Dialogue.* New York: Macmillan, 1989.

Knitter, Paul. *No Other Name? A Critical Study of Christian Attitudes towards the World Religions.* Maryknoll, N.Y.: Orbis, 1985.

Küng, Hans, et al. *Christianity and the World Religions: Paths of Dialogue with Islam, Hinduism, and Buddhism.* Tr. Peter Heinegg. Garden City, N.Y.: Doubleday, 1986.

Phan, Peter, ed. *Christianity and the Wider Ecumenism.* New York: Paragon, 1990.

Rahner, Karl. "Christianity and the Non-Christian Religions." In *Theological Investigations*, vol 5. Tr. Karl-H. Kruger. Baltimore: Helicon, 1966. 115-134.

Tracy, David. *Dialogue with the Other: The Inter-Religious Dialogue.* Grand Rapids: Eerdmans, 1991.

2. Buddhism, Taoism

Dumoulin, Heinrich. *Christianity Meets Buddhism.* LaSalle, Ill.: Open Court, 1974.

Geffre, Claude, and Mariasusai Dhavamony, eds. *Buddhism and Christianity. Concilium* 116. New York: Seabury, 1979.

Johnston, William. *The Still Point: Reflections on Zen and Christian Mysticism.* New York: Harper, 1971.

Lee, Chen Jiuan A., and Thomas G. Hand. *A Taste of Water: Christianity Through Taoist-Buddhist Eyes.* New York: Paulist, 1990.

Mitchell, Donald W. *Spirituality and Emptiness: The Dynamics of Spiritual Life in Buddhism and Christianity.* New York: Paulist, 1991.

Pieris, Aloysius. *Love Meets Wisdom: A Christian Experience of Buddhism.* Maryknoll, N.Y.: Orbis, 1988.

Waldenfels, Hans. *Absolute Nothingness: Foundations for a Buddhist-Christian Dialogue*. Tr. J. W. Heisig. New York: Paulist, 1980.

Yagi, Seiichi, and Leonard Swidler. *A Bridge to Buddhist-Christian Dialogue*. New York: Paulist, 1990.

3. Hinduism

Abhishiktananda. *Saccidananda: A Christian Approach to Advaitic Experience*. Rev. ed. Delhi: I.S.P.C.K., 1984.

Clooney, Francis X. *Theology after Vedānta: An Experiment in Comparative Theology*. Toward a Comparative Philosophy of Religions. Albany, N.Y.: SUNY Press, 1993.

Griffiths, Bede. *Christian Ashram: Essays toward a Hindu-Christian Dialogue*. London: Darton, Longman, and Todd, 1966.

Panikkar, Raimundo. *The Unknown Christ of Hinduism: Towards an Ecumenical Christophany*. Maryknoll, N.Y.: Orbis, 1981.

VonBruck, Michael. *The Unity of Reality: God, Experience and Meditation in the Hindu-Christian Dialogue*. New York: Paulist, 1990.

4. Islam

Borelli, John. "The Goals and Fruit of Catholic-Muslim Dialogue." *The Living Light* 32,2 (Winter 1995): 51-60.

———. "This Rapid Period of Development in Catholic-Muslim Relations." *Origins* 21 (1991): 535-38.

Borrmans, Maurice, et al. *Guidelines for Dialogue between Christians and Muslims: Interreligious Documents*. New York: Paulist, 1990.

Gerry, Joseph. "What the Purpose of Catholic-Muslim Dialogue Is and Is Not." *Origins* 21 (1991): 538-39.

Mallon, Elias. "The Challenges in Catholic-Muslim Dialogue." *Origins* 21 (1991): 531-34.

XVII. Philosophy

Copleston, Frederick. *A History of Philosophy*. 9 vols. Garden City, N.Y.: Doubleday Image Books, 1962-77.

Gadamer, Hans-Georg. *Truth and Method*. Second, revised edition. Translation [by Wilhelm Glen-Doepel] revised by Joel Weinsheimer and Donald G. Marshall. New York: Continuum, 1993 [1960].

Lonergan, Bernard J. F. *Insight: A Study in Human Understanding*. Third edition. New York: Philosophical Library, 1970.

Marcel, Gabriel. *The Mystery of Being*. Tr. G. S. Fraser and René Hague. 2 vols. Chicago: Regnery, 1960.

Maritain, Jacques. *Distinguish to Unite or The Degrees of Knowledge*. Tr. under the direction of Gerald B. Phelan. New York: Scribner, 1959.

——. *Integral Humanism*. Tr. Joseph W. Evans. New York: Scribner, 1968 [1936].

Rahner, Karl. *Hearer of the Word*. Tr. Joseph Donceel. New York: Continuum, 1994.

——. *Spirit in the World*. Tr. William Dych. New York: Herder and Herder, 1968 [1939].

XVIII. Catholicism and Culture

A. General Works

Ong, Walter. *Faith and Contexts*. Ed. Thomas J. Farrell and Paul A. Soukup. 2 vols. South Florida-Rochester-St. Louis Studies on Religion and the Social Order. Atlanta: Scholars, 1992.

B. Architecture

Krautheimer, Richard. *Early Christian and Byzantine Architecture*. 4th ed. Revised by Richard Krautheimer and Slobodan Curcic. The Pelican History of Art. New York: Penguin, 1986.

Norman, Edward. *The House of God: Church Architecture, Style and History*. London: Thames and Hudson, 1990.

Wilson, Christopher. *The Gothic Cathedral: The Architecture of the Great Church 1130-1530*. London: Thames and Hudson, 1990.

C. Art

Apostolos-Cappadona, Diane. *Dictionary of Christian Art*. New York: Continuum, 1995.

Beckwith, John. *Early Christian and Byzantine Art*. 2d ed. the Pelican History of Art. New York: Penguin, 1979.

Belting, Hans. *Likeness and Presence: A History of the Image before the Era of Art*. Tr. Edmund Jephcott. Chicago: University of Chicago Press, 1994.

Dillenberger, John. *A Theology of Artistic Sensibilities: The Visual Arts and the Church*. New York: Crossroad, 1986.

Newton, Eric, and William Neil. *2000 Years of Christian Art*. New York: Harper and Row, 1966.

Nichols, Aidan. *The Art of God Incarnate: Theology and Image in Christian Tradition*. London: Longman and Todd, 1980.

U.S. Bishops' Committee on the Liturgy. *Environment and Art in Catholic Worship*. Washington, D.C.: U.S. Catholic Conference, 1978.

Weitzman, Kurt. *The Icon: Holy Images—Sixth to Fourteenth Century*. New York: Braziller, 1978.

D. Music

Apel, Willi. *Gregorian Chant*. Bloomington: Indiana University Press, 1958.

Day, Thomas. *Why Catholics Can't Sing: The Culture of Catholicism and the Triumph of Bad Taste*. New York: Crossroad, 1990.

Fellerer, Karl Gustav. *The History of Catholic Church Music*. Tr. Francis A. Brunner. Baltimore: Helicon, 1961.

Funk, Virgil C., ed. [Bishops' Committee on the Liturgy.] *Music in Catholic Worship, Revised Edition: The NPM Commentary* [with text]. Washington, D.C.: Pastoral Press, 1983.

Gelineau, Joseph. *Voices and Instruments in Christian Worship: Principles, Laws, Applications*. Trans. Clifford Howell. Collegeville, Minn.: Liturgical, 1964.

Hayburn, Robert F. *Papal Legislation on Sacred Music, 95 A.D. to 1977 A.D.* Collegeville, Minn.: Liturgical, 1979.

Hiley, David. *Western Plainchant: A Handbook*. New York: Oxford University Press, 1993.

Nemmers, Erwin Esser. *Twenty Centuries of Catholic Church Music*. Milwaukee: Bruce, 1949.

Poultney, David. *Dictionary of Western Church Music*. Chicago: American Library Association, 1991.

Quasten, Johannes. *Music and Worship in Pagan and Christian Antiquity*. Tr. Boniface Ramsey. Washington, D.C.: Pastoral Press, 1983.

Robertson, Alec. *Christian Music*. The Twentieth Century Encyclopedia of Catholicism. New York: Hawthorn, 1961.

Winter, Miriam Therese. *Why Sing? Toward a Theology of Catholic Church Music*. Washington, D.C.: Pastoral Press, 1984.

E. Literature

Fraser, Theodore P. *The Modern Catholic Novel in Europe*. New York: Twayne, 1994.

Giles, Paul. *American Catholic Arts and Fictions: Culture, Ideology, Aesthetics*. New York: Cambridge University Press, 1992.

Lynch, William F. *Christ and Apollo: Dimensions of the Catholic Literary Imagination*. Notre Dame, Ind.: University of Notre Dame Press, 1960.

Sparr, Arnold. *To Promote, Defend, and Redeem: The Catholic Literary Revival and the Cultural Transformation of American Catholicism, 1920-1960*. New York: Greenwood, 1990.

F. Science

Haught, John F. *The Cosmic Adventure: Science, Religion, and the Quest for Purpose*. New York: Paulist, 1984.
———. *Science and Religion: From Conflict to Conversation*. New York: Paulist, 1995.
Tracy, David, and Nicholas Lash, eds. *Cosmology and Theology*. *Concilium* 166. New York: Seabury, 1983.

Index

This is not a complete index. It is primarily confined to secondary definitions and identifications within dictionary articles. *It does not include any name or term to which a dictionary entry is devoted.*

cincture, 424
Cistercians, 10, 27, 74, 279
Clare of Assisi, St., 168
Clement of Alexandria, 39, 83
cloister, 388
Clovis, 9, 26
coadjutor bishop, 81
college, 418
Committal, Rite of, 172
Compline, 196
Comunione e liberazione, 224
conclave, 89, 337
congregation, religious, 361
consecration (of a bishop), 304
consensus of the faithful, 382
Copernicus, Nicholas, 172
Coptic Christianity, 40, 60, 138, 281, 307
Courage (organization), 191
Cyril of Alexandria, 39

dalmatic, 424
Darwin, Charles, 157
Daughters of Charity, 382, 425
Day, Dorothy, 95, 312
decretal, 85
deism, 145
de Maestre, Joseph, 417
demythologization, 290
despair, 192
deterrence, nuclear, 297
deuterocanonical books, 50, 76
dignity, human, 197
Dignity (organization), 191
domestic prelate, 281
Donation of Pepin, 27, 313
Douay-Rheims version, 76
Duff, Frank, 240

Edict of Milan, 111
Egeria, 162
Ember Days, 161
England, John, 17
eparchy, 127
Essenes, 122
Eunomius, 57
Eutyches, 280-1
Evangelical Protestants, 347

evangelists, 176
Evening Prayer, 196
ex cathedra, 207
exorcist (minor order), 304

Fatima, 54
Feast of Orthodoxy, 310
Fénelon, François, 349
Ferrara, Council of, 71, 165
First Friday, 371
form criticism, 78
Formula of Union, 146-7
fortitude, 89
fresco, 60
friar, 269
fruits of the Spirit, 188

Gilson, Etienne, 409
Gioberti, Vincenzo, 301
Good Friday, 137
Gothic, 55, 61
Gratian, 85
Great Week, 189
Gregory of Nazianzus, St., 88
Gregory of Nyssa, St., 88
Griffiths, Bede, 187
Guadalupe, 54
guardian angels, 44
Guéranger, Prosper, 249
Gutiérrez, Gustavo, 245
Guyon, Madame Jeanne, 349

Hadewijch, 72
Halloween, 40
Healy, James A., 37
Hecker, Isaac T., 42, 319
hegumen, 33
heterodoxy, 310
holocaust (sacrifice), 372
Holocaust, the, 225
Holy Office, 109, 209
Holy Saturday, 137
Holy Thursday, 137
homoousios, 57, 295
Hus, Jan, 110
hypostatic union, 98

iconostasis, 199

The Author

William J. Collinge received a bachelor's degree from Georgetown University in 1969 and a Ph.D. in philosophy from Yale University in 1974. Since 1980 he has taught at Mount Saint Mary's College, Emmitsburg, Maryland, where he is Professor of Theology and Philosophy. With John A. Mourant, he coauthored *Augustine: Four Anti-Pelagian Writings* (Washington, D.C.: The Catholic University of America Press, 1992), a volume in the series, The Fathers of the Church. He lives in Gettysburg, Pennsylvania, with his wife, Susan Collinge, and their three sons.